"Very impudent
when drunk or sober"

# Delaware Runaways,
## 1720-1783

Compiled by
Joseph Lee Boyle

CLEARFIELD

Copyright © 2014 by Joseph Lee Boyle
All Rights Reserved

Printed for Clearfield Company by
Genealogical Publishing Company
Baltimore, Maryland
2014

ISBN 978-0-8063-5694-5

## INTRODUCTION

One of the many neglected episodes of American history is that of the many thousands of white Europeans who did not come to the colonies as free men and women. Instead they came as indentured servants, political exiles, or transported convicts. White servitude was a major institution of the social and economic fabric of colonial British America. Bound whites preceded the use of black slaves in every colony. It is estimated that from 350,000 to 500,000 servants were imported through 1775. Though by the start of the eighteenth century the importation of black slaves increased dramatically in the Chesapeake and southern colonies, white bound labor remained significant until the American Revolution.

There were thousands of white people who wanted to leave their home countries, but were unable or unwilling to pay the cost of their passage, so as "free-willers" they became servants for a period of years to a colonial master who purchased them. Others were convicts or exiles. More than half the whites who came to the colonies south of New England were servants. Those who came voluntarily hoped for a better life. Most indentures were from four to seven years, though this varied over time.

Some were abducted to the colonies, as made famous in Robert Louis Stevenson's *Kidnapped*, but many are likely to have made the claim of being kidnapped to escape the terms of their indenture. Others may have runaway from home to leave families, debt, or other personal problems.

Of course the numbers of both free and indentured immigrants depended on economics. For example, the Irish came in a wave in 1770-1775 due to the collapse of the linen industry. Crop failures, wars, and economic disruptions in general added to the level of immigrants.

Underwriting of transportation was sometimes assumed by the planter, or more often by English merchants specializing in the sale of indentured servants. Recruiting agents called "crimps" hired drummers to recruit, sometimes making extravagant promises about the good life in the colonies. Illiterates were likely the most easily taken advantage of.

Though convicts were sent to the colonies before, the Transportation Act of 1718 opened the floodgates for exiled criminals, those convicted of minor crimes could be sent to the colonies for seven year terms. Capital crimes meant terms of fourteen years. After serving their time, they were eligible for royal mercy, and could return to England, but returning early was a capital offense. Convicts were attractive as they were relatively cheap, their sales prices were about one-third that of African slaves, and female felons sold for only two-thirds the price of males. From 1718 to 1773, some 50,000 convicts from all parts of Europe, largely Great Britain, were sent to America.

Benjamin Franklin noted convicts that "must be ruled with a Rod of Iron" and considered the British "emptying their jails into our settlements is an insult and contempt, the cruellest, that ever one people offered to another." While the colonists were incensed about receiving so many convicts, surviving court records do not show that they committed an inordinate number of crimes. Perhaps the lack of large towns, commercial activity, and general lack of opulence did not lend themselves to crimes the way the cities of England did, nor was there an existing criminal subculture

In the early days of the Delaware colony, Indians were enslaved, but they soon died off, or left for better places. The first black slave was brought to Delaware in 1639. In 1776 the state constitution ended the slave trade, but slavery continued to exist until the national adoption of the Thirteenth Amendment in December 1863. The first ad in this collection which specifically mentions a slave as a runaway does not appear until 1755. The majority of the ads which mention negroes and mulattoes simply say that they ran away, not stating whether they were slaves or indentured laborers. An interesting 1760 ad is that for the "villainous Affair" that Robert Caten committed when "took, some Time ago, a free born Mulatto Woman, and sold her for a Slave." Delaware residents sometimes paid slave owners for manumissions in order that the freedmen might be indentured.

In the decade before the American Revolution an estimated 20-25 percent of the Delaware colony's population was enslaved. Much higher than the northern colonies, but lower than the southern ones, including Maryland. The 1790 census showed 70 percent of the state's black population were slaves, and slaves were 15 percent of the state's total. The first federal census in 1790 showed that there was a total of 59,096 people total, with 3,899 free blacks and 8,887 black slaves.

There were also "redemptioners," initially German, and then British. They promised to pay ship captains on their arrival in America. If they could not pay, or find a relative or countryman to do so, the captain was free to dispose of them for a number of years, (usually two to seven) to defray the cost of their passage. For many this must have been a distress sale, as they could not return to Europe. Coming in family or large groups, they sold their own, or their children's labor for the cost of passage. The redemptioners were often called "free-willers."

These potential immigrants had the opportunity to negotiate the cost before they embarked. The time involved varied, depending on the amount owed. Upon arrival the immigrant usually had up to fourteen days to negotiate a sale of his services. If he could not do so, the shipper recovered his costs by selling the indenture to the highest bidder, the immigrant having no choice what work he might have, or where he would go.

The Chesapeake colonies received the highest number of servants, followed by Pennsylvania. So many Irish Catholics came to Maryland, that the Protestants became alarmed and a duty was imposed on them, while Protestant servants came in free. The Irish were more likely to come than the English as they were not bound to their parishes by the Poor Laws, which also provided the English with a meager sustenance.

There was money to be made at multiple levels. The contractor who arranged the transportation profited, the ship owner and captain profited, and if the transport involved convicts, the county sheriff in England or Ireland had his palm out to facilitate the process. At one time Irish sheriffs received five pounds a head for convicts sentenced to transportation, but paid out only three pounds to the merchant transporters. Subject to supply and demand at the ports, agents would sometimes keep servants on shipboard or in houses until a sale at a good price could be arranged. Once in America, if the servant ran away, local officials were eager to earn rewards for their capture.

There were financial risks at all levels of the investment. Some individuals absconded before boarding the ship. While ship captains wanted to make as much as possible from transportation the servants, the less they paid for food, the more they made. Though high shipboard mortality was regrettable, some deaths always occurred after six to eight weeks at sea. While convict cargoes were generally chained, there were cases of uprisings with the ship's crew being overpowered.

Ship arrivals in the colonies tended to be seasonal, with the fall preferred, so that ships could take cured tobacco back to Europe, and new arrivals would have cooler weather to adjust to their new environment. The term "seasoning" was applied to newcomers, whose death rate varied, but was rarely less than ten percent, and as high as forty percent. Malaria in particular was a chronic problem in the Chesapeake area.

Masters purchased their labor, not their bodies, but it was a risky investment. Death, injuries, chronic maladies, running away, or a shirking worker could mean loss of income. But cheap labor was more important than quality labor.

While the terms of indentures varied a great deal, the master was usually required to provide his servants with "sufficient meat, Drink, Apparell, Washing and Lodging." Of course what was "sufficient" from the master's view, was often not deemed such by the servant. White servants had the right to go appeal their treatment to the courts. Maryland courts often took masters to task for the denial of rest, sleep, food, drink, and lodging. A third offense by a master was grounds to set a servant free.

On the other hand, colonial courts could impose servitude on any citizen, usually for larceny or debt, if restitution could not be made, and fines and court costs paid. A 1723 Delaware law required that illegitimate mulatto children of white mothers should be bound out until they reached the age of 31, ten years longer than white children. The mothers of these children were sentenced to 39 lashes, to be exposed in the pillory, and to be fined. The mothers also had five years added to their indentures. In 1760 the General Assembly moved to allow children of such unions to petition for their freedom as they were often held as slaves.

Of course if servitude was to be a significant source of reliable labor, runaways could not be permitted to go free with impunity. As might be expected most runaways departed April through October, staying closer to home during winter weather. Non-English speakers might have runway less, whereas the Irish might have runaway more, due to the general anti-Irish feelings of the time. The not infrequent references to iron collars in these ads, show that running away was common. The collars were intended to make an example of the truants and to make identification easier. Servants were sometimes dangerous individuals. In 1770 "a Runaway Servant Man (who pretended to be dumb) belonging to Mr. Richard Lemon, of Newark, Newcastle County, was on Saturday committed to Gloucester Goal, for the barbarous Murder of a Woman, in New-Jersey, whose Husband had met this Murderer and sent him to his House for Entertainment." But then masters could be capricious. In 1737 Charity Brinckle of Dover was jailed for beating and starving an Irish servant girl named Mary Riley, which led to her death.

Passes were required for those more than a certain distance away from home. Those who appeared to be suspicious characters, or could not give satisfactory accounts of themselves were committed to jail and held temporarily. Even if no master appeared to pay the costs of the man being held, he still might be remanded to servitude for failure to pay the costs of his own incarceration.

Unsuccessful flight also added to the time of servitude. This was done partly as punishment, and partly to compensate for the costs of capture, reward and return. On the other hand bad or abusive masters were sometimes punished by the judicial system with the shortening or cancelling of indentures.

Many children were bound out to learn a trade. There were often orphans, but self-sufficient parents sometimes bound out their children to learn a trade. Beginning in 1752, indentures created in Delaware required the approval of a Justice of the Peace.

For those fulfilled the terms of their indentures "well and faithfully [in] such employments as the master may assign" for a set period of time, the average man had a better chance of attaining a decent standard of living than he did in Europe. The master had paid for passage to the colonies, and for food, drink, clothing and shelter during the time of the indenture, and depending on the individual transaction, some form of "freedom dues," which could be money, land, tools, livestock, etc.

For the ambitious servant, the term of servitude was a time of preparation. He was used to the climate and ways of the new land. He learned farming or another skill as practiced in the New World. He made contacts in the area he lived, and if an artisan, might have a list of customers when on his own. Abbott Emerson Smith estimated that one in ten would take up land and become prosperous, and that one in ten would become an artisan. The other eight died in servitude, returned to England, and or became "poor whites."

The American Revolution stopped the transport of convicts and regular migration, as well as slave importation. Though regular immigration resumed after the war, with limited importation of indentured servants, convicts were not permitted. Botany Bay in Australia became the dumping ground for those undesirables beginning in 1786.

Immigrant servitude was not in fact abolished until 1785, and servitude among American residents remained long after immigrant servitude disappeared, with apprenticeships for indigent children being the most common form. In Delaware the last officially recorded servant contract for an indigent child was record in 1930.

These ads include all descriptions of runaways and criminals in Delaware or who were born or had contacts in there. The provide a first-hand view of history, as well as valuable demographic information with the age, sex, height, place of origin, clothing, occupation, speech, as well as physical imperfections, etc. They often display attitudes of the owners, and personality traits of the runaway, such as a common affection for alcohol. Some ads give extensive vignettes of individuals with their perceived idiosyncrasies. They provide a bonanza of information for the social historian. Those interested in tracking their ancestors will also find a goldmine of details.

It is impossible to know how many runaways there really were. Escapees of low value or close to the end of their terms may not have been advertised. Given that so many of the servants appear to be scapegraces, one wonders why their masters spent money to advertise for them, let alone pay a reward for their return. Those who were useful workers with lots of time remaining were likely to be the most sought after. Masters were likely to ignore those who left for a few days of dissipation, particularly planters during the agricultural slow season.

Is it likely there were far more runaways than are represented in these ads. Delaware had no newspapers for the entire time period in this compilation, and New Jersey did not have one until 1777. While Maryland had two newspapers for much of the period, they were located in Annapolis and Baltimore, but many of the issues did not survive. As nearly all the land boundary of Delaware is shared with the Eastern Shore of Maryland, which had no newspapers, masters in the lower part of Delaware in particular would not be inclined to pay the cost of the ads. Between September 3, 1777, and April 22, 1778, no ads were found in any newspapers for Delaware people. This was due in part to the to the British invasion and occupation of Philadelphia.

The *Virginia Gazette* was not included in this compilation as it is online. I have retained the original spelling, punctuation, and capitalization of the ads. Illegible words or letters are in brackets.

This compilation lists all men and women with Delaware connections. This includes some who are referenced as having lived in Delaware or such as Jacob Carvel, who ran from Burlington County, New Jersey, and "the said boy's father lives at Duck-Creek, and it is supposed he has gone that way." Black men and women are indexed as Negroes, including those listed as Molatto, Malatto, Molattoe, etc.

Sometimes the ads in different papers are very similar and only the ad which occurs first in time is included, with references to the later ones. Minor differences in the advertisements are considered to be capitalization, spelling such as trousers/trowsers and 7/seven. If the ads are substantially different, each appears at the time it is first run. The majority are advertised in only one paper, many in two. Advertisements that are largely illegible are not included.

It will be noticed that far more men were runaways than women. In part this was due to the imbalance in the ratio of those who were indentured.

There are numerous variations in the spelling of names such as Swain/Swen Colesbery/Colesberry/Colesbury. In the same ad one man appears as John Gardner/Gardiner/Garner. In addition to creative spelling, the use of aliases was common. Good luck to the genealogist attempting to trace the line of "JAMES WILSON; he is well known by different names in different parts of the country, viz. in Chester county by Simson, at New York by Stenson, and Belcher and Brown elsewhere."

**For further reading:**

See the periodicals: *Papers of the Historical Society of Delaware* and *Delaware History*, though articles on runaways are few.

Blumenthal, Walter Hart. *Brides From Bridewell: Female Felons Sent to Colonial America,* 1962, reprint, Westport, Conn.: Greenwood Press, 1973.

Coldham, Peter Wilson. *Emigrants in Chains: A Social History of Forced Emigration to the Americas of Felons, Destitute Children, Political and Religious Non-Conformists, Vagabonds, Beggars and Other Undesirables, 1607-1776.* Baltimore: Genealogical Publishing Company, 1992.

Ekirch, A. Roger. *Bound for America: The Transportation of British Convicts to the Colonies, 1775-1778.* Oxford: Clarendon Press, 1987.

Emmer, P. C. ed. *Colonialism and Migration Indentured Labour Before and After Slavery.* Boston, 1986.

Essah, Patience, "Slavery and Freedom in the first State: The History of Blacks from the Colonial Period to 1865." Ph.D. dissertation, University of California at Los Angeles, 1985.

Fogleman, Aaron S. "From Slaves, Convicts, and Servants to Free Passengers: The Transformation of Immigration in the Era of the American Revolution," *The Journal of American History* 85 (1998): 43-76.

Galenson, David W. *White Servitude in Colonial America: An Economic Analysis.* Cambridge: Cambridge University Press, 1981.

"Servant Auction Records and Immigration into the Delaware Valley, 1745-1831: The Proportion of Females Among Immigrant Servants," *Proceedings of the American Philosophical Society,* 133 (June 1989): 154-169.

Grubb, Farley. "The Trans-Atlantic Market for British Convict Labor," *Journal of Economic History,* 60, 1 (March 2000): 94-122.

Hancock, Harold N. "The Indenture System in Delaware, 1681-1921," *Delaware History* 16 (April 1974): 47-59.

Heinegg, Paul. *Free African Americans of Maryland and Delaware from the Colonial Period to 1810.* Baltimore: Genealogical Publishing, 2000.

Meaders, Daniel. *Dead or Alive: Fugitive Slaves and White Indentured Servants Before 1830.* New York: Garland Publishing, 1993.

Menard, Russell R. "From Servants to Slaves: The Transformation of the Chesapeake Labor System," *Southern Studies,* 16 (1977): 355-388.

Miller, William. "The Effects of the American Revolution on Indentured Servitude." *Pennsylvania History,* 7, 3 (July 1940): 131-41.

Prude, Jonathan. "To Look Upon the "Lower Sort": Runaway Ads and the Appearance of Unfree Laborers in America, 1750-1800," *The Journal of American History* 78 1 (June, 1991): 124-159.

Reed, H. Clay. *Delaware: A History of the First State,* 2 vols. New York: Lewis Historical Publishing, 1947.

Salinger, Sharon V. "Labor, Markets, and Opportunity" Indentured Servitude in Early America," *Labor History,* 38, 2/3 (Spring/Summer 1997): 311-338.
Scharf, J. Thomas. *History of Delaware, 1609-1888,* 2 vols. 1888; reprint Port Washington, N.Y.: Kennikat Press, 1972.

Smith, Abbot Emerson. *Colonists in Bondage: White Servitude and Convict Labor in America, 1607-1776,* 1947; reprint; Gloucester, Mass.: Peter Smith, 1965.

Tomlins, Christopher L. *Reconsidering Indentured Servitude: European Migration and the Early American Labor Force, 1600-1775.* American Bar Foundation Working Paper #9920 American Bar Association, 1999.

Williams, William H. *Slavery and Freedom in Delaware, 1639-1865.* Wilmington, Del.: Scholarly Resources, 1996.

**Newspapers Consulted:**

It should be noted that none of these newspapers had a complete run for the period. Also, there were no newspapers published in Delaware or New Jersey for the entire period, colonies where ads for Maryland runaways might have been numerous. Even in Maryland the first surviving newspaper was not published until 1728, so the researcher must rely on a Pennsylvania newspaper for the first seven years of runaway advertisements.

*The American Weekly Mercury*
*The Boston Gazette*
*The Boston News-Letter*
*The Boston Post-Boy*
*Dunlap's Maryland Gazette*
*The Maryland Gazette*
*The Maryland Journal and Baltimore Advertiser*
*The New-England Courant*
*The New-England Weekly Journal*
*The New-Hampshire Gazette*
*The New-London Summary*
*The Newport Mercury*
*The New-York Evening Post*
*The New-York Gazette*
*The New-York Gazette, or Weekly Post-Boy*
*The New-York Mercury*
*The New-York Weekly Journal*
*The Pennsylvania Gazette*
*The Pennsylvania Journal, or Weekly Advertiser*
*The Providence Gazette*
*Weyman's New-York Gazette*

## 1720

RUN away from his Master *Cornelius Williams* of *Appaquimena* in *New-Castle* County a Servant Man named *Nicholas Howell* of a Middle Stature Well Set (he is a *Welsh* Man) Black short Bushy hair and Pock freten in the Face a Lightish Broad Cloth Vest and Britches Trimed with Red a Light Coloured Great Coat, Linnen Drawers over his Britches, a pair of yearn Stockins, He took from his Master an Iron Gray Horse branded on the near Shoulder with **I H** Whosoever shall take up said Servant and bring him to his said Master, or secure him and give Notice thereof so that he may be had again, shall have Three Pounds as a Reward, with Reasonable Charges.
*The American Weekly Mercury*, May 5, 1720; May 19, 1720.

RUN away on the Second of this Instant *July*, from *Griffeth Jones*, High Sheriff of *Kent* County upon *Deleware*, a Servant Man Named *Marmaduke Coulton*, of a short stature, thin pale Visiage, light Hair, redish Beard, short thick leggs, something lame in his Hipps aged between forty and fifty, had on an Old Gray Duroy Coat, trimmed with black, white linnen Vest, Ozenbriggs Shirt and Breeches, Carry'd away with him a Small Boat, and was accompany'd by three or four Servants, or Sailors, unknown. whoever can Secure him shall receive has a Reward the Sum of Forty Shillings, with Reasonable Charges.
*The American Weekly Mercury*, July 21, 1720; July 28, 1720.

## 1722

Caecil County, Maryland, June 15.
*RUN away from his Master William Cox, at the Head of North-East in Maryland, a Servant Man named* Henry Tuffo, *a Swede, Newcastle County born. A little short Man, having on a Felt Hat, Ozenbrig Shirt, blue Jacket and old Drugget Breeches, with his Hair lately cut off.*

*Whoever takes him up and secures him, so that his said Master may have him again, shall have a Pistole Reward.*
*The American Weekly Mercury*, From Thursday June 14th, to Thursday June 21st, 1722; From Thursday July 12th, to Thursday July 19th, 1722.

## 1723

March the 24th, 1722. [*sic*]
RUN away from the Rev. Daniel Magil of London-Tract, in New-castle County, a Servant-Lad named Denish Macanoully about 18 Years of Age, of

a swarthy Complexion, with a brown Coat and a Sailor Jacket, a Bever-Hat, Leather Breeches, Canvass-Drawers under them without any Hair on his Head. Whoever shall secure the said Run-away, and bring him to his said Master, shall have 20 Shillings Reward besides the Allowances according to the Laws of the Country.

*The American Weekly Mercury*, From Thursday March 21, to Thursday March 28, 1723; From Thursday April 11, to Thursday April 18, 1723; From Thursday April 25, to Thursday May 2, 1723.

RUN away from John Gooding of Ready-Island in the County of New-Castle, a Servant Lad aged about 18 or 19 Years, Swarthy Complexion and slender, having Short Hair, an old Hat, Homespun grey Cersey Coat and Breches, and a blakish Vest with Pewter Buttons, Whoever shall take up the said Run-away, and secure Him so that his Master may have him again shall have 40 *s*. and Reasonable Charges paid by, *John Gooding.*

*The American Weekly Mercury*, From Thursday March 28, to Thursday April 4, 1723; From Thursday April 11th, to Thursday April 18th, 1723; From Thursday April 25th, to Thursday May 2d, 1723.

RUN away from William Whittet of Appaquinamank in New-Castle County, a Servant Man named James Tomson aged about 20 Years, of Middle stature, well set, brown Complexion, his Hair is cut off, he hath on a Camblet Coat and blew Cloth Breeches, and several other Sea Cloaths. Whoever shall take up the said Servant and secures him and gives Notice to his said Master so that he may be had again shall have 40 *s*. as a Reward and reasonable Charges.

*The American Weekly Mercury*, From Thursday June 27th, to Thursday July 4th, 1723; From Thursday July 4th, to Thursday July 11th, 1723.

RUN away from John Keyll on Cristeen Creek in New Castle County, on the 18th of this Instant a Servant man named James *M*<sup>c</sup> Curdey, aged about 21 Years, a little *M*an, fair Complexion, pretty fresh Coloured, fair short Hair, he had on a grey Frys Coat, a brownish Cloth Jacket and *M*ohair Buttons, a pair of Buck-skin Breeches and brownish Stockings, a felt Hat. Whosoever takes up the said Servant and conveys him to his said *M*aster shall have a Pistole Reward and Reasonable Charges.

paid by me *John Keyll.*

*The American Weekly Mercury*, From Thursday August 22d, to Thursday August 29th, 1723; From Thursday September 19th, to

Thursday September 26th, 1723; From Thursday October 3d, to Thursday October 10th, 1723.

RUN away the 5th of this Instant November, from William Hugh of White-Clay Creek Hundred, in the County of New-Castle, a Servant Man named Charles May, aged about Thirty Years, of a middle Stature, Black hair and a large Crooked Nose, having on a Loose Coat and another loose Coat of an Ash Colour, and a gray homespun Wast-Coat a new Ozenbrig Shirt, and Course Linen Breeches, a pair of new Shoes with Round tooes and a new pair of Gray stockings, a new Felt Hatt. Whosoever Takes up the said Runaway and brings and brings him to his said Master, living near John Evans's Mill or secures him so that his Master may have him Forty shillings as a Reward besides Reasonable Charges.
*The American Weekly Mercury*, From Thursday November 7, to Thursday November 14, 1723.


RUN away from his Master *Nathaniel Caruther*: near *New-Castle*, the 28th Instant, a Servant Man named *Joseph Vanable*, Aged about Twenty nine Years, Black bushey Hair, black Eyes, a large old Beaver Hat, a brown Cloath Coat with leather Buttons, a brown Broad Cloath Jacket, Ozenbrigs Britches, black yarn Stokings and round too'd Shoes, he is a Black-Smith by Trade, and formerly belonged to *Hugh Lowdon*. Whosoever shall take up and secure the said *Joseph Vanable*, so that his Master may have him again, shall have Twenty Shillings as a Reward with reasonable Charges.
*The American Weekly Mercury*, From Thursday December 24, to Thursday December 31, 1723; From Tuesday January 7, to Tuesday January 14, 1724.

## 1724

ON the 16th. of this Instant January William Sinton, Committed to the County Goal of New-Castle, for Forgeing the Paper Currency of this Government, Broke the said Goal and made his escape; the said Sinton being a short fresh Coulered Man, about Twenty three Years of Age, wears a light Bobb Wigg and Cinamon Coulered Cloaths, by Profession a *Quaker*. Whoever shall apprehend the said Sinton, and bring him to the Sheriff of New-Castle aforesaid, shall receive the Reward of Ten Pounds
from *Rowland Fitz Gerald*, Sheriff.
*The American Weekly Mercury*, From Tuesday January 21, to Tuesday January 28, 1724; From Tuesday January 28, to Tuesday February 4, 1724; From Tuesday February 4, to Tuesday February 11, 1724.

## 1725

RUN away from *James Sykes* and *Jehu Curtis* of the City of *New-Castle*, two Servants, the one a lusty tall Fellow, named *Mathias Barry*, his Hair frisly and Sun Burnt, he had on a good brown Kersey Pea Jacket with flat white Mettle Buttons, Breeches of the same, a pair of white Stockings and new Shoes, Aged about 25 Years. The other a short wellset Fellow, named *Stephen Ouldisworth* aged about 25 Years, very short Hair having lately wore a Wigg, having Jacket and Breeches the same as the other, brown Stockings, good Shoes with Hobnails in the Soles, he pretends to be a Clock-maker by Trade. 'Tis supposed they have stolen a bright Bay Horse with a bob Tail, branded on the near Buttock with the Letter N, a new Saddle with Broad-Cloth Housing, also a grey Mare. Whoever takes up the said Servants, or either of them, so that they be delivered to their said Master, shall have Forty Shillings as a Reward of each, and reasonable Charges.

*The American Weekly Mercury*, From Tuesday February 2, to Tuesday February 9, 1725; From Tuesday February 9, to Tuesday February 16, 1725; From Tuesday February 23, to Thursday March 4, 1725.

RUN away the 19th of *January* last, from *Thomas Parke* of *Kent-County*, two Servant Men, the one named Richard Burk an Irish Man, aged about 26 Years, of short Stature, short dark brown Hair, fresh Complection; he had on him a yellowish Drugget Vest, and under it a Course blue serge Wast-Coat, with Eyelit Holes laced to his Body, a pair of Leather Breeches, an old Hat, round Toe'd Shoes, white yarn Stockings, and two new Ozenbrigs Shirts. The other named *Peter Barber*, an English Man, Aged about 22 Years, of short Stature, short black Hair, and fresh Complection; his Apparel is a dark Colour'd Drugget Vest, and a striped Holland Vest and Breeches, and a striped Ticking Vest, a pair of new Ozenbrigs Trousers, & a new Shirt of the same, an old Hat narrow Brim'd, round Toe'd Shoes and a pair of dark Coloured yarn Stockings. They have Stolen a new dark Colour'd Kersey Jockey Coat, a large Silver Spoon, and several other things.

Whoever secures the said Servants, so that I may have them again, shall have 5 *Pounds* Reward, or 50 *Shillings* for each of them,
paid by me *Thomas Parke*.

*The American Weekly Mercury*, From Tuesday January 26, to Tuesday February 2, 1725; From Tuesday February 16, to Tuesday February 23, 1725; From Thursday March 11, to Thursday March 18th, 1725.

## 1726

*RUN away on the 8th of this Instant* May, *from* Edmond Farrel *Tanner, of* Philadelphia, *two Servant Men, one is named* Peter Clare, *Aged about* 24 *Years, of a middle Stature, a Tanner by Trade, his Face thin and Freckl'd, he has streight brown Hair, an old Felt Hat, a brown Cloath Coat and a Fustin Jacket. The other named* John Hynes, *of a middle Stature, Aged about* 20 *Years, a Skynner by Trade, he has very short Hair, a black Fustin Frock with Mother of Pearl Buttons, and a white Flannen Jacket.*

*Run away in Company with the above two Servants, from* Lawrence Reynolds *Currier, a Servant Man named* John Willson, *Aged about* 20 *Years, by Trade a Butcher, of a small Stature, with short brown Hair, he has an old Pea Jacket, a striped Flannel Jacket under it, and an old Felt Hat. They are all Irish Men, and was lately brought into* New-Castle, *by Mr.* Patterson *Merchant, from* Dublin. *Whoever takes up the said Servants or either of them, so that they may be had again, shall* have 40 Shillings *as a Reward for Each, with reasonable Charges.*

*The American Weekly Mercury*, From Thursday May 5, to Thursday May 12, 1726.


*RUN away the 25th Day of* August *last, from* Sapins Harison *of* New-Castle *County, near* Duck Creek, *a Servant Man named* Richard Moor, *of a middle stature, with short thin curl'd Hair, an old Hat with a slit down the Crown which was sowed up again, he has a Yelow Lincey-woolsey Jacket, and grey Breeches with one Button on each Knee, a course shirt, a pair of large grey Home spun stockings, and a pair of Leather Heel'd shoes; he professes himself a Sergent, he is an* Irish *Man, and can write a little. Whoever takes up said servant, and secures him to his Master, shall have* 40 Shillings *as a Reward, and reasonable Charges.*

*The American Weekly Mercury*, From Thursday September 29th, to Thursday October 6th, 1726; From Thursday October 6th, to Thursday October 13th, 1726.


THAT there is in the Custody of *William Battell* Sheriff of the County of *New-Castle* on *Delaware*; a very likely Negroe Man, who was taken up and Committed as a runaway, he calls himself *Toby*, and says his Masters name is *Captain Bond*, but he has not *English* enough to discribe where his Master Lives. Whoever can make a legal Claim to the said Negroe and will pay the Lawful Charges, may have him delivered by the above Sheriff.

*The American Weekly Mercury*, From Thursday September 1, to Thursday September 8, 1726; From Thursday September 8, to Thursday

September 15, 1726; From Thursday September 22, to Thursday September 29, 1726; From Thursday October 6, to Thursday October 13, 1726.

## 1727

RUN away the 3d Instant *May*, from *John Macdaniel* of *New-Castle* County near *Christeen*, a Servant Man named *Timothy Murry*, aged 40 Years, with a gray Homespun Cloath Coat, trim'd with the same, the Ratts has Eaten the lower part of one of the Cuffs, a pair of Linnen Drawers patch't, he has dark thin Hair and Bald on the Crown, he is very Hairy in his Body. Whoever secures said Servant so as his said Master may have him again, shall have *Forty Shillings* Reward and all reasonable Charges.

*The American Weekly Mercury*, From Thursday May 11, to Thursday May 18, 1727


RUN away on the 12th of this Instant, from *John Bryan* senr. living near *New-Castle*, a Servant Woman named *Margaret Murphy*, she is of low Stature, and much Freckled and goes in Company with a young Man, named *John Bryan* a Freeman. Whoever apprehends the said Servant Woman, and returns her to her said Master, shall have 30 Shillings paid as a Reward, by me       *John Bryan*, senr.

*The American Weekly Mercury*, From Thursday August 17, to Thursday August 24, 1727; From Thursday August 31, to Thursday September 7, 1727.


RUN away the 2d of *October* from *John Goure* at *New-Castle*, a Servant Man named *Vallentine Dempsy* aged about 18 Years, a Rope maker by Trade, he is a well set fresh coloured Young Lad with fair Hair, when he left his Master he wore a light coloured Cloth Jacket and Breeches, blew Stockings and new Shoes, He was lately imported with Capt. *King* from *Ireland*. Whoever takes up the said the said Servant and brings him to *James Sykes* in *New-Castle*, or *Alexander Frame*, in *Philadelphia*, shall have *Forty Shillings* Reward & reasonable Charges paid by       *John Goure*.

*The American Weekly Mercury*, From Thursday October 5th, to Thursday October 12th, 1727; From Thursday October 12th, to Thursday October 19th, 1727; From Thursday October 19th, to Thursday October 26th, 1727.

## 1728

RUN away on the 27th of May last from *Richard Lawden* Shoe-maker, in *Chester*, a Servant Man, named *William Smith*, who served his Time at *Dublin*, in *Ireland*, to a Clog and Patten-maker, properly belonging to one *Duncan Dummond* Mercht. in the County of *New-Castle*; of a middle stature, with black Hair, pretty fresh Complection, aged about 23 or 24 Years, having on darkish coloured Cloaths trimm'd with Black, Linnen Drawers, gray Yarn Stockings, pretty good Shoes, with small Brass Buckles in them; he is an *Irish-man* born, and supposed to be gone to *New-York*. Whoever takes up the said Servant and secures him so that his said Master may have him again, shall have Three Pounds as a Reward and reasonable Charges.
    *The American Weekly Mercury*, From Thursday July 18, to Thursday July 25, 1728.


RUN away the 24th of *June*, from *Thomas Yeatman* of *New-Castle* County, near *Ellis Lewis* Mill. A Servant Man named *James Gibbs*, he is of a very short stature, with short Dark Curl'd Hair, a large mould on the right side of the Chin, a tow Shirt and Draws old leggins and Shoes. Whoever takes up the said Servant and secures him, so that his master may have him again, shall have reasonable Satisfaction paid him by me
*Thomas Yeatman.*
    *The American Weekly Mercury*, From Thursday August 1st, to Thursday August 8th, 1728; From Thursday August 8th, to Thursday August 15th, 1728; From Thursday August 15th, to Thursday August 22d, 1728.


RUN away the 21st of *November* from *William M'Dowell*, of *White-Clay-Creek*, in *New-Castle*-County, a Servant Man named *William Callsey*, he is a Tall well set Man, pale Complection'd, full Fac'd, a Gray full Eye, light Brown short Hair, some times wears a light short Wigg, a Suit of half worn Cloaths of a darkish Brown colour, Trim'd with small Mohair Buttons, a Pair of Gray Yarn Stockings, single soal'd Pumps, with a piece of a Black Scarf about his Neck Aged about Twenty years, an *Irishman* born: Whoever secures the said Servant, or gives Notice thereof, so that the said Master may have him again, shall have Forty Shillings reward and reasonable Charges bore.    *Carriage paid by*     *William M'Dowell.*
    *The American Weekly Mercury*, From Thursday November 21st, to Thursday November 28th, 1728; From Thursday December 24th, to Thursday December 31st, 1728.

## 1729

RUN away the 25th. of *January*, 1728-9. from *Thomas John*, of *New-Castle* County, Farmer; a Malatto Man, named *Joseph Williams*, about 24 Years of Age, having on an Ozenbrug Jacket and Breeches, and a Gray Homespun outside Jacket, Gray Yarn Stockins, and New Shoes; a White Woman went away with him, which he calls his Wife, named *Bridget*: Whoever secures the said Malatto Man, shall have *Thirty Shillings* Reward pay'd by
*Thomas John.*

*The American Weekly Mercury*, From Tuesday March 27th, to Thursday [*sic*] April 3, 1729; From Tuesday April 3d, to Thursday [*sic*] April 10, 1729.

*New-Castle upon Delaware*, March 20, 1728-9.
RUN away from Mrs. *Aves French*, and *William Battell*, Two Servants, on the Fourth of *February* last; one is a Man, born in *Staffordshire*, named *Richard Cook*, a Brick-maker by Trade, and a bold pretending Fellow, had on a Felt Hat, Light Wig, short Black Hair, a Homespun Gray Jockey's Coat, with Pewter Buttons, a Black Jacket, with other under Apparel necessary; the other an *Irish* Woman, named *Bridget Duncan*, who passes with him as his Wife; she is a well Set short Woman, downlook'd, took with her a Riding-Hood and Cloak. of a Yellowish colour, Fac'd with a Persian suitable; a Silk Gown of an Ash colour, with small dark Stripes, a Drugget upper Petty-Coat, &c. Whosoever will take up, and secure both, or either of the said Parties, so that they, or either of them may be had again; shall Receive *Thirty Shillings* as a reward for each, and reasonable Charges from
*William Battell.*

*The American Weekly Mercury*, From Tuesday March 27th, to Thursday [*sic*] April 3, 1729; From Tuesday April 3d, to Thursday [*sic*] April 10, 1729.

ON Tuesday the 2d: of this Instant *July*, One *John Shrennan*, [*sic*] a Prisoner to *William Read*, Sheriff of *New-Castle* County on *Delaware*, and in Execution for sundry Debts, due to divers Persons; Deserted from the said Sheriff, and made his Escape: The said *John Shennan*, is an *Irishman*, but speaks good English, he is a Tall, proper Man, and well Limb'd, fair spoken, aged about Twenty eight Years, wearing his own Black bushey Hair: Whoever takes up, and secures the said *John Shennan*, so that the Sheriff shall have him again, shall have *Five Pounds* reward, and all reasonable Charges paid by
*William Read Sheriff* of New-Castle-County.

*The American Weekly Mercury*, From Thursday June 26, to Thursday July 3, 1729; From Thursday July 3d, to Thursday July 10th, 1729; From Thursday July 17th, to Thursday July 24th, 1729; From Thursday July 24th, to Thursday July 31th, 1729. See *The Maryland Gazette*, July 8, 1729, to July 15, 1729.


ON *Tuesday* the first of this Instant *July*, One *John Shennan*, a Prisoner to *William Read*, Sheriff of *Newcastle* County on *Delaware*, (and in Execution for sundry Debts due to divers Persons) deserted from the said Sheriff, and made his Escape. The said *John Shennan*, is an *Irish* Man, but speaks good *English*, is a tall, proper, well limb'd, and fair spoken Man. Whosoever takes up and secures the said *John Shennan*, so that the Sheriff may have him again, shall have five Pounds Reward, and reasonable Charges paid by me
*William Read.*
*The Maryland Gazette*, July 8, 1729, to July 15, 1729; July 15, 1729, to July 22, 1729. See *The American Weekly Mercury*, From Thursday June 26, to Thursday July 3, 1729.


*New-Castle*, July *the* 10th. 1729.
RUN away from his Master the 6th. of this instant *July*; a Servant Man Aged about Eight and Twenty, of a Sandy Complexion, short Hair, or rather Shaved, a New Homespun Kersey Coat with no Lining, and Mohair Buttons, Ozenbrig Breeches, an Old Linnen Shirt, New Shoes, and several Pair of Stocking, of a Tall Stature, an *Irishman*, and is in Company with a *Welshman*, a Servant also, a short well set Fellow; they have Stolen a Pass formely belonging to one *Rger O'Dough[ir]t*, [sic] of which Name it is supposed one of them has Borrow'd: Whoever shall take, and secure, or convey the said *Hodgins* to his said Master, in *New-Castle*, shall have *Forty Shillings* Reward, and all reasonable Charges Paid by me,
*Thomas Williams.*
*The American Weekly Mercury*, From Thursday July 10, to Thursday July 24, 1729.


RUN away from *Simon Hadly*, Esq; of *New-Castle* County, the 28th of *October*, 1729, a Servant Lad, named *Edward Kenny*, about Eeighteen [sic] Years of Age, of a Middle Stature, of a Fair Complexion, Light Brown Hair, goes close with his Knees, and out with his Toes; having on when he went away an Old Beaver Hat, a Brown English Drugget Jacket, a Homespun Coat of Dark colour, with broad Pewter Buttons on it, a Homespun Shirt, a Linnen Draws, Old Shoes and Stockings: Whosoever takes up said the Servant, and

bring him to his Master, or secures him, so that he may be had again, shall have Thirty Shillings Reward, paid by me.
*Simon Hadly.*
*The American Weekly Mercury*, From Thursday October 23, to Thursday October 30, 1729; From Thursday October 30th, to Thursday November 6th, 1729. See *The American Weekly Mercury*, From Thursday November 6th, to Thursday November 13th, 1729.


RUN away from *Simon Hadly*, Esq; of *New-Castle* County, the 28th of *October*, 1729, a Servant Boy, named *Edward Kenny*, about 18 Years of Age, of a Middle Stature, of a Fair Complexion, Light Brown Hair, goes close with his Knees, and out with his Toes; having on when he went away an Old Beaver Hat, a Homespun Shirt, a Brown English Drugget Jacket, a Homespun Coat, of Dark colour, with Broad Pewter Buttons, he has on a Pair of Linnen Draw's, Old Shoes, and Stockins; he took with him, when he went away, a Spoon Mould, and likely Gray work'd Horse, Branded on the Shoulder, and on the near Buttock with *I. W.* Whosoever takes up said Servant, and brings him to his Master, or secures him, so that he may be had again, shall have Five Pounds Reward; and if they secures the said Horse, so that he may be had again, shall have Twenty Shillings Reward, Paid by me.
*Simon Hadly.*
*The American Weekly Mercury*, From Thursday November 6, to Thursday November 13, 1729; From Thursday November 13, to Thursday November 20, 1729. See *The American Weekly Mercury*, From Thursday October 23, to Thursday October 30, 1729.


*New-Castle* County, ss.
ON the 13th day of *October* last, a Strange Negroe Man, was taken up as a Run-away, in *Miln Creek* Hundred in this County; He is a Low sized Slender and nimble Fellow, seems to be about Twenty five Years old; has a large Head, small Hands and Legs, looks Wild and Staring, wears a Brown Jacket, ragged black Shirt, short Ozenbriggs Trowsers, with a Pair of Leather Breeches underneath; he seems, as if he cannot Speak or understand English, or the Language of any of the Negroes of this Place; so that 'tis not yet known here, to whom, or where, he belongs. Whoever know's the said Negroe, or his Oyner; are desired to make the same known to the Sheriff of the said County, *Wm. Read.*
*The American Weekly Mercury*, From Thursday November 6th, to Thursday November 13th, 1729; From Thursday November 13, to Thursday November 20, 1729; From Thursday November 20, to

Thursday November 27, 1729. See *The American Weekly Mercury*, From Thursday, July 16, to Thursday, July 23, 1730.

RUN away from the Widow *Anne John's*, of the *Welsh-Tract*, in *New-Castle-*County, the 2d of this Instant *December*, 1729. a Servant Man named *John Macquire*, of a Middle Stature, with a Fresh Countenance, a Grey full Eye, with Brown short Hair a little Curled, he goes Stooping in the Shoulders, about 20 Years of Age; having on a Brown Broad-Cloth Coat, the fore Part Lined with Brown Shalloone, a Linnen and Woollen Blew Jacket, Lin'd with Course Tow-Linnen, with Brass Buttons, a good Fine Shirt, a Felt Hat, a Pair of Dark coloured Stockings, and good Shoes. Whoever shall take up the said Servant, and secure him, or convey him to his said Mistress, or give Notice to *Thomas John's* of the *Welsh Tract*, shall have Forty Shillings Reward, and reasonable Charges, paid by me      *Thomas John's*.

*The American Weekly Mercury*, From Thursday December 4, to Tuesday December 9, 1729; From Tuesday December 9, to Tuesday December 16, 1729.

## 1730

*Apoquinomy, February* 24, 1729-30.
Stolen from the Subscriber, about a Month ago, by two Men that run away from these Parts, the one named — *Parker*, the other *Thomas Anderson*, and were seen in *Baltimore* County, a bright Bay Horse, branded on the Buttock with O, and has a white Spot on one of his Cheeks, shod all round, (tho' they may be pull'd off,) with a thin Main hanging smooth over to the right Side, and paces very well, near Fourteen Hands high. Whoever secures the said Horse, so that the Owner may have him again, shall have Two Pistoles Reward, paid by      *Richard Cantwell*.

*The American Weekly Mercury*, From Tuesday, February 24, to Tuesday, March 3, 1729-30; From Tuesday, March 3, to Tuesday, March 10, 1729-30.From Tuesday, March 10, to Tuesday, March 17, 1729-30.


RUN away on the 5th of this Instant from *Samuel Eves*, near *New-Castle* on *Delaware*, Sadler, a Servant Man named *Benjamin Berry*. He is of middle Stature but slender, of a fair Complexion, short brown Hair, somewhat ruddy in his Cheeks; speaks very plain English, but somewhat drawing. He had on a half-wore Raccoon Hat; white corded dimmity Jacket, too long for him; two homespun Shirts and a short brown Jacket with him; a whitish Coat much worn, Leather Breeches, black and white Stockins and good Shoes. Whoever

secures the said Servant, and brings him home to his said Master, or gives Notice at the *New Printing-Office* in *Philadelphia*, shall have *Twenty Shillings* Reward and reasonable Charges paid,
                                    by *Samuel Eves.*
   *The Pennsylvania Gazette,* From Thursday, May 7, to Thursday, May 14, 1730; From Thursday, May 14, to Thursday, May 21, 1730; From Thursday, May 21, to Thursday, May 28, 1730. See *The Pennsylvania Gazette,* From Tuesday, January 19, to Tuesday, January 26, 1730-31, *The Pennsylvania Gazette,* From Tuesday, February 23, to March 4, 1730-31, and *The Pennyslvania Gazette,* From May 13, to May 20, 1731.

                                                 *July* 20. 1730.
Whereas Notice was published in the *American Weekly Mercury,* and the *Maryland Gazette,* in the Months of *November* and *December* last, concerning a strange Negroe Man, in the Custody of the Sheriff of *New-Castle* County, which Negro was taken up as a Runaway, in *Mill=Creek* Hundred, in said County, on the Thirteenth Day of *October* last; and no Person has since that Time, claim'd the said Negroe, or brought any Account of him, but, by all that can be discovered, from the Account the Negroe gives of himself; it seems, his Master is a practicioner of Physick or Surgery, in some part of *Maryland* or *Virginia*. These are therefore to give Notice, That, if there be no further Account of the Master, or Owner of the said Negroe, before the Twentieth Day of *August* next, the said Negroe is to be Sold for Payment of his Prison Charges, &c. He is a short small Limb'd nimble Fellow, about Twenty five Years of Age, has a great Head, wide Mouth, and large Eyes, looks wild and staring; seems as if he cannot speak or *understand English,* nor the Language of any of the Megroes [sic] about *New*=Castle.
                      *Charles Read, Sheriff of New-Castle.*
   *The American Weekly Mercury,* From Thursday, July 16, to Thursday, July 23, 1730; From Thursday, July 30, to Thursday, August 30, 1730; From Thursday, August 6, to Thursday, August 13, 1730; From Thursday, August 13, to Thursday, August 20, 1730. See *The American Weekly Mercury,* From Thursday November 6th, to Thursday November 13th, 1729.

 

RUN away the 21st of this Instant *July*, from his Master, *James Johnson,* near *White Clay Creek,* a Servant Man named *Timothy Sullivan,* a well-set stong [sic] Man, had a small Piece cut off his right Ear, he wears a Dark Coloured Kearsey Coat, a *B*lue Jacket, and *B*uckskin Breeches, with *B*uttons of Mother of Pearl. Whoever secures the said Servant, shall have Twenty Shillings, with reasonable Charges, paid by said *Johnson,*

or by Mr. *John Henry*, at *Whiteclay*-Creek.
*The American Weekly Mercury*, From Thursday, July 23, to Thursday, July 30, 1730; From Thursday, July 30, to Thursday, August 6, 1730; From Thursday, August 6, to Thursday, August 13, 1730; From Thursday, August 13, to Thursday, August 20, 1730.


RUN away on the 17th Instant, from *James Armitage*, Esq; of the County of *New-Castle* on *Delaware*, an Irish Servant Man, named *Richard Hall*, about 22 Years of Age, pretty tall and slender, strait black Hair if not cut off, a piece cropt off one of his Ears, brownish great Coat, close-bodied Coat, Wastecoat and Breeches, with Mohair Buttons, new Shoes full of small Nails; it is supposed he hath a counterfeit Pass with his Masters Name to it: He took with him a little young Bay Mare, shod before, branded S L on the near Buttock; with a Saddle and snaffle Bridle with twisted Bitts; a small Gun, and several other things. RUN away at the same time (supposed to be in Company) an Irish Servant Boy about 18 Years of Age, belonging to the Widow *Watson* of the Place aforesaid; he is short and well sett, short light-colour'd curled Hair, named Charles Levett; has with him a whitish great Coat with brass Buttons, Leather Breeches; took with him a black Horse with a Star in the Forehead, not shod, branded with **T** on the near Shoulder, and **W** on the near Buttock, with a breasted Saddle, and several other things. Whoever secures the said Servants, so that they may be had again, shall have *Fifty Shillings* Reward, for each, and reasonable Charges
paid by *James Armitage*.
*The Pennsylvania Gazette*, From Thursday, November 12. to Thursday, November 19. 1730; From Thursday, November 19. to Thursday, November 26. 1730; From Thursday, November 26. to Thursday, December 3. 1730. See *The American Weekly Mercury*, From Thursday, November 26, to Thursday, December 3, 1730.


*November* 24.
RUN the 17th Day of this Instant, November, from *James Armitage*, Esq; of the County of *Newcastle* on *Delaware*, an *Irish* Servant Man, named *Richard Hall*, aged about 22 Years, pretty tall and slender, strait black Hair if he hath not cut it off since he went away; he hath a piece cropt off one of his Ears; Had on a brownish Great Coat, Close Bodied Coat, Wastcoat and Breeches with Mohair Buttons, new Shoes full of small Nails in the Soles; It is supposed he hath a Counterfeit Pass with his Master's Name to it. He took away with him a little young Bay Mare with two Shoes before, branded with **S. L.** on the near Buttock, a Saddle and Snaffle Bridle with twisted Bitts; a small Gun, and several other Things. Run away at the same Time and

supposed to be in Company with him, an *Irish* Servant Boy about 18 Years of age, named *Charles Lovett*, belonging to the Widow *Watson* of the Place aforesaid; he is a thick short well sett Boy, with short lightish Coloured Hair, he had on a whitish Coloured Great Coat, with Brass Buttons, a grey Coat and Wastcoat with Brass Buttons, and Leather Breeches. He took also from his Mistress a Black Horse with a Star in his Forehead, branded with the Letter **T** on the near Shoulder, with **W** on the near Buttock, having no Shoes, a Breasted Saddle and old Bridle, with several other Things. Whoever secures the said Servants, and gives Notice to their said Master, shall have Forty Shillings Reward and Reasonable Charges,
                    paid by me, *James Armitage.*

    *The American Weekly Mercury,* From Thursday, November 26, to Thursday, December 3, 1730. See *The Pennsylvania Gazette,* From Thursday, November 12, to Thursday, November 19, 1730.

                                      *New Castle, Decem.* 30.
RUN away from *Abraham Gudding*, Coroner of this County, a Servant Man named *John Fryer*, formerly Servant to Col. *French*, deceas'd, a middle siz'd Man, well set, black complection, wears his own Hair which is strait and black, has a Scar under his Chin having once attempted to cut his Throat: His Cloaths are dark colour'd and made fashionable, with a great Coat of the same colour, and probably for want of Shoes wears his Boots. He was sold out of this Prison by the Sheriff on the 24th Instant, having been try'd for breaking open the Store of Mr. *John Read*, out of which he stole sundry Goods. Whosoever secures him will do good Service to the Publick and shall have *Forty Shillings* Reward with reasonable Charges paid, by *Abraham Gudding.*

    *The Pennsylvania Gazette,* From Tuesday December 29, to January 5, 1730-31; From Tuesday January 5, to Tuesday January 12, 1731; From Tuesday January 12, to Tuesday January 19, 1730-31; From Tuesday January 19, to Tuesday January 26, 1730-31.

## 1731

RUN away on the 12th of the Instant, from *Samuel Eves,* near *New- Castle,* Sadler, two servant men, viz. *Benjamin Berry,* of middle stature, but slender; speaks good English, but somewhat drawing; fresh fair complection, grey eyes, short strait brown hair: had on an old beaver hat with large brims, a blueish grey home-spun plain-made coat much worn, with brass buttons set with glass; old leather breeches patch'd on both knees, yarn stockings; and old shoes, with a hole cut in the instep, and nails in the soal. The other is a middle-siz'd man, fresh full face, much pock-broken, wears a cap, and an old felt hat, ozenbrigs shirt, a light-colour'd drugget coat, broke on the shoulders,

with mohair buttons, leather breeches; yarn stockings much darn'd, old shoes, with nails. They have a counterfeit pass with them: it is thought they will change their names and alter their habit. Whoever secures them shall have *Three Pounds* Reward and reasonable charges
paid, *by Samuel Eves.*
*The Pennsylvania Gazette,* From Tuesday, January 19, to Tuesday, January 26; From Tuesday, January 26, to Tuesday, February 2, 1731. See *The Pennsylvania Gazette,* From Thursday, May 7, to Thursday, May 14, 1730, *The Pennsylvania Gazette,* From Tuesday, February 23, to March 4, 1730-31, *The Pennyslvania Gazette,* From May 13, to May 20, 1731, for Berry.


RUN away the 26th of *December*, 1730, from Hugh Durborow of the County of *Kent*, on *Delaware*, a Servant Man named *James Cahoone*, aged about 18 Years, of Middle Stature, fair Complexion, round full Visage, much sign of the Small-Pox, strait Hair of a brown or a light brown colour, a small stoppage in his Speech, which causeth him to shut his Lips and Eyes close sometimes before he utters his Words; had on when he went away, new Shoes, new Stockings made of natural black Wool, new Vest and Breeches of Linsey Woolsey, the Vest strip'd the Breeches light colour, (a black Coat, which 'tis said he has not now with him) an old Hat. Any Person securing the said Servant, so that his Master may have him again, shall have Twenty Shillings Reward and reasonable Charges, paid by me,
*Hugh Durborow,* jun.
*The American Weekly Mercury,* From Tuesday, January 26, to Tuesday February 2, 1731; From Tuesday, February 2, to Tuesday February 9, 1731; From Tuesday, February 16, to Wednesday, February 24, 1731.


RUN away on the 22d of *February* past, from *Samuel Eves* near *New-Castle*, Sadler, a Servant Man named *Benjamin Berry*, middle siz'd, but slender, fresh-colour'd, his Hair lately cut off, speaks good English but somewhat drawing, has grey Eyes, Nose somewhat sharp and a little dropping. Has on an old Beaver Hat, with large Brims, an ozenbrigs Shirt with Buttons of the same, a blueish grey homespun Coat very ragged, leather Breeches patch'd on both Knees, black worsted Stockings much broken, old Shoes. He ran away the 12th of *January* last, and was enter'd in this *Gazette*, taken, and was but 2 days out of Prison before he went away again. Whoever secures him so that his Master may have him again, shall have *Twenty Shillings* Reward, and reasonable Charges paid by me    *Samuel Eves.*
*The Pennsylvania Gazette,* From Tuesday, February 23, to March 4, 1730-31; From Thursday, March 4, to Thursday, March 11. 1730-31;

From Thursday, March 11. to Thursday, March 18. 1730-31. See *The Pennsylvania Gazette*, From Thursday, May 7, to Thursday, May 14, 1730; *The Pennsylvania Gazette*, From Tuesday, January 19, to Tuesday, January 26, 1730-31, and *The Pennyslvania Gazette*, From May 13, to May 20, 1731.

RUN away on the 26th of March past, from Edward Thomas, of Red lion Hundred in the County of New-Castle, a Servant Man named Owen Jones a Welshman, of a middle Stature, about 25 Years of Age, is indifferent fat and well set, and hath no Beard. He had on two homespun dark colour'd Jackets, coarse Linen Breeches, a coarse Shirt, black and white mixed yarn Stockings, good Shoes, an old Hat and Cap. Whoever secures the said Servant so that his Master may have him again shall have Twenty Shillings Reward, and reasonable Charges paid, by me,      Edward Thomas.
*The Pennsylvania Gazette*, From Thursday April 1, to Thursday April 8, 1731; From Thursday April 8, to Thursday April 15, 1730; From Thursday April 15, to Thursday April 22, 1731.

RUN away on the 5th Instant from *Samuel Eves* near *New-Castle*, Sadler, a Servant Man named *Benjamin Berry*, of middle size but slender, fresh fair Complexion, speaks good English but a little drawing; grey Eyes, sharp Nose a little dropping, his hair brown about an inch long. Has with him a old Beaver Hat, a brown great Coat torn up the back, with some Holes, and a double cape; homespun Shirt, ozenbrigs Trowsers, white stockings, good shoes without buckles. Also a Duroy Coat of a dirty grey colour, about half-worn, made very plain, much too short for him, which he stole since he went away. He is wont to change his Name to *George Grub* or *John Hart*, can write a good Hand, and perhaps has made a counterfeit Pass. 'Tis thought he is gone towards *Durham Iron Works* or *Sopus*. Whoever secures the said Servant, so that his Master may have him again, shall have Forty Shillings Reward, and reasonable Charges paid by
Samuel Eves.
*The Pennsylvania Gazette*, From May 13, to May 20, 1731; From May 20, to May 27, 1731; From May 27, to June 3, 1731. See *The Pennsylvania Gazette*, From Thursday May 7, to Thursday May 14, 1730; *The Pennsylvania Gazette*, From Tuesday January 19, to Tuesday January 26, 1731; *The Pennsylvania Gazette*, From Tuesday February 23, to March 4, 1731, *The Pennsylvania Gazette*, From May 13, to May 20, 1731 for Berry.

## 1732

RUN *away the* 21*st of this Instant, from Thomas Smith, Shopkeeper, at New-Castle, a Servant Man of middle Stature, with light short Hair, a Mole on his left Cheek, pale Complexion. Has with him an old ruffel'd Shirt, a striped Jacket, and a red & white Handkerchief. 'Tis supposed that he has a false Pass, and that he has taken a Horse with him. Whoever secures the said Servant so that his Master may have him again, shall have Twenty Shillings Reward, and all reasonable Charges paid,*
      *by me* Thomas Smith.
 *The Pennsylvania Gazette*, From September 18, to September 26, 1732; From September 26, to October 5, 1732.

RUN away, the 3d of this Instant *Nov.* from *William Battell*, Post-Master, in *New-Castle*, a Servant Woman named *Christian Read*, about 20 Years old, red Hair, Fat and well Complexion'd, speaks fast and bold, is fond of her Singing and Dancing; she had on when she went away a new Plat Bonnet lined with red Silk which she stole in *New-Castle* Fair, a small flower'd Calico round Gown red and white, and other under Cloaths convenient. She went in Company with one *Ann Bargain*, a little hump back'd Woman, who Travels with a Brief and intends for *Brunswick* and *New-York*. Whoever will secure the said Servant and give Notice so that she may be had again, shall have *Forty Shillings* and all reasonable Charges,
    paid by *William Battell.*
 *The American Weekly Mercury*, From Thursday November 16, to Thursday November 23, 1732; From Thursday November 23, to Thursday November 30, 1732; From Thursday December 7, to Tuesday December 12, 1732.

## 1733

RUN *away* March 15. *from* Thomas Moore *of Brandewyne Hundred in New-Castle County, a Servant Man named* Joseph Knight, *a short, thick, well-set Fellow, longish thick black Hair, fresh coloured, and very bold spoken. He had on a new Kersey double breasted Jacket faced with red, with brass Buttons, a new Felt Hat, Leather Breeches, and blackish brown Stockings. Whoever secures the said Servant, so that he may be had again, shall have Twenty-five Shillings Reward, and reasonable Charges*
     *paid, by* Tho. Moor.
 *The Pennsylvania Gazette*, From March 15, to March 22, 1733; From March 22, to March 29, 1733.

*RUN away from* Kent *upon* Delaware, *last Sunday, one* Timothy Packom, *a Blacksmith by Trade, a Tall Man much Pockfretten. Had on when he went away a darkish coloured Coat, a blueish Duroy Coat under it, Leather Breeches, white Thread Stockings, and new Hat. Any Person that secures the said* Timothy Packom *in any Prison, or sends him to* Evan Jones *in* Kent *upon* Delaware, *or gives Notice so that he may be had again, shall have* Five Pounds *reward and reasonable Charges*
*paid by Evan Jones.* April 5.
*The Pennsylvania Gazette,* From April 5, to April 12, 1733; From April 12, to April 19, 1733.


RUN away from *Peter Henrickson* of *Christeen* Hundred in *New-Castle* County, the 6th of *May* last, a Servant Lad about 16 Years old, named *Robert Baird,* of short Stature, thin Vissag'd, short brown Hair, had on a Linsey Wolsey Jacket, Felt Hat, homespun Shirt and Drawers, black Stockings and half worn Shoes. He formerly belonged to Capt. *Abel Cane* and *George Mifflin* of *Philadelphia.* Any Person that brings the said Servant to his Master, or secures him so that he may have him, again, shall have *Forty Shillings* Reward and reasonable Charges,
paid by me *Peter Henrickson.*
*The American Weekly Mercury,* From Thursday June 7, to Thursday June 14, 1733; From Thursday June 14, to Thursday June 21, 1733.


Dover in *Kent-County* on *Delaware, Sept,* 8, 1733.
WHEREAS one *George Helm,* an *Irishman,* of small Stature, much Pock-pitted, of a ruddy Complexion, speaks fast and thick, and has a blemish on one Eye, broke out of the Goal of *Dover* on the 6th Instant and made his Escape. He had on a gray Broadcloath Jacket, a pair of Trousers and a half worn Felt Hat.

Whoever takes up the said *George* and secures him so that he may be had again, shall have *Five Pounds* Reward,
paid by *Thomas Tarrant.*
*The American Weekly Mercury,* From Thursday August 6, to Thursday September 13, 1733 [*sic*]; From Thursday September 13, to Thursday September 20, 1733; From Thursday September 20, to Thursday September 27, 1733.

## 1734

RUN away from *Cornelius Toby* of *New-Castle* County, a Servant Named *John Gallaway,* a slender young Fellow, fair hair'd, with a large Nose, he is

about 19 or 20 Years of Age, had on when he went away a new Felt Hat, a course Shirt, a half worn Duroy Coat, striped Ticken Jacket much worn, an old pair of Buckskin Breeches, Yarn Stockings and course Shoes Whoever takes up said Servant and secures him so that his Master may have him again, shall have *Fifteen Shillings* as a Reward and all reasonable Charges,
paid by me     *Cornelius Toby.*
*The American Weekly Mercury*, From Thursday March 24, to Thursday April 4, 1734; From Thursday April 18, to Thursday April 25, 1734.


RUN away from *Alexander Draper* of *Sussex* County on *Delaware*, a Negro Man named *David*, he is about 30 Years of Age, had on an old whiteish colour'd Jacket and a pair of Linnen Breeches with open Knees. He says he can Read and Wright, [*sic*] and that he is a Carpenter by Trade. He took with him a broad Ax. Whoever takes up the said Negro and secures him so that he may be had again shall have *Four Pounds* Reward, and reasonable Charges,
paid by     *Alexander Draper.*
*The American Weekly Mercury*, From Thursday May 30, to Thursday June 6, 1734; From Thursday June 13, to Thursday June 20, 1734; From Thursday June 27, to Thursday July 4 1734.


RUN away from *Stephen Lewis*, Tanner, in *New-Castle*, Servant Man named *Morgan Jones*, of a midling Stature, pretty long sandy colour'd Hair, red Beard, long Vizag'd and very homely, he has an old look tho' he is but 25 Years of Age, by Trade a Tenner, [*sic*] he is a Welch Man and speaks English broad; had on when he went away a half worn Felt Hat, new Ozenbrigs Shirt, an old grey Kersey Coat, plain, without Pleats and Brass Buttons on it, pretty good Leather Breeches with Strings at the Knees had no Buttons, old leggings of Tow Cloath and a pair of half worn strong Shoes.
Whoever takes up the said Servant and secures him so that his Master may have him again, shall have *Forty Shillings* Reward and reasonable Charges, paid by     *Stephen Lewis.*
*The American Weekly Mercury*, From Thursday May 30, to Thursday June 6, 1734; From Thursday June 13, to Thursday June 20, 1734; From Thursday June 20, to Thursday June 27, 1734.


RUN away from *Edward Jones* of *Appoquinimank*, on the 2d of this Instant *August*, (being then at *Philadelphia*) a Servant Lad named *Benjamin Nichol*s, aged 18 or 20 Years, of slender middle Stature, had on when he went away a Kersey great Coat of a light colour, Ozenbrigs Shirt and Trowsers, an old small trim'd Hat. 'Tis supposed he is gone over the River towards *New-York*.

Whoever takes up the said Servant and brings him to *Owen Meredith* in *Front*-street, or to *John Croker* in *Strawberry*-Alley, shall have *Thirty Shillings* as a Reward besides reasonable Charges,
paid by *Edward Jones* or *Owen Meredith.*
*The American Weekly Mercury*, From Thursday August 1, to Thursday August 8, 1734; From Thursday August 15, to Thursday August 22, 1734; From Thursday August 29, to Thursday September 5, 1734.

## 1735

RUN away, sometime last Week, from *Jonathan Rayman's* Shallop lying at *Philadelphia*, an Irish Servant Man named *Andrew Dowdall*, aged 28 or 30 Years, of a middle Stature, a dark brown Complexion, wearing his own Hair and a Suit of homespun or Country made Cloth. Whoever shall take up the said Servant and deliver him to his Master dwelling at *Duck*-Creek, or to *James Steel* in *Philadelphia*, shall have *Forty Shillings* Reward,
*May* 14. 1735.
*The American Weekly Mercury*, From Thursday May 8, to Thursday May 15, 1735; From Thursday May 22, to Thursday May 29, 1735.


RUN away, the 24th of *April* last, from *John Whitside*, at *Duck-Creek* in *New-Castle* County, a Servant Man named *Robert Clark*, about 20 Years of age, an *Irishman*, he is a good Scholler and pretends to the Sea, he is pretty tall and straight, of a ruddy Complexion, and short brown Hair or a fair Natural Wig, had on a blue Coat and Vest, brown Stuff Breeches, gray Yarn Stockings and Shoes with picked Toes. [sic] Whoever takes up and secures the said Servant so that his Master may have him again, shall have *Twenty Shillings* Reward and reasonable Charges,
paid by me    *John Whitside.*
*The American Weekly Mercury*, From Thursday May 15th, to Thursday May 22, 1735; From Thursday May 22 to Thursday May 29, 1735; From Thursday May 29, to Thursday June 4, 1735.


ON the 9*th* of *Dec.* Inst. the Store House of *John Read* in *New-Munster*, near the Head of *Elk*-River, was broken up, and sundry Valuable Goods taken out. It was done by two transient Fellows, suppos'd to come from *Marshy-hope*, in *Kent* County, upon *Delaware.*

The one a Tall Fellow, of a *Swedish* swarthy Complexion. Had on a light colour'd great Coat with Brass Buttons, a blue strait Coat with broad white metal Buttons, a Pair of red Indian Leggings. The fore part of his Head shav'd, and on the remainder of his Head long brown Hair. He has large heavy Brows.

The other a middle siz'd Fellow of a sowre down look, has black frizzel'd Hair: Had on an old blue great Coat bound about the Edges with blue Quality binding, and a blue strait Coat with metal Buttons without sleeves; a pair of Sliders and Buskins button'd down to his Shoes.

They both had old Shoes ty'd with Thongs, and sometimes wear Caps

One goes by the Name of *John Smith*, and the other by the Name of *James Duddley*.

They have taken with them some remarkable Goods, viz. One piece of Cinnamon colour'd narrow Persian, one piece of dark Ratteen, one Dozen of fine gray Stockings, one piece of fine Chints, fine Hats, one Remnant of blue Broad Cloth, with several other Goods.

Whoever takes up said Robbers, with said Goods shall have *Five Pounds* Reward and reasonable Charges
                paid by me    *John Read*.

*The American Weekly Mercury*, From Tuesday December 18, to Tuesday December 23, 1735; From Tuesday December 23, to Tuesday December 30, 1735; From Tuesday December 30, to Tuesday January 5, 1735-36; From Tuesday January 6, to Tuesday January 13, 1736. See *The Pennsylvania Gazette*, From December 18, to December 24, 1735.

## 1736

RAN-away the 24th of *Jan.* past, from *Thomas Tarrant* of *Dover*, in *Kent* County on *Delaware*, an Irish Servant Boy named *Michael Brown*, a Taylor by Trade, about 16 Years of Age. He is smooth Fac'd, and bandy Leg'd; and took with him when he went away, a grey broad Cloth great Coat with flat carv'd Brass Buttons, a blue broad Cloth Coat lin'd with brown Holland, a striped Linen Vest, green Callimanco Breeches much worn, and blue worsted Stockings. It is supposed that he has taken with him a natural pacing Bay Mare with a short switch Tail.

Whoever secures the said Servant, and gives Notice thereof to his said Master, or to *Samuel Parr* of *Philadelphia*, so that he may be had again, shall have *Three Pounds* Reward and reasonable Charges
                paid by me    *Thomas Tarrant*.

*The American Weekly Mercury*, From Tuesday February 3, to Tuesday February 10, 1736; From Tuesday February 10, to Tuesday February 17, 1736; From Tuesday February 17, to Tuesday February 24, 1736.

*Run away, 2d of this Instant May a Servant Man named John Watson aged about* 40 *Years, is a short thick Man, fair Complexion, born near New-*

*Castle on Delaware lately redeemed out of Bergin County Goal by Cornelius Wynkoop and Elizabeth Anthony, storekeepers, in the said County, for a Considerable Sum of Money, he had on when he went away a Duroys Coat light brown, a Kersey Coat dark Brown, with Brass Buttons, a Striped Holland Wastcoat and Britches of the same, wears a Wigg or Cap, is very subject to Drink, it is supposed that he has with him a Negro Man named Johnny a middle Sized slender Fellow, Pock broken, about 35 Years of Age, is a very good Cooper, speaks English, French and Dutch and can read and Write, had on an torn Gray Great Coat, who other Cloath is uncertain, his Masters Name is Peter Valleau. There is also with them another Negro Fellow, named Cato, aged about 22 Years, a likely Fellow,—some thing taller than the above described and some thing thicker a Native of Madagascar, speaks good English and Dutch had on when he went away, a black homespun Coat with Brass Buttons, a striped homespun jacket and homespun Stockins, had with him two aair [sic] of new Shooes.*
  *The New-York Journal, May 10, 1736; May 17, 1736.*


*RUN away from* Richard James *of* Kent *County on* Delaware, *three Servants, viz. A Man* 30 *odd Years, and his two Sons, the name of the eldest is* Daniel, *and the other* John, *their Father's name is* Robert Roberts, *tho' he often changes his name, he is a lusty Man of a swarthy Complexion, long brown Hair, he lives with his Wife and two Sons on the Widow* Newberry's *Plantation, near* Benjamin Moor's *at* Ancocus-Creek *in* Burlington *County, but sheltered by some so that their Master cannot get them. His Wife is very near her time but it is supposed they will soon move from thence. Whosoever secures and brings them to the Sheriff in* Philadelphia, *or to their Master, shall have Five Pounds reward, and reasonable Charges*
  *paid, by* Richard James.
  *The Pennsylvania Gazette,* From May 20, to May 27, 1736; From May 27, to June 3, 1736; From June 3, to June 10, 1736. The second and third ads shows the father as "aged 35 Years".


*RUN away from* William Beeks *of* New-Castle, *an* English *Servant Man named* William Darlington, *formerly a Servant to* Jacob Metcalf, *opposite to* Philadelphia, *and afterwards to* George Hargrave *back of* Burlington, *aged about* 30 *Years, of middle Stature, light brown strait Hair, brown Complexion, down look, wheyish Beard; Had on when he went away, a white corded Fustian Jacket, much worn and too big for him, good ozenbrigs Shirt, new ozenbrigs Trowsers, Felt Hat. Note, He was sent to Town with Horses to return to* New-Castle, *and has absented himself from the Three Tuns.*

*Whosoever secures the said Servant so that he may be had again, shall have* Thirty Shillings *Reward and reasonable Charges paid.*
William Beeks.
*The Pennsylvania Gazette*, July 8, to July 15, 1736; From July 15, to July 22, 1736.


*RUN away on the 6th Inst. from Archibald Beard of* Mill-Creek Hundred *in the County of* New-Castle, *a Servant Man named Dennis O Loug, he squints with one Eye, and has a swell'd sore Leg: Had on a Felt Hat, a brownish Coat and Jacket, coarse Shirt and Trowsers of Tow Cloth, and single Pumps. Whoever secures the said Servant so that he may be had again, shall have Forty Shillings Reward and reasonable Charges paid by*
Philad. Sept. 16, 1736.    Archibald Beard.
*The Pennsylvania Gazette*, From September 9, to September 16,1736; From September 16, to September 23, 1736; From September 23, to September 30, 1736; From September 30, to October 7, 1736.


TAken up on the 19*th* of *November*, in St George's Hundred, in the County of *New-Castle*, a tall lusty Negro Man, who talks little or no English, and so cannot give an account of who he belongs to; but (by what can be found out by his Motions) it is thought he came lately by Water from some Part. He was found quite Naked, and his Beard was as long as the Wooll on his Head.
Whoever has lost such a Negro may apply to *Garret Dushen*, at the Trap, in the Hundred and County aforesaid, who has taken him up, and if they can prove their Right to him they may have him again.
*The American Weekly Mercury*, From Thursday December 9, to Thursday, December 16, 1736; From Thursday December 16, to Thursday, December 23, 1736.

## 1737

RAN-away, about the 28*th* of *December* last, from his Master the Subscriber, in *New-Castle*, a servant Boy named *Thomas McBride*, last Fall imported from *Ireland*, aged about 13 Years, well set, black Eyes, yet having a Pearl in one of them, at first Sight he seems to Squint, looks staring, is of a swarthy Complexion, forward, talkative, and fond of Singing; had short dark brown Hair, and wore a coarse worsted single English Cap, linsey woolsey brown Jacket with brass Buttons and red stuff Lining, brown Cloth or Kersey Breeches unlin'd, having brass Buttons and the back part of the Waistband mended with old Doe skin, white yarn Stockings, one of his Shoe-Buckles Brass the other Iron.

Whoever takes up and brings him to his Master, shall be well Rewarded,
By *Henry Gonne.*

*The American Weekly Mercury,* From Thursday January 13, to Tuesday January 18, 1736; [*sic*] From Tuesday January 18, to Tuesday, January 25, 1737; From Thursday February 3, to Tuesday, February 8, 1737.


RAN-away (about Three Months since) from *William Howel,* living at *Christiana* Bridge, an Irish Servant Man named *James MacMullen,* about 40 Years of Age, a short well-set Fellow, but of thin Visage. He had on when he went away, a light colour'd Irish Kersey Coat, dark gray Jacket, Buck-skin Breeches, white Stockings, and good Shoes.

It is supposed that he is gone towards *Connestogoe.*

Whoever takes up said Servant and returns him to his said Master, shall have *Forty Shillings* Reward and all reasonable Charges,
paid by *William Howell.*

*The American Weekly Mercury,* From Thursday April 14, to Thursday April 21, 1737; From Thursday April 21, to Thursday April 28, 1737; From Thursday April 28, to Thursday May 5, 1737.


RAN-away from *David Cloyd* of *Mill-Creek-Hundred,* in the County of *New-Castle,* (a few days since) a Servant Man named *Alexander MacCurdey,* about 19 Years of Age, of middling Stature, has fair Hair and a down Look. He had on a new brown Coat, with flat Metal Buttons, had no Jacket, a pair of large Trowsers and dirty Drawers, and dirty Shirt, and an half worn Felt Hat. He has Stole two Linen Shirts, one of them fine, and the other Coarse, and a pair of Womens Shoes with flat Leather Heels.

Whoever shall take up said Servant, (if above 5 Miles from home) and return him to his said Master shall have *Thirty Shillings* Reward and all reasonable Charges paid       By *David Cloyd.*

*The American Weekly Mercury,* From Thursday May 19, to Thursday May 26, 1737; From Thursday May 26, to Thursday June 2, 1737; From Thursday June 2, to Thursday June 9, 1737.


WENT from on board the *St. Andrew,* at *New-Castle,* on the 24th of *November* last, a Servant Man named *Nathan MacClure,* belonging to *William Hartley.* He is about 30 Years of Age, of middling Stature; has a broad Face, red Hair (but sometimes wears a Cap or Wig) and is much Pock Fretten. He had on a blue Coat, his other Cloaths unknown.

Whoever secures the said Servant and brings him to *Walter Denny* in *Lancaster* County and Township of *Dromore,* or to *William Hartley* at

*Matthias Alpden's,* Merchant in *Philadelphia,* shall have *Thirty Shillings* Reward and reasonable Charges paid
  By *Walter Denny,* or *William Hartley.*
  *N. B.* If the said *Nathan MacClure* will come of his own accord, immediately after the publication hereof, to the said *Denny* or *Hartley,* he shall be used with Civility, paying them their just Demands: But if any Persons shall Entertain or Conceal him, they shall be prosecuted according to Law.
  *The American Weekly Mercury,* From Thursday June 9, to Thursday June 16, 1737; From Thursday June 16, to Thursday June 23, 1737; From Thursday June 23, to Thursday June 30, 1737.


RAN-away on the 12th of *November* past, from the Subscriber, of *Sussex* County on *Delaware,* an Irish Servant Man named *David Finly,* by Trade a Blacksmith, is of middling Stature, has short dark Hair, and a Scar on the right side of his upper Lip, about an Inch long, which is almost right up and down. He had on when he went away, a checquer'd Shirt, a blue & white strip'd Flannel Jacket, a seersucker Vest lin'd with Linnen, a white Duroy close bodied Coat, a white old Great Coat, a pair of white Stockings newly footed, and a pair of Oznabrigs Trowsers. He rode on a white Horse that had but one Eye.
  Whoever takes up the said Servant and secures him so that the Subscriber may have him again, shall have *Three Pounds* Reward, and all reasonable Charges, paid  By *John Shankland.*
  *The American Weekly Mercury,* From Thursday November 24, to Thursday December 1, 1737; From Thursday December 1, to Thursday December 8, 1737; From Thursday December 8, to Thursday December 15, 1737. See *The Pennsylvania Gazette,* November 24, to December 1, 1737.


*RUN away on the* 12*th of Novemb. past, from the Subscriber, living in* Sussex *County, an* Irish *Servant Man named* David Finly, *by Trade a Blacksmith, of middle Stature, short dark Hair, and hath a scar on the right side of his upper Lip about an Inch long, which scare is up and down or Perpendicular: Was Clothed when he went away, with a checker'd Shirt, a blue and white stripp'd flannel Jacket, a seersucker Vest lin'd with Linnen, a white duroy close bodied Coat, a white old great Coat, a pair of white stockings newly footed, and a pair of ozenbrigs Trowsers, He rode on a white Horse, that has but one Eye.*
  *Whoever secures the said Servant , so that his Master may have him again, shall have Three Pounds Reward, and reasonable Charges*

*paid by* John Shankland.

*The Pennsylvania Gazette*, November 24, to December 1, 1737; December 1, to December 8, 1737. See *The American Weekly Mercury*, From Thursday November 24, to Thursday December 1, 1737.

## 1738

*RUN away from Capt.* James Chalmers *of* Willingtown *in the County of* New-Castle *upon* Delaware, *an English Servant Man, named* William Alton, *a short well set Man, pock mark'd, grey ey'd, short brownish Hair, his Nose somewhat crooked: Had on when he went away a brown cloth Coat lin'd with red, a dark-colour'd homespun Coat lin'd with a Linseywoolsey of a yellowish colour, Scotch Plad Breeches with Straps and Knee-Buckels, two pair of Stockings the one white yarn the other of a brownish colour, a pair of Pumps with plain brass Buckels in them, two ozenbrigs Shirts and a check'd one, a Felt Hat, sometimes wears a Cap, a Silk Handkerchief about his Neck, he is a Brickmaker by Trade, but can Weave and work well at the Smith's; he is inclinable to Drink and is Quarrelsome.*

*Any Person that secures the said Servant so that his Master may have him again, shall have* Forty Shillings *Reward and reasonable Charges paid by* Jenet Chalmers.
Willingtown Feb. 2 1737.8

*The Pennsylvania Gazette*, From February 7, to February 15, 1738; From February 15, to February 21, 1738; From February 21, to February 28, 1738; From February 28, to March 7, 1738; From March 7, to March 14, 1738.


RAN-away from *Thomas Noxon* of *New-Castle* County, on the 29th of *January* last, a Servant Man named *Thomas Loe*, aged about 21 Years. He is of a middling Stature and Slender, very smooth Fac'd, has black Hair a little Bushy, and scarce any Beard. He took with him, amongst other Things, a new pair of Leather Breeches, a cloth pair with Scraps at the Knee-bands: He wore a pair of large brass plain Shoe-buckles, and had divers sorts of good Apparel with him. He has also with him, an Indenture, by which he served a Time in the upper part of *Chester* County in *Pennsylvania*, with a Discharge thereon, in which he became Bound in the City of *Bristol* in *Great-Britain*.

Whoever takes up the said Servant, & brings him to the aforesaid *Thomas Noxon*, or commits him to the Gaol at *New-Castle*, shall have *Thirty Shillings* paid him as a Reward.

By *Thomas Noxon*.

*The American Weekly Mercury*, From Tuesday February 21, to Tuesday February 28, 1738; From Tuesday February 28, to Tuesday March 7,

1738; From Tuesday March 7, to Tuesday March 14, 1738; From Tuesday March 14, to Thursday March 23, 1738.


RAN-away on the 3d Instant, from *Wm. Patterson*, at *Christiana* Bridge, a Servant Man nam'd *John McDowell*, about 20 Years of Age, well Set, and fresh colour'd, and has short black Hair. He had on when he went away, a double breasted Ratteen Jacket with a brownish one under it, Leather Breeches, coarse Shirt, old Shoes, and a Felt Hat.

Whoever secures the said Servant so that his said Master may have him again, shall have *Twenty Shillings* Reward, and reasonable Charges paid by *Thomas Williams*, Hatter, in *Philadelphia*, or at *Christiana*
     By *William Patterson.*
*The American Weekly Mercury*, From Thursday March 30, to Thursday April 6, 1738.


*RUN away on the* 28*th inst. from the Subscriber hereof at Christiana Bridge, a Servant Man named* James Downing, *an* Irish *Man, he is short of Stature, black Complexion, broad Shoulders, bandy Legs, hopper-arsed, walks as if he was Hip shot: Had on when he went away, a good Felt Hat, white quilted Cap, an old drab-colour'd Broad Cloth Coat full trimm'd with open Sleeves, and no Pockets, an old reddish-colour'd Waistcoat without Sleeves, old coarse Kersey Breeches, two pair of bluish Stockings, good Shoes and Buckles, he formerly was a Servant to* Joseph Thomas *of* Pencader *Hundred in* New-Castle *County, afterwards went to* Ireland, *and came back again last Fall a Servant with Mr.* James Johnson; *he knows all Parts of the Country and is an abominable Lyar. Whoever takes up the said Runaway and brings him to his Master, or secures him so that he may be had again, shall have Twenty Shillings Reward and reasonable Charges*
March 29. 1738.    *paid by John Read.*
*The Pennsylvania Gazette*, From March 30, to April 6, 1738; From April 6, to April 13, 1738.


RUN away on the 14th of *March* past, from *David Niven* of *Mill-Creek* Hundred in *New-Castle* County, an Irish Servant Woman, named *Mary Aloan*, aged about 26 Years, short and well-set, of a swarthy Complexion, something long-visag'd, with grey Eyes: Had on when she went away, a new linsey Gown strip'd with black, blue, and white Stripes, a blue Apron, new Shoes and Stockings. Whoever secures the said Servant so that she may be had again, shall have *Forty Shillings* Reward and reasonable Charges
    paid by *David Niven.*

*The Pennsylvania Gazette*, From April 13, to April 20, 1738; From April 20, to April 27, 1738; From April 27, to May 4, 1738; From May 11, to May 18, 1738.

ON the 24th Inst. the Dwelling-House of *Benjamin Ford*, of *Brandywine* Hundred, in *New-Castle* County, was broke open, and about Two or Three and Thirty Pounds of Paper Currency and about Three Pounds in Copper stolen therefrom; and 'tis suppos'd to be done by one *John Kelly*, an Irishman, middle siz'd, with no Hair; wears a blue and white Cap, dark brown Jacket, with large brass Buckles in his Shoes, and has taken with him a little Bay Horse mark'd upon the near Buttock with *E K*.

Whoever takes up and secures the said Thief, so that he may be brought to Justice, shall have *Ten Pounds* Reward and reasonable Charges,
          paid by *Benjamin Ford*.

*The Pennslvania Gazette*, From July 27, to August 3, 1738; From August 3, to August 10, 1738.

BROKE out of the Goal at *Dover* in *Kent* County, on the 3d Inst. at Night, the two following Persons, *viz*.

*Thomas Johnson*, an Irishman, by Trade a Blacksmith, short and well set, reddish Complexion, short brown bush Hair.

*William Spencer*, by Trade a Joyner, slim in Body, of middle Stature, smooth fac'd, and clear skin'd; wears a Cap and a blue Jacket.

Whoever secures the said Persons, so that they are had again, shall have *Thirty Shillings* Reward each, and reasonable Charges,
          paid by    *Daniel Robinson*.

*The Pennsylvania Gazette*, From October 5, to October 12, 1738; From October 12, to October 19, 1738; From October 19, to October 26, 1738.

*RUN away on the 4th Inst. from John Housman, of Kent County, on Delaware, the two following English Servant Men, viz One named* John Rachford, *a lusty Fellow, pock broken, light grey Eyes, brown curl'd Hair, and stammers and swears much when in a Passion: The other named* Joseph Clay, *alias* Clayton, *a lustly broad shoulder'd Fellow, flat faced, down Look, very short black Hair. The Cloaths they took with them are mostly stolen, viz. A new Cloth colour'd German Searge Coat well trimm'd, a brown Holland Coat, green Dammask Jacket with Mother of Pearl Buttons, new Doe-skin Breeches and new Sheep-skin ones lined, good Shoes, coarse Hats, good Stockings, a Pair of Boots, and a Fowling Piece. They likewise stole a large* black Stallion, four Years old this Fall, a white Snip down his Nose, and a Flesh Diamond at the Bottom close to his Mouth, one white Foot, a large Main and Foretop; also a bright bay Gelding, about 7 Years old, of a neat Hunting Make, about 14 Hands high, branded on the near Shoulder I and near Buttock C, his Feet white, also russet-colour Saddles and Bridles.

Whoever takes up the said Servants with the Cloaths, Horses, Saddles, and Bridles, and delivers them to the Keeper of the King's Goal, at Dover, or secures them so that they are had again, shall have Ten Pounds Reward, and so in Proportion for either of the said Men, Cloaths, &c.

       *paid by*  John Housman.
October 26, 1738.

*The Pennsylvania Gazette*, From October 19, to October 26, 1738; From October 26, to November 2, 1738; From November 2, to November 8, 1738.


RUN away from *William Draper* of *Sussex* County, a Servant Man named *Henry Wingate*, Aged about 22 Years, of a tall Stature, on his left Ancle is a remarkable Scar, a brown colour'd Camlet Coat lin'd with red, a red Jacket with Silver twist Buttons.

Whoever takes up the said Servant, and brings him to his said Master, or secure him in the next County Jail, and give Notice thereof to his said Master, shall have Forty Shillings Reward, and reasonable Charges paid by *William Draper*.

*The American Weekly Mercury*, From Thursday November 16, to Thursday November 23, 1738; From Thursday November 23, to Thursday November 30, 1738; From Thursday December 7, to Thursday December 14, 1738.


# 1739

STOLEN from the Plantation of *Alexander Farquhar*, two Horses, one a dark Bay, no Brand, has a small black Spot on the nigh side of his Face: The other, white, and fleabitten, no brand; also a small Saddle of a russet colour. It is supposed that are stolen by one *Moses Lewis*, he and his Wife being seen to ride the said Horses, and a small Boy with them; the said *Lewis* is of a middle Stature, black bushy Hair much like a Wig, he is a House-Carpenter by Trade, and understands keeping a Grist Mill, he is a *New-England* Man Born.

Whoever takes up and secures the said *Lewis* so that he may be brought to Justice, shall have *Forty Shillings* Reward; and for the two Horses *Twenty Shillings* each, and reasonable Charges,

       paid by *Alexander Farquhar*.
*Kent* County on *Delaware, Jan.* 7, 1738,9.

*The Pennsylvania Gazette*, From January 4, to January 11, 1738-39; From January 11, to January 18, 1738-39; From January 18, to January 25, 1738-39.

*RUN* away on the 3d Instant, from *Thomas Thomas* of *Welch-Tract* in the County of *New-Castle* upon *Delaware*, a Servant Man, named *Charles Mc'Carter*, a Highlandman, of short stature, well set, round Visage, fresh complexion, and somewhat tawny, strait blackish Hair, his fore-Finger on both Hands turns over the others, between 35 and 40 Years of Age, talks broken *English*: Had on, a wide Coat much wore, of a darkish colour'd Cloth, a new close-bodied Coat of the same colour with Buttons of the same, new felt Hat, old blue Breeches striped with red and white, Highland plad Stockings, new Shoes, with brass Buckles not fellows, two new homespun Shirts, one with Buttons on, and the other without.

Whoever secures the said Servant so that his Master may have him again, or brings him to *Owen Owen* at the Indian King in *Philadelphia*, shall have *Four Pounds* Reward, and reasonable Charges,
           paid by    *Thomas Thomas.*

*The Pennsylvania Gazette*, From March 1, to March 8, 1738,9; From March 8, to March 15, 1738,9; From March 15, to March 22, 1739; From March 22, to March 29, 1739; From March 29, to April 5, 1739.

RUN away on the 31st of *March* past, from *Caleb Perkins* of *Brandywine Hundred* in *New-Castle* County, an *Irish* Servant Man, named *Nicholas Mc'Guire*, aged about 40 Years, a lusty well set Fellow, of a reddish Complexion, with curl'd bushy Hair, has a large Dint on one of his Cheeks, and a Wart on the other: Had on when he went away, a brownish cloth Vest, a pair of tow Trowsers, brown Cloth Breeches, yarn Stockings, good Shoes, and a felt Hat. He belong'd to *Samuel Harrison*, Esq; of *Glocester* County, *West New-Jersey*, and ran away from him.

Whoever secures the said Servant, so that his Master may have him again, shall have *Forty Shillings* Reward, and reasonable Charges,
           paid by    *Caleb Perkins.*
*Philad. April* 5. 1739.

*The Pennsylvania Gazette*, From March 29, to April 5, 1739; From April 5, to April 12, 1739; From April 12, to April 19, 1739.

RAN-away on the 25th of *March* from *William Hicklen*, in *Brandy-wine* Hundred, in *New-Castle* County, a Servant Man named *John Stevilen*, about 24 Years of age, of a midling Stature, of a very pale Complection, short brown Hair but 'tis believed he will cut it off for he has with him a light brown Wig, his under Lip is very thick and hands down a little: He had on when he went away, a new Coat and Jacket, full trim'd, of a light Colour and lined with white Linen, a pair of new Breeches but not the same of his Coat with Pewter Buttons, a felt Hat, two pair of Stockings the one white and the other a blue grey, and good Shoes.

Whoever secures the said Servant so that his Master may have him again, shall have *Three Pounds* Reward and all reasonable Charges paid by *William Hicklen.*

*The American Weekly Mercury,* From Thursday March 29, to Thursday April 5, 1739; From Thursday April 5, to Thursday April 12, 1739; From Thursday April 12, to Thursday April 19, 1739; From Thursday April 19, to Thursday April 26, 1739.


*RUN away on the 6th Inst. from the Subscriber at* Christiana *Bridge, an English Servant Man named* Abraham Lay, *a lusty well set Man, aged about 30 Years, his Hair cut off. Had on when he went, a coarse light grey doublebreasted Pea Jacket and Breeches with white metal Buttons, old Felt Hat, speckled or homespun Shirt, yarn Stockings, and old Shoes. Has lately been a fighting and is very much bruised in the Face.*

*Whoever takes up and secures the said Servant in any Goal so that his Master may have him again, shall have* Forty Shillings *Reward, and reasonable Charges paid by* Lewis Howell.

*N. B. He pretends to be a Carpenter by Trade, and is very talkative about all Affairs.*

*The Pennsylvania Gazette,* From April 5, to April 12, 1739; From April 12, to April 19, 1739; From April 19, to April 26, 1739. See *The Pennsylvania Gazette,* October 23, 1740.


*RUN away on the 19th Inst. from* Thomas Emson *at Duck-Creek, in Kent County on Delaware, a Negro Man named Caesar, a lusty well-set Fellow, complexioned something like a Molatto: Had on a flesh-colour'd Duroy Coat and Vest, old Leather Breeches, and thin broad striped Cotton Breeches under them, old homespun Shirt, old Shoes and Stockings, a new Felt Hat, and sometimes wears a black Wig. Whoever takes up and secures the said Negro in Goal, so that his Master may have him again, shall have Thirty Shillings Reward,      paid by* Thomas Emson. May 24. 1739.

*The Pennsylvania Gazette,* From May 17, to May 24, 1739; From May 24, to May 31, 1739; From May 31, to June 7, 1739; From June 7, to

June 14, 1739; From June 14, to June 21, 1739; From June 21, to June 28, 1739.

*RUN away on the* 15*th Inst. from John Huey of Mill Creek Hundred, New-Castle County, a Native Irish Servant Man, named Hugh O'Neil, about* 30 *Years of Age, six feet high, a smooth Face, of a dark Complexion, and no Hair: Had on, a white worsted Cap, new felt Hat, dark whitish colour'd Coat, spotted with Pitch or Tar, one of the fore Lappets eaten short off, Jacket of the same, with cloth Buttons, patch'd on the Breast, with a red Jacket under it, two check'd Shirts, a pair of brownish cloth Breeches, and a pair of dark olive Green, with cloth Buttons, dark grey yarn Stockings, narrow toe'd Shoes, has upon the Joints of both his great Toes Lumps greater than ordinary. Whoever secures the said Servant so that his Master may have him again, shall have Forty Shillings Reward, and reasonable Charges,*
*paid by* John Huey.
*The Pennsylvania Gazette,* October 18, 1739; October 25, 1739; November 1, 1739.

*Absconded from his Bail in* Kent *County on* Delaware, *on the* 22*d of* Octob. *one* James Williams, *aged* 22 *Years, of middle Stature, light Complexion, smooth Face with some Freckles: Had on a beaver Hat, old light colour'd Duroy Coat, two pair of Trowsers, a Jacket made of a turn'd Coat. He took with him, belonging to* Daniel Rodeney, *a small bay Horse, with a croppd Ear, and an old Saddle. Whoever secures him so that he may be had again, shall have* Forty Shillings *Reward,*
*paid by* Daniel Rodney *or* Robert Basil.
*The Pennsylvania Gazette,* November 1, 1739; November 8, 1739; November 15, 1739; November 22, 1739.

RAN-away the 10th Instant, from *Joseph Underwood,* of *Christiana Hundred,* near *Brandiwine,* a Servant Man, named *Joseph Slauter,* aged about 18 years, he is well set, very much pock fretten, has a piece of his Ear off, short black Hair, and a scold [*sic*] Head, had on when he went away, a light colour'd homespun new Coat, Jacket and Breeches, with a light colour'd great Coat, good Shoes and Stockings, and has a Gun with him. He rides on a little light grey Mare, between four and five Years old, shod before, trim'd Mane, and no mark, has an old Russel leather Saddle, and a good Bridle.

Whoever takes up and secures said Servant so that his Master may have him again, shall have *Forty Shillings* Reward and reasonable Charges
paid By *Joseph Underwood.*

*The American Weekly Mercury*, From Thursday December 13, to Thursday December 20, 1739; From Thursday December 20, to Thursday December 27, 1739; From Thursday December 27, to Thursday January 3, 1739. [*sic*]

## 1740

RUN away on the 21st Inst. from *Valentine Robinson*, of *Brandewyne Hundred*, *New Castle* County, a Mulatto Girl, named *Rose Hugin*, aged about 26 Years, of middle Stature and slender, long visag'd, and well featur'd, with two or three of her fore upper Teeth out. Had on an ash-coloured homespun Gown of worsted Drugget, a striped linsey-wolsey Petticoat, good Stockings and wooden heel'd Shoes, a Platt Bonnet lined with light red Silk, good linnen Shifts, Aprons and Handkerchiefs.
Whoever takes up said Mulatto and delivers her to *Owen Owen*, in *Philadelphia*, shall have *Twenty* Shillings Reward and reasonable Charges paid by *Valentine Robinson*.
*January* 29, 1739,40.
*The Pennsylvania Gazette*, January 29, 1740; February 7, 1740; February 21, 1740.


*THomas Thomas* went away from *Lewis-Town*, in Sussex County, on *Delaware*, on the 6th of this Instant, he is of middle Stature, and pretty clear Complection, Pockfretten, and a Hair Mole on his Left Check; he had on a Check Shirt, a light colour'd Cloth Coat, a double-breasted Jacket of a Drab colour, old Breeches of Saganet, and a pair of Boots. He is round Shouldred [*sic*] and wears a white Wigg, he has the Itch and walks much like one that has the Pox. He goes by several Names unknown to us.
Whoever secures the said Man in some Goal, and gives Notice thereof to Christopher *Toppam* at *Lewis-Town*, shall have *Forty Shillings* Reward and all reasonable Charges.
*The American Weekly Mercury*, From Tuesday March 11, to Thursday, March 20, 1739, 40; From Thursday March 20, to Thursday, March 27, 1740; From Thursday March 27, to Thursday, April 3, 1740; From Thursday April 3, to Thursday, April 10, 1740; From Thursday April 10, to Thursday, April 17, 1740.


RUN away the 20th Inst. from *Thomas Barr*, of *Millcreek* Hundred, *Newcastle* County, an *Irish* Servant Lad, named *William Mourton*, aged about 23 Years, of middle stature, well set, of a red Complexion, and no Hair; had on when he went away, a narrow brimm'd felt Hat, white linnen Cap, a brown cloth Coat, without Lining and bound round the Neck with Red, a Tow Shirt and Trowsers, blue yarn Stockings, and good new Shoes.

Whoever takes up and secures the said Servant so that he may be had again, shall have Thirty Shillings Reward and reasonable Charges,
paid by *Thomas Barr.*

*The Pennsylvania Gazette*, July 31, 1740; August 7, 1740; August 14, 1740.


RUN away the 7th Inst. out of Capt. *Jenkins's* Company at *New-Castle*, from *William Berry* of *Motherkill* in *Kent* County, a Servant Man named *James Cosway*, aged about 20 years, a small spare Man, thin Visage, short black Hair, a Wart on one of his Eyes; had on a lightish colour'd Cloth Jacket, an old Felt Hat, striped Trousers, an old coarse Shirt, is bare-footed, and can play several Tumbler's Tricks. Whoever secures the said Servant, so that he may be had again, shall have Twenty Shillings Reward, and all reasonable Charges, paid by *William Berry.*

*The Pennsylvania Gazette*, August 21, 1740; August 28, 1740; September 4, 1740.


STOLEN, Stray'd, or Run-away, on the 12th from Dr. *John Finney* in *New-Castle*, a Negro Woman, named *Betty*, aged about 18 Years, of small Stature, round Face, has been about a Month in this Country, speaks very little *English*, has had one Child: Had on, the Body of an old Gingham Gown, and an ozenbrigs Petticoat. She is supposed to have been taken from hence by an Oyster Shallop, *Benj. Taylor* Master, bound for *Philadelphia*, and may be sold on some Part of the River.

Whoever brings her to the Subscriber in *New-Castle*, and discovers the Person who carries her off, shall have *Forty Shillings* Reward, and reasonable Charges, paid by *John Finney.*
*Philad. Sep.* 14. 1740.

*The Pennsylvania Gazette*, September 18, 1740


*RUN away in the Night Time, between the* 18*th and* 19*th Inst. from John Gooding, of Reden Island, in New-Castle-County, a Servant Man, named Abraham Lay, an Englishman, about* 27 *Years of Age, of middle Stature, well set, full fac'd, and fresh Complexion: Had on when he went away, an ash colour'd Wastcoat, ozenbrigs Shirt, coarse Country-made Trowsers, a pair of linnen Breeches, lin'd with fustian, a pair of Country-made Shoes, patch'd, grey Country-made Stockings, and a pair of worsted Stockings mich darned: He has also stolen a liver coloured Cloth Coat, full trimmed, a red Camblet*

*Jacket, several Shirts, a new Beaver Hat, small brim'd, also a Pocket Book with several Papers in it belonging to one Elias or Haley Demerist; it is supposed he will change his Name answerable to those Papers; the Jacket he stole is too short and too narrow for him; He has also taken a great Coat of Devonshire Kersey of a deep drab colour.*

*Whoever takes up and secures the said Servant so that his Master may have him again, shall have Five Pounds Reward, and Reasonable Charges paid by         John Gooding.*
*Philadelphia, Octo. 19th, 1740.*

The *Pennsylvania Gazette*, October 23, 1740; October 30, 1740; November 6, 1740. See *The Pennsylvania Gazette*, From April 5, to April 12, 1739.


RUN away from the Subscriber, the 4th Day of November last, a Servant Woman, aged about 28 Years, fair Hair'd, wants some of her Teeth before, a little deafish, named Susannah Wells, born near Biddeford, in England: She had on when she went away, a Callico Gown, with red Flowers, blue Stockings, with Clocks, new Shoes, a quilted Petticoat, Plat Hat. Whoever secures said Servant, and delivers her to said Subscriber at Wilmington, or to Robert Dixson in Philadelphia, shall have Twenty five Shillings Reward, and reasonable Charges paid by Robert Dixon, or Thomas Downing.
Philad. December 4. 1740.
N. B. It's believed the said Servant was carried from New Castle in the Ship commanded by Capt Lawrence Dent, now lying at Philadelphia.

*The Pennsylvania Gazette*, December 4, 1740; December 11, 1740; December 18, 1740; January 1, 1741.

## 1741

RAN-away on the 22d Day of May last, from William Burton, of Lewes-Town, a Servant Man, named John Day, an English Man, of small Stature, he has a wry Mouth and a blasted Eye.

Whoever takes up said Servant and secures him so that his Master may have him again, shall have *Forty Shillings* Reward and reasonable Charges paid         By William Burton.

*The American Weekly Mercury*, From Thursday January 8, to Thursday, January 15, 1741; From Thursday January 15, to Thursday, January 22, 1741; From Thursday January 22, to Thursday, January 29, 1741; From Thursday January 29, to Thursday, February 5, 1741.

RUN away on the 18th of this Instant January, from John Trimble, of Wilmington, an Irish Servant Man named William Anderson, Aged about Eighteen Years, by Trade a Taylor, of middle Stature, Slender, and of a thin white Complexion, short black Hair, and stoops as he goes, wears a new Felt Hat with a piece torn out of the brim, a new brown Coat with slash Sleeves, Jacket and Breeches of the same trimmed with Mohair, the Coat having two buttons on each Sleeve, one blue Jacket, both Jackets have no Sleeves, a pair of yarn Stockings of a dark Colour, and a white Shirt. Whoever takes up said Servant and secures him so that his Master may have him again, shall have Twenty Shillings Reward, and reasonable Charges paid by John Trimble. Wilmington , Jan. 19. 1740,1.

N. B. It is supposed that the said Servant will Enquire for one Andrew Love.
*The Pennsylvania Gazette*, January 22, 1741; January 29, 1741. See *The American Weekly Mercury*, From Thursday February 19, to Thursday, February 26, 1741.


RAN-away on the 18th of January, from John Trimble of Wilmington, In New-Castle County, an Irish Servant Man named William Anderson, aged about 18 Years, of middle Stature and thin, white Complexion, short black Hair, and stoops as he goes, by Trade a Taylor, wears a new Felt Hat with a small snip out of the Brim, a new brown Coat with slash Sleeves, Jacket and Breeches of the same two Buttons on each Knee, all trim'd with Mohair, a blue under Jacket, both Jackets without Sleeves, a pair of good dark colour'd Yarn Stockings, good Shoes with large Brass Buckels, and a white Shirt.

Whoever takes up and secures said Servant so that his Master may have him again, shall have Thirty Shillings Reward and reasonable Charges paid    By John Trimble.
*The American Weekly Mercury*, From Thursday February 19, to Thursday, February 26, 1741; From Thursday March 5, to Thursday, March 12, 1741; From Thursday March 12, to Thursday, March 19, 1741; From Thursday March 19, to Thursday, March 26, 1741; From Thursday April 9, to Thursday, April 16, 1741; From Thursday April 16, to Thursday, April 23, 1741. See *The Pennsylvania Gazette*, January 22, 1741.


*RAN-away on Friday the 19th of June. from on board the Snow Ann and Mary, Samuel Hodson, Commander, now lying at Wilmington, David Pits, an Indented Servant for four Years, by Trade a Nailor, born in England Speaks broad English, of low Stature, thin Body, redish beard, thin Visag'd, on his Arms and Legs just healing, had on when he went off, an old outside Body dark Frize Coat, broke on the Elbows and split on the Back, a thin blue*

*Vest without Lining, a new felt Hatt, a worsted Cap, his hair Cut, two blue and white Shirts, a frize pair of Breeches, coarse Yarn Stockings, and a pair of half worn shoes made fast with strings.*
  *Whoever secures the said Servant so that he may be had again, shall have Twenty Shillings Reward and reasonable Charges paid by said Samuel Hodson, or David Bush at Wilmington,*
                 *or Edward Bridges, in Philadelphia.*
  *The American Weekly Mercury*, From Thursday June 18, to Thursday, June 25, 1741; From Thursday June 25, to Thursday, July 2, 1741; From Thursday July 2, to Thursday, July 9, 1741. See *The Pennsylvania Gazette*, June 25, 1741


RUN away the 19th Inst. from on board the Snow Ann and Mary, Samuel Hodson Master, now lying at Wilmington, an indented Servant named David Pitts, by Trade a Nailer, born in England, speaks broad English, of low stature, thin Body, reddish beard, thin visag'd, blotches on his arms and legs just healing; had on when he went away, an old dark frize coat, broke on the elbows and split on the back, a thin blue vest without lining, a new felt hat, a worsted cap, his hair cut, two blue and white shirts, a frize pair of breeches, coarse yarn stockings, and half worn shoes tied with strings. Whoever secures the said Servant so that he may be had again, shall have Twenty Shillings reward, and reasonable charges paid by the said Samuel Hodson or
         David Bush at Wilmington, or Edward Bridges in Philadelphia.
  *The Pennsylvania Gazette*, June 25, 1741; July 2, 1741; July 9, 1741. See *The American Weekly Mercury*, From Thursday June 18, to Thursday, June 25, 1741.


R*AN away, the 1st of this Instant, from* Valentine Robinson *of* Brandy Wine Hundred *in* New-Castle *County, a Negro Man named Caesar, about 21 Years of Age, of Middle Stature, well set, and Large Boned, this Country Born. Had on when he went away, a gray Kersey Coat with Pewter Buttons, a pair of New Buckskin Breeches, new blew and white Worsted Stockings, a pair of new Pumps, a good Felt Hat, a good Linen Cap, a Linen Shirt and 2 tow Shirts. He took with him a Gun with Brass mounting.*
  *Whoever takes up and secures said Negro so that his Master may have him again, shall have* Thirty Shillings *and all reasonable Charges,*
             *Paid by*     Valentine Robinson.
  *The American Weekly Mercury*, From Thursday July 30, to Thursday August 6, 1741; From Thursday August 6, to Thursday August 13, 1741; From Thursday August 13, to Thursday August 20, 1741.

RUN away the 30th past, from New-Castle Prison, a Man named Daniel Kelly, aged about 26 Years, a lusty Fellow, about six foot high, of a swarthy Complexion, a scar on his Forehead, black curl'd Hair: Had on when he went away, a coarse check Shirt and Trowsers, a white linnen Coat, an old felt Hat. He lived in East-Jersey and was lately taken up and put in Prison on suspicion of running from his Master there. Whoever takes up and secures said Run away, so as the Subscriber shall have him again, shall have as a Reward Twenty Shillings with reasonable Charges, paid by
August 6. 1741.          Robert Gordon, at New-Castle.
  *The Pennsylvania Gazette*, August 6, 1741; August 13, 1741; August 20, 1741.


RUN away the 19th of September, sometime before Day, from William Selthridge, of Cedar Creek, in Sussex County, a Irish Servant Man, named James Reily, a Weaver, aged about 30 Years, a pretty lusty Fellow, somewhat long visaged, a mould on one of his Cheeks, some Freckles on his Face and Hands, straight bodied, dark Hair but lately cut, and wears a Cap, has sore Legs: Had on when he went away, a fine broad cloth Coat of a bluish colour, lines with dark blue Shalloon, a homespun Shirt, and three fine Shirts, a coarse cloth Vest lined with red Bays, brown holland Breeches, two pair of Ozenbrigs Trowsers, a pair of new Shoes peaked toe'd, with large Brass Buckles, he can Sing well, and says he can play on the Violin, can read and write tolerably well, has picked the Lock of a little Trunk, and Stole his Indenture, which was assigned over to me by Capt. Pardue, before three Magistrates, two of them being Mr. Kollock and Mr. Holt of Lewestown. Likewise another Man went away along with him, one Patrick M'Clane, an Irish Man, a well set Fellow, wears a shagged Cotton Cap, a homespun Shirt, a whitish coloured Vest with brass Buttons, have taken with them a broad cloth double breasted Jacket of a drab colour, trim'd with Mohair, two Sheets, one coarse and the other fine, and several other things; they went to Muspillion Creek, and broke the Chain or Lock of John Walton's Canoe, and took it away with them. Whoever takes up and secures either of them, shall have Thirty Shillings Reward for each, and all reasonable Charges, paid by me the Subscriber,     William Selthridge.
N. B. He sometimes calls himself Patrick M'Lone.
  *The Pennsylvania Gazette*, October 1, 1741; October 8, 1741.


RUN away on the 3d Inst. from Thomas Clark, of the Welsh Tract, near Mr. Evans Meeting House, in New-Castle County, two Servant Men, both from the North of Ireland, viz.

The one named William Skanlon, a tall lusty Man, about 20 Years of Age, smooth faced, brown short Hair that dont cover his Ears, with a great long Nose, and has one Leg much thicker than the other; had on when he went away, a white fustian Coat, an old stuff Jacket of a lightish colour, two pair of Shoes, the one round toe'd and the other peaked, a pair of light blue Stockings, a pair of oznabrigs Trowsers, a pair of dark brown Breeches, two white Shirts of Irish Linnen, and a coarse felt Hat.
The other John Hutcheson, a little Man, about 20 Years of Age, very smooth round faced; had on when he went away, a light brown Coat of Irish homespun Cloth, a white Jacket of very fine English Cloth, lined with fine Serge of the same colour, and trim'd with Mohair and Buttons suitable to the Cloth, Breeches of the same with the Coat; two old brown Jackets of Irish Cloth, three of four pair of coarse Stockings, five or six white linnen Shirts, of Irish Cloth, a pair of old Pumps, and it's suppos'd has taken a single Blanket, has a brown Wig and a grey one, a coarse Felt Hat, a red and yellow printed Handkerchief about his Neck; they both came in this Year, and speak much scotchified. Whoever secures them, or either of them, so as their Master may have them again, shall have Thirty Shillings Reward for each, paid by James Claxton, next Door to the three Tons in Chesnut-Street, Philadelphia, or Thomas Clark.
*The Pennsylvania Gazette*, November 12, 1741; November 19, 1741; November 26, 1741.

## 1742

RUN away last Night, from James Bennett, near Concord, Chester county, three servants, One named Patrick M'Guire, (who lived sometime ago with one Jones, a shallop-man, at Apoquiminy,) aged about 21, a lusty fellow, swarthy complexion, without hair, speaks bad english; had on when he went away, a dove-colour'd homespun coat, trim'd with mohair buttons, but almost wore out, a brown kersey jacket with brass buttons, leather breeches, and new shoes; he has a large scar on one of his legs cut with an ax. The other named John Fowler, an irish man, by trade a taylor, aged about 21, of low stature, and limps very much, caused by a weakness in his knee; had on a new felt hat, an old brown coat, striped linnen jacket, leather breeches and trowsers, good shoes, speaks but indifferent english.

The third a servant woman, named Margaret M'Collister, aged about 25, of low stature, brown hair, swarthy complexion; took with her two gowns, one a brown linsey, pretty good; the other an old lead-colour'd stuff gown, and an old brown drugget quilted petticoat. Whoever secures the said Runaways, so that their master may have them again, shall have Twenty Shillings reward for each, and reasonable charges, paid by James Bennett.

*The Pennsylvania Gazette*, May 20, 1742; May 27, 1742.

THERE was committed to the County Goal, in New-Castle, on the 25th of June last, a certain William Carter, upon Suspicion of being a Runaway-Servant; he is a well-set Man, about 24 Years old, an Irishman, marked on the left Arm with W, and on the right Arm with three: Had on a new castor Hat, seersucker Cap, an old ash-coloured Jacket lined with olive-coloured Shaloon, an old Shirt and Trowsers, new Shoes. Any Person that has a just Claim to the above said Man, is hereby desired to come for him by the third Tuesday of this Instant, at which Time, he will be discharged if no Master appears.          John Gooding, Sher.
August 6, 1742.

    *The Pennsylvania Gazette*, August 5, 1742; August 12, 1742; August 19, 1742; August 26, 1742.


*Kent County on Delaware, ss.*
ON the 20th of July past was committed to the Goal of this County, a Person taken up on suspicion of being a Runaway: He refuses to give an Account of himself, otherwise, than that his Name of John Mc'Rabbie, and came in a Servant for four Years, two of which he serv'd with Ephraim Mc'Dowel, near Lemington River, in East New-Jersey, and the other Part he purchased and paid his Master for: He is a Scotchman, about five Feet and an half high, of a ruddy Complexion, has lost the Sight of his right Eye; and is almost naked. If any Person has a Property to him, they are desired to pay the Charges, and take him away.          SAMUEL ROBINSON, Sheriff.
*August* 20, 1742.

    *The Pennsylvania Gazette*, September 9, 1742; September 16, 1742.


RAN-away, about 2 Weeks ago, from *Anthony Dushane*, Store-keeper, near *St. George's*, in *New-Castle* County, a Servant Man named *James M'Carlin*, by Trade a Taylor, a tall young Man, pretty well set, much Pock-mark'd, wears a Wig or Cap; had on a dark brown homespun Cloath Coat lined with blue Shalloon, a pair of light colour'd German Sarge Breeches with 3 Buttons at the Wasteband, a pair of new Cotton Stockings and a pair of new Pumps. He may produce his old Indenture, but has been since judg'd out for longer Time.

    He went away in Company with a short well-set Man, with a long Nose and Chestnut brown Hair.

    Whoever takes up and secures the said Servant so that his Master may have him again, shall have *Four Pounds* Reward; and if they take up the other (his pretended Couzen) shall have *Twenty Shillings* more, and reasonable Charges.          paid by          Anthony Dushane.

*The American Weekly Mercury*, From Thursday September 9, to Thursday September 16, 1742; From Thursday September 23, to Thursday September 30, 1742; From Thursday September 30, to Thursday October 7, 1742. Second and third ads show he ran away "about 4 Weeks ago."


There is in New-Castle Goal, one Robert Cormely, a lusty well set English Man, and one Emanuel Taylor, looks like an Indian, but says he is a Portuguese, both appear like Sailors.

Also Richard Lovelock, who formerly belonged to one John Bowen of Baltimore, in Maryland, he is a tall raw boned Englishman, and says he came into the Country a Convict. The Owners if any they have, are desired to come or send for them in one Month after the Date, otherwise they will be discharged paying their Fees.
New-Castle, Dec. 9. 1742.	Samuel Bickley, Sher.
*The Pennsylvania Gazette*, December 21, 1742; December 30, 1742.


*TAKEN up on the first of this Inst. and committed to the Prison at Burlington, one who confesses that he is a Servant to Joseph Briggs or Boggs, living in or near New-Castle. His said Master is desired to pay the Charges, and fetch him away, within three Weeks after the Date hereof, otherwise he will be discharged, paying his Fees.*
*Burl. Dec. 25. 1742.	Thomas Hunloke, Sheriff.*
*The Pennsylvania Gazette*, December 30, 1742; January 4, 1743; January 13, 1743.

## 1743

THERE was lately commited to the Goal of Sussex County, upon Delaware, two Men, suspected to be Servants, *viz*. John Williams, a West Country man, aged about 32 Years, says he came into the Western part of Virginia with one Capt. Taylor, from Bristol: He is a lusty Man, wears his own Hair, ozenbrigs Shirt, yarn Stockings, old brown Coat, very much patch'd, an old felt Hat, leather Breeches, white homespun twiled Jacket, metal Buttons of several Sorts upon all his Cloathing. And Thomas Rogers, of middle Stature, who says he came with the above Williams from Bristol, aged about 25 Years, wears his own Hair, black and white homespun Breeches, white yarn Stockings, an old brown Holland double breasted Jacket, old white kersey great Coat, black and white kersey Jacket, and a Piece of an old Hat. They say they came in Freemen. The Owners (if any they have) are desired to come or send for them, in one Month's Time after this Date, otherwise they will be discharged paying their Fees.

    PETER HALL, Sher. Lewestown, March 9. 1742,3.

*The Pennsylvania Gazette*, March 17, 1743; March 24, 1743; March 31, 1743.

                  *Lewestown, Sussex* County, on *Delaware, April* 30. 1743. RUN away from the Subscriber, on the 25th of April past, at Night, two Servant Men, Blacksmiths by Trade: One named Thomas Hanson, a thick short Fellow, aged about 24 Years, this Country born: Had on a light colour'd duroy Coat, flower'd worsted damask Vest, striped Trowsers, a pair of Pumps, good narrow brim'd Hat, fine Shirt, ruffled with Muslin, and check Shirts. The other named John Mines, an Irishman, about 20 Years of Age, of middle Stature, pretty much pockbroken, long Visage: Had on, a grey duroy Coat, flower'd worsted damask Breeches the same as the Vest aforesaid, Calf-skin Shoes, soal'd. They have other Cloathing with them, not inserted. 'Tis supposed they stole a Canoe out of Mispelion Creek, with Oars and Sails, and are gone over the Bay. Whoever takes up the said Servants, and secures them so that they may be had again, shall have Three Pounds Reward, and reasonable Charges,       paid by PETER HALL.

*The Pennsylvania Gazette*, May 12, 1743; May 19, 1743; May 26, 1743; June 2, 1743.


RUN away on the 4th of this Inst. from Samuel Thompson, of New-Castle-Hundred, an Irish Servant Man, named William Wall, a well set young Fellow of very fair Complexion, has a little of the Brogue on his Tongue, a little sower look'd, he pretends to be a Shoemaker and several other Trades: Had on when he went away a brown slip-over-coat a little too long for him, a brown Jacket, a new linen Shirt, old leather Breeches badly mended, grey yarn Stockings, and half worn Shoes one has a Hole in the Soal, an old Castor Hat, linen Cap made out of an old Shirt, a cotton Handkerchief about his Neck. He has a Scar on his Forhead. Whoever takes up and secures said Servant so that his Master may have him again, shall have Twenty Shillings Reward, and reasonable Charges, paid by
*May* 18. 1743.                 SAMUEL THOMPSON.

*The Pennsylvania Gazette*, May 19, 1743; May 26, 1743; June 2, 1743; June 9, 1743.


RUN away from Andrew Jolley, of Wilmington, an Apprentice Lad, named Charles Tilden, about 16 Years old, of fair Complexion, and battle-knee'd: Had on an olive colour'd cloth Coat, a linen Jacket, a new castor Hat, a silk

Cap, and worsted stockings; and he took with him a Bundle of Cloaths, and a Gun. Whoever takes up and secures the said Lad so that his Master may have him again, shall have Twenty Shillings Reward, and reasonable Charges, paid by      Andrew Jolley.
May 23. 1743.
*The Pennsylvania Gazette*, May 26, 1743; June 2, 1743; June 9, 1743; June 16, 1743.


MADE his Escape from the Subscriber, Constable of Apoquinomy Hundred, one Charles Cavenor, who stood committed for House-breaking: He is a Fellow of middle Stature, bandy leg'd, and walks reeling, stoops something in his Shoulders, and of black Complexion: Had on, a cinamon coloured Waiscoat, and the rest of Cloathing very mean. After he had made his Escape, he broke into the House of Thomas Lewis, and stole a black Gown, a pair of leather Breeches, a Shirt and three Yards of Linnen. He also took from the said Lewis, a bright bay Horse, with a black Mane and Tail, a Star in his Forehead, and two white Feet.
Whoever takes up and secures the said Robber, so that he may be brought to Justice, shall have Five Pounds Reward, and reasonable Charges; and whoever secures the Horse, shall have Twenty Shillings,
       paid by      EDWARD RICHARDSON.
*The Pennsylvania Gazette*, June 9, 1743; June 16, 1743.


LAST WEEK was taken up and committed to the Goal of New-Castle, one William Waters, he is a little Man, thin Visage, sandy Complexion, and much freckled, has with him, good felt Hat, two ozenbrigs Shirts, and 2 pair of Trowsers of the same, one white Shirt, a half worn blue broadcloath Coat, an old red Jacket, 2 pair of leather Breeches, a double breasted white Jacket, 2 pair of blue rib'd Stockings, and half worn Shoes, and good worsted Cap and black Wig. Any Person that has any thing to say to the said Waters, are hereby desired to appear within six Weeks after the Date, otherwise he will be discharged paying the Charges.
       SAMUEL BICKLEY, Sher.
N. B. The said Waters says he serv'd his Time with William Rodgers of Baltimore County, Maryland.    July 4.
*The Pennsylvania Gazette*, July 14, 1743; July 21, 1743; July 28, 1743; August 4, 1743; August 11, 1743.


THIS DAY was committed to the Goal of New-Castle, one by the Name of Richard Homes an Englishman, he is a lusty tall Man of dark Complexion, no Hair, wears a white Cap, good felt Hat, with a black Scarf, good check Shirt, Sailors Trowsers, and blue Jacket with a list of Canvas on the seams, & a brown broad cloth Coat about half worn. About a Week before he was taken up, burnt his Leg with Gun-powder in the Woods, as he says. His Master is any he has, is desired to appear in 6 Weeks, otherwise he will be set free at Liberty, paying his Charges.

Two Days before there was one Joshua Bevan, a Servant to one Abraham Ingram, of Somerset County Maryland, taken up and committed to the Goal aforesaid. SAMUEL BICKLEY, Sheriff.

*The Pennsylvania Gazette*, July 21, 1743; July 28, 1743; August 4, 1743; August 11, 1743; August 18, 1743; August 25, 1743.

*This is to give NOTICE,*
THAT there is a lusty well set Negro Man, committed to New-Castle Goal; Had on when taken up, an old brown Great Coat, coarse white Shirt, old ragged Trowsers, very broad fore Teeth, and shews them very much when he talks, says he belongs to one Benjamin Hill, of North Carolina, his Master (if any he has) is desired to come within three Months, otherwise he will be Sold to pay his Charges.
August 10. Samuel Bickley, Sheriff.

*The Pennsylvania Gazette*, August 18, 1743; August 25, 1743; September 1, 1743; September 8, 1743.

RUN away on the 17th of August last, from John Dodd, of St. George's Hundred, in the County of New-Castle, an Irish Servant Man, named John Hawksford, aged about 25 Years, of short Stature, well set, his Collar Bone being sometime since broke near the Shoulder, it sticks up near an Inch; and the Shoulder is fallen from it. Had on when he went away, a narrow brim'd felt Hat, a cotton Cap, seersucker Jacket lin'd with Linnen, a check Shirt and Trowsers, thread Stockings, new peaked to'd Shoes, and large Copper Buckles marked R L. He took some other Clothes in a Wallet. 'Tis suspected he has a Counterfeit Pass or Clearance said to be from his Master. Whoever takes up and secures said Servant, so that his Master may have him again, shall have Three Pounds Reward, and reasonable Charges,
paid by John Dodd.

*The Pennsylvania Gazette*, October 13, 1743; October 20, 1743; October 27, 1743; November 3, 1743; November 10, 1743.

RUN away on Monday Night last, from James Baxter of Apoquinimy in New-Castle County, a Servant Man, named Patrick Edonovan, about 21

Years of Age, a lusty Fellow, about 5 Foot and 7 Inches high, fulfac'd, and mark'd with the small pox, swarthy Complexion, short brownish Hair: Had on a short brown old Wig, and a Felt Hat, a broad cloth Coat and Jacket of light greyish colour, lined with red; a short coarse brown Jacket without lining, much worn; new ozenbrigs Shirt, brown mill'd linsey-woolsey Breeches with Knee buckles, brown yarn Stockings, and half-soled Shoes. He is suspected to have taken with him a Horse, Saddle and Bridle. He is a Taylor by Trade.

Whoever secures the said Servant so that his Master may have him again, shall receive a Reward of Thirty Shillings, and reasonable Charge, paid by James Baxter,
or Mr. Mollen, of Philad. Taylor,
Dec. 27 or Anthony Duchee, Tavernkeeper
at Apoquinimy.

*The Pennsylvania Gazette*, December 29, 1743; January 3, 1744; January 11, 1744; January 19, 1744.

RUN away from the Ship Catharine, in the Bite of New-Castle, Joseph Bowle and Mathew Chambers (Sailors) the latter a Guernsey Man. Whoever takes up said Sailors, shall have Six Pounds Reward, or for any one of them Four Pounds. Davey and Carsan.

*Note*, The said Ship's Yaul was stolen or drove from the Wharff about three Weeks ago: Any Person who takes her up and returns her, shall have Twenty Shillings from
Dec. 27. 1743. Davey and Carsan.

*The Pennsylvania Gazette*, December 29, 1743; January 3, 1744; January 11, 1744; January 19, 1744.

## 1744

Run away on the 20th of April from George and Valentine Robinson, of Brandywine Hundred, New-Castle County, two Mulatto Men, named George and William Hugill, two Brothers, this Country born; one a lusty able Fellow, and the other a slender long-limbed, spare thin faced Fellow; their Cloathing made of home-spun gray Cloth, leather Breeches, check Trowsers, linnen Shirts, gray yarn Stockings, and Thread ones, with Country-made Shoes and Pumps, felt Hats; they wore their own Hair; it's supposed they took with them two Periwigs, of different Colours, and each of them a Gun. Whoever secures the said Servants, and what Things they have with them, committing them to the first Goal, and there well secur'd, and sending Account to their Masters, shall have Three Pounds Reward, for each Man, paid by us,
George Robinson, Valentine Robinson.

*The Pennsylvania Gazette*, April 26, 1744; May 3, 1744; May 10, 1744; May 17, 1744. See *The Pennsylvania Journal, or, Weekly Advertiser*, April 26, 1744.

*RUN away this Day from* George *and* Valantine Robinson, *two Mulatto Men, named* George *and* William Hugill *Brothers, this Country born. The one a lusty able Fellow, about thirty Years of Age, the other, a slender long-limb'd, spear [sic] thin fac'd Fellow; aged about twenty four. Their Cloathing made of Homespun Grey Cloth, Leather Breeches's, Check'd Trowsers, Linen Shirts, Grey Yarn and Thread Stockings, this Country made Shoes and Pumps, Felt Hats; they had their own Hair on when they went away, but are suppos'd to have two Perukes of sundry Colour, and each of them a Gun. Whoever secures the said Servants, and what Things they have with them, committing them to the next Goal, and there well secur'd, and send Notice to their before mentioned Masters, shall have Three Pounds Reward, for each Person, paid by us,* George Robinson, Valantine Robinson.
New-Castle County, Brandywyne Hundred
*April* 20, 1744.

*The Pennsylvania Journal, or, Weekly Advertiser*, April 26, 1744; May 3, 1744; May 10, 1744. See *The Pennsylvania Gazette*, April 26, 1744.

RUN Away on the 30th of May, from Walter Thetford, of Newcastle County, a Servant Man, named Henry Radmont, fair Hair, whitish Complexion. Had on when he went away, a blue Jacket, and another of Huckaback double breasted Drawers of the same, half peak toe'd Shoes. There went away with him, a Freeman, called Patrick Silver, native Irish; he deluded him away, and it is thought took some Goods with him that was not his own. Had on a brown Coat of broad cloth, a Jacket of the same of the others and same Fashion both Jacket and Drawers. Any Person that takes up said Servant, and brings him to Joseph Ramage, or secures them, so that they may be had, shall have Three Pounds, and reasonable Charges,
paid by Walter Thetford.
*The Pennsylvania Gazette*, June 14, 1744, June 21, 1744; June 28, 1744.

RUN-away, on the 2d Inst. from David Marshall, of Duck-Creek, in Kent County, a Servant Man, named Samuel Forrist, aged about 22 Years, a short well-set Fellow, with pretty long yellow Hair, but perhaps has cut it off and wears a Worsted Cap: Had on when he went away, a double-breasted Kersey

Jacket with brass Buttons, and a Linen Jacket under it, good Leather Breeches, Ozenbrigs Trowsers, blue Stockings, old Shoes, and good Felt Hat. Whoever takes up and secures the said Servant, so that his Master may have him again, shall have Forty Shillings Reward, and reasonable Charges,
   paid by  DAVID MARSHALL.
*The American Weekly Mercury*, From July 5, to July 12, 1744.


*RUN away on the 18th of July, from the Subscriber, living near Christine Bridge, New-Castle County, an Irish Servant Man, named Robert M'Fee, about 22 Years of Age, by Trade a Cooper, short Stature, long sandy colour'd Hair. He was seen on the Road towards Philadelphia, and may be at Work in the City or gone towards New-York. Had on, a Coat of blue Stuff almost new, a blue and white Jacket of raised Work like Diaper, white cotton and linnen Drawers, worsted Stockings of two Threads blue and white, one white Shirt, but may have purchased more, pretty good Shoes. Whoever takes up said Servant, and secures him in any County Goal, so that I may have him again, shall have Forty Shillings Reward,*
   *paid by*  John Hawthorn.
*The Pennsylvania Gazette*, July 26, 1744; August 2, 1744.


*RUN away the 17th of June, from John Prosser and James Downey, near Wilmington, in New-Castle County, a Servant Man named Patrick O-Caden, a native Irishman, about 25 Years of Age, well set, about 5 Feet four Inches high, fresh Complexion, and a little freckled, has one of his Teeth in the upper Jaw out. Had on, a homespun Snuff-coloured kersey Coat, good homespun Shirt and Trowsers, good strong Shoes, with brass Buckles in them.*
  *Whoever takes up said Servant and secures him, so that his Master may have him again shall have* Twenty Shillings *Reward, and reasonable Charges, paid by*
   John Prosser, or James Downey.
*The Pennsylvania Gazette*, August 2, 1744; August 9, 1744; August 16, 1744; August 23, 1744; August 30, 1744; September 6, 1744.


*RUN away the 12th of September, from William Berry, in Kent County, on Delaware, a native Irish Convict Servant Man, named Michael Doyle, a thin spare Man, looks sickly, and pretends to be a Black-smith: Had on when he went away, a cotton Cap, a half worn Hat, light coloured linsy-woolsy Jacket, and Breeches, thickned in the Mill, with two pair of coarse tow Trowsers, old Shoes.*

*Whoever takes up and secures the said Servant, so that his Master may have him again, shall have Ten Shillings Reward, more than the Law allows paid by      William Berry.*
*N. B. It's suppos'd he will go on board some Vessel.*
*The Pennsylvania Gazette*, September 20, 1744; September 27, 1744.


Newcastle County, October 10. 1744.
*THIS Day was taken up and committed to goal, one by the name of John Pusell, a short man, of about thirty three years of age, an Englishman, born in Warwickshire, as he says, wears his own hair, which is thin, and of a lightish colour: Has on an old patch coat of a light colour, with white metal buttons, brown Jacket, and old leather breeches, with some brass buttons, old grey stockings, coarse tow shirt, and good shoes; says he is a miller and a baker by trade. If he is an indented servant, or made his escape from any officer, they are desired to appear in six weeks, otherwise he will be discharged paying his fees.*
Samuel Bickley, *Sheriff.*
*The Pennsylvania Gazette*, November 15, 1744; November 22, 1744.

## 1745

New-Castle County, Feb. 25, 1744-5.
*THis Day was taken up and committed to Goal, one by the name of Thomas George, a Welshman; wears his own Hair, good new red Great Coat, good Shoes, Stockings and Hat; says he served his Time with James Powel, of Baltimore County, in Maryland. All Persons who have any Claims on said Thomas George are desired to appear at Newcastle within one Month after Date, otherwise he will be discharged, paying his Fees.*
Sam. Bickley, Sheriff.
*The Pennsylvania Gazette*, March 5, 1745; March 12, 1745; March 19, 1745.


Run away, on the 22d of May last, from Thomas Allfree, of Thoroughfare Neck, Newcastle County, an Irish Servant Man, named John Wilson: He is a middle sized Fellow, about 20 Years of Age, has no Beard, and curled yellowish Hair; and had on when he went away, an old brown Jacket, Double breasted, with flat Metal Buttons, a Homespun Linen Shirt and Trowsers, and an old fine Hat, without Shoes or Stockings. Whoever takes up and secures said Servant, so that his Master may have him again, shall receive Forty Shillings Reward, and reasonable Charges, paid by THOMAS ALLFREE.

*The Pennsylvania Gazette*, June 6, 1745; June 13, 1745; June 20, 1745.


RUN away about the 8th of June last, from George Monrow, of Newcastle, a Servant Man, named John Evans, of a brown Complexion, about 5 Foot 8 Inches high, well made, and about 25 Years of Age: Had on when he went away, an old brown Coat, with a Cape. Whoever takes and secures said Runaway, so as his Master may have him again, shall have THREE POUNDS Reward, and reasonable Charges,
          paid by    GEORGE MONROW.
*The Pennsylvania Gazette*, June 27, 1745; July 4, 1745. See *The Pennsylvania Gazette*, July 11, 1745.


RUN away the 8th of June last, from George Monro, of Newcastle, an Irish Servant Man, named John Evance, aged about 25 Years, of middle Stature, well set, brown Complexion, long Visage, and a little hollow-eyed: Had on when he went away, an old brown Coat, with slash Sleeves, and blue Cloath Vest, without Sleeves, a Felt Hat, Woollen Cap, gathered at the Crown, Check Shirt, new Ozenbrigs Trowsers, made Petticoat Fashion, or greasy Sheep-skin Breeches, coarse Shoes and Stockings, unless he has stolen others, which'tis supposed he has. Whoever takes up and secures said said Runaway, so as his Master may have him again, shall have Forty Shillings Reward, and reasonable Charges,
          paid by    GEORGE MONRO.
*The Pennsylvania Gazette*, July 11, 1745; July 18, 1745; July 25, 1745. See *The Pennsylvania Gazette*, June 27, 1745.

                        *Newcastle, August* 19. 1745.
*This Day was taken up, and committed to this Goal, one by the Name of John Coulton, an Irishman, something more than five Foot high, pretty well set, about Twenty eight Years of Age: Has on a good brown Drugget Coat, with a Cape, and large round Sleeves, brown Breeches, blue ribbed Stockings, old Pumps, with Brass Buckles, a good white Shirt, and Worsted Cap. Any Person who has any Demand against him as a Servant, are desired to appear within six Weeks from the Date, otherwise he will be set at Liberty, paying Charges.*        *SAM. BICKLEY, Sheriff.*
*The Pennsylvania Gazette*, September 12, 1745; September 19, 1745.


RUN away from Robert Nivin, of Whiteclay Creek, near Christine-Bridge, two Servant Men; one named Patrick Kerlan, an Irish Man, about nineteen

Years of Age: Had on when he went away a brown Coat, with Slash Sleeves, and Brass Buttons and Oznabrigs Trowsers, his Hair cut off, and wears a Cap. The other born in Maryland, named Josiah Kincoval; and had on when he went away a white Coat, full trim'd, Linnen Trowsers, half worn Shoes, and is of middle Stature. Whoever takes up and secures them, so as their Master may have them again, shall have Five Pounds Reward, and reasonable Charges, and Fifty Shillings for any one of them,
   paid by  Robert Nivin.
*The Pennsylvania Gazette*, September 19, 1745; September 26, 1745; October 3, 1745.


RUN away on Saturday the 14th Instant from John Reed, sen. of Christine Bridge in Newcastle County, an Irish Servant Lad, named Briant Conely, about 17 Years of Age, dark Complexion, down Look. Had on when he went away, a dark grey Coat, too big for him, a Cinnamon colour'd Jacket, a pair of Trowsers, with Leather Breeches under them, old Stockings, new Shoes, and an old Hat. Whoever takes up and secures the said Servant, and brings him to John Reed, sen. of Christine Bridge, or to John Harding at the lower End of Market Street, Philadelphia, shall have Twenty Shillings Reward, and reasonable Charges, paid by
   *JOHN READ*, sen. or, *JOHN HARDING*.
*The Pennsylvania Gazette*, December 17, 1745; December 24, 1745; December 31, 1745.

## 1746

*WHEREAS JOHN M'COLUM, late of St. George's Hundred, in Newcastle County, upon Delaware, hath run away from those parts on the 13th of December last, and hath left one John M'Farland, who was his special Bail, and will suffer much by his going off. He is an Irishman, middle siz'd, thick of hearing, speaks thick, and has short brown Hair. Had on when he went away, a light coloured Cloth Coat, green Jacket with Brass Buttons, old Leather Breeches, Yarn Stockings, and good Shoes, and a good Hat. He took with him a grey Horse, which paces, but is very poor. Whoever takes up the said John M'Colum, and commits him to Newcastle Goal, or secures him, so that the said John M'Farland may have him brought to Justice, shall have Three Pounds Reward, and reasonable Charges,*
   paid by me  *JOHN M'FARLAND.*
*The Pennsylvania Gazette*, January 21, 1746; January 28, 1746; February 4, 1746.

*Dover, April* 27, 1746.
NOTICE is hereby given, that there is in this goal, a man that goes by the name of James Young, an Englishman, is about 5 feet 9 inches high, of a ruddy complexion, well set, has black curl'd hair, long visage, high thin nose, a learing down look, and is about 40 years of age. 'Tis thought he is the person that made his escape in August last, from Anthony Tate, near Newtown goal, Bucks county, as he has confessed he had an ax with him, when he made his escape some time ago, from some body in Bucks county, but does not know from whom. If he is the person, it is desired he should be speedily taken away. *THOMAS GREEN*, Sheriff.
*The Pennsylvania Gazette*, May 8, 1746.

*Philadelphia, July* 3. 1746.
RUN away from John Buckingham, of Newcastle County, the 28th of June last, one John Hutchison, a short, well set Fellow; he took with him 3 Coats and a Waistcoat, and one Pair of Breeches, all of brownish Colour, 3 Shirts, 2 Pair of Trowsers, 2 Pair of Shoes, and 1 Pair of Hose. Whoever takes up and secures said Hutchison, so that he may be had again, shall have Thirty Shillings Reward, and reasonable Charges,
   paid by *JOHN BUCKINGHAM.*
*The Pennsylvania Gazette*, July 3, 1746; July 10, 1746; July 17, 1746; July 24, 1746.

*Philadelphia, July* 17. 1746.
RUN away the 7th Instant, from Samuel Ralston, of Whiteclay-creek Hundred, New-castle County, an Irish Servant Lad, about 17 Years of Age, named Nicholas M'Entire, short, thick and well set, brown Complexion, black bushy Hair, Pock-mark'd, short Nose, and has one of his Foreteeth broke: Had on when he went away, a good Hat, Homespun Shirt, brown Coat, coarse Trowsers, brown Stockings, and good Shoes. Whoever takes up and secures said Servant, so that his Master may have him again, shall have Twenty Shillings Reward, and all reasonable Charges,
   paid by *SAMUEL RALSTON.*
*The Pennsylvania Gazette*, July 17, 1746; July 31, 1731; August 7, 1746.

*Philadelphia, July* 24. 1746.
*RUN away from the Subscriber, on Whiteclay Creek, in Newcastle, on Delaware , a Negroe Man, named Ned, of short Stature, but well set, speaks very abruptly and broken. Had on when he went away, a Linsey Wolsey Coat, with Buttons of the same, a striped Linnen Jacket, striped Woolsey Trowsers,*

black and white, old Shoes, a good Felt Hat, white Cotton Cap, with red Stripes. Whoever takes up the said Negroe, and secures him, so that he may be had again, shall have Twenty Shillings Reward, with reasonable Charges, paid by    REYNOLD HOWELL.

*The Pennsylvania Gazette*, July 24, 1746; July 31, 1746; August 7, 1746.

*Philadelphia, July 24. 1746.*
RUN away, about a Fortnight ago, from the Subscriber, in Dover, Kent County, on Delaware, a Servant Man, named David Price, about 24 Years of Age, born in Somerset County, Maryland; he is well set, but very short, fresh colour'd, has short Fingers, brown Hair, lately cut off, talks little, and very low, and is much given to Drinking. Had on when he went away, a Country Cloth grey Jacket, lined with blue and white striped Linsey Woolsey, old Leather Breeches, Oznabrigs Trowsers and Shirt, with brown Linnen Gussets, old Felt Hat, old Shoes, and a Worsted Cap. 'Tis thought he intends to inlist in some of the Companies designed against Canada by some other Name. Whoever brings him back, or secures him, so that he may be had again, shall have Forty Shillings Reward, and reasonable Charges,
       paid by    THOMAS NIXON.

*The Pennsylvania Gazette*, July 24, 1746; July 31, 1746; August 7, 1746; August 14, 1746.

*Philadelphia, July 31. 1746.*
RUN away the 2d of July from Richard Colegate, of Kent County on Delaware, a Molatto Man, named James Wenyam, of middle Stature, about 37 Years of Age, has a red Beard, a Scar on one Knee: had on when he went away, a Kersey Jacket, a Pair of plain Breeches, a Tow Shirt, and a Felt Hat. He swore when he went away to a Negro Man, whom he wanted to go with him, that he had often been in the back Woods with his Master, and that he would go to the French and Indians, and fight for them. Whoever secures the said Molatto Man, and gives Notice thereof to his master, or to Abraham Gooding, Esq; or to the High Sheriff of Newcastle County, so that his Master may have him again, shall have Three Pounds Reward, and reasonable Charges,   paid by    RICHARD COLEGATE.

*The Pennsylvania Gazette*, July 31, 1746; August 7, 1746; August 21, 1746.

*Philadelphia, August 7. 1746.*
FROM Thomas Clemson ran away,
One Evening on a Saturday,
The Six and Twentieth Day of July,
If that I am informed truly;

A Man, one Joseph Willard call'd,
His Hair is brown, he is not bald;
His Visage long, and wou'd you know
His Colour, it is swarthy too;
His Hat, it is of an antient Date,
Which keeps the Weather from his Pate;
A yellow Jacket, old and torn,
His wretched Carcase doth adorn;
A Homespun Shirt, and look below,
You'll find his Trowsers made of Tow,
And also coarse; and for his Shoes,
He did the same this six Months use;
They ragged are: He with him took
(If that you will be pleas'd to look)
A Handsaw, made of London Steel,
And stamped with White, near to the Heel;
A Broad-ax, of an ugly Shape,
A Justice made it, near to Gap;
And other Clothes, perhaps may have,
That he may better play the Knave.
By Calling, he pretends to be
A Person used to the Sea,
A Millwright, Carpenter, and all
The Crafts which you to Mind can call.
If you shou'd happen for to be
By Chance drawn into his Company,
You'll find him lye at such a Rate,
You can't conceive it in your Pate.
His Birth Bucks County did adorn.
To all his Friends he is a Scorn;
His Father left him an Estate
Enough, with Care, to make him great;
He wasted it, and then he went
To Lancaster, with Intent
His ragged Fortune to repair,
And soon was made a Servant there.
If you'll expect to have a Fee
For taking up this Man for me,
Full TWENTY SHILLINGS I will give,
And truly pay it, as I live;
Provided, that you will not fail,
To cast him in the nearest Goal,
And send me Word, you need not doubt,

I'll quickly lug the Money out:
In Christine Hundred, there you may
Soon find me out, on any Day;
I at John Heath's doth make my Home.
It will please me, if you hither come;
Pray use your Skill, to help your Friend,
And I'll conclude, and make an End.
      THOMAS CLEMSON.
*The Pennsylvania Gazette*, August 7, 1746; August 14, 1746.


      Ogeltown, new New-Castle, June 30. 1746.
*RUN away from the Subscriber, an Apprentice Lad, named John Bennett, aged* 19, *Country born, took with him, a convict Servant Man, somewhat tall, long Visage, thin Face, pale Complexion, his Hair cut off, his Arms hang very odd, his Voice pretty coarse, walks very upright; he is an Englishman, and a Brass Founder by Trade: Took with him an old blue Broad Cloth Coat, a Hat almost new, a Pair of coarse Trowsers, midling good Shoes, and some small Tools. Bennett took with him a light-coloured Drugget Coat, a Vest much of the same Colour, a Pair of Leather Breeches, a Deer Skin Apron, white Stockings, and a good new Hat; he is midling tall, long Visage, and grim look'd, by Trade a Brass Founder. They were seen going through Woodberry in Gloucester County, and 'tis supposed they will go to Egg Harbour or New-York. Whoever secures the said Servants, so that their Master may have them again, shall have* FIVE POUNDS *Reward, and reasonable Charges,*
   *paid by*  CHARLES MILLER.
*The Pennsylvania Gazette*, August 14, 1746; August 21, 1746.


      *Philadelphia, Sept.* 25. 1746.
*RUn away, about a Fortnight ago, from William Armour, of Newcastle, Edward Macgunnigan, a native Irish Servant man, about 22 years of age, of small stature, dark complexion, a little pitted with the small-pox, freckled, has strait black hair, pretty much of the brogue, and a large scar on one of his legs. Had on when he went away, a new felt hat, brown homespun coat, pretty much worn, linsey woolsey jacket, with buttons of the same stuff, new dark coloured Breeches, much too big for him, with wrought pewter buttons, new dark coloured stockings, and good shoes. Whoever takes up and secures said servant in any goal, so as his master may have him again, shall have Thirty Shillings reward, and reasonable charges,*
   *paid by*  WILLIAM ARMOUR.

*The Pennsylvania Gazette,* September 25, 1746; October 2, 1746; October 9, 1746.

## 1747

Philadelphia, March 3. 1746-7.
RUN away on the 16th of February last, from Walter Thetford, of Mill-creek hundred, in New-Castle county, an Irish servant man, named Patrick Carril, of low stature, sandy complexion: Had on when he went away, two jackets, one a dark grey, with metal buttons, the other mixt blue and white, with carved metal buttons, leather breeches, with the seams much ript, old stockings, and brogues almost new, no hat nor coat, except he stole them since he went away. Whoever takes up and secures said servant, so that his master may have him again, shall have Forty-shillings reward, and reasonable charges, paid by WALTER THETFORD.
N. B. he speaks broken English, or much with the brogue on his tongue.
*The Pennsylvania Gazette,* March 3, 1747; March 10, 1747; March 16, 1747.

Philadelphia, March 16, 1746-7.
RUn away, the 8th instant, from Jonathan Woodland, of St. George's Hundred, Newcastle county, an Irish servant man, named John Carroll, about forty years of age, of middle stature, and well-set, sandy complexion, and dark coloured hair: Had on when he went away, a greasy, old hat, coarse worsted coat, something of an orange colour, old olive green jacket, old leather breeches, old grey stockings, and old shoes. Whoever takes up said servant, and secures him, so as his master may have him again, shall have Thirty Shillings reward, and reasonable charges, besides what the Law of the place where taken allows,
paid by JONATHAN WOODLAND.
*The Pennsylvania Gazette,* March 16, 1747; March 24, 1747.

St. George's, N. Castle county, March 16. 1746-7.
RUN away on the 13th inst. from the subscriber, a native Irish servant man, named Laughlin O Dennysey; he is 6 foot high, 30 years of age, fat and full faced, long visage, brown eyes, thick lips, and his mouth a little on one side, sandy beard, speaks good English, nothing on the brogue, but rather on the Scotch tongue, by reason of his living in the north of Ireland: Had on, a light coloured jockey coat, a brown jacket with some brass buttons, a pair of new olive coloured breeches, with pewter buttons on each knee; he had a brown wig, and a new grey wig, a felt hat, two white shifts, half worn shoes and

stockings. Whoever takes up and secures said servant, so that his master may have him again, shall have Three-pounds reward, paid by
David Witherspon, Esq; or WILLIAM MOORE.
*The Pennsylvania Gazette*, March 24, 1746-7; April 2, 1747; April 9, 1747.

*New-Castle, March* 13, 1746-7.
THIS day was taken up and committed to this goal (on suspicion of being a runaway) one Thomas Gilpin, of a low Stature, has on a felt hat, light coloured jersey coat, country cloth jacket, grey breeches with brass buttons, white cotton stockings, and old shoes with white metal buckles, says he is a shoemaker by trade, and has some tools with him. His master, if any he has, is desired to come and discharge him in six weeks from the date, otherwise he will be disposed of for his charges.
GIDEON GRIFFITH, Sheriff.
*The Pennsylvania Gazette*, March 24, 1747; April 9, 1747.

Philadelphia, May 14. 1747.
RUN away from Mr. John Read's, at Christine Bridge, on Thursday the 23d of April, a negro man, call'd Stephen, late the property of Dr. Thomas Bond, of Philadelphia: He is of a middle size, well set, and hath a sower countenance. Had on when he went away, a cloth colour'd kersey jacket, lined with red, a pair of leather breeches, and very large pewter buckles in his shoes. He was seen to go towards Philadelphia.
Whoever takes and delivers him to Mr. James Mathews, in Chester, or to Mr. Shelley, at the work house, in Philadelphia, shall have Ten Shillings, and reasonable charges,
paid by    GEORGE ROCK.
*The Pennsylvania Gazette*, May 14, 1747; May 21, 1747; May 28, 1747.

Philadelphia, July 9. 1747.
RUn away, about a Fortnight ago, from the widow Price, in Kent County, a Negroe fellow, named Cesar, about 30 years of age, middle sized, speaks good English, has lost two of his foreteeth, has a scar above each temple, and remarkably small feet. Had on an old linsey woolsey jacket, old leather breeches, and a half worn large felt hat. Whoever takes up said Negroe, and brings him to John Booth, in Kent county, or secures him, so as he may be had again, shall have Fifty Shillings Reward, and reasonable charges,
paid by    John Booth.
*The Pennsylvania Gazette*, July 9, 1747; July 16, 1747.

Philadelphia, August 13. 1747.
RUN away on the 10th of this instant, from Isabella Nevins, of Mill Creek Hundred, in New-Castle county, a Irish servant man, named Francis Grachams; he is a short lad, about 21 or 22 years of age, short red hair, and talks English short and quick, and passionately, as if angry. Had on when he went away, an old hat, a whitish coloured coat, of Irish cloth, with whitish mohair buttons, lin'd with linsey woolsey, strip'd white and blue, pretty broad new homespun linnen shirts, he had 2 if not 3 when he went away; one pair of trowsers and drawers of brown linnen, one pair of light blue worsted stockings, middling new, a good new pair of shoes, with brass buckles in them; he hath but a very little foot to be a man. Whoever takes up said servant, and secures him in any goal, so that his mistress may have him again, shall have Twenty Shillings reward and reasonable charges,
      paid by    ISABELLA NEVINS.
N. B. 'is suppos'd that he hath a pistol and ammunition with him. Masters of vessels are desired not to carry him off, on pain of being prosecuted.
*The Pennsylvania Gazette*, August 13, 1747; August 20, 1747; August 27, 1747.


              SIX POUNDS Reward.
              Philadelphia, August 20. 1747.
Run away, on Sunday night last, from the subscribers, in Wilmington, the two following Irish servant men, viz. from Robert Lewis, a thick set man, named John Powell, about 20 years of age, round visage, much freckled, down look, red eye- brows, and red hair, cut short, and perhaps may wear a wig over his hair: Had on when he went away, 'tis thought, a homespun drugget or plain cloth jacket, lined, and brass buttons, check trowsers, a homespun shirt, and a fine one, the buttons of the collar on the left-side, felt hat, with a large brim, and very meally, and a pair of old round toed shoes; he may be certainly proved by the drawing of his breath in a very hard and uncommon manner from other people, and is a very good scholar, and will undoubtedly write himself and his fellow runaway a pass; he is hard of hearing, will pass for a miller or schoolmaster, and is supposed to have much better clothes with him than those here described.
    The other from Edward Hopkins, ship carpenter, a short small man, named John Pendegrass, fair complexion, round visage, and freckled: Took with him a blue serge coat, a bird's eye vest, a homespun drugget coat, a red and black flower'd stuff vest, very remarkable, a pair of large check trowsers, a pair of ozenbrigs ditto, and leather breeches, check shirt, yarn stockings, and spotted thread ones, almost new, single soiled shoes, good castor hat, and commonly wears a wig. 'Tis supposed he will pass for a sailor or ship carpenter, and says he has been a privateering. Whoever takes up and secures

said servants, or either of them, so as their masters may have them again, shall have Three Pounds reward for each, and reasonable charges,
                paid by     *Robert Lewis*, and *Edward Hopkins*.
*The Pennsylvania Gazette*, August 20, 1747; August 27, 1747; September 3, 1747.

                                          Philadelphia, October 1. 1747.
RUn away, on the 19th of September last, from Francis Graham, of Millcreek Hundred, Newcastle county, a servant man, named James Paterson, about 25 years of age, of middle stature, fresh complexion, and his hair cut off: Had on when he went away a good felt hat, and a cap, a dark coloured coat, with pewter buttons, lined with striped linsey, coarse shirt, much worn, coarse trowsers, black yard stockings, and good shoes. Whoever takes up and secures said servant, so that his master may have him again, shall have Forty Shillings reward, and reasonable charges,
                paid by     FRANCIS GRAHAM.
N. B. He pretends to be a blacksmith.
*The Pennsylvania Gazette*, October 1, 1747; October 8, 1747; October 15, 1747. See *The Pennsylvania Journal, or Weekly Advertiser*, October 8, 1747.

                                          *Philadelphia, October* 8, 1747.
RUN-away on the 19th of *September* last, from *Francis Graham*, of *Mill-Creek-Hundred*, and County of *New-Castle*, a Servant Man named *James Patterson*, aged about 20 Years, of middle Stature, fresh Complexion, had on when He went away, a good felt Hat, short Hair, coarse Linnen Trowsers, and a dark brown Coat with pewter Buttons, lined with a striped lincewoolsey Cloth, an old Shirt, good Shoes, and a pair of black yarn Stockings. This Man pretends to be a Black Smith, and can do a little at the Trade; he has been in the Country about Sixteen Months. Whoever takes up and Secures the said Servant, so that his Master may have him again, shall have *Forty Shillings* Reward and reasonable Charges
                paid by,    FRANCIS GRAHAM.
*The Pennsylvania Journal, or, Weekly Advertiser*, October 8, 1747; October 15, 1747; October 22, 1747; October 30, 1747; November 5, 1747; November 12, 1747; November 19, 1747; November 26, 1747; December 3, 1747; December 10, 1747; December 15, 1747; December 22, 1747; December 29, 1747; January 5, 1748; January 12, 1748; January 19, 1748; January 26, 1748; February 2, 1748. See *The Pennsylvania Gazette*, October 1, 1747.

*Philadelphia, October* 8. 1747.
RUN away from Francis Mines, in Appoquinimy, Newcastle county, a servant woman name Ann Wainrite: She is short, well-set, fresh-colour'd, of a brown complexion, round visage, was brought up in Virginia, speaks good English and bold. Had one when she went away, a blue linsey-wolsey gown, a dark-brown petticoat, and a Bath bonnet. She hath taken with her a striped cotton shirt, and some white ones, a drab-colour'd great coat, a silver-hilted sword, with a broad belt, and a cane; with a considerable parcel of other goods: Also a large bay pacing horse, roughly trimm'd, shod before, and branded on the near buttock **SR**. There went away with her a Negroe woman belonging to Jannet Balvaird, named Beck; she is lusty, strong, and pretty much pock-broken; had on when she went away, a brown linnen gown, a striped red and white linsey-wolsey petticoat, the red very dull, a coarse tow petticoat, and callicoe one, with a great piece tore at the bottom, and stole a black cape gown: Also a bay horse, with three white feet, a blaze down his face, and a new russet bunting saddle. Whoever takes up the abovementioned women and horses, and secures them, so as they may be had again, shall have Four Pounds reward, and reasonable charges,
   paid by *Francis Mines, Jannet Balvaird.*
*The Pennsylvania Gazette,* October 8, 1747; October 15, 1747; October 22, 1747.

Philadelphia, December 15. 1747.
Run away from his bail, one Peter Fitzpatrick, from Newcastle county, on the eighteenth of November last, an Irishman, of middle stature, brisk and lively, fair complexion; he wore a wig, and took with him a black horse. Whoever secures said man in any goal on the continent, shall have Three Pounds reward, paid by PATRICK CONNER.
*The Pennsylvania Gazette,* December 15, 1747; December 22, 1747; December 29, 1747; January 5, 1748; July 19, 1748.

# 1748

Philadelphia, March 22. 1747-8.
Run away on the 22d of January last from Andrew M'Clement, of Kent county on Delaware, an Irish servant man, named Patrick Hopkins, of about 30 years of age, a low well set fellow, black bushy hair, full faced, pitted with the small-pox, had a hole under the left Jaw, occasion'd by the King's evil, a large flat foot, and big heels. Had on when he went away, a dark grey coat of manks cloth, and an old bluish drugget coat under it, and old linnen jacket, brown coloured kersey breeches, patched with white cloth, a good felt hat, coarse grey yarn stockings, a pair of good shoes, with leather shoe strings; he also took with him two linnen shirts. Whoever brings the above servant to his

master, or secures him, so as he may have him again, shall have Forty shillings reward, and reasonable charges, paid by Andrew M'Clement.

N. B. It is supposed he has an old Indenture, whereby he was bound to his former masters. Andrew Bandy, and Richard Bandy, which 'tis likely he may produce, in order to make people believe he is a freeman.

*The Pennsylvania Gazette,* March 22, 1747-8; April 5, 1748; April 16, 1748.

*Philadelphia, April* 21. 1748.
*RUN away from the subscriber, an Irish servant man, named John Newland, aged about 26 years, of middle stature, fresh complexion, long visage, no hair on, wore a worsted cap, took with him one fine shirt, and one coarse ditto: had on when he went away, a light coloured broad cloth coat, with round cuffs, let out at the sides, with mohair buttons, half worn, an homespun jacket, black and white, with a striped linsey woolsey jacket, without sleeves, under it, with buttons of the same, a pair of new buckskin breeches, with one button at each knee, homespun stockings, shoes half worn, with brass buckles. Whoever secures said servant, so as his master may have him again, shall receive Forty-shillings reward, and reasonable charges; and if brought to the subscriber, living in Dragon's neck, near the Red lion, Newcastle county, shall have Three Pounds reward, and all reasonable charges,*
    *paid by*   *John Hance.*

*The Pennsylvania Gazette,* April 21, 1748; April 28, 1748; May 5, 1748; May 12, 1748.

*Philadelphia, May 26.* 1748.
RUn away from the subscriber, living near St. George's Newcastle county, on the first of February last, a Negroe man, named Dick, alias Harry, a thick, well-set fellow, somewhat bandy legg'd, about 40 years of age: Had on when he absconded two jackets, one of cloth, the other of linsey woolsey; and took with him a good ax, stamped on one side Wallace. Whoever takes up and secures said Negroe, so as his master may have him again, shall have *Three Pounds* reward, and reasonable charges,
    paid by   *Valentine Dushane.*

*The Pennsylvania Gazette,* May 26, 1748; June 2, 1748; June 9, 1748.

*Philadelphia, June* 23, 1748.
RUN away on the Twenty-first Instant from the Subscribers, living at Christiana-Bridge, Newcastle-County, two Irish Servant Man, one named Edward Gillan, of a middle Stature, aged about 19 Years, pale-faced, speaks a little upon the Brogue, and is a Cooper by Trade: Had on when he went away, a light colour'd Coat with flat metal Buttons, and old beaver Hat, and

a pair of Trowsers. The other named Thomas Steel, much of the same Stature and Age of the former, speaks good English: Had on when he went away, a white linen Jacket, an old Coat, and a pair of Trowsers, he is marked with the Small-Pox pretty much and is suppos'd to have taken some Money from his Master. Whoever takes up and secures said Servants so as their Masters may have them again, shall Forty Shillings [sic] Reward for each, and reasonable Charges, paid by       HANCE RUDULLPH, or
                              JOHN M'CARTEY.
    *The Pennsylvania Journal, or, Weekly Advertiser*, June 23, 1748; June 30, 1748; July 14, 1748; July 21, 1748; August 4, 1748; August 11, 1748.

                                *Philadelphia, August 4. 1748.*
RUN away on the twenty seventh of July last, from Robert Arthur, of Little-Creek-Hundred, Kent county, two servant lads; one an Irishman, Abraham Long, about 18 years of age, a short, well-set fellow, round shoulder'd, fair complexion, short black hair, talks pretty good English, can read and write well, & knows something of the Latin. The other a Scotch lad, named Duncan Campbell, about 16 years of age, short and slim, of a yellowish complexion, and talks good English. Abraham Long had on a blue cloth homespun jacket, lined with bluish coloured linsey woolsey, homespun tow trowsers, two homespun shirts, old blue yarn stockings, and pretty good shoes, with white-metal buckles in 'em. Duncan Campbell had on and took with him, a whitish coloured homespun cloth jacket, with a shag on it, lined one half with blue camblet, the other with linsey woolsey, with flat white-metal buttons, homespun shirt, tow trowsers, and old shoes, with brass buckles in them that are not fellows. They have taken some money with them, but how much uncertain. Whoever takes them up, and secures them in any goal, so as they may be had again, shall have Five Pounds reward for both, or Fifty shillings for each, and reasonable charges,
         paid by    ROBERT ARTHUR.
N. B. They took their Indentures with them.
    *The Pennsylvania Gazette*, August 4, 1748; August 11, 1748; August 18, 1748; August 25, 1748.

                            Philadelphia, November 17. 1748.
RUn away, the beginning of last month, from Thomas Collins, of Thoroughfare Neck, in Apaquimiay Hundred, Newcastle county, near Bombahook, a Negroe fellow, named Jack, formerly belong'd to Mr. Andrew Hamilton, and commonly went by the name of Whitehall Jack: Had on when he went away, an orange colour'd close bodied coat, blue jacket, half worn beaver hat, and trowsers, He is a lusty, well-set fellow, about 32 years of age,

of a yellowish colour, was born in Philadelphia, brought up in Kent county, speaks good English, and has a brother that lives with John Palmer, of Philadelphia, bricklayer. Whoever takes up said Negroe, and secures him, so as his master may have him again, shall have Three Pounds reward, and reasonable charges,

        paid by    THOMAS COLLINS.

*The Pennsylvania Gazette*, November 17, 1748; November 24, 1748; December 8, 1748.

## 1749

Philadelphia, January 3. 1748-9.
ABsented from his master, of Wilmington, New Castle county, on the 7th of December last, one Henry Shafter, by trade a shoemaker: had on when he went away, a suit of light blue colour'd French serge cloth, is an English-man by birth, has been on the expedition to Canada; he stole from his master a beaver hat, and several things not yet known. Whoever secures the said Shafter, in any county goal, so that he may be had again, shall have Thirty Shillings reward, paid by    JOHN CHAMBERLAIN, or
                    GOLDSMITH EDWARD FOLWELL.

*The Pennsylvania Gazette*, January 3, 1749, January 10, 1749; January 17, 1749. See *The Pennsylvania Gazette*, January 31, 1749.

Philadelphia, January 17. 1748-9.
RUn away, the 13th instant, from Jacob Lewis, of the city of Philadelphia, carpenter, an apprentice lad, named Abraham Wood, a tall well-set fellow, about nineteen years of age: Had on when he went away, a bearskin coat, with slash sleeves, and a vest of the same, leather breeches, grey worsted stockings, a pair of pumps, with large brass buckles, and generally wears a cap. He is supposed to be gone in company with a sort of molattoe, named George Shirley, servant to Samuel Rowland, of Lewes-town. Whoever takes up said apprentice, and secures him, so as his master may have him again, shall have, if taken in town, *Twenty Shillings* reward, and if any distance from town, *Three Pounds*, and reasonable charges,

        paid by    JACOB LEWIS.

N. B. Said Lewis will likewise give Forty Shillings reward, and reasonable charges, for the above George Shirley.

*The Pennsylvania Gazette*, January 17, 1749; January 24, 1749; January 31, 1749.

*Philadelphia, January* 31. 1748-6. [*sic*]
ABsented from his master, of Wilmington, Newcastle county, on the 7th of December last, one Henry Shafter, by trade a shoemaker: had on when he went away, a suit of light blue colour'd French serge cloth, is an English-man by birth, has been on the expedition to Canada; he stole from his master a beaver hat, and several things not yet known. Whoever secures the said Shafter, in any county goal, so that he may be had again, shall have Thirty Shillings reward, paid by     JOHN CHAMBERLAIN, or
DANIEL GOLDSMITH.
*The Pennsylvania Gazette*, January 31, 1749; February 7, 1749; February 14, 1749; February 21, 1749. See *The Pennsylvania Gazette*, January 3, 1749.

*Philadelphia, February* 14. 1748-9.
RUn away, on the sixth instant, from the subscriber, living in Mill-creek Hundred, Newcastle county, an Irish servant man, named Francis Grimes, about 22 years of age, and about 5 feet 6 inches high, sandy beard, reddish complexion, thin visage, speaks a little on the brogue, a smart, lively, active fellow: Had on when he went away a felt hat, a whitish colour'd coat and jacket, woollen breeches, and new shoes. Whoever takes up and secures said servant, so that his master may have him again, shall have Fifty Shillings reward, and reasonable charges,
    paid by     HUGH RENDELS.
*The Pennsylvania Gazette*, February 14, 1749; February 21, 1749; March 7, 1749.

*Philadelphia, April* 20. 1749.
RUN away the 6th inst. from the subscriber, of Red-lion hundred, Newcastle county, a short well-set Negro man, near 40 years of age, bandy legged: Had on when he went away, a blue great coat, a light coloured kersey jacket, old leather breeches, tow shirt, and an old felt hat; took with him, a gun, powder-horn, shot-bag, and a good twill'd bag. Whoever takes up and secures the said Negro, so that the owner may have him again, shall have Thirty-shillings reward, and reasonable charges,
    paid by     VALENTINE DUSHANE, junior.
*The Pennsylvania Gazette*, April 20, 1749; April 27, 1749; May 4, 1749.

*Philadelphia, April* 20. 1749.
Run away, on the 28th of March last, from Abraham Humphries, tanner, of St. George's hundred, Newcastle county, a negro man, named Dick, about 28 years of age, a stout well-set fellow, country born, and talks good English:

Had on when he went away, a light colour'd jacket, and striped linsey woolsey under jacket, a pair of half worn leather breeches, with brass buttons, good shoes, and black stockings, a good homespun shirt, and old felt hat; he is supposed to have gone over to the Jerseys. Whoever takes up said negro, and brings him to the subscriber, or secures him in any goal, so that his said master may have him again, shall have, Forty Shillings reward, and reasonable charges, paid by     *Abraham Humphries.*

*The Pennsylvania Gazette*, April 20, 1749; April 27, 1749; May 4, 1749.

RUn away, on the 30th of last month, from Daniel Howell, living in the Welsh Tract, Newcastle county, an Irish servant man, named John Fitzgerald, has much of the brogue on his tongue, and is about 20 years of age: Had on when he went away, a bluish colour'd homespun cloth vest, tow shirt and trowsers, old yarn stockings, old shoes, and an half-worn rackoon hat; he took from his master upwards of *Eighty Pounds*, in gold, silver, paper, and brass; he has also with him, besides what he had on, one linnen vest, two shirts, one pair drawers, one pair old leather breeches, and one pair pumps.

Also run away, at the same time and place, from David John, a ship mate of said Fitzgerald's, who is supposed to be gone with him, and had on an old blue coat, too large for him, and a check shirt, without sleeves; he is a slim fellow, about 23 years of age, or thereabouts. Whoever take sup said servants, and secures them so as they may be had again, with the money, shall have *Ten Pounds* reward,
    paid by     *Daniel Howell,* or *David John.*

*The Pennsylvania Gazette*, May 4, 1749; May 11, 1749; May 18, 1749.

Philadelphia, May 18. 1749.
RUn away, the 16th instant, from the subscriber, living in White-clay Creek hundred, Newcastle county, an Irish servant man, named John Gilespy, well set, fair complexion, with very short black hair, about twenty one years of age, had on when he went away, a whitish broadcloth coat, much worn, brown linnen jacket, coarse tow trowsers, two shirts, one a ten, and the other an eight hundred, fine black worsted stockings, almost new, coarse shoes, almost new, with founders buckles in them. Whoever takes up and secures said servant, so as his master may have him again, shall have Three Pounds reward, and reasonable charges, paid by     ROBERT NIVIN.
N. B. He inclines to the sea, and pretends to be a drummer.

*The Pennsylvania Gazette*, May 18, 1749; May 25, 1749; June 1, 1749.

RUn away from John Sparling, of the corporation of New-Brunswick, New-Jersey, an indented servant man, named William Thompson, born at Duckcreek, Newcastle county, and is short and thick: Had on a blue coat, a white cloth jacket, with the buttons on the left side, a felt hat, linnen drawers, no shoes; he is bow legg'd, and his eyes much sunk in his head. Whoever secures the said servant, so that his master may have him again, shall have Three Pounds reward, and reasonable charges,
    paid by  JOHN SPARLING.
*The Pennsylvania Gazette*, July 6, 1749; July 13, 1749; July 20, 1749.


RUn away from Reas Thomas, in Pencader hundred, New Castle county, upon Delaware, an Irish servant man, named Morgan Murphy, of middle stature, about 20 years of age swarthy complexion, pock marked, black hair, and has a great scar upon his leg: Had on when he went away, a large felt hat, a homespun grey colour'd coat, with pewter buttons, homespun linnen shirt, and tow trowsers. Whoever takes up and secures said servant in any goal, so as his master may have him again, shall have *Forty Shillings* reward, and reasonable charges, paid by  REAS THOMAS.
*The Pennsylvania Gazette*, July 13, 1749; July 27, 1749; August 3, 1749.


Run away the sixth day of April last past, from the subscriber, living near St. George's, in Newcastle county, a Negro man, call'd Dick; a short well-set fellow, bow legg'd, of a tawny complexion, and took with him a pair of buckskin breeches, kersey jacket, a blue great coat, two coarse shirts, and two pair of trowsers; he also took a gun and ammunition with him. Any person securing the said Negro, and letting his said master have him again, shall have Forty Shillings reward, and reasonable charges,
    paid by  VALENTINE DUSHANE.
*The Pennsylvania Gazette*, November 2, 1749; November 9, 1749; November 16, 1749; November 23, 1749; November 30, 1749; December 5, 1749; December 19, 1749; December 26, 1749; January 2, 1750; January 9, 1750; January 16, 1750; January 23, 1750; February 6, 1750; February 13, 1750; February 20, 1750.


RUn away from Thomas Collins, near Bombahook, an Irish servant man, named John Hughes, about 22 years of age, a short well set fellow, fresh complexion, pretty much pock broken, black short hair: Had on, an olive green cloth coat, lined with dark shaloon, grey kersey jacket, homespun shirt,

narrow trowsers, purple yarn stockings, good shoes, and felt hat, Whoever takes up said servant, and brings him to his said master, or secures him, so that he may be had again, shall have Five Pounds reward, and reasonable charges,   paid by   THOMAS COLLINS.
N. B. He took with him a canoe, sharp at stem and stern, and crack'd in the bottom, and perhaps may go by the name of John Still, as he has often done before.
*The Pennsylvania Gazette*, November 2, 1749; November 9, 1749; November 16, 1749.

## 1750

RUn away from the subscribers, of Mill-creek hundred, Newcastle county, two Irish servant men; one named Mark Lolor, a strait, tall, smart fellow, about six foot high: Had on when he went away, a light brown jacket, a striped one, and a flannel one, buckskin breeches, check shirt, and a woollen cap. The other named John Beady, a short well-set fellow, about five foot eight inches high, and has a down look: Had on when he went away, a light blue colour'd coat, and stole from his master an olive colour'd coat, and three shirts; he wore a felt hat, and black wig. Whoever takes up said servants, and secures them, so that their masters may have them again, shall have Twenty shillings reward, and reasonable charges,
paid by HUGH CLARK, or WALTER THEADFORD.
*The Pennsylvania Gazette*, February 13, 1750; February 20, 1750; February 27, 1750. See *The Pennsylvania Gazette*, August 23, 1750.


RUN away from the house of James M'Connell, of Sadsbury township, in Lancaster county, a servant lad, belonging to Joshua Wood, of New-castle county, named Aaron Allen, aged about 17 years, about 5 foot high, brown complexion, black eyes: Had on when he went away, an old felt hat, old worsted cap, an old light colour'd cloth jacket, strip'd linnen trowsers, and a pair of old Indian stockings, old shoes, and ozenbrigs shirt; and has been among the Indians, and pretends to talk Indian. Whoever takes up the said servant, and secures him, so that his master may have him again, shall have Thirty Shillings reward, and reasonable charges,
paid by   JAMES M'CONNELL.
*The Pennsylvania Gazette*, April 5, 1750; April 12, 1750.


*Philadelphia, March* 28. 1750.
RUN away on *Monday* the 26th Inst. from *Thomas Ogle* of *New-Castle* County, a servant Man named *Christopher Welch*, about twenty-five Years

of age, of low Stature, had on a light coloured Coat with a Cape to it, a blue waist Coat with pewter Buttons, old leather Breeches, old Shoes and Stockings. Said Servant is supposed to be gone in Company with one *William Waller*, who is a Hired Servant to said *Ogle*, said *Waller*, is a middle sized Man, had on when he went away, a blue Coat with blue Lining, and has a scare [*sic*] on his Nose. Whoever takes up said Servants, and secures them so that their Master may have them again shall have *Thirty Shillings* for each, and reasonable Charges
              paid by    THOMAS OGLE.
*The Pennsylvania Journal, or, Weekly Advertiser*, April 5, 1750; April 12, 1750; April 19, 1750; April 26, 1750; May 3, 1750; April 10, 1750.


Run away, on the 4th inst. from David Wilkin, of Noxonton, New-castle county, an Irish servant woman, named Mary Conolly, about 23 years of age, about 5 feet 4 inches high, fair complexion, is very slim, and looks sickly, stoops pretty much when she walks: Had on when she went away, a red duffil jacket, an old cotton and linnen bed gown, an old straw hat, 2 linsey woolsey petticoats, coarse apron, and shirt. She broke open a store and took several sorts of goods away, and may probably change her name van apparel. Whoever takes up said thief, and secures her so that she may be brought to justice, shall have Five Pounds reward, and reasonable charges,
            paid by    John Jones, in Noxonton.
*The Pennsylvania Gazette*, May 17, 1750; May 24, 1750; May 31, 1750.


RUN away on the 8th of this Instant, from *John Grubb*, of *Brandeywine Hundred*, in the County of *New-Castle*, on *Delaware*, a Negro Man named *Cesar*, some what yellowish in Complection, short and well set; Had on when he went away, a homespun Shirt and Trowsers, a dark grey homespun Jacket, and an old Hatt. Whoever takes up, and secures said Negro, so that his Master may have him again, shall have *Forty Shillings* Reward, and reasonable Charges paid by    JOHN GRUBB.
*The Pennsylvania Journal, or, Weekly Advertiser*, June 26, 1750; July 19, 1750.


RUn away, on the 20th inst. from George Monro, of Newcastle, an Irish servant man, named Hugh Kelly, aged about 21 years, a lusty clumsy made fellow, his hair cut off, and has a very little beard: Had on when he went away, a wool hat, somewhat worn, a white cap, a light coloured cloth jacket, lines with blue bayes, and very tarry, a homespun shirt, and trowsers, likewise he has others to shift, and has taken with him a cedar whale boat, a hammock, an old scarlet jacket, with metal or silver buttons, and sundry other things. Whoever secures said servant, if taken above Philadelphia, shall have Forty Shillings reward, and reasonable charges,

   paid by  GEORGE MONRO.

*The Pennsylvania Gazette*, June 28, 1750; July 5, 1750; July 12, 1750.

          New-castle on Delaware, June 30, 1750. THis is to give notice of the 3 following persons being taken up and committed to this goal, viz. William Davis, aged about 40 years, short brown hair, has on a tow shirt, and ozenbrigs trowsers, a pair of red breeches, old felt hat, new dogskin shoes, and a coat of Maryland kersey, fit for Negroes wear, a pair of worsted stockings, about 5 feet 10 inches high.

 George Griffin, a well-set fellow, about 22 years old, of a brown complexion, has on a tow shirt, and ozenbrigs trowsers, old felt hat, but neither shoes nor stockings.

 James Burns, about 5 feet high, somewhat freckled in the face, or mark'd with the small pox, in the same habit as the above George Griffin, all but a linsey woolsey jacket, with stripes across the body. Their masters, or master, if any they have, are desired to appear and discharge them, otherwise they will be set at liberty in 6 weeks, paying their charges.

   *Caleb Pusey*, deputy sheriff.

*The Pennsylvania Gazette*, July 5, 1750; July 12, 1750; July 19, 1750.

RUn away from John Juquat, of Swannack, Newcastle county, on the 3d inst. a Dutch servant man, named Frederick Vandyke, about 30 years of age, of middle size, dark complexion, dark brown hair, speaks tolerable good English, and can talk French: Had on when he went away, a coarse shirt, with half sleeves put to it, coarse trowsers, and an old felt hat. Whoever takes up and secures said servant, so as he may be had again, shall have Thirty Shillings reward, and reasonable charges, paid by John Juquat, or Caleb Pusey, deputy sheriff of Newcastle .

 *The Pennsylvania Gazette*, July 19, 1750; July 26, 1750; August 2, 1750; August 9, 1750.

*RUn away from the subscriber, living in Miln-Creek hundred, New-castle county, an Irish servant man, named Mark Lolar, a smart likely fellow, about 5 foot 9 inches high, had short curl'd hair, or perhaps hath cut it off: Had on when he went away, a felt hat, a white cloth jacket, lin'd with brown, two coarse pair of tow trowsers, and shirts of the same, one pair of new stockins,*

*a pair of calfskin pumps, and silver buckles: There was another fellow in company with him, named Morris Welch, a short well set fellow: Had on when he went away, a light olive colour'd coat, and blue jacket, 3 pair of white stockings; he had also two black wigs, and perhaps hath given the other one of them, and perhaps the other hath given him the silver buckles, and they may have changed clothes for disguise. Whoever takes up said fellows, and secures them, so that they may be brought to their master, shall have Forty Shillings reward, and reasonable charges,*
    *paid by*    HUGH CLARK.
The Pennsylvania Gazette, August 23, 1750; August 30, 1750; September 6, 1750. See *The Pennsylvania Gazette*, February 13, 1750.


*RUn away on the 6th instant, from the subscriber, near St. George's, Newcastle county, a Negroe man, named Sam, about 30 years of age, about 6 foot high, is a likely fellow, took with him a blue duroy coat, a brown drugget coat, with white metal buttons, check trowsers, old leather breeches, shoes and stockings, a fine shirt, a new raccoon hat, and an old ditto, and has a fiddle with him: Also a Negroe woman, about the same age, she is short and thick, and is not as black as the man: She took with her, a good calico gown, a linsey do. a red quilt, shoes, and stockings, and good linnen. Whoever takes up said Negroes and sends them home, or secures them in any goal, so that the owner may have them again, shall have Three Pounds reward, and reasonable charges,*
    *paid by*    JAMES JAMES.
The Pennsylvania Gazette, September 13, 1750; September 20, 1750; October 11, 1750.


RUn away on the 5th instant, from Archibald Little, of Wilmington, Newcastle county, two Irish servants, viz. a man and his wife; the man's name Nicholas Welsh, the wife's name Mary, and have with them a young child, about two months old; the man is about 40 years of age, of middle stature, of a pale complexion, has dark colour'd hair, and speaks pretty good English. Had on when he went away, a light colour'd cloth coat and jacket, both patched on the back, coarse shirt, old leather breeches, and check trowsers, dark grey yarn stockings, old shoes, and pretty good felt hat. The woman is between 20 and 30 years of age, is pock-mark'd, of a sandy complexion; had on a crape gown, and the child has a striped gown. Whoever takes up and secures said servants, so as their master may have them again, shall have Three Pounds reward, and reasonable charges, paid by Joseph M'Dowell, of East Marlborough township, Chester county.

*The Pennsylvania Gazette*, October 25, 1750, November 1, 1750; November 8, 1750; November 15, 1750.

## 1751

RUN away the 11th inst. from John Henderson, of Welch-Track, Newcastle county, a native Irish servant man, named Charles Connor, about 20 years of age, speaks pretty good English, a slim fellow, about 5 foot high, pock-mark'd, short black hair, if not cut off: Had on when he went away, a coarse felt hat, a diaper cap, a striped linsey jacket, a white cloth ditto, with brass buttons, a blue coat, made the new fashion, a check short, blue breeches, grey stockings, new shoes, with brass buckles. Whoever takes up and secures said servant in any goal, so as his master may have him again, shall have Three Pounds reward, and reasonable charges,
   paid by JOHN HENDERSON.
N. B. It is supposed he hath taken a gun with him, and a new coarse linnen shirt, and a pair of blue worsted stockings; they all being stole the night he run away.
 *The Pennsylvania Gazette*, January 22, 1751; January 29, 1751; February 5, 1751; February 12, 1751. See *The Pennsylvania Gazette*, August 8, 1751.


         Philadelphia, January 29, 1750-1.
RUn away on the 20th inst. from the subscriber, living in Mill-Creek Hundred, Newcastle county, an Irish servant man, nam'd Bartholomew M'Guire, about 25 years of age, well-set, fresh colour, black hair: Had on when he went away, a good felt hat, dark brown wig, blue cloth coat, lined with blue, a napp'd ratteen jacket, without lining, striped linsey jacket, blue cloth breeches, good shoes and stockings; has several shirts, check and white, and other clothes not here mentioned. Whoever takes up and secures said servant in any goal, so that his master may have him again, shall have Twenty Shillings reward, if taken in Newcastle county, and if in any other County, Forty Shillings, and reasonable charges,
   paid by FRANCIS GRAHAM.
N. B. All masters of vessels or others, are forbid to harbour, conceal, or carry him off, at their Peril.
 *The Pennsylvania Gazette*, January 29, 1751; February 5, 1751; February 12, 1751; February 19, 1751.


RUn away on the 19th of this inst. from the subscriber, living in Newcastle county, an Irish servant man, named Manus Harly, about 25 years of age, a short well-set fellow, pock-marked, brown curled hair: Had on when he went

away, an old blue camblet coat, patch'd on one shoulder, a dark grey vest, and a grey under ditto, with two sorts of brass buttons, and also a striped holland jacket and breeches, and a blue cloth jacket, one coarse shirt, and 'tis likely a fine one, also a middling fine hat, old shoes, one half soled; looks thin in the face, being lately under a salivation. [sic] Whoever takes up and secures said servant, so as his master may have him again, shall have Three Pounds reward, and reasonable charges,
            paid by    JOHN EDWARDS.
N. B. 'Tis supposed that he took with him, a small black stallion; he went from the doctor before he was well cured of the pox.
    *The Pennsylvania Gazette*, February 26, 1751; March 5, 1751; March 12, 1751; March 28, 1751.


*RUN away from* James Lefferty, *Cordwainer, of* Apoquimony, *in the County of* Newcastle *on* Delaware, *the* 17*th of* February *last, an Irish Servant Man named* William Waffen, *aged about* 27 *Years, thin Vissage, and limps with his right Leg; and had blue Cloaths on: He went off with one* George Kelley, *a short Man, and very impudent. Also one* Mary Fitzgerald, *a young Woman of about* 17 *Years of Age, large Nose, down Look, and pock-mark'd; as also* Catharine Lefferty, *Mother to the said* Mary Fitzgerald: *They have stole two Horses and two Mares, and sundry other Goods, to the Value of above Ninety Pounds: The said* Catharine Lefferty *is well dress'd, and the others pass for her Relations and Servants. They pass'd through* New-York *about* 10 *Days ago, in their Way designing for* Boston, *and are Roman Catholicks. Whoever takes up and brings the said Run-aways and Thieves to* Newcastle *Jail, shall have* TWENTY-FIVE *Pounds Reward,* Philadelphia *Currency, or shall bring only the said* Waffen *and* Fitzgerald *to said Jail, shall have* SIXTEEN POUNDS *Reward, and reasonable Charges,*
            *paid by*    JAMES LEFFERTY.
    *New-York Gazette Revived in the Weekly Post-Boy*, March 4, 1751; March 11, 1751; March 18, 1751.


                            Philadelphia, March 28, 1751.
RUn away from the subscriber, the 2d inst. near St. George's in Newcastle county, a Dutch servant man, named Thomas Anslow, bred up in England, he is about 25 years of age, about 5 feet 8 inches high, fresh coloured, red hair, but cut off, and wears a cap: Had on when he went away, a large grey jacket, and a black one under it, old leather breeches, two shirts, blue and white yarn stockings, rackoon hat, about half-worn, a cotton culgee handkerchief, but may perhaps have changed his apparel; he is a thick well-set fellow. Whoever takes up and secures the said servant, so that his master

may have him again, shall have Three Pounds reward, and reasonable charges, paid by me       JAMES JAMES.

*The Pennsylvania Gazette,* March 28, 1751; April 4, 1751; April 18, 1751; May 2, 1751.


*RUn away the* 17*th of this inst. March, from the subscribers Uriah Blue, and Henry Bishop, living near White-Clay-Creek, in Mill-Creek hundred, and county of Newcastle,* 2 *servant men, the one an Irish man, named Thomas Donaldson, about* 6 *foot high,* 35 *years of age, and supposed to have his indentures with him, being an old soldier, and has lost one eye, and has a Certificate, intitling him to a pension from the King, for the loss of it: Had on when he went away, a lightish colour'd coat, old red jacket, striped flannel ditto, breeches of the same of his coat, mounted with white metal buttons, carved on the top, a check shirt, and a white one, grey yarn stockings, good shoes, sharp toe, a pretty good wool hat.*

*The other a native Irish-man, named Thomas Ryan, about* 22 *years of age, about* 5 *foot* 6 *inches high, talks quick and broken English, has short black hair: Had on when he went away, an old blue jacket, and a striped linnen ditto, coarse two shirt, old leather breeches, has a hole on the right knee, and has a paid of lightish colour'd worsted stockings, and a pair of mixed yarn stockings with him, a pair of duck-bill'd shoes, half-worn, a new wool hat, large in the brim. Whoever takes up and secures said servants, so that their said masters may have them again, shall have Three Pounds for both, or Thirty Shillings for either of them, paid by us.*
       URIAH BLUE, and HENRY BISHOP.

*The Pennsylvania Gazette,* March 28, 1751; April 4, 1751; April 11, 1751. See *The Pennsylvania Gazette,* September 12, 1751, for Ryan.


                              Christine-Bridge, March 26. 1751.
*RUn away from the subscriber, a servant man, named John Clark, a small man, about* 35 *years of age, a thin faced man, of a brown complexion, wore a blue and white cotton cap, has a small cast with his eyes: Had on when he went away, a snuff coloured jacket, with metal buttons, a pair of old leather breeches, very much broke at the knees, check shirt, yarn stockings, a pair of shoes, tied with strings, an old felt hat. Whoever takes up the said servant and brings him to the subscriber, shall have Forty Shillings reward, and all reasonable charges*
             paid by     CATHERINE KIRKPATRICK.

*The Pennsylvania Gazette,* April 4, 1751; April 11, 1751; April 25, 1751.

Whereas John Rodman made his escape from William Bradshaw, constable of Christine Hundred, Newcastle county, on the 27th of February last, who had him in custody for debt; he is a New-England man, about 25 years of age, a shoemaker by trade, of a middle size, slender, pock-mark'd, and his nose turns remarkably up: Had on a bearskin coat, with white metal buttons, wears a cap, and has long black hair. Whoever takes up and secures said Rodman, so as said Bradshaw may have him again, shall have Three Pounds reward, and reasonable charges,
          paid by    WILLIAM BRADSHAW.
*The Pennsylvania Gazette*, May 9, 1751; May 23, 1751; May 30, 1751; June 6, 1751.


*RUn away from the subscriber, of St. Georges's hundred, in the county of Newcastle, upon Delaware, an indented servant man, about 25 years of age: Also an apprentice, about 20 years of age, both weavers by trade; the servant's name is John Graham, an Irish man born, but speaks good English, about 5 feet 5 inches high, a well set fellow, full faced, bold spoken, and pretty much pock-mark'd; Had on when he went away, a blue and white homespun jacket and breeches, a pair of brown cloth breeches, a new felt hat, a black wig, and white linnen cap, old blue worsted stockings, and good shoes. The apprentice's name is William Seers, a likely black ey'd fellow, country born: Had on when he went away, a brown homespun cloth jacket, much worn, with black linsey woolsey lining, ozenbrigs shirt, a pair of brown yarn stockings, old shoes, a hat, half-worn, a white linnen cap, and an old brown wig; but may either of them change their names, as well as their apparels.*

    *Whoever takes up the said servant and secures him, so as his master may have him again, shall have Four Pounds for the servant man; and Twenty Shillings reward for the apprentice, and reasonable charges,*
          paid by    BOAZ BOYCE.
*The Pennsylvania Gazette*, June 6, 1751; June 13, 1751; June 20, 1751.


                                     *Philadelphia, July* 25. 1751.
*Run away on the* 19*th inst. from the subscriber, living in Newcastle county, an Irish servant man, named Michael Brannen, about* 20 *years of age, of a middle stature, and sandy complexion, speaks pretty much with the brogue on his tongue (and what is very remarkable) one joint of his left hand thumb is cut off, and also one of his fingers on said hand is crooked, as the effect of a cut; Had on when he went away, an old felt hat, a whitish colour'd jacket, and brass buttons, a new shirt, a pair of trowsers, and a pair of new shoes, with brass buckles; and it is thought that he hath taken some of his master's clothes with him.*

*Whoever takes up and secures said servant, so as his master may have him again, shall have Five Pounds reward, and reasonable charges,*
        paid by   DANIEL BRITT.
*The Pennsylvania Gazette,* July 25, 1751; August 1, 1751; August 15, 1751.

                                    Philadelphia, July 19. 1751.
RUn away, on Monday last, from George Bratten, of Brandywine Hundred, Newcastle county, a native Irish servant lad, namd Patrick Connolin, about 17 years of age, about 5 foot 5 inches high, has black streight hair, lately trimm'd, one of his upper teeth grows remarkably over the tooth next to it, and he has a little of the brogue on his tongue: Had on when he went away, a brownish colour'd homespun jacket, lined with thick blue Cloth, and pewter buttons on it, old homespun flax shirt, the collar much too wide for him, old tow trowsers, patch'd before, half worn shoes, with straps; he has also two new castor hats, and it is supposed he took a good deal of money with him. Whoever takes up said servant, and secures him, so as his master may have him again, shall have Forty Shillings reward,
        paid by   GEORGE BRATTEN.
N. B. All masters of vessels are forbid to carry him off at their peril.
*The Pennsylvania Gazette,* July 25, 1751; August 1, 1751; August 15, 1751.


RUn away on the 4th inst. from John Henderson, of Welch Tract, Newcastle county, A native Irish servant man, named Charles Conner, about 20 years of age, speaks pretty good English, is a slim fellow, about 5 feet high, pock-mark'd, pale visage, down look, black bushy hair, the top of one of his fore fingers crooked: Had on when he went away, a coarse felt hat, light colour'd cloth jacket, with brass buttons, coarse tow shirt and trowsers of the same, old shoes, with brass buckles. Whoever takes up and secures said servant in any goal, so as his master may have him again, shall have Three Pounds reward, and reasonable charges,
        paid by   JOHN HENDERSON.
N. B. Said servant run away last February, and was put in Newtown goal, and from thence made his escape, and was secured in Philadelphia goal. All masters of vessels and others are forbid to carry him off at their peril.
*The Pennsylvania Gazette,* August 8, 1751; August 22, 1751; September 5, 1751. See *The Pennsylvania Gazette,* January 22, 1751.

Christine-Bridge, August 18, 1751.
RUn away last Saturday night, from John Simkin, at the house of Thomas Williams, at Christine-bridge, in New-castle county, A convict servant man, named John Piercy, with a pair of hand-coofs on; he has lost his right thumb, close to his hand: Had on, a half-worn castor hat, black curl'd hair, a blue jacket, a dirty check shirt, a pair of sailors wide trowsers, and old shoes. He passes for a distressed sailor, and was whipt in Philadelphia last week. Whoever takes up and secures said servant in goal, so as his master may have him again, shall have Twenty Shillings reward, and reasonable charges,
          paid by    THOMAS WILLIAMS.
*The Pennsylvania Gazette*, August 22, 1751; August 29, 1751; September 5, 1751.


      St. George's Hundred, Newcastle County, August 22. 1751.
RUn away from the subscriber, on the 12th inst. an Irish servant man, nam'd Patrick White, about 23 years of age, five feet nine inches high, fresh colour'd, has black hair, and had on when he went away, a felt hat, dark brown plain coat, with red lining, round cuffs, lin'd with red, flat metal buttons on it, a jacket of the same, with coat buttons on it, lined with old stuff, and ozenbrigs shirt and trowsers. he has a scar on his chin. Whoever takes up said servant, and secures him, so as his master may have him again, shall have Forty Shillings reward, and reasonable charges,
          paid by me.    JOHN CLARK.
*The Pennsylvania Gazette*, August 29, 1751; September 5, 1751; September 12, 1751.


RUn away on the 8th inst. from the Subscriber, living near White-Clay-Creek, in Newcastle county, A native Irish servant man, named Thomas Ryan, about 5 feet 6 inches high, fresh colour'd, talks quick, and has short hair: Had on when he went away, a lightish colour'd camblet jacket, lined with deep blue shaloon, tow petticoat trowsers, tow shirt, and a half-worn wool hat, large brimm'd, and has a large light colour'd dog with him. Whoever takes up and secures said servant, so as his master may have him again, shall have Thirty Shillings reward, and reasonable charges,
          paid by    HENRY BISHOP.
*The Pennsylvania Gazette*, September 12, 1751; September 19, 1751; September 26, 1751. See *The Pennsylvania Gazette*, March 28, 1751.


RUn away on the 8th inst. from John Logue, of Christine hundred, Newcastle county, A servant man, named Jeremiah Sullivan, about 22 years of age: Had on when he went away, a blackish coat, and a jacket, without sleeves, a pair of old breeches, mended in the seat, shoes and buckles, a wool hat, and a black wig: He is of a middle stature, and pale complexion. Whoever takes up and secures said servant so as his master may have him again, shall have Twenty Shillings reward, and reasonable charges,

            paid by    JOHN LOGUE.

*The Pennsylvania Gazette*, September 12, 1751; September 19, 1751; September 26, 1751.


RUn away on the 16th instant, from James Moore, of Mill-Creek hundred, Newcastle county, a native Irish servant man, named Dudley Hanley, about 20 years of age, of a dark complexion, round visage, and speaks pretty good English: Had on when he went away, a woollen jacket, striped with blue, red and yellow, new buckskin breeches, brown linnen shirt, coarse yarn stockings, new shoes, with large carv'd buckles, and a large brimm'd felt hat. Whoever takes up and secures said servant, so as his master may have him again, shall have Forty Shillings reward, and reasonable charges.

            paid by    JAMES MOORE.

*The Pennsylvania Gazette*, September 19, 1751; September 26, 1751; October 3, 1751.


                                Philadelphia, September 26. 1751.
Runaway the 16th inst. an Irish servant lad, named Alexander Steel, about 19 years of age, was formerly a drummer in the army, and speaks good English: Had on when he went away, a black frize jacket, and a calicoe under jacket, regimental breeches, check shirt, two pair worsted stockings, one a light blue colour, half worn, and a coarse hat. He is smooth faced, has long black hair, sometimes plaited with a black ribbon. Whoever takes up said servant , and brings him to his masters at Rariton, in Millcreek Hundred, Newcastle county, or secures him, so as they may have him again, shall have Forty Shillings reward, and reasonable charges, paid by us,

            HUGH KELLY, WALTER THETFORD.

*The Pennsylvania Gazette*, September 26, 1751.


ON Monday the 18th of November last, between three and four a clock in the morning the house of George Adams, at Christine-bridge, Newcastle county, was broke open, and robbed of money to the value of about Two Pounds Ten Shillings, in small tickets, pennies, and some small pieces of silver, also a small trifle of goods; said Adams on hearing a noise in his shop, got up to see what it was, when the thief threatened to shoot him, and accordingly snapp'd a pistol several times at him, and then made his escape, leaving his shoes behind, and several sorts of carpenters tools, with which 'tis supposed he opened the door; the same morning a man came barefoot and bare legg'd to one Adam Marley, a shoemaker at Newport, and got a pair of shoes, which person is supposed to be the thief, having his stockings and a large pair of silver shoe-buckles in his pocket; said fellow has been shot thro' the small of his left leg, which causes a lump on his shin, and has also been shot thro' one of his thighs, is a middle aged man, about five feet nine inches high: Had on three bluish colour'd jackets, a light colour'd surtout coat, wide ticken trowsers, and a half worn hat, with a ribbon band. Whoever takes up and secures said fellow in any goal in Newcastle county, Pennsylvania, or Maryland, so that he be brought to justice, shall have Thirty Shillings reward, and reasonable charges, paid by     GEORGE ADAMS.

*The Pennsylvania Gazette*, December 5, 1751; December 10, 1751; December 17, 1751.

## 1752

STray'd or stolen, on the 25th of last month, from William Tussey, of Brandywine Hundred, Newcastle county, a large roan mare, four years old, about 15 hands high, all her feet white, and black at the knees, a white streak down her face, grey mane and tail, both paces and trots, and suckled a colt when she stray'd, or was stolen, has neither brand nor ear mark; if stolen, it is supposed to have been by one Alexander Davis, who was formerly a servant in that Hundred, and has lately been lurking about that neighbourhood, but is now gone off; he appear'd in several sorts of dress, sometimes in his own hair, at other times in a wig, with his hair tuck'd up under it, and sometimes wears a black velvet hunting cap. Whoever secures the said mare and thief, so that he may be brought to justice, shall have Five Pounds reward, and reasonable charges, and for the mare alone Forty Shillings, paid by     WILLIAM TUSSEY.

*The Pennsylvania Gazette*, January 7, 1752; January 14, 1752.

RUn away on the 15th instant, from John Lettimore, of Pencader hundred, in Newcastle county, an Irish servant man, named James Boucher, by trade a shoemaker, of a middle size, wears his own short black hair: Had on when he went away a reddish colour'd [f]lip coat dark colour'd cloth jacket, old buckskin breeches, black stockings, new shoes, with large pewter buckles, and a half-worn castor hat: Also took with him, a lead colour'd strait coat, lined with light blue linsey, a green double-breasted jacket, check trowsers, two setts of shoemakers tools, two lasts, a pair of mens shoes, and two calf-skins. Whoever takes up and secures said servant, so that his master may have

him again, shall have FIVE POUNDS reward, and reasonable charges,
             paid by   JOHN LETTIMORE.
    N. B. It is thought he will endeavour to pass for a free man, he having an old indenture with him, dated August 24, which was made before Thomas James, Esq; He also took a very good hat with him, besides that he had on.
    *The Pennsylvania Gazette*, January 21, 1752; January 28, 1752; February 4, 1752; February 11, 1752; February 18, 1752.


    RUn away from Vincent Lockerman, of Dover, a Negroe man, named Dick, about 26 years of age, 5 feet 6 or 8 inches high, a slim likely fellow, by trade a chocolate grinder, lately belonging to Conrad Whitaker, butcher in Philadelphia: Had on when he went away, a bear-skin great coat, trimm'd with white metal buttons, with cat-gut eyes, and brown jacket and breeches, his shoes hob nail'd all round, worsted cap, and an old castor hat. Whoever takes up the said Negroe, and secures him in any Goal, or brings him to his said master, shall have Twenty Shillings reward, besides what the law allows, and reasonable charges,
             paid by   VINCENT LOCKERMAN.
    *The Pennsylvania Gazette*, April 2, 1752; April 9, 1752; April 16, 1752; April 23, 1752.


    Stolen from Bermudian Settlement, Cumberland county, on the 29th of April last, from the subscriber, A small black horse with a star in his forehead, one of his hind feet white, a white mark on the inside of one of his thighs, his sides shaved with geers, paces and trots, short bob tail. Supposed to be stolen by one Joseph Henchy, an Englishman, pretends to be a mason, about 50 years of age, 5 feet 6 inches high: Had on A blue coat, grey jacket, and ragged cloth breeches. Whoever secures said horse and thief, so that he may be brought to justice, shall have Forty Shillings reward, and if the horse only Twenty Shillings, and reasonable charges, paid by George Henry, Blacksmith, near New-castle, on Delaware.
    *The Pennsylvania Gazette*, May 21, 1752; June 4, 1752.


    RUN away from the subscriber, living at Cool-spring, Sussex county, upon Delaware, A servant man, named Edward Proger, by trade a Taylor, about 20 years of age, about 5 feet and a half high, swarthy complexion, his lips are very thick, and his face somewhat bump'd, born in England: Had on when he went away, A blue waistcoat, without sleeves, white ruffled shirt, black wig, new felt hat, new shoes, one brass buckle, and one steel ditto, and grey yarn stockings. 'Tis suppos'd he went abroad of a vessel bound to Rhode-

Island, Joseph Hadley, commander. Whoever takes up and secures said servant, so as his master may have him again, shall have Forty Shillings reward, and reasonable charges,
   paid by  JAMES M'ILVAINE.
*The Pennsylvania Gazette*, July 9, 1752; July 16, 1752; July 23, 1752.

*Newcastle*, July 13, 1752.
Notice is hereby given, that on the 18th of June last was taken up, and committed to Jail, a Negroe fellow, nam'd Ned: Had on a good linen jacket, and a strip'd ditto, with broad brass buttons; says he belongs to Mr. John Elsey, of Summerset county, Maryland. Also on the 10th inst. James Coldren, and Ann Cortney, were committed, on suspicion of being runaways; the man is of a middle size, says he married the woman lately in Philadelphia, has on a half worn wool hat, brown wig, check shirt, grey worsted stockings, pretty good shoes, with white metal buckles, red jacket, without sleeves, and a green coat, with blue lining, and says he came from Accamack, in Virginia. The woman has on an old linen shift, blue quilted petticoat, blue stockings, and old shoes, a short calico bed-gown, and red cloak; she is an Irish woman, and says she serv'd her time in Philadelphia. There is also in same Jail one John Phillips; has on a good castor hat, white linnen shirt, blue sailor jacket, brown coat, with red lining to the collar, old check trowsers, grey stockings, old shoes, and old brass buckles in them; is thin visag'd, has short black hair, and is about 24 years of age. The owners of the white people are desir'd to appear in six weeks after this date, otherwise they will be discharg'd on paying charges.  CALEB PUSEY, Deputy Sheriff.
*The Pennsylvania Gazette*, July 16, 1752; July 23, 1752; August 6, 1752.

*Philadelphia, July* 30, 1752.
Run away from the subscriber, of Thoroughfare Neck, New-castle county, a servant man, nam'd William Charlton: had on when he went away, old shoes, and two pair blue stockings, two pair petticoat trowsers, tow and tear, [*sic*] two shirts, one of them new, both tow and tear, two jackets, one new, one strip'd red, black and white, the other black, and old beaver hat. He is of a dark complexion, has light colour'd hair, and has a scar on one of his cheeks: Had with him a twill'd bag, mark'd I E. He is supposed to have gone by water in a canoe. Whoever takes up said servant, and secures him, so that his master may have him again, shall have Five Pounds reward, and reasonable charges,
   paid by  JAMES EGBURTS.
N. B. The above servant ran away the second of June last.
*The Pennsylvania Gazette*, July 30, 1752; August 13, 1752.

RUN away on the 8th instant, at night, from the subscriber, living at the Red Lion, in Newcastle county, a Dutch servant man, nam'd Matthias Ambruster, about five foot six inches high, about 36 years of age, pale complexion, with long strait fair colour'd hair: Had on when he went away, a blue cloth coat, made Dutch fashion, one of the sleeves much chaw'd by a creature, red cloth jacket, without sleeves, old striped cotton trowsers, leather breeches, half worn shoes, with small carv'd buckles, and a half worn felt hat; he can scarce speak any English, is a mason by trade, and when talking, or looking earnestly at any thing, commonly shuts one eye. Whoever takes up said servant , so that his master may have him again, shall have Forty Shillings reward, if taken out of the said county,
    paid by  OBADIAH ELLIOT.
*The Pennsylvania Gazette*, August 13, 1752; September 14, 1752. Second ad has "Philadelphia, August 16, 1752." at the top.

RUN away, on the 19th inst. at night, from George Crow, of the borough of Wilmington, Newcastle county, An English servant man, named Henry Bimpson, a clock-maker by trade, about 5 feet 8 inches high, and about 30 yearss of age, thin visage, much pitted with the small-pox, is pretty slender, and walks briskly: Had on when he went away, A blue broad-cloth coat, with slash sleeves, lined with blue shaloon, old buckskin breeches, that has been dy'd purple, grey mill'd stockings, old half soaled shoes, with brass buckles, an old weather-beaten wig. Whoever takes up and secures said servant in any goal, so as his master may have him again, shall have Five Pounds reward,
    paid by  GEORGE CROW.
*The Pennsylvania Gazette*, September 28, 1752; October 5, 1752; October 12, 1752.

RUn away from the subscriber, living in Red Lion hundred, in Newcastle county, on the 20th of September last, a Negroe-man, named Gregg, aged 23 years, about 5 feet high, of a very black colour, hollow eyes, strait small legs, and little feet, had a sore on the upper part of his left foot, and talks pretty good English: Had on when he went away, a brown cloth jacket, double breasted, with brass buttons, but he may probably change it, a tow shirt, and trowsers of the same, and a half-worn felt hat. Whoever takes up and secures said Negroe, so that his master may have him again, shall have Forty Shillings reward, and reasonable charges,
    paid by  JAMES DAVIES.
*The Pennsylvania Gazette*, October 12, 1752; October 19, 1752; November 2, 1752; November 16, 1752; November 30, 1752.

*Philadelphia, October* 19, 1752.
RUN away on the 25th of last month, from the subscriber, living in Whiteclay creek hundred, Newcastle county, near Christine Bridge, An Irish servant man, named Robert Cleary, about 22 years of age, about 6 feet high, and well proportioned according to his height, is much pock-mark'd. He writes a good clerk's hand, and understands the five common rules in cyphering; and has kept a school. Had on when he went away, A London brown cloth coat, not half-worn, without lining, mohair buttons, and a striped linnen jacket; and took with him, striped drawers, old cloth breeches, yarn stockings, and a half-worn felt hat.
Whoever takes up and secures said servant, so as his master may have him again, shall have Forty Shillings reward, and reasonable charges
          paid by    DAVID EVANS.
*The Pennsylvania Gazette,* October 19, 1752; November 9, 1752; November 16, 1752.


RUn-away the 18th of *September* from the subscriber, living in Wilmington, New Castle county, a negro woman about 30 years of age small stature, marked much with the small-pox, subject to talk much and fast in her own praise, had on or with her a green cloth jacket and camblet quilt, and coarce cloath jacket, and light coloured camblet quilt, and coarse cloath petticoat near the colour, shalloon cloath with lining the same, without a cape to it, and straw hat. when she is closely examined she is subject to shut her eyes and wink much. she formerly belonged to mr. Turner in Philadelphia and lately to mr. Duff of Newport. Whosoever takes up and secures said wench so that her master may have her again shall have forty shillings reward and all reasonable charges paid by    JOHN ECCLES.
*The Pennsylvania Journal, and Weekly Advertiser,* November 30, 1752; December 6, 1752; February 20, 1753.


Philadelphia, December 14, 1752.
There is in Newcastle goal at present, three servant men, viz. One James Caddle, about 35 years of age, about 5 feet 7 inches high, sandy complexion, pock-marked, and very bare of clothes, and says he belongs to one James Chestnut, at Sasquehanna. Another named John Campbell, about 30 years of age, and the same size and complexion, with red jacket and trowsers, and says he belongs to Capt. John Richey. And one J — Thomson, a weaver, a little crooked faced fellow, dark complexion, and says he came in with Capt. Archibald Stewart from Newry. These are therefore to warn all their masters, that they will be sold out for their charges, in a very short time, if they are not redeemed, of which take notice,

from *George Monro*, sheriff.
*The Pennsylvania Gazette*, December 14, 1752; December 19, 1752; January 2, 1753.

## 1753

RUn away from Wilmington, in Newcastle county, the 10th of December last, One Joseph Wilson; country born, of middle stature, long and thin visag'd, about 30 years old; by trade a sadler; but of late a carter; apt to talk, and has lost his upper fore-teeth; his hair cut off, and wears a cap or wig: Wore a leaden colour'd great coat, and a jacket of the same colour, a close-bodied coat, of camblet or duroy, of a brown colour, beaver hat, but not new, fine shirt, and more with him, and both shoes and boots; and feloniously took away the following creatures, viz. A bright sorrel gelding, with a large white mane and tail, trimmed just under the bridle, his mane hangs chiefly on the off side, shod all round, about 14 hands high, about 8 years old, neither brand nor earmark, goes very free and well on a swift pace, and carries himself high, but travels ill on a slow pace, and is apt to trot. A sorrel mare, 3 years old last spring, 14 hands high or upwards, well-set, a small switch tail, small mane, of a reddish colour, hangs on both sides, a broad white spot in her face, which runs in a small strip almost to the end of her nose, one hind foot white, neither brand nor ear-mark, natural trotter, and not broke to ride, but will draw well, and lead a team, shod all round. Whoever takes up and secures said Wilson and creatures, and brings them to Edward Dawes, tavernkeeper, in Wilmington, or Joseph Cobourn, in Philadelphia, or sends word, so that the owner may have his creatures, and the felon brought to justice, shall have Eight Pounds reward, or Three Pounds for each of the creatures, either separate or together, and Forty Shillings for the felon by himself,
    paid by    *Thomas Lewis*, or *Griffith Minshall*.
*The Pennsylvania Gazette*, January 2, 1753; January 9, 1753; January 16, 1753; January 23, 1753; January 30, 1753; February 6, 1753; February 13, 1753; February 20, 1753; February 27, 1753; March 6, 1753; March 13, 1753.

Philadelphia, January 30, 1753.
RUn away from his bail, on Monday the 22d instant, one John Kearns, a cooper by trade, about five feet eight inches high, is a very likely young man, about 23 years of age: Had on when he went away a light brown camblet coat, with a piece on the back of a dark colour, green cloth jacket, two shirts, one check the other white, two pairs of breeches, the uppermost buckskin, white yarn stockings over another pair, white metal buckles in his Shoes, a large fur hat without loops, a striped silk cap, of different colours, striped silk

handkerchief, a greyish great coat, with large metal buttons. Whoever secures said Kearns, so that his bail, Isaac Hersay, of Mill-Creek hundred, in Newcastle county, may have him again, shall have Three Pounds reward, Pennsylvania currency, and reasonable charges,
   paid by ISAAC HERSAY.
 *The Pennsylvania Gazette*, January 30, 1753; February 6, 1753.


Run away, on the 15th instant, from his bail, living at Christine-bridge, New-Castle county, one William Dunn, an Irishman, about 25 years of age, about 5 feet 7 inches high, pock-mark'd; he has formerly followed horse-jockying, but is a weaver by trade: Had on when he went away, a new lead colour'd jacket, with metal buttons, old blue stuff coat, buckskin breeches, blue yarn stockings, old beaver hat, and a silk Handkerchief about his neck. Whoever takes up said William Dunn, and secures him, so as his bail may have him again, shall have Three Pounds reward, and reasonable charges,
   paid by WILLIAM WILSON.
 *The Pennsylvania Gazette*, February 27, 1753; March 6, 1753; March 13, 1753.


Run away on the 12th inst. from James Few, and Nicholas Wilson, of Wilmington, the following servant men, viz. The one named Edward Westward, a Black-smith, or Lock-maker, by trade, an Englishman, about 6 feet high, talks broad West-Country; his upper-lip stands much out: Had on when he went away, A sort of grey bearskin coat, with flat metal buttons, old snuff colour'd jacket, with brass buttons, old greasy leather breeches, old hat and shoes. The other named Patrick Gill, a native Irish-man, speaks tolerable English, a bricklayer or mason by trade, of a middle stature: Had on when he went away, a bearskin jacket, with brass buttons, check shirt, old leather breeches, grey yarn stocking, old shoes, black hair, broad face, with little or no beard; they both stoop as they walk. Whoever takes up and secures said servants so that their masters may have them again, shall have Three Pounds reward, or Thirty Shillings for either,
   paid by JAMES FEW, or NICHOLAS WILSON.
N. B. It is supposed they have got false passes with them.
 *The Pennsylvania Gazette*, March 13, 1753; March 20, 1753; April 5, 1753.


RUN away from his bail, on the 28th ult. One Murtha Denn, a native Irishman, has the brogue on his tongue, thick lips, down-look, and is a lusty well-set fellow: had on when he went away, A camblet coat and jacket, the coat has a large piece set in below the pocket, good castor hat, silk cap, new check shirt, and a white ditto, old breeches, good yarn stockings, half-worn shoes, with brass buckles in them, white cloth jacket, with white metal buttons. Likewise stole, and took with him, A pair of grey cloth breeches, new grey worsted stockings, good check petticoat trowsers, and a blue and white spotted silk handkerchief. Whoever takes up and secures said fellow, so as he may be brought to justice, shall have Three Pounds reward, and reasonable charges, paid by the subscribers hereof, living at Whiteclay creek, near Christine-bridge, in New Castle county,

    *Joseph Rotheram,* or *Joseph England*
   *The Pennsylvania Gazette,* April 5, 1753; April 12, 1753.


RUN away from the subscriber, living in Brandywine Hundred, New-Castle county, on the 23d of April last, a Dutch servant man, named John Schluter, about 48 years of age, middle size, of a thin visage, and long nose: Had on when he went away, a half-worn castor hat, large brown jacket, with brass buttons, lined with striped linsey, brown cloth breeches, seated with blue, black worsted stockings, and a large pair of coarse half-worn shoes. Whoever secures said servant, so that his master may have him again, shall have Thirty Shillings reward, and reasonable charges,

    paid by JASPER POLESON.
 *The Pennsylvania Gazette,* May 3, 1753; May 10, 1753; May 17, 1753.


RUN away on the 10th instant, from the subscriber, living near Christine ferry, in New-Castle hundred, an Irish servant man, named Richard Dalton, about 23 years of age, about 5 feet 4 inches high, well-set, of a black complexion, and has tender eyes: had on when he went away, a grey homespun double breasted jockey coat, pretty old, with small pewter buttons, light colour'd homespun jacket, with white metal buttons, brown homespun breeches, light colour'd stockings, good shoes, with steel buckles, a half-worn felt hat, and a brown wig. Whoever takes up and secures said servant, so that his master may have him again, shall have Thirty Shillings reward, and reasonable charges,

    paid by *Peter Sigfreidusalrichs.*
N. B. Said servant is pretty handy on board a vessel: All masters of vessels are forbid to carry him off at their Peril.
 *The Pennsylvania Gazette,* May 17, 1753; May 24, 1753.


           Philadelphia, May 31, 1753.
Broke out of New-Castle jail, on Wednesday, the 16th inst. A convict man, named Henry Barlow, an Englishman, is a likely well-set fellow, about 30

years of age, and wants the fore-finger of his left hand: Had on when he went away, A blue coat, with broad metal buttons, blue jacket, the holes wrought with silver twist. Whoever secures said servant in any jail, so as his master may have him again, shall have Thirty Shillings reward, paid by George Monrow, Sheriff, of said County, or by William Hodge,
or Alexander Lunan, in Philadelphia.
*The Pennsylvania Gazette*, May 31, 1753; June 7, 1753; June 14, 1753.


Philadelphia, June 21, 1753.
RUN away on the 10th inst. in the morning, from John Robinson, living in Mill-creek hundred, New-Castle county, a Dutch servant man, named Augustine Stahl, aged about 20 or 25 years, a well set man, pretty fair complexion, and black hair, about five feet six inches high: Had on when he went away, a whitish broadcloth coat, with old silk lining, a red cloth jacket, without sleeves, a fine shirt, with ruffles down the bosom; it is supposed he has also a tow shirt with him, an old felt hat, and a buckling comb under his hat, a pair of leather breeches, new whitish colour'd silk stockings, and a pair of new shoes, with brass buckles. Whoever secures said servant, so that his master may have him again, shall have Three Pounds reward, and reasonable charges, paid by    JOHN ROBINSON.
N. B. The said run-away is a mason and stone-cutter by trade, and is supposed to have taken some tools with him.
*The Pennsylvania Gazette*, June 21, 1753; June 28, 1753; July 12, 1753.


Philadelphia, June 21, 1753.
RUN away from Thomas Ogle, of New-Castle county, near Christiana-bridge, two men, one, named John Connor, aged about 25 years, of a middle stature, and well-set, has short black hair, and has lost one of his toes; and, on one of his arms, has letters set in with gun-powder: The other, named Thomas Johnston, aged about 20 years, of a middle stature, well-set, and wears a cap, took his wife, a little boy, about 4 or 5 years of age, with him; also a small black horse, with some grey hairs, and white about his face: Said men stole from Thomas Ogle a beaver hat, little worn, and sundry other goods. Whoever takes up and secures said men, so as they may be brought to justice, shall have Thirty Shillings reward, and reasonable charges, for each, paid by    THOMAS OGLE .
*The Pennsylvania Gazette*, June 21, 1753; June 28, 1753; July 12, 1753.


Philadelphia, June 28, 1753.
RUN away from the subscriber, living in St. George's Hundred, New-Castle county, on the 24th of June instant, an Irish convict servant man, named Hugh

Mulvehill, about five feet sex inches high, sell set, fresh colour'd, with short curled brown hair, but it is supposed he will cut it off, and change his name, having got a pass from some other person, with which it is supposed he will travel: Had on and took with him, two coats, one brown, lined with red shaloon, with flat metal buttons, the other a lightish colourcoat, lined with light colour'd shaloon, with mohair buttons, two ozenbrig shirts, one fine, white ditto, two pair of ozenbrig trowsers, a pair of half-worn leather breeches, grey yarn stockings, a pair of shoes lately half soaled, and a striped linen jacket. Whoever takes up and secures said servant , so that his master may have him again, shall have three Pounds reward,
    paid by  DAVID CLEMENT.
*The Pennsylvania Gazette*, June 28, 1753; July 5, 1753; July 12, 1753.

               Philadelphia, August 16, 1753.
RUN away, on the sixth of this instant August, from his bail, living at Dover, in Kent county, on Delaware, one Joseph Carlisle, this country born, a ship-joiner by trade, about thirty years of age, thin visag'd, long black hair, if not cut off, pitted with the small pox, round shoulder'd, Roman nosed, walks light, and bending forward: had on when he went away, a paid of black leather breeches, white shirt, an old brown coat, with a long darn down the back, ribb'd stockings, of a light colour: Whoever takes up said runaway, and brings him to the subscriber, shall have Three Pounds reward, and reasonable charges, paid by  THOMAS ALFORD.
 *The Pennsylvania Gazette*, August 16, 1753; August 23, 1753; August 30, 1753.


RUN away on the 26th of August last, from the subscriber, living in Mill-creek Hundred, New-Castle county, near Newport, an Irish servant girl, named Jean M'Clellan, of a low stature, very thick, of a dark complexion, black eyes, and black hair, not long enough to tie up, speaks very improper, between Scotch and English: Had on when she went away, a linsey woolsey petticoat, of a dunnish colour, and a bed-gown of the same, a flag handkerchief, with small brown and yellow figures. Whoever takes up and secures said servant, so as her master may have her again, shall have Twenty Shillings reward, and reasonable charges,
    paid by  JAMES WALKER.
 *The Pennsylvania Gazette*, September 6, 1753; September 13, 1753; September 20, 1753.

*RUN away from his bail, in April last, A man named Jonathan Smith, about 40 years of age, near 6 feet high, pretends to be a Carpenter by trade, of a*

*dark complexion, and lived in the Jerseys, near Salem; it is said he was well dressed when he went off. Whoever takes up said Smith, and brings him to his bail, or the Sheriff of Newcastle, shall have Six Pounds reward, and reasonable charges,*
*paid by* THOMAS CANBY, *in Wilmington.*
*The Pennsylvania Gazette,* September 20, 1753; September 27, 1753; October 4, 1753; October 11, 1753; October 18, 1753; October 25, 1753.

Philadelphia, November 8, 1753.
RUN away last night, from the subscriber, living in Mill-Creek hundred, New-Castle county, An Irish servant man, named Samuel Allison, about 30 or 40 years of age, of middle stature, has very black curled hair, with a ring worm on his beard: Took with him, Three linen shirts, a short blue jacket, without lining, a pair of brown cloth breeches, with cloth buttons, a brown coat, lined with flannel, two pair of shoes, one pair new, the other old, old fine hat, and a pair of thread stockings. Whoever secures said servant, so as his master may have him again, shall have Three Pounds reward, and reasonable charges, paid by me DAVID ENGLISH.
N. B. He professes to be fit for land or sea service. 'Tis likely he will change his name. All masters of vessels are forbid to carry him off.
*The Pennsylvania Gazette,* November 15, 1753; November 22, 1753; November 29, 1753.

## 1754

RUN away the 16th of December last, from Boaz Boyce, in New-Castle county, St. George's Hundred, an Irish servant woman, named Agnes Fee, of a low stature, brown complexion, pretty much pitted with the small-pox, bold spoken, and loves a dram very well: Had on when she went away, a black silk hat, a red cloak, lead colour'd stuff gown, blue quilted petticoat, half-worn, an old black quilted ditto, blue yarn stockings, high heel'd shoes, likewise a calicoe bed gown. Whoever takes up said servant woman, and secures her, so that her master may have her again, shall have Thirty Shillings reward, besides what the law allows, paid by the said subscriber,
BOAZ BOYCE.
N. B. She may change her clothes, as well as her name.
*The Pennsylvania Gazette,* January 29, 1754; February 5, 1754; February 12, 1754.

RUN away on the 17th instant, from the subscriber, living in Red-lion hundred, Newcastle county, a servant man, named Matthew Morrison, a short

well-set fellow, with brown bushy hair, about 23 years of age: Had on when he went away, a lightish colour'd coat, with white metal buttons, a white flannel jacket, with flat brass buttons, two homespun shirts, an old felt hat, a pair of blue camblet breeches, two pair of stockings, one pair blue worsted, the other mixed yarn, a pair of old shoes, half soaled, with brass buckles; he formerly served Nathaniel Grub, in Chester County. Whoever takes up and secures said servant, so that his master may have him again, shall have Forty Shillings reward, and reasonable charges,
    paid by JOHN TAYLOR, or ALEXANDER MONTGOMERY.
*The Pennsylvania Gazette*, February 26, 1754; March 5, 1754; March 19, 1754.

              Philadelphia, May 30, 1754.
RUN away on the 15th inst. from Anthony Whitely, tavern-keeper, living in New Castle, An Irish servant man, named William M'Analty, about 23 years of age, of a sandy complexion, much pock marked, with a small flesh mole on his left cheek: Had on when he went away, A new coarse felt hat, country cloth shirt, whitish colour'd fustian jacket and breeches, with white metal buttons, and an under jacket, of twilled flannel, and wears a linen cap, a pair of shoes with straps, but tied with strings, a pair of old white stockings, much darned, and a pair of wide trowsers. 'Tis supposed he will get on board some vessel as a seaman, but he is none. Whoever takes up and secures said servant, so as his master may have him again, shall have Twenty Shillings reward, and reasonable charges,
    paid by  ANTHONY WHITELY.
N. B. All masters of vessels are forbid to carry him off at their peril.
 *The Pennsylvania Gazette*, May 30, 1754; June 6, 1754; June 13, 1754.


              Philadelphia, June 6, 1754.
RUN away from the subscriber, living in St. George's hundred, New-Castle county, about the first of February, A Negro fellow, named Sip, of a low stature, about 48 or 49 years of age, pretty much pock mark'd, had some grey hairs in his head: Had on when he went away, Two brown jackets, with metal buttons, the one without sleeves, and the other with, and lining in it, leather breeches, felt hat double soaled shoes, coarse woolen stockings; he talks good English, is a little tawney, one of his legs a little shorter than the other, and limps a little in his walk.
  Whoever takes up and secures the said Negro, so as his master may have him again, shall have Forty Shillings reward,
    paid by  JAMES ANDERSON, sen.
 *The Pensylvania Gazette*, June 6, 1754; June 13, 1754; June 20, 1754.

RUN away, on the 18th ult. from the subscriber, living in Mill-creek Hundred, Newcastle county, a Negroe woman, about 28 years of age, nam'd Kate, smooth faced, a good black, 5 feet 6 inches high: Had on, when she went away, a calicoe gown, blue quilted petticoat, and carried off with her several other clothes. Whoever takes up and secures said Negroe woman, so as her master may have her again, shall have Thirty Shillings reward, and reasonable charges, paid by      JOHN MONTGOMERY.
*The Pennsylvania Gazette*, July 4, 1754; July 11, 1754.


RUN away from Thomas Montgomery merchant, near Christine bridge, in Newcastle county, a servant man, nam'd Thomas Hoyd, middle siz'd, thin visage, and has fair hair: Had on when he went away, a grey coat, with a rent in the back, and metal buttons, red cloth breeches, or coarse linen trowsers, woollen yarn stockings, narrow toed shoes, felt hat, and coarse lien shirt, and is thought to have gone towards Mr. Daniel Lawrie's, Indian trader in Donegall, Lancaster county, with whom he says he formerly serv'd his time, and was in that time taken by the French, and afterwards got to Liverpool in England, and came from thence in the ship Susanna, Moses Rankin master, in the month of May last, and has gone in a shalop of said Montgomery's since, until he absented himself the 20th ult. in Philadelphia. Whoever takes up said servant, and brings him to said Montgomery, or secures him in any goal, so that his master may have him again, shall have Forty Shillings reward, and reasonable charges,
            paid by    THOMAS MONTGOMERY.
*The Pennsylvania Gazette*, August 1, 1754; August 8, 1754; August 15, 1754; August 22, 1754; August 29, 1754.


RUN away on the 31st of the Seventh Month, called July, from James Hicklin, of Christiana hundred, New-Castle county, A native Irish servant girl, named Mary Neal, speaks pretty good English, and at times speaks loud and fast, and may be perceived to stutter a little, of a ruddy complexion, pretty full breasted, thick black bushy hair, chunky and well-set, short legs, and pretty thick: Took with her when she went away, A new linsey petticoat, striped purple and yellow, and a blue and white strip'd petticoat, no gown, bare footed when she went away, supposed to be about 20 years of age. Whoever takes up and secures said servant Girl, so as her master may have her again, shall have Forty Shillings reward, and reasonable charges,
            paid by    JAMES HICKLIN.
N. B. Perhaps she may pass by the name of O'Neal, but in her indenture she is call'd Mary Neil or Neal, and may probably change her name and apparel.

*The Pennsylvania Gazette*, August 8, 1754; August 15, 1754; August 22, 1754.

*Philadelphia, August 12, 1754.*
RUN away last night from the subscribers hereof, living in Wilmington, two Irish servant men; the one nam'd John Hennen, by trade a spinning-wheel maker, a man of middle stature, fair complexion, well set, and talks somewhat short and surly: had with him and on him when he went away, a bluish cloth coat, red vest and breeches; likewise a white linen vest, and new ozenbrigs trowsers, his stockings thread or worsted, or both; a new coarse felt hat, and a dark brown wig, and sometimes wears a white cap, and middling fine white shirts.

The other nam'd Philip Fitzpatrick, of a dark complexion, and freckled face: had on a black vest, and homespun trowsers, made of tow cloth, a check shirt, and check handkerchief, old shoes, and a new castor hat. Whoever takes up the said servants, and secures them in any goal, so that their masters may have them again, shall have *Three Pounds* reward for both, or *Thirty Shillings* for either of them, and reasonable charges,
      paid by    THOMAS CANBY, and HENRY TROTH.
N. B. All masters of vessels are forbid to carry them off at their peril.
*The Pennsylvania Gazette*, August 15, 1754; August 22, 1754; August 29, 1754. See *The Pennsylvania Gazette*, January 14, 1755, *The Pennsylvania Gazette*, March 18, 1755, and *The Pennsylvania Gazette*, May 1, 1755, for Fitzpatrick.

RUN away on the 25th of last month, from Jacobus Hains, at the Mouth of Christine creek, New Castle county, An Irish servant lad, named James M'Laughlin, but it is thought will go by the name of Jeremiah Connor, having a pass with that name in it, about 19 years of age, 5 feet 6 inches high, and has short dark brown hair; Had on, a new linsey woolsey jacket, without buttons, with eyelit-holes made for lacing, tow petticoat trowsers, shoes, with strings in them, old felt hat, and old ozenbrigs shirt. He has a double tooth in the upper part of his mouth, and squints a little in one of his eyes. Whoever takes up and secures said servant, so as his master may have him again, shall have Forty Shillings reward, and reasonable charges,
      paid by    JACOBUS HAINS.
*The Pennsylvania Gazette*, September 12, 1754; September 19, 1754; September 26, 1754. See *The Pennsylvania Gazette*, June 26, 1755.

**THREE POUNDS** Reward.
RUN away from captain Blair's ship, at Lewes-Town, in Sussex county, and province of Pennsylvania, on the 5th of this inst. Two Negroe men, one about

5 feet 7 inches high; the other a likely fellow, near 6 feet high, about 35 years of age each, and both very ordinary cloathed. Whoever secures the above Negroes in any goal, and gives notice to John Spafford, in Philadelphia, or Thomas Cooch, Miller, on Christine creek, New-Castle county, shall have Three Pounds reward for both, or Thirty Shillings for either, and reasonable charges, paid by      JOHN SPAFFORD, or THOMAS COOCH.
N. B. Run away from the above Thomas Cooch, last spring, A Negroe man, named Sam, a tall slim fellow, near 50 years of age, pretty grey hair'd; he was taken up sometime ago at Burlington, and discharg'd as a free Negroe, by a false pass which he had procured. Whoever secures the said Negroe in any goal, or brings him to his master, shall have Twenty Shillings reward, and reasonable charges, paid by THOMAS COOCH.
*The Pennsylvania Gazette*, September 19, 1754; September 26, 1754; October 3, 1754. See *The Pennsylvania Gazette*, January 28, 1755, for Sam.


RUN away on the 19th of September last, from the subscriber, living at the Red Lion, in New-Castle county, An Irish servant man, named Patrick Wall, talks good English, has been in the country about three months, and was sickly most part of the time, looks very pale, has a sharp thin nose, spare made, about five feet eight inches high, pretends to be a slater and plaisterer by trade: Had on when he went away, a grey kersey jacket, and a linsey woolsey jacket under it with stripes across the breast, two check shirts, a pair of blue cloth breeches, blue yarn stockings, and old shoes, with old steel buckles; also a pair of two linen trowsers, which he made into a wallet, and carried a blanket in it. Whoever takes up and secures said servant, in any goal, so as his master may have him again, shall have Forty Shillings reward,
paid by      OBADIAH ELLIOT.
N. B. All masters of vessels are forbid to carry him off.
*The Pennsylvania Gazette*, October 10, 1754; October 17, 1754; October 24, 1754.

Wilmington, October 15, 1754.
RUN away from Amos Jones, master of the Ship Recovery, of Wilmington, an apprentice lad, named Thomas King, about 18 years of age, he is short, well-set, and bow legged, clear grey eyes, and large nose, pretty much marked with the small-pox. Whoever secures the said Apprentice, so that his master may have him again, shall have Five Shillings reward. All masters of vessels and others, are desired not to ship or carry him off, as they will be proceeded against according to law.    AMOS JONES.
*The Pennsylvania Gazette*, October 24, 1754; October 31, 1754; November 7, 1754.

Lewis-town, Sussex county, October 15, 1754.
WHEREAS *a certain Person, who saith he came from Stafford County, in Virginia, and calls himself Samuel Beverton, was taken up, and committed to his Majesty's Goal of this County, for travelling without a Pass: he is a short Man, of a dark Complexion, short black Hair; he had on when taken up, a brown Jacket, a Pair of old Trowsers, an Ozenbrigs Shirt, Shoes, with Pewter Buckles, no Stockings, &c. Any Person who hath any Claim to said Servant Man (as supposed) are desired to repair to the Subscriber in 30 Days, otherwise said Beverton will be sold for the Payment of Fees, according to law,* by JACOB KOLLOCK, sheriff.

*The Pennsylvania Gazette*, October 24, 1754; October 31, 1754; November 7, 1754.

Wilmington, Nov. 18, 1754.
RUN away from the owners of the ship Recovery, of this port, on the 16th inst, the two following German servants; Ludwick Hofman, about 20 years of age, middle stature, fair or pale complexion, light brown curl'd hair, and stutters a little: Had on when he went away, A blue cloth coat, with metal buttons, a green jacket, linen breeches, and light grey worsted ribb'd hose. He has been in the country before, speaks tolerable English, and likely may attempt to ship himself, or pass for a linguist or newlander. And George Millar, about 25 years of age, by trade a stocking weaver, tall, slender, thin and long visage, black complexion, wears a cap over short black hair, with a large broad brimm'd hat, speaks no English: Had on when he went away, A blue cloth coat, jacket and breeches, check shirt, and yarn stockings. Whoever takes up the said servants, or either of them, and secures them in any county jail, so that said owners may have and again, shall, on notice thereof, receive Three Pounds reward for each, with all reasonable charges, paid by us, Griffith Minshall, Robert Lewis.

*The Pennsylvania Gazette*, November 21, 1754; November 28, 1754; December 5, 1754.


RUn away on the 24th of November last, from the subscriber, living at Christine Bridge, an Irishman, named Henry Walkens, of a middle stature: Had on when he went away, a blue cloth coat, with yellow metal buttons, light colour'd cloth breeches, new shoes, grey stockings, wears a cap, and took sundry good with him in a clandestine manner. Likewise went with him, one Robert Faries, of a fair complexion, about 20 years of age: Had on, a light colour'd cloth coat and jacket, fustian or cloth breeches, new single channel pumps, with bend-leather soles, a pale wig, and a new felt hat. Whoever takes up said men, and brings them to Christine-bridge, or secures them in any goal, so as they may be brought to justice, shall have Three

Pounds reward, or Thirty Shillings for either, and reasonable charges, paid by     WILLIAM SMITH.
N. B. All masters of vessels are forbid to carry them off at their peril.
*The Pennsylvania Gazette*, December 5, 1754; December 12, 1754; December 19, 1754.


There is committed to the goal of New-Castle county, A New Negroe man, about 24 years of age, of a slender body, about 6 feet high, can't speak proper English. His master coming and paying the charges, may have him again.     JOHN THOMPSON, Goaler.
*The Pennsylvania Gazette*, November 28, 1754; December 12, 1754.


RUN away on the 11th inst. from the subscriber, living in New-Castle, An Irish servant man, named Hugh Carberry, of a middle stature, about 20 years of age, is very talkative: Had on when he went away, A blue jacket, without lining, with brass buttons, an under jacket, of striped stuff, with white metal buttons, check shirt, felt hat, worsted cap, buckskin breeches, white woollen stockings, and good shoes; his eye brows is remarkable for heaviness. He has been used to the sea, and it is supposed he will endeavour to get on board some vessel. He is a good deal acquainted in the upper counties. Whoever takes up and secures said servant, so as the subscriber may have him again, shall have Twenty Shillings reward if taken in New-Castle county, and Forty Shillings if in any other county, paid by     *John Thompson.*
N. B. The breeches are remarkable, being pieces all round between the thighs and waistband.
*The Pennsylvania Gazette*, December 19, 1754; December 26, 1754; December 31, 1754; January 14, 1755; January 21, 1755; January 28, 1755.

## 1755

ON Friday the 27th of December last, broke out of Dover goal, a young man, named Ithiel Reed, a tall slim fellow: Had on, a blue cloth coat and jacket. Also a woman, named Mary Tool. Whoever takes up and secures said Reed, and Tool, shall have Forty Shillings reward, paid by the goal keeper of Dover.
*The Pennsylvania Gazette*, January 14, 1755; January 28, 1755.


RUN away on the 28th of November last, from the subscriber, living near Dover, in Kent county, on Delaware, two Negroes, a man and a woman; the man is a lusty yellow fellow, about 36 years old: had on when he went away,

A homespun blue coat and jacket, leather breeches, new shoes, a castor hat; has with in a fiddle, on which he can play. He is country born, speaks good English, and is called Cap. The woman is about 40 years old; had on when she went away, A striped linen gown and petticoat, and a short gown; she is called Rane. Whoever takes up said Negroes, if taken up out of the counties of New-Castle, Kent and Sussex, and delivered to their master, living as above, shall have the sum of Four Pounds reward for each, and reasonable charges; and it taken within the aforesaid counties, the sum of Twenty-five Shillings for each, paid by me    RICHBELL MOTT.

*The Pennsylvania Gazette,* February 4, 1755; February 11, 1755; February 18, 1755; February 25, 1755; March 4, 1755; March 18, 1755.

Run away on the 20th of December last, from the subscriber, living in Wilmington, an Irish servant man, named Philip Fitzpatrick, a cooper by trade, a short well-set fellow, with short black hair, freckled face, and looks pale with the ague: Had on when he went away, a felt hat, old grey homespun jacket, a black ditto, and a striped under jacket, homespun tow shirt, old patch'd leather breeches, blue grey stockings, and new shoes. Whoever takes up and secures the said servant, so that his master may have him again, shall have Thirty Shillings reward, and reasonable charges,
        paid by    THOMAS CANBY.

*The Pennsylvania Gazette,* January 14, 1755; January 21, 1755, January 28, 1755. See *The Pennsylvania Gazette,* August 15, 1754, *The Pennsylvania Gazette,* March 18, 1755, and *The Pennsylvania Gazette,* May 1, 1755.

RUN away from Thomas Cooch, Miller, on Christine creek, New-Castle county, in the province of Pennsylvania, A Negro man, named Sam, a pretty tall, slim fellow, near 50 years of age, and pretty grey headed. He was brought from Amboy jail last fall, and had with him there a pass, and went for a free Negro; he a probably have the same pass with him now. Whoever takes up and secures said Negro in any goal, so that his master may have him again, shall have Twenty Shillings reward, and reasonable charges,
paid by    *Thomas Cooch,* or Mr. *John Spafford,* in Philadelphia.

*The Pennsylvania Gazette,* January 28, 1755; February 11, 1755; February 18, 1755; February 25, 1755; March 4, 1755; March 18, 1755; March 25, 1755; April 3, 1755; April 17, 1755. See *The Pennsylvania Gazette,* September 19, 1754.

*Lancaster, January* 31, 1755.
THIS day was committed to the goal of this county James Hamilton, an Irish lad, about 18 or 19 years of age, 4 feet [sic] 11 inches high, and says he

belongs to Moses Rankin, who is Captain of the ship William, from Londonderry, and that he left the ship at New-Castle. This is to desire Mr. Rankin, or some other in his behalf, to come and pay his fees, otherwise he will be sold for the same in six weeks after the date of this advertisement,
   by JOHN CLARK, Goaler.
*The Pennsylvania Gazette*, February 18, 1755.

*Philadelphia, February* 25, 1755.
RUN away, on the 26th of January last, from the subscribers, living near Blackbird Creek, in New-Castle county, two native Irish servants, one nam'd James M'Daniel, the other Robert Barry. M'Daniel is a well set fellow, much pock mark'd, given to liquor, and quarrelsome, has a scar on his upper lip: Had on when he went away, a blue fearnothing jacket, a flannel under jacket, fine hat, linen cap, coarse shirt, leather breeches, grey stockings, and half worn shoes, tied with strings.

  Barry is a swarthy fellow, about five feet five inches high: had on when he went away, a new coarse jacket, old felt hat, worsted cap, ozenbrigs shirt, leather breeches, yarn stockings, and old shoes; he is very apt to take the name of Jesus in vain. Whoever takes up and secures said servants, so as their masters may have them again, shall have Four Pounds reward for both, or Forty Shillings for either, and reasonable charges,
   paid by JAMES MARTIN, or WILLIAM WOODCOCK.
*The Pennsylvania Gazette*, February 25, 1755; March 4, 1755; March 11, 1755.

*Wilmington*, in *New-Castle* County, *March* 13, 1755.
RUN away last night, from the subscribers, living in Wilmington, two Irish servant lads, viz. Patrick Gile, by trade a bricklayer, of middle stature, well-set, fair complexion, brown hair, and talks pretty much with the brogue: had on when he went away, a blue jacket, and a white ditto under it, half-worn felt hat, tow shirt, leather breeches, black stockings, old shoes. Took with him, a scale and dividers, Patoun's treatise of navigation, a parcel of furrs, a cheese; and understands navigation, writes a good hand, and it is supposed will forge passes.

  Philip Fitzpatrick, by trade a cooper, a well-set Fellow, of a middle stature, dark complexion, black hair, and talks much with the brogue: Had on when he went away, an old black Irish jacket, or a homespun yellow sea jacket, much tarr'd, old felt hat, coarse tow shirt, old leather breeches, black yarn stockings, newly footed, half-worn shoes; he took with him, an old great coat, and a cooper's adze. 'Tis supposed they are gone towards New-York, and will endeavour to go to sea; therefore, all masters of vessels are forbid to harbour them, or carry them off, at their peril. Whoever takes up and secures

the said servants, so as they may be had again, shall have *Three Pounds* reward, or *Thirty Shillings* for each, and reasonable charges,
        paid by       THOMAS CANBY, and NICHOLAS WILSON.
*The Pennsylvania Gazette*, March 18, 1755; March 25, 1755; April 10, 1755. See *The Pennsylvania Gazette*, August 15, 1754, *The Pennsylvania Gazette*, January 14, 1755, and *The Pennsylvania Gazette*, May 1, 1755 for Fitzpatrick.

                              *Lancaster, March 10, 1755.*
*This day was committed to the goal of this county, one John Ross, on suspicion of being a runaway servant; he is about five feet seven inches high, of a fresh complexion, with short black hair, his cloathing but ordinary, about 19 or 20 years of age, and understands something of the taylors trade; he says, he came in with Captain M'Carty, from Dublin to New Castle, that he swam on shore and made his escape from the vessel, and has been in the Jerseys, and was some time near Schuylkill, where he was taken up, and discharged again; he says it is five years next July since he came to this country, and that the vessel was consign'd to one Mr. Wakely, in Philadelphia: These are to desire Mr. Wakely, or any other person who may have any demands against him to come and pay his fees, otherwise he will be sold in six weeks after the date hereof,*
        by JOHN CLARK, *goaler.*
*The Pennsylvania Gazette*, March 25, 1755; April 17, 1755; May 8, 1755.

RUN away on the 14th of April inst. from the subscriber, living in Wilmington, a Dutch servant lad, named George Michael Dunabour, about 19 years of age, has black curled hair, long visage, down look, stoops as he walks, and is pock-marked: Had on, an old blue coat, fustian breeches, yarn stockings, half worn country shoes, and a good felt hat. Whoever takes up and secures said servant, so as his master may have him again, if taken ten miles from home, shall have Forty Shillings reward, and reasonable charges,
        paid by     JOSHUA LITTLER.
N. B. 'Tis thought that he cannot get away, unless secreted or carried off by some person; whoever will discover any person so secreting or carrying him off, shall have the above reward.
*The Pennsylvania Gazette*, April 24, 1755; May 1, 1755; May 15, 1755.

                                Philadelphia, April 18, 1755.
RUN away from Thomas Canby, living in Wilmington, in New-Castle county, on the seventh instant, An Irish servant man, named Philip Fitzpatrick, about 20 years of age, short and set, of a black complexion, with

black hair; he's a cooper by trade, and has much of the brogue on his tongue: Had on when he went away, A tow shirt, yellowish jacket, and a black one under it, yellowish kersey breeches, old felt hat, dark grey stockings, and old shoes. Took with him an adze and drawing knife. Whoever takes up and secures said servant, so as his master may have him again, shall have Thirty Shillings reward, and reasonable charges,
                   paid by    THOMAS CANBY.
*The Pennsylvania Gazette,* May 1, 1755; May 8, 1755; May 15, 1755. See *The Pennsylvania Gazette,* August 15, 1754, *The Pennsylvania Gazette,* January 14, 1755, and *The Pennsylvania Gazette,* March 18, 1755.

                              Philadelphia, May 15, 1755.
*ON the 14th of February, was committed to the Workhouse of this city, a boy about 15 or 16 years of age, who called himself John Perkinson, but has since confess'd his name is John Collings, and that he ran away from James Clark, living in New-Castle county: the master hath been wrote to several times, but no answer is come to hand; the boy says he has two sisters, one living at Newport, the other at Fogs-manor; these are to desire any person that has any demand on the said John Perkinson, alias Collings, to come and pay his charges, or he will be sold out of the workshop for the same, by the first of June.*    JAMES WHITEHEAD.
*The Pennsylvania Gazette,* May 15, 1755; May 29, 1755.


                              Philadelphia, May 22, 1755.
RUN away, on the 14th instant, in the evening, from on board the ship Susannah, Moses Rankin master, an Irish servant man, who goes by the name of John Nicholls, and pretends to be a joiner, about 24 years of age, about five feet eight inches high, smooth face, and brown complexion: had on when he went away, a striped jacket, blue and white cotton cap, check shirt, brown cloth breeches, and a pair of grey yarn stockings. Whoever takes up and secures said servant, so as he may be had again, shall have *Forty Shillings* reward, and reasonable charges, paid by Mr. Thomas Montgomery, merchant at Christine-Bridge, or Captain John Mitchell, in Front-street, Philadelphia.
    *The Pennsylvania Gazette,* May 22, 1755.


                              Philadelphia, May 22, 1755.
RUN away from the subscriber hereof, living in Whiteclay Creek Hundred, New-Castle county, on the 20th instant, an Irish servant man, nam'd John Kelly: Had on when he went away, a tow shirt and trowsers, a brown cloth jacket, without sleeves, blue yarn stockings, and calf-skin shoes, with brass

buckles in them, a felt hat, and it is thought stole a light blue drugget coat. Whoever takes up and secures said servant, so that his master may have him again, shall have Twenty Shillings reward, and reasonable charges,

   paid by me  ROBERT ENGLISH.

*The Pennsylvania Gazette*, May 22, 1755; May 29, 1755; June 12, 1755.

RUN away on the 15th of May at night, Jacobus Hines, near Christine-ferry, an Irish servant lad, named James M'Laughlin, about 19 or 20 years of age, five feet six inches high, has dark brown hair, of a fresh complexion, has a double tooth in the upper part of his mouth, and a small cast with one eye: Had on when he went away, an old beaver hat, home made brown colour'd cloth coat, pretty much worn, lined with brown linen, old petticoat trowsers, pretty much worn, with old blue breeches under them, neats leather shoes, tied with strings, white and black woollen stockings. Whoever takes up and secures said servant, so as his master may have him again, shall have Forty Shillings reward, and reasonable charges,

   paid JACOBUS HINES.

*The Pennsylvania Gazette*, June 26, 1755; July 10, 1755. See *The Pennsylvania Gazette*, September 12, 1754.

STOLEN or deluded away, on the 9th of this instant, from the subscriber, living in Chester, Pennsylvania, an apprentice lad, named John Ryan, about 14 years of age, well grown, full round fac'd, of a brown complexion, and thin dark brown hair: had on when he went away, a striped homespun flannel jacket, check shirt, tow trowsers, old beaver hat. He is supposed to be taken away by an idle woman, named Nancy Wainwright, who keeps about the Welsh track, New-Castle county, urged thereto by the boy's mother, named Mary Ryan, living at the same place, who is a lame woman, and teaches school on the Great Road leading from New-Castle to Elk-River; she has been whipt several times at Chester, for pilfering and house breaking, and once tryed for her life, for burglary, but escaped the gallows, by the death of the prosecutor, before her tryal. Whoever takes up and secures said apprentice in any goal, and gives notice to his master, shall have Thirty Shillings, and if brought home Forty Shillings reward,

   paid by  DENNIS M'LOGHLIN.

*The Pennsylvania Gazette*, July 17, 1755; July 24, 1755.

           New-Castle, August 4, 1755.

Committed to the goal of New-Castle county, on suspicion of being a runaway servant, a man, who calls himself William Davies, about 28 years of

age, about five feet ten inches high, slender in body, of a fair complexion, and wears his hair, has on, white yarn hose, a red flannel jacket, and an old hat. If he be a servant, his master is hereby desired to come, take him out, and pay his charges, before the tenth of September next, otherwise he will be sold for the same by     JOHN THOMPSON, sub-sheriff.
*The Pennsylvania Gazette*, August 7, 1755; August 14, 1755; August 21, 1755.


RUN away, on the 28th of July last, from the subscriber, living in New Castle, a short, well set, stout, sly looking Molattoe slave, about 32 years of age: Had on when he went away, a little old beaver hat, a shirt white woolen jacket, without sleeves, tow cloth shirt, and ozenbrigs petticoat trowsers. He had cut his fore-finger whetting his scythe. He sometimes changes his name to Guy, James, &c. Whoever secures said fellow, so that his master may have him again, or brings him to the subscriber, shall he sufficiently rewarded, and all reasonable charges paid by     GEORGE MONRO.
*The Pennsylvania Gazette*, August 7, 1755; August 14, 1755.


RUN away on the 10th instant, from Thomas Ogle, of Ogle-Town, in New-Castle county, one Thomas Francis, a freeman; he is of low stature, has sore legs, and black hair: Had on a brown coat and jacket. Went away with him a servant man, named David Ecklin, an Irishman, of a pale complexion, and has much of the brogue on his tongue: Had on a striped linsey woolsey jacket, and an old hat. They took with them a large bay horse, that has the pole-evil, and a lump on his side. It is supposed they stole a suit of brown broadcloth clothes. Whoever takes up and secures said Men, shall have Three Pounds reward, and reasonable charges, paid by
    THOMAS OGLE, JOHN SCOTT, or DANIEL WORMS.
*The Pennsylvania Gazette*, August 14, 1755; September 4, 1755; September 11, 1755. Second and third ads show "10th ult." for the runaway date. See *The Pennsylvania Gazette*, October 9, 1755.


RUN away from the subscriber, living near Christine Bridge, a servant man, named Richard Faulkner, but may change his name; he is a painter and carver by trade, about 5 feet 6 inches high, well-made, smooth faced, has a mould [*sic*] on his cheek, much given to drinking and talking: Had on, when he went away, a fustian coat, white jacket, and leather breeches. Whoever takes up and secures said servant, so as his master may have him again, shall receive Four Pistoles reward, and reasonable charges,
        paid by    JOHN SINGLETON.

*The Pennsylvania Gazette*, August 21, 1755; September 4, 1755; September 11, 1755.

New-Castle, August 25, 1755.
ON the 18th of this inst. August was committed to the goal of New Castle county, on suspicion of a run away servant, Thomas Matthews, an Englishman born, aged about 24 years, about 5 feet 6 inches high. He says he served his time in Maryland, near Annapolis. If he be a servant, his master is hereby desired to come and pay his charges in a month after this date, otherwise he will be sold for the same
by JOHN THOMPSON, goaler.

*The Pennsylvania Gazette*, August 28, 1755; September 4, 1755; September 11, 1755; September 18, 1755. See *The Pennsylvania Gazette*, September 25, 1755.

THREE POUNDS Reward.
ESCAPED out of the goal of New-Castle county, on the 21st of September inst. a certain Thomas Matthews, about 23 years of age, five feet five inches high, a well set, full faced pale looking fellow, and has a small scar on some part of his face, has his hair, which is dark colour'd, cut, and wears a white cap: Had on an old dark colour'd coat, a pair of long narrow white trowsers, old shoes, &c. Stole and took with him, a light colour'd napt cloth coat, trimm'd with brass carved buttons, and lined with red shaloon, plain made, and somewhat worn, a light colour'd serge ditto, lined with blue shaloon, a linen jacket, with ten flat silver buttons on the breast, laced on with a cotton lace, a pair of black buckskin breeches, faded in the colour, with flat clear metal buttons, a pair of blue worsted stockings, and two pairs of new shoes, sundry fine holland shirts, and a new check ditto, some linen caps, a muslin cravat, &c. he is a simple looking fellow, and 'tis tho't has procured some sort of a pass, he may probably change his name and apparel, and 'tis thought will endeavour to get himself inlisted. Whoever takes up and secures said fellow, so that the subscriber may have him again, shall have Three Pounds reward, and reasonable charges,
paid by JOHN THOMPSON, goaler.
N. B. If he be put in any goal, the goaler is requested to give the subscriber notice.

*The Pennsylvania Gazette*, September 25, 1755; October 2, 1755; October 23, 1755; October 30, 1755; November 13, 1755; December 4, 1755. See *The Pennsylvania Gazette*, August 28, 1755.

Philadelphia, September 25, 1755.
RUN away from the subscriber, living near Red-Lyon, in New-Castle hundred and county, on Delaware, An Irish servant man, named James Jones, about 5 feet 5 inches high, well set, has a thin oval face, fair hair, very talkative, about 20 years of age, pitted a little with the small-pox: Took and had on when he went away, A fine half worn large hat, with silk broad cocks, about Forty shillings price, blue ratteen fly coat, linen jacket, with a false breast, buckskin breeches, thread stockings, half-worn shoes, with steel buckles, and a flag handkerchief. He has very large feet, with lumps on the joints of his toes; he had a little money with him: Took with him a little jet black horse, with a switch tail, and a trotter, also an old saddle, much broken, with two fine shirts. Whoever secures said servant, so as his master may have him again, shall have Forty Shillings reward, and if man and horse Three Pounds, paid by Patrick Flynn, living near the Red-Lyon as abovesaid, or Patrick Flynn, living with Mr. John Inglis, Merchant, near the Draw-bridge, Philadelphia.
N. B. All masters of vessels, and others, are forbid to carry said servant off at their peril.
*The Pennsylvania Gazette*, October 2, 1755; October 9, 1755; October 16, 1755.


RUN away on the 3d instant, at night, from the subscriber, living in Wilmington, an English servant man, named Eustatius Broker, about five feet nine inches high, used to drive a cart, pretty full faced, has light clay coloured hair, and very thin, something pock-marked: Had on, a whitish cloth coat, made frock fashion, with flat metal buttons, ozenbrigs shirt, old tow trowsers, old shoes, and a felt hat, which he wears close cock'd; has been a soldier in Ireland, and 'tis supposed will endeavour to enlist. Whoever takes up and secures said servant, so as his master may have him again, shall have Twenty Shillings reward, and reasonable charges,
     paid by ROBERT LEWIS.
*The Pennsylvania Gazette*, October 9, 1755.


STOLE from the subscriber, living in East Fallowfield, Chester county, on the 12th of August last, a mixt colour'd grey horse, five years old, a natural pacer, shod before, very flat footed, with a white face, three white feet and legs, white under the jaws, has a trimmed mane, neither brand nor ear mark. he was stole by two runaways from Thomas Ogle, of Ogletown, in New Castle county, one named Thomas Francis, a free man, of low stature, has sore legs, and black hair: Had on a brown coat and jacket; the other named David Ecklin, an Irishman, of a pale complexion, and has much of the brogue on his tongue; they took with them a suit of brown broadcloth clothes, but cannot easily be described by their apparel or horses, they are so much given to stealing and swapping. Whoever takes up and secures said men, and horse, so as their masters may have them again, shall have a Pistole for the horse, and Three Pounds for the men, and reasonable charges,

    paid by  THOMAS OGLE, or GEORGE BENTLEY.

N. B. They are supposed to be gone into the Jerseys.

*The Pennsylvania Gazette*, October 9, 1755. See *The Pennsylvania Gazette*, August 14, 1755.


BROKE out of the publick goal of Kent county, on Delaware, on the 2d of September, a certain Isaac Gray, a thick well set fellow, about five feet eight inches high, pretty much marked with the small-pox, an Irishman born, was committed to goal on his being charged with counterfeiting Pennsylvania bills of credit, and uttering the same. Also a runaway servant, belonging as he said, to Thomas Sands, of Queen Ann's county, Maryland, called himself David Williams, a Welch man born, a thick set fellow, about five feet six inches high; had on a linen waistcoat, homespun trowsers, one homespun shirt, a check ditto; his hair cut off, and wore a linen cap. Whoever takes up said prisoners, and secures them, or either of them, so as the subscriber may have them again, shall have Three Pounds reward for Isaac Gray, and Forty Shillings for David Williams, and reasonable charges,

    paid by  JOHN CLAYTON, Sheriff.

*The Pennsylvania Gazette*, October 9, 1755; October 16, 1755; October 23, 1755.


              New-Castle, Nov. 12, 1755.

IN October last was committed to the goal of New Castle county, on suspicion of being runaway servants, James Farrow, a lusty young fellow, supposed to belong to Mr. Randle Johnston, of Talbot county, Maryland; and in company with him a certain John Sharp, a little man, supposed to belong to some gentleman in said county; likewise a certain John Ridgeway, an old man, supposed to belong to Mr. Nathaniel Grubb, in Chester county; and a certain James Johnston, a short well-set young fellow, with blue clothes. Any person or persons having any demands against said runaways, or either of them they are desired to come in five weeks after this date, and pay their fees, otherwise they will be sold for the same

      by JOHN THOMPSON, Sub-Sheriff.

*The Pennsylvania Gazette*, November 20, 1755; December 4, 1755.

*Newcastle, December* 6, 1755.
COMMITTED to the goal of New-Castle county, a certain Peter Carr, an old man, servant to Andrew Ball, in Maryland; and a certain Mary Crummell, a servant to Henry Ferson, in Kent county. Their masters are hereby desired to come in a month after this date, and pay their fees, otherwise they will be sold for the same,   by JOHN THOMPSON, Goaler.
*The Pennsylvania Gazette*, December 18, 1755; January 1, 1756.

## 1756

*Chester Town, Kent County, Maryland, January* 1, 1756.
RUN away from the subscriber, living near Chester-Town, in Kent county, on Thursday, the 18th day of December last, a servant man, named Robert Jones, but passes by the name of Robert Williams, 19 years of age, about 5 feet 2 inches high, well set, has short brown hair, and a fair complexion: Had on when he went away, a brown cloth jacket, pretty much patched, and under it a country cloth jacket, without sleeves, buckskin breeches, and country made shoes and stockings, his shoes tied with leather. Whoever takes up and secures said servant, so that his master may have him again, shall have Twenty Shillings reward, besides what the law allows,
   paid by   WILLIAM FRAY.
*The Pennsylvania Gazette*, January 8, 1756; January 22, 1756.

Philadelphia, January 29, 1756.
RUN away from the subscriber, in Christine hundred, New-Castle county, on the 20th of this inst. An Irish servant lad, named Samuel Dickson, says he was born in England, about 18 years of age, about 5 feet 6 inches high, a thick clumsey fellow, full faced, black hair and eyebrows, pitted with the smallpox, small eyes and very talkative when in drink, which he is apt to get; pretends to be a sailor, but may incline to list as a soldier: Had on when he went away, A pale bluish homespun cloth jacket, with broad leather buttons, the fore parts lined with red worsted, and the back with striped linsey, tow shirt, buckskin breeches, much greased, two metal buttons and strings at the knees, pale red coarse yarn stockings, old shoes, half soled upon the old soles, with strings, and a patch on one of them, old wool hat, with a patch of black buckskin on the top. Took with him a young brownish dog, of the bull breed, has some white on his neck and breast, and a large scar on his breast, near one of his fore legs. Whoever takes up the said servant, so that his master may have him again, shall have Two Pistoles reward,
   paid by   ROBERT ROBINSON.
*The Pennsylvania Gazette*, January 29, 1756; February 12, 1756.

*New-Castle*, January 31, 1756.

RUN away last night from George Monro, of New-Castle, an Irish servant man, aged about 27 years, named Philip Harrison; had on, when he went away, an old hat, cock'd sharp, a Germantown blue and white cap, a light colour'd homespun cloth cloak, with mohair buttons, and dark jacket of ditto, with metal buttons, a tow shirt, leather breeches, brown yarn stockings, good shoes, with brass buckles, and pretends to have been a soldier. Whoever secures said fellow, so that his master may have him again, shall have Thirty Shillings reward, and reasonable charges, paid by GEORGE MONRO.

N. B. If any gentlemen who is recruiting should enlist him, this information will save further trouble.

*The Pennsylvania Gazette*, February 5, 1756. See *The Pennsylvania Gazette*, February 12, 1756.

*New-Castle*, January 31, 1756.

RUN away last night from George Monro, of New-Castle, An Irish servant man named Philip Harrison, aged about 27 years, about 5 feet 3 inches high, well-set, of a fresh sandy complexion; Had on, when he went away, An old hat, cock'd up sharp, a light colour'd homespun cloth coat, with mohair buttons, a dark colour'd ditto jacket, with metal buttons, coarse shirt, leather breeches, brown yarn stockings, good shoes, with brass buckles. Whoever takes up and secures said fellow, so that his master may have him again, shall have Thirty Shillings reward (and any person that will prove his being inlisted in his majesty's service, shall have Ten Shillings) and reasonable charges, paid by     GEORGE MONRO.

*The Pennsylvania Gazette*, February 12, 1756; February 19, 1756; February 26, 1756; March 4, 1756; March 11, 1756; March 25, 1756. See *The Pennsylvania Gazette*, February 5, 1756.


RUN away on the 15th of March, from the subscriber, living in Wilmington, a servant woman, this country born, near 30 years of age, of a dark complexion, with black hair: Had on when she went away, an old homespun worsted gown, a striped linsey bed gown, and a pretty good flag silk handkerchief. Whoever takes up and secures said servant in any goal, so as her master may have her again, shall have Twenty Shillings reward, and reasonable charges, paid by     DANIEL FEW.

*The Pennsylvania Gazette*, April 1, 1756; April 15, 1756.


Philadelphia, May 24, 1756,

RUN away on the 20th inst. from the subscriber, living in Wilmington, New-Castle country, An Irish servant girl, named Frances Mercer, about 22 years

of age, about 5 feet and a half high, pretty lusty, has black hair and black eyes, has a broad full face, and speaks pretty good English: Had on, and took with her, when she went away, A petticoat and gown, of new dark striped linsey, and an old striped linen petticoat and gown, with sundry other cloathing. Whoever takes up and secures said servant, so as her master may have her again, shall have Thirty Shillings reward, and reasonable charges
    paid by  RICHARD CARSAN.
*The Pennsylvania Gazette,* May 27, 1756; June 10, 1756.


RUN away on the 27th of last month, from James Edwards, of Duck creek hundred, A native Irish servant man, named Thomas Welch, speaks good English, about 25 years of age, 5 feet 6 inches high, of a pale complexion, with sandy colour'd hair: Had on, A striped linsey jacket, with patches of blue cloth on the fore parts of it, felt hat, long tow trowsers, and shirt of the same. Whoever takes up and secures said servant in any jail, or brings him to his master, shall receive Forty Shillings reward, and reasonable charges,
    paid by  JAMES EDWARDS.
*The Pennsylvania Gazette,* June 3, 1756; June 10, 1756; June 17, 1756.

### THREE POUNDS Reward,
*RUN away about the middle of April last, from the Sheriff of Kent county on Delaware, (being then under execution) a certain James Fulton, by trade a weaver, but has for some time past followed pedling, and horse-jockeying, north of Ireland born, speaks broad, about five feet six inches high, thin visaged, and has a roman nose. Whoever takes up and secures said James Fulton in any of his majesty's goals, shall receive the above reward of Three Pounds, and all other reasonable charges,*
    *paid by*  CAESAR RODNEY.
*The Pennsylvania Gazette,* June 10, 1756; June 24, 1756.

*Borough of Wilmington, June 28, 1756.*
*WHEREAS Humphrey Jones has advertised a Negroe girl, called Bess, in the news; these are to certify, that the said Negroe girl was taken up, and brought to Wilmington, and delivered to her master, Peter Gantbony, and the said Humphrey Jones is desired to come to Wilmington, and produce his right to said Negroe. And as the said Humphrey Jones did, in a clandestine manner, take said Negroe from the house of John Springer, of Wilmington, and has kept her from her master three years and upwards, these are to forbid any person or persons whatever to take up or molest said Negroe girl on their peril, she being the property of PETER GANTHONY.*
  *The Pennsylvania Gazette,* July 1, 1756; July 15, 1756.

TAKEN up, and secured in Dover goal, in Kent county, on Delaware, on the first of January last, one Jonathan Boort, an Englishman, about 5 feet 2 inches high. Also one William Brown, an Englishman, taken up on the first of March last, about 5 feet 9 inches high, both supposed to be runways. Their masters are desired to come speedily, and take them out, or they will be sold to discharge their fees, by     JAMES WELLS, Goaler.
*The Pennsylvania Gazette,* July 8, 1756; July 29, 1756.


Run away the 22d of June, from Anthony Whitley, of New-Castle, a servant woman, named Mary Cromel, born in Ireland, of a middle size, pretty fat, broad face, flat nose, has a lump above one eye, black hair, which she wears down her neck: Had on when she went away, a linsey woolsey petticoat, with broad stripes of black and white, and is suspected of having some stolen goods with her. Whoever secures her in any goal, so as her master may have her again, shall have Twenty Shillings reward, and reasonable charges,
paid by     ANTHONY WHITLY.
*The Pennsylvania Gazette,* August 5, 1756; August 19, 1756.


New-Castle, July 23, 1756.
THIS day was committed to the goal of this county a certain James Smith, about 25 years of age, who says he is a servant to James Black, farmer, living in Middletown township, Chester county. And a Negroe slave who calls himself Ming, and says he belongs to John Calley, tanner, in Middletown township, Bucks county. Their masters are hereby desired to come in six weeks after this date, and pay their fees, otherwise they will be sold for the same, by     JOHN THOMSON, goaler.
*The Pennsylvania Gazette,* August 5, 1756.


New-Castle county, August 28, 1756.
FIFTEEN POUNDS Reward.
WHEREAS Godfrey Brown, late of Christiana Hundred, and county aforesaid, a German, but talks tolerable English, nigh Sixty years of age, about five feet three inches high, slender in body, has short brown frizley hair, small face, and little hollow eyes, his chin stands remarkably out, and his mouth far in, so that his chin and nose almost meet, seems to lisp when he speaks, from his want of teeth, and is of a swarthy complexion, is absconded from his usual place of abode, and is strongly suspected to have murdered a certain Mary Reel, and her son, whose bodies are found on his plantation. These are to give notice, that whoever will apprehend said Godfrey Brown, and secures him, so that he may be brought to justice, shall

have Fifteen Pounds reward, which reward is offered by Col. William Armstrong, David Bush and Richard M'William, Esquires, three of his majesty's justices for said county.

N. B. There are in the goal of this county, a white man, named Arthur M'Claskin, and a Negroe man, named James Hoburn, they both say they are free: M'Claskin is a short well-set fellow, wears his own black hair, is of a black complexion; has on, a coarse shirt and trowsers. The Negroe is slender in body, about 40 years of age, and says he was set free by Henry Rennalds, of Chester county. Any person having any demands against said persons, are desired to come in four weeks after this date, and take them out, otherwise they will be sold for their charges,

by    JOHN THOMPSON, Sub-Sheriff.

*The Pennsylvania Gazette*, September 9, 1756; September 23, 1756; September 30, 1756.

Philadelphia, August 26, 1756.

RUN away from his bail, living in New-Castle county, some time this month, one John Ganduett, by trade a ship carpenter, about 28 years of age, 5 feet 10 inches high, of a swarthy complexion, and very much pitted with the small-pox: Had on a dark coloured coat, and a brown wig. Whoever takes up and secures the said Ganduett in any goal of the province of Pennsylvania, or in the Counties of New-Castle, Kent, or Sussex, whereby he may be brought to justice, shall have EIGHT POUNDS reward,

paid by   CORNELIUS CARTY.

*The Pennsylvania Gazette*, August 26, 1756; September 2, 1756; September 9, 1756.

RUN away on the 11th day of September last, from the subscriber, living in Red-Lion Hundred, New-Castle county, a Mulattoe man, named Ned, 23 years of age, about 5 feet 8 inches high, of a pretty dark colour, is this country born, and talks good English, and is a very smart, active, cunning fellow: Had on when he went away, a coarse tow shirt and trowsers, and a new 20 Shilling hat, but the rest of his apparel not known. As he has several times expressed a desire of going to sea, it is probable he may endeavour to get on board some privateer, or other vessel, and for that end may pretend to be a free man, and no doubt will produce some counterfeit pass or certificate; therefore all masters of vessels are requested not to carry him off. Whoever apprehends the said slave, and brings him to his master, or secures him in any county goal, so that his master may have him again, shall have Three Pounds reward,

paid by    VALENTINE DUSHANE.

*N. B. It is probable he will change both his name and apparel.*

*The Pennsylvania Gazette*, October 21, 1756; November 4, 1756.

New Castle, September 24, 1756.
THIS day was committed to the goal of this county, a Negroe woman, who called herself Judith, and either cannot, or will not, tell who she belongs to. She appears to be about thirty years of age, seems to be an ideot, and it is thought came from Maryland. Her owner is hereby desired to come in six weeks from this date and take her out, otherwise she will be discharged.
JOHN THOMPSON, Goaler.
*The Pennsylvania Gazette*, October 21, 1756; November 4, 1756.

TWENTY-FIVE POUNDS REWARD.
A *Person who calls himself* John Pattison, *with short hair, an olive colour thick-set coat, a pair of short check trowsers, yarn stockings, and has an impediment in his speech, about 32 years old, is five feet 6 inches high, of a slender make, and has told others he has two sisters married in or about* Prince-Town; *sold a person on wednesday last was se'nnight, to the subscriber, as a servant, who called himself* Edward Brewer, *a house-carpenter by trade, born in* Ireland, *pock fretten, well-set, has black eyes, about 5 feet 4 inches high, with an old striped jacket, a check shirt, short narrow dirty ozenbrigs trousers; and as there is great reason from the said* Pattison's *informing the subscriber that he lived in* East-Jersey, *when in fact his place of residence is on or near* Duck-Creek, *in the lower counties on* Delaware, *and his being seen lurking about the vessel that the said* Brewer *was on board of, the day following, and both disappearing the same day, that they are gone off together; the subscriber will pay any person that takes up and secures the said* Edward Brewer, *if out of this government,* FIVE POUNDS; *and also* FIFTEEN POUNDS *for taking up the said* Pattison, *provided such person can prove that the said* Pattison *was in any respect aiding or assisting the said servant in making his elopement as aforesaid.*
WILLIAM KELLY.
N: B. *Run-away also another servant man named,* Walter Cook, *aged 35 years, about 6 feet high, of a long thin visage, and wears his own light-coloured hair. For him there is* FIVE POUNDS *Reward.*
*The New-York Mercury*, October 11, 1756; October 18, 1756; October 25, 1756; November 1, 1756; November 8, 1756; November 15, 1756. The last ad lacks the paragraph beginning "N: B." See *The Pennsylvania Gazette*, November 4, 1756 and *The Pennsylvania Journal, and Weekly Advertiser*, November 4, 1756.

New York, October 11, 1756.
TWENTY-FIVE POUNDS Reward.
A Person who called himself John Pattison, having short hair, an olive coloured thick set coat, a pair of short check trowsers, yarn stockings, and

has an impediment in his speech, about 32 years old, is 5 feet 6 inches high, of slender make, and has told others he has two sisters married in or about Prince-Town; sold a person on Wednesday last was se'ennight to the subscriber, as a servant, who called himself Edward Brewer, and a housecarpenter by trade, born in Ireland, pock-mark'd, well-set, black eyes, about 5 feet 4 inches high, with an old striped jacket, a check shirt, and short narrow dirty ozenbrigs trousers; and as there is great reason, from the said Pattison's informing the subscriber that he lived in East-Jersey, when in fact his place of residence is on or near Duck-creek, in the lower counties on Delaware, and his being seen lurking about the vessel that the said Brewer was on board of on the Day following, and both disappearing the same day, that they are gone off together; the subscriber will pay any Person that takes up and secures the said Edward Brewer, if out of this government, Five Pounds; and also Fifteen Pounds for taking up the said Pattison, provided such person can prove that the said Pattison was in any respect aiding or assisting the said servant in making his elopment as aforesaid.
       WILLIAM KELLY.
N. B. The said Pattison and Brewer came to this Town from the southward, by the stage last Wednesday was se'ennight.
The above reward will be paid by Townsend White, in Philadelphia, if the persons are brought to him.
 *The Pennsylvania Gazette*, November 4, 1756; November 11, 1754; November 25, 1756. See *The New-York Mercury*, October 11, 1756 and *The Pennsylvania Journal, and Weekly Advertiser*, November 4, 1756.

<br>

Twenty-Five Pounds Reward.

A Person who calls himself himself John Pattison, with short hair, an olive colour thick-set coat, a pair of short check trowsers, yarn stockings, and has an impediment in his speech, about 32 years old, 5 feet 6 inches high; of a slender make, and has told others he has two Sisters married in or about Prince-Town; sold a person on wednesday last was se'nnight, to the subscriber, as a servant, who called himself Edward Brewer, and a house carpenter by trade, born in Ireland, pock fretten, well set, black eyes, about 5 feet 4 inches high, with an old striped jacket, a check shirt, and short narrow dirty ozenbrig trousers; and as there is the greatest reason from the said Pattison's informing the subscriber that he lived in East-Jersey, when, in fact, his place of residence is on or near Duck-creek, in the lower counties on Delaware, and his being seen lurking about the vessel that the said Brewer was on board of, the day following, and both disappearing the same day, that they are gone off together; the subscriber will pay any person that takes up and secures the said Edward Brewer, if out of the government, Five Pounds; and also Fifteen Pounds for taking up the said Pattison, provided such person

can prove that the said Pattison was in any respect aiding or assisting the said servant in making his elopement as aforesaid.
                WILLIAM KELLY.
*The Pennsylvania Journal, and Weekly Advertiser*, November 4, 1756. See *The New-York Mercury*, October 11, 1756 and *The Pennsylvania Gazette*, November 4, 1756.

                                  New-Castle, October 20, 1756.
THERE are now in the goal of this county three Negroe men, committed some days ago as runaways. One, who calls himself Ben, says he belongs to Mr. Rhody Neil in Virginia. Another, who calls himself Jem, says he belongs to Mr. Spencer Smith in Virginia. They seem both to be new Negroes, and can read. The other calls himself James, and says he belongs to Samuel Blunt, captain of a company of foot living in Kent Island, Maryland. The owners of said Negroes are hereby desired to come in six weeks from this date, and take them out of goal, otherwise they will be sold for their fees,
                by JOHN THOMPSON, Goaler.
*The Pennsylvania Gazette*, November 11, 1756; December 2, 1756.

## 1757

RUN away from the subscriber, living at Christiana Bridge, in New-Castle County, on Delaware, an Irish Servant Girl, named Honor Bryant, of a short Stature, black Hair, down Look, speaks much with the Brogue, has remarkable large Breasts, aged about 20 Years: Had on when she went away, a Calicoe Gown, and a Linsey Petticoat, but it is thought she will change both her Name and Apparel. She was taken up at Wilmington, and rescued from the Constable by the Grenadiers of Capt. Porter's Company, belonging to the third Battalion of the Royal Americans, and put on board a Shallop for Trenton, and there concealed and protected by Lieutenant Willington, of said Company, contrary to law, and the Perswasions of the Burgess then present, and against an Order from Major Provost, and supposed she is still in said Company, in keeping of said Willington. Whoever takes up and secures said servant, so that her Master may have her again, shall have Forty Shillings Reward, and reasonable Charges
                paid by    JOHN M'CARTY.
*The Pennsylvania Gazette*, April 7, 1757; April 21, 1757.

                        FOUR PISTOLES Reward.
*RUN away about the first of April last, from his Bail, living in the Colony of Virginia, on the Eastern Shore, a certain Samuel Kirkpatrick, a short well set Fellow, fresh Complexion, full Face, large Eyes, formerly lived near the*

*Head of Elk River, and has been Pedling last Winter and Spring in Worcester, Somerset and Dorset Counties, in Maryland, and is supposed to have crossed from Kent island to Annapolis, in order to go Back. Whoever takes up said Kirkpatrick and secures him in any Goal, and sends Word to the Subscriber, living in Dover, in Kent County, on Delaware, who is properly impowered by George Matthews, shall receive the above Reward, and if brought to Dover, reasonable Charges,     paid by    HUGH PARKE.*
*The Pennsylvania Gazette,* May 19, 1757; June 2, 1757.

TEN PISTOLES Reward.
RUN away from the Sheriff of Kent County, on Delaware, about the first of May last, a certain Tobias Gilder, who is well known for a considerable Time past, to have follow the Shalloping Business from Duck-Creek and Appoquiminy to Philadelphia. He is a lusty fat well set Man, about 5 Feet ten fifty inches high, of a sandy Complexion, and remarkable for having one Ancle considerably bigger and the other. Any Person that will take up and secure the said Tobias Gilder,, so that the said Sheriff may have him again, shall have Ten Pistoles, and if brought to Dover, in said County, shall likewise have reasonable Charges paid them,
by    CAESAR RODENEY, Sheriff.
*The Pennsylvania Gazette,* June 16, 1757; June 30, 1757.

*New-Castle, August 23, 1757.*
*NOW in the Goal of this County two Negroe Men; one calls himself Peter, and says he belongs to a certain Mr. Andrews, living in Baltimore County, about five Miles from Joppa, in Maryland; the other calls himself Tom, and says he came from on board of a Ship, and that his Master's Name is Pollien, The Owners of said Negroes are desired to come or send for them,*
by    JOHN THOMPSON, Sub-sheriff.
*The Pennsylvania Gazette,* September 1, 1757; October 27, 1757.

*Newport, New-Castle County, September 24, 1757.*
*RUN away on Friday Night, the 23d Instant, from the Subscriber, a Servant Girl, named Catherine Preden, lately come from Ireland; she is a short thick chunky Girl, and had on when she went away, a striped Calicoe Gown, with Shells between the Stripes; also a striped Linen Gown, and a Linsey Petticoat, striped yellow and black, and a brown Linsey Ditto, white Yarn Stockings, and old Shoes, without Buckles. Whoever takes up said Girl, and brings her to her Master, or secures her in any Goal, and sends Notice thereof, shall have Twenty Shillings Reward, and reasonable Charges,*

*paid by me*     JAMES BROOM
*The Pennsylvania Gazette*, September 29, 1757; October 20, 1757.


New-Castle, December 14, 1757.
NOW in the Goal of this County, a Negro Fellow, named Dick, who says he belongs to Mr. Edward Shippen, in Philadelphia; likewise a new Negro Man, who was committed in August last, speaks broken English, and says he came from on board of a Ship, and does not know who his Master is. Any Persons having Demands against the above Negroes, are desired to come in four Weeks after this Date, and take them away, otherwise they will be discharged, on paying their Fees,
       by    JOHN THOMPSON, Sub-sheriff.
*The Pennsylvania Gazette*, December 15, 1757; December 29, 1757.

## 1758

March 20, 1758.
RUN away from the Subscriber, living in Lewes Town, in Sussex County, on the 17th Day of October last a Molattoe Slave, named Sam, about five Feet ten Inches high, full faced, and has a large Scar on his Right-thigh. Whoever takes up the said Slave, and secures him, so that his Mater may have him again, shall have Seven Pistoles Reward,
       paid by me.     STEPHEN GREEN.
*The Pennsylvania Gazette*, March 30, 1758; April 6, 1758; April 13, 1758.


RUN away from the Subscriber, THOMAS ADAMS, of White-clay Creek, New Castle-County, on the second of this instant July, a Servant Woman, named Diana Lawson: Had on when she went away, a new Linsey Petticoat and Bedgown, is a middle aged Woman, came from Lancaster, speaks broad, and I believe has had the King's Evil. Whoever secures the said Servant, shall have Twenty Shillings Reward, and reasonable Charges,
       paid by    THOMAS ADAMS.
*The Pennsylvania Gazette*, July 20, 1758; August 3, 1758.


RUN away from the Subscriber, on the 19th inst. November, A Servant Man, named John Endless, an Englishman, speaks broad, about 40 Years of Age, 5 feet 8 Inches high, pretty lusty, brown Hair, swarthy Complexion, and wants most of his fore Teeth: Had on when he went away, A whitish coloured full trimmed Cloth Coat, blue Broad-cloth Breeches with Shammy Lining, a

Pair of green Ditto, a red Jacket, black ribbed Stockings, and a Pair of grey Ditto. He was inlisted last April in the Delaware Government service, but got his Discharge. Whoever apprehends the said Servant, and secures him in any Goal, so that the Subscriber may have him again, shall be paid Three Pounds as a Reward,   by William Hay,
                              at Christine Ferry, New-Castle County.
N. B. It is supposed he is gone towards Maryland.
*The Pennsylvania Gazette*, November 30, 1758; December 7, 1758; December 28, 1758; January 4, 1759; January 18, 1759; January 25, 1759; February 15, 1759; February 22, 1759; March 15, 1759. See *The Pennsylvania Journal, and Weekly Advertiser*, February 22, 1759.

## 1759

STOLEN from the Subscriber, out of a Stable in Newark, on white Clay Creek, New Castle County, on Delaware, the 27th of last Month, a bay Horse, 14 Hands high, branded on the near Shoulder, with the figure 2, and some Saddle Marks on his Back, and his mane hangs on the off Side, shod before, natural Pacer, the Hair worn off under the Crupper, long bob Tail. He is supposed to be taken away by a Runaway Negroe Man, who had on a light coloured Coat, broad Metal buttons, and a light coloured Jacket; the said Negroe had a Gun, a Cutlass, and a Wallet with him. Whoever takes up the said Horse, and brings him to the Owner, or secures him, so that the Owner may have him again, shall have Twenty Shillings Reward, and reasonable Charges,   paid by me     HUGH GLASFORD.
*The Pennsylvania Gazette*, February 8, 1759; March 8, 1759.

                                        Burlington, February 14, 1759.
WHEREAS one JOHN ANDREWS, is now confined in the County of Burlington, on suspicion of his being a servant to one William Hay, at Christian Ferry in the County of New-Castle, in pursuance of an advertisement by him the said Hay, published, this is therefore to notify to all whom it may concern, that if no person appears to prove him the said Andrews a servant, in one Month after the date hereof, he will be discharged on paying fees, agreeable to any orders made the last sessions at Burlington for that purpose.     JOSEPH IMLAY, Sheriff.
*The Pennsylvania Journal, and Weekly Advertiser*, February 22, 1759; March 1, 1759; March 8, 1759; March 15, 1759. See *The Pennsylvania Gazette*, November 30, 1758.

THREE POUNDS Reward,
RUN away from his Bail, out of St. George's Hundred, New Castle County,

upon Delaware, a certain Thomas M'Lane, born in Ireland, is about five Feet four Inches high, has black curled Hair, broad Face, speaks tolerable good English, is very talkative, and pretends to tell Fortunes: Had on, when he went away, an old brown Coat and Jacket, Leather Breeches, Shoes and Stockings, and an old Felt Hat. He served his Time in Chester County, in the Province of Pennsylvania, has been in the Back Country, and fond to boast that he has been in several Skirmishes with the Indians. Whoever takes up the said Thomas M'Lane, and secures him in any Goal, shall be intitled to the above Reward of Three Pounds,
    paid by  HENRY VANBEEBER.
*The Pennsylvania Gazette*, June 14, 1759; June 21, 1759; July 19, 1759; August 2, 1759; August 23, 1759.

RUN away from the Subscriber, living in Duck Creek Hundred, Kent County, on Delaware, A Servant Woman, named Mary Armstrong, about 5 Feet 2 Inches high, fair Complexion: Had on when she went away, A striped Linsey Gown and Petticoat, black Bonnet, half-worn Ozenbrigs Shift, and stole sundry Sorts of small Clothes. Whoever secures the said Servant and Clothes, shall have Forty Shillings Reward, and all reasonable Charges,
    paid by me  JOHN REES.
*The Pennsylvania Gazette*, July 12, 1759; July 19, 1759; August 2, 1759; August 23, 1759. See *The Pennsylvania Gazette*, December 20, 1759.

RUN away from his Bail, in Kent Count, on Delaware, on the 28th Day of May, 1759, one John Miller, a Dutchman, of short Stature, brown Complexion, by Trade a Cooper, but pretends to be a Brewer, and several other Trades; is a smart lively young Fellow, of about 25 Years of Age, is very much given to lying, and served his Time in Philadelphia, but since free, has been in several parts to the Northward of this Country: Had on when he went away, a new Hat, a white Cap, a new home made Cloth Coat, of a light blue Colour, with Metal Buttons, a thickset Jacket, Fustian Breeches, new white Cotton Stockings, new Calf Skin Pumps, with new Buckles. Whoever takes up said Miller, and secures him in the nearest Goal, so his Bail may have him again, shall have Three Pounds Reward, and reasonable Charges,
    paid by  JOHN SUTTON, and PETER DUNLAP.
*The Pennsylvania Gazette*, August 16, 1759; August 23, 1759.

*RUN away from the subscribers, living between Christine Ferry and the town of New Castle, in the county of New Castle, on the 19th of July, An Irish*

Servant Woman, about 30 years of age, middle stature, thin visage, and has a remarkable short chin, is a great talker, and served some part of her time with Francis Thornton, near Reedy island, in said County; she calls herself Grace Rogers: Had on when she went away, A striped linen gown, black and white striped linsey petticoat, and sundry old clothes. Whoever takes up and secures said servant in any goal, so that her master may have her again, shall have Forty Shillings reward, paid by* John Jaquet.
  The Pennsylvania Gazette, September 20, 1759; September 27, 1759; October 11, 1759. See The Pennsylvania Gazette, June 12, 1760.


RUN away from the House of Matthew Cannan, on Christine Road, about two Miles from New-Castle, about four Weeks ago, one Charles M'Kay, supposed to be out of his Senses, is about 30 Years of Age, 5 Feet 8 Inches high, has short brown Hair, and a red Beard; and had on a light coloured Ratteen Coat, red Jacket, Buckskin Breeches, a Pair of old Shoes, and blue Germantown Stockings. He speaks good English, and followed the Pedlar's Business some time ago in the Jerseys. Whoever brings said M'Kay to said Cannan, shall have Forty Shillings Reward, and reasonable Charges,
        paid by    MATTHEW CANNAN.
  The Pennsylvania Gazette, September 27, 1759; October 4, 1759; October 11, 1759.


*RUN away, on the 8th of October last, from the Subscriber, living in Dover Hundred, in Kent County on Delaware, a Negro Man, named Abraham: Had on and with him, a blue Camblet Coat, lined with red Shaloon, a green Waistcoat, and red Breeches, with several other Clothes, but may have changed them; he is of a yellowish Colour; about 5 Feet 6 Inches high, a lively Fellow, and takes Delight in Singing; it is supposed he has crossed Delaware and gone into the Jerseys. Whoever takes up and secures the said Fellow, in any Goal, or brings him to his Master, shall have Forty Shillings Reward, and reasonable Charges,    paid by    CALEB LUFF.*
  The Pennsylvania Gazette, December 13, 1759; December 20, 1759; December 27, 1759.


*RUN-away from the Subscriber, living at the Cross Roads, in Duck-creek Hundred, Kent County, on Delaware, a Servant Woman, named Mary Armstrong, about five Feet four Inches high: Had on when she went away a Calicoe Gown, black Bonnet, and high heel'd Shoes: Took with her a small black Horse, with a Star in his Forehead, paces a Travel; she also stole sundry Clothes, such as Shirts, Shifts, Stockings and other small Clothes.*

*Whoever secures the said Woman and Horse, so that her Master may get her again, shall have Forty Shillings Reward, and reasonable Charges,*
    paid by  JOHN REES.
*The Pennsylvania Gazette,* December 20, 1759; December 27, 1759; January 3, 1759. See *The Pennsylvania Gazette,* July 12, 1759.

## 1760

RUN away the second of this instant January, from the Subscribing, living in Brandiwine Hundred, New-Castle county, at Naaman's Creek Mills, an Irish Servant Girl, about 26 Years of Age, middle Stature, black Hair, dark Complexion, much given to Talking and strong Drink, and is apt to swear; she went away with a Soldier belonging to the 44th Regiment: Had on when she went away, a striped Linsey-woolsey Jacket and Petticoat, a whitish coloured Cloak, one red Cloak, and black Bonnet, good Shoes and Stockings, with two good Aprons. Whoever takes up and secures said Servant in any Goal, so that her Master may have her again, shall have Thirty Shillings Reward, and reasonable Charges,
    paid by me.  JAMES CUMMINS.
*The Pennsylvania Gazette,* January 10, 1760; January 17, 1760.

RUN away from the Subscriber, living in New-Castle, on the 31st of December last, a likely Negroe Fellow, about five Feet six Inches high: Had on when he went away, a new brown Coat, or Country Cloth, lined with red Shaloon, mounted with broad white Metal Buttons, a white Fustian Jacket, good Buckskin Breeches, with Metal Buttons, covered with Leather, white Yarn Stockings, and Shoes tied with Leather Whangs, [sic] one of them patched on the Toe, a Felt Hat, and Cotton Cap. He has on one of his great Toes a Lump of Flesh, as large as a small Bullet; his Name Sharper. It is supposed he had several other Things with him. Whoever secures said Negroe, so that his Master may have him again, if out of the County, shall have Forty Shillings Reward, and reasonable Charges, or Twenty Shillings in the County.  ROBERT M'LONEN
N. B. He came from Barbados about two Years ago, and did work a little at the Bricklayer's Business, speaks broken English.
 *The Pennsylvania Gazette,* January 10, 1760; January 17, 1760.

RUN away from his Bail in New-Castle, on the 20th of this instant January, an Irishman, named John Connor, about five Feet five Inches high, and has red Hair: Had on when he went away, a green Coat, red Jacket, and Buckskin Breeches; he also picked a recruiting Sergeant's Pocket of Four Pounds Four

Shillings. Whoever takes up said Connor, and confines him in any of his Majesty's Goals in America, so as he may be brought to Justice, shall have Forty Shillings Reward, paid by ABIGAIL WHITELY, Tavern keeper, in New-Castle.—Said Connor was out this last Campaign, in Capt. Vanbebber's Company.

*The Pennsylvania Gazette*, January 31, 1760; February 14, 1760.

*FIVE POUNDS* Reward,
RUN away some Time in November last, from his special Bail, living near Dover, in the County of Kent, upon Delaware, a certain John Boyd, about five Feet six Inches high, well set, black Hair and Eyes, born in Scotland, by Trade a Weaver: Had on when he went away, a white Cloth Coat, full trimmed, white Jacket, and a small red Ditto: He has lived near Lancaster, and is a very remarkable Person, having a Mole on the Top of his Nose, and a small Wen, or a Thing like a Teat, on the Top of his Head. Whoever delivers the said Boyd to the Sheriff of the County aforesaid, shall have the above Reward, or Forty Shillings for securing him in any Goal, so as the Subscriber may have him again. WILLIAM LEVICK.

*The Pennsylvania Gazette*, February 7, 1760; February 14, 1760; February 21, 1760.

February 2, 1760.
RUN away on Monday last from the subscriber, living at the Cross roads, near Duck Creek, a mulatto fellow, a slave for life, about 40 years old, about five feet eight inches high, and has a down look: Had on when he went away, a half worn bearskin coat, with broad metal buttons, the fore part lined with blue, a new jacket of light coloured napt cloth, lined with tammy, an ozenbrigs shirt, leather breeches, old felt hat, white yarn stockings, old shoes, with copper buckles; he worked two years at the tanners trade, and his clothes are coloured yellowish; his name is Jim, but likely may change it and his clothes. Whoever takes up and secures the said fellow, so as his master may have him again, shall have Fifty Shillings reward, and reasonable charges,
paid by WILLIAM MORRIS, Tanner.
N. B. All masters of vessels, and recruiting officers, are forbid to carry him off at their peril.

*The Pennsylvania Gazette*, February 7, 1760; February 14, 1760; February 21, 1760.

FORTY SHILLINGS Reward.
*BRoke out of the Goal at New Castle, the 31st Day of December last, at Night, a certain David Morgan, about 30 years of Age, about five Feet six Inches*

high, *of a sandy Complexion, small Eyes, and short curled Hair, professes to be a carpenter by Trade; his Parents now live at Christiana Bridge, in New Castle County. Whoever apprehends the said Prisoner, and brings him to the Goal at New-Castle, or secures him in any other Goal, so that the Subscriber may have him again, shall receive the above Reward, and reasonable Charges, paid by* JOHN GARRITSON, *Goaler.*

*N. B. All Ship-masters, Masters of Stage boats, &c. are forbid to carry him off at their Peril.*

*The Pennsylvania Gazette,* February 21, 1760; February 28, 1760; March 13, 1760.

Christiana Bridge, March 10, 1760.
RUN away from the subscriber, on Monday morning, a Molatto slave, named George, he is a lusty young fellow, about 5 feet 11 inches high, 20 years of age, a very white Molatto, and has short black curled hair: Supposed to have on when he went away a brown coat, full trimmed, and buckskin breeches, with many other clothes, and is supposed to have made for Philadelphia. Whoever secures the said slave in any goal, shall receive forty shillings reward, and reasonable charges,

paid by me    WILLIAM PATTERSON.

N. B. All masters of vessels and others are forewarned not to carry him off at their peril.

*The Pennsylvania Gazette,* March 13, 1760; March 20, 1760; April 3, 1760.

RUN away from the subscriber, living between the town of New Castle and Christine ferry, in the county of New Castle, on the 15th of May, an Irish servant woman, calls herself Grace Rogers, about 30 years of age, middle stature, thin visage, and has a remarkable short chin, is a great talker, and served some part of her time with Francis Thornton, near Reedy Island in said county: Had on when she went away, a stamped linen bed gown, striped linen petticoat, and a striped linsey one with three colours, also a white linsey petticoat, a flowered gauze handkerchief, and an old black bonnet. Whoever takes up and secures said servant, in any goal, so that her master may have her again, shall have Thirty Shillings reward,

paid by    JOHN JAQUET.

*The Pennsylvania Gazette,* June 12, 1760; June 19, 1760; June 26, 1760.
See *The Pennsylvania Gazette,* September 20, 1759.

RUN away from John Hall, of New-Castle County, upon Delaware, an Irish Servant Man, named Daniel Raredon, about 24 or 25 Years of Age, a short

well set Fellow; had with him a new Thickset Coat, of a light Cloth Colour, lined with Red, and Breeches of the same, two Hats, the one old, and the other new, Worsted Stockings, a Pair of Pumps, one check, one Ozenbrigs, and one fine Shirt, a Calicoe Jacket, and sundry other Cloaths, and has his old Indenture with him, that he served his Time in Maryland with one John Tucker. Whoever takes up said Servant, so that his Master may have him again, shall have Forty Shillings Reward, and reasonable Charges,
    paid by  JOHN HALL.
*The Pennsylvania Gazette*, July 3, 1760; July 10, 1760; July 17, 1760; August 7, 1760.

               Philadelphia, July 21, 1760.
RUN away, on the 17th Instant, from on board the Sloop Recovery, Lawrence Brice Commander, now lying at Wilmington, four Men, all Irishmen, viz. Patrick Brown, talks broad, about 5 feet 9 Inches high, wears a green Jacket, and black Wig. Thomas M'Bride, smooth faced, about 5 Feet 7 Inches high. William Bowman, about 5 Feet 4 Inches high, Thomas Healy, about 19 Years of Age, has a smooth Face, and stammers much in his Speech. They had all taken a Month's Pay, and broke open the Captain's Chest, out of which they took 20 Dollars, a Watch, and a Gold Ring. Whoever takes up and secures said Men, so as they may be had again, shall have Six Pounds Reward, or thirty Shillings for each, and reasonable Charges,
    paid by  CONYNGHAM and NESBITT.
*The Pennsylvania Gazette*, July 24, 1760; July 31, 1760; August 21, 1760.

                *August* 16, 1760.
      *TWENTY POUNDS REWARD.*
RAN away on Tuesday, the 12th Day of this Instant *August*, from the County of *Kent*, upon *Delaware*, a certain *Robert Caten*, born in the said County; he is a short well built Fellow, his upper Teeth ride over each other; he had on when he went away, a blue Coat, a cock'd Hat, and ties his Hair behind; he took with him Four Negroes, Three of which he stole, they being taken in Execution by me the Subscriber; these Three are, a Wench about 40 Years of Age, named *Kate*; a Girl about 9 or 10 Years of Age, named *Sue*; and a Boy about 2½ Years old, named *Toney*; the other a young Child, in the Wench's Arms. He is supposed to have gone to the Back Wood, somewhere near Patowmack, he being acquainted there, and has a Brother living there, named *Thomas Caten*; he rode a Roan Mare. Any Person, who may have the Opportunity of apprehending him, and the said Negroes, are desired to take very good Care of them, as he will perhaps make fair Promises, and thereby deceive them. I would likewise inform the Public, that the Debt for which the Execution arose, was, That the said *Robert Caten* took, some Time ago, a

free born Mulatto Woman, and sold her for a Slave; which villainous Affair he was obliged to compound, by giving a Judgment Bond, upon the abovementioned Execution issued; therefore People may judge was Sort of Person he is. The above Reward shall be paid on the Delivery of the aforesaid Three Negroes, *Kate*, *Sue* and *Toney*, at *Dover*, in the County aforesaid, or in Proportion for any of them, and reasonable Charges,
        by   THOMAS PARKE, Sheriff.
*N. B.* All person are forbid buying them.
    *The Maryland Gazette*, August 28, 1760; September 4, 1760; September 11, 1760.

                    *Three* POUNDS *Reward.*
RUN away from the Subscriber, living near Duck-Creek, in Kent County upon Delaware, on the 24th of this Instant August: An English Servant Man, named THOMAS HUMPHRIES, a lusty tall Fellow, six Feet high; of a dark Complexion, with streight black Hair; he has a large Scar on his right Cheek, and has lost some (or all) of his upper fore Teeth. He is 41 Years of Age, by Trade a Black-smith, and speaks in the West-Country Tongue. Had on when he went off, an old Felt Hat, a lightish colour'd cloth Jacket, lined with Shalloon of the same Colour; old Camblet Breeches, ozenbrigs Shirt and Trowsers, old grey yarn Stockings, and half worn Shoes. It is however supposed that he has changed his dress, and cut off his hair. Whoever takes up and secures said Humphries, so as his Master may have him again, shall have Three Pounds Reward, and all reasonable charges
        paid by me    JOHN COOK.
N. B. The Public is forbid to harbour the said Servant at their Peril; And all Masters of Vessels warn'd not to carry him off, as they wou'd avoid Prosecution.
    *The Pennsylvania Journal, and Weekly Advertiser*, September 4, 1760; September 11, 1760; September 18, 1760; September 25, 1760; October 2, 1760; October 9, 1760; October 16, 1760; October 23, 1760; October 30, 1760. See *The Pennsylvania Gazette*, October 9, 1760, and *The Pennsylvania Gazette*, December 4, 1760.

                    THREE POUNDS Reward.
RUN away from the Subscriber, living near Duck Creek, in Kent County, upon Delaware, on the 24th of August last, an English Servant Man, named Thomas Humphries, a lusty tall Fellow, six Feet high, of a dark Complexion, with straight black Hair; he has a large Scar on his right Cheek, and has lost some (or all) of his upper fore Teeth; he is 41 Years of Age, by Trade a Blacksmith, and speaks in the West Country Tongue: Had on when he went

off, an old Felt Hat, a lightish coloured Cloth Jacket, lined with Shaloon of the same Colour, old Camblet Breeches, Ozenbrigs Shirt and Trowsers, old grey Yarn Stockings, and half worn Shoes. It is, however, supposed that he has changed his Dress, and cut off his Hair. Whoever takes up and secures said Humphries, so as his Master may have him again, shall have three Pounds Reward, and all reasonable Charges, paid by me
JOHN COOK.
N. B. The Public is forbid to harbour said Servant, at their Peril; and all Masters of Vessels warned not to carry him off, as they would avoid Prosecution.
*The Pennsylvania Gazette*, October 9, 1760; October 16, 1760; October 23, 1760. See *The Pennsylvania Journal, and Weekly Advertiser*, September 4, 1760, and *The Pennsylvania Gazette*, December 4, 1760.

*FIFTEEN POUNDS* Reward.
RUN away from the Subscriber, near Lewis-Town, about the 20th of November last, a Negroe Man, named Will, about 30 Years of Age, six Feet high, well set, speaks good English, he formerly belonged to Captain Charles Ratcliffe, in Senepuxtion, Worcester County, Maryland. The said Negroe was seen several Times in Senepuxtion, after he ran away; but as it is some Time since he has been seen there, it is imagined he is transported to some other Part. Whoever takes up said Negroe, and secures him, so as the Subscriber may have him again, shall have Ten Pounds Reward, and reasonable Charges, or whoever will give the Subscriber Intelligence where the said Negroe is harboured, shall be reasonably satisfied. Likewise run away, on the 4th of September last, a Negroe Man, named Toppen, about five Feet ten Inches high, speaks good English, plays on the Violin, formerly belonged to the aforesaid Ratcliffe, and is suspected to make towards Senepuxtion. Whoever takes up said Negroe, and secures him, as aforesaid, shall have Five Pounds Reward, and reasonable Charges,
      paid by   JOSEPH SHANKLAND.
*The Pennsylvania Gazette*, October 9, 1760; October 16, 1760; October 23, 1760.


RUN away from the Subscriber, living near Duck-Creek, in Kent County, on Delaware, on the 24th of August, an English Servant Man, named Thomas Humphreys, near six Feet high, remarkable strait, of a dark Complexion, has strait black Hair, long and thin Visage, and looks sickly, has lost most of his upper fore Teeth, a large Scar on his Right Cheek, occasioned by a Burn or Scald, carries his Head high, has a Cast upwards with his Eyes, is full breasted, rocks in his Walk, speaks in the West Country Dialect about 41

Years of Age, by Trade a Blacksmith, and Gardiner: Had on when he went away, a light coloured Cloth Jacket, old Camblet Breeches, Ozenbrigs Shirt and Trowsers, old grey Yarn Stockings, old Shoes, and old Felt Hat. Whoever takes up and secures said Servant, so as his master may have him again, shall have Three Pounds Reward, and reasonable Charges, paid by JOHN COOK. N. B. Said Servant was taken upon the first of October, above Octerara-Creek, and brought within 18 Miles of Home, but got away, and is supposed to be gone upwards again.

*The Pennsylvania Gazette*, December 4, 1760; December 11, 1760; December 25, 1760. See *The Pennsylvania Journal, and Weekly Advertiser*, September 4, 1760, and *The Pennsylvania Gazette*, October 9, 1760.

RUN away, on the 25th of last Month, from the Subscriber, living near Christiana Creek, in Chester County, a Servant Man, lately from Ireland, named James M'Filie, about 20 Years of Age, has short black Hair, dark Complexion, slender, about 5 Feet 8 Inches high, grey Eyes; had on a Castor Hat, an old blue Cloth Coat, patched at the Elbows, an old Velvet Waistcoat, old Cloth Breeches, Check Shirt, a Pair of white Stockings, and another Pair of grey, and a pair of Shoes; he pretends to be a Dancer. Whoever takes up and secures said Servant, so as his Master gets him again, shall have Three Pounds Reward, and reasonable Charges,
   paid by  ANDREW M'DOWELL.

*The Pennsylvania Gazette*, December 4, 1760; December 11, 1760; December 25, 1760.

## 1761

New-Castle, January 24, 1761.
STOLEN last Night from the Stable of Elizabeth Boggs, in New-Castle, a black Mare, about 13 Hands and an Half high, paces, trots and hand-gallops, has a short switch Tail, a white Spot on each Side of her Back, under the Saddle, but no white Feet, nor Star. Also a half worn Saddle, with blue Housing, edged with Leather, and a new double reined Bridle, that had been chewed in the Reins; a blue Cloth Surtout Coat, lined with Shaloon, and has yellow Buttons. Likewise a Pair of black Saddle-bags, containing a ruffled Shirt, and a Check Ditto, a Pair of black Worsted knit Breeches, a Pair of black Worsted Stockings, two Pocket Handkerchiefs, and a Boatswain's Call. The Person who is supposed to have stolen the above, is a Recruit, named George Long, a tall lusty likely Fellow, about 5 Feet 10 Inches high, fair Complexion, much Pock marked, with short light brown curled hair, has a large Dimple in his Chin, wears a short blue Coat, with white Metal Buttons,

a short white Flannel Jacket, with black Spots, and Buckskin Breeches. Whoever takes up and secures the above Mare and Goods, so that the Owner may have them again, shall have Three Pounds Reward, and Three Pounds more for apprehending the Thief, paid by HENRY DUFF, in Black-horse-Alley, in Philadelphia, or by the Subscriber in New-Castle.
    ELIZABETH BOGGS.
*The Pennsylvania Gazette*, January 29, 1761; February 5, 1761; February 12, 1761; February 19, 1761. See *The Pennsylvania Gazette*, May 28, 1761.

    Philadelphia, January 23, 1761.
RUN away from James Brown, Cordwainer, living in Spruce-street, at the Sign of the Shoe and Boot, near the Drawbridge, an Apprentice Boy, named Cornelius Conaway, about 18 Years of Age, five Feet six Inches high, a down looking Face, and of a dark Complexion, one of his fore Teeth broke, full faced, black coloured Hair; had on when he went away, a Suit of greyish coloured Clothes a new Check Shirt, and a new Hat, a Pair of round toed Pumps, and a Pair of carved Buckles. He has a Mother living in the lower Part of New-Castle County, who keeps Tavern, and two Uncles near the same Place. Whoever takes up the said Apprentice, and secures him, so that his said Master may have him again, shall have Forty Shillings Reward, and Ten Shillings Charges, paid by me.     JAMES BROWN.
*The Pennsylvania Gazette*, January 29, 1761. See *The Pennsylvania Journal, and Weekly Advertiser*, January 29, 1761.

RUN-away from James Brown, Cordwainer, living in Spruce-street, at the sign of the shoe and boot, near the Drawbridge, an apprentice boy, named Cornelius Conaway, about eighteen years of age, five foot six inches high, a down look face, and of a dark Complexion, one of his fore-teeth broke, full faced, black coloured hair; had on when he went away, a suit of greyish coloured cloath, a new check shirt, and a new hat, a pair of round toed pumps, and a pair of carv'd buckles; he has a mother living in the lower part of New-Castel county, who keeps Tavern, and two uncles near the same place. Whoever takes up the said apprentice, and secures him, so that his said master may have him again, shall have FORTY SHILLINGS Reward, and TEN SHILLINGS Charges, paid by me.     JAMES BROWN.
*The Pennsylvania Journal, and Weekly Advertiser*, January 29, 1761; February 5, 1761; February 12, 1761; February 26, 1761. See *The Pennsylvania Gazette*, January 29, 1761.

*TEN POUNDS* Reward,

MADE his Escape from the Subscriber hereof, being Petit Constable of the Borough of Wilmington, in the county of New-castle on Delaware, a certain Richard Hall, who left Chester County when a Child, and hath lived ever since in Lunenburgh County, in Virginia, aged about 25 years, 5 feet 6 or 7 inches high, brown Hair, well countenanced and made, who had been examined, and was going to be committed to the Goal of the County by one of the Burgesses of said Burrough, for uttering Counterfeit Bills of Credit of the Colony of Virginia, of Forty Shillings and Ten Pounds; whereof were found about him, when examined, to the Sum of Four Hundred and Thirty-four Pounds, all dated June 8, 1757. Both Margin and Printing are pretty well done, except such Words as are attempted in old English Letters, which are very base, and the Signer's Name Peyton Randolph in the Genuine, reads like Tryton in the Counterfeit. 'Tis probable he has passed a great many, and that he has several Accomplices, whereof the Public is cautioned to beware. Whoever apprehends said Hall, so that he may be committed to the Goal of the County aforesaid, shall be paid the above Reward of TEN POUNDS
by    JOHN CARTER.

N. B. He has left a small bay Horse, which he said belonged to one Jacob Hugins of York County, with whom he left his own. If the Owner does not come and claim said Horse in three Weeks, he will be sold to pay Charges.

*The Pennsylvania* Gazette, March 19, 1761; The *Pennsylvania Journal, and Weekly Advertiser*, March 19, 1761; April 1, 1761; April 16, 1761. Minor differences between the papers.

New-Castle, March 16, 1761.

RUN away from Abigail Wheatly, of New Castle, an Irish Servant Man, named John Horan, about 35 Years of Age, of low Stature, and black Complexion: Had on when he went away, a Felt Hat, dark brown Wig, dark coloured coarse Cloth Coat, with flat white Metal Buttons, old red Jacket, Ozenbrigs Shirt, new Leather Breeches, coarse ribb'd Yarn Stockings, and old Shoes, by Trade a Miner; he pretends to pass by a Certificate from William Allen, Esq; at Philadelphia, but has been since that sold out of New-Castle Goal for his Fees. Whoever takes up and secures said Servant, so as his Mistress may have him again, shall have Twenty Shillings Reward, and reasonable Charges, paid by    ABIGAIL WHEATLY.

N. B. He run away the 15th Instant.

*The Pennsylvania Gazette*, March 26, 1761; April 2, 1761; April 23, 1761.

RUN away from the Subscriber, in New Castle, on Saturday the 28th of March, an Irish Servant Lad named Michael M'Cane, about sixteen or

seventeen Years of age, has dark brown Hair which he ties behind, and wears his Hat smartly cock'd; had on when he went away, an old brown cloth Coat, with red Cuffs and Cape, and yellow metal Buttons, a spotted flannel lapell'd Jacket, old leather Breeches and yarn Stockings. Whoever takes up and secures said Servant, so that his Master may have him again, shall receive a Reward of TWO PISTOLES, to be paid by Lathim and Read,
 Merchants in Philadelphia, or GEORGE READ.
*The Pennsylvania Journal, and Weekly Advertiser*, April 2, 1761; April 23, 1761; *The Pennsylvania Gazette*, April 16, 1761; April 30, 1761; May 21, 1761. Minor differences between the papers


RUN away from the House of the Subscriber, in Brandywine Hundred, on the 1st Instant, a Servant Girl, born in England, named Elizabeth Allmark, aged 19 Years, of a middle Stature, and swarthy Complexion: Had on, when she went away, a good Ozenbrigs Shift, a greenish Quilt, has been mended round the Bottom with green Shaloon, a striped Linen Jacket, and Check Linen Bonnet; she took with her two new Check Aprons, and two blue and white Cotton Handkerchiefs, a white Holland one, a Damask Cap, Cambrick Ditto, fine Linen Ditto, two coarse ones, new Shoes, and good blue Yarn Stockings. Whoever takes up said Servant, and secures her, so that her Master may have her again, shall have Twenty Shillings Reward,
 paid by JOHN BUCKLEY.
*The Pennsylvania Gazette*, April 9, 1761; April 23, 1761; April 30, 1761.

             New Castle, April 6, 1761.
      FIVE POUNDS Reward.
THIS Day made his Escape from the Goal of this County, a Mulattoe Fellow, named John Miller, his Mother lives in, or near Philadelphia, married to Henry Heany, at whose Suit he was committed; he is a short, impudent Fellow, big Lips and Mouth, his Right-leg shorter than the other: Had on an old blue Jacket, Leather Breeches, black Stockings, new Pumps, and large Brass Buckles. Whoever secures the said Fellow, so that he may be had again, shall receive the above Reward,
   from SWAIN COLESBERRY, Goaler.
*The Pennsylvania Gazette*, April 16, 1761; April 30, 1761.


      TWO PISTOLES REWARD.
RUN away, on Monday the 13th Inst. from the Subscriber, living in Kent County, on Delaware, near Dover, a Country born Servant Man, named James M'Kinley, 22 Years of Age, about five Feet six Inches high, wore his

own Hair, which is not very long, and of a dark brown Colour; he has a bad Countenance, and is smooth faced: Had on an old Hat, a half worn County Cloth Fly Coat, a white Jacket, red Everlasting Breeches, new Worsted Stockings, and old Shoes, with Brass Buckles; and had with him one fine Shirt, and one coarse Ditto. Whoever takes up the said Servant, and secures him, so that his Master may have him again, shall have the above Reward, and all reasonable Charges, paid by     JAMES CLAYTON.

*The Pennsylvania Gazette*, April 23, 1761; May 21, 1761.


New-Castle, May 17, 1761.
BROKE out of the Goal of this County, last Night, the following Prisoners, viz. a certain George Long, about 5 Feet 10 Inches high, a lusty fat Fellow, fresh Complexion; had on and took with him, when he made his Escape, a dark drab strait Coat, white flannel Jacket, old check Shirt, old Leather Breeches, old Stockings and Shoes. Also a certain David Anderson, about 5 feet 7 or 8 Inches high, fair Hair, and fair Complexion; had on when made his Escape a Bearskin grey Coat, old check Shirt, old Leather Breeches, old Shoes and Stockings, they were both tried lately for criminal Causes. Also a certain Mulattoe Fellow, named John Miller, who made his Escape some Time ago from said Goal; he is remarkable, one Leg being stiffer and shorter than the other, and appears when he walks to have one Side foremost; had on and took with him two blue Jackets, old check Shirt, Leather Breeches, black Stockings, and Pumps with large Brass Buckles. Whoever apprehends the said Fellows, and brings them to the Subscriber, shall have Ten Pounds Reward, or Three Pounds for each and reasonable Charges,
         paid by     SWEN COLESBERRY, Goaler.
N. B. All Masters of Vessels are forbid to carry them off at their Peril.

*The Pennsylvania Gazette*, May 28, 1761; June 11, 1761; July 16, 1761; July 23, 1761; August 6,1761; August 13, 1761; August 20, 1761; August 27, 1761; September 3, 1761. *The Pennsylvania Gazette*, January 29, 1761, for Long.


RUN away from the Subcriber, living in Kent County, on Delaware, an English Convict Servant Man, named Joseph Burroh, aged 21 Years, five Feet eight Inches high, or thereabouts, fair Hair, somewhat Pock marked; had on a white Lincey Jacket, new Homespun Shirt, old Trowsers, Leather Breeches, new Shoes, old blue clouded Yarn Stockings, old felt Hat; his Right Arm somewhat withered, and stiff in the Elbow Joint, by being formerly broke. Whoever secures the said Servant, so that his Master may have him again, shall have Twenty-five Shilling Reward, more than the Law allows, and reasonable Charges,

          paid by me    MICHAEL FURBEE.
*The Pennsylvania Gazette*, May 28, 1761; June 11, 1761; June 18, 1761.
See *The Pennsylvania Gazette*, September 3, 1761.


RUN-away, the 17th of this month, from the subscriber, living at Christiana bridge New-Castle County a slim middle sized man named Henry Tizdel, a sadle-tree maker by trade, had on when he went away, a light coloured broad cloath coat, a new brown calimanco jacket, a pair of red breeches, and single channel pumps, he took with him a watch without a Christal, it is supposed he is gone towards New-York. as he was seen near Chester on his road to Philadelphia, whoever takes up said Tizdel or secures him, shall have THREE POUNDS paid by me    JOHN CUSTOLOW.
N. B. Said Tizdel hath long brown hair tyed with a ribbond, he has been a soldier in the Eastern and Western expeditions, and when he went away rode a dark brown mare a trotter.
    *The Pennsylvania Journal, and Weekly Advertiser*, June 6, 1761; June 11, 1761.


RUN away from the Subscriber, living in Whiteclay Creek Hundred, New-Castle County, An Irish Servant Man, named Cornelius Healy, about 5 Feet 8 Inches high, with short curly Hair: Had on when he went away, a Snuff coloured Thickset Coat, a Calico Jacket, Thickset Breeches, Worsted Stockings, and good Shoes, with Steel Buckles, and sundry Clothes not well known. He has been inlisted in the regular Service, and has his Discharge from the Regiment, which he has for his Pass. Any Person that secures the said Servant in any Goal, so that his Master may have him again, shall have Forty Shillings Reward, and reasonable Charges,
          paid by me    GEORGE EVANS.
*The Pennsylvania Gazette*, July 23, 1761.


                              Wilmington, August 28, 1761.
RUN away, in the Night, between the 26th and 27th instant, from on board the Sloop Speedwell, John Lockhart Master, for Providence, lying at Wilmington, a certain John James, a Sailor, after receiving one Month's Advance, born in Wales, but bred, as he says, in the North of Ireland; a well set Down looking Fellow, about 5 Feet 10 Inches high, wears a Wig, his other Clothes cannot be described. He has a Pearl over one of his Eyes, but not readily discerned. Whoever brings, or secures said Fellow in any goal, so that he may be brought to Justice, shall have Five Pounds Reward,
          paid by    THOMAS DOWDLE, in Wilmington.
*The Pennsylvania Gazette*, September 3, 1761.

New-Castle, August 20, 1761.
COmmitted to the Goal of this County, the 20th of July last, on Suspicion of being a Runaway, a certain Joseph Borrough, of a fair Complexion, about 5 Feet 8 Inches high; had on, when committed, a coarse Linsey Jacket, coarse Shirt and Trowsers. His Master (if he has any) is hereby desired to come in four Weeks after the Date hereof, pay Charges, and take him away, otherwise he will be sold for the same,
by SWEN COLESBERY, Goaler.

*The Pennsylvania Gazette*, September 3, 1761; October 8, 1761. See *The Pennsylvania Gazette*, May 28, 1761.


RUN away from the subscriber living in New Castle County, in Whitley Creek hundred, a servant man named Thomas M'Gill, about 5 foot 10 inches high and about 18 years of age, he wears his own hair (which is of a black colour) tied behind, and has the fore-part cut off, is pitted with the small-pox, and has grey eyes: He had on, a new felt hat, a new coat, of home-spun whitish coloured cloth, with broad metal buttons, a dark colour'd fustian jacket and breeches, the jacket has blue lining, but no sleeves, blue worsted stockings, old shoes, with brass buckles; he wears a short black line ribbon about his neck. He is supposed to be gone on board of Capt. M'Pherson's privateer. Any person taking up and securing said servant, so that the owner may have him again, shall have *Forty Shillings* Reward, and reasonable Charges, paid by    ROBERT M'ANTIER.
N. B. All masters of vessels are forbid either to harbour or conceal him, at their peril.

*The Pennsylvania Journal, and Weekly Advertiser*, September 3, 1761; September 10, 1761.


FIVE POUNDS Reward.
RUN away, about the latter End of August, from the Subscriber, living at Little-Creek, in Kent County, on Delaware, a Servant Man, named Robert Pierce, about 48 Years of age, a short tick Fellow, professes to be a good Sawyer with a Whip-saw, or for Ship-carpenters Work; also speaks much of his working and managing a Plantation, loves Liquor, and looks like a clumsy hard-working Fellow: Had on and took with him a dark coloured Thickset Jacket and breeches, white and check Shirts; it is thought he has Plenty of Silver and Paper-money, as he is supposed to have broke open and robb'd John Lock's Shallop of 70 l. he was born in the West of England, and speaks a little of the West Country Dialect, but has been several Years in this Country, and lived in different Parts of Maryland, but last in Queen Ann's or Talbot County. Whoever takes up and secures said Servant, so as he may be

had again, shall have the above Reward, and reasonable Charges,
paid by    MARY HUNTER.
*The Pennsylvania Gazette,* September 24, 1761; October 8, 1761; October 15, 1761; October 29, 1761; November 5, 1761.


New-Castle, Sept. 21, 1761.
COMMITTED to the Goal of this County the 5th Inst. on Suspicion of being a Runaway, a Negroe Man, who calls himself William Wilson, about 5 Feet 7 Inches high, wears a Bonnet, blue Jacket, coarse Shirt and Trowsers; his Master (if he has any) is hereby desired to come, pay Charges, and take him away in four Weeks after the Date hereof, otherwise he will be sold for the same by    SWEN COLSBERRY, Goaler.
*The Pennsylvania Gazette,* October 1, 1761; October 22, 1761. See *The Pennsylvania Gazette,* November 12, 1761.


RUN away, the 4th of this instant October, from the Subscriber, in Kent County, on Delaware, near Dover, a certain William Brown, who the under named was Bail for; he is about 5 Feet 9 Inches high, wears his Hair, middling short, curls, and is inclined to brown, is full faced, and of a red Complexion: Had on when he went away, a bluish coloured Coat, trimmed with large Block-tin Buttons, a striped or Calicoe Cotton Jacket, with the Stripes round his Body, and a Pair of half-worn Leather Breeches, with carved white Metal Buttons, and sometimes wears wide Sailors Trowsers over them. He has the Brogue pretty much, and his upper Teeth are rotten up to the Gums. Went away with him a Woman, whom he has kept about six Months, and a Girl, about six Years old. It is supposed they will pass for Man and Wife. Whoever takes up the said Man, and secures him, so that his Bail may have him again, shall have Three Pounds Reward, and reasonable Charges,
paid by    JOSIAH WALLACE.
N. B. All Masters of Vessels are forbid to carry him off at their Peril.
*The Pennsylvania Gazette,* October 22, 1761; November 5, 1761; November 12, 1761. See *The Pennsylvania Gazette,* September 9, 1762.


New-Castle County, Nov. 7, 1761.
Broke out of the Goal of this County last Night, the 3 following Persons, viz. one named David Anderson, a thick set Fellow, fair Hair; had on when he went away, a lightish coloured Coat, old Shirt, Leather Breeches. Another named Arthur Kelly, a tall ill looking Fellow, wears his own Hair; had on a grey Rateen Jacket, old Shirt and Breeches. The other a Negroe Fellow, committed on Suspicion of being a Runaway, calls himself William Wilson;

he is a short Fellow, much bandy leg'd, and little on the yellowish Colour. Whoever apprehends said Fellows, and secures them so that they may be had again, shall have Six Pounds, or Forty Shillings for each,
           paid by SWEN COLESBURY, Goaler.

*The Pennsylvania Gazette*, November 12, 1761; November 26, 1761; December 3, 1761. See *The Pennsylvania Gazette*, October 1, 1761, for Wilson.


RUN away from the Subscriber, living at White-Clay-Creek, New-Castle County, on Wednesday the 21st of October, the following Apprentices (Ship Carpenters) viz. Robert Carr, about 20 years of age, about 5 Feet 10 Inches high, round shouldered, well set, of a fresh Complexion, long Chin, wears his own fair Hair, is an imperious Fellow; had on when he went away, a very short Thickset Coat, white Cloth Jacket, new Thickset Breeches, Thread Stockings, good Shoes, a good Castor Hat, and took a Bundle of other Cloaths, such as Jackets, Trowsers, Shirts and Stockings. The other named Barney Couzens Harris, about 17 Years of Age, very much freckled, wears his own black Hair, not very big of his Age, has lost one of two Joints of his Fingers, and has a crooked Thumb, but on which Hand not known; had on when he went away a dark grey Coat, trimmed with black, a red Halfthick Jacket, and a white Cloth Ditto, the same of the others, with turn-up Cuffs, Leather Breeches, Check Shirt, Worsted Stockings, good Shoes, Castor Hat, and took with him a Bundle of other Cloaths. Whoever takes up and secures said Apprentices in any Goal, shall have Forty Shillings for each, or if brought Home Fifty Shillings for each, and reasonable Charges,
           paid by    RICHARD DENNIS.

*The Pennsylvania Gazette*, December 17, 1761; December 24, 1761; December 31, 1761.


RUN away from the Subscriber, living in Brandywine Hundred, New-Castle County, an Englishman, named John Jones, a thick set Fellow, about 50 Years of Age, long visaged, wears his own Hair, of brownish Colour: had on and carried with him, three brown Coats, one new, with carved Metal Buttons, a red jacket, old Buckskin Breeches, a good Beaver Hat, three Paid blue Stockings, one Pair Worsted, the rest of his Apparel unknown, and it is supposed he took with him a Silver Watch, the Property of the Subscriber. Whoever apprehends the said Jones, in any of his Majesty's Goals in this Province, shall have Three Pounds Reward,
           paid by    CALEB PERKINS.

*The Pennsylvania Gazette*, January 28, 1762; February 5, 1762. See *The Pennsylvania Journal, and Weekly Advertiser*, January 28, 1762.

# 1762

*FORTY SHILLINGS Reward.*
RUN away, the 16th of this Instant, from the Subscriber, living in Dover, Kent County, on Delaware, a Mulattoe Servant Man, named Francis Miller, about 34 Years of Age, about 5 Feet 11 Inches high, slim built, walks loose in his Knees, pretty much pock-broken, and a large Beard: Had on when he went away, A blue Kersey Jacket, lined with ozenbrigs, old Check Shirt, old breeches, good Shoes, milled Stockings, and, it is believed, he stole, and took with him, two Great Coats, one old blue Cloth, the other light coloured. It is supposed he is gone up the Country to one Joseph Cookson's, living in Lancaster County, near the Head of Pequea. Whoever takes up said Servant, and bring him Home to his Master, shall have the above Reward, and reasonable Charges; or if secured in any goal, so that he may be had again, shall have what the Law allows, paid by THOMAS PARKE.
N. B. All Persons are forbid harbouring or concealing him, as they will answer the fate at their Peril.
*The Pennsylvania Gazette*, January 28, 1762.

*January* 28.
RUN-away from the Subscriber, living in Brandywine Hundred, New-Castle County, an English Man named John Jones, a thick set Fellow, about 50 Years of Age, long visag'd, wears his own hair of a brownish colour, he has on and carried with him, three brown Coats, one whereof is new, with carved mettle Buttons, likewise a red Jacket and old Buck-skin Breeches, and a good Beaver Hat, likewise three pair of blue Stockings, one pair worsted, the rest of his apparel unknown, (and supposed to have taken a watch with him.) Whoever takes up said Jones and secures him in any of his Majesty's Goals in this Province, so that the subscriber man have him, shall be paid the sum of THREE POUNDS,    by CALEB PERKINS.
*The Pennsylvania Journal, and Weekly Advertiser*, January 28, 1762; February 4, 1762. See *The Pennsylvania Gazette*, January 28, 1762.

RUN away on the 7th Instant, from the Subscriber, living in Christiana Hundred, New-Castle County, an Apprentice Lad, named Shadrach Lee, about 19 Years of Age, 5 Feet 8 or 9 Inches high, with black Hair, and is a sour looking ill-natur'd Fellow, much given to Lying, a Shoemaker by Trade: Had on when he went away, an Olive coloured Cloth Coat, Linsey Jacket, white Shirt, light coloured Cloth Breeches, a blue Silk Handkerchief, with white Spots, grey Stockings, footed with blue, old Shoes, and steel Buckles. Whoever takes up said Apprentice, and brings him to the Subscriber, shall

have Forty Shillings Reward, and reasonable Charges,
        paid by    WILLIAM UNDERWOOD.
N. B. As his Mother and Brother live in Leacock Township, Lancaster County, it is supposed he is gone that Way.
*The Pennsylvania Gazette*, February 18, 1762.

### FIVE POUNDS Reward.

RUN away the 18th ult. from the Subscriber, living near Wilmington, New-Castle County, A Servant Man, named Richard Ryan, about 30 Years of Age, near or quite six Feet high, of a fresh colour, remarkable for being handy about cooking, Washing or Ironing, as well as for being inclinable to Finery: Had on, and took with him, when he went away, Two coats, one a blue Broadcloth, full trimmed, open cuffed, the other of a light coloured Fustian; four Jackets, one a Scarlet Broadcloth, one a greenish cut Velvet, one a brown coloured cloth, and a striped one; two Pair of Breeches, one Leather, and the other lightish coloured cloth; several Pair of Stockings, some are white, and has very large Clocks; [*sic*] two Pair of Shoes, one of Neats-leather, and the other of Calf-skin, with Straps and white Metal Buckles; has a great Quantity of fine Linens, such as ruffled Shirts, and Petticoat Trowsers, on which he frequently pinned a Number of black Silk Ribbons; sometimes wore a brown Wig, and sometimes a ruffled Linen Cap; had two Hats, one of which of Beaver, quite new. Whoever takes up and secures said Servant, and gives Notice, thereof to the Subscriber, or to Joseph Musgrove in Kennet, Chester Country, shall have five Pounds Reward, and reasonable Charges,
        paid by    MORRIS CONER.
*The Pennsylvania Gazette*, March 4, 1762; March 11, 1762.

### FIVE POUNDS Reward.

Made his escape from the subscriber, the 26th of last month, at night, a certain James Senix, a Ship-carpenter by trade, who lived with Griffith Thomas at that time; he is about five feet ten inches high, full fac'd, and is remarkable, by reason of a large mole near the right side of his nose. Whoever apprehends said prisoner, and secures him in New-Castle Goal, or any of his Majesty's goals, shall receive the above reward, from
        ANDREW JUSTIS, Constable.
N. B. All masters of vessels are forbid to carry him off, at their peril.
*The Pennsylvania Gazette*, April 1, 1762; April 15, 1762; April 22, 1766.

### FORTY SHILLINGS Reward.

RUN away from the Subscriber, living at Duck-Creek Landing, Kent County, on Delaware, on the 25th of March in the Morning, a Negroe Man, named

Pompey, about 32 Years of Age, about five Feet four Inches high, a well set Fellow, took with him three Jackets, one of a lightish Colour, of plain Cloth, one a red Halfthick, and one a black and white Calicoe, mostly black; also a Pair of good Leather Breeches, with a Flap before, buttoned up near each Hip, dark grey Stockings, old Shoes, with carved Metal Buckles, middling good Wool Hat, and Ozenbrigs Shirt. Whoever secures said Negroe in any Goal, and gives Notice thereof to the Subscriber, shall have the above Reward, paid by     JOHN BLACKSHER.
All Masters of Vessels are forbid to carry him off at their Peril.
*The Pennsylvania Gazette*, April 1, 1762; April 15, 1762; April 22, 1762; April 29, 1762.

THIRTY PISTOLES REWARD.
Wilmington, April 8th, 1762.
*RUN-AWAY on or about the 27th of last Month from his Bail, and in Debt to sundry Creditors, to the Amount of several Thousand Pounds, a certain Robert Middleton, about 35 Years old, 5 Feet 5 or 6 Inches high, of a dark Complection, middling round Vissage, sharp Nose, dark Eyes, chearful Countenance, much pitted with the Small-pox, middling well built, is free and agreeable in Company, forward in talking, Card-playing, and drinking, but not apt to be drunk, snuffs and sings well, but with a strong Voice; when he went-away wore a short black Wig, his Apparel uncertain: It is supposed he will endeavour to get to his Partner James Weir, who sailed from this Port last Spring, to Tortola, with Captain Joell, and is not yet returned. Whoever takes up said Middleton, and secures him in any Gaol on this Continent or elsewhere, so that his Bail and Creditors may have him again, shall have the above Reward, paid by us the Subscribers*, James Bratten, George Thompson, John Miller, *Esq*; Isaac Richardson, *Esq*: William Clingan, *Esq*; John Douglass, *Esq*; Robert Karree, John Fleming, Thomas Karling.
N. B. *Said* Middleton *followed shalloping from* Wilmington *to Philadelphia. All Masters of Vessels are forewarned not to carry him off.*
*The New-York Gazette*, April 12, 1762; April 19, 1762. See *The Pennsylvania Gazette*, April 22, 1762.

THIRTY PISTOLES *Reward.*
Wilmington, April 8, 1762.
RUN away on or about the 27th of last Month, from his Bail, and in Debt to sundry Creditors, to the Amount of several Thousand Pounds, a certain ROBERT MIDDLETON, about 35 Years old, five Feet five or six Inches high, of a dark Complexion, middling round Visage, sharp Nose, dark Eyes, chearful Countenance, much pitted with the Small pox, middling well built,

is free and agreeable in Company, forward in talking, Card playing and Drinking, but not apt to be drunk, snuffs, and sings well, but with a strong Voice; when he went away wore a short black Wig, his Apparel uncertain. It is supposed he will endeavour to get to his Partner James Wier, who sailed from this Port last Spring to Tortola, with Captain Joel, and is not yet returned. Whoever takes up said Middleton, and secures him in any Goal on this Continent, or elsewhere, so that his Bail and Creditors may have him again, shall have the above Reward, paid by us the Subscribers, James Bratten, George Thompson, John Miller, Esq; Isaac Richardson, Esq; William Clingan, Esq; John Douglass, Esq; Robert Karree,
    John Fleming, Thomas Karling.
N. B. Said Middleton followed Shalloping from Wilmington to Philadelphia. All Masters of Vessels are forewarned not to carry him off.
 *The Pennsylvania Gazette*, April 22, 1762. See *The New-York Gazette*, April 12, 1762.


RUN AWAY on the 4th of this Inst. from the Subscriber, living in Noxontown, in New-Castle County on Delaware, A Servant Man, named Samuel Bateman: Had on when he went away, A new blue Coat, made short, with a small Cape on it, an old Pea Jacket, with a Pair of blue Breeches of the same of the Coat, and sundry other Jackets and Breeches, a Pair of broad ribbed Stockings, of a blue grey Colour, with sundry others, &c. Had also a Parcel of new checked Shirts, with some white Ditto. He is an Englishman born, of a redish Complexion, with red Hair, generally tied behind, has been 5 or 6 Years in the Provincial Service, of which he brags pretty much; he is very subject to drink, and when talking seems to have a Twist in his Face. He was seen at Christine Ferry, it is thought making for Philadelphia, and supposed to be there at present, waiting to get on board a Privateer. Whoever takes up the said Servant, and secures him in any Goal, so that his Master may have him again, shall have Three Pounds Reward, paid them by
    HENRY VANBEBBER, senior.
 *The Pennsylvania Gazette*, May 13, 1762.


      New-Castle, May 25, 1762.
Committed to the Goal of this County, on the 17th Instant (on Suspicion of being a Runaway) a likely Negroe Boy, about 12 or 13 Years of Age, says he belongs to one James Anderson, jun. who lives near the Manor Church, Cecil County, Maryland, that his Master took him to George Town to lead a Horse there, and that he lost his Way going home. His master, if he has any, is hereby desired to come in four Weeks after the Date hereof, pay his Charges,

and take him away, otherwise he will be sold for the same,
by ALEXANDER HARVEY, Goaler.
*The Pennsylvania Gazette*, May 13, 1762.


RUN away from his Bail, on Saturday the 15th Day of this inst. May, a certain Thomas Dixon, a Weaver by Trade, about 25 Years of Age, low Stature, Pock marked, has a Mole under one of his Ears, an Irishman born: Had on when he went away, a red Jacket and Breeches, a dark brown Broadcloth Coat, Check Leggings gathered round the Knees, and has light brown Hair tied; he likewise took with him a dark sorrel Mare, with a Star in her Forehead, and shod before it is supposed he will make towards Carolina. whoever takes up and secures the said Dixon, so as the Subscriber may get him again, shall have Ten Pounds Reward, paid by CATHERINE REDICK,
living in Kent County, on Delaware.
*The Pennsylvania Gazette*, May 27, 1762.

June 10.
*Three Pistoles Reward.*
RUN-away from the Subscriber living in Noxon-town, a Servant Girl named Mary Stanley, tall, & black hair, and some marks of the small pox, had on when she went aways a dark cotton chintz gown, red cloth shoes, white worsted hose; she has a bashful and down looking countenance. Went with her one Anne Smith, a short set girl with pale hair, and in sundry debts fraudulently contracted; she has a very bold countenance, large eyes, with much white in them, leers or look. [*sic*] with a side look. she had on when she went away a yellow persian gown, red shoes, with several other gowns. Whoever takes up and secures said Mary Stanley in any Goal, so that her Master may have her again, shall have Three Pounds Reward, and one Pound for said Ann Smith, paid by     ANDREW M'GAUGTY.
N. B. They were seen at New Castle Fair and at Court; and it's supposed they are gone to Philadelphia.
*The Pennsylvania Journal, and Weekly Advertiser*, June 10, 1762; June 24, 1762.

June 17.
RUN-away last night from the subscriber living in Christiana Hundred New-Castle county on Delaware. a Mulato slave named John, born (he says) in one of the Spanish Islands, aged about eighteen years. five feet six Inches high, a Slender active fellow, speaks plain, apt to smile; had on when he went away an old light colour'd stuff Coat, a red Jacket, the fore Parts of Plush, old Breeches, one Pair of striped Trowsers, very narrow, one pair of ditto. of corse Linnen, wider and shorter than the others, one check Shirt, several ditto

of corse Linnen, worsted Stockings, old Shoes, an old castor Hat, with a black Ribbon buckled round it, &c. It is supposed he will endeavour to go out in one of the Privateers, he had been in that way before and beats on the Drum. Whoever takes up and secures said Slave, so that his Master may have him again, shall have TWO POUNDS Reward, and reasonable Charges
paid by    GEORGE CRAGHEAD,
*N. B*, All Masters of Vessels, and others, are forbid to take him off, as they will answer for it.

*The Pennsylvania Journal, and Weekly Advertiser*, June 17, 1762; June 24, 1762; July 1, 1762. See *The Pennsylvania Gazette*, June 24, 1762.

*FORTY SHILLINGS Reward.*
RUN away, on the 14th of this instant June, from the Subscriber, living in Christiana Hundred, New-Castle County, A Mulattoe Slave, named John, 18 Years of Age, about 5 Feet 6 Inches high, a slender made active Fellow, and says he was born in one of the Spanish Islands. He took with him a lightish coloured Stuff Coat, red Jacket, the fore Parts Plush, old Breeches, long narrow striped Trowsers, Tow Ditto, wider and shorter; Check, white Linen, and coarse Shirts; Worsted Stockings; old Shoes; an old Castor Hat, with a black Ribbon buckled round it; can beat on a Drum; and it is thought he will make towards Philadelphia or New-York, in order to get off in some Vessel. Whoever takes up and secures said Slave, so that his Master may have him again, shall have Forty shillings Reward , and reasonable Charges,
paid by    GEORGE CRAGHEAD.
N. B. All Masters of Vessels, and others, are forbid to take him off at their Peril. He is suspected of having a forged Pass.

*The Pennsylvania Gazette*, June 24, 1762. See *The Pennsylvania Journal, and Weekly Advertiser*, June 17, 1762.


RUN-AWAY on the 26th ult. from the Subscriber, living in Wilmington, An indented Servant BOY, named THOMAS TOTTAN, about 15 Years of Age, 4 Feet and an Half high, of a fair Complexion, has a Scar over his left Eye, and has sandy Hair; having on when he went away, A Pair of coarse Trowser, &c. Whoever takes up and secures said Servant Boy, so that his Master may have him again, shall have ONE PISTOLE REWARD, and all reasonable CHARGES, paid by    ANDREW BORELL.
N. B. All Masters of Vessels are forbid to carry him off at their Peril.

*The Pennsylvania Gazette*, July 1, 1762; July 8, 1762 .

*Five Pistoles* Reward.
New-Castle County, on Delaware, June 26.
RUNaway from his special Bail, on Tuesday the 14th Inst. a certain Eleazer David, aged 25 Years, about five Feet eight Inches high, of a fair complexion, somewhat pitted with the Small-pox, and wears a Cap, a Carpenter by Trade; had on when he went away, a lightish coloured Homespun cloth Coat, with yellow buttons, and a lightish Camblet Ditto, lined with red Shaloon or Tammy, a blue Camblet Waistcoat, old Leather Breeches, and an old Fur Hat; he is remarkable for playing on the Violin, Left handed; it is supposed he intends to make his Escape towards North Carolina, as he has Relations living there. Whoever takes up and secures him in any of His Majesty's Goals on the Continent, and sends Word to the Subscriber, living in Pencader Hundred, and County aforesaid, and reasonable Charges,
  paid by  ALEXANDER GIBSON.
N. B. All Masters of Vessels are forbid to carry him of at their Peril.
*The Pennsylvania Gazette*, July 8, 1762.


THREE POUNDS *Reward.*
RUN away from the Subscriber, of Kent County, on Delaware, the 4th of this Instant, a Servant Man, named John Wilson; it is supposed he will go toward Sasquehannah Ferry, as his Father, Charles Wilson, lives near said Ferry: Had on when he went away, a dark grey Bearskin Coat, no Jacket, Ozenbrigs Trowsers, Homespun Shirt, Felt hat, no Shoes nor Stockings; and is supposed to be seventeen Years old. Whoever secures said Servant in any Goal in the Province of Pennsylvania, or in any of the three lower Counties, so that his Master may have him again, shall have the above Reward,
  paid by  HENRY STEVENS.
*The Pennsylvania Gazette*, August 19, 1762; September 9, 1762.


TEN DOLLARS Reward.
RUN away from the Subscriber, the Fourth Day of this instant August, a Servant Man, named John Price, born in England, aged about 24 Years, 5 Feet 7 Inches and a Half high, a thin spare Fellow, has black hair, if not cut off: Had on, when he went away, an Olive coloured Thickset Coat, and leather Breeches. He is very remarkable, by having the first Joint of his Left Thumb cut off, and may wear a Glove to hide it. He is supposed to have gone up the Country, or may cross Delaware to the Jerseys. Whoever takes up said Servant, and secures him, so that his Master may have him again, shall have Ten Dollars Reward, and reasonable Charges,
 paid by  THOMAS RATLIDGE, living near Dover, in Kent County, on Delaware.

N. B. All Masters of Vessels are forbid carrying him off at their Peril.
*The Pennsylvania Gazette*, August 26, 1762.

*August* 19.
RUN-AWAY from the Subscriber, living at Mr. David Weatherspoons, New-Castle county, on the 15th of August, an Irish Servant lad named John Mc.Collough, about five feet Eight inches high of a fair complexion, lightish brown hair, had on when he went away, a felt Hat, a white Dowles shirt, a brown cloth Coat Lapeled with a cut and slash sleeve but does not fit him, with mohair buttons of the same colour, no waist-coat, brown linen breeches, white Stockings, a pair of pumps, with steel Buckles in them. Whoever takes up and secures said Servant in any Goal, so that his Master may have him again, shall have Forty Shillings Reward, besides what the Law allows, and Reasonable charges
   paid by  JOSEPH JAQUES.
*The Pennsylvania Journal, and Weekly Advertiser*, August 19, 1762; August 26, 1762; September 2, 1762; September 19, 1762.


RUN away, on the 17th of last Month, from James Colgan, of the Town of Dover, in Kent County, on Delaware, two Servant Men, the one named John Duell, born in Maryland, 26 Years of Age, about 5 Feet 9 Inches high, fair Complexion, wears a Cap; his Apparel is uncertain, as he took several Changes along with him, particularly a Scarlet Jacket, lined with white Flannel, dark striped Holland Trowsers, and an old blue Great Coat. He is a great Chewer of Tobacco. Whoever secures the said Duell in any of His Majesty's Goals in North-America, so as his Master may have him again, shall have Five Pounds Reward, and reasonable Charges, as his said Master has entered Bail in a Sum of Money on his (the said Duell's) account.—The other named John M'Que, born in Ireland, about 22 Years of Age, about 5 Feet 5 Inches high, Pock marked, wears long black Hair, not tied: Had on when he went away, A blue Cloth Coat, half-worn, a Crimson cut Velvet Jacket, with small high Crown Silver Buttons, blue Saggathy Breeches, without Lining, and black ribbed Stockings. H is very much given to Liquor, chewing Tobacco, and quarrelsome. Whoever secures said M'Que, shall receive Four Pounds Reward, or Nine Pounds for apprehending both said Runaways,  paid by  JAMES COLGAN.
N. B. All Masters of Vessels are forbid to carry them off at their Peril.
*The Pennsylvania Gazette*, September 2, 1762.


RUN away from the Subscriber, on the 28th of last Month, a Mulattoe Man, named George, about 23 Years of Age, 5 Feet 9 Inches high; had on, when

he went away, a black Jacket, red Breeches, white Stockings, and wears his own Hair, tied. Whoever takes up the said Mulattoe, and secures him, so that his Master may have him again, shall have THREE POUNDS Reward, and reasonable Charges, paid by ARCHIBALD GARDNER, of Philadelphia, or WILLIAM PATTERSON, of Christine Bridge.
N. B. All Masters of Vessels are forbid to carry him off at their Peril.
*The Pennsylvania Gazette*, September 2, 1762; September 16, 1762. See *The Pennsylvania Journal, and Weekly Advertiser*, September 2, 1762, and *The Pennsylvania Journal, and Weekly Advertiser*, September 9, 1762.

*September 2.*
RUN away, on Saturday last, from William Patterson, of Christeen-Bridge: A Mulatto Man, named George, aged about 23 years, about 5 feet 9 inches high, with short black hair tied behind Had on whan he went away, a black Waistcoat, red Breeches, white Stockings, long striped Trowsers, and had a Bundle with him so that it is supposed he may change his Cloaths, and 'tis tho't he designs to go on board some Vessel. Whoever takes up and secures the said Mulatto, so that his Master may have him again, shall have THREE POUNDS Reward, and reasonable Charges,
paid by    WILLIAM PATERSON, or
       Capt. ARCHIBALD GARDNER in Philadelphia.
N. B. All Masters of Vessels are forbid taking him off at their Peril.
*The Pennsylvania Journal, and Weekly Advertiser*, September 2, 1762. See *The Pennsylvania Gazette*, September 2, 1762, and *The Pennsylvania Journal, and Weekly Advertiser*, September 9, 1762.

*THREE POUNDS REWARD.*
RUN away from the Subscriber, living in Kent County on Delaware, near Dover, a Servant Man, named William Brown, about 35 Years of Age, about 5 Feet 8 Inches high, well set, wears his own brown Hair, red Face, when he talks fast is apt to stutter, and his Teeth rotten before: had on when he went away, a blue grey Cloth Coat, old Felt Hat, long Check Trowsers, and good Pumps: He went away on Saturday Night the 28th of August, in a Boat, in Company with John Delong, whose Wife was with them: Said Brown took his Wife with him, she had a young Child with her, and a small Girl about six Years old. They took two or three Guns with them, and it is supposed they will go over the Bay into the Jerseys: The said Brown was taken out of Salem Goal last Winter, by his Master. Whoever takes up and secures the aforesaid Servant, so that his Master may have him again, shall have Three Pounds Reward, and all reasonable Charges,
       paid by    JOSIAH WALLACE.

*The Pennsylvania Gazette*, September 9, 1762; September 30, 1762; *The Pennsylvania Gazette*, October 22, 1761.

September 9.
On the 28th day of August last, Run away from William Patterson, of New-Castle county, a mulatto man, named George, about 21 years of age, a lusty strong fellow: Had on when he went away, a black jacket, a pair of striped trowsers, white stockings; took also with him a brown (or) yellowish homespun jacket, made almost after the manner of a plain coat; supposed to have also with him a pair of red breeches, with other clothes in his bundle: He is also supposed to have taken with him a quantity of money among which are some £ 5 Bills. Whoever secures him so as I may have him again, shall have Five Pounds reward, and charges paid.

*The Pennsylvania Journal, and Weekly Advertiser*, September 9, 1762; September 16, 1762; September 23, 1762; September 30, 1762; October 14, 1762; October 28, 1762. See *The Pennsylvania Gazette*, September 2, 1762, and *The Pennsylvania Journal, and Weekly Advertiser*, September 2, 1762.

Philadelphia, Ninth Month, 12, 1762.
*Three Pounds Reward.*
Run away last Night from the Subscriber, living near Wilmington, New-Castle County, A native Irish Servant Lad, named Patrick Hartin, about 16 Years of age, 5 Feet high, has short red Hair, and something of a redish Complexion, freckled in the Face, and pretty much so on his Breast and Stomach, Clumsy built, and walks so; has several remarkable Scars, viz. one over his Eyebrow, one on the back Part of his Head, and a very large one on the Inside of his right Leg: Had on when he went away, An old brownish coloured Coat, with whitish coloured Sleeves, and a Patch on each Shoulder and Hip, of the Colour of the Sleeves, a yellow Jacket without Sleeves, old Felt Hat, old Tow Shirt, short Tow Trowsers, Pair of old Mockasons with Strings, a Pair of blue grey Yarn Stockings, mended at the Heels: He inclines to Gaming, and is a great Liar. Whoever takes up said Servant, and brings him to his said Master, or secures him in any Goal, so as he may have him again, shall have Thirty Shillings, if not above ten Miles from Home, and if further, the above Reward, and reasonable Charges,
paid by    JOSEPH NEWLIN.
N. B. He had the Ague and Fever when he went away.
*The Pennsylvania Gazette*, September 16, 1762.

Christiana Bridge, Sept. 8, 1762.
RUN away from the Subscriber, living at Christiana Bridge, New-Castle County, on the 2d Instant, a Servant Woman, named Margaret Bennett, a

lusty fat Woman, full-faced, long visaged, heavy-browed, remarkable for large Legs; had on when she went away, a brown Stuff Gown, a striped Linen Bed-gown, two Petticoats, the one yellow Shaloon, and the other red Cloth Serge, a Check Apron. a Pair of new Shoes, and black Yarn Stockings: She came from Ireland with Capt. Miller, in the Ship Phoenix, from Londonderry. Whoever takes up and secures the said Servant in any Goal, so that her Master may have her again, shall have Forty Shillings Reward, and reasonable Charges, paid by JOHN READ,
or ALEXANDER MONTGOMERY.
*The Pennsylvania Gazette*, September 23, 1762.

*EIGHT DOLLARS Reward.*
RUN away from the Subscriber, in New-Castle County, the 20th of August last, an Irish Servant Lad, named John M'Cullough, five Feet nine Inches high, wears his own Hair, speaks a little on the Scotch Accent, swarthy Complexion, his Clothes uncertain, as he was two Weeks with his Aunt in Philadelphia, and is said to have left her last Friday; he had the Fever and Ague, and is apt to get in Liquor, and loves Gaming. Whoever takes up said Servant, and secures him in any Goal, so that his Master may have him again, shall have the above Reward, paid by          JACOB PATTERSON, Esq;
*The Pennsylvania Gazette*, September 23, 1762; October 7, 1762. See *The Pennsylvania Journal, and Weekly Advertiser*, September 23, 1762, and *The Pennsylvania Gazette*, October 28, 1762.

September 23.
EIGHT DOLLARS Reward.
RUN-away from the Subscriber in Newcastle County, an Irish Servant Lad, named John M'Cullough, five Foot nine Inches high, wears his own Hair, speaks a little Scotchfied, swarthy Complexion, his Cloaths uncertain as he has been this two Weeks with his Aunt in Philadelphia and is said to have left her last Friday, he has the Fever and Ague, is subject to get in Liquor and gaming at Cards. Whoever takes up said Servant, or secures him in any Goal, so that his Master may have him again, shall have the above Reward
paid, by JACOB PETTERSON, Esq;
*The Pennsylvania Journal, and Weekly Advertiser*, September 23, 1762; September 30, 1762; October 21, 1762. *The Pennsylvania Gazette*, September 23, 1762, and *The Pennsylvania Gazette*, October 28, 1762.

Philadelphia, Oct. 27, 1762.
NOW In the Goal of this City, a certain John M'Cullough, who says he is a Servant to Jacob Peterson, Esq; in New-Castle County, to whom repeated

Notice has been sent of his being confined here: These are once more to desire him to come and take him out, or he will be sold in two Weeks from this Date, by      JOHN MITCHELL, Goaler.

*The Pennsylvania Gazette*, October 28, 1762. See *The Pennsylvania Gazette*, September 23, 1762, and *The Pennsylvania Journal, and Weekly Advertiser*, September 23, 1762.

October 28.

RUN-away from the subscriber, a Mulatta Boy on the 19th day of August last; named William Francisco, about seventeen years of age, well grown, about five feet six or seven inches high, round Visag'd, had on a half worn felt Hat cut about the brim, a grayish coloured home-spun Jacket, two home-spun Shirts; and a home-spun pair of Trowsers, a grey pair of Stockings, a new pair of Shoes, with a pair of square buckles in them, he cut of [sic] his hair in the Spring and left a lock behind his Head. Whosoever takes up the said Boy, and secures him in any Goal, or bring him home or so that I may have him again shall have THREE POUNDS Reward, and all reasonable Charges paid, by me Living in Little-Creek Hundred, in the County of Kent upon Delaware.       JOHN WHITE.

*The Pennsylvania Journal, and Weekly Advertiser*, October 28, 1762; November 11, 1762; December 2, 1762.

New-Castle, December 2, 1762.

NOW in the Goal of this County, A Negroe Fellow, calls himself Caesar, says he belongs to John Hall, Esq; in Cecil County, Maryland; his master is hereby desired to come, in four Weeks after this Date, pay Charges, and take him away, otherwise he will be sold for the same,
      by    ALEXANDER HARVEY, Goaler.

*The Pennsylvania Gazette*, December 23, 1762.

RUN away from William Sutton, of Newport, Christiana Hundred, in New-Castle County, an English Servant Man, named William Rowan, of a sandy Complexion, well set, about five Feet six Inches high, walks quick, loves Drink, very handy about Womens Work, such as washing Dishes, and the like; if anything disturbs him when in Liquor he will cry like a Child; pretends to be a Blacksmith, but is a bad Workman: Had on when he went away, a white Country made twilled Coat, red Everlasting jacket without Sleeves, Check Shirt, Leather Breeches with Check Trowsers over them, blackish Country made Stockings, good Shoes, with Brass Buckles, old Racoon Hat, and short sandy Hair. He was sold out of New-Castle last February for his Fees, and worked some Time till he paid Part of the Money; and afterwards work'd with Henry Colesbury, of New-Castle Hundred, to pay the

Remainder; but after staying a small Time, and getting some Shirts, Shoes and Stockings from said Colesbury, he pretended to be sick, and asked Leave to go to a Doctor to get some Medicines, but never went. Whoever brings said Servant to the Subscribers, or secures him in any Goal, so as he may be had again, shall have Forty Shillings Reward, and reasonable Charges,
        paid by    WILLIAM SUTTON, or HENRY COLESBURY.
All Masters of Vessels are forbid to carry him off.
*The Pennsylvania Gazette*, December 30, 1762.


RUN away, last October, from Archibald Getteys, at New-Castle, a Servant Man, named Nicholas Garland, by Trade a Taylor, about 24 Years of Age, and about six Feet high, of a fair Complexion, long Visage, and has some Pock-marks: Had on when he went away, a darkish Snuff-coloured Broadcloth Coat and Jacket, white Drawers, Check Jacket, light blue Stockings, and a lightish coloured Wig. It is thought he has stole his Indentures. Whoever takes up and secures said Servant, so as his Master may have again, shall have Three Pounds Reward, and reasonable Charges, paid by SAMUEL GETTEYS, living at Marsh-Creek,
        in Cumberland Township, York County.
*The Pennsylvania Gazette*, December 30, 1762.

## *1763*

RUN away from the Subscriber, of Mill Creek Hundred, New-Castle County, an Apprentice Boy, named Samuel Magee, aged about 13 Years; but it is supposed he will alter his Name: Had on when he went away, a light coloured Jacket, old Breeches, old Shoes and Stockings, and an old Hat. He is of a sandy Complexion, much given to lying, and has worked at the Shoemaker's Trade some Time. Any Person taking up the said Apprentice, and bringing him to me, or securing him in any Goal in this Province, shall have Twenty Shillings Reward, and all reasonable Charges from
        ABRAHAM YARNALL.
*The Pennsylvania Gazette*, January 6, 1763; January 13, 1763.


FIVE POUNDS REWARD.
RUN away from New-Castle, a Servant man, named John Adair, about five Feet ten Inches high, born in Ireland, and came over with Capt. Osborn this last Fall: Had on when he went away, a grey Frize Surtoot Coat, with a long Tail, yellow carved Buttons, and double frogged Button Holes, blue Jacket, old Leather Breeches, white Thread Stockings, and old Shoes, with black rusty Steel Buckles; and took with him three Shirts, two were white, the other

brown, and a Pair of Breeches made Trowsers. He is likely, of a fresh colour, fair faced, and fair long Hair, tied behind, and is very remarkable for a great Deal of short curled Hair under the other. Whoever takes up said Servant, and secures him in any Goal, so as his Master may have him again, shall the above Reward, paid by me     JAMES M'CONNELL.
N. B. All Masters of Vessels are forbid to carry him off at their Peril.
*The Pennsylvania Gazette*, January 13, 1763; January 20, 1763.

Christiana Hundred, New Castle County, Feb. 1, 1763.<br>
FIVE POUNDS REWARD.

MADE his Escape from John Garretson, on the 27th of last Month, a certain JOSEPH WOODS, about Twenty two Years of Age, about five Feet seven Inches high, Pockmarked about his Nose, a slender Man, thin Visage, grey Eyes, and brown Hair: Had on, when he went off, a brownish Thickset Coat and Vest, Leather Breeches, Yarn Stockings, thick heavy Shoes, is a great Talker, has been in the Country from Ireland a Year the last Fall, and worked with the said John Garretson the last Winter, and the last Summer followed Ditching between Philadelphia and Schuylkill, and is supposed to be gone that Way again. Any Person or Persons apprehending the said Joseph Woods, and bringing him to the Subscribers, in Christiana Hundred, New Castle County, or to the County Goal, so that he may be brought to Justice, shall have the above Reward, and reasonable Charges,
paid by JOHN GARRETSON, or ZACHARIAH DERECKSON.
*The Pennsylvania Gazette*, February 10, 1763.

FIVE POUNDS Reward.

STOLEN from Jacob Rothwell, of New-Castle County, in the Night of the First Instant, a brown Horse, with an old Leather Saddle, and snaffle Bridle; the Horse about 14 Hands high, with a Star and Blaze in his Forehead, both his hind Feet and one fore Foot white, shod before, branded O on the near Shoulder and Buttock. The said Horse was stolen by a Person who called himself John Williams, of middle Age, well-set, by Trade a Taylor, about five Feet four Inches high, his Right Leg has been broke a little above the Ancle, which is not yet well, loves Drink, born in New England, wears a Silk Cap: Had on, when he went away, a light coloured Broadcloth Coat, Claret-coloured Broadcloth Jacket, Buckskin breeches, with covered Buttons, black Stockings, half-worn Shoes, with large carved Metal Buckles, and a blue great Coat. Whoever secures said Williams in any of his Majesty's Goals, shall have the above Reward, or Three Pounds for the Horse only, and reasonable Charges, paid by
March 7, 1763.     JACOB ROTHWELL.

*The Pennsylvania Gazette*, March 17, 1763. See *The Pennsylvania Journal, and Weekly Advertiser*, March 17, 1763.

March 17.
FIVE POUNDS Reward.
WAS stolen from Jacob Rothwell, of the County of Newcastle, the first of this Inst. at night, a brown Horse, an old leather Saddle, and snapple Bridle; the Horse is about fourteen Hands high, has a Star and Blaze in his Forehead, branded with the Letter O on his near Shoulder and another on the near Buttock, both hind Feet and one fore Foot is white, shod before. The Person who stole the said Horse, says his Name is John Williams, born in New-England, he is middle aged, about five Foot four Inches high, a well set Fellow, has had his right Leg broke a little above the Ancle, and is not yet well, and apt to get it Drink, he is a Taylor by Trade; wore when he went away, a Silk Cap, cock'd Hat, a light coloured broad cloth Coat, a clarret coloured broad cloth Jacket, buckskin Breeches, with covered Buttons, black Stockings, half worn Shoes, large carved mettal Shoe Buckles, and a blue great Coat. Any Person who secures the said Williams in any of his Majesty's Goals, so that he may be brought to Justice, shall have the above Reward; for the Horse only THREE POUNDS, and reasonable Charges,
    paid by    JACOB ROTHWELL.
*The Pennsylvania Journal, and Weekly Advertiser*, March 17, 1763; March 24, 1763; April 14, 1763; April 28, 1763. See *The Pennsylvania Gazette*, March 17, 1763.

New-Castle County, February 10.
SIX POUNDS Reward.
WAS broke open, the House of the Subscriber, on the great Road, between Christiana Ferry and New Castle; on Saturday night last, and stolen from thence the following articles, viz. one broad cloth Coat, light coloured, with mohair buttons, lined with white Shalloon, and a small Collar, claret coloured, one manchester velvet Jacket without sleeves lined with the same as the Coat, one pair of black stocking Breeches lined with Home spun linnen, and sett buttons, one new pair of Shoes, one new pair of blue Stockings, one Half worn beaver Hat, one fine Shirt, one home spun Ditto. Also one new blue home spun Coat lined with blue worsted, metal buttons. Also nine yards of Blanketing dressed at the Mill, the old half fill'd with black. Whoever apprehends the Thief with the Goods, and secures him in any of his Majesty's Goals, shall have the above Reward, if the Thief only, FOUR POUNDS paid by    CORNELIUS HAINS.
    N. B. The Person suspected to commit the above Robbery is west of England born, and speaks much on the west Country tongue, he says his name is John Downon, but may change his name, he has on a white long strait

Bodied cloth Coat, blue Jacket, Buckskin Breeches, wears a brown cut Wig, smooth faced, his teeth bears out before; he is about five feet Eight Inches high.
*The Pennsylvania Journal, and Weekly Advertiser*, March 24, 1763.

STOLEN from the Subscribers, living near Blackbird Bridge, in New-Castle County, sundry Men and Womens Wearing Apparel, viz. a Snuff coloured Coat and Waistcoat, light coloured Suit of Broadcloth, a new Snuff coloured Thickset Coat, and a light coloured Waistcoat, Mens Shoes, and seven Pair of Stockings, two Chints Gowns, a Lincey Woolsey Ditto, a new Pair of Stays, five Mens Shirts, two Shists, four Aprons, several Womens Caps, Neckcloths, two Sheets, four Yards of new brown Linen, and sundry other Things, too tedious to mention. They are supposed to be taken away by a middle sized Man, of a thin Visage, with black Hair, and blue Eyes; he was seen riding a white Horse, with a Woman not known, and tis thought they have more Confederates. Whoever takes up and secures the Thieves, with the said Goods, in any Goal, so as they may be brought to Justice, and the Goods restored, shall have Five Pounds Reward, paid by THOMAS MURPHY,
THOMAS BARTLEY, and WILLIAM WELDON.
*The Pennsylvania Gazette*, April 14, 1763.

WHEREAS one Robert White, a Taylor, eloped from Mill Creek Hundred, in the County of New-Castle, on or about the 15th of March last and, to defraud his Creditors of their just Debts, carried off with him an Apprentice Lad, bound to him for seven Years, the Indenture bearing Date the 13th of August, 1760, named Samuel Woods, about 16 Years of Age, of a tall slender Growth, has pretty long fair Hair, and long Visage. Whoever secures said Robert White in any Goal, so as he may be brought to Justice, shall have Forty Shillings Reward, and reasonable Charges, paid by the Subscriber, living in New London Township, Chester County.
GEORGE CURREY.
N. B. All Persons are hereby forewarned not to purchase the remaining Time of said Samuel Woods's Apprenticeship from said Robert White, as he is bound only to said White, and not to his Assigns.
*The Pennsylvania Gazette*, April 21, 1763.

RUN away from the Subscriber, in the Town of St. George, New-Castle County, on Delaware, a Servant Man, named William Evans, by Trade a Taylor, born in Dublin, of middle Size, strong, and well set, has black Hair, well shaped Legs, and is a spry Fellow; has been in the Northern Expedition, and since worked at his Trade in Philadelphia, where he shipped himself aboard a Privateer, but was put in Goal at New-Castle, and sold to James Armstrong Taylor, of the Town and County aforesaid. Had on a Claret or Copper coloured Coat, his other Clothes not well known; he writes a very good Hand, is given to Drink, and Company keeping. Whoever secures the said Servant in any Goal in any Part of His Majesty's Dominions, so that he may be had again, or in his Stead the Sum of FIFTEEN POUNDS, Pennsylvania Currency, shall have THREE POUNDS Reward, and reasonable Charges, paid by     ISAAC DUSHANE.

*The Pennsylvania Gazette*, May 19, 1763; June 2, 1763; June 23, 1763. See *The Pennsylvania Journal, and Weekly Advertiser*, May 19, 1763.

May 19.
### THREE POUNDS REWARD.
RUN-away from the Subscriber in the Town of St. Georges and County of Newcastle on Delaware, a Servant Man named William Evans, by Trade a Taylor, born in Dublin, middle Size, strong, well set, black Hair, handsom leg'd sprie Fellow; has been in the Northern Expedition and since work'd at his Trade in Philadelphia, from thence ship'd himself for Privateering, but was put in Goal at Newcastle and sold to James Armstrong, Taylor of the Town and County aforesaid; had on a claret or copper coloured Coat, his other Cloaths not well known, he writes a very good Hand, is given to Drink, and Company keeping. Whoever secures the said Servant in any Goal, in any part of his Majesty's Dominions so that he may be had again, or in his stead the Sum of FIFTEEN POUNDS, Pennsylvania Currency, shall have the above Reward and reasonable Charges
             paid by     ISAAC DUSHANE.

*The Pennsylvania Journal, and Weekly Advertiser*, May 19, 1763; May 26, 1763; June 2, 1763; June 9, 1763; June 16, 1763; June 23, 1763. See *The Pennsylvania Gazette*, May 19, 1763.

RUN away from the Subscriber, a Servant Man named Joseph Townsend, a Brick Maker and Layer by Trade, about 5 Feet 10 Inches high, between 23 and 24 Years of Age: Had on, when he went away, a blue Broadcloth Coat, with an old white Great Coat over it, a Pair of Leather Breeches, Half worn, with grey Yarn Stockings, old Shoes, drawls when he speaks, and has Moles in his Face, and his Hair cut off. It is supposed he made towards Baltimore County. Whoever secures him in any Goal, and sends me word, or brings him to me, shall have Forty Shillings Reward, and reasonable Charges, paid by me     JOSEPH TAYLOR, living near Dover, in Kent County.

*The Pennsylvania Gazette*, June 9, 1763.

New-Castle, May 26, 1763.
NOW in the Goal of this County, A certain Mary Downs, says that she is a Servant to Mr. Carson, Merchant, in Philadelphia, and that she was sent from thence, in a Shallop, to be sold in Maryland, and being unwilling, made her escape at Christine. Her Master is hereby desired to come, pay Charges, and take her away, otherwise she will be sold for the same, by
ALEXANDER HARVEY, Goaler.
*The Pennsylvania Gazette*, June 9, 1763.


THREE POUNDS Reward.
RUN away from his Bail (John O'Donnelly, living at Samuel McClintoc's, in Brandywine Hundred, New-Castle County) on the third Day of February last, a certain Owen Ogorman, an Irishman, about 26 Years of Age, about five Feet five Inches high, wore long black Hair, has a down Look, and smoaks Tobacco: Had on, when he went away, a brown Coat and Breeches, a Claret Coloured Jacket, blue Stockings, new Shoes, and an old Furr Hat. Whoever takes up said Runaway, and secures him, so as his Bail may have him again, shall have the above Reward, and all reasonable Charges,
paid by me    JOHN O'DONNELLY.
*The Pennsylvania Gazette*, June 23, 1763.


THREE POUNDS Reward.
RUN away, on the Ninth of this instant July, from Christine Bridge, an Irish *Servant* Man, named Robert M'Culey; he came in from Dublin last May, in the Brig Sally, Captain Dougherty, is near 6 Feet high, well made, round shouldered, his Hair tied behind, pretends to be a Sailor and Soldier; he had on a Frize Jacket, white Drawers and Stockings, and had a Bundle of other Clothes with him; has been under the Doctor's Hands, and is not well. He stole, and took with him, a Silver Watch, with a Steel and Silver Chain. Whoever secures him in any Goal, so that the Subscriber may have him again, shall have the above Reward, paid by us,
JOHN SINGLETON, and ALLAN GILLESPIE.
N. B. If any Gentlemen enlists him, and would direct a Line to us where he is, he may have him to serve the Time he inlists for.
*The Pennsylvania Gazette*, July 14, 1763.


New-Castle, July 13, 1763.
NOW in the Goal of this County, a certain Francis Richard, aged about 45 Years, about six feet high, says he is a Blacksmith by Trade, and that he was a servant to Mrs. Mary M'Cay, in Georgetown, but got his Freedom. His

Master or Mistress (if he has any) is hereby desired to come pay Charges, and take him away, otherwise he will be sold out for the same, by
ALEXANDER HARVEY, Goaler.
*The Pennsylvania Gazette*, July 21, 1763.


RUN-away on the 27th of the 7th Month, 1763, from the Service of the Subscriber, living near Wilmington, New-Castle County, A certain John Gausling, who embezzled Goods out of his Master's House and Mill, and hath likewise taken up Money where it was owing, without Orders: Had on, and took with him, An old Castor Hat, green Jacket, a light coloured Fustian ditto, new Check Shirts and Trowsers, and turn'd Pumps. He is about 23 Years of Age, 5 Feet 9 Inches high, and of a dark Complection; used to drive a Team, and subject to drinking, swearing, and boasting of his Wrestling and Jumping. Any Person securing the said Gausling in any of the Goals of New-Castle, or Kent on Delaware, or Philadelphia, Chester, Lancaster, or Buck Counties, in Pennsylvania, so that he my be brought to Justice shall have Thirty Shillings Reward, paid by     VINCENT GILPIN.
*The Pennsylvania Gazette*, August 11, 1763.


THREE POUNDS Reward.
RUN away from his Bail, in Kent County, on Delaware, on the 19th Day of July last, a certain William M'Bride, a Weaver by Trade about 5 Feet 7 Inches high, pretty well set, full faced, has black straight Hair, walks close with his Knees, very apt to get drunk, and then very quarrelsome: Had on, when he went away, a Claret coloured Broadcloth Coat and Breeches, a Jacket much of the Colour of his Coat, and took with him two Pair of Trowsers, one Pair coarse, and the other Pair striped; had one Silver and one Copper Buckle in his Shoes, both small; he was out privateering last Summer, in the Brig Grace, Capt. Taylor, from Philadelphia. Whoever takes up and secures said William M'Bride, so that the Subscriber may get him again, shall have the above Reward, and reasonable Charges, paid by   WILLIAM CARTER .
*The Pennsylvania Gazette*, August 18, 1763.


RUN away, on the First of August, from the Subscriber, living in Christeen Hundred, New-Castle County, an Irish Servant Man, named Andrew Brann, about 20 Years of Age, five Feet eight Inches high, has fair Hair, much pitted with the Small Pox, walks strait kneed, can discourse properly, is a Weaver by Trade: Had on when he went away, a brown Coat, Silk Jacket, striped yellow and red, brown Breeches, grey Yarn Stockings, and strong coarse Shoes, with Brass Buckles, also a Wool Hat, with Silk Loops. Whoever takes

up and secures said Servant, so as his Master may have him again, shall have Three Pounds Reward, paid by Alexander Johnson, Esq; or Alexander Moore, or by Jacobus Hines, in Wilmington.
*The Pennsylvania Gazette*, September 1, 1763.

New-Castle, August 23, 1763.
NOW in the County Goal, a certain James M'Knight, who is advertised in the Pennsylvania Gazette by John Crosby, living in Ridley Township, Chester County, as a Runaway; his Master is hereby desired to come and pay Charges, and take him away, otherwise he will be sold for the same in six Weeks after the Date hereof, by
ALEXANDER HARVEY, Goaler.
*The Pennsylvania Gazette*, September 1, 1763.
Another ad by John Crosby in *The Pennsylvania Gazette*, September 8, 1763, stated that the above fellow was not his man.

New London, in Chester County, August 30, 1763.
THREE POUNDS REWARD.
RUN away, about two Weeks ago, an ill-natured, scolding, cursing, swearing, thieving servant Woman (who has been with 5 or 6 Masters, and in several Prisons and Workhouses within two Years, in Bucks County, New-Castle, and this County) named Eleanor Ferrel, about 35 Years of Age, low of Stature, black haired, thin Visage, and talks with the Brogue: had on and took with her, a coarse Calicoe Gown, with dark coloured Cuffs, a spotted Calicoe Bed gown, a white Petticoat, with a Calicoe border, a striped Linsey ditto, a Pair of white Ticken Shoes, green Worsted Stockings, a black Silk Bonnet, with Gimp round the Edge; she is supposed to be gone to Philadelphia, or Bucks County, near Bristol. Whoever imprisons, or send her Home, the Favour will be gratefully acknowledged, beside the above Reward paid by    ABRAHAM EMMIT.
N. B. She is a great Snuffer.
*The Pennsylvania Gazette*, September 8, 1763.

New Castle, September 5, 1763.
Committed to the Goal of this County, as a Runaway, a certain Terence Carabery; his Master, if he has any, is desired to come in six Weeks after the Date hereof, pay Charges, and take him away, otherwise he will be discharged, paying his Fees, by
ALEXANDER HARVEY, Goaler.
*The Pennsylvania Gazette*, September 15, 1763.

New Castle, September 20, 1763.
Committed to the Goal of this County, on Suspicion of being Runaway Servants, George Chubb, and William Chubb, both Englishmen, wear brown Coats, blue Jackets, white Shirts, Leather Breeches, Worsted Stockings, good Shoes, and White-metal Buckles; they are about 5 Feet 10 Inches high, and say they are Brothers.

Also a Negroe Lad, who says he belongs to John Shaw, in George Town, wears a light coloured Jean Coat, Broad Cloth Jacket, Check Shirt, Broad Cloth Breeches, coarse white Yarn Stockings, half worn Shoes, and Brass Buckles. Their Masters are hereby desired to take them away in six Weeks after the Date hereof, otherwise they will be sold for their Fees, by
    ALEXANDER HARVEY, Goaler.
*The Pennsylvania Gazette,* September 29, 1763.

September 7, 1763.
RUN away Last Night, from Deep-Creek Furnace, near the Head of Nanticoke River, Four Native Irish Men, viz. John Kittle, Martin Kelly, Patrick M'Nealy, and Thomas Clinton; they are all of middle Stature, of fair Complexion, and each of them more or less pitted with the Small-pox; they wore striped Linsey Caps or short Hair; Felt Hats, almost new; check or Ozenbrigs Shirts, and Ozenbrigs Trowsers; about half-worn Shoes: One of them had a Scar above his Eye-brow on his Forehead: Another has a Scar or Blister near his Ear; the same is broke out with several Sores on his Legs, Arms, and some Parts of his Body: One of them had a light-coloured Cloth Jacket, the others striped Lincey Ones. It is thought they will endeavour to pass for Sailors. Whoever takes up and secures the said Servants in any Goal, or brings them to the said Furnace, shall have Thirty Shillings Reward for each, paid by    JONATHAN VAUGHAN.

N. B. These Fellows are expected to make to Philadelphia, or New York, or up that Way.—All Masters of Vessels, and others, are forbid to harbour, or carry them off, at their Peril.
*The Pennsylvania Gazette,* September 29, 1763.

New-Castle, October 7, 1763.
RUN away from the Subscriber, the Second instant, a Negroe man, named Sharper; he is a well made Fellow, about 5 Feet 8 Inches high, pitted with the Small-Pox: Had on, when he went off, a blue Cloth Jacket without Sleeves, fine white Shirt, Snuff coloured Cloth Breeches, and Trowsers over them, old Shoes and Stockings; he may be distinguished by a Lump he has on the big Toe of the Right Foot. Whoever takes up said Negroe Man, and secures him, so that his Master may have him again, shall have Twenty Shillings Reward,
    paid by    ROBERT M'LONEN.
*The Pennsylvania Gazette,* October 20, 1763.

RUN-AWAY from the Subscriber, living in Christine Hundred, New-Castle County, on Monday Morning, the 22d ult. A Servant Man, a Blacksmith by Trade, can read and write, is a cunning Fellow, and I bought him by the Name of Daniel Dorthety, but has since changed his Name to William Armstrong, and it is likely he may change it again; he was born in the County of Donegall, near Belemefye, in Sonarlin, and brought into this Country from Ireland by Thomas Maglaery, Master of the Ship King of Prussia, from Dublin, but may change both the Name of Captain and Ship. The said Daniel Dorthety is a grim looking Fellow, has short black hair, which turns into his Neck straight limbed, about 5 feet 5 Inches high, and has thick Lips: had on, and took with him, A white Shirt, and a Check Ditto, Cloth Breeches, with Horn Buttons, a striped Vest, with the Stripes across, and blue Buttons, of divers Sizes, new Shoes, with gilt Buckles, a Pair of Stockings, near a Squirrel Colour, and a Silk Handkerchief. He broke open a Lock, and took out of a Chest the following Things, viz. One new brown Coat, with a falling Cape, a new Fur Hat, white Shirt, and a Pair of long white Trowsers. Whoever takes up and secures said Servant, so as his Master may have him again, shall have Three Pounds Reward, and reasonable Charges,
           paid by    THOMAS OGLE, jun.
N. B. He was seen near Lancaster, and is supposed to be gone back.
*The Pennsylvania Gazette*, November 10, 1763.


           TWENTY SHILLINGS Reward.
RUn away on the 22d of October, from the Subscriber, living in New Castle County and Hundred, A Negroe Man, named Ben, about 30 Years of Age, this Country born, talks good English, of a middle Stature, has an agreeable Countenance as most of his Colour, with a small Dimple on his Chin, is a smart, active, brisk Fellow: Had on when he went away, A light coloured Cloth Coat and Waistcoat, Tow Trousers and Shirt, old Shoes and Stockings, an old Hat, cut in Form of a hunting Cap, &c. Whoever apprehends said Slave, and secures him, so that his Master may have him again, shall have the above Reward, with reasonable Charges, if taken on the Continent, if off it Five Pounds, paid by    ALEXANDER EAKIN.
N. B. He has been used to Shalloping, and it is supposed he will endeavour to get out to Sea; all Masters of Vessels are forbid to carry him off at their Peril.
    *The Pennsylvania Gazette*, November 10, 1763. See *The Pennsylvania Journal, and Weekly Advertiser*, November 10, 1763.

           TWENTY SHILLINGS Reward.
RUN-away on the 22d of October, from the subscriber living in New-Castle county and hundred, a negro man named BEN, about thirty years of age, this

country born, talks good English, of a middle stature, has an agreeable countenance as most of his colour, with a small dimple on his chin, he is a smart, active fellow. Had on when he went away, a light coloured cloath coat and waistcoat, tow trowsers, old shoes and stockings, tow shirt, an old hat cut in form of a hunting cap. Whoever apprehends said slave, and secures him so that his master may have him again, shall have the above reward with reasonable charges, if taken on the continent, if off it, FIVE POUNDS
paid by    ALEXANDER EAKIN.
N. B. He has been used to Shalloping, and 'tis supposed he will endeavour to get out to Sea.
All Masters of Vessels are forbid to carry him off at their Peril.
*The Pennsylvania Journal, and Weekly Advertiser*, November 10, 1763; November 17, 1763; November 24, 1763. See *The Pennsylvania Gazette*, November 10, 1763.


RUN away from the Subscriber, living in Mill-creek Hundred, New-Castle County, an Irish Servant Man, named William Graham, about 30 Years of Age, middle Stature, red haired, tender eyed, one of which he is blind of; is an ill-looking Fellow, extremely given to Lying, and has been in the Provincial Service: Had on, when he went away, an old Felt Hat, old dark coloured Bearskin Coat, Snuff coloured Thickset Jacket, Buckskin Breeches, &c. All Masters of Vessels are forbid to carry him off. Whoever takes up and secures said Servant , so as his Master may have him again, shall have Twenty Shillings Reward, and reasonable Charges,
November 8, 1763.        paid by JOHN MONTGOMERY.
*The Pennsylvania Gazette*, November 24, 1763; December 29, 1763.


New-Castle, Nov. 21, 1763.
NOW in the Goal of this County, a certain Bryan Doran, taken up as a Runaway Servant; says he came into the Country this Fall, with Capt. Fussell, from Newry; wears a blue Sea Jacket, blue Breeches, and good Shoes.
Also a Negroe Man, calls himself Jack, says he ran from William Corsa, of Queen Anne's County, Wye River, near Queen's Town, wears a white Cotton Jacket and Breeches, Ozenbrigs Shirt, and old Felt Hat. Their Masters are hereby desired to pay Fees, and take them away, otherwise they will be sold for the same, by    ALEXANDER HARVEY, Goaler.
*The Pennsylvania Gazette*, December 1, 1763.


FIVE POUNDS Reward.
RUN away from the Subscriber, living in St. George's Hundred, New-Castle County, on Delaware, a Negroe Man, called Tom, six Feet high, well

proportioned, a very likely sensible Fellow, this Country born, walks remarkable lofty, and appears hollow backed when walking, used to comb up the Hair or Wool on his Forehead in a fashionable Manner. Took with him two coarse and two fine Shirts, two Pair of Trowsers, a Pair of new Buckskin Breeches, an old Pair of Plush Ditto, old Beaver Hat, and old Boots, but 'tis thought he will buy Shoes, as he took Money with him; he also took a light coloured Saggathy Coat, and sundry other Clothes, not remembered; it is imagined he will endeavour to pass for a free Negroe, and probably will try to ship himself as a Piece of a Sailor in some Vessel. Whoever takes up said Negroe, and brings him home, or secures him in any Goal, shall have Three Pounds Reward, if taken in the County, or Five Pounds if out of it,
    paid by  JAMES SHAW.
N. B. All Masters of Vessels are forbid, at their Peril, to employ or carry off said Negroe.
*The Pennsylvania Gazette*, December 1, 1763.


               New-Castle, Nov. 30, 1763.
       FIVE POUNDS Reward.
MADE his Escape from the Goal of this County, on Tuesday, the 29th Inst, a certain Henry Cast, born of Dutch Parents, served his Time to the House Joyner Trade with Mr. John Gooding, near the New Quaker Meeting, on Society-Hill, in Philadelphia: Had on when he went off, a blue Coat, black Velvet Jacket, Beaver Hat, &c. he may change his Cloathing when he gets to Philadelphia, if he went there. Whoever apprehends said Cast, and secures him in any Goal, so that the subscriber may have him again, shall have the above Reward, and if brought to New-Castle Goal, reasonable Charges with the Reward, paid by  ALEXANDER HARVEY, Goaler.
N. B. Said Cast has a Brother in some of the West India Islands, and may endeavour to get to him, all Masters of Vessels are requested not to carry him off.
*The Pennsylvania Gazette*, December 15, 1763; January 5, 1764.

## 1764

RUN away, on the 21st of December, from the Subscriber, living in New-Castle, a French Servant Man, named Joseph Duffore: Had on when he went away, an old brown Broadcloth Coat and Jacket, old Leather Breeches, grey Yarn Stockings, old Shoes, Ozenbrigs Shirt, old Hat, and his Hair tied behind, the middle Finger, and the one next the little one, on both Hands, grow together. Whoever secures said Servant; so that his Master may have him again, shall have Thirty Shillings Reward, or if brought to New-Castle Forty Shillings, and reasonable Charges,

paid by   THOMAS LENNON.
*The Pennsylvania Gazette*, January 12, 1764.


ABSENTED from the Subscriber, living near Newport, New Castle County, a likely Negroe Man, about 23 Years of Age, about 6 Feet high: Had on, when he went away, a blue Coat, and a new red Jacket, old Leather Breeches, old Shoes and Stockings, with a Felt Hat; his name is Sam, well known in Philadelphia, formerly belonging to Rudeman Robinson. Whoever secures said Negroe, so that his Master may have him again, shall have Twenty Shillings Reward, if taken in, or near Philadelphia, but if 40 Miles Distance, Forty Shillings Reward, and reasonable Charges,
paid by   DAVID REYNOLDS.
N.B. He has Liberty of his Master to go and see his Friends at Philadelphia, to return in two or three Days, but has now been about 16 Days.
*The Pennsylvania Gazette*, January 26, 1764.


York Goal, March 6, 1764.
WAS committed to the Goal of this County, three young Men, on suspicion of being Runaways, viz. Elijah Davis, born in West Jersey, and brought up in Cumberland County, a Shoemaker by trade, about 26 Years old, of a ruddy Complexion, about 5 Feet 11 Inches high, wears a light coloured lappeled Jacket, with Whitemetal Buttons, as under half worn red Flannel Ditto, Buckskin Breeches, blue Stockings, new Shoes, and Pewter Buckles. John M'Peters, born in Kent County, on Delaware, a Cooper by Trade, aged 23 Years, of a swarthy Complexion, about 5 Feet 6 Inches high, wears a dark Bearskin Great Coat, red Flannel Jacket, old Buckskin Breeches, old blue Stockings and Shoes; they both say they are free. Joseph Thomas, born in Philadelphia, a Hatter by Trade, and served his Time to George Owen, of said Place, about 5 Feet 7 Inches high, aged about 30 Years, wears a dark Coat, blue knit Breeches, brown Stockings, and halfworn Shoes. Their Master or Masters, if any such there be, are desired to come and take them away, paying Charges, otherwise they will be sold in 30 Days from the Date hereof for the same, by   JACOB GRAYBILL, Goaler.
*The Pennsylvania Gazette*, March 29, 1764; April 12, 1764; April 19, 1764.


RUN away from the Subscriber, living in Christine Hundred, New-Castle County, an Irish Servant Man, named James M'Gradie, about 20 Years of Age, something pitted with the Small-pox, about 5 Feet 4 or 5 Inches high; much given to Drink, and very talkative: Had on, when he went away, an old

Wool Hat, pretty much worn, which he keeps generally cocked, black curled Hair, and two old Jackets, one coarse Cloth, of a brownish Colour, the under one Worsted, very ragged, of a redish Cinnamon Colour, two good Tow Shirts, two Pair of Breeches, very much worn, one Pair Leather, the other Cloth, and it is probable he will wear the Leather Ones, as they are the best; he has also two Pairs Yarn Stockings, one grey, the other blue, and coarse Shoes, tied with Strings. It is thought he will go towards Carlisle or Philadelphia. Whoever takes up and secures the said Servant, so as his Master may have him again, shall have Four Dollars Reward, and reasonable Charges, paid by me    SAMUEL CLENEAY.

N. B. All Masters of Vessels are forbid to carry him off at their Peril.

*The Pennsylvania Gazette*, April 5, 1764; April 19, 1764.


RAN-AWAY last night from Ralph Walker, living at Wilmington in New-Castle county: A negro man named Ned Lamy, aged about twenty-six years, about 5 feet 6 inches high, is a very black well set fellow, has lost several of his fore teeth, has a lump near as big as a marble on his forehead. Had on an old brown coat, an old brown jacket, long red trowsers, blue and white worsted cap, shoes and stockings, and has been used to flatting in the river. Whoever takes up and secures said negro, so that his master may have him again, shall receive FORTY SHILLINGS reward, and all reasonable charges March 30.    paid by me    RALPH WALKER.

*The Pennsylvania Journal, and Weekly Advertiser*, April 5, 1764; April 12, 1764; April 19, 1764; April 26, 1764.


RUN away on the 18th of March, from the Subscriber, living in Little-Creek Neck, Kent County, a Servant Man, named John Moor, a West Countryman, about five Feet eight Inches high, 45 Years of Age, a thick well set man, the Bridge of his Nose has been broke, of a pale Complexion, and brown Hair, mixwith grey: Had on when he went away, a Felt Hat, coarse brownish grey Country made Cloth Coat, without Lining, a light coloured Kersey Jacket not lined, and Breeches of the same; he took a short thick Woman with him (whom he calls Wife) she has a sharp thin Visage, and is very apt to get disguised with Liquor. Whoever takes up and secures said Servant Man, so that his Master may have him again, shall have Forty Shillings Reward,
    paid by    CLAYTON LEVICK.

*The Pennsylvania Gazette*, April 12, 1764; April 19, 1764.


RUN away, on the 30th of March, from the Subscriber, in Mill-Creek Hundred, New Castle County, an Irish Servant Man, named John Morrow,

about 21 Years of Age, about five Feet nine or ten Inches high: Had on when he went away, an old Wool Hat, blue Coat and Jacket, white Shirt, two Pair of Trowsers, one of Tow, made Petticoat Fashion, the other narrow Stripe, long Fashion, three Pair of black Stockings, one Pair ribb'd, new Shoes, with carved white Metal Buckles; he is a down looking Fellow, with black Hair, smooth Face, has a Mark on one of his Cheeks something like a Half moon. Whoever takes up and secures said servant, in any of His Majesty's Goals, so that his Master may have him again, shall have Forty Shillings Reward, and reasonable Charges, paid by   WILLIAM KELLEY.
N. B. All Masters of Vessels are forbid to carry him off.
  *The Pennsylvania Gazette*, April 12, 1764; April 19, 1764.


RUN away from his Bail the 28th Day of March last, one Andrew Parks, about 5 Feet 10 Inches high, of a brown Complexion: Had on when he went away, a lead coloured homespun Coat, blue Jacket, and old Buckskin Breeches. It is likely he is gone to Philadelphia. Whoever takes up and secures the said Andrew Parks, so that he may be brought to Justice, shall receive 12 Dollars Reward, and all reasonable Charges,
     paid by George Clark, of Dragon Neck, New-Castle County.
  *The Pennsylvania Gazette*, April 12, 1764.


RUN away on the 17th of March, from the Subscriber, living in Dover Hundred, Kent County, on Delaware, a Servant Man, named James Kinley, about 26 Years of Age, of a middle Stature, with a Scar on one of his Cheeks: Had on when he went away, a white Fustian Coat, old light coloured Broadcloth Jacket, red and white striped Lincey Do. old black Everlasting Breeches, old dark Wig, new fine Hat, new Shoes, and blue Stockings. Went away with one James Swetman, a well set Fellow, about 22 Years old. Whoever takes up and secures said Servant, so that his master may have him again, shall have Forty Shillings Reward, and reasonable Charges,
     paid by   JOHN MEQUE.
N. B. He was formerly a Servant to Matthew Manlove, and has that Indenture with him, from which likely he will endeavour to pass for a free Man.
  *The Pennsylvania Gazette*, April 12, 1764; April 19, 1764.


                            Philadelphia, May 16, 1764.
SINCE the 19th of January last has been committed to the public Goal of this City, the following Persons, who have confessed themselves Runaway Servants, viz. James Hamilton, the Property of William Boon, of Berks County—John Morrow, the Property of William Kelley, of New Castle—

And Benjamin Newport, the Property of John M'Duff, of Caecil County, Maryland. The Masters of the above Servants are desired to take them away within then Days from the Date hereof, otherwise they will be sold to pay Charges, by    JOHN MITCHELL, Goaler.
*The Pennsylvania Gazette*, May 17, 1764; May 24, 1764.

New-Castle, May 25, 1764.
NOW in the Goal of this County, a certain George Rankin, committed there as a Runaway Servant; his Master (if he has any) is desired to come in 6 Weeks after this Date, pay Charges, and take him away, otherwise he will be discharged, paying his Fees, by ALEXANDER HARVEY, Goaler.
*The Pennsylvania Gazette*, May 31, 1764.

May 31.
MADE his escape from the subscriber, high sheriff of Kent county on Delaware, the 24th of April last, a certain Benjamin Arrowsmith, taken by a Cassa, he is about five feet ten inches high, slender withal: Had on when he made his escape, a suit of green cloth: His usual place of abode is supposed to be in the Jersies. Whoever takes up the said Benjamin Arrowsmith, and delivers him to the subscriber, shall have the Reward of THIRTEEN POUNDS, TEN SHILLINGS current lawful money of this government,
       paid by    THOMAS COLLINS, Sheriff.
*The Pennsylvania Journal, and Weekly Advertiser*, May 31, 1764; June 21, 1764; July 5, 1764.

June 7.
RUN away last Sunday Night from Mr. Hunter's boat about 10 Miles above New-Castle, a Negro man named Bazil, about 5 feet 9 or 10 Inches high, speaks bad English, has been at sea, and is a tolerable cook; he was a French Negro, and pretends to be free. Whoever takes up and secures said Negro so that I may have him again, shall have FIVE POUNDS Reward by applying to me at Philadelphia.    DAVID HAY.
All Masters of Vessels are forbid to carry him off.
*The Pennsylvania Journal, and Weekly Advertiser*, June 7, 1764; June 21, 1764; June 28, 1764; July 5, 1764; July 12, 1764; July 19, 1764; July 26, 1764; August 2, 1764. See *The Pennsylvania Gazette*, June 14, 1764.

FIFTY SHILLINGS, Reward.
RUN away, on the 4th inst. June, from the Subscriber, living in Brandywine Hundred, near the Upper End of New-Castle County, an Irish Servant Man, named James Cotter, about 20 years of Age: Had on, when he went away, an

old brown homespun Coat, with broad hard Metal Buttons, and slash Sleeves, an under Jacket of white Flannel, long coarse Tow Trowsers, bare footed, and bare legged; he is about 5 Feet 10 Inches high, of a swarthy Complexion, and pretty much Pock-marked, something stoop shouldered, and a down sour-like Look, with dark brown Hair, and scalped on the Crown, but likely he will cut it all off, and wear a Cap, with an old Felt Hat: He came into the Country last Fall with one Captain Welsh, and says he is a Weaver by Trade, he probably may make towards Crown Point, as he says his Father is about there among the Soldiers. Whoever takes up and secures said Servant, so that his Master may have him again, shall have the above Reward, and reasonable Charges, paid by      MARK ELLIOT.
*The Pennsylvania Gazette*, June 14, 1764.


RUN away on Sunday Night, the 3d inst. June, from Mr. Hunter's Boat, about 10 Miles above New Castle, a Negroe Man named Bazil, about 5 Feet 9 or 10 Inches high, speaks bad English, has been at Sea, and is a tolerable Cook; he is a French Negroe, pretends to be free. Whoever takes up and secures said Negroe, so that I may have him again, shall have Five Pounds Reward, by applying to me at Philadelphia. DAVID HAY.
N. B. All Masters of Vessels are forbid to carry him off.
*The Pennsylvania Gazette*, June 14, 1764. See *The Pennsylvania Journal, and Weekly Advertiser*, June 7, 1764.


FORTY SHILLINGS Reward.
RUN away from the Subscriber, living in Newport, New-Castle, on the 29th Day of May last, a Negroe Man, called Julius, aged 22 Years, about 5 Feet 3 Inches high, straight and well made, and bred to the Biscuit baking Business; Had on, when he went away, a light coloured Ratteen Coat, cut short in the Skirts, Petticoat Trowsers, and red Breeches under, a striped Linsey Jacket, without Sleeves; he is of a yellowish Cast in Colour. Whoever takes up said Negroe, and puts him again, shall receive the above Reward, and reasonable Charges,  paid by     THOMAS DUFF.
N. B. All Masters of Vessels are forbid to carry him off.
*The Pennsylvania Gazette*, June 21, 1764; July 5, 1764.


TWELVE DOLLARS Reward.
RUN away from the Subscriber, living in Redlion Hundred, New-Castle County, on Delaware, on the 10th of May last, a Servant Man, named James Robinson, about 35 Years of Age; had on, when he went away, a Felt Hat, blue Broadcloth Coat, red Serge, double breasted Jacket, without Skirts,

yellow knit Breeches, light coloured Worsted Stockings, and good Shoes, with Brass Buckles. Wears his Hair, of a brown Colour, and very remarkable by a Scar under his right Eye; has been in the Regular Service in North America, and is acquainted with the Fortresses to the Northward; his Back is very much mark'd by being often whipt in the Army, and is much given to strong Drink. Whoever takes up said Servant, and secures him in any of His Majesty's Goals, so that the Owner may have him again, shall have the above Reward, paid by JOHN CLARK.

*The Pennsylvania Gazette*, July 5, 1764.


Absented himself from his Father, on the Second of July, a Boy about 17 Years of Age, named Jacob Sauter: Had on when he went away, a striped Calimancoe Jacket without Sleeves, a red one with Sleeves, which reaches but to his Breeches Waistband, Check Trowsers, a Pair of Pumps, with large Brass Buckles, Silver Sleeve Buttons, and a Silver Broach in his Shirt; he took a Sickle with him, and went away with another Boy that is supposed to be likewise run away. Whoever takes up said Boy, and brings him to his Father, or secures him in any Goal, so that he may be had again, shall have Thirty Shillings Reward, and reasonable Charges,
     paid by JOHN SAUTER, in Christine Hundred,
New-Castle County, near Newport.

*The Pennsylvania Gazette*, July 12, 1764.


RUN away on Saturday Evening, the 30th of June last, from the Subscriber, living in New-Castle County, St. George's Hundred, a Mulattoe Fellow, named Frank, about 20 Years of Age, about five Feet five Inches high, well set, round faced, short curled black hair, cut off the Crown of his Head: Had on, when he went away, an old blue Broadcloth Coat, brown Serge Jacket, and a white Woollen home made One, new Shirt and Trowsers of Tow and Flax Linen, an Ozenbrigs Shirt, coarse white Woollen Stockings, a new Felt Hat, old Shoes and Buckles; of a bashful Countenance, very apt to swear when angry, Jersey born, a Slave for Life. Any Person taking up and securing said Mulattoe in any Goal in this Government, or elsewhere, or brings him to his Master, shall have Thirty Shillings Reward, beside reasonable Charges,
     paid by THOMAS WITHERSPOON.

*The Pennsylvania Gazette*, July 19, 1764. See *The Pennsylvania Gazette*, November 22, 1764.


TEN DOLLARS Reward.

RUN away from the Subscriber, living in Dover, Kent County, on Delaware, an Apprentice Lad, named Ebenezer Manlove, a Shop-Joiner by Trade, about

5 Feet 4 Inches high, about 19 Years of Age, a full-faced chunky Lad, has straight light coloured Hair, tied behind: Had on when he went away, an old superfine Cloth Jacket, without Sleeves, of a mixed Colour, Check Shirt, striped Trowsers, Shoe and Stockings, and old Castor Hat. It is supposed he will cross Delaware to the Jerseys. Whoever takes up said Apprentice, and brings him to the Subscriber, or secures him, so as his Master may have him again, shall have the above Reward, and reasonable Charges, if brought home, paid by    JOHN GORDON.
*The Pennsylvania Gazette*, August 2, 1764; August 16, 1764; August 23, 1764.


RUN away from the Subscriber, living in Christiana Hundred, and County of New-Castle, on Delaware, a Servant Lad, named Amos M'Gloughlin, about 18 Years of Age, 5 Feet 6 or 7 Inches high, pretty long visaged. Pock marked, has black Hair, which curls a little, has a lazy Way of walking, and is a great Observer of Things of little Consequence; Hand on, when he went away, a half-worn Felt Hat, a new light coloured Cloth Waistcoat, lined with Linsey, round Cuffs to it, & Whitemetal Buttons, white Shirt, long Check Trowsers, and halfworn Shoes, with Whitemetal Buckles. He has been used to tend a Merchant-Mill, Saw-Mill and making Flour Casks. Any Person that takes up and secures the aforesaid Lad, so that his Master may have him again, shall have Forty Shillings Reward, and reasonable Charges,
          paid by me    VINCENT GILPIN.
*The Pennsylvania Gazette*, August 9, 1764; August 23, 1764; August 30, 1764.

                              New-Castle, August 10, 1764.
COmmitted to the Goal of this County, on Suspicion of being a Runaway Servant, a certain Richard Welch; he is about 50 Years of Age, about 5 Feet 7 or 8 Inches high, wears a light coloured Great Coat, blue Body Coat, Check Shirt, Buckskin Breeches, old Shoes. Large Silver Buckles, stamped I B, were found on him when taken up, 23 Spanish Dollars, 1 Pocket Piece, 52 English Shillings, 23 English Six-pences, and 2 Quarter Dollars. Any Person having any Property to said Welch or Money, is desired to make it known in six Weeks after the Date hereof, otherwise he will be discharged, paying his Fees, by    ALEXANDER HARVEY, Goaler.
*The Pennsylvania Gazette*, August 16, 1764; September 6, 1764; September 20, 1764.


RUN away, on the 6th of this instant August, from Thomas Morton, living near New-Castle, a Negroe Man, named Dick, a well set Fellow, thick Legs,

and pretty fleshy, talks something broken, in the Negroe Way; says he was born in Morocco, and that he is a Freeman: Had on, when he went away, a Thickset Coat, and Leather Breeches, but perhaps may change both his Clothes and Name. He has a Scar on one of his Hands (thought to be the Right Hand, but not certain) which looks as if his Thumb had been almost cut off. Whoever takes up and brings home said Negroe, or secures him in any Goal, so that his Master may have him again, shall have Five Dollars Reward, paid by me THOMAS MORTON.
*The Pennsylvania Gazette*, August 16, 1764; August 30, 1764; September 6, 1764.


RUN away from the Subscribers, living near Witherspoon's, in New-Castle County, on the Borders the Maryland, two Servant Men, one named George Rankin, about 35 Years of Age, five Feet seven Inches high, long Visage, dark Complexion, black Hair: Had on when he went away, an old Felt Hat, Linsey Jacket, trimmed with Brass Buttons, old Cloth Breeches, new blue home made Stockings, and old Shoes; took with him, a Pair of long Ozenbrigs Trowsers, a fine Shirt, and a half worn coarse ditto, is apt to get drunk at every Opportunity, and is very talkative: He came from Ireland about ten Months ago, and formerly served his Time in this Country. The other named William Price, about 40 Years of Age: Had on when he went away an old light coloured Coat, with white Metal Buttons, with a Hole burnt in one of the Sleeves, a Cloth under Jacket, two home made Shirts, two Pair of Trowsers, old Shoes tied with Strings, old Cotton Cap, and an old Felt Hat. He is of a sandy Complexion, and is remarkable by having two Thumbs on his Right Hand, and is blind of the Left Eye, is apt to get drunk, and squeaks when he speaks high: He ran away in the Year 1762, and says he drove a Team at Pott's Ironworks, and called himself John Reese. Whoever secures said Servants in any Goal, so as their Masters may have them again, shall have Five Pounds Reward for both, or Fifty Shillings for either,
       paid by    JAMES WILSON, and JOHN DOBBINS.
N. B. All Masters of Vessels are forbid to carry them off at their Peril.
*The Pennsylvania Gazette*, September 13, 1764; September 27, 1764; October 25, 1764. See *The Pennsylvania Gazette*, May 31, 1764, for Rankin.


MADE his Escape, the 14th of August last, from Samuel Enos, Constable of Whiteclay Creek Hundred, New-Castle County, a Prisoner, named Daniel M'Collister, about 5 Feet 7 Inches high, of a swarthy Complexion, thin faced, black Hair, tied behind with a black Ribbon; had on when he went away, a Check Shirt and Trowsers, a halfworn Hat, cocked upright, and no other

Clothing; as he was at that time committed for stealing, it is expected he will steal again, having been guilty of robbing Mr. Adams's Store, at Christine Bridge, of several Articles, and broke open a Trunk for another Person. Whoever brings said Prisoner to New-Castle Goal, shall have Four Pounds Reward, and reasonable Charges, paid by  SAMUEL ENOS.
*The Pennsylvania Gazette,* September 27, 1764; October 11, 1764; October 18, 1764.

October 18.
RUN-AWAY
From the subscriber living in Brandywine Hundred and New-Castle county.

AN Irish servant man, named James M'Swine, or Sweney, he is about 5 feet 6 or 7 inches high, he is of a redish complexion, wears his own black hair club'd behind, with tuskers [sic] down his cheeks: Had on when he went away, a light coloured broad cloth coat, an old blue jacket, both pretty much wore, an old felt hatt, tow shirt and trowsers, a pair of channel'd pumps with three soals, he is round shouldered, and has pretty much of a down look. Whoever takes up and secures said servant in any of his majesty's goals, so that his master may have him again, shall have THREE POUNDS reward and reasonable charges paid by  WILLIAM ROBESON.
*The Pennsylvania Journal, and Weekly Advertiser;* October 18, 1764; November 1, 1764.

September 27.
RUN-away the 21st inst. from on board the shallop Hannah, Ralph Walker master, now lying in Philadelphia, A negro man named Ned Lamme, about 26 or 27 years of age, about 5 feet 6 or seven inches high, has lost most of his fore teeth, has a large bump on his forehead as large as a marvle and speaks good english; had on when he went away an old great coat, a pair of red breeches and trowsers over them, and wears a cap. Whoever takes up said negro and secures him in any goal, or brings him to Peter Sutter, in Strawberry Alley, or to his said master in Wilmington, shall have FORTY SHILLINGS reward and reasonable charges paid by RALPH WALKER.
N. B. All masters of vessels and others are desired not to Harbor or carry him off at their peril.
*The Pennsylvania Journal, and Weekly Advertiser;* October 18, 1764; November 1, 1764.

RUN away from the Subscriber, living in Newport, in New-Castle County, a Negroe Man, called Cudjoe Briens, about five Feet five Inches high, with a Blemish on his Right eye, about Thirty Years of Age; he is bandy legged, and

has a Lump on the Inside of his Left-ancle; had on, when he went away, a blue Surtout Coat, a Linen Jacket, lined with Lincey, and a Pair of Tow Trowsers, and a good Hat. Whoever takes up the said Negroe, and secures him, so that the Subscriber may have him again, shall receive the Sum of Three Pounds, paid by
October 24, 1764        CONRAD GRAY, in Newport.
*The Pennsylvania Gazette*, November 1, 1764; November 15, 1764; November 22, 1764.

November 8.
RUN-away from the subscriber, living in New-Castle Hundred and County, on the 2d day of August, a servant man named John Brown, about 50 years of age, about 5 feet 6 inches high, of a black complexion, and has a mole on his left cheek as large as a pea, he speaks broken english, has sore legs and one of them is pretty much swelled about the ancle: Had on and took with him when he went away, a short coat and a new jacket of grey home-spun cloth, one coarse white and one check shirt, one pair of new petticoat trowsers, one pair of old shoes, and an old wool hat, he is busten'd [*sic*] and stole a steel belt to support his disorder, besides several other things too tedious to mention. Whoever takes up secures said servant or brings him to Matthew Cannan in New-Castle hundred and County, or to Randall M'Killip in Philadelphia, shall receive FORTY SHILLINGS reward, paid by either of the said persons.
*The Pennsylvania Journal, and Weekly Advertiser*; November 8, 1764; November 22, 1764; December 6, 1764; December 13, 1764; December 20, 1764.

FIVE POUNDS Reward.
RUN away from the Subscriber on Saturday, the 30th of June last, a young Mulattoe Fellow, about 20 years of Age, named Frank, about five Feet five Inches high, well set, full faced, short black curled Hair, very apt to swear when angry; had on and with him, when he went away, a coarse home made Tow Shirt and Trowsers, a Woollen Jacket, home-made, old Hat and Stockings; it is supposed he has changed his Clothes, and perhaps his Name by this Time; it also is supposed he is some where in the Cedar Swamps in the Jerseys, down Delaware River, as his Mother, and others of his Acquaintance, live near Cohansey, where the Fellow I believe was bred. Whoever secures said Mulattoe in any Goal, or brings him to his said Master, shall have the above Reward, besides reasonable Charges,
           paid by      THOMAS WITHERSPOON.
*The Pennsylvania Gazette*, November 22, 1764. See *The Pennsylvania Gazette*, July 19, 1764.

November 24.
RUN away from the subscriber living at Reedy island, New Castle county, an apprentice, on Friday the 4th day of November, at the county of Cape May, named David Foster, twenty one years of age or there abouts, a well set fellow, down look he has black strait hair, and is a talkative fellow of a swarthy complexion; had on when he went away, a red jacket, and a pair of blue trowsers, or red plush breeches, a flopped hat, and a new pair of shoes with broad rimmed brass buckles. Whoever takes up said apprentice, and secures him in any of his majesties goals so that I may get him again, shall have FORTY SHILLINGS reward if taken in this county, or FIFTY SHILLINGS if taken else where, and reasonable charges
          paid by   HENRY TUDER, Pilot.
N. B. All Persons are forwarned of entertaining said apprentice.
*The Pennsylvania Journal, and Weekly Advertiser*; November 24, 1764; December 1, 1764; December 8, 1764.


New-Castle, November 20, 1764.
NOW in the Goal of this County, a Negroe Man, can speak little or no English, has on an old Flannel Jacket, two old white Shirts, old Hat, wears a Blanket about him; he is a great Smoaker, &c. His master, if he has any, is desired to come in six Weeks after the Date hereof, pay Charges, and take him away, otherwise he will be sold for the same,
          by ALEXANDER HARVEY, Goaler.
*The Pennsylvania Gazette*, November 29, 1764; January 10, 1765.

## 1765

RUN away, on Friday, the 30th of November last, from the Subscriber, living in Christine Hundred, New-Castle County, upon Delaware, a Servant Girl, named Jane Winsant, born near Newtown, in Maryland, aged about 28 Years, a short thick Girl, of a pale Complexion, long Visage, and black Eyes, the Middle Finger of her Left hand had a Lump on it; had on, when she went away, a Calicoe Bed-gown, striped Linsey Petticoat, blue Stockings with red Clocks in them. Whoever takes up said Jane Winsant, and secures her in any Goal, so that her Master may have her again, shall have Forty Shillings Reward, and reasonable Charges,
          paid by   JEREMIAH SMITH.
N. B. One of her upper Teeth is rotted out.
*The Pennsylvania Gazette*, December 20, 1764; January 3, 1765; January 17, 1765.

FIVE POUNDS Reward.

RUN away from the Subscriber, living near Dover, in Kent County, on Delaware, on Saturday, the 2d inst. March, two Men, one from his Bail, and the other an indented Servant; the former named John Wotterson, this Country born, about 20 Years of Age, of a fair Complexion, with short Hair; had on, when he went away, a light coloured Nap Great Coat, a white coloured Cloth straight Ditto, a red Nap Jacket, with a Calicoe one under it, and Leather Breeches; and took with him other Cloaths, sorts unknown. The latter named John Story, alias John Morton, an Englishman, about 20 Years of Age, of a fair Complexion, with short black Hair, which he ties; he professes to be a School master, and sometimes a Merchant, had on, when he went away, a Snuff coloured cloth Coat, and a white Cloth Jacket, both lined with brown Damask, a Pair of red Stocking Breeches, with flowered Knee Garters, a ruffled Shirt, and a new Hat; and took with him besides, another ruffled Shirt, a Pair of Boots, almost new, a Pair of Pumps, and several Things unknown. Whoever takes up and secures the above described Men, so that the Subscriber can have them again, shall have the above Reward for both, or Fifty Shillings for each, and reasonable Charges,

   paid by  JOSEPH CALDWELL.

N. B. Said John Story lately married a Wife in this City, under the Name of John Morton. All Masters of Vessels, and others, are forbid to harbour or carry them off, as they will answer it at their Peril.

*The Pennsylvania Gazette*, March 14, 1765; May 2, 1765; May 9, 1765.


March 9, 1765.

RUN away last Night, from Alexander Miller, of Newport, New-Castle County, a Servant Man, named Charles Black, about 5 Feet 8 Inches high, 25 Years of Age, wears dark brown Hair, cut on the Crown, has some Scars in his Face, and came into this Country a few Weeks ago, with Captain Edgar, from Belfast, had on, when he went away, a grey Coat, black Broadcloth Jacket, Cream coloured Rig-and-Fur Stockings, old Wool Hat, and old Pumps. Whoever takes up and secures said Servant, so that his Master, may have him again, shall have Three Pounds Reward, and reasonable Charges,

   paid by  ALEXANDER MILLER.

*The Pennsylvania Gazette*, March 14, 1765; April 18, 1765; April 25, 1765.


RUN away the 14th of this instant March, from the Reverend Mr. David Davis, of Newark, New-Castle County, an Irish Servant Man, named Patrick Gillespy, about 5 Feet 9 or 10 Inches high, abut 26 Years of Age, remarkably broad shouldered, and has light curled Hair, generally well curled: Had on a light coloured Bearskin Jacket, and an under One of nearly the same Colour;

his other Cloathing uncertain; he is an ill looking Fellow, has a good Deal of the Brogue, and fond of bad Company and strong Liquor. Whoever takes up said Servant, and secures him, so that his Master may have him again, shall have Thirty Shillings Reward, and reasonable Charges,
   paid by DAVID DAVIS.
*The Pennsylvania Gazette*, March 21, 1765; April 4, 1765; April 11, 1765.


RUN away from the Subscriber, living in Brandywine Hundred, the 24th of April last, an Irish Servant Man, named James Walker, about 5 Feet 6 Inches high, black Hair, and thin visaged; had on, when he went away, a brown Cloth Coat, stripped Linsey Jacket, striped Trowsers, blue Breeches, old black Worsted Stockings, old Felt Hat, old patched Pumps, and an old white shirt. Whoever takes up said Servant, and secures him, so that his Master may have him again, shall have Thirty Shillings Reward,
   paid by JAMES HUSTIN.
*The Pennsylvania Gazette*, May 2, 1765; May 16, 1765; May 23, 1765.
See *The Pennsylvania Journal, and the Weekly Advertiser*, February 19, 1767.

       THREE POUNDS Reward.
RUN away, on Sunday, the 28th of April last, from the Subscriber, living in Newark, New-Castle County, an Apprentice Man, named Michael Boyl, about 20 years of Age, of a thin Visage and loves strong Drink; had on and took with him, a half worn Castor Hat, a home made Cloth Coat, of a yellowish Colour, a striped Linsey Jacket, red Plush Breeches, blue Worsted Stockings, and a Pair of half worn Shoes. Whoever takes ups said Apprentice, and secures him in any of his Majesty's Goals, so as his Master may have him again, shall have the above Reward, and all reasonable Charges,
   paid by JOHN M'CLEAN.
N. B. Said Apprentice is a Blacksmith by Trade.
*The Pennsylvania Gazette*, May 9, 1765. See the following ad.


              April 30, 1765.
COmmitted to the Goal of Lancaster, a certain Michael Boyl, who says he is a Servant to John M'Clane, in Newark Town, New-Castle County; these are to desire his Master to come, pay Charges, and take him away, otherwise he will be sold in four Weeks from this Date, for his Fees, by me
     FELIX DONNALLY, Goal-keeper.
*The Pennsylvania Gazette*, May 9, 1765; May 16, 1765; May 23, 1765.
See the foregoing ad.

New-Castle, May 10, 1765.
NOW in the Goal of this County, the two following Prisoners, committed on Suspicion of being Runaways, viz. Edward Boss, alias William Burnet, about 55 Years of Age, has on a Castor Hat, brown Jacket, and a green one under it, Check Shirt, Leather Breeches, old Stockings, Neats Leather Shoes, and Brass Buckles. Also a Negroe Man, who calls himself Jacob, says he run from Joseph Sadler, in Dorset County. Their Masters, if they have any, are hereby desired to come, in six Weeks from the above Date, pay Charges, and take them away, otherwise they will be sold for the same,
by ALEXANDER HARVEY, Goaler.
*The Pennsylvania Gazette*, May 16, 1765; May 30, 1765; June 6, 1765.

New-Castle, June 3, 1765.
FIVE POUNDS Reward.
MADE his Escape from the Goal of this County, on the 28th of May inst. a certain John Carroll, about 25 or 30 Years of Age, wears his own Hair, which is short, fair and curly, and is pitted with the Small-pox; his Clothing uncertain; but he may be easily known, as when he offers to speak, he gapes and stutters. Whoever apprehends said Carroll, and secures him, so that I may have him again, shall have the above Reward, with reasonable Charges, if brought to New-Castle, and delivered to me,
paid by ALEXANDER HARVEY, Goaler.
N. B. There are now in said Goal the two following Prisoners, committed on Suspicion of being Runaways, viz. John Clarkson, a white Man, has on an old Felt Hat, Check Shirt, brown Jacket, blue Woollen Trowsers, &c. Null, a Negroe, says he belongs to William Wilson in Kent on Delaware. Their Masters are desired to send for them in six Weeks after the Date hereof, to prevent their being sold for their Fees.
*The Pennsylvania Gazette*, June 13, 1765; June 20, 1765; June 27, 1765.
See *The Pennsylvania Gazette*, May 22, 1766.

Philadelphia, June 5, 1765.
RUN away, last Night, from Captain Hugh Wright's Ship, a Mulattoe Fellow, named Dick, about 5 Feet 6 Inches high, well set, very crafty, talks much, and is remarkable for a Cast in his Right Eye; he wears a red Jacket, white Breeches, Check Shirt, new Shoes and Stockings, and an old Beaver Hat. It is supposed he is gone to Dover, as he has a Wife there. Whoever secures said Fellow in any Goal, or brings him to JAMES HARDING, in Philadelphia, shall have Forty Shillings Reward, beside Charges.
N. B. Masters of Vessels are cautioned against taking him away.
*The Pennsylvania Gazette*, June 13, 1765; June 27, 1765. See *The Pennsylvania Gazette*, July 4, 1765.

New Castle, June 19, 1765.
IN Custody of the Subscriber, a Mulattoe Fellow, named Dick, advertised by Mr. James Harding, in Philadelphia. His Master is desired to send for him,
        by ALEXANDER HARVEY, Goaler.
*The Pennsylvania Gazette*, July 4, 1765. See *The Pennsylvania Gazette*, June 13, 1765.


RUN away from the Subscriber, living in New-Castle Hundred and County, near Christiana Bridge, on Monday, the 24th of June last, a Servant Man, named Robert M'Cully, aged about 25 Years, a thick set Fellow, has black Hair, and wears it tied; he is about 5 Feet 7 Inches high; had on, when he went away, a red and white striped Linsey Jacket, with the Stripes cross the Body, a Felt Hat, and short Town Trowsers patched; he was lately bought out of New-Castle Goal. Whoever takes up said Runaway, and secures him in any of His Majesty's Goals, so that his Master may have him again, shall receive Four Dollars Reward, and reasonable Charges,
        paid by    SAMUEL PORTER.
*The Pennsylvania Gazette*, July 18, 1765; August 8, 1765; August 15, 1765.


ABSCONDED from the Subscriber, living at Christiana Bridge, New-Castle County, on Sunday, the 21st of July last, an Apprentice Lad, named Andrew Kinkaid, about 19 Years of Age, a tall slender young man, of a fair Complexion, with his Hair curled; had on, and took with him, a brown coarse Frock, a spotted Flannel Jacket, Buckskin Breeches, two Pair of Ozenbrigs Trowsers, two white Shirts, a Pair of ribbed Cotton Stockings, new Shoes, and plated Buckles; also wears a black Neckcloth; he has served a Time to the Blacksmith's Trade, and bound himself with me about two Months ago, and says the Blacksmith's Trade did not agree with him, and that he left his Parents with their Consent, who live in Carlisle. Whoever takes up said Apprentice, and secures him in any of His MajestyGoals, so that his Master may have him again, shall have a Reward of Twenty Shillings, and reasonable Charges, paid by    DAVID SMITH, COOPER.
*The Pennsylvania Gazette*, August 1, 1765; August 8, 1765; August 15, 1765.


        FOUR POUNDS TEN SHILLINGS Reward.
STolen from the Subscriber, living in New-Castle County, near Duck-Creek, the 27th of July last, a large light coloured bay Horse, with a small Star in his Forehead, a very small Snip betwixt his Nostrils, the near hind Foot white as far as the Foot lock, marked on the same Buttock with a dim S, natural Pacer,

drags his hind Feet, so that his Hoofs are much worn. A Saddle, Cloth and Bridle, were likewise stolen the same Night in the Neighbourhood, supposed to be carried along with said Horse; the Saddle not much worn, large and full, the Cloth blue, but fades, bordered with green Tape, partly worn off, with a Snaffle Bridle. Whoever takes up said Horse, Saddle and Bridle, so that the Owner may have them again, and secures the said Thief in any Goal, shall have the above Reward, or for the Horse and Saddle Thirty Shillings,
        paid by    CHARLES CARSON.
N. B. The Thief is supposed to be one John Moorand, a low set Man, swarthy Complexion, freckled, black Hair tyed, a Silver Button to his Hat, brown coloured Coat, prodigal to Appearance, was a Soldier, and has a Discharge, which serves as a Pass.
*The Pennsylvania Gazette*, August 8, 1765; August 22, 1765; August 29, 1765.

August 12, 1765.
RUN away last night from the subscribers, living in Newport, New-Castle county, the following persons, viz. Charles Black, an Irishman, about 5 feet 5 or 6 inches high, well set. with a down look, and dark brown hair; had on an old hat, old dirty shirt, wide short trowsers of Russia sheeting, with a patch on one leg, a dark brown jacket, above half worn, new pumps, old buckles, one Pinchbeck, and one brass. The other an Irishman, about 5 feet 3 or 4 inches high, speaks very bad English, a tanner by trade; had on, when he went away, a dark grey cloth coat and jacket, a check shirt, pretty much dyed with tan, long trowsers, white thread stockings, old shoes, brass buckles, half worn wool hat, and short brown hair. Whoever takes up and secures said men in any goal, so that their masters may have them again, shall have Five Pounds reward for both, or Fifty Shillings for each, paid by
        ALEXANDER MILLER, ROBERT SLATER.
*The Pennsylvania Gazette*, August 15, 1765; August 22, 1765; August 29, 1765.

EIGHT DOLLARS Reward.
RUN away, on the 20th of August, an Irish Servant Man, named Patrick Gillespie, about 5 Feet 9 or 10 Inches high, very stout built, remarkably broad shouldered, a little knock-kneed, grey Eyes, short brown curled hair: had on, when he went away, a blue Cloth Coat, a coarse grey Jacket, the Back and Foreparts of different Cloths, an old Castor Hat, that has been cut in the Brim, and mended again, Petticoat Trowsers, Check Shirt, grey ribbed Stockings, black grained Leather Shoes, with large Pewter carved Buckles. Whoever takes up said Servant, and secures him, so that his Master may have him again, shall receive the above Reward, from
        PATRICK M'COLGAN, living at Newark.

*The Pennsylvania Gazette,* August 29, 1765; September 12, 1765; September 19, 1765.


RUN away, on the 25th Instant, at Night, from the Subscriber, living in Brandywine Hundred, New-Castle County, an English Servant Man, named John Gray, 21 years of Age, speaks proper, and walks very upright, wears his own dark brown Hair, which he generally keeps in good Order, and tied, about 5 Feet 8 or 9 Inches high: Had on, and took with him a blue Sailor's Jacket, lined with striped Linsey, one Ozenbrigs, and one Check Shirt, long Trowsers, made of Top sail Duck, a small Felt hat, bound with Firreting, new Shoes, with square Pewter Buckles. Whoever takes up said Servant, and secures him so as his Master may have him again, shall have Forty Shillings Reward, and reasonable Charges, paid by   JACOB FORWOOD.
N. B. All Masters of Vessels are requested not to carry him off.
*The Pennsylvania Gazette,* August 29, 1765; September 12, 1765; September 19, 1765.


RUN away from the Subscriber, of Muspilion Hundred, Kent County, on Delaware, the 20th of August last, a Mulattoe Slave, named Joe, about 5 Feet 8 Inches high, slim Legs and Thighs, and has an Indian Look; had on, when he went away, an old Beaver hat, with a Hole on the Crown, old white Jacket, made of Blanketing, new homemade tow Shirt and Trowsers, old Shoes; also took with him two Shirts, one new tow, and the other an old fine one, an old white cotton Jacket; he can read Print, and will try to pass for a Freeman. Whoever takes up the said Slave, and secures him, so as his Master may have him again, shall have a satisfactory Reward, more than is allowed by the Law, and all reasonable Charges paid by   GEORGE MANLOVE.
N. B. All Masters of Vessels are forbid to carry off the said Slave at their Peril.
*The Pennsylvania Gazette,* September 5, 1765; September 12, 1765; September 19, 1765.

THREE POUNDS Reward.
RUN away, on the 17th of last Month, from the Subscriber, living in St. George's Hundred, New-Castle County, a Servant Man, named William Gordon, born in Scotland, about 23 years of Age, five Feet eight or nine Inches high, has a round full Face, ruddy Complexion, with some Freckles, brown sandy Hair, very long, and tied behind, but it is supposed he has cut it off; he is a smart pert looking Fellow, very talkative, and a good deal on the Scotch Accent; it is like he may forge a Pass, as he writes a good Hand; Had on when he went away, a new Felt Hat, Check Shirt, black Neckcloth, old

light coloured Broadcloth Coat and Jacket, both much worn, old Leather Breeches, very dirty grey Yarn Stockings, and old Shoes, but may probably change his Clothes, as he has a Supply at some Distance. Whoever takes up and secures said Servant, so as his Master may have him again, shall have the above Reward, and reasonable Charges,
          paid by    SAMUEL SMITH.
*The Pennsylvania Gazette*, October 3, 1765; October 10, 1765; October 17, 1765.

                        New-Castle Goal, October 2, 1765.
IN Custody of the Subscriber, the two following Persons, viz. John Bambridge, committed as a Runaway Servant, is about 5 Feet 5 Inches high; has on a white Coat, blue Jacket, white Shirt, white thread Stockings, Leather Breeches, &c. Also Elizabeth Gold, says that she is a Servant to Thomas Spry Morgan, near Chester Church, Maryland. Their Masters, if any, are desired to pay Charges, and take them away in 6 Weeks from this Date, otherwise they will be sold for the same by    ALEXANDER HARVEY, Goaler.
*The Pennsylvania Gazette*, October 10, 1765; October 17, 1765; October 24, 1765. See *The Pennsylvania Gazette*, May 8, 1766, for Bambridge.

                        New Castle Goal, December 16, 1765.
IN Custody of the Subscriber, the two following Prisoners, both committed as Runaways, viz. Pompey, a Negroe Man, says he belongs to Mr. Isaac Briscow, in Steelpone, Maryland; Thomas Hughes, a young Negroe Fellow, says he came away from Captain Colburn, at Wilmington. Their Masters, (if any they have) are hereby desired to come, pay Charges, and take them away, otherwise they will be sold for the same,
          by ALEXANDER HARVEY, Goaler.
*The Pennsylvania Gazette*, December 26, 1765; January 9, 1765; January 16, 1766.

# 1766

RUN away, on the 29th of October last, from Wilmington, in New-Castle County, one John Mills, a Shoemaker by Trade; had on, and took with him, when he went away, a short brown Jacket, a white Linen one under it, a black Calimancoe, and a striped Lincey Ditto: He is about 5 Feet high, was born in England, about 34 Years of Age, his Hair black, and curled a little. Whoever secures him in any Goal, or brings him to John M'Donnald, in Mill-Creek Hundred, New-Castle County, shall have Three Pounds Reward, and reasonable Charges.
N. B. He stole a Watch from said M'Donnald.

*The Pennsylvania Gazette*, January 2, 1766; January 9, 1766; January 16, 1766.

RUN away, on the 31st of December last, from the Subscriber, living in Front-street, three Doors below Chestnut street, an Apprentice Lad, named Daniel Britt, by Trade a Taylor, about 14 Years of Age, born at St. George's, in New Castle County, Pennsylvania, of a low Stature, fair Hair, tied behind, and of a fair Complexion; had on, when he went way, an old blue Coat, with red Lining, an old red Flannel Jacket, lappelled, a Pair of blue Plush Breeches, and a Pair of blue Yarn Stockings, but had no Hat on. Whoever secures said Apprentice, so as his Master may have him again, shall have One Shilling Reward, paid by  JOHN GRANT.
*The Pennsylvania Gazette*, January 16, 1766; January 23, 1766.


TEN POUNDS Reward.
Broke out of Goal, at Dover, in Kent County, on Delaware, on the 18th of this Instant, two Irishmen, named William M'Laughlin and Patrick Gillaspy; the said William is a lusty Man, but looks very poorly having been in Goal some Time; had on, when he went away, a Saggathy Coat and Breeches, very much worn, and took with him a Pair of blue Breeches, and old Shoes and Stockings; wears his Hair which is black, bushy or curled, and is very much Pock-marked. Patrick is a stout well set Fellow, born in Dublin, said to be a Servant, and very impertinent; both of said Men are very much given to Drink, and have stole, or took out of Goal two new Negroes, which they will sell, if they meet with an Opportunity, likewise a Gun, and sundry other Things, to the Amount of four or Five Pounds: Said Patrick had on, when he went away, a blue Coat and Breeches, a large Racoon Hat, a cut Wig, new Shoes and Thread Stockings, which he stole. By his Looks he may be supposed to be a Robber or Highwayman. Whoever takes up the said Irishmen and Negroes, and secures them so as the Goaler may have them again, shall have the above Reward,
paid by  JOHN WINTERTON.
*The Pennsylvania Gazette*, February 6, 1766; February 13, 1766; February 20, 1766. See *The Pennsylvania Gazette*, April 3, 1766.


FIVE POUNDS Reward.
RUN away, on the 11th of July last, from the Subscriber (their Bail) living near New-Castle, the following Persons, viz. a certain James Carson, a Weaver by Trade, about five Feet eight or nine Inches high, of a fair Complexion; had on when he went away, a coarse Country mixed Cloth Jacket, Buckskin Breeches, white ribbed Linen Stockings, and a coarse Shirt.

He is supposed to be gone towards Carlisle. Also a certain Archibald M'Vaugh, about five Feet six Inches high, has strait Hair, and squints much with both Eyes: Had on when he went away, a black Calimancoe Jacket, without Sleeves, and a coarse Shirt and Trowsers; he served his Time about Pequea-Creek, and is supposed to be gone that Way. Likewise went away on the 12th of March instant, a certain James Cannon, a Weaver by Trade, but may pass for a Sailor; had on a new Felt Hat, a coarse Blanket Jacket, with Leather Buttons, coarse Shirt, and old Trowsers, and white Yarn Stockings. He is an Irishman, and has the Brougue on his Tongue and is supposed to be gone to Philadelphia. Whoever takes up and secures the above Persons in any of His Majesty's Goals, and gives Notice thereof in the publick Papers, so that the Subscriber may get them again, shall have Forty Shillings for Carson, and for M'Vaugh and Cannon thirty Shillings each,
   paid by me  SAMUEL RUTH.
*The Pennsylvania Gazette*, March 20, 1766; March 27, 1766; April 3, 1766.

Dover, March 25, 1766.
NOTICE is hereby given, that there is now confined in the Goal of the County of Kent on Delaware, a certain Man, named Patrick Gilaspy, but called himself John Dougherty, committed on suspicion of being a Run-away Servant. His Master is desired to come, pay the Charges, and take him away, otherwise he will be sold for his Fees, as the Law directs.
   JOHN WINTERTON, Goaler.
N. B. There were also taken up in Muspelion Neck, about the latter End of September 1765, and committed to this Goal, two New Negroes, viz. a Man, named Jack, and a Woman, named Jane. Their Masters are desired to come and take them away, otherwise they will be sold out for their Fees, as the Law directs.
*The Pennsylvania Gazette*, April 3, 1766; April 10, 1766; April 17, 1766. See *The Pennsylvania Gazette*, February 6, 1766

New-Castle, March 27, 1766.
NOW in the Custody of the Subscriber, a certain Person, who calls himself Samuel Hughes, committed on Suspicion of being a Run-away Servant; he is about five Feet nine or ten Inches high, wears a blue Jacket, old grey under Ditto, new Check Shirt, old Leather Breeches, half worn Shoes and Stockings, and a small Felt Hat, bound round the Edge with black Tape. His Master (if he has any) is desired to come in six Weeks after Date, pay Charges, and take him away, otherwise he will be sold for the same, by
   ALEXANDER HARVEY, Goaler.

*The Pennsylvania Gazette*, April 3, 1766; April 10, 1766; April 17, 1766.

New-Castle, April 24, 1766.
FORTY SHILLINGS Reward.
MADE his Escape from the Goal of this County, the 21st Instant, a certain John Bambridge, an Englishman, he is a little slim Fellow, his Cloathing uncertain, only a Pair of blue Breeches, red shirt Jacket, and double channelled Pumps; he went away with a little Woman, named Catherine Oharro, alias Catherine Thomas; she is native Irish, and speaks but bad English, both much given to Drink, and may pass for Man and Wife. Whoever secures said Bambridge in any Goal, so that the Subscriber may have him again, shall have the above Reward, and if brought to New-Castle, reasonable Charges, paid by ALEXANDER HARVEY , Goaler.
N. B. Now in the Subscriber's Custody, a certain Timothy Kelly, confesses himself to be a Servant to William Snodgrass, of Mount Mebas, Lancaster County. His Master is hereby desired to send for him in six Weeks, or he will be sold for Charges, by    ALEXANDER HARVEY, Goaler.
*The Pennsylvania Gazette*, May 8, 1766; May 15, 1766; May 22, 1766.
See *The Pennsylvania Gazette*, October 10, 1765.


Chester Goal, April 28, 1766.
WAS taken up last Week, and committed as Runaways, the two following Negroes, viz. the one named Jem, who says he belongs to Alexander Scott, in Lancaster County. The other named Charles, who says he belongs to Joseph Tatloe, near New-Castle. Their Masters are desired to come and pay Charges, and take them away.    JOSEPH THOMAS, Goaler.
*The Pennsylvania Gazette*, May 8, 1766.

FIVE POUNDS Reward.
RUN away, on the 12th Instant, from on board my Shallop, three Servant Men, native Irish; one a Cooper, named Dennis Murphy, of a brown Complexion, wore a Wig, very ordinary Clothes, a coarse white Coat. Another a Shoemaker, of a fair Complexion; wore a Wig, ordinary Clothes, coarse black outside Jacket, and perhaps has a full Kit of Tools. The other a remarkable ordinary Fellow, no Trade; wore his Hair, short Face, and more out-shinned than any Negroe, with a coarse black Coat or Jacket. They all had striped Jackets, and very coarse Yarn Stockings; they were all grey-eyed, about five Feet six Inches high, and well set. They stole two Pieces of Irish Linen, some Womens Velvet, and other Goods. Whoever takes them up, and secures them in any of his Majesty's Goals, shall have Five Pounds Reward for all of them, or a Third of that Sum for either,

paid by DAVID VANDYKE, of Apoquiminy.
*The Pennsylvania Gazette*, May 15, 1766; May 29, 1766; June 5, 1766.
See *The Pennsylvania Journal, and the Weekly Advertiser*, May 22, 1766.

RUN away from the Subscriber, living near New Castle, on Sunday Night last, the 18th of this instant May, an Irish Servant Man, named Henry Cowan, about 24 Years of Age, dark Complexion, about 5 Feet 6 Inches high, pretty fat; had on when he went away, a light blue Serge Coat, Nankeen Jacket and Breeches, white Linen Shirt, white Thread Stockings, new Pumps, and wears his own black Hair; came from Ireland last Fall, in the Ship Marquis of Granby, Captain Macilvaine, and as he is a tolerable Good Scholar, may forge a Pass, perhaps; from under the Captain's Hand. Whoever takes up and secures said Servant, so that his Master may have him again, shall have Five Pounds Reward, and reasonable Charges, paid by MATTHEW CANNON. N. B. All Masters of Vessels are forbid to carry him off at their Peril.
*The Pennsylvania Gazette*, May 22, 1766; June 5, 1766; June 12, 1766.
See *The Pennsylvania Journal, and the Weekly Advertiser*, August 9, 1766.

RUN away, on the 11th of this instant May, an indented Servant Man, named John Carroll, stutters very much, was bought out of New-Castle Goal, by Joshua M'Dowell, the 3d of this Month; had on, when he went away, a Snuff coloured Coat, blue Jacket, old Snuff coloured Breeches, he stole and took with him, a black cut Velvet Jacket, new Shoes, white Linen Shirt, almost new, and broke open a Desk, and tore a Lock to pieces; therefore it is hoped all Person will exert themselves in apprehending him. Whoever takes up said Servant, and secures him in any of His Majesty's Goals, or brings him to the Subscriber living in Chester County, near the Brick Meeting House, shall have Forty Shillings Reward, and reasonable Charges,
paid by   HENRY EWING.
*The Pennsylvania Gazette*, May 22, 1766; May 29, 1766; June 5, 1766.
See *The Pennsylvania Gazette*, June 13, 1765.

May 22.
RUN away the 12th inst. from on board my shallop, three servant men, native Irish, the one named Dennis Murphy, brown complexion, wore a wig, very ordinary cloaths, coarse white coat: The other a shoe maker, fair complexion, wore a wig, ordinary cloths, course black outside jacket, & perhaps has a full kit of tools with him: The other a remarkable ordinary fellow, wore his hair, short fac'd, and more out shin'd than any Negro, a coarse black coat or jacket,

they all had striped jackets and very coarse yarn stockings, they were all grey eyed, about five feet six inches high, well set, they stole two pieces of Irish linnen, some women's velvet and other goods. Whoever takes them up and secures them in any goal, shall have FIVE POUNDS reward for all of them, or a third of that sum for either, paid by
     DAVID VANDIKE of Apoquonamia.
*The Pennsylvania Journal, and the Weekly Advertiser*, May 22, 1766; May 29, 1766. See *The Pennsylvania Gazette*, May 15, 1766; May 29, 1766.

     Christiana Bridge, New-Castle County, May 24, 1766.
STRAYED or stolen about the Middle of April last, a bright bay Horse, with a Blaze in his Face, black Mane and Tail, paces, trots, and hand gallops very free, was trimmed under the Bridle only, four Years old this Spring, 14 Hands high, and shod before. It is supposed he was stolen by a certain Man, who called himself William Floyd, who came from about Albany some Time ago, with his Wife and one Child. Said Floyd is about 5 Feet 11 Inches high, brown Hair, bad Countenance, and his Nose inclining to one Side; his Cloaths not known; he also took with him another Horse, and two Saddles, at the same Time. Whoever takes up and secures said Horse, so as the Subscriber may get him again, shall receive Thirty Shillings Reward, if in Possession of said Floyd, for Horse Thief, Five Pounds,
  paid by  WILLIAM M'MECHEN.
*The Pennsylvania Gazette*, June 5, 1766; June 12, 1766.

     FORTY SHILLINGS Reward.
RUN away, in the night of the 8th inst. June, from Mr. Isaac Janvier's, at Christiana Bridge, a certain John Heran, a bricklayer by trade, about 5 feet 9 inches high; had on a white country made jacket, leather breeches, has a very remarkable red spot above his right brow; he has been inlisted with the Royal Americans, and deserted, and was taken up by them again, and put into Philadelphia goal, and taken out of the same by the subscriber, his master of Baltimore, and come with him his said master as far as Christiana Bridge homewards, but went off with a pair of iron hand-cuffs. Whoever takes up the said servant, and puts him in any of his Majesty's goals, or brings him to Mr. Isaac Janvier, or to his said master, shall have the above reward, and reasonable charges, paid by  CONRAD SMITH.
*The Pennsylvania Gazette*, June 12, 1766; June 26, 1766; July 3, 1766.

     New-Castle, May 20, 1766.
NOW in the Subscriber's Custody, the following Persons, viz. Robert Dunavin, a white Man, committed as a Runaway Servant, says he was

formerly an Apprentice to one Davis, a Carver in Philadelphia, he is about 5 Feet 7 Inches almost naked. Dick, Negroe Man, belonging to John Douglass, in Pequea. A Negroe Man, calls himself John Montgomery, says he belongs to John Keay, near Annapolis. Their Masters are desired to come, pay Charges, and take them away in six Weeks after this Date, otherwise they will be sold for the same, by    ALEXANDER HARVEY, Goaler.

*The Pennsylvania Gazette*, June 19, 1766; June 26, 1766; July 3, 1766.

New-Castle, July 10, 1766.
IN Custody of the Subscriber, the following Prisoners, committed on suspicion of being Runaway Servants, viz. William King, about 5 Feet 10 Inches high, has on a Shirt and Trowsers of home-made Tow cloth. Darby Leonard, says he lived in Kent County, on Delaware; he is about 5 Feet 8 Inches high, has on a Shirt and Trowers of home-spun Linen. Their Masters, if they have any, are hereby desired to come in six Weeks, from the Date hereof, pay charges, and take them away, otherwise they will be sold for the same.        ALEXANDER HARVEY, Goaler.

*The Pennsylvania Gazette*, July 17, 1766; August 14, 1766.

Newcastle, July 23, 1766.
RUN away from the subscriber, living in Newcastle, a servant man, named John Wright, alias John Holderness, I am told he calls himself a four year servant, a well set fellow, fair complexion pock-marked, with short light brown hair, almost flaxen; had on, when he went away, a white flannel jacket, with four or five horn buttons on the breast of it, an ozenbrigs shirt, a pair of coarse striped ticken breeches, a pair of white yarn stockings, his shoes tied with strings, an old felt hat, by trade a weaver, and seems to be a very innocent fellow. Whoever takes up and secures said servant in any of his Majesty's goals, as the subscriber may have him again, shall receive THIRTY SHILLINGS reward, if taken up after the publication of this advertisement, paid by        JACOB LEMMON.

*The Pennsylvania Gazette*, July 23, 1766; July 31, 1766; August 7, 1766; August 21, 1766. See *The Pennsylvania Gazette*, September 18, 1766.

New-Castle, July 30, 1766.
*COMMITTED to the Goal of this County, a certain Henry Lloyd, an Englishman, about 30 Years of Age, 5 Feet 8 or 9 Inches high; has on an old Felt Hat, Ozenbrigs and Striped Ticken Trowsers, and Flannel Jacket. His Master (if he has any) is desired to come, pay Charges, and take him away, otherwise he will be sold for the same, by*
            ALEXANDER HARVEY, Goaler.

*The Pennsylvania Gazette,* August 7, 1766; August 14, 1766; August 21, 1766; September 4, 1766.


*RUN away, in the Night of the 27th of July, from the Subscriber, living in Brandywine Hundred, New-Castle County, an Irish Servant Man, named John M'Dermont, about 25 Years of Age, and about 5 Feet 6 Inches high; had on a blue Cloth lappelled Jacket, without Sleeves, Tow Shirt, and Trowsers, and took with him a Hemp Shirt, a pair of turned Pumps, and a Pair of blue Worsted Stockings. He is a down looking Fellow, of a sandy Complexion, his Hair cut off, and has with him an old brown Wig, and old Felt Hat; he is much addicted to strong Drink, and has a large Scar under one of his Jaws, which has been a running Sore. Whoever takes up said Servant, and secures him in any of his Majesty'sGoals, so as his Master may have him again, or brings him to his said Master, living within two Miles of Wilmington, shall have Three Pounds Reward, and reasonable Charges,*
   *paid by me*   PAUL RALSTON.
*The Pennsylvania Gazette,* August 7, 1766; August 14, 1766; August 28, 1766. See *The Pennsylvania Gazette,* April 21, 1768.

May 29.
RUN away from the subscriber, living in New-Castle county and hundred upon Delaware, an Irish servant man, named Henry Cowan, has served about 8 months; had on when he went away, a pale blue serge coat with yellow mettal buttons, boot sleeved, buff coloured nankeen jacket and breeches, also a pair of buckskin breeches, thread stockings, calfskin pumps, and a pair of carved brass buckles, one of them broke, and has four shirts, three of them check'd, had on an old beaver hat, and an old silk handkerchief about his neck: he is about 5 feet 6 inches high, he is a little set man, with pretty long dark brown hair, he is about 24 years of age, swarthy complexion a good scholar and a small fellow, perhaps may counterfeit a pass from some of the captains which came in last fall or this year, as a discharge from them for his passage. Whoever takes up the said servant and secures him in any gaol so that his master may have him again shall have FIVE POUNDS reward and reasonable charges paid by me   MATTHEW CANNAN.
*The Pennsylvania Journal, and the Weekly Advertiser,* August 9, 1766. See *The Pennsylvania Gazette,* May 22, 1766.


THREE POUNDS Reward.
RUN away on the 18th of last month, from the subscriber, living in St. George's, New-Castle county, a Scotch servant man, named John Young, about 25 years of age, about 5 feet 8 or 9 inches high, is stoop shouldered,

has sandy coloured hair, is smooth faced, and has a red beard; had on, when he went away, only a shirt of flax and tow linen, and old tow linen trowsers. As he had some discourse with some Recruiting Officers that came down the country, it is thought that he may endeavour to meet with them at Philadelphia. Whoever takes up said servant and secures him, so that his master may have him again, shall receive the above reward

    from SAMUEL SMITH.

N. B. All masters of vessels are forbid to carry him off at their peril.

 *The Pennsylvania Gazette*, August 14, 1766; August 28, 1766; September 11, 1766.

    THREE POUNDS Reward.

RUN away, on the 12th inst. from the Subscriber, living in Christiana Hundred, New-Castle County, an Irish Servant Man, named Peter Purcell, lately came in with Captain Murphy, from Dublin; a well set Fellow, of a fair Complexion, by Trade a Weaver, about five Feet three Inches high, has red Hair, which he commonly wears tied: Had on and took with him, a grey Bearskin Jacket, two Linsey Jackets, both lapelled, a half-worn Felt Hat, and old Trowsers. Whoever takes up and secures said Servant, so as his Master may have him again, shall have the above Reward, if ten Miles from Home, if under, Thirty Shillings, and reasonable Charges,

   paid by  CORNELIUS STIDHAM.

It is supposed he is gone towards Philadelphia, or Lancaster.

 *The Pennsylvania Gazette*, August 21, 1766; September 4, 1766; September 11, 1766.

           August 28th, 1766.

RUN away from the Subscriber, living in New-Castle county, in Appoquiminy hundred, the 26th instant, a servant man, named John Moore, about 23 years of age, had on, when he went away, a dirty shirt, and a pair of new ozenbrigs trowsers, and an old felt hat, he wears his own hair, and commonly wears it tied, it curls at the end, is of a fair colour, he hath grey eyes, and the little finger of his left hand stands quite straight, which came by the cut of a sickle last harvest, and hath a small scar below his left nostril, is about 5 feet 6 inches high, a pale looking fellow; he served his time, till he was of age, with Mr. Andrew Metere, in Chestnut Level; he is this country born, and pretends to know something belonging to the carpenter's trade; whosoever takes up, and secures the said servant, so that his master may have him again, shall have three pounds reward and reasonable charges,

   paid by me  ROBERT MURPHEY.

N. B. The said Master was special bail to the sheriff of the said county, for twenty pounds penalty; and therefore all persons are forwarned not to harbour him at their peril.

*The Pennsylvania Gazette*, September 11, 1766; September 18, 1766; September 25, 1766.

TWENTY POUNDS Reward.
Newcastle, September 13, 1766.
BROKE out of the Goal of this County last Night, the two following Prisoners, to wit, Daniel Alexander, a tall slim Fellow, about 30 Years of Age, about 6 Feet high, his Clothing uncertain, as he may be assisted in changing them, it is probable he may push toward Carolina, as he has Friends there. The other named William Bowen, about 35 Years of Age, 5 Feet 8 or 9 Inches high; he is a simple looking Fellow. Whoever apprehends said Prisoners, and secures them, so that the Subscriber, may have them again, shall have the above Reward, or fifteen Pounds for Alexander, and five Pounds for Bowen, and reasonable Charges,
        paid by    THOMAS DUFF, Sheriff.
*The Pennsylvania Gazette*, September 18; 1766; September 25, 1766; October 2, 1766; December 4, 1766; December 18, 1766; January 1, 1767; January 15, 1767; January 22, 1767.


STOLEN from the Subscriber, living in Mill-Creek Hundred, Newcastle County, on Delaware, the following Articles, viz. Fourteen Pounds Currency, in Bills of Twenty Shillings each, Six Pounds in British Coin, such as Crowns, Half Crowns, and Shillings, with two Pieces of gold, Value Thirty Shillings. Likewise a Gown of Sattin Silk, striped white, yellow and red, lined with Sarsnet, with a petticoat of the same; together with several other Articles. The thief supposed to be an Irish Woman, named Mary Hart, about 5 Feet 2 Inches high, well set, sandy coloured hair, of a fair complexion, talks much, and is apt to drink freely. She is supposed to have gone towards New York, as she had contracted an Acquaintance with one Cummings, who she called Cousin, who, it is alledged, is confederate with her, and said he was a going that way; he says he is a Seaman, is about 5 Feet 8 Inches high, of a dark Complexion, speaks a good deal of the Irish tone, and is remarkable for using the Expression, Great Luck to me. These are therefore to inform the Public, that if any Person shall apprehend said Mary Hart, with any of the above mentioned Articles, in her Custody, and commit her to any of his Majesty's Goals, shall have FIVE POUNDS Reward and reasonable Charges, paid by      MARY HAMELON.
*The Pennsylvania Gazette*, September 18, 1766; October 2, 1766.

Newcastle, September 2, 1766.
RUN away from the Subscriber, John Wright, a well set Fellow, about 5 Feet 7 or 8 Inches high, fair faced, a little pock marked, with light brown Hair,

almost a Flaxen; had on, when he went away, a white Flannel Jacket, with four or five Horn Buttons on the Breast, an Ozenbrigs Shirt, a Pair of coarse striped ticken Breeches, an old Felt Hat, and was barefooted; he says he is an English Man, a Weaver by Trade, and pretends to be a very innocent Fellow; this is twice he has run away; he is a four Year Servant, and lately came in with Capt. M'Carty, from Dublin. The above Servant has a Way of putting his Hand in a crooked Form, like as if he had not the Use of it, and one of his Fellow servants says he intends to travel as a Cripple, till he gets quite away. Any Person who will take up said Wright, and lodge him in any of his Majesty's goals, so that his Master may have him again, shall have Twenty Shillings Reward, paid by       JACOB LEMMON.

*The Pennsylvania Gazette,* September 18, 1766; September 25, 1766; October 2, 1766. See *The Pennsylvania Gazette,* July 23, 1766.


New-Castle, September 4, 1766.
COMMITTED to the goal of this county, a negroe man, who says he belongs to Thomas Bishop, speaks bad English, about 40 years of age, about 5 feet 7 inches high; had on, when brought here, an old felt hat, home-made tow shirt and trowsers, negroe kersey jacket, with large brass buttons. His master is hereby desired to come, pay charges, and take him away, otherwise he will be sold for the same by      ALEXANDER HARVEY, goaler.

*The Pennsylvania Gazette,* September 18, 1766; October 2, 1766.


Newcastle, October 4, 1766.
FIVE POUNDS Reward.
BROKE out of the goal of this county last night, a certain Francis Consiglio, a slim fellow, about 5 feet 8 or 9 inches high, a Shop Joiner by trade; has lived in Philadelphia, Newport, and Wilmington had on, a blue coat, red jacket, long trowsers, has a droll way of speaking, was committed for divers felonies. Whoever apprehends said prisoner, and secures him, so that the subscriber may have him, shall have the above reward, paid by
            THOMAS DUFF, Sheriff.
N. B. He is an Englishman, and a very great villain, was connected with a knot of thieves at Philadelphia, therefore I think it every man's duty, whom he falls in the way of, to apprehend him.

*The Pennsylvania Gazette,* October 9, 1766; October 16, 1766. See *The Pennsylvania Gazette,* December 18, 1766.


RUN away from the Subscriber in Newport, an Irish Servant Man, named John Purday, and Mary, his Wife, the said John Purday is about 5 Feet 9

Inches high, and about 27 Years of Age, is pitted with the Small pox, has strait pale Hair commonly tied behind; had on, when he went away, a light coloured Coat, and Thickset Jacket and Breeches, Worsted Stockings, his Hat sharp cocked, and appears very neat in his Clothes, has been a Soldier in Flanders, speaks very good English, a little inclined to the Scotch Accent. His Wife is a little short thin woman, dark Complexion, dark frizled hair, speaks broad Scotch. They are about 6 Weeks in from Ireland, and came in the Ship Marquis of Granby. Whoever takes up the said John Purday, so as his Master may have him again, shall have Twenty Shillings Reward, and reasonable Charges, paid by me ROBERT ALL, or by applying to Mr. JAMES ALEXANDER, Merchant in Water street, Philadelphia.
    ROBERT ALL.
*The Pennsylvania Gazette*, October 30, 1766; November 20, 1766; December 11, 1766.


RUN away, on Thursday, the 23d of October last, a Servant Man, named Alexander Hamilton, aged about 35 Years, a well set Fellow, and smooth faced; had on, a blue Broadcloth Coat, and a blue Jockey Coat, wears a Wig, and has a Brother living near New York, or in New England; he came over last September from Londonderry, in the Ship Marquis of Granby. Whoever secures said Servant, so that either of the Subscribers may have him again, shall have Three Pounds Reward, and reasonable Charges, paid by JOHN SINGLETON, or RICHARD M'WILLIAMS, Esq; in New Castle County,
    or JAMES M'MULLEN, in York County.
N. B. He has been in this Country before, a Soldier.
*The Pennsylvania Gazette*, November 6, 1766; November 20, 1766; December 11, 1766.


RUN away, the 29th of October, from the Subscriber, living at Christine Bridge, Newcastle county, a convict servant woman, named Alice M'Carty, alias Eleanor Brown, about 35 years of age, born in Ireland, has brown hair, very lusty and fat; had on, and took with her, an old brown camblet gown, 2 short gowns, the one white linen, the other dark calicoe, both new, a cream coloured skirt, a red quilt, 2 check aprons, a pair of neat made mens shoes, and a pair of diamond cut silver buckles, marked E. H. a linen handkerchief, spotted red and white, coarse sheet and blanket, and a pair of womens shoes, all which she stole when she went away; it is supposed she is in company with a man, his name unknown. Said servant has been several times whipped in the workhouse, in Philadelphia, and whipped for theft at the public post.
N. B. The master of the servant forgot to put his name to his advertisement.

*The Pennsylvania Gazette,* November 13, 1766; November 20, 1766; November 27, 1766. Second and third ads omit the line beginning N. B. and end with: "Whoever takes up and secures said servant, so as her master may have her again, shall have FORTY SHILLINGS reward, paid by     WILLIAM HENDERSON."

*EIGHT DOLLARS Reward.*
RUN away, on Saturday, the 22d of November, an apprentice boy, about 19 years of age, a shoemaker by trade, about 5 feet 8 inches high, has brown hair, tied behind, of a yellow complexion, and a down look; had on a brown outside jacket, a green waistcoat, old leather breeches, yarn stockings, old shoes, and a half worn hat. He is a Swede, but many take him for a Dutchman: He has three letters of his name marked on one of is arms, I. S. B. Whoever takes up and secures said apprentice, so that his master may have him again, shall have the above reward, and reasonable charges,
          paid by     THOMAS ROBINSON, *in Wilmington.*
*The Pennsylvania Gazette,* November 27, 1766; December 11, 1766; December 18, 1766.


RUN away, on the 18th of November, from the Subscriber, living in Christine, New Castle County, a Servant Man, named James Sweney, about 5 Feet 6 or 7 Inches high, took with him a brown or Snuff coloured Cloth Coat, a grey Jacket, with a turn-up Cuff, with three Buttons on the Cuff, a Pair of Buckskin Breeches, a Pair of ribbed Stockings, and a Pair of Channel Pumps, and a Half-worn Castor Hat. He is a down looking Fellow, about 18 Years of Age, with dark coloured Hair; he has likewise some old Cloths with him. Whoever takes up said Servant, shall have Three Pounds Reward, and reasonable Charges, paid by     STEPHEN MENDENHALL.
*The Pennsylvania Gazette,* November 27, 1766; December 11, 1766; December 18, 1766. See *The Pennsylvania Gazette,* February 12, 1767.


                    New Castle County, Dec. 5, 1766.
NOW in the custody of the subscriber, the three following persons, viz. Samuel Galloway, about 35 years of age, about 5 feet 9 inches high, wears a cap, a blue cloth coat, with white metal buttons, thickset waistcoat, and light coloured cloth breeches, was committed the 10th of July last as a vagrant, and on suspicion of horse stealing, and it is suspected that he has escaped from some goal.
    Also a certain William Muheaw, about 20 years of age, about 5 feet 4 inches high, light brown hair, by trade a tinker; had on, when committed, a brown broadcloth coat and waistcoat, with mohair buttons, striped Holland

trowsers, white worsted stockings, and half boots, committed 21st of October last as a runaway; says his master's name is Thomas Beech, and lives in Arundel County, in the province of Maryland.

Also a negroe lad, about 19 years of age; about 5 feet 6 inches high, slender made, speaks bad English, pretends to be foolish, to obtain his freedom, calls himself Cato, and says he belongs to Samuel Jones, at Grubb's Iron Works, in Lancaster County; had on, when committed, an Indian blanket coat, ragged tow trowsers, and old shoes, with strings. Their masters (if any they have) are desired to come, pay charges, and take them away in six weeks, or they will be sold out for the same by

                THOMAS PUSEY, Goaler.

*The Pennsylvania Gazette*, December 11, 1766; December 18, 1766; January 1, 1767; January 15, 1767; January 29, 1767; February 26, 1767.

                            *Philadelphia, December* 17, 1766.
BROKE out of the Goal of this City last Night, the following Persons, viz. David Smith, aged 36 Years, about 5 Feet 5 Inches high, dark thin visage, his Hair lately cut off; had on a light brown Coat, red Jacket, and black Stockings; he lately kept Store at Reckless Town, New-Jersey.

John Morrison, aged about 30 Years, 5 Feet 8 Inches high, of a sandy Complexion; had on a brown Cloth Coat, striped Cotton Jacket, Leather Breeches, and black Stockings.

William Bowman, about 28 Years old, 5 Feet 10 Inches high, of a dark Complexion, long black Hair, long visaged, a little Pock-marked; had on a light blue grey Coat, red Jacket, Stocking Breeches, and white Thread Stockings.

Francis Consiglio, 25 Years old, about 5 Feet 7 Inches high, wears his own long black Hair, mostly tied behind; had on two red Jackets, Buckskin Breeches, and white Thread Stockings.

Michael Haggerty, about 25 Years old, 5 Feet 6 Inches high, knock kneed; had on a striped Woolsey Jacket, with Sleeves, a black Velvet Jacket, old buff coloured Stocking Breeches, and black Stockings.

John Fitzgerald, about 5 Feet 7 Inches high, about 40 Years old; had on a Flannel Jacket, old Leather Breeches, wore his own black short Hair, and is of a very dark Complexion.

James Price, about 5 Feet 3 Inches high, about 30 Years old.

Oliver Moles, about 5 Feet 11 Inches high, about 34 Years old.

William Conway, about 5 Feet 5 Inches high, about 27 Years old.

Alexander Auckintack, an Irishman, about 5 Feet 5 Inches high, about 30 Years old. Whoever takes up the above Persons, shall have the following Rewards, viz. Ten Pounds for David Smith; Five Pounds for Francis

Consiglio; and Forty Shillings for each of the others, and reasonable Charges, paid by　　　　WILLIAM PARR, Sheriff.
*The Pennsylvania Gazette*, December 18, 1766. See *The Pennsylvania Gazette*, October 9, 1766, for Consiglio.

## 1767

Carlisle Goal, Cumberland County, Jan. 24, 1767.
NOW in the said Goal, on Suspicion of being Runaways, the two following described Fellows, viz. Daniel Edwards, a Molattoe, near six Feet high, a very stout well built Fellow, about 35 Years of Age, plays on the Fiddle, says he is a free Man, and was born in the City of Boston. James Sweney, a young slim Lad, says he belongs to, and run away from, Stephen Mendenhall, of New Castle County, near Wilmington. Their Masters (if any they have) are hereby notified to come and take them away, otherwise they will be sold out for their Fees within six Weeks from the Date hereof,
by HENRY CUNNINGHAM, Goaler.
*The Pennsylvania Gazette*, February 12, 1767; February 26, 1767; March 12, 1767. See *The Pennsylvania Gazette*, November 27, 1766.


RUN away, on the 10th of January, from the Subscriber, living in St. George's Hundred, New-Castle County, a Servant Man, named William Hewes, born in Philadelphia, about 5 Feet 4 Inches high, fair Complexion, round Face, about 21 Years of Age, has lost a Joint of the fore Finger of his Left Hand: Had on, when he went away, a knit Cap, with brown, red and white Diamonds, coarse homespun Cloth Jacket, and a brown under Jacket, Buckskin Breeches, blue Yarn Stockings, and good Shoes, with Brass Buckles. He has been in several parts of Europe, and came last from Ireland, says he served some time with James Chattin, Printer. He is supposed to be gone toward Philadelphia. All Masters of Vessels are desired not to harbour or carry him off. Whoever takes up said Servant, and secures him, so as his Master may have him again, shall have Thirty Shillings Reward, and reasonable Charges, paid by　　　　HENRY WALL.
*The Pennsylvania Gazette*, February 19, 1767; February 26, 1767; March 12, 1767.


*RUN away from the subscriber, living in St. George's hundred, New-Castle county, on the 21st of February, an apprentice lad, named John M'Clean, country born, about 18 years of age, middle sized, full faced, black hair; had on, when he went away, a light coloured country cloth coat and breeches, with metal buttons, and has with him sundry clothes in a bundle, amongst*

which are two new home made shirts, one fine ditto, a new fine hat, &c. &c. supposed to be in company with a certain John Edger, a Thresher. If they are both taken together, and secured, so that they may be brought to justice, the person so apprehending them shall receive Three Pounds reward, or Forty Shillings, with reasonable charges, for securing M'Clean,
        paid by   JAMES LATTOMUS.
*The Pennsylvania Gazette*, March 5, 1767; March 19, 1767; April 2, 1767.

                                                                          February 19.
RUN AWAY, on Wednesday the 11th of this instant February, from the subscriber, living in Brandewine hundred, county of New-Castle, an Irish servant man named James Walker, about twenty-eight or thirty years of age, about 5 feet 5 inches high, a slim fellow, small boned, down look, dark complexion, wears his own dark hair, which is but thin and strait; had on when he absconded, a half worn cloth coat of a whitish colour, made jacket fashion, with an old jacket under, and buckskin breeches almost new, with strings at the knees, yarn stockings with one thread black, the other white, an old white shirt, old shoes which were soaled, copper buckles, and an old wool hat: he is much given to strong drink, and says he was some years aboard of a man of war; it is supposed that he took some cash with him, and may change his cloathing and name. Whoever takes up and secures said servant, so that his master may have him again, shall have FORTY SHILLINGS reward
        paid by       JAMES HUSTON.
N. B. All masters of vessels are forbid to harbour or carry him off at their peril.
   *The Pennsylvania Journal, and the Weekly Advertiser*, February 19, 1767; February 26, 1767; March 5, 1767. See *The Pennsylvania Gazette*, May 2, 1765.


RUN away, the 17th of March last, from the subscriber, living in St. George's hundred, New-Castle county, a Negroe man, named Tom, about 30 years of age, 5 feet 6 or 7 inches high, a remarkable hollow spot on one of his cheeks, big lips, with his teeth standing out, a sly artful fellow when sober, and a great fool when in liquor, which he is very subject to be; had on, when he went away, a lead coloured pair of breeches, three jackets, one blue, without sleeves; one black and white mixed in the loom, and the other brown colour, black and white stockings, a new shirt of tow linen, half-worn shoes, a felt hat, and worsted cap; it is supposed he will make for Somerset County, in Maryland, being born there. Whoever takes up and secures the said slave in any county goal, or other wise, so that his master may have him again, shall have Forty Shillings reward, and reasonable charges,

paid by ANDREW BRYAN.
*The Pennsylvania Gazette*, April 2, 1767; April 16, 1767; April 30, 1767.

RUN away from the Subscriber, living in White-clay Creek Hundred, New Castle County, on the 30th of March, an Apprentice Man, named Thomas Martin, about 25 Years of Age, and about 5 Feet 6 Inches high, full faced, fresh coloured, thick set, down looking, red Beard, brown Hair, cut short on the top of his Head: Had on and took with him, when he went away, a light coloured Cloth Coat and Jacket, with Metal Buttons, a short white Napt Jacket, with Leather Buttons, Leather Breeches, Check Shirts, Stockings both Worsted and Yarn, one Paid of white Yarn Ditto, a new coarse Hat, and old Ditto, new Winter Shoes, double soaled, stitched through the Soles as double-channelled Pumps in several Rows, an old Pair of Ditto, Steel Buckles, and sundry other Clothes; he is subject to Drink, and took with him a new Canoe, newly paid with Turpentine and Tar all over, and a Rope spliced at both Ends, with Eyes, and in her Bow. Whoever takes up and secures the said Fellow, so that he may be had again, shall have Forth Shillings Reward, and reasonable Charges, and for the Canoe Five Shillings,
paid by RICHARD DENNIS.
*The Pennsylvania Gazette*, April 9, 1767; April 23, 1767; April 30, 1767.

RUN away from the Subscriber, in Newark, New-Castle County, last Night, a Servant Man, named Samuel Rice, an Irishman, about 50 Years of Age, about 5 Feet 10 Inches high, has short brown Hair, mixed with grey, his Features surly and roguish, swears horridly, is a Wool-Comber by Trade, very handy about a House, and can do most Sorts of Country Work: Had on, when he went away, a light coloured short Coat, brown Jacket, both with Horn Buttons, brown Breeches, of Country made Cloth, brown Worsted Stockings, a fine Tow Cloth Shirt, and a Pair of Shoes; he took with him a Check Shirt, and a Pair of Shoes; it is very probable he will change his Name, as he has already, having assumed the Name of John Brown; he tells a deal about his being at the Havannah, and on board Ship the last War; he was taken up last Fall in the Jerseys, and brought to Philadelphia Goal. Whoever takes up said Servant, and brings him to his Master, in Newark aforesaid, or secures him, so that his Master may have him again, shall have Forty Shillings Reward, and reasonable Charges, paid by
*April* 17. JAMES POPHAM.

*The Pennsylvania Gazette,* April 23, 1767; April 30, 1767; May 7, 1767; May 28, 1767; June 4, 1767; June 11, 1767. See *The New-York Mercury,* April 27, 1767.


RUN-away from the Subscriber, in the Night of the 16th of April Instant, living at Newark, Newcastle County, and Province of Pennsylvania, [sic] a Servant Man named Samuel Rice, an Irishman: he is about 50 Years of Age, 5 Feet 10 Inches high, has short brown hair, mixed with grey, his Features surly and rough, swears horridly, a Wooll-comber by Trade, very handy about a House, and can do most Sorts of Country Work: Had on when he went away, a light-coloured short Coat, a brown Jacket, both with Horn Buttons, brown Breeches of Country Cloth, brown Worsted Stockings, a fine Tow Cloth Shirt, and a Pair of Shoes; he took with him a Check Shirt, and a Pair of Shoes; and it is very probable he will change his Name, as he has already done, having assumed the Name of John Brown; he talks much about his having been at the Havannah, and at Sea the last War, was taken up last Fall in the Jersies, and bro't to Philadelphia Goal. Whoever takes up said Servant, and brings him to his Master, at Newark aforesaid, or secures him so that his Master may have him again, shall have *Forty Shillings* Reward, and reasonable Charges paid, by     JAMES POPHAM.

*The New-York Mercury,* April 27, 1767; May 4, 1767; May 18, 1767; June 1, 1767. See *The Pennsylvania Gazette,* April 23, 1767.


RUN away from the subscriber, living at the Cross Roads, near New-Castle, a servant man, named Samuel Smith, about 34 years of age, about 5 feet 7 inches high, pock-marked, short black hair, and a Roman nose; he speaks Erse, [sic] is much given to drink, swears much when in liquor, and came from Ireland last fall with Capt. M'Ilvaine; had on a brown cloth coat and jacket, buckskin breeches, and new shoes. There is supposed to be with him a servant, named Samuel Price, a Woolcomber, and has been long in this country. Whoever takes up said servants, and secures them, to that their masters may have them again, shall have Four Pounds for both, or Forty Shillings for each, with reasonable charges, paid by ANDI M'BAY,
or JOHN SINGLETON.

*The Pennsylvania Gazette,* April 30, 1767; May 14, 1767; May 21, 1767.

RUN away, on Thursday, the 30th of April last, from the subscriber, a servant man, named Thomas Tolbot, a lusty well set fellow, about 5 feet 8 inches high, wears straight hair, is slow of speech, and addicted to drinking: Had on, when he went away, a light coloured Wilton coat, much worn, a double

breasted white waistcoat, and buckskin breeches; he is supposed to have taken with him a servant woman, called Eleanor Clemens, a short good looking woman, about 28 or 30 years old; she has with her a brown stuff, and 2 or 3 calicoe gowns, and a good black silk cloak and a hat. It is probable they have taken more clothes than are here described. Whoever secures the above servants, shall have TWENTY SHILLINGS, reward for each, and reasonable charges, paid by        WILLIAM NEWNAN.
    *The Pennsylvania Gazette*, May 14, 1767; July 9, 1767; September 10, 1767; September 17, 1767. All but the first ad end with the line: "N. B. It is supposed he has a forged pass."


RUN away, on the 23d Instant, at Night, from the Subscribers, living near Christiana Ferry, in New-Castle County, a Servant Man, named John Johnson, born in this Country, about 22 Years of Age, 5 Feet 8 Inches high, and well set, of a fair Complexion, wears his own fair Hair, is very talkative in Company, inclinable to Merriment, and has a remarkable Scar on his Nose; had on, when he went away, a light spotted Coat, blue Jacket, made in the Sailors Fashion, Leather Breeches, Tow Trowsers, one Check and one white Shirt, pretty good Shoes and Stockings, and a good Beaver Hat, but it is supposed he may have changed his Clothes. Whoever takes up said Servant, and secures him, so as his Owners may have him again, shall have Forty Shillings Reward, and reasonable Charges, paid by
    ANDREW STALCOP, and THOMAS SUTHERLAND.
N. B. All Masters of Vessels are forbid to carry him off at their Peril.
    *The Pennsylvania Gazette*, May 28, 1767; June 4, 1767; June 11, 1767.

FIVE POUNDS Reward.
STOLEN from the Subscriber, living in Newark, New-Castle County, on Saturday Night, the 27th of June, a bay Horse, with a Star in his Forehead, half of his Mane lately cut, but grown again, shod all round, paces and trots, thick and well made, 6 years old, about 15 hands high, supposed to be stolen by a Man, who calls himself John Williams, wore a blue Surtout Coat, had Check or striped Trowsers on, black Hair, and is a sour looking Fellow. Whoever secures the said Horse and Thief, so as he may be brought to Justice, shall receive the above Reward, or Thirty Shillings for the Horse only,
    paid by     SAMUEL PLATT.
    *The Pennsylvania Gazette*, July 9, 1767; July 16, 1767; July 30, 1767.

Wilmington, New-Castle county, June 28, 1767.
THEN left the house of BENJAMIN ENOCH, in Wilmington, one Hannah Abraham, alias Hannah Stalcop, a lunatick, far advanced in years, and talks

both Dutch and English; had on only her common wearing apparel, no shoes, or any thing worth mentioning, is about 5 feet high, and has short hair: These are therefore to desire she may be stopt and kept, so as the subscribers may have an account of her; for which, or the bringing her home, a reasonable reward will be paid by
      BENJAMIN ENOCH, or ANDREW CRIPS.
*The Pennsylvania Gazette*, August 20, 1767; September 3, 1767; September 10, 1767.

                    August 13.
RUN-away, on the 11th day of September last, from the subscriber at Princeton, New-Jersey, An Irish servant girl named Mary Croane, about 26 years of age, a middle sized woman, was supposed to be secreted by Robert Nemins at Princeton, and by him conveyed to his son William Nemins living at Brandywine Rocks near Christeen Ferry, and there it's said passed for said William's servant, was challenged by James Saunders the forepart of April last, at the house of Henry Bracken, about five miles from New-Port in New-Castle County, but he, the said Saunders, being detained by said Bracken and his sons till said Mary made her escape. Whoever takes up said servant and secures her in any of his Majesty's goals, so that her master may have her again, shall have THIRTY SHILLINGS reward, and all reasonable charges paid by Daniel Balis at the Head of Elk, or
      WILLIAM MOUNTEER.
*The Pennsylvania Journal, and the Weekly Advertiser*, August 13, 1767; August 20, 1767.

       SIX POUNDS Reward.
RUN away, on Monday, the 17th instant, from the subscriber, living near Newark, New-Castle county, the following servants, viz. One named JOHN BRYAN, about 25 years of age, an Irishman, 5 feet 8 inches high, an arch fellow, being an old soldier, and a rope-maker by trade, given much to drink and swearing, cannot see with his left eye, his hair newly cut very short before; had on a tow shirt, striped linsey trowsers, no shoes known of. The other, an Irishman, named JOHN MILIGEN, aged about 26 years, about the same height of the other; had on a tow shirt, tow petticoat trowsers, supposed to have a good pair of shoes, has a down look when spoke to, with often repeating his Words, hat off, and stroking his hair back, and very complaisant, often repeating the word, Sir.—They took with them each a bundle of womens clothes, and it is supposed has a woman in company with them, who is of a small size, and very brazen in countenance and behaviour; it is thought they will make for New York and Albany. Those apprehending the said servants, shall have the above reward,
    paid by  JOSHUA M'DOWELL.

*The Pennsylvania Gazette*, August 27, 1767; September 3, 1767; September 10, 1767. See *The Pennsylvania Gazette*, October 15, 1767.

Chester goal, August 22, 1767.
THIS day was committed to my custody, as a runaway, a certain TOBIAS STEDHAM, who says he is a servant to Matthew Crips, of the borough of Wilmington; also a negroe lad, named JACK, who says he belongs to Mr. Thomas Burke, in Philadelphia. Their masters are desired to come, pay charges, and take them away, by     JOSEPH THOMAS, goaler.

*The Pennsylvania Gazette*, August 27, 1767; September 3, 1767; September 17, 1767.

*Sussex County, on Delaware, Three Run Mills,*
*September* 22, 1767.
TEN POUNDS Reward.
RUN away, from the Subscriber, on the 13th instant, a Mulatto slave, named HARRY, about 40 years of age, 5 feet 6 inches high, and well-set: Had on when he went away, a brown cloth coat, white linen jacket, and brown breeches; he was bred a miller, and understands very well how to manufacture flour, and can invoice the same; is much given to strong drink, and playing on the violin; understands the carpenter's and mill wright's business middling well; was removed from East-New-Jersey in the year 1762, by one Nicholas Veight, who lived at Rocky-Hill, and kept a mill; and the said fellow has a free Mulatto wife, named Peg, and two children.— I expect they will endeavour to get together (though they did not run away at one time)—it is expected they will endeavour to get to the Province of East New-Jersey; it is imagined said Mulatto has a pass.
Any person or persons that takes up and secures the said Mulatto, and delivers him to CHARLES WHARTON, Merchant, in Philadelphia, or to the subscriber, shall have the above reward of Ten Pounds, if taken in the province of New-Jersey, and Six Pounds if in the province of Pennsylvania,
          paid by     LEVIN CRAPPER.
N. B. The said Mulatto woman, named Peg, has run away from her bail, at Lewis Court, in Sussex county.

*The Pennsylvania Chronicle, and Universal Advertiser*, From Monday, September 21, to Monday, September 28, 1767. See *The Pennsylvania Gazette*, October 1, 1767, *The Pennsylvania Gazette*, June 30, 1768, and *The Pennsylvania Chronicle, and Universal Advertiser*, From Monday, June 27, to Monday, July 4, 1768.

Sussex county, on Delaware, Three Run Mills, Sept. 22, 1767.
TEN POUNDS Reward.

RUN away, from the subscriber, on the 13th instant, a mulattoe slave, named HARRY, about 40 years of age, 5 feet 6 inches high, and well set. Had on, when he went away, a brown cloth coat, white linen jacket, and brown breeches; he was bred a miller, and understands very well how to manufacture flour, and can invoice the same; is much given to strong drink, and playing on the violin; understands the carpenter's and mill-wright's businesses, middling well was removed from East New-Jersey in the year 1762, by one Nicholas Veight, who lived at Rockey-Hill, and kept a mill. The said fellow has a free mulattoe wife, named Peg, and two children, and I expect they will endeavour to get together (though they did not run away at one time) it is expected they will endeavour to get to the province of East New-Jersey; it is imagined said mulattoe has a pass. Any person or persons that takes up and secures the said mulattoe, and delivers him to CHARLES WHARTON, merchant, in Philadelphia, or to the subscriber, shall have the above reward of Ten Pounds, if taken in the province of New-Jersey, and Six Pounds if in the province of Pennsylvania, paid by LEVIN CRAPPER.
N. B. The said mulattoe woman, named Peg, has run away from her bail, at Lewis Court, in Sussex county.

*The Pennsylvania Gazette*, October 1, 1767; October 8, 1767; October 22, 1767. See *The Pennsylvania Chronicle, and Universal Advertiser*, From Monday, September 21, to Monday, September 28, 1767; *The Pennsylvania Gazette*, June 30, 1768, and *The Pennsylvania Chronicle, and Universal Advertiser*, From Monday, June 27, to Monday, July 4, 1768.

SIX POUNDS Reward.

RUN away, on Monday, the 17th of August, from the subscriber, living near Newark, New-Castle county, the following servants, viz. John Bryn, an Irishman, aged about 25 years, 5 feet 7 or 8 inches high, an arch fellow, being an old soldier in the American expeditions, both to the westward and northward, a ropemaker by trade, given much to drink and swearing, and trembles very much with his hands, blind of the left eye, but open and clear; and as he is a tolerable good scholar, probably will write passes for himself and the other, and will be apt to talk about New-Castle and Wilmington, as he is well known in both places, has short black hair, lately cut short before, a midling slim built fellow; had on a tow shirt, striped linen trowsers, an old spotted jacket, no shoes nor hat known of. The other an Irishman, named John Milighen, aged about 26 years, 5 feet 9 or 10 inches high, given to drink, and swears when in liquor, is a good butcher, having served a time to that trade in Ireland, a midling set fellow, thin faced; had on a tow shirt, tow petticoat trowsers, striped linen jacket, and a pair of new shoes, tied with thongs, has a down look when spoke to, with often repeating the word Sir, and stroking his hair back, with his hat off, and looking downwards. Whoever takes up

and secures said servants, so as their master may have them again, shall have the above reward, paid by JOSHUA M'DOWELL.
*The Pennsylvania Gazette*, October 15, 1767; October 22, 1767; November 5, 1767. See *The Pennsylvania Gazette*, August 27, 1767.

RUN away from the subscriber, about two weeks ago, an Irish servant man, named John Morrow, about 5 feet 10 inches high, aged about 20 years; had on, when he went away, a blue coat, lined with white shalloon, new shoes, trowsers, and sundry other cloathing, and collected upwards of Eight Pounds of his master's money; he has a scar on his cheek, like a half moon. Whoever secures said servant, and brings him to New-Castle goal, shall have Five Pounds reward, and reasonable charges, or Three Pounds, if secured in any other goal, so that his master may have him again,
   paid by THOMAS MOODY.
*The Pennsylvania Gazette*, October 15, 1767; October 29, 1767; November 12, 1767.

     FIFTY SHILLINGS Reward.
RUN away from the subscriber, on the 27th ult. an Irish servant man, named John Ryan, he is about 30 years of age, 5 feet 6 or 7 inches high, fresh complexion, thin black hair; had on, when he went away, an old felt hat, commonly wears the fore part down, an old brown coat, broke at the elbows, with plaits behind, and different sorts of metal buttons, spotted flannel jacket, half worn, coarse shirt, long trowsers, broke at the knees, and old black stocking breeches, under them, half worn shoes; he was sold out of Caecil goal, and stole his indentures; he lived some time with Dr. Vanlier, above Chester. Whoever takes up said Servant, and secures him in any goal, so that the subscriber may have him again, shall have the above reward, and reasonable charges, if brought to New-Castle,
   paid by CORNELIUS DEVENNY.
*The Pennsylvania Gazette*, November 19, 1767; December 3, 1767.

RUN away from the subscriber, an Irish servant lad, named MICHAEL CANNAN, about 17 or 18 years of age, about 5 feet 2 or 3 inches high, black complexion, wears his own short black hair, trimmed before, but supposed to be somewhat grown; has on, when he went away, a striped linsey jacket, with a white flannel under jacket, a pair of leather breeches, too long for him, and patched at the knees with white cloth, a small coarse hat, tow short, much worn, a pair of new shoes, with odd buckles, and black stockings. Whoever takes up said servant, and secures him in any of his Majesty's goals within this province, shall have Twenty Shillings reward; and if out of the province,

Thirty Shillings, and all reasonable charges, paid by JOHN CON, in Brandywine Hundred or MATTHEW BIAYS, in the district of Southwark, near the blue bell, on Society Hill.
*The Pennsylvania Gazette*, December 24, 1767; December 31, 1767; January 7, 1768.

## 1768

RUN away, on the third instant, from the subscriber, living in Christiana Hundred, New-Castle county, an Irish servant man, named WILLIAM LEE, about 21 years of age, about 5 feet 3 inches high, fair complexion, with light strait hair, cut pretty close on the top of his head, and has a stammering in his speech: Had on, and took with him, two shirts, one fine, the other coarse, two coats, one of a snuff colour, almost new, with carved yellow buttons; the other a light colour, pretty much worn, without buttons; two jackets, one the same colour, pretty much worn, without buttons; two jackets, one the same cloth as the first-mentioned coat, the other striped flannel, the stripes crossways, two pair of buckskin breeches, one pair almost new, the other pretty much worn, blue and white yarn stockings, old shoes, pieced, with carved yellow buckles, an old castor hat, that has been cut in the brim, and sewed up again, and a black silk handkerchief about his neck. He served four years with one Christopher Wilson, in New-Castle county, and may probably have his old indentures with him, or may change his name to Brian Daily. Whoever takes up and secures said servant, so that his master may have him again, shall have Forty Shillings reward, and reasonable charges,
   paid by  DAVID SCHOLEFIELD.
*The Pennsylvania Gazette*, January 7, 1768; January 14, 1768; January 21, 1768.

FORTY SHILLINGS Reward.
RUN away from the subscriber, living in Dover, Kent county, on Delaware, a certain JOHN HIRON, an apprentice to HUGH PARKE, hatter, of the said town of Dover, aged about 20 years, a well set fellow, with brown hair, fair complexion; had on, when he went away, a brown broadcloth coat, with gilt buttons, a white demity jacket, one white shirt, one check ditto, some coarse ones, and a pair of green halfthick trowsers. He stole and carried off, a blue surtout coat, pretty much worn, a black velvet jacket, not half worn, and a pair of blue knit breeches; he went away with a certain John Goforth, an apprentice to a certain James Bellach, of the same town, shop joyner. Whoever takes up, and secures the said John Hiron, so that his master may have him again, shall have the above Reward,
   paid by  HUGH PARKE.

*The Pennsylvania Gazette*, January 14, 1768; January 21, 1768; January 28, 1768.

FIVE POUNDS Reward.

Newcastle County, December 30, 1767.
ABSCONDED yesterday, a certain man, who called himself HUGH WILSON, was born in Ireland, and appears to be about 30 years of age; he is a tanner by trade, is about 5 feet 3 or 4 inches high, well set, has black hair, marked with the small-pox, a pleasant countenance, lived some time ago in the Jerseys, near Haddonfield: Had on, when he went away, a new blue surtout coat, blue broadcloth close-bodied coat, snuff-coloured waistcoat, leather breeches; and had some other half-worn clothes with him. He took with him a brown Gelding, 4 years old, about 14 and a half hands high, paces some, but most natural to trot; and a new saddle, with a hogskin seat, and plad cloth housings. It is thought he took with him a quantity of money, chiefly gold. Whoever takes up the said Hugh Wilson, and secures him, so that he may be had, shall receive the above reward,
    paid by    HARMON YEATS.

*The Pennsylvania Gazette*, January 14, 1768; January 21, 1768.


WILMINGTON, January 11, 1768.
WHEREAS Catharine my wife lives in adultery with a man in Philadelphia; and, notwithstanding I have for more than two years tenderly and repeatedly entreated her to return to her duty, yet she persists in running me in debt, and refusing to live with me, wherefore I am under the painful necessity of publishing her crimes to the world, and of desiring the public not to trust her on my account, for I will pay no debts of her contracting after the date hereof.
    ANTHONY REDMAN.

*The Pennsylvania Chronicle, and Universal Advertiser*, From Monday, January 11, 1767, to Monday, January 18, 1768; From Monday, January 18, 1767, to Monday, January 25, 1768.


RUN away from the subscriber, living in Brandy-wine Hundred, New-Castle county, a servant girl, named ELIZABETH BARNES, this country born, pretty thick and chunkey, her eyes look sore, has a hollow mouth, wears her own hair tied behind; had on a striped linen gown, and white bed-gown, linsey petticoat, check linsey apron, a white handkerchief, a pair of old shoes, lately soled and capt, with carved buckles, plated with silver; she took with her a light bay mare, with a large mane and tail, trots and paces, shod before, and has a small star on her forehead. Whoever takes up and secures said servant and mare, so as they may be had again, shall have Forty Shillings

reward, or Twenty Shillings for each, paid by JOSEPH DUTTON,
or ROBERT HODGEN.
*The Pennsylvania Gazette*, January 21, 1768; January 28, 1768; February 4, 1768.

Philadelphia, February 1, 1768.
WHEREAS JACOB DECAMP, servant to John Beale Boardley, Esq; of Baltimore town, Maryland; GEORGE JACK, servant to Henry King, of Chestnut Ridge, Baltimore county, Maryland; THOMAS WILKINSON, alias SOUTH, servant to Cornelius Robbins, of Amwell, New Jersey; JOHN FREDERICK HARBURN, servant to Thomas Robinson, of Wilmington, Brandywine Hundred; JOHN M'DERMOTT, servant to Paul Rolston, near Wilmington, New Castle county; JOHN CARROLL, servant to Robert Fulton, in Lancaster county; ISAAC BEATE, servant to Philip Levingston, in New York; and ANDREW PEELE, servant to Dr. Boyd, of Baltimore; being confined in the public goal of this county, as runaway servants, public notice is hereby given to the masters of the said servants, that I intend to apply to the court of quarter sessions, to be held in the city of Philadelphia, for the county of Philadelphia, on Monday, the 7th day of March next, for an order to sell the said servants for their fees, unless their masters redeem them before that time.     JEHU JONES, goaler.
*The Pennsylvania Gazette*, February 4, 1768; Febuary 11, 1768; February 25, 1768.


RUN away the 31st of January last, at night, from the subscriber, living in Christiana Hundred, New-Castle county, an Irish servant man, named JOHN SHEEHAN, born in Cork, and came in last fall with Captain Rankin, about 18 or 20 years of age, 5 feet 8 inches high, of a fair complexion, wears his own brown hair, tied behind, and cut before; had on, when he went away, a fine broadcloth coat, of a light colour, and broke in the sleeves, an old blue jacket, blue plush breeches, new ozenbrigs shirt, a pair of Germantown stockings, of a lightish colour, a pair of soaled shoes, well hob-nailed, with a pair of brass or copper buckles, and a small wool hat, cocked much in the beau order; speaks much of his learning, and values himself highly for his dancing and singing. Whoever takes up said servant, and brings him to his master, or secures him in any goal, so that he may have him again, shall have Twenty Shillings if 10 miles from home, Forty Shillings if 20 miles, and Three Pounds if 60 miles, paid by     SAMUEL MEANS.
*The Pennsylvania Gazette*, February 4, 1768; Febuary 11, 1768; February 18, 1768.

St. George's Hundred, New-Castle County, Jan. 16, 1768.
TEN POUNDS Reward.

WHEREAS, on Sunday evening, the 22d of November last, was set on fire, the barn, stack yard, and fodder house, of the subscriber, supposed to be done by a certain JAMES WILSON; he is well known by different names in different parts of the country, viz. in Chester county by Simson, at New York by Stenson, and Belcher and Brown elsewhere; has had several wives, two of which are in this neighbourhood, the latter was the Widow Bumgardain, who he posted the 17th of April 1766 in the Pennsylvania gazette, No. 1947; he is a middle sized fellow, pocked-marked, wants some of his fore teeth, short nose, small red eyes, short neck, short black hair, wears a white cap, a home-made strait bodied coat, light coloured, a striped lincey jacket, leather breeches, brass buckles, a home-made blue great coat, with small red spots from the mixture of the wool, speaks thick and somewhat through his nose, or as if he had a cold; spiteful, blood-thirsty and revengeful against those he has any ill will, which may be easily perceived by his conversation; a horrid swearer, mostly every word by his Maker; is very artful and cunning to contrive or conceal mischief; has been charged with several crimes in this neighbourhood which would convict him, besides the present, viz. for an intention and attempt to poison his last wife, also the altering the present currency of this government, in parting Twenty Shilling bills, and passing the same; he has repeatedly threatened the lives and properties of many in this neighbourhood, as well as mine, and others, from whence he came. No less than the lives and properties of all those in general he had any difference with on the most trifling occasions. Any person securing said fellow, and bringing him to me, or New-Castle goal, shall have the above reward, and reasonable charges, paid by    THOMAS WITHERSPOON.

*The Pennsylvania Gazette*, February 4, 1768; Febuary 18, 1768.

*Gloucester county, New Jersey, February* 13, 1768.
TEN POUNDS Reward.

BROKE out of the goal of the county of Gloucester, this morning, the following prisoners, viz. HUGH WILSON, born in Ireland, about 30 years of age, a tanner by trade, 5 feet 3 or 4 inches high, well set, has black hair, a pleasant countenance, marked with the small-pox, has lived lately in Chester and New-Castle counties; had on, a good blue surtout, a light coloured broadcloth jacket, and swanskin waistcoat with black spots, a pair of good leather breeches, and a good hat. It is thought he has a large quantity of money with him, chiefly gold. And DAVID COCHRAN, born in Ireland, about 25 years of age, 5 feet 6 inches high, has a freckled face, and red short hair, a fuller by trade, and has lived in Allentown and Haddonfield; had on, a light coloured homespun cloth coat, a striped jacket, cloth breeches, a pair of half-

boots, and an old hat; also took a pair of shoes with him; it is supposed he is gone towards Lancaster. They are both much inclined to strong liquor, and apt to be intoxicated. Whoever takes up the above prisoners, and secures them in any goal in New-Jersey, Pennsylvania, or the lower counties on Delaware, and gives notice to the subscriber, so that he may have them again, shall receive for Hugh Wilson, Six Pounds reward, and for David Cochran, Four Pounds, and reasonable charges from
SAMUEL BLACKWOOD, Sheriff.
*The Pennsylvania Gazette*, February 18, 1768; February 25, 1768. See *The Pennsylvania Chronicle, and Universal Advertiser*, From Monday, February 14, to Monday, February 22, 1768.

TEN POUNDS REWARD.
BROKE out of the gaol of the county of *Gloucester*, this morning, the two following prisoners, to wit, *Hugh Willson*, born in *Ireland*, about thirty years of age, a tanner by trade, five feet three or four inches high, well set, has black hair, a pleasant countenance, marked with the small-pox, has lived lately in *Chester* and *New-Castle* counties; had on a good blue surtout, a light-coloured broadcloth jacket, and swanskin waistcoat, with black spots; a pair of good leather breeches, and a good hat. It is thought he has a large quantity of money with him, chiefly gold. And *David Cochran*, born in *Ireland*, about twenty-five years of age, five feet six inches high, has a freckled face, and red short hair, a fuller by trade, and has lived in *Allen-Town* and *Haddonfield*; had on, a light-coloured homespun cloth coat, a striped jacket, cloth breeches, a pair of half boots, and an old hat; he took a pair of new shoes with him, it is supposed he is gone towards *Lancaster*. They are both much inclined to strong liquor, and apt to be intoxicated. Whoever takes up the above prisoners, and secures them in any goal in *New-Jersey*, *Pennsylvania*, or the lower counties on *Delaware*, and gives notice to the subscriber, so that he may have them again, shall receive the above reward, and all reasonable charges, of      S. BLACKWOOD, Sheriff
*Feb.* 13, 1768.

*The Pennsylvania Chronicle, and Universal Advertiser*, From Monday, February 15, to Monday, February 22, 1768. See *The Pennsylvania Gazette*, February 18, 1768.

To be LETT....apply to the subscriber, living in New Castle, upon Delaware, THOMAS M'KEAN.
RUN away from the said THOMAS M'KEAN, about a month ago, a servant boy, named PHILIP COWDEN, about 17 years of age, of a fair complexion, pale yellow coloured strait hair; took only his common apparel, having no change of linen, &c. with him; he appears to be a soft simple

fellow, and may be easily known by a scar under the waistband of his breeches, in the middle of his back, which was occasioned by a wound received on a short stump, by a fall from a horse last year. Whoever apprehends him, and confines him in any goal, so that his master may have him again, shall receive FORTY SHILLINGS reward.

*The Pennsylvania Gazette*, February 18, 1768; February 25, 1768; April 21, 1768.


RUN away from the Subscriber, at Witherspoon's Tavern, in New-Castle County, on the 2d Day of March instant, an English Servant, named David Williams, 25 Years of Age, a short thick Man, black curled Hair, dark Complexion, full faced, pitted with the Small-Pox, his right Leg and Hand withered, and his little Finger bent in the Palm of his Hand: Had on when he went away, a dark coloured Jacket, lined with striped Linsey, an under Ditto of blue Cloth, a Pair of Leather Breeches, and a light coloured Great Coat. Whoever secures the said Servant, so that his Master may have him again, shall receive SIX DOLLARS Reward, and reasonable Charges,
   paid by  JAMES COCKRAN.

*The Pennsylvania Gazette*, March 10, 1768. See *The Pennsylvania Gazette*, August 18, 1768.


February 18, 1768.
RUN away, last night, from the subscriber, living in Wilmington, a girl, who calls herself SARAH WILSON, and stole the following things, viz. A double callicoe gown, a red shaloon quilt, a striped woollen petticoat, very much of a blue, a home spun sheet, a black peeling bonnet, and a striped linsey bed gown; likewise several other things, too tedious to mention. The girl is a thick short body, has very small grey eyes, and squints very much with both eyes. Whoever takes up said thief and things, so that the owner may have them again, shall have Fifteen shillings reward, and reasonable charges,
   paid by  EDWARD MOON.

*The Pennsylvania Gazette*, March 10, 1768; March 17, 1768; March 31, 1768.


### THREE POUNDS Reward.

RUN away from the subscriber, last January, a servant woman, called Mary Diggens (has since changed it to Mary Morgan) pretty lusty, with large features, and light hair; had on, when she went away, a brown worsted damask gown, with velvet cuffs, a pink durant quilt, and a white silk bonnet. As she has stolen a quantity of cloaths, perhaps she will change them. When she served her time in Maryland, she had her toes frost-bitten, which may be discovered by her walk; she is extremely artful, and will deceive almost any

person with an appearance of the utmost innocence and simplicity. Whoever apprehends said servant, so that her mistress may have her again, shall have the above reward, and reasonable charges; or if taken with the goods, Five Pounds, paid by ANDREW DOZ, in Philadelphia, or the subscriber, in Dover, ANN PARKE.
N. B. As she has stolen from her mistress money sufficient to pay her passage to Wales, the place of her nativity, all masters of vessels are forbid to carry her off.
*The Pennsylvania Gazette,* March 10, 1768; March 17, 1768; March 21, 1768.

Newark, in New-Castle county, March 9, 1768.
RUN away from the subscriber, on the 8th instant, Joseph Priestman, by trade a breeches-maker, and understands something of shammy dressing. He is about 24 years of age, 5 feet 5 inches high, well made, round faced, and pockmarked, with long brown hair, tied behind: Had on when he went away, a blue body coat, a blue surtout, buckskin breeches, and good white linen shirts. He had also check linen with him, a white fustian body coat, and a new pair of doe skin gloves, of the best kind. Whoever apprehends him, so as the subscriber may get him again, shall receive a reward of THREE POUNDS, from       JACOB LEMMON.
N. B. He can write well, and is supposed to be now in Philadelphia, most probably intending for New York.
*The Pennsylvania Gazette,* March 17, 1768; March 24, 1768; March 31, 1768; April 7, 1768; *The Pennsylvania Journal, and the Weekly Advertiser,* March 17, 1768; March 24, 1768; March 31, 1768; April 7, 1768; *The New-York Journal; or the General Advertiser,* March 24, 1768; March 31, 1768; *The-New York Gazette or The Weekly Post-Boy,* March 21, 1768; March 28, 1768. Minor differences between the papers. See *The Pennsylvania Gazette,* March 24, 1768.

*Okessin, March 17.*
TEN DOLLARS REWARD.
*RUN-AWAY on the 12th of this inst. from the subscriber, living in Okessin, New-Castle county, Mill-creek Hundred—an Irish servant man, named RICHARD BLOCK, about 21 years of age, about 5 feet 8 or 9 inches high, is well set, fresh coloured, lightish hair; had on when he went away, a red broad-cloth under jacket, with a stocking sleeve, and two cloth coloured ones over it, the uppermost tore behind and on the shoulders, old leather breeches, shoes without buckles. Whoever takes up and secures said servant so that his master may have him again shall receive the above reward, and all reasonable charges, paid by me     JOHN WAY.*

N. B. *It is supposed this servant is gone towards Philadelphia, and intends to go off in some vessel. All masters of vessels are forwarned to carry him off at their peril.*
    *The Pennsylvania Journal, and the Weekly Advertiser*, March 17, 1768; March 24, 1768; March 31, 1768. See *The Pennsylvania Gazette*, March 31, 1768, and *The Pennsylvania Chronicle, and Universal Advertiser*, From Monday, July 25, to Monday, August 1, 1768.

                        Newark, in New-Castle county, March 9, 1768.
RUN away from the subscriber, on the 8th instant, Joseph Priestman, by trade a breeches-maker, and understands something of shammy dressing. He is about 24 years of age, 5 feet 5 inches high, full round faced, well skinned, and pock-marked, with light brown hair, inclined to flaxen, tied behind, his legs a little bandy, his toes turns in as he walks, and his shoulders are roundish, is an Irishman, and speaks good English: Had on when he went away, a white fustian body coat, a blue turned surtout, with a double cape, one of which is velvet, buckskin or black leather breeches, and a good white linen shirt. Whoever apprehends him, so as the subscriber may get him again, shall receive a reward of THREE POUNDS,
                      from JACOB LEMMON.
N. B. He can write well, and is supposed to be now in Philadelphia.
    *The Pennsylvania Gazette*, March 24, 1768; March 30, 1768; April 7, 1768. See *The Pennsylvania Gazette*, March 17, 1768.

                      *TWO PISTOLES Reward.*
RUN away from the subscribers, a servant man, named LEWIS REED, born in Germany, but came into America when young, and speaks English distinctly; he is about 30 years old, 4 feet [*sic*] 4 or 5 inches high, and one or both his knees bend much inward, his hair long and black, which he ties behind; had on when he went away, a green jacket and trowsers, made of half thicks, and an under jacket of brown cloth; he is very vain and talkative, pretending to understand the carpenter's trade in all its branches. He was seen a few days since in the Bordentown stage boat, going from Philadelphia with his wife, a short, thick, red haired woman. Whoever will take up the said servant, and bring him to either of the subscribers, at New-Castle, on Delaware, shall receive the above reward, and reasonable charges.
                GEORGE READ, JOHN DOWNING.
    *The Pennsylvania Gazette*, March 24, 1768; March 31, 1768; April 7, 1768.

Okessin, March 17, 1768.
TEN DOLLARS Reward.
RUN away on the 12th of this inst. from the subscriber, living in Okessin, New-Castle county, Mill-creek Hundred, an Irish servant man, named RICHARD BLOCK, about 21 years of age, about 5 feet 8 or 9 inches high, is well set, fresh coloured, lightish hair; had on when he went away, a red broadcloth under jacket, with a stocking sleeve, and two cloth coloured ones over it, the uppermost tore behind, and on the shoulders, old leather breeches, shoes without buckles. Whoever takes up and secures said servant, so that his master may have him again, shall receive the above reward, and all reasonable charges, paid by me    JOHN WAY.
*The Pennsylvania Gazette*, March 31, 1768; April 7, 1768. See *The Pennsylvania Journal, and Weekly Advertiser*, March 17, 1768, and *The Pennsylvania Chronicle, and Universal Advertiser*, From Monday, July 25, to Monday, August 1, 1768.


RUN away from his Bail, out of New-Castle, on the 30th of March last, one John Meshefrey, born in the North of Ireland, a thick well set Fellow, about 5 Feet 7 Inches high, of a black Complexion, and talks broad: Had on, when he went away, a blue Coat, whitish Jacket, Buckskin Breeches, grey Stockings, a Pair of Brass Buckles, and an old Felt Hat, tarred on the Top of the Crown. Whoever takes up said Runaway, and secures him in any Goal in this Province, so that I may have him again, or brings him to me in New-Castle, shall have Forty Shillings Reward,
            paid by    JAMES CAMBLE.
*The Pennsylvania Gazette*, April 7, 1768; April 21, 1768.


RUN-away, with his father, from the subscriber, living in Wilmington, New-Castle county, the 10th of April, an apprentice lad named Joseph Elliott (son of Obadiah Elliott, who formerly kept the tavern at Red Lion, between New-Castle and St. George's) about 18 years of age, 5 feet 6 or 7 inches high, long visaged, has a condemned downcast countenance, dark brown hair, wears it tied sometimes. Had on and took with him, a half-worn castor hat, old short lead-coloured cloth coat, snuff-coloured jacket, gilt buttons on both, a pair of brown plush breeches and brown ribb'd stockings, a pair of new shoes and old half boots, large carved shoe and knee buckles, one white shirt and one check'd ditto.
    Said lad having been at the silver-smith's trade for some time, may endeavour to get employ in that business in Lewis-Town or Maryland; 'tis thought they are gone that way, as his father has a wife living near Dover;

but probably may do her and the neighbours the kindness of pursuing his journey farther with his son.

Whosoever takes up the said apprentice only, (his father can be spared) and secures him so that his master may have him again, shall have Forty Shillings reward, and reasonable charges,

paid by me, JOSEPH WARNER.

All masters of vessels are forbid to harbour or carry off said apprentice, at their peril.—They may take the father and welcome.

*The Pennsylvania Chronicle, and Universal Advertiser*, From Monday, April 11, to Monday, April 18, 1768.

RUN away, from the Subscriber, in Brandywine Hundred, New-Castle County, on the Tenth of this instant April, an Irish Servant Man, named John M'Dermont, but probably may change his Name; he is about 5 Feet 6 Inches high, of a sandy Complexion, about 30 Years of Age, has a Down-look, and a Scar under his Chin: Had on, an old Hat, two white Flannel Jackets, old greasy Leather Breeches, Tow Shirt, blue Yarn Stockings, and old Shoes. Whoever takes up said Servant and secures him in any Goal, so as his Master may have him again, shall have Forty Shillings Reward, and reasonable Charges, paid by     PAUL RALSTON.

*The Pennsylvania Gazette*, April 21, 1768; May 5, 1768. See *The Pennsylvania Gazette*, August 7, 1766.


Sussex County on Delaware, Three-Run Mills, June 24, 1768.

RUN away, from the subscriber, on the 13th of September last, one Mulattoe slave, named HARRY, about 40 years of age, 5 feet 6 inches high, and well set. Had on, when he went away, a brown cloth coat, white linen jacket, and brown breeches; he was bred a miller, and understands very well how to manufacture flour, and can invoice the same; is much given to strong drink, and playing on the violin; understands the carpenter's and millwright's businesses middling well; was removed from East New-Jersey in the year 1762 by one Nicholas Veight, who lived at Rockey-Hill, and kept a mill. The said fellow has a free wife, named Peg, and two children, which are supposed to be somewhere in the province of East New-Jersey. I am told the said Mulattoe has got a pass. Any person or persons that will secure the said Mulattoe in any of his Majesty's goals, so that the owner may have him again, shall have TEN POUNDS reward, and reasonable charges, paid by Mr. CHARLES WHARTON, merchant, in Philadelphia;

or by LEVIN CRAPPER.

*The Pennsylvania Gazette*, June 30, 1768; July 14, 1768. See *The Pennsylvania Chronicle, and Universal Advertiser*, From Monday,

June 27, to Monday, July 4, 1768, *The Pennsylvania Chronicle, and Universal Advertiser*, From Monday, September 21, to Monday, September 28, 1767, and *The Pennsylvania Gazette*, October 1, 1767.

*Sussex county, on Delaware, Three Run Mills,*
*June 23, 1768.*
TEN POUNDS Reward.

RAN away, from the subscriber, on the 13th of September, 1767, a Mulatto Slave, named HARRY, about 40 years of age, 5 feet 6 inches high, and well set: Had on when he went away, a brown cloth coat, white linen jacket, and brown breeches. He was bred a miller, and understands very well how to manufacture flour, and can invoice the same; is much given to strong drink, and playing on the violin; understands the carpenter's and mill-wright's business middling well; was removed from East-New-Jersey in the year 1762, by one Nicholas Veghte, who lived at Rocky-Hill, and kept a mill; and the said fellow has a free Mulatto wife, named Peg, and two children. I expect they will endeavour to get together, though they did not run away at one time. It is expected they will endeavour to get to the province of East New-Jersey. It is imagined said Mulatto has a pass.

Any person or persons that takes up and secures the said Mulatto, so that the owner can have him again, shall have Five Pounds Reward, and all reasonable Charges, by applying to CHARLES WHARTON, Merchant, in Philadelphia, or to the subscriber, living at the aforesaid mills.
LEVIN CRAPPER.

*The Pennsylvania Chronicle, and Universal Advertiser*, From Monday, June 27, to Monday, July 4, 1768; From Monday, July 4, to Monday, July 11, 1768. See *The Pennsylvania Chronicle, and Universal Advertiser*, From Monday, September 21, to Monday, September 28, 1767, *The Pennsylvania Gazette*, October 1, 1767, and *The Pennsylvania Gazette*, June 30, 1768.

New-Castle County, July 2, 1768.
RUN away from the Subscriber, living in New-Castle County, on Delaware, on Thursday, the 16th of June last, a Negroe Man, called SHARPER, a slim smart Fellow, about 5 Feet 10 Inches high, very black, pitted with the Small-pox, can read, and is very talkative: Had on, an old Felt Hat, Tow Shirt and Trowsers, and a grey Cloth Jacket; took with him a Tow Shirt and Trowsers. It is very probable he will change his Dress, and endeavour to pass for a free Negroe. Whoever secures the said Negroe in any Goal, so that his Master may have him, or brings him to his Master, shall have Forty Shillings Reward, and reasonable Charges,
paid by ALEXANDER PORTER.

*The Pennsylvania Gazette*, July 14, 1768; July 28, 1768; *The Pennsylvania Journal, and the Weekly Advertiser*, July 14, 1768; July 21, 1768; July 28, 1768. Minor differences between the papers. See *The Pennsylvania Chronicle, and Universal Advertiser*, From Monday, July 11, to Monday, July 18, 1768.

Newcastle County, July 3, 1768.
*RAN away from the subscriber, living in Newcastle county, on Delaware, on Thursday the 16th ult. a Negro Man, called SHARPER; he is a slim smart fellow, about four [sic] feet ten inches high, very black, pitted with the small pox, can read, and is very talkative. He had on an old felt hat, tow shirt and trowsers, and a grey cloth jacket; he also took with him a tow shirt and trowsers. It is probable he will change his dress, and endeavour to pass for a free Negro. Whoever secures the said Negro in any goal, so that his master may have him, or brings him to his master, shall have FORTY SHILLINGS reward, and reasonable charges,*
    *paid by ALEX. PORTER.*
*The Pennsylvania Chronicle, and Universal Advertiser*, From Monday, July 11, to Monday, July 18, 1768; From Monday, July 18, to Monday, July 25, 1768; From Monday, July 25, to Monday, August 1, 1768. See *The Pennsylvania Gazette*, July 14, 1768.


RAN away, last night, from the subscriber, living in Mill-Creek Hundred, Newcastle county, an Irish servant-man, named *Richard Block*, about 22 years of age, pale complexion, smooth faced, about five feet eight inches high, wears his own short brown hair: Had on, and took with him, a felt hat pretty much worn, a lightish mixed with red blue and white homespun coat, with a collar turned back, two homespun flaxen shirts, two pair of tow trowsers, a pair of yarn stockings, and a pair of neats leather shoes, tied with strings; he pretends to be a painter and glazier by trade, and is left handed. Whoever takes up and secures the said servant, so that his master may have him again, shall have THIRTY SHILLINGS reward, and reasonable charges paid by   July 19, 1768.   JOHN WAY.
*The Pennsylvania Chronicle, and Universal Advertiser*, From Monday, July 25, to Monday, August 1, 1768. See *The Pennsylvania Journal, and the Weekly Advertiser*, March 17, 1768, and *The Pennsylvania Gazette*, March 31, 1768.


       St. George's hundred, New-Castle county.
RUN away, the first day of March last, a servant man, named DAVID WILLIAMS, about 5 feet 5 inches high, short black curled hair, a few small pock-marks in his face, his right hand is withered, and his fingers turn in the

palm of his hand, his right leg is smaller than the other; had on, when he run away, a dark coloured kersey jacket, with metal buttons, a pair of old leather breeches, grey yarn stockings, an old light coloured great coat, and half-worn felt hat; it is supposed he went to Philadelphia, and continues about the town: Whoever secures said servant in goal, or any place else, so as his master may have him again, shall have Six Dollars reward, and reasonable charges,
paid by me    JAMES COCHRAN.
If he is taken any where near Philadelphia, call on Joseph Yeates, at the sign of the Three Tons, in Chestnut-street, and he will pay the reward.
*The Pennsylvania Gazette*, August 18, 1768; September 1, 1768; September 8, 1768. See *The Pennsylvania Gazette*, March 10, 1768.


WHEREAS a certain young Man, named HANS ADAMS, between 18 and 19 Years of Age, hath absconded from the Subscriber, living in Wilmington, New-Castle County, and it is possible will want to borrow Money on his Account, or crave some of his outstanding Debts; these are therefore to forbid those with whom the Subscriber has any Dealings, or others, not to let him have any, on any Account.    JAMES ADAMS.
*The Pennsylvania Gazette*, September 8, 1768; September 15, 1768.


Newcastle County, September 24, 1768.
WAS committed, to the goal of said county, on the 13th instant, JOHN MARROW, a servant lad, about 18 years of age, who says he left Captain William Burns, of the ship Buff and Bull, on the first instant; he is of a fair complexion, has fair hair, about 5 feet 2 inches high, slim made, and a little marked with the small-pox; had on, when committed, a brown lincey-woolsey coat, and coarse homespun shirt and trowsers. Also was committed, on the 22d instant, ROGER EGAN, a lad, about 5 feet high, well set, brown hair, had on, when committed, an old blue coat, black stocking breeches, old shoes and stockings. Their masters, if any they have, are desired to come and pay their charges, and take them away, in six weeks from this date, or they will be sold for the same, by    THOMAS PUSEY, Goaler.
*The Pennsylvania Gazette*, September 29, 1768; October 6, 1768; November 3, 1768; November 10, 1768; November 24, 1768.

## 1769

RUN AWAY from the subscriber, living in Dover, in Kent County, on Delaware, on the 28th of Marsh last, a servant Man named STEPHEN TURNER, about 50 years old, about five feet eight or nine inches high, a well set fellow, of a Brown complexion, wears his own hair, but the fore part of his head is quite bald, he came from the West of England and talks very bad English and is by trade a shoemaker. Had on and took with him a brown cloth vest with sleeves of a darker brown, a linsey one and a scarlet one, an old raccoon hat, a tow linen and an oznabrigs shirt, a pair of leather breeches full short for him and a pair of old red plush ones, and took with him a parcel of shoemaker's tools and lasts and two leather aprons. Any person or persons apprehending him and bringing him to the subscribers, or securing him in any gaol, shall receive THIRTY SHILLINGS reward if taken within this county and THIRTY SHILLINGS if taken out of it, and reasonable charges paid by JOSEPH GOODFELLOW. April 6.

*The Pennsylvania Journal, and the Weekly Advertiser*, April 6, 1769; April 13, 1769; April 20, 1769.

April 27.

RUN-AWAY, from the subscriber, living in the Welsh Tract, Penkader Hundred, New-Castle county, an Irish servant man, named Daniel Murphy, about 5 feet 4 inches high, dark complexioned, black curl'd hair, about 25 years of age, round shoulder'd, has something of the brogue on his tongue: Had on a blanket coat, a white flannel vest, with black horn buttons, a pair of blue breeches half worn, blue or white yarn stockings, good shoes and brass buckles: He also stole and took with him, a white broad cloth coat, lined with a dark shalloon, and mohair buttons, a dark coloured fustian jacket, new buckskin breeches, a pair of buckskin gloves, two silk handkerchiefs, and a pair of ribb'd thread stockings. Whoever takes up and secures the said servant, so that his master may have him again, shall receive, if taken within this county, FORTY SHILLINGS, and if out of the county, THREE POUNDS reward, and reasonable charges,
paid by DAVID LEWELLIN.

*The Pennsylvania Journal, and the Weekly Advertiser*, April 27, 1769; May 4, 1769; May 11, 1769.

EIGHT DOLLARS Reward.

RUN away from the Subscriber, living near Indian River, an indented Servant Man, named PURMOTT LEE, about 6 Feet high, 25 Years of Age, and a little hard of Hearing, was born at Egg-Harbour, where it is supposed he is now, as his Wife and Father were seen travelling the Road that leads to that Place. Whoever takes up the said Servant, and brings him to John Mifflin, Merchant in Philadelphia, or to his Master at Indian River, shall receive the above Reward, from JOHN JONES

*The Pennsylvania Gazette*, April 27, 1769.

RUN away last night, from Newport, New-Castle county, upon Delaware, an Irish woman, named CATHERINE M'CLURE, a short thick set woman, black hair, full eyes, has a kind of lisp in her speech, about 23 years of age; had on, and took with her, when she went away, a brown camblet gown, about half worn, a striped linsey bed gown, one of striped linen and cotton, and one of white linen, one striped linsey petticoat, and one ditto of blue calimancoe, a chip hat, linen bonnet, and two pair of shoes. She had a young child, about 6 weeks old, and came in the night into an out kitchen of mine, and left the child, which was almost perished with cold, before it was perceived. Whoever takes up said Catherine M'Clure, and secures her in any of his Majesty's goals, so that she may be brought to justice, shall have Twenty Shillings reward, and reasonable charges,
   paid by me  ROBERT SLATER.
*The Pennsylvania Gazette,* May 4, 1769; May 18, 1769.


RUN away from the subscriber, living at Newark, two servant men; one named JOHN DAILY, a well set young fellow, about 5 feet 9 or 10 inches high, black hair, tied behind, about 25 years of age; had on, when he went away, an old white cloth coat, a redish brown cloth jacket, blue breeches, broken at the knees, grey stockings, old shoes, old striped linen shirt, and a red handkerchief; professes to be a Miller by trade, and has been in this country for some time; The other, named JOHN JONES, about 5 feet 8 inches high, a slim fellow, blind of one eye, and about 40 years of age; had on, when he went away, a little bound hat, a thin Wig, with one curl at bottom, and old mixt purple coloured coat, broken at the arms, shoes, and old buckles, not fellows; he professes Horsemanship. Whoever takes up, and secures said servants in any of his Majesty's goals, or brings them to their master in Philadelphia, living in Second street, on Society-Hill, at the Blue Bell, shall have Three Pounds reward for John Daily, and Twenty Shillings for John Jones, and reasonable charges,
   paid by me  JOSEPH ANDERSON.
*The Pennsylvania Gazette,* May 4, 1769.

           New Castle County, May 9 1769.
      *THREE POUNDS Reward.*
RUN-away from the Subscriber, the 7th instant, a servant Man, named LUKE SWAINEY, about 30 years of age, and about 5 feet 5 inches high, of a brown complexion, somewhat pitted with the smallpox, wears his own hair, had on, and took with him, a blanket coat, with a blue cap to the cape of it, and bound with red tape; a blue jacket that has had the sleeves torn out, and has small mettal buttons on the breast; a wool hat, an old pair of buckskin breeches; two shirts, one new of coarse linen, the other old of check; two pair of

trowsers, one pair of duck, almost new, the other of Russia sheeting, much patched; one pair of old blue stockings, with the feet cut off, one pair of new black grained pumps, and one pair of shoes cut down the instep below the buckle; two pair of silver buckles, one pair a carved pattern, the other round marked 11 on the side of each: he feigned himself to be lately from Ireland, but it is now well known that he was lately taken out of Philadelphia gaol. Whoever takes up said servant, and secures him in any of his Majesty's gaols, shall have the above reward, and reasonable charges

paid by me    JOHN JOHNSON.

N. B. All masters of vessels are forbid to take him off at their peril. The Subscriber gave a note for the above servant, payable to a certain George M'Dowell and Joseph Anderson, and he hereby forewarns all persons from taking an assignment of said note, as he is determined to dispute the payment of it.

*The Pennsylvania Journal, and the Weekly Advertiser,* May 18, 1769; May 25, 1769; June 8, 1769.

Pencader Hundred, New-Castle County, May 6, 1769.
SIX POUNDS Reward.

*RUN away, the 24th of April last, from the Subscribers, two Irish indented servants. Daniel Murphy, between 25 and 30 years of age, about 5 feet 5 inches high, has the brogue on his tongue, fresh coloured, black curly hair, round shouldered, thin sharp nose, has a hobbling walk; had on a flannel vest, with black horn buttons, ozenbrigs shirt, &c. stole and took with him, a lightish coloured broadcloth coat, lined with dark shaloon, mohair buttons, dark fustian jacket, black horn buttons, new buckskin breeches, white ribbed thread stockings, bluish yarn ditto, good shoes, brass buckles, new holland shirt, ditto of 12 hundred, country make, red and yellow silk handkerchief, black silk gauze ditto, felt hat, &c. James Field, born in Dublin, 20 years of age, about 5 feet 4 or 5 inches high, full freckled face, marked with the small-pox, short nose, large greyish eyes, blackish hair, round shouldered, &c. stole, and took with him, a darkish coloured broadcloth coat, lined in the fore parts with green stuff, big leather pockets, old red and black flannel vest, buckskin breeches, bluish worsted stockings, good shoes, check shirt, black silk handkerchief, felt hat, with white bowlings &c. Whoever takes up said servants, and secures them in any goal, so that their masters may have them again, shall have the above reward or Three Pounds for either,*

paid by    DAVID LLEWELIN, JOHN JONES.

*N. B. They were seen together, within 8 miles from Lancaster, going upwards. It is likely they will change their names and apparel, as said Field did before. All masters of vessels, and others, are forbid to harbour to take them away, at their peril.*

*The Pennsylvania Gazette,* May 25, 1769.

RUN away, on the 16th of last month, from the Subscriber, living in Pencader Hundred, New-Castle county, a servant man, named RICHARD SEBLEY, a woman's heel maker by trade; he is a thick short fellow, about 5 feet 4 inches high; had on, when he went away, a blue-grey broadcloth coat, a cotton and linen jacket, a pair of serge-denim breeches, almost new, and a castor hat; he wears his own hair, has short legs, and very flat footed; he is given to strong drink, and when in liquor talks much; and generally has a large quid of tobacco in his mouth. He was born in the west of England, and talks generally in that dialect. Whoever takes up the said servant, and sends him to WILLIAM HEMPHILL, at Wilmington, shall have Fifty Shillings reward; or if taken at Philadelphia, and put in that goal, Forty Shillings,
         paid by me    CHARLES WILSON.
*The Pennsylvania Gazette*, June 1, 1769; June 29, 1769.


                THREE POUNDS *Reward*.
RUN-AWAY from the subscribers, the 9th instant, living at Christiana-bridge; an Irish servant named THOMAS NOADS, aged about 19 years, is about five feet five inches high, fair complexion, short straight dark hair, and speaks with a good deal of Irish dialect; had on when he went away, a new hat, a jean coat, striped damascus jacket, and Russia drilling breeches, new shoes with silver buckles: he also took with him a sorrel mare, between thirteen and fourteen hands high, half worn saddle and new crupper, a pair of saddle bags, the contents therein unknown, and two or three surtout coats. Said servant the day before he run away, picked the subscribers drawer and took from thence a £3 bill, Jersey money. There is likewise gone in company with him, a certain WILLIAM HENDERSON, much about his age, who followed school keeping in Christiana, has been formerly employed to write for a merchant in Joppa, Baltimore county, is about five feet eight inches high, slender made, dark hair tied behind and curled at each ear: it is supposed he has one of the surtouts on him, as he took none of his own with him: he has also a spotted flannel jacket, with black breeches or striped trowsers, he being concerned in the felony with Noads and deluding [sic] him off. Whoever takes up said runaway, and secures him in any of his Majesty's gaols, or brings him to the subscriber, shall have the above-mentioned reward for Noads, and reasonable charges paid by us
        HANNAH WALL,    ELIZABETH JANAURY. [sic]
N. B. It is supposed they are gone to Egg Harbour.
*The Pennsylvania Journal, and the Weekly Advertiser*, June 15, 1769; June 22, 1769; July 6, 1769.

*Sussex County, on Delaware.*
ON the sixth day of June instant, was taken up a Negroe BOY, by John Wood, of Lewis Town, on Suspicion of being a runaway, and committed to the goal of the county aforesaid; and upon examination, he is found to answer every description (except his cloathing, which he says is changed) of a boy advertised in the Pennsylvania Gazette, No. 2110, by John Brockenbrough, of Hobb's Hole, in Virginia. His master may have him again, by applying to
     BOAZ MANLOVE, Sheriff.
*The Pennsylvania Gazette,* June 22, 1769; June 29, 1769.

*New-Castle, July* 20, 1769.
NOW in the goal of this county, a certain Thomas O Shocknecy, who was committed on suspicion of being a runaway servant of Joseph Richardson, of Chester county; he is about 5 feet 8 or 9 inches high, slender made, about 30 years of age, of a black complexion; had on, when committed, a blanket coat, linen drawers, old shoes and yarn stockings. His master (if any he has) is desired to come in three weeks, pay his fees, and take him away, otherwise he will be sold out for the same by
     THOMAS PUSEY, Goaler.
*The Pennsylvania Gazette,* July 27, 1769; August 10, 1769.

*RUN away from the Subscriber, living in Evesham, Burlington county, West-Jersey, on the 8th instant, a servant lad, named Jacob Carvel, about 5 feet 5 or 6 inches high, about 18 years of age, well set, of a yellowish complexion, coarse harsh hair, a kind of flax colour, cut very close on the top, is very much hump skinned; had on, and took with him, two shirts, one ozenbrigs, the other fine linen, two pair of tow trowsers, and one pair of striped ditto, four jackets, two bearskin, one lead coloured, the other black and white, a good broadcloth one, light coloured, lined with striped woollen, and bound before, one cotton and woollen striped ditto, a new black neckcloth, two hats, one an old beaver the other plat, a new pair of neats leather shoes. He also took with him a large brindle dog; the said boy's father lives at Duck-Creek, and it is supposed he has gone that way. Whoever takes up and secures said servant in any goal, so that his master may have him again, shall receive Thirty Shillings reward, and Five Shillings for the dog, with reasonable charges,  paid by* NATHAN HAINES.
*The Pennsylvania Gazette,* August 10, 1769.

*Reading Goal, in Berks County, June* 27, 1769.
THIS *day was committed to my custody, a young Negro* GIRL, *named Esther, who says she belongs to one John Jackson, of Duck-Creek, in Kent county; had a striped linsey petticoat, homespun shift, calicoe bed gown, no shoes.*

*Her master is desired to come and pay the said Negroe's charges, and take her away, otherwise she will be sold out for her fees, in six week after date hereof, by* GEORGE NAGEL, *Goaler.*
   *The Pennsylvania Gazette,* August 10, 1769.


FIVE POUNDS Reward.
RUN away, last night, from the Subscriber, living at Christiana Bridge, an Irish servant man, named Robert Jones, about 5 feet 8 or 9 inches high, a well set and stout fellow, wears his short brown hair, inclining to curl, stoops much when he walks, his legs have been lately sore, and are not quite well; had on, and took with him, a blue cloth coat, white jacket, buckskin breeches, new long check trowsers, half worn shoes, and plain silver buckles. Whoever takes up said servant, and secures him in any goal so that his master may have him again, shall have the above reward, paid by
*August* 31, 1769.            ALLEN GILLESPIE.
N. B. All masters of vessels, and others, are forbid to harbour or carry him off at their peril. He was chiefly concerned in breaking a store, and taking out a great many goods.
   *The Pennsylvania Gazette,* September 7, 1769. See *The Pennsylvania Journal, and the Weekly Advertiser,* September 7, 1769.


FIVE POUNDS Reward.
RU-AWAY on the 30th of August, at night, from the subscriber, living at Christiana-bridge; an Irish servant man named ROBERT JONES, about five feet eight or nine inches high, a well set stout fellow, wears his short brown hair inclining to curl, stoops much when he walks, his legs have been lately sore, and are not quite well yet: Had on and took with him, a blue cloth coat, white jacket and buckskin breeches, new long check trowsers, half-worn shoes and plain silver buckles. Whoever takes up said servant, and secures him in any goal, so that his master may have him again, shall have the above reward, paid by            ALLEN GILLESPIE.
N. B. All masters of vessels, and others are forbid to harbour or carry him off at their peril. He was chiefly concerned in breaking a store and taking out a great many goods.
   *The Pennsylvania Journal, and the Weekly Advertiser,* September 7, 1769; September 14, 1769; September 21, 1769. See *The Pennsylvania Gazette,* September 7, 1769.


*RUN away the 15th of August last, from the subscriber, living in Mill Creek Hundred, New Castle county, an Irish servant man, named JOHN FORAN,*

*about* 30 *years of age, about* 5 *feet high, of a thin complexion, light brown hair, cut before; had on, when he went away, a short sheep grey coloured jacket, coarse tow trowsers, old shirt patched before, old shoes, but no buckles, and a good felt hat. Whoever takes up and secures said servant, in any of his Majesty's goals, so as the owner may have him again, shall have Three Pounds reward, and reasonable charges,*
     *paid by*  *ISAAC HEWES.*
*The Pennsylvania Gazette*, September 14, 1769.

         *New-Castle County, October* 3, 1769.
WAS committed to the goal of this county, upon suspicion of being runaway servants, to wit. JOHN MONEY, born in Ireland, about 5 feet 6 inches high, black hair, pale complexion, by trade a weaver; had on, when committed, a light coloured homespun cloth coat, linsey waistcoat, and coarse tow trowsers. ELIZABETH MOORE, a native Irish woman, about 30 years of age, fair complexion, brown hair; had on, when committed, a stampt cotton gown, of a purple colour, a linsey petticoat, shoes, and stockings. Their masters (if any they have) are desired to come, pay their cost, and take them away, in 6 weeks from this date, or they will be sold for the same
    by THOMAS PUSEY, Goaler.
*The Pennsylvania Gazette*, October 12, 1769.


     Kent County of Delaware, December 14, 1769.
RUN-AWAY, from his bail the subscriber of Kent-County on Delaware aforesaid, about the first of this inst. a certain JOHN EVERET, about five feet ten inches high, 22 years of age; had on when he went away, and oldbrown broad-cloth coat, a c[ut]veleet waistcoat, brown broad cloth breeches, blue and white yarn stockings, a new pair of shoes, a pair of large carved silver buckles, and a white flannel shirt. Whoever will take up the said JOHN EVERET, and secure him so that the subscriber may have intelligence thereof, shall have FIVE POUNDS reward, and all reasonable charges paid.
     ROBERT HALL.
  *The Pennsylvania Journal, and the Weekly Advertiser*, December 21, 1769; December 28, 1769; January 4, 1770.

             December 17, 1769.
*RUN away from the Subscriber, living* 4 *miles below New-Castle, a servant man, named William Blaney, born in this country,* 17 *years of age, about* 5 *feet* 6 *or* 7 *inches high, of a fair complexion, wears his own dark brown hair: Had on, an old superfine blue broadcloth coat, a blue cloth jacket, broke about the breast, an old blue and white linen jacket, an old narrow brimmed beaver hat, without loops, new buckskin breeches, and new shoes. He halts a*

*little, occasioned by a cut on his great toe. The coat and jackets do not fit him well, being his master's clothes.* Whoever takes up said servant, and secures him, so that his master may have him again, shall have TWENTY SHILLINGS reward, or FORTY SHILLINGS, if taken more than 20 miles from New Castle, and reasonable charges,
    paid by  JOHN KING.
*The Pennsylvania Gazette,* December 28, 1769; January 4, 1769. See *The Pennsylvania* Gazette, July 12, 1770, and *The Pennsylvania Journal, and the Weekly Advertiser,* August 2, 1770.

## 1770

    New-Castle county, December 28, 1769.
NOW in the goal of said county, a certain Elizabeth Berry, about 20 years of age, born in Ireland, a low thick set woman, fair complexion, brown hair, and speaks much like an English woman; she says she served her time with Jacob Philimon, in Frederick county, Maryland; had on, when committed, a linsey coat, and coarse homespun shift, without shoes or stockings. Also Thomas Bolton, born in England, about 30 years of age, 5 feet 2 or 3 inches high, brown hair, and red beard, by trade a taylor; had on, and with him, when committed, two suits of cloaths, one of a light cloth colour, and one blue, the waistcoat of the latter, full trimmed, with yellow gilt buttons. Likewise Mary Watson, born in Ireland, 25 years of age, fair complexion, sandy hair, and a little pock-marked; had on, when committed, a striped stuff gown, a purple calicoe ditto, high heeled leather shoes, white metal buckles, and worsted stockings; says she came into this country with Captain Burn, about two years ago, and belongs to John Doyle, of the city of Philadelphia. Likewise a Negroe man, named Cuff, about 25 years of age; he says he was born in Barbados, and lived with Jonathan Smith, of Philadelphia; had on, when committed, a blue waistcoat, with a short swanskin ditto, long trowsers, and brown great coat; his cloathes much worn. Since his confinement, says he belongs to Thomas Saven, in Maryland. Their masters, if any they have, are desired to come and pay their charges, in six weeks from the date, and take them away, or they will be sold for the same,
    by THOMAS PUSEY, Goaler.
*The Pennsylvania Gazette,* January 11, 1770.


RUN away, on the 9th Instant, from the Subscriber, living in Newark, New Castle County, an Irish Servant Man, named Cadry Leary, about 5 Feet 5 Inches high, chunky made, black Hair, Pock marked, has a down grum Look, broad Face, a Hollow in his Nose, and a Lump on one of his Legs, above the Ancle; had on, a Beaver Hat, short dark grey lapelled Coat, with Horn

Buttons, buckskin Breeches, blue Worsted Stockings, and turned Pumps; he speaks very bad English, was seen going towards Philadelphia, and acted as a dumb Man by Signs. Whoever takes up and secure said Servant, so that his master may have him again, shall have Twenty Shillings Reward, and reasonable Charges, paid by      RICHARD LEMMON.

*The Pennsylvania Gazette*, January 18, 1770. See *The Pennsylvania Journal, and the Weekly Advertiser*, January 18, 1770 and *The New-York Gazette; and the Weekly Mercury*, February 5, 1770.

Newark, Newcastle county, January 12.
RAN-AWAY from the subscriber, an Irish servant man named CADRY LEACY; he is about five or six inches high, black hair, pock marked, has a surly down look, broad face, hollow in his nose and a lump on one of his legs above the ancle; he had on a beaver hat, a short gray lapelled coat, and black horn buttons on it with wire shanks to them, buckskin breeches, blue worsted stockings, and turned pumps; speaks very bad English: He was seen going towards Chester, and acted as a dumb man, by signs. Whoever takes up said servant, so that his said master may have him again, shall receive TWENTY SHILLINGS reward, paid by me     RICHARD LEMON.

*The Pennsylvania Journal, and the Weekly Advertiser*, January 18, 1770; January 25, 1770. See *The Pennsylvania Gazette*, January 18, 1770 and *The New-York Gazette; and the Weekly Mercury*, February 5, 1770.

### PHILADELPHIA, JANUARY 29.

We just now hear the one Cadry Leacy, a Runaway Servant Man (who pretended to be dumb) belonging to Mr. Richard Lemon, of Newark, Newcastle County, was on Saturday committed to Gloucester Goal, for the barbarous Murder of a Woman, in New-Jersey, whose Husband had met this Murderer and sent him to his House for Entertainment. This attrocious Action was attended with many extraordinary Circumstances, which we have neither Time nor Room to insert at present.

*The New-York Gazette; and the Weekly Mercury*, February 5, 1770. See *The Pennsylvania Gazette*, January 18, 1770, and *The Pennsylvania Journal, and the Weekly Advertiser*, January 18, 1770

### FORTY SHILLINGS Reward.

RUN away from the subscriber, in Frederick county, Maryland, in August last, a country born NEGROE fellow, named JUPITER, about 35 years of age, 5 feet 9 or 10 inches high, stout and well made, slow of motion and speech, but a very handy fellow at all kinds of farming business, has a small

scald or bare place on his head, and one of his little fingers stiff, his clothes uncertain; he has, since his elopement, been some time confined in New-Castle goal, and escaped with a pair of hand-cuffs on, from a person attempting to bring him home; he was born in New-Castle county, and it is thought will try to conceal himself there, until an opportunity of going off by water may offer, of which all masters of vessels will please take notice. Any person securing said Negroe, in any goal, so that his master may have him again, shall be entitled to the above reward, from
*January*, 1770.  WILLIAM BUCHANAN.
*The Pennsylvania Gazette*, February 15, 1770.


THREE POUNDS Reward.
RUN away the 16th instant, from Isaac Bailey, living in West Marlborough, in Chester county, one THOMAS LITTLE, who was judged out of New-Castle goal, for a debt due to one John Underhill, living in Kennet; he was born in Ireland, is about 5 feet 8 or 9 inches high, of a sandy complexion, wears his own hair, of a sandy colour, cut short on the top of his head, a thick well set fellow, and talks good English; can do something at the weaving business; had on, when he went away, a grey homespun jacket, grey yarn stockings, velvet breeches, and supposed to have with him a velvet jacket, and light coloured broadcloth coat, a lapelled striped jacket, black knit breeches, and a grey surtout; he is supposed to have gone towards the Lower Counties, or the Jersies. Whoever takes up the said Thomas Little and brings him to the said Bailey, or Underhill, shall have the above reward, and reasonable charges, paid by
*March* 21, 1770.  JOHN UNDERHILL.
*The Pennsylvania Gazette*, March 29, 1770.


FIFTY DOLLARS Reward.
*RUN away last night, from the subscriber, living at Christiana Bridge, in New-Castle county, a servant man, named William Watters, a shoemaker by trade, a likely well set fellow, about 25 years of age, 5 feet 8 inches high, smooth face, very talkative, and amorous with women; he has been in the country several years, and well acquainted in Philadelphia, and several parts of the country; it is likely he will endeavour to get towards New-York, Boston, or some part to the northward. Whoever takes up the said servant, and brings him to me, shall receive, if taken in this government, Six Dollars; if in the province of Pennsylvania, Twelve Dollars; if in the Jerseys, Twenty Dollars; if in New York, or Boston, Fifty Dollars, paid by me*
*March* 20, 1770.  ALLEN GILLESPIE.
*N. B. He went off in company with another runaway man, named Thomas*

Littler, a lusty likely man, 5 feet 8 inches high. As the above Watters has been guilty of every base crime, excepting murder, I make no doubt but every good man will exert himself, in detecting such a villain. I do forewarn all persons from harbouring or dealing with the above Watters.
                    Allen Gillespie.
*The Pennsylvania Gazette*, March 29, 1770. See *The Pennsylvania Chronicle, and Universal Advertiser*, From Monday, April 2, to Monday, April 9, 1770.


RUN away from the Subscriber, living in New Castle, a Servant MAN, about 23 Years of Age, 5 Feet 7 Inches high, thick bushy Hair, large Eyes: had on, a grey coloured cloth Surtout Coat, with a fall-back Cape, spotted Jacket, Check Shirt, yellow Velvet Breeches, new Shoes and Stockings. Whoever takes up said Servant, and secures him, so as his Master may have him again, shall have TWENTY SHILLINGS Reward. It is imagined he is gone to Philadelphia.          THOMAS PUSEY.
*The Pennsylvania Gazette*, March 29, 1770.


MADE his Escape out of New-Castle Goal, on the 28th of March, a certain John Thomas, otherwise Richard Smith, an English Convict Servant Man, aged about 21 Years, about five Feet 8 or 9 Inches high, brown Complexion, and short brown Hair; had on, a Hat bound round the Brim, an old light coloured Drab Coat, with broad Metal Buttons. Whoever apprehends said Servant, and secures him in any of his Majesty's Goals, so as the Subscriber may have him again, shall have Thirty Shillings Reward, paid by
          ROBERT MACK, *Goal-keeper of New-Castle.*
N. B. He seems a very innocent Fellow, but is a great Rogue; one Skirt of his Coat is very greasy; and he talks in the West Country Dialect.
*The Pennsylvania Gazette*, April 5, 1770.


### FIFTY DOLLARS REWARD.
RAN away last night from the subscriber, living at Christiana-Bridge Newcastle County, a servant man named WILLIAM WATERS, a shoemaker by trade; he is a likely well set fellow, about twenty-five years of age, five feet eight inches high, smooth faced, very talkative, and amorous with women, he has been in the country several years and is well acquainted in Philadelphia and several other parts of the country. It is likely he will endeavour to get towards New-York, Boston, or some part of the northward. Whoever takes up the said servant, and brings him to me, shall receive, if taken in this government, Six Dollars, if in the province of Pennsylvania,

Twelve Dollars, if in the Jerseys, Twenty Dollars, if in New-York or Boston, Fifty Dollars, paid by me  ALLEN GILLESPIE.

N. B. He went off in company with another Runaway man, named THOMAS LEITLER, a lusty likely man, five feet eight inches high. As the above Waters has been guilty of every beastly crime, excepting murder, I make no doubt, but every good man will exert himself in detecting, such a villain. I do forward all persons from harbouring or dealing with the above Waters.

*The Pennsylvania Chronicle, and Universal Advertiser*, From Monday, April 2, to Monday, April 9, 1770. See *The Pennsylvania Gazette*, March 29, 1770.

*EIGHT DOLLARS Reward.*

RUN away, on the 25th of February last, from the Subscriber, living in Duck Creek Hundred, Kent County, on Delaware, a dark Mulattoe Servant Fellow, named George Duffee, aged about 25 Years, about 5 Feet 6 or 7 Inches high, thick set, of a down Look, with a Scar over his Eye; had on, when he went away, a homespun cloth Jacket, of a light colour, an old Felt Hat, a striped blue and white Linsey under Jacket, half worn, a new Tow Linen Shirt, two Pair of Trowsers, one of which striped Linsey, the other Tow Linen, and old Shoes and Stockings. Whoever takes up and secures said Servant, so that his Master may have him again, shall have the above Reward, with reasonable Charges, paid by
March 29, 1770.  JOSEPH MEREDITH.

N. B. All Masters of Vessels are forbid to carry him off at their Peril.

*The Pennsylvania Gazette*, April 12, 1770.

*FOUR DOLLARS Reward.*

RUN away, on Sunday evening, the 20th instant, from the subscriber, living in Brandywine Hundred, New-Castle county, HUGH DOUGHERTY, an Irish servant, by trade a weaver, about 35 years of age, 5 feet 4 or 5 inches high, red faced, and much addicted to drink strong liquor; had on, a blue broadcloth coat lappelled, with old white metal buttons, a red lapelled jacket, leather apron, cloth breeches, light blue ribbed yarn stockings, good shoes, and a half worn hat. He was seen at the barracks in Philadelphia, on Wednesday evening last, enquiring for work at his trade, and is supposed to have gone towards Trenton. He was bought out of Chester goal, about three weeks ago. Whoever secures said servant in any of his Majesty's goals, and gives notice to the subscriber shall have the above reward, paid by me
ROBERT JACK.

N. B. Masters of vessels, and others, are forbid to harbour him at their peril. Perhaps he may change his apparel, as he did at the barracks.
May 25, 1770.

*The Pennsylvania Gazette*, May 31, 1770; June 14, 1770.

Chester County, June 8, 1770.
NOW in the goal of this county the following persons, committed on suspicion of being runaway servants, viz. John Daily, *about 50 years of age, 5 feet 9 or 10 inches high, of a black complexion, wears a brown Wig; had on, when committed, a brown coat, a blue striped flannel jacket, with the stripes across, a check shirt, old leather breeches, coarse shoes and stockings.* James Farrall, *about 30 years of age, of a dark complexion, wears a grey wig, a brown coat, a blue cloth jacket, a blue striped flannel ditto, with the stripes across, a white shirt, old leather breeches, coarse shoes and stockings.* Patrick Reiley, *is about 30 years of age, about 5 feet 7 inches high, of a fair complexion, wears his own sandy coloured hair; had on a grey fearnought sailor's jacket, a blue striped flannel ditto, the stripes across, a white shirt, ozenbrigs breeches, coarse shoes and stockings.* John Mullagan, *about 21 years of age, 5 feet 9 or 10 inches high, of a fair complexion, wears his own hair; of a lightish colour; had on a blue and red striped flannel jacket, with the stripes across, a check shirt, ozenbrigs breeches, coarse shoes and stockings. The above described persons are all native Irishmen, and say they came into New-Castle about 3 weeks ago, with one Captain Norris, from Ireland, but don't know the vessel's name. Their masters, if any, are desired to come, pay charges, and take them away, or they will be discharged in 6 Weeks from the date hereof.*

Likewise committed to the said goal, the following runaway servants, viz. William Tiday, *who says he is a servant to John Dorsey, in Baltimore county.* Weldon Dunbar, *who says he is a servant to Josiah Dellum, of Baltimore county. And* Edward Clemmons, *who says he is a servant to James Hinchmam, in Gloucester county, in the Jerseys. Their masters are desired to come, pay charges, and take them away.*
JOSEPH THOMAS, *Goaler.*

*The Pennsylvania Gazette*, June 14, 1770; June 28, 1770.

New-Castle Hundred, June 6, 1770.
RUN away from the subscriber, the 5th instant, an apprentice lad, named STEPHEN PIKE, about 18 years of age; had on, when he went away, an old castor hat, with a patch on the crown, light coloured home made jacket, homespun shirt and trowsers, shoes not fellows, with square brass buckles; took with him some of his master's bricklaying tools, has two particular marks on him, to wit, on the inside of his left knee, the mark of a bile, and on the outside of his right knee, the mark of a cut of an ax. Whoever apprehends said apprentice lad, and secures him in any of his Majesty's goals, so that his

master may have him again, shall have Ten Shillings reward, and all reasonable charges, if brought home, paid by CORNELIUS HAINS.
  *The Pennsylvania Gazette,* June 14, 1770. See *The Pennsylvania Gazette,* September 19, 1771.

TEN DOLLARS Reward.
*RUN away, on Monday, the 26th of June, from the subscriber, living in New-Castle, an Irish servant man, called John Teernan, about 5 feet 8 inches high, well made, is marked with the small- pox, has black hair, tied behind, and talks much with the brogue; had on, and took with him, a light coloured nap coat, with Pinchbeck buttons, inlaid with steel, two striped silk damascus jackets, Russia drilling breeches, good shoes and stockings, silver shoe and knee buckles. Whoever takes up said servant, and secures him, so that the subscriber may get him, shall receive the above reward, and reasonable charges, if brought home, paid by     ROBERT MACK.*
*N. B. He took with him an old dun coloured horse, with saddle and bridle; he also had several advertisements with him, and may pretend to be going after runaways. All masters of vessels are forbid taking him off at their peril.*
  *The Pennsylvania Gazette,* July 5, 1770; August 30, 1770.


*RUN away from the subscriber, living four miles below New-Castle, a servant lad, named William Bleany, this country born, about 18 years of age, about 5 feet 8 inches high, with dark brown hair; had on and took with him, a darkish coloured cloth lapelled jacket, home made, lined with striped linsey, and had pewter buttons, a flowered worsted jacket, without sleeves (called Mechlenburg) one coarse and one fine shirt, a pair of check trowsers, and a pair of tow ditto, calf-skin shoes, almost new, with broad founders buckles, and a good coarse hat. Whoever takes up said servant, and secures him, so as his master may have him again, shall have Thirty Shillings reward, and reasonable charges, paid by     JOHN KING.*
*N. B. He took a sickle with him, marked W. B. and is supposed to be gone towards Maryland to reap.*
  *The Pennsylvania Gazette,* July 12, 1770; August 9, 1770; August 16, 1770. See *The Pennsylvania Gazette,* December 28, 1769, and *The Pennsylvania Journal, and the Weekly Advertiser,* August 2, 1770.

*Easton Goal, in Northampton County, July 2,* 1770.
COMMITTED to my custody, on Saturday, the 30th day of June last, a certain Negroe man who calls himself Charles Hamilton, says he belongs to Joseph Garrison, of Newberry township, New-Castle county; he is about 30

years of age, and about 5 feet 5 inches high; these are therefore to desire his said master to come, or send for the said Negroe, and pay what reasonable charges are accrued on him. JOHN SPEARING, Goaler.

*The Pennsylvania Gazette*, July 19, 1770. There was no township of that name in Newcastle County.


RAN away July the fourth, from the subscriber, living four miles below New-Castle, a servant lad named WILLIAM BLEANY, this Country born, 18 years of age, 5 feet 7 or 8 inches high, short dark brown hair, smooth faced, one of his great toes is much larger than the other, occasioned by the cut of an ax, had on and took with him, a darkish coloured cloath lapelled jacket home made, lined with striped lincey with pewter buttons, a flowered worsted jacket without sleeves, called mecklingburg, one course and one fine shirt, one pair of check trowsers and one pair of tow ditto, calf skin shoes, with broad founders buckles, a good coarse hat. Whoever takes up and secures said servant in any goal, so that his master may have him again, shall have THIRTY SHILLINGS reward & reasonable charges paid,
by JOHN KING.
N. B. He took one baby's silver spoon, marked T
T B
One silver tea spoon, marked M+T
One sickle marked W B
All masters of vessels are forbid to carry him off. Aug. 2.

*The Pennsylvania Journal, and the Weekly Advertiser*, August 2, 1770; August 9, 1770. See *The Pennsylvania Gazette*, December 28, 1769, and *The Pennsylvania Gazette*, July 12, 1770.


SIX DOLLARS Reward.

RUN away from the subscriber, in Dover, Kent county, on Delaware, on Wednesday, the 18th of July last, a country born servant man, named DAVID MARKER, about 21 years of age, a house-carpenter by trade, about 5 feet 9 inches high, well set, fresh coloured, slow of speech, and little to say; had on, when he went away, a half worn claret coloured saggathy coat, buckskin breeches, half worn beaver hat; it is very probable he may change his apparel. Whoever takes up and secures said servant man, so that his master may have him again, shall have the above reward, and reasonable charges
paid by JOHN BANNING.

*The Pennsylvania Gazette*, August 9, 1770; August 23, 1770.

## Twenty-Six Dollars Reward.

Run away from his bail, in the borough of Wilmington, in the county of Newcastle, on Delaware, the 26th of this instant (July) ROBERT HILBURN, a man of about 30 years of age and about 5 feet 7 or 8 inches high, straight black hair, and a very remarkable redness about his mouth and nose, much resembling a great drinker; by trade a cooper, but of late hath followed butchering, he hath a smo
oth deceitful tongue, by which he hath insinuated himself into people's favour, and thereby got considerably in debt: His own wearing apparel was a white linen frock, a jean jacket, new castor hat, and new buckskin breeches, remarkable for having but one pocket and only three buttons on each knee, silver knee and shoe buckles, rode a chesnut sorrel horse, about 10 years old, about 12 hands high, and an old saddle and bridle, a silver watch, maker's name not known.

Also HENRY WILBY, a short well set fellow, dirty brown hair and look, about 5 feet 6 inches high, of Dutch extraction; his wearing apparel is not known to be any more than a shirt and pair of trowsers, a striped linen jacket which he had made a few days before, he likewise had a watch, maker's name not known, silver shoe buckles, and rode a small black horse of about 12 or 13 hands high, and about 4 years old, and stole a saddle from William Jones, with a pair of double stirrup irons, blue plush seat and a blue cloth with red binding: As the horses and watches were fraudulently obtained, it is supposed they robbed a shallop which was broke open a few nights before; out of which was taken, one light coloured cloth coat with mohair buttons almost new, one dark brown sagathy ditto, one thick brown cloth jacket lined with blue, lappeled and slash sleeves, one pair of brown velvet breeches which have been seated, and one pair black ditto half worn, one beaver hat almost new, with sundry other things. Whosoever secures the said villains, so that they may be brought to justice, shall have the above reward, with all reasonable charges, or one half for either,

        paid by us,    WILLIAM JONES,
                           FRANCIS ROBINSON.

*The Pennsylvania Chronicle, and Universal Advertiser*, From Monday, August 6, to Monday, August 13, 1770 From Monday, August 13, to Monday, August 20, 1770.


ON the 30th of July last, was stolen from William Patterson, near Christiana Bridge, New-Castle County, a middle sized, well made horse, of a dark bay colour, about 9 years old, in very good order; he is a natural pacer, with a long switch tail, a hanging mane, shod before, and some white hairs on his neck. It is fully believed that the said horse was stolen by a servant lad, named ROBERT M'DERMED, belonging to Mr. James Partrige, living at the

aforesaid place; he, said servant, being seen (in company with another man) to have said horse in his custody. As a considerable quantity of clothes were stolen at the time the aforesaid M'Dermed ran away, his apparel cannot fully be described, but was seen to have on a bluish dark outside coat, with a striped jacket, bluish breeches, and blue ribbed stockings. Who ever takes up and secures said horse, so that I may have him again, shall receive Forty Shillings reward; also *Forty Shillings* for the thief, so that he may be brought to justice,
    paid by  WILLIAM PATTERSON.
N. B. It is supposed that the above M'Dermed intended to cross Sasquehannah, near Peach Bottom.
 *The Pennsylvania Gazette*, August 16, 1770; August 30, 1770.

              Wilmington, September 10.
ABSENTED herself from her Master's service in Wilmington, on the 8th day of August last, an apprentice Girl, named MARY HAWKS, the daughter of Jane Hawks, of Penn's Neck, Salem county, West New Jersey. The mother had on a short gown and petticoat of dark blue broad striped linsey the daughter had a new shift, two tow ditto, linsey short gown and petticoat, is about nine years old, full face, black eyes, and large teeth. It is supposed she is with her mother in Philadelphia, as they were lately seen there. Any person taking up the said apprentice, so that her master shall have her again, shall have TWENTY SHILLINGS Reward, and reasonable charges
    paid by  JOHN GYLESE.
 *The Pennsylvania Journal, and the Weekly Advertiser*, September 20, 1770; September 27, 1770.

              *September* 14, 1770.
WAS left at the subscriber's, in Newport, New-Castle county, on Delaware, on the first instant, by a person who called himself *John Morgan*, a bright bay mare, about 13 or 14 hands high, her hind feet white, supposed to have a Colt, also a saddle and bridle. The man who left said mare was well set, pock marked, about 5 feet 6 inches high; had on a blue coat, grey flip, and striped trowsers. The owner of said mare is desired to come, pay charges, and take her away, in 4 weeks from this date, or she will be sold by
      CONRAD GRAY.
 *The Pennsylvania Gazette*, September 27, 1770.

      Mill-Creek Hundred, New-Castle County, October 29, 1770.
RUN away from the subscriber, an Irish servant woman, named Elizabeth Bryan, had on, when she went away, an old black quilted petticoat, old black cloak, calicoe short gown, striped silk handkerchief; she is about 35 years of

age, 5 feet 4 inches high, a large scar on her right wrist, dark brown hair, and talks much with the brogue. Whoever secures said servant, so as her master may have her again, shall have Twenty Shillings reward, and reasonable charges, paid by     MATTHEW GIFFEN.
*The Pennsylvania Gazette*, November 15, 1770.


*Wilmington, New Castle county, the tenth of* 12*th month*, 1770.
TWENTY SHILLINGS Reward.
RUN away from the subscriber, yesterday, a servant boy named William Patterson, about 16 years of age, a cooper by trade, fair hair and complexion, down look, walks stooping; had on, when he went away, a light coloured home-made cloth coat, linen jacket, nankeen breeches, a new hat, John Clark's make, new shoes, and two homespun shirts; he took with him an old cloth jacket, with new sleeves of a different colour, and old leather breeches. Whoever takes up the said servant, and secures him, so that his master may have him again, shall have the above reward, and reasonable charges,
          paid by     HENRY REYNOLDS.
N. B. All masters of vessels are forbid to harbour or take him away at their peril.
*The Pennsylvania Gazette*, December 13, 1770.


*MADE his escape last night, a certain Negroe man, called BRISTOR, committed to my custody as a runaway, said his master lived at St. George's Hundred, New-Castle county; he is about 5 feet 5 inches high, well set, very apt to smile when spoke to; had on, when he went away, a white hat, white cloth jacket, homespun shirt, blue trowsers, good shoes, with brass buckles in them. Whoever takes up and secures said Negroe, shall have, if taken in this province,* Forty Shillings, *and if out of the Province,* Three Prounds *[sic] with reasonable charges, paid by*
Salem, November 9, 1770.          JOSEPH BURROUGHS.
*The Pennsylvania Gazette*, December 13, 1770. See *The Pennsylvania Chronicle, and Universal Advertiser*, From Monday, December 17, to Monday, December 24, 1770.


FIVE POUNDS Reward.
RUN away on the 22d of April last, from the subscriber, living in Kent county, on Delaware, a Mulattoe slave, named JOE, a slim Indian made fellow, has had 5 fingers on each hand, which is visible to be seen; had on, and took with him, a jacket and breeches of mixed Negroe cloth, a snuff coloured broadcloth coat, a blue and yellow damask jacket, tow trowsers,

good shoes, and stockings. Whoever takes up said slave, and secures him, so that his master may have him again, shall have the above reward,
   paid by  HENRY STEVENS.
*The Pennsylvania Gazette*, December 20, 1770.


RUN away the 4th day of this instant December, from the subscriber, living in Brandywine Hundred, New-Castle county, a servant girl, named MARTHA EYERS, about 22 years of age, fair hair; had on, when she went away, a brown bonnet, a blue cloak, and a white linen short gown, a striped linsey woolsey petticoat, and a pair of leather heeled shoes. It is thought she went to Philadelphia. Whoever takes up the said servant girl, and secures her, so that her master may have her again, shall have Ten Shillings reward, and reasonable charges, paid by  ANDREW M'KEE.
*The Pennsylvania Gazette*, December 20, 1770.


      FORTY SHILLINGS Reward.
RAN-AWAY on the 29th of November, an Irish Servant Man, named JAMES O'HERRIN, about 25 years old, by trade a Black Smith, about 4 feet 6 inches high, a down look, wears his own brown hair, coarse spoken, had on when he went away, a Russia linen shirt, two pair of trowsers of the same, yarn stockings, a pair of half worn shoes, two blue broad-cloth jackets, and a half worn felt hat. Whoever takes up said servant, and secures him in any gaol, so that his Master shall get him again, shall receive the above reward from the subscriber, living at Duck Creek in Kent County on Delaware.
   WILLIAM REES.
*The Pennsylvania Journal, and the Weekly Advertiser*, December 20, 1770; December 27, 1770; January 3, 1771.


MADE his escape, last night, a certain negro man called Bristol, committed to my custody as a run-away, said his master lived in St. George's hundred, Newcastle county; about 5 feet 5 inches high, well set and apt to smile when spoke to; he had on when he went away, a white hat, a white cloth jacket, homespun shirt, blue trowsers, and good shoes with brass buckles in them. Whoever takes up and secures said negro, shall have, if taken in this province, FORTY SHILLINGS, and if out of the Province, THREE POUNDS, with reasonable charges, paid by    JOSEPH BURROUGHS.
Salem, November 9, 1770.
 *The Pennsylvania Chronicle, and Universal Advertiser*, From Monday, December 17, to Monday, December 24, 1770. See *The Pennsylvania Gazette*, December 13, 1770.

# 1771

TEN DOLLARS Reward.
*Purchased by Doctor* Bouchell, *as he runs*, [sic]
A Pale Mulatto Man (a Slave for Life) named *Joe*, but now passes by the Name of *PRINCE ORANGE*, and often changes his name. Was seen in April last, at Blackford Town, and worked near that place for some weeks. Was born at Cambridge, in Dorset county, and sold in Kent, on Delaware. He is a tall, slender, boney fellow; about thirty years old; very talkative when in drink; can read a little; and pretends to be a seaman; has a small stoop in his shoulders, thin face, high nose, a little pitted with the small-pox; is a drunkard, swearer, and liar; had on a whitish brown country cloth jacket, and red under ditto. Whoever delivers the said fellow at Mr. WITHERSPOON'S, in New-Castle County, shall receive the above reward, and all reasonable charges paid by            SLUYTER BOUCHELL.
Jan 10.

*The Pennsylvania Journal, and the Weekly Advertiser*, January 10, 1771; January 24, 1771; *The Pennsylvania Gazette*, March 7, 1771. Minor differences between the papers.


FORTY SHILLINGS Reward.
RAN-AWAY on the 9th instant, from the subscriber, an Apprentice LAD, named TAGUE RIGGON, about 17 years of age, near five Feet two Inches high, had on and took with him, a felt hat, new light coloured sagathy coat, without lining; striped lincy jacket, white shirt, buckskin breeches, light blue worsted stockings, black grain pumps, and plain brass buckles; It is supposed he is gone to his Parents, living near Indian River. Whoever takes up said Apprentice, and secures him in any Goal, so that his master may get him again, shall receive the above reward, and reasonable charges, paid by DAVID WARE, Shoemaker; living in Front-street, a little below Pine-street, Philadelphia.       Jan 10.

*The Pennsylvania Journal, and the Weekly Advertiser*, January 10, 1771; January 24, 1771.


Kent-County, Feb, 8, 1771.
THERE is now in gaol, in the town of Dover, a certain Negro Man named JAMES, who says he belongs to one John Emory, in the island of St. Christophers, in the West-Indies: Also, one WILLIAM MILLS, a White Man, who says he belongs to one William Anders, of Joppa, in Maryland.

*The Pennsylvania Journal, and the Weekly Advertiser*, February 14, 1771; February 21, 1771. See *The Pennsylvania Gazette*, May 2, 1771.

*Christiana Bridge, February* 13, 1771.
*RUN away from the subscriber, last Sunday, a certain* EDWARD M'COLGAN, *born in Ireland, aged 32 or 33 years, about 5 feet 6 inches high, fresh coloured, has long blackish hair, a little marked with the smallpox, and rocks in his walking: Had on, when he went away, a light grey napped duffil coat and waistcoat, bound and lined, tape the same colour as the coat, the waistcoat wore a good deal below his breast, light coloured cloth breeches, old blue yarn stockings, new shoes, one buckled with a broad brass buckle, the other tied with a leather string. Whoever takes up and secures said servant, so that his master may have him again, if within the county of New-Castle, shall receive the sum of* Forty Shillings, *or out of said county,* Three Pounds, *on confining him in any of his Majesty's goals, or* Three Pounds, *and reasonable charges, upon delivering him to*
PATRICK M'GONNEGAL.
*The Pennsylvania Gazette*, March 7, 1771.


RUN-AWAY from the subscriber, in New-Castle county, an Irish SERVANT MAN, named JOHN M'DANIEL, aged about 20 years, about 5 feet 10 inches high, stoops forward, has a hump back, short black hair, and fair complexion; had on when he went away, and took with him, an old blue great coat, a close body coat of superfine cloth much wore, when new of a claret colour, white flannel jacket, one coarse shirt, two pair of old white woollen stockings, old shoes, with pewter buckles, and an old hat. Whoever takes up said servant, and secures him in any gaol, so that his master may have him again, shall have THIRTY SHILLINGS reward, and reasonable charges, paid by me   CORNELIUS ARMSTRONG.
March 7.
*The Pennsylvania Journal, and the Weekly Advertiser*, March 14, 1771.


FOUR DOLLARS Reward.
*RUN away about the* 1st *of March,* 1771, *from the subscriber, living in Christiana Hundred, New-Castle county, an Irish servant man, named John Shehan, about* 20 *years of age, about 5 feet* 10 *or* 11 *inches high, dark streight brown hair, cut on the top of his head, has a sharp nose, a wide mouth, grey eyes, a small beard, fresh coloured, walks very stately, talks a little on the Irish accent; had on, and took with him, a light coloured homespun cloth surtout, with mohair buttons with a red and white cotton jacket, and a grey cloth ditto, without sleeves, and horn buttons,* 2 *homespun linen shirts, halfworn buckskin breeches,* 1 *pair blue worsted stockings,* 1 *pair grey ribbed yarn ditto, a half-worn beaver hat, a black handkerchief, good new shoes, with steel buckles, and had with him a China faced watch; he is very apt to*

*swap away his clothes, and perhaps may change them; he is much given to strong liquor, had no money with him, but perhaps he may sell his watch. Whoever takes up and secures him in any goal, so that his master may have him again, shall have the above reward, and reasonable charges,*
*paid by* WILLIAM CLENFAY.
*The Pennsylvania Gazette,* March 28, 1771.


*RUN away from the subscriber, on the 26th day of November,* 1770, *a young Negroe man, called Spencer, about* 24 *years of age, supposed to have altered his name to that of* Harman Blake; *had on when he went away, and carried with him, two tow linen shirts, one pair of tow trowsers, one old linsey-woolsey jacket, one old superfine broadcloth ditto, cloth coloured, one pair of thread stockings, a pair of new pumps, and a half-worn felt hat. Whoever takes up the said fellow, and secures him in any goal, and sends the subscriber word, shall have Three Pounds reward, paid by William Holland, on the south side of Indian River.*
*N. B. The above said Negroe is a middling tall fellow, somewhat of a yellowish complexion, full eyed, out mouthed, and plays on the violin.*
March 26, 1771.
*The Pennsylvania Gazette,* March 28, 1771.

*New-Castle County, on Delaware, April* 16, 1771.
*NOW confined in the goal of said county as runaways, viz. A certain* Betty Berry, *as she calls herself, about* 20 *years of age, says she is servant to Mr. Daniel Turner, of the county aforesaid; a certain* Polly Matthews, *a likely young girl, says she belongs to Mr. Thomas Davis, Inn-holder, at Frederick-Town, Caecil county, Maryland; a certain* Sanders Bickham, *a lusty young fellow, wears a bonnet, and says he belongs to Duncan Caudon, of Sword's-Town, near Charles-Town in Maryland.*

*A Negroe man, named* Jack, *and* Prudence, *his wife, who say they belong to James Cronkelton, of New Castle county; a Negroe man, named* Tom, *says he belongs to Widow Bayard, of Philadelphia; a Negroe man, named* Jack, *says he belongs to Francis Holland, of Holland's Island, in Maryland.*

*Their masters are desired to come in ten days from the date hereof, pay charges, and take them away, otherwise they will be sold out for the same, without further notice, by* ROBERT MACK, Goaler.
*The Pennsylvania Gazette,* April 18, 1771.


RUN away, on the 26th of last month, a certain MICHAEL CONNOR, by trade a Barber; he has a very great stoppage in his speech; had on, when he

went away, a Wilton coat, without lining; a white dimity jacket, new shoes, with a pair of silver buckles; he is supposed to be gone to New-York; he stole several articles out of my house. Any person taking up the said Michael, and securing him, so that I may have him again, shall have Forty Shillings reward,
paid by me      JOSEPH RUTH,
living at Christiana Bridge, New-Castle county.
*The Pennsylvania Gazette,* May 2, 1771.

Kent County, on Delaware, April 16, 1772, THIS is to give notice, that there was committed to Dover goal, in October last, a certain WILLIAM MILLS, who says he is a servant to William Anders, or Andrews, living at Joppa, in Maryland; and unless his said master applies for him, he will be sold to pay charges, in four weeks from this date. This is the second time of his being advertised.
HENRY WELLS, Goaler.
*The Pennsylvania Gazette,* May 1, 1771. See *The Pennsylvania Journal, and the Weekly Advertiser,* February 14, 1771; February 21, 1771.

THREE POUNDS Reward.
RUN away, on the 21st of this instant May, from the subscriber, living in Whiteclay-creek Hundred, New-Castle county, a servant lad, this country-born, named MOSES COCHRAN, about 19 years of age, 5 feet 10 inches high, wears his own brown straight hair, parted before, of a very dark complexion, much pitted with the small-pox; had on, when he went away, a new hat, light coloured cloth jacket, with cuffs to it, a linsey lappelled waistcoat, with wooden buttons, check shirt and trowsers, blue and white thread stockings, good shoes, and brass buckles; he is remarkably stoop shouldered; he served a part of his time with Thomas Lunn;—has been uneasy some time past, and signified he wanted a new master; but it is supposed he will enlist, if he meets with an opportunity. Whoever takes up said servant, and brings him home, or secures him in and goal, so that his master may get him again, shall have the above reward,
paid by    JOHN CHAMBERS.
*The Pennsylvania Gazette,* May 30, 1771.

EIGHT DOLLARS Reward.
*RUN away, the 15th of May last, one* William Marshall, *a young man, who bound himself apprentice after he was of age, to Isaac Cox, near Dover town, in Kent county, on Delaware, to learn the trade of chaise and chair-making; he is about 5 feet 8 inches high, and well proportioned to his heighth, has a down look, and pale countenance, has long straight brown hair, tied or cued behind, though it is likely he may cut it off, to disguise himself; had on, and*

*took with him, a blue broadcloth coat, full trimmed, with carved gilt buttons, 2 pair of breeches, one of blue worsted plush, the other black knit pattern, both half-worn, 2 red broadcloth vests, one of which is almost new, long skirts, and mohair buttons, but no sleeves; the other a short skirted vest, lappelled, about half-worn, with new sleeves put in, and has gilt buttons; he had a pair of fine white cotton ribbed hose, 2 pair of new shoes, 1 ditto of pumps, carved silver buckles, a silver watch, with a china face, a steel chain, and white stone seal, made by J. Jones; he took up sundry goods in Dover, a few days before he went off, such as check linen, white linen, stockings, and sundry other things; and went in company with one Charles Hirons, a young man, a blacksmith, about 5 feet 7 inches high, brown or swarthy complexion, middling slim, wears his own brown hair; had on, a brown fustian coat, &c. It is reported they took pistols with them, and an old bayonet, to defend themselves; the said apprentice can talk Dutch, he is very ingenious, and can do almost anything belonging to the aforesaid trade, also can do carpenters and coopers work middling well. Whoever takes up the said apprentice, and secures him, so that his master may have him again, shall have the above reward, and reasonable charges,*
          *paid by    ISAAC COX.*
*All masters of vessels are forbid to carry him off at their peril.*
   *The Pennsylvania Gazette,* June 13, 1771.


RUN away from the subscriber, living at Christiana Ferry, in New-Castle county, on the 8th of this instant June, a servant lad, named WILLIAM PHILLIPS, about 5 feet high, 19 years of age, pock-marked, a flat nose, of a brown complexion, has the mark of a cut of an axe on his right foot, and walks a little lame; had on, when he went away, a striped linen jacket, without sleeves, and a striped linsey ditto, with sleeves, a coarse homespun shirt, woollen trowsers, with a patch on each knee, and a blue Scotch bonnet; he says he has been to sea with Captain Macpherson; it is likely he will endeavour to go to sea again, to make his escape, therefore all masters of vessels are forbid to carry him off. Whoever takes up said servant, and secures him, so that his master may have him again, shall have Two Dollars reward, and reasonable charges,
          paid by    CORNELIUS HAINS.
   *The Pennsylvania Gazette,* June 20, 1771.


RUN away, the 5th of this instant June, from the subscriber, living in Christiana Hundred, New-Castle County, an Irish servant man, named ROBERT FRAIM, has been about 4 years in this country, about 5 feet 7 or 8 inches high, wears his own dark brown curled hair, round shouldered, has

middling thick lips, a grim look, but fresh coloured, and a little freckled, is very apt to swear and drink too much, and rocks a little when walking; he is a well limbed fellow, inclining to a claret colour, a lapelled jacket, the fore parts of the same, the hind parts blue, two fine shirts, and one coarse ditto, a red jacket, a half-worn raccoon hat, with a large brim, buckskin breeches, almost new, silver fleece buttons, marked H.S. white cotton ribbed stockings, black yarn ditto, turned pumps, not much wore, and Pinchbeck buckles, two silk handkerchiefs, one black, the other a flag; it is possible he may change his name. Whoever takes up said servant, and secures him, so that the subscriber may get him again, shall have FIVE POUNDS reward, and reasonable charges, paid by    JOHN MACKEY.
N. B. All masters of vessels are forbid to carry him off, at their peril.
*The Pennsylvania Gazette*, June 20, 1771.


EIGHT DOLLARS Reward.
RUN away, the 12th of this instant June, from the subscriber, living at Mill-Town, near Newport, in New-Castle county, upon Delaware, a certain JAMES M'LAUGHLIN, a slim man, about 5 feet 8 inches high, about 22 years of age, long red hair, tied behind, wants two of his upper fore teeth, he is a Cooper by trade, and carried an adze with him; is very much given to liquor, and fractious in his cups; had on, when he went away, a light coloured country cloth jacket, double breasted, with yellow lackered buttons, new striped linen trowsers, calf-skin shoes, patched on one side, a half worn wool hat, cocked on all sides, and wears it high up before; he stole a Wilton cloth coat, and a pair of olive coloured velvet breeches. Whoever takes up said person, and secures him in any of his Majesty's goals, shall receive the above reward, and reasonable charges,
         paid by me    WILLIAM FOOTT.
*The Pennsylvania Gazette*, June 20, 1771.


RUN away from the subscriber, being one of the Constables of Kent county on Delaware, in Murtherkill Hundred, from under an arrest at sundry suits, one LAWRENCE M'WHIGGON, an Irishmen, about 23 years of age, a weaver and blue-dyer by trade, a short, thick, well set fellow, middling likely, marked pretty much with the small-pox; he has been in the country about one year; had on, when he went away, a short blue jacket, striped trowsers, mixed with cotton and thread, the cotton white, thread stockings, and black grained pumps. Whoever takes up the said fellow, secures him, and brings him to me, shall have THREE POUNDS, and reasonable expences, paid by me
*June* 24, 1771.        BENJAMIN JONES, junior, Constable.
*The Pennsylvania Gazette*, July 4, 1771.

FORTY SHILLINGS Reward.

A CERTAIN *Patrick Braidy*, alias *Baity*, on the 5th of 6th of June last, did take, in a felonious manner, from the subscriber, certain goods (not yet all known.) Whoever takes up said *Braidy*, alias *Baity*, and secures him in any of his Majesty's goals in this government, or will bring him to New-Castle goal, shall receive the above reward, and all reasonable charges, for bringing him to the aforesaid goal, or delivering him to
WILLIAM GOLDEN.
*The Pennsylvania Gazette*, July 4, 1771.


FORTY SHILLINGS Reward.
*RUN away, in the night of the 9th of July inst. from the subscriber, living in Mill-creek Hundred, New-Castle County, a servant man, named WILLIAM M'WHORTER, born in Scotland, and came in the ship Philadelphia, Captain Malcom, from Belfast, the beginning of this month; he is about 19 years of age, five feet five inches high, squint-eyed, pitted with the small-pox, and has black curled hair; had on, and took with him, a new broad cloth coat, jacket and breeches, one dozen or more of good shirts, one pair of tow trowsers, and a shoe and a pump. He said he had some relations in Philadelphia of the name of Shepperd, who would set him free, and it is supposed he is gone that way. Whoever takes up and secures the said servant in any of his Majesty's goals, so as his master may have him again, shall have the above reward, and reasonable charges,*
     paid by     MICHAEL RANKIN.
*The Pennsylvania Gazette*, July 25, 1771. See *The Pennsylvania Gazette*, September 12, 1771.


*Philadelphia, July* 25, 1771.
SIX DOLLARS Reward.
RAN away, last night, from the subscriber, living in Strawberry-Alley, an apprentice lad, named NAZARETH FREELAND, 20 years of age, 5 feet 7 or 8 inches high, is a well-set fellow, has clumsey legs, and walks lame, occasioned by his thigh being broke when young, has dark bushy hair, which he generally wears tied, is of a swarthy complexion, was born in Mushmellon Hundred, Kent County, by trade a taylor: Had on, and took with him, a good beaver hat, brown cloth coat, with yellow metal buttons; thread stockings, good shoes, with plain Pinchbeck buckles in them; he has also one white and 2 check shirts. Whoever takes up and secures said lad, so that his master may have him again, shall receive the above Reward, and reasonable Charges, paid by me     STEPHEN PHIPPS.
N. B. All Masters of Vessels, and others, are hereby forwarned not to habour or carry him off, at their peril.

*The Pennsylvania Gazette,* August 1, 1771; August 15, 1771; *The New-York Journal; or, the General Advertiser,* August 8, 1771; August 15, 1771; August 22, 1771. The *New-York Journal* shows his place of birth as "Muskmelon" Hundred.

Wilmington, July 29. 1771.

THREE POUNDS Reward.

RAN AWAY on Tuesday morning last, an indented Irish servant woman called JANE KAIRNS, about 30 years of age, of a middling stature, rather low, a little marked with the small-pox, and long vissage, fat and clumsey in body, and walks heavy: She took with her a black silk bonnet lined with red, a striped stampt cotton gown, also a blue and white striped bed gown, a striped stuff petticoat, a black quilted ditto, a red cloth cloak with a hood to it, a pair of stays, and other wearing apparel tied up in a bundle. Whoever takes up and secures said woman in any of his Majesty's gaol, or brings her home to the subscriber, shall receive the above reward, and all reasonable charges, paid by        JAMES MOULSDALE.

N. B. She has remarkable black hair and black eyebrows.

*The Pennsylvania Journal, and the Weekly Advertiser,* August 3, 1771; August 10, 1771.

FORTY SHILLINGS Reward.

RUN away from the subscriber, at James Latimer's, Esq; at Newport, New-Castle county, a NEGROE man, named CATO, speaks bad English, about 21 or 22 years of age, 5 feet 9 or 10 inches high, well built, and a good deal wrinkled in the forehead, with several scars on his cheeks, which are his country marks; had on, when he went away, a check shirt, and a pair of white ozenbrigs trowsers. Whoever apprehends said Negroe, and will bring him to me at Newport, or secure him in any of his Majesty's goals, giving notice thereof, shall have the above reward, and reasonable charges,

paid by        RICHARD LATIMER.

N. B. He made his escape the 23d day of July last, and has been seen since his elopement, with a case-knife in his hand, at Newark, and at Mr. Alexander Steel's tavern, at the head of Christine.

*The Pennsylvania Gazette,* August 8, 1771.

New Castle county, August 7, 1771.

NOW confined in the Goal of said county, a certain WILLIAM WILEY, a young lad, who says he is a servant to ZACHARIAH NIEMAN, that lives about a mile from Philadelphia. Also a certain MARTIN M'ANALY, who says he is a servant to JOSEPH BILDERBANK, of New-Castle county, on Delaware. Likewise a certain MARGARET SMITH, that says she belongs to WILLIAM GODARD, of Philadelphia, and lives in Front-street, near Race-

street. Their masters are desired to come, pay charges, and take them away, otherwise they will be sold for their fees,
                    by    ROBERT MACK, Goaler.
*The Pennsylvania Gazette*, August 15, 1771.

                          RUN-AWAY,
        From the subscriber on the first of this Instant,
AN Apprentice black-smith lad, named JOSEPH LEA, about 19 years of age, 5 feet 4 inches high, has brown hair cut on the top, he is a down looking, round shoulder'd slovenly fellow, has a remarkably bad walk. Had on when he went away, an old beaver hat, lately cut round the edge, and is very thick, a coarse blue cloth Jacket lined with oznabrigs, double brested, with yellow mettal buttons, peiced on the elbows Sailor's fashion. He went in company with one MICHAEL MORRIS, an apprentice tanner lad, about the same age and height, is streight and slender, is an impudent hardened fellow, had on a half worn racoon hat, home made linen shirt and trowsers, the rest of his cloaths unknown; whoever takes up and secures the said JOSEPH LEA, in any of his Majesty's gaols, so that his master may have his again shall have Forty Shillings Reward, and reasonable charges paid by
Dover, August 14th, 1771.                JOHN WINTERTON.
    *The Pennsylvania Journal, and the Weekly Advertiser*, August 20, 1771; August 29, 1771; September 5, 1771.

                        *Christiana Bridge, August* 19, 1771.
RUN away from the subscriber, a native Irish servant Boy, named *Patrick Ferrell*, about 18 years of age, 5 feet 3 or 4 inches high, black hair and eyes, broad fore teeth, and has a little of the brogue on his tongue: Had on, and took with him, when he went away (the 12th of this instant August) a blue coat, yellowish striped linsey jacket, the stripes of which go across, or round his body, a pair long, and a pair short trowsers, and shoes full of nails, much worn, the hind part of them ript, and sewed up with twine; three shirts, two of which are coarse Irish brown linen, the other Russia sheeting. He left his hat behind, but possibly may have procured one. He writes a tolerable hand, and may forge some kind of pass. Whoever secures the above servant in any of his Majesty's goals, and gives me notice, shall receive Twenty Shillings, and if brought home, reasonable charges,
                  paid by    JAMES PARTRIDGE
*The Pennsylvania Gazette*, August 22, 1771.

                            *York Goal, August* 9, 1771.
COMMITTED to my custody, a certain John Day, about 5 feet 2 or 3 inches high, about 22 or 23 years of age; had on, when committed, a red and white coloured coat, an old lead coloured jacket, without sleeves, an old shirt and

trowsers, and a pair of old shoes; his master (if any he has) is desired to come, pay charges, and take him away.

As also, Thomas Holme, about 4 feet high, about 14 or 15 years of age; had on, when committed, a fearnought jacket, ozenbrigs shirt, coarse trowsers, and an old hat. Likewise, a Negroe man, who calls himself *Cedo* (and says his master lives in Newport, New-Castle county) about 6 feet high, and has 3 marks on each cheek, which are supposed to be marked in his own country; had on, when committed, a check shirt and ozenbrigs trowsers, and a blanket with him. Their masters are desired to come, within four weeks, and pay their charges, and take them away.

JACOB GRAYBIL, Goaler.
*The Pennsylvania Gazette*, August 22, 1771.


FOUR DOLLARS Reward.
*RUN away on the 19th of August, from the Subscriber, living in the Borough of Wilmington, in New-Castle County, on Delaware, an Apprentice Lad, named Hugh M'Callion, by Trade a Shoemaker, about 20 Years of Age, five Feet 8 or 9 Inches high, a pretty slim Fellow, thin Face, pale Complexion, and has dark long Hair: Had on when he went away, a light blue Lincey Jacket, a Pair of Check Trowsers, Tow Shirt, old Pumps, patched at the Toes, with Buckles in them, and a deep crowned Wool Hat. Whoever secures said Apprentice, so that his Master may get him again, shall have the above Reward, and reasonable Charges,*
*paid by    ANDREW CRIPS.*
*N. B. He pretended to go with the Soldiers.*
*The Pennsylvania Gazette*, September 5, 1771.


FORTY SHILLINGS Reward.
RUN away, in the night of the 9th of July last, from the subscriber, living in Mill creek Hundred, New Castle County, a servant man, named WILLIAM M'WHORTER, born in Scotland, and came in the ship Philadelphia, Captain Malcom, from Belfast, the beginning of said month; he is about 18 years of age, five feet five inches high, squint-eyed, pitted with the small-pox, and has black curled hair; had on, and took with him, a new broadcloth coat, jacket and breeches, one dozen or more of good shirts, one pair of tow trowsers, and a shoe and a pump. He said he had some relations in Philadelphia of the name of Shepperd, who would set him free, and it is supposed he is gone that way. Whoever takes up and secures the said servant in any of his Majesty goals, so as his master may have him again, shall have the above reward, and reasonable charges, paid by    MICHAEL RANKIN.

*The Pennsylvania Gazette*, September 12, 1771. See *The Pennsylvania Gazette*, July 25, 1771.

FOUR DOLLARS Reward.
*RUN away from the Subscriber, living in Brandywine Hundred, New-Castle County, a native Irish Servant Man, named Thomas Gearran, about* 21 *and* 22 *Years of Age,* 5 *Feet* 6 *or* 7 *Inches high, stoops a little as he walks, of a fresh Complexion, fairish straight Hair, whitish Eyes, one of them whiter than the other, he has the Marks of a Scar over one of them, and a down Look, and had the great Toe of his right Foot split with an Axe; had on, when he went away, an old Russia Shirt, and coarse Trowsers; he attempted to kill his Master in the Night, without any Provocation in the least, but was frustrated of his Design, which caused him to run off in so bare a Habit, but may have stole more. Whoever takes up said Servant, and secures him in any of his Majesty's Goals, so that his Master may have him again, shall have Thirty Shillings Reward, and reasonable Charges,*
 *paid by me* WILLIAM M'CLURE.
*The Pennsylvania Gazette*, September 19, 1771.


RUN away the 9th of this instant September, at night, from the subscriber, living at Christiana Ferry, in New-Castle county, a servant lad named STEPHEN PIKE, country born, about 20 years of age, 5 feet 1 inch high, or thereabouts, short brown curled hair, of a brown complexion; had on, when he went away, a grey bearskin jacket, a coarse homespun shirt, patched a little, a pair of new blue and white striped ticken trowsers, grey ribbed stockings, his shoes and hat unknown; has, on the inside of his left knee, the mark of a bile, very plain, and on the outside of his right leg, near his knee, the mark of a cut of an ax: He stole, from his said master, to the amount of Three Pounds, and upwards. Whoever takes up the said servant, and secures him in any of his Majesty's goals, and sends word to his master, so that he may get him again, shall receive THIRTY SHILLINGS reward, and all reasonable charges, paid by CORNELIUS HAINS.
*N. B.* All masters of vessels, and others, are forbid to harbour or carry him off, at their peril.
 *The Pennsylvania Gazette*, September 19, 1771. See *The Pennsylvania Gazette*, June 14, 1770.


RUN away, the 3d of this instant October, from the subscriber, living at Christiana Ferry, in New-Castle county, a Dutch servant lad, named GEORGE WILLIAMS, of a very brown complexion, has a scald head, about 5 feet 1 or 2 inches high; had on, when he went away, a blue and white striped lincey jacket, the stripes across, a white linen cap, an old hat, with a hole in the crown, a green and white striped silk handkerchief, old check shirt, patched on both shoulders, with new blue and white striped ticken trowsers,

a pair of home-made thread stockings, and half-worn shoes. Whoever takes up said servant, and secures him in any of his Majesty's goals; and sends word to his master, so that he may get him again, shall receive FOUR DOLLARS reward, and all reasonable charges,
    paid by  CORNELIUS HAINS.
N. B. All masters of vessels, and others, are forbid to harbour or carry him off, at their peril.
 *The Pennsylvania Gazette*, October 10, 1771. See *The Pennsylvania Journal, and the Weekly Advertiser*, October 10, 1771.


   RAN AWAY, Yesterday, from the Subscriber, living at
     Christiana Ferry, in Newcastle County,
A Dutch Servant LAD, named GEORGE WILLIAMS, of a very brown complexion, has a scald head, and generally wears a cap over it, about 5 feet 1 or 2 inches high: Had on when he went away, a blue and white striped linsey jacket, the stripes across, a white linen cap, an old hat, with a hole in the crown, a green and white stripe silk handkerchief, old check shirt, patched on both shoulders, with new blue and white striped ticken trowsers, a pair of home-made thread stockings, and half worn shoes. Whoever takes up said servant, and secures him in any of his Majesty's gaols, and sends word to his master, so that he can get him again, shall receive FOUR DOLLARS reward, and all reasonable charges, paid by me
      CORNELIUS HAINS.
N. B. All masters of vessels, and others, are forbid to harbour or carry him off at their peril.    October 4.
 *The Pennsylvania Journal, and the Weekly Advertiser*, October 10, 1771. See *The Pennsylvania Gazette*, October 10, 1771.


     TEN POUNDS Reward.
WHEREAS the Swedish Church, called Trinity Church, in Wilmington in Newcastle county, was broke open in the night between the last day of September and first of October, and robbed of the following articles, viz— Two new large hangings belonging to the pulpit and the communion table; a cushion, all of green broadcloth, garnished with fringes; a white fine diaper linen table-cloth; a pair of bellows, for the stove in the church, quite new. The church wardens and vestrymen of said church offer the above reward to any person or persons, who shall be able to discover this sacrilege, so that the villain or villains may be apprehended, convicted, and for such an atrocious crime duly punished.
 N. B. The person suspected is one who calleth himself WILLIAM DAVIS, came from Philadelphia last Friday, went to Newcastle on Sunday,

and as it is very probable, committed the robbery in that church on Sunday night, came to Wilmington on Monday, was seen very early on Tuesday morning, walking with a pair of bellows in his hand, on board of Mr. George Gordon's shallop; in which he also had a man's and a woman's saddle, a calicoe pillow case and some other bundles supposed to contain stolen goods, as the saddles and some other things were stolen in Wilmington that night. He left Mr. Gordon's shallop in Philadelphia on Wednesday, taking the above-mentioned goods along with him, in order to carry them on board the Burlington stage.—This man then had on and wore, an old blue great coat, a lightish grey under coat, a striped calicoe jacket, striped ticken trowsers; was about 5 feet 8 inches high, fair complexion, sandy hair, red locks, middling large, one each side of his face, and had one of his hands very much cut, as it is supposed, from breaking the window of the church.
October 10.

*The Pennsylvania Journal, and the Weekly Advertiser*, October 10, 1771; October 24, 1771. See *The Pennsylvania Packet, and the General Advertiser*, November 18, 1773.


THREE POUNDS Reward.
RAN AWAY from Dover, the 21st ult. from the subscriber, living in this city, an Irish servant man named JAMES M'BRIDE, by trade a shoemaker, about 23 years of age, 5 feet 5 or 6 inches high, of a fair complexion, and a little pitted with the small-pox: Had on when he went away, blue coat and jacket, strip'd trowsers, and good stockings and shoes. He will probably change his apparel, as it is supposed he has other clothes with him. He was adjudged at the last court of Dover for debtors, to be the property of the subscriber. Whoever takes up said runaway, and secures him in any of his Majesty's goals, so that his master may receive him again, shall have the above reward, and reasonable charges, paid by
October 24.     ALEXANDER RUTHERFORD.
N. B. All masters of vessels, and others, are forbid to harbour or carry him off.

*The Pennsylvania Journal, and the Weekly Advertiser*, October 24, 1771; November 14, 1771.

*October 19.*
*RUN AWAY, from the subscriber, living in Newark, New-castle county, on Friday the 18th instant;*
*A New Irish SERVANT MAN, named JOHN CARTER, of a pale complexion, being just got out of the ague, his hair black, and curls. Had on an old wool hat, a whitish half-worn coat, old grey jacket, and an old red sailor's ditto, old ticken breeches, very dirty, grey rib'd stockings, and old shoes. He took*

with him a new Irish SERVANT MAN, belonging to James M'Cullough, named JOHN LAVERY, who had on a blue coat without cuffs, old striped linsey jacket, old tow trowsers, and old shoes. Whoever takes up said servants, and secures them, so that their masters may get them again, shall receive for the first described FORTY SHILLINGS reward, and for the other TWENTY SHILLINGS, and reasonable charges,
    paid by   ALLEN GILESPIE.
N. B. John Carter is about 5 feet 7 inches high, well made, smooth tongued, about 30 years of age, stole and took with him a pair of new plain silver buckles, of an oval round, likewise a homemade cloth coat, deep blue mixed with red, and several other things.
  *The Pennsylvania Journal, and the Weekly Advertiser*, October 24, 1771; October 31, 1771.

            *Burlington, October 21, 1771.*
THIS is to give notice, that on the 20th day of September last, was committed to the goal of Burlington, a Mulattoe man, aged about 26 years, says he was born in New-England, and brought up to the seas, he calls himself by the name of Jeremiah Clark, and says he is a servant to one Robert Robertson, in Brandywine Hundred, New-Castle county, about 4 miles from Wilmington; had on, when committed, a dark brown double breasted jacket, with brass and metal buttons; and says he left him in June last; his master, if any he has, is desired to come, or send, by the 12th day of November next; otherwise I shall apply to the court, to get him sold out for his charges.
     EPHRAIM PHILLIPS, Goaler.
  *The Pennsylvania Gazette*, October 31, 1771.


              *September*, 1771.
    THREE POUNDS REWARD.
 *RAN AWAY, on Friday the 27th instant, from the subscriber,*
      *living at Duck-Creek;*
A NEGROE MAN, about 30 years of age, country born, called BOB, about 5 feet 6 inches high, hollow-faced, his upper lip a little turn'd, has two teeth out before; had on when he went away, a light fustian white short coat lapell'd, wide-brim'd coarse hat, grey broadcloth breeches, and black stockings. He took a mare-colt, two years old, with a long tail, with him, and a bundle of sundry cloaths, so that it's probable he will change his dress and endeavor to pass for a free person. Whoever takes up said negroe, and secures him any of his majesty's goals, so that his master may have him and the mare again, shall have the above reward, and all reasonable charges, paid by William Griffin, miller, at Duck-Creek.
  *The Pennsylvania Journal, and the Weekly Advertiser*, October 31, 1771.

*Philadelphia, Nov.* 16. 1771.
ON Monday evening the 11th instant, ST. PAUL'S CHURCH in this city, was robbed of all its Hangings (being of rich Crimson Silk Velvet,) for the Communion Table, Pulpit and Desks, with Cushions trimmed with very rich Gold Lace about one inch broad, Tassels of Gold; the front part of the Pulpit Cloth is embroidered with
S
gold, with letters I†H in a circle, representing the rays of the sun. The above sacrilege was committed by William Davis, *alias* David Williams, a person about five feet nine or ten inches high, born in England, wears his own broad hair, sometimes with a false tail, pock marked, limps a little in his walking; his clothes were, a short green coat with metal buttons, a calicoe jacket, and green breeches, but may since have changed. The above William Davis robbed the church in Wilmington of its hangings, (out of which his green coat is made) and a reward of Ten Pounds is offered by the congregation of said church for apprehending of him. Whoever apprehends the said William Davis, who was seen yesterday in this city, so that he may be brought to justice, and the good restored, shall have the above reward paid by
    EPHRAIM BONHAM,   Wardens
    JOHN WOOD.
    N. B. A warrant is obtained from William Allen, Esq; Chief Justice of the province of Pennsylvania, requiring all sheriffs and constables in the said province, to use their utmost endeavours for apprehending the said William Davis.
*The Pennsylvania Packet, and the General Advertiser*, November 18, 1773. See *The Pennsylvania Journal, and the Weekly Advertiser*, October 10, 1771.


*RUN away, on the 30th of October last, from the subscriber, living in Apoquiminy Hundred, New-Castle county, an Irish servant lad, named* RICHARD ANDREW, *about 19 years of age, 5 feet 8 or 9 inches high, short thick pale hair, of a fair complexion, long visaged, slow of speech; had on, when he went away, a new felt hat, coat, jacket and breeches, of blue kersey, brass knee buckles, brown and white mixed woollen stockings, good shoes, with carved brass buckles; very remarkable for having the two first letters of his name wrote in blue on the thumb of his right hand, pretends to weaving, but is not tractable. Whoever takes up said servant, and secures him in any of his Majestygoals, so as his master may have him again, shall have EIGHT DOLLARS reward, and reasonable charges,*
    *paid by*   JACOB M'COMBS.
*The Pennsylvania Gazette*, November 28, 1771.

RUN AWAY from his master, JAMES ANDERSON, living at the head of Indian River; a NEGRO MAN, on the yellowish cast, named AMES; he is a well-set thick full-faced fellow, about 5 feet 8 inches high, apt to laugh; had on a blue coat: It is supposed that he will pass for a free mulatto of the name of JOHN PARKESON, as a free one of that name got a pass, and was in company with him into Philadelphia, and returned home. It is supposed he is somewhere in Philadelphia. Whoever shall take up said fellow, and bring him to the subscriber, shall have a reward of SIX DOLLARS, if taken in this province, if elsewhere FIVE POUND, [sic] and all reasonable charges paid by           HENRY HARPER.
N. B. All masters of vessels are forbid to carry him of [sic] at their peril.
*The Pennsylvania Journal, and the Weekly Advertiser*, December 5, 1771; December 12, 1771.

## 1772

TEN POUNDS Reward.

BROKE out of the goal of this county, on the 31st of December last, the two following persons, viz. WILLIAM BROWEN, about 5 feet 7 inches high, a likely young fellow, said he was born in New England, of a black complexion, black hair, and wore black clothes. JOHN PENROSE, an Irishman, a likely young fellow, very active, speaks good English, about 5 feet 8 inches high, of a brown complexion; had on brown clothes. Whoever apprehends said villains, and secures them in any of his Majesty's goals, and gives information to the subscriber, shall be intitled to the above reward, or Five Pounds for either of them, lawful money of Pennsylvania. Given under my hand,      ROBERT MACK, Goaler of New-Castle.
N. B. The above Browen followed knitting of silk purses, and ladies mittens, and they were both criminals; it is very likely they will change their names.
*The Pennsylvania Gazette*, January 9, 1772.

New-Castle County, on Delaware, March 23, 1772.
EIGHT DOLLARS Reward.

*RUN away from his bail, about the first of this instant, a certain PATRICK HART, about 5 feet 6 or 7 inches high, of a coarse complexion, well set, has red hair and beard, and appears to be about 30 years of age; had on, when he went away, a brown coat, red jacket, yarn stockings, and felt hat; is fond of strong liquor, and is supposed will seek employment at ditching, as he has followed that business for several years past. Whoever secures the said Hart, in any of his Majesty's goals, so as the subscriber may have him again, shall receive the above reward, to be*
              *paid by me*     THOMAS TOBIN.

*The Pennsylvania Gazette,* April 2, 1772; April 16, 1772. See *The Pennsylvania Packet; and the General Advertiser,* April 6, 1772

Newcastle County, on Delaware, March 23d, 1772.
EIGHT DOLLARS Reward.
RUN away from his bail, about the 1st of this instant, a certain PATRICK HART, about five feet six or seven inches high, of a coarse complexion, well set, has red hair and beard, and appears to be about thirty years of age. Had on when he went away, a brown coat, red jacket, yarn stockings, and felt hat: He is fond of strong liquor, and is supposed will seek employment at ditching, as he had followed that business for several years past. Whoever secures said Hart, in any of his Majesty's goals, so that the subscriber may have him again, shall receive the above reward. THOMAS TOBIN.
*The Pennsylvania Packet; and the General Advertiser,* April 6, 1772; April 13, 1762; April 20, 1762. See *The Pennsylvania Gazette,* April 2, 1772.

RUN-AWAY from the subscriber, living in New-Castle county, near Noxontown, the 29th of April, 1772, a Negro man, who calls himself JOHN SHARPER, and a Negro wench, named NAN, who took with her a Negro boy, about three years old, named ISHMAEL. The Negro man is about 5 feet 4 inches high, well-set, pock-marked, his fingers and toes appear to be hurt with the frost, born, as he says, in Barbados, pretends to be a bricklayer: Some years ago he belonged to Thomas Lennon, at Christina ferry, near Newcastle, and serv'd as Ferryman for said Lennon. Had on when he went away, an old pair of shoes, white yarn stockings, old blue breeches, fearnought jacket, tow shirt, and old hat. The said Negro is about 35 years of age, talks bad English. The wench is likely, tall and slim, black, smooth skinned, about 21 years of age, country born, talks good English; had on when she went away, an old linsey petticoat, and a white linen ditto, linsey bed gown, tow shifts, & white caps. The Negro boy is small of his age, and very bow-legged, but lively and smart. 'Tis supposed they will pass for free Negroes. Whoever takes up the said Negro man and wench, with the child, and brings them to the subscriber, shall have FIVE POUNDS reward, and reasonable charges,
   paid by   ARNOLD NAUDAIN.
*The Pennsylvania Journal, and the Weekly Advertiser,* May 7, 1772; May 14, 1772; May 21, 1772.

FOUR DOLLARS Reward.
RUN AWAY *from the subscriber, living in Kent county, near the province Bridge, an apprentice lad, named JOSHUA REW, aged* 17, *about* 5 *feet* 6

inches high; had on, and took with him, a lightish brown coat, of coating, an unfulled kersey jacket, with sleeves, a blue cloth jacket, without sleeves, old buckskin breeches, an oxenbrigs shirt, mixed blue yarn stockings, and a new felt hat. Whoever takes up and secures said servant, so that his master may have him again, shall have the above reward, and reasonable charges,
     paid by  JOHN LEWIS.
N. B. He was born in Bucks county, but I suppose is gone to some part of Queen-Anne's. He is a well set fellow, but a remarkable sloven.
 The Pennsylvania Gazette, May 7, 1772.


      FIFTY POUNDS Reward.
MADE his escape from Dover goal, in the county of Kent, upon Delaware, on the 21st of May instant, JOHN WINTERTON, who was committed on a charge of murder; he is a tall raw boned person, of a pale complexion, thin visage, wears his own hair, of dark colour, generally ties behind, and has a large scar upon his nose. Had on, when he made his escape, a blue great coat, a blue close bodied coat and waistcoat, his other apparel unknown. Whoever apprehends the said John Winterton, within the county aforesaid, and brings him to the subscriber, shall receive the sum of Twenty five Pounds,
 paid by   JAMES CALDWELL, Sheriff.
Dover, May 21, 1772.
 The Pennsylvania Gazette, May 28, 1772; June 4, 1772.


        NEWCASTLE, May, 26th, 1772.
COMMITTED to the goal of this county, Two Negro Man; one called JACK, and says he belongs to James Pearce, of George-Town; the other calls himself CHARLES, and says he belongs to David Foset of Snowhill. They are both likely negroes. Their Masters are desired to pay charges and take them away, otherwise they will be sold out for the same, by
    ROBERT MACK, Goaler.
 The Pennsylvania Packet; and the General Advertiser, June 1, 1772.


THIS day was committed to the public Goal of Kent county, on Delaware, on suspicion of being a runaway servant, a young fellow, about 20 years of age, tall and slim, smooth faced, dressed in a sailorshort waistcoat of swanskin, a woollen cap, and blue and white striped long trowsers. He at first called himself JOHN THARP, but has since declared his name to be EDMUND PRICE, and that he ran away from his Master Captain JOHN HAILY, of New-York, about four months ago, at Charlestown, South Carolina. His Master is desired to pay charges, and take him away, or he will, in six weeks, be sold for his prison fees, by

*Kent County Goal, May* 25, 1772.   JOHN BULLEN, Goaler.
*The Pennsylvania Gazette,* June 4, 1772.


RAN away from the subscriber, on Tuesday evening the 19th of May, an indented servant woman, named ANN WASSON, much marked with the small-pox, has a hole or dent in one of her wrists, is a tall lusty woman; had on when she went away, a blue and white linsey petticoat, blue and white figured callico gown, a pair of leather pumps; has a hole or dent in her nose, and is newly come from Ireland. Whoever takes up and secures said servant, so that her master may get her again, shall have THIRTY SHILLINGS reward, paid by
          THOMAS COOCH, jun. (living near Christiana-Bridge.)
*The Pennsylvania Chronicle, and Universal Advertiser,* From Monday, June 1, to Monday, June 8, 1772; From Monday, June 8, to Monday, June 15, 1772. See *The Pennsylvania Journal, and the Weekly Advertiser,* June 25, 1772.

THIRTY SHILLINGS Reward.
RUN AWAY from the subscriber, on Tuesday, the 19th of May last, an indented servant woman, named ANN WASSON, much marked with the small-pox, has a hole or dent in one of her wrists, and a large indentation on her nose, is a tall lusty woman, and lately came from Ireland: Had on when she went away, a blue and white linsey petticoat, a blue and white bed gown, a calicoe gown, a pair of leather pumps, and took with her a brown cloak, with a cap to it. Whoever takes up said run-away, and brings her to the subscriber, living near Christiana-Bridge, shall have the above reward, paid by      THOMAS COOCH, jun.
N. B. All person are forbid harbouring or concealing said run-away at their peril.    June 25.
*The Pennsylvania Journal, and the Weekly Advertiser,* June 25, 1772; July 2, 1772. See *The Pennsylvania Chronicle, and Universal Advertiser,* From Monday, June 1, to Monday, June 8, 1772.


FOUR DOLLARS Reward.
RUN away from the subscriber, living near Christiana Bridge, on the 21st day of June last, a servant GIRL, named MARGERY DIAMOND, but may possibly change it to ROANY; had on, when she went away, a linsey petticoat, a striped linen bed gown, no shoes; black haired, much freckled, and looks a squint with both eyes, very much given to drink and loose company, about 25 years of age, this country born. Whoever takes up said girl, and secures her in any of his Majesty's goals, or brings her home to the

subscriber, shall receive the above reward, and all reasonable charges,
paid by    HENRY BRAKEN.
N. B. All masters of vessels, or others, are forbid to harbour or carry off said servant, of their peril.
*The Pennsylvania Gazette*, July 16, 1772

FIVE POUNDS REWARD.
RUN AWAY from the Subscriber, living in Kent county, on Delaware, on the 18th of May, 1771, an indented servant man, named JOHN HARWOOD, by trade a taylor, born in England, about five feet six or seven inches high, is a very smooth faced fellow, wears his own hair sometimes tied behind is very black, and has a pretty large scar upon his face. Had on when he went away, a large blue jacket made out of an old superfine cloth coat, an under cloth coloured bath coating jacket, reddish coloured wilton breeches, a new raccoon fur hat, had very good shoes and stockings, and took with him some good shirts of different sorts. He has work'd in many places of America, viz. in New-York, in Baltimore and Newton in Maryland, in Salem in the Jersies, in Wilmington in New-Castle county, and in Virginia: He loves drink very much, and when in liquor swears and sings: He has a large Roman nose. Whoever takes up said servant, and secures him, so that his master may have him again, shall receive the above reward
paid by    JOSEPH CALDWELL.
N. B. He has been seen in Philadelphia about a month
*The Pennsylvania Packet; and the General Advertiser*, July 20, 1772; July 27, 1772; August 10, 1772; August 24, 1772.


FOUR DOLLARS Reward.
RUN away from the subscriber, living in New-Castle County, Pencader Hundred, on Friday, the 10th of July inst. an Irish servant lad, named *Thomas Gore*, between 16 and 17 years of age; had on, when he went away, an old felt hat, a half-worn flax shirt, tow trowsers, a pair of shoes, with leather strings; is of a sandy complexion, wears his own curled hair, and when he laughs shews his eye teeth, as they stick pretty much out; took a sickle with him; loves liquor, and has a down look. Whoever takes up and secures said fellow, so that this master may have him again, shall have the above reward, and reasonable charges, paid by    NATHAN BOLDEN.
N. B. All masters of vessels are forbid to carry him off, at their peril.
*The Pennsylvania Gazette*, July 23, 1772.

THREE POUNDS Reward.
RUN away from the subscriber, living in St. George's, an indented servant man, named JACOB JOHNSTON, by trade a Taylor, born near Philadelphia,

5 feet 6 or 7 inches high, black bushy hair, down look, wants some of his fore teeth, very yellow complexion, and has a large mark or scar on his cheek; took with him a light coloured coat, of fine cloth, and jacket, made plain, the coat has been torn, but neatly sewed between the shoulders, with facing, double shelled buttons; also took with him a piece of homespun drugget, twilled, of a grey mixture, 3/4 of scarlet nap, a pair of white worsted stockings, and several other things, too tedious to mention. Whoever takes up said servant, shall have the above reward,
    paid by me  WALTER FULLAM.
*The Pennsylvania Gazette*, August 26, 1772.


RUN away from the subscriber, living in New-Castle on Delaware, as indented servant man, named JAMES M'KNIGHT, 5 feet 7 inches high, dark complexion; had on, when he went away, a short light coloured coat, an old hat, and old ozenbrigs trowsers; he is about 35 years of age, given very much to strong liquor, and apt to get drunk, has been in his Majesty's service, some years ago, and received a wound in one of his knees; he is a great liar, has a large mouth, and chews tobacco to excess; he pretends to know all sorts of work, and it is thought he had made towards Philadelphia. Whoever takes up said servant, and secures him in any of his Majesty's goals, so that his master may get him again, shall have THREE POUNDS reward, and all reasonable charges, paid by me  PATRICK HART
*New-Castle, August* 21, 1772.
*The Pennsylvania Gazette*, August 26, 1772.


      FOUR DOLLARS Reward.
RUN AWAY, *about the middle of June last, from the subscriber's plantation, near New-Castle, an Irish servant LAD, named* GEORGE HENRY, *about 20 years of age, about 5 feet 3 inches high, of a yellowish complexion, has light brown curly hair, large nostrils, and a small scar on his upper lip; had on, when he went away, a tow shirt and trowsers, a felt hat, a dark grey kersey jacket, light coloured yarn stockings, and shoes, almost new. Whoever apprehends the said servant, and delivers him to the subscriber, at New-Castle, shall receive the above reward, and reasonable charges, paid by August* 24, 1772. RICHARD M'WILLIAM.
\*\*\* He is now supposed to be about Christiana Bridge.
 *The Pennsylvania Gazette*, September 2, 1772. See *The Pennsylvania Gazette*, June 2, 1773, *The Pennsylvania Gazette*, September 1, 1773, and *The Pennsylvania Gazette*, August 17, 1774.

## THREE POUNDS Reward.

RUN away from the subscriber, living near the town of New-Castle, on the road leading from thence to Christiana Ferry, an Irish servant man, named GEORGE PARKS, about 20 years of age, near 5 feet 8 inches high, of a sandy complexion, and somewhat marked with the small-pox; had on, when he went away, a half-worn wool hat, and old blue coat, and jacket, of broadcloth, a striped shirt, and tow trowsers, with old shoes, and brass buckles, but may change them the first opportunity; it is supposed he will go to Shippen's town, having enquired the way at his departure. Whoever takes up the said servant, and brings him to the subscriber, or secures him in any of his Majesty's goals, shall receive the above reward, and reasonable charges.       CHRISTIANA JACQUET. *Sept.* 14, 1772.

*The Pennsylvania Gazette*, September 23, 1772.

## FIFTEEN PISTOLES REWARD.

RUN AWAY *from the subscriber's plantation, in Murtherkiln Hundred, in Kent county, on Delaware, on Wednesday, the 2d of this instant, September, Two Men, by profession ditchers, (who are under articles to the subscriber) the one named* JAMES DICKSON, *alias* EDWARD ROGERS, *and for whom I stand bail, and took out of Queen Anne's county goal, in the province of Maryland; he is about 5 feet 6 inches high, supposed to be between 32 and 35 years of age, smooth faced, a well made squat fellow, is very talkative, boasts much of knowledge in his business, and reports himself to be the heir of a very considerable estate in England. The other, named* JOHN COLE, *about 5 feet 7 inches high, a well made fellow, and bump backed. Their wearing apparel cannot be well described, as they took with them a change of clothes. It is supposed they will make for the Jerseys. Whoever will take up the said two fellows, and secure them in any goal, within the province of Maryland, shall have, for* Dickson, TEN PISTOLES, *and for* Cole, FIVE PISTOLES *reward,*
*paid by*       JAMES HUTCHINGS, *junior.*

*The Pennsylvania Gazette*, September 23, 1772. See *The Pennsylvania Packet; and the General Advertiser*, September 28, 1772.

## TWO DOLLARS Reward.

RUN AWAY from the subscriber, in June last, living at Wilmington, JOHN MACCLEAN, he is about 5 feet 8 inches high, and has an iron coloured face: Had on brown clothes, and wore a wig, or a cap; but the wig was a little weather-beaten, or turned brown. Whoever takes up said servant, and brings him to Mr. JOHN TAYLOR, Merchant, in Front-street, Philadelphia, or secures him in any of his Majesty''s gaols, so that his Master may have him again, shall receive the above reward,

paid by  CHARLES WILSON.
*The Pennsylvania Journal, and the Weekly Advertiser*, September 23, 1772; September 30, 1772.

FIFTEEN PISTOLES REWARD.
MARYLAND, *Queen Anne's county, Sept* 11, 1772.
RUN AWAY from the Subscriber's plantation, in Murtherkiln Hundred, in Kent county, on Delaware, on Wednesday, the 2d of September inst. (who are under articles to the Subscriber) two men, by profession ditchers; the one named JAMES DICKSON *alias* EDWARD ROGERS, and for whom I stand bail, and took out of Queen-Anne's county goal, in the province of Maryland: he is about five feet six inches high, supposed to be between thirty-two and thirty-five years of age, smooth faced, a well made square fellow: He is very talkative, boasts much of knowledge in his business, and reports himself to be the heir of a very considerable estate in England. The other, named JOHN COLE, about five feet seven inches high, a well made fellow, and hump backed. Their wearing apparel cannot be well described, as they took with them change of clothes. It is supposed they will make for the Jerseys.— Whoever will take up and secure the said two fellows in any goal within the province of Maryland, shall have for Dickson, Ten Pistoles, and for Cole, Five Pistoles reward, paid by  JAMES HUTCHINGS, Jun.
*The Pennsylvania Packet; and the General Advertiser*, September 28, 1772; October 5, 1772. See *The Pennsylvania Gazette*, September 23, 1772.

THREE POUNDS Reward.
RAN AWAY from the subscriber, living in Kent county, on Delaware, A servant man named ROBERT RICHARD PYE, born in England; he is a short, thick, well set man, about five feet high, and has remarkable bow legs, yellow hair and thin beard: Had on when he went away a fearnought jacket, coarse home-spun shirt, oznabrig trowsers, and a half worn hat. Whoever takes up and secures the said servant, so that his master may get him again, shall have the above reward, paid by  RICHARD SMITH.
*The Pennsylvania Packet; and the General Advertiser*, October 19, 1772; October 26, 1772; November 2, 1772.

FOUR DOLLARS REWARD.
NEWARK, *Sept.* 15, 1772.
MADE his escape from the Constable, a certain JOHN DOLAN, a short set fellow, upwards of twenty years of age, has dark brown hair, a wide mouth, large nose, is a bold impudent fellow, much given to strong drink, and is very apt to swear. Had on when he made his escape, a short brown jacket lined with striped lincey, or a striped jacket under it, coarse white shirt and

trowsers, good shoes and stockings. Any person that will apprehend said fellow, shall have the above reward
    paid by  JOHN DODDS, Constable.
*The Pennsylvania Packet; and the General Advertiser*, November 2, 1772.

      SIX DOLLARS REWARD.
RAN AWAY from the subscriber, about two years ago, a servant man named JAMES ADAMSON, about twenty-eight years of age, five feet 8 or 9 inches high, slim made, stoop shouldered, has a stoppage in his speech, dark skin, brown hair, pock-marked, and is a weaver by trade. Whoever takes up the said servant, and secures him in any gaol, so that his master may get him again, or brings him to SAMUEL BRADFORD, near Wilmington, in Newcastle county, shall have the above reward, and reasonable charges, paid by me  JOHN HEARSHA.
*The Pennsylvania Packet; and the General Advertiser*, November 16, 1772; November 23, 1772; November 30, 1772.


RAN AWAY from the subscriber, living in Kent county upon Delaware, near Johnny-cake landing, on the night between the 15th and 16th instant (November) a servant man named WILLIAM DYAL, country born, about five feet five or six inches high, long black hair tied behind, and ruddy complexion; had on a new beaver hat, a blue surtout, the fore part of the lining black and the hind part blue; likewise sundry other cloathing which are not particularly known: He also took with him a chesnut sorrel mare, about nine years old, one hind foot white, a star in her face, about thirteen hands and an half high, paces and trots, and a remarkable old saddle with a woman's stirrup to it. Whoever takes up the said servant and secures him in any gaol, so that his master may have him again shall have *THREE POUNDS* reward; and *THREE POUNDS* for the mare, and reasonable charges,
    paid by  JAMES REED.
*The Pennsylvania Packet; and the General Advertiser*, November 30, 1772; December 7, 1772.

            *Wilmington, December* 3, 1772.
RUN away last night, from the subscribers, living in Wilmington, New Castle county, two servant lads, country born, one named JAMES M'KEVER, about 18 years of age, 5 feet 4 or 5 inches high, strong and well set, a little marked with the small-pox, brownish curled hair, of a churlish sour countenance, apt to speak short, and is an intolerable liar; had on, and took with him, a half-worn castor hat, a dark coloured cloth coat, lately turned, a cloth jacket, near the same colour, newly turned, a blue jacket, without

sleeves, a new coat of a redish brown, lately altered to fit him, and before altered was full trimmed, with buttons on the sleeves, but now left off, &c. two new homespun shirts, the collars made two little, but now pieced on the button side, old fine shirt, buckskin breeches, mended with a new piece between the legs, a pair of cotton velvet ditto, one pair of strong new shoes, and one pair of slim ditto, Pinchbeck shoe buckles and silver knee ditto, a yellow checked silk handkerchief, somewhat stained with red paint, 3 pair of yarn and worsted stockings. The other, named WILLIAM PATTERSON, about the same age and height of M'Kever, a Cooper by trade, long thin pale visage, light coloured straight hair, stoop shouldered, down look, seems simple, but is a very great rogue, having run away about two years ago, and was then away 16 months, at *York-town, Baltimore- town*, and divers other places; had on, a light coloured thickset coat, with wooden buttons, nankeen jacket, white corded linen breeches, old red under jacket, rather too large for him, one old homespun shirt, the tail newly turned up, half-worn castor hat, rather too little for him, pale blue yarn stockings, newly footed with deep blue; he took with him a suit of blue and red superfine broadcloth clothes, much too long for him, as they were made for another person, the breeches pretty much worn and dirty, also a silver watch, with a silver chain; the watch opens with a pin in the end of the key, a dent in the outside case, old seal, the number and maker's name unknown: They also took with them a short gun, some powder, shot and bullet moulds, and some bar lead; the shotbag is made of old sheepskin, English dressed; they may forge a pass, and change their names, as *M'Kever* writes a good hand. Whoever secures the said lads, so that their masters may have them again, shall have THREE POUNDS reward for *McKever*, and FIVE POUNDS for *Patterson*, and the clothes and watch, or for the watch and clothes THREE POUNDS, and for him FORTY SHILLINGS, and if brought home reasonable charges,
   paid by JOHN STAPLER, and HENRY REYNOLDS.
N. B. All masters of vessels, and others, are forbid to carry them off or harbour them, at their peril. Any person giving information of their being harboured at any particular place, will be paid, as a reward, Twenty Shillings.
 *The Pennsylvania Gazette*, December 9, 1772; December 16, 1772; December 23, 1775.


RUN AWAY from the subscriber, living in Mill-creek Hundred, New Castle County, an Irish servant MAN, named JAMES ADAMS; he is about 5 feet 7 inches high, has a swarthy complexion, full face, wide mouth, and grey eyes, with an uncommon white in them when he particularly looks at any object; had on, when he went away, a cloth coloured outside jacket, with broad metal buttons, breeches of the same, an under jacket, of striped worsted, much worn, black sheepwool stockings, a pair of shoes, almost new, a half-worn

felt hat, bound round the edge with black binding, and an old coarse shirt; he is knock-kneed, and very active in handling his knife and fork; he pretends a great deal to religion. Whoever takes up and secures said servant, so that his master may have him again, may have FOUR DOLLARS reward, and reasonable charges, paid by
JOHN JAMES.    December 17.
*The Pennsylvania Gazette*, December 23, 1772; January 6, 1773.

WAS COMMITTED to my custody, on the 28th day of October last, one JOHN RUSSELL, who says he is a servant to William Baker, at Duck creek, in Kent county, on Delaware. Likewise, on the 3d day of this instant, one WILLIAM GALLASPEY, on suspicion of being a runaway servant. Their masters are desired to come, pay the charges, and take them away, within three weeks after this date, or they will be discharged, on paying their fees. *Chester, December* 23, 1772.    JOEL WILLIS, Goaler.
*The Pennsylvania Gazette*, December 23, 1772; December 30, 1772.

## 1773

Salem, New-Jersey, January 10, 1773.
EIGHT DOLLARS REWARD.
RAN AWAY from the subscriber, about the 15th of July last, an indented Irish servant man, named MICHAEL WHEALON, but has changed his name to WILLIAM YOUNG; he has been working in Newcastle county, near Saint Georges, and left that about two months ago and said he was going down to Maryland to work; he is about five feet six or seven inches high, of a pale complexion, a little pock marked, a down look, has light sandy hair, stoops a good deal in his walk, talks much on the brogue, is fond of liquor, and is very impudent when drunk or sober; he took with him a blue cloth sailor's jacket, a pair of blue plush breeches, white thread stockings, a red and white narrow striped linen jacket without sleeves, made very long waisted, a red short cloth jacket, the fore parts of which is very fine and the back is Bath coating; he had got a few yards of white linen at St. Georges, in pay for his work, which it is likely he will offer for sale; his other cloaths uncertain: He has been in Newfoundland, and says he intends going there next spring, and is very apt to talk of it. Whoever takes up and secures said servant, so that his master may have him again, shall receive the above reward, and if brought home FOUR POUNDS, from    CURTIS TRENCHARD.

*The Pennsylvania Packet; and the General Advertiser*, January 18, 1773; January 25, 1773; February 1, 1773; February 8, 1773; February 15, 1773; February 22, 1773. See *The Pennsylvania Gazette*, January 20, 1773, *The Pennsylvania Journal, and the Weekly Advertiser*,

January 20, 1773, *The Pennsylvania Packet; and the General Advertiser*, August 23, 1773, and *The Pennsylvania Journal, and the Weekly Advertiser*, August 25, 1773.

EIGHGT [sic] DOLLARS REWARD.
RUN AWAY from the subscriber, about the 15th of July last, an indented Irish servant man, named MICHAEL WHEALON, (but has changed his name to WILLIAM YOUNG,) he has been working in New-Castle county, near Saint Georges, and left that about two months ago, and said he was going down to Maryland to work; he is about 5 feet 6 or 7 inches high, of a pale complexion, a little pock-marked, a down look, has light sandy hair, and stoop's a good deal in his walk, talks much on the brogue, is fond of liquor, and is very impudent when drunk or sober; he took with him a blue cloth sailor's jacket, a pair of blue plush breeches, white thread stockings, a striped linnen jacket without sleeves, the stripes red and white, and very narrow, made very long waisted, a red short cloth jacket, the fore parts of which is very fine, the back is Bath coating, (he had got a few yards of white linnen at Saint Georges, in pay for his work, which it is likely he will offer for sale) his other cloaths uncertain: He has been in Newfoundland, and says he intends going there next spring, and is very apt to talk of it. Whoever takes up, and secures said servant, so that his master may have him again, shall receive the above reward, and if brought home FOUR POUNDS,
from CURTIS TRENCHARD.
Salem, N. Jersey, January 10, 1773.
*The Pennsylvania Journal, and the Weekly Advertiser*, January 20, 1773; January 27, 1773; February 10, 1773; February 17, 1773; March 3, 1773; March 10, 1773; March 17, 1773; April 21, 1773; May 12, 1773. See *The Pennsylvania Packet; and the General Advertiser*, January 18, 1773, *The Pennsylvania Gazette*, January 20, 1773, *The Pennsylvania Packet; and the General Advertiser*, August 23, 1773, and *The Pennsylvania Journal, and the Weekly Advertiser*, August 25, 1773.

*Salem, New Jersey, January 10, 1773.*
EIGHT DOLLARS Reward.
*RUN AWAY from the subscriber, about the 15th of July last, an indented Irish servant man, named MICHAEL WHEALON (but has changed it to William Young) he has been working in New- Castle county, near St. George's, and left that about two months ago, and said he was going down to Maryland to work; he is about 5 feet 6 or 7 inches high, of a pale complexion, a little pock-marked, a down look has light sandy hair, stoops a good deal in his walk, talks much on the brogue, is fond of liquor, and is very impudent when drunk or sober; he took with him, a blue cloth sailor's jacket, a pair of blue plush*

breeches, white thread stockings, a striped linen jacket, without sleeves, the stripes red and white, and very narrow, made very long waisted, a red short cloth jacket, the fore parts of which are very fine, the back is Bath coating; he had got a few yards of white linen at St. George's, in pay for his work, which it is likely he will offer for sale; his other clothes uncertain. He has been in Newfoundland, and say he intends going there next spring, and is very apt to talk of it. Whoever secures said servant, so as his master may have him again, shall receive the above reward, and if brought home,

FOUR POUNDS, from CURTIS TRENCHARD.

The *Pennsylvania Gazette*, January 20, 1773. See *The Pennsylvania Packet; and the General Advertiser*, January 18, 1773, *The Pennsylvania Journal, and the Weekly Advertiser*, January 20, 1773, *The Pennsylvania Packet; and the General Advertiser*, August 23, 1773, and *The Pennsylvania Journal, and the Weekly Advertiser*, August 25, 1773.

*January* 26, 1773.
FOUR DOLLARS REWARD.

RUN AWAY from the subscriber, living in Kent county. Little Creek Hundred, a Negro man named TONEY, about 27 years of age, five feet seven or eight inches high; had on and took with him when he went away, a large light coloured jacket, made of Kersey, with white flannel lining, Buckskin breeches, a pair of blue duffil trowsers, an old blue coat, home-spun shirt, coarse yarn stockings, old shoes, and an old felt hat: He plays well on the violin, is pretty talkative, and is addicted to drink. He formerly belonged to JOHN DICKENSON, Esq: of Philadelphia, and perhaps may pass himself for a freeman. Whoever takes up and secures said negro, so that his master may have him again, shall have the above reward and reasonable charges, paid by            CHRISTOPHER DENNY.

The *Pennsylvania Packet; and the General Advertiser*, February 15, 1773; February 22, 1773; March 1, 1773; March 8, 1773.


RUN AWAY, *on the 10th of February instant, from the subscriber, living in Wilmington, New Castle county, an Irish servant girl, named ANN LISTON, her age not known, has black hair; had on, when she went away, a home made linsey bed gown, and two petticoats, one striped, the other brown, the same of the bed gown. Whoever takes up the said girl, and secures her, so as her master may have her again, shall have FOUR DOLLARS reward, and reasonable charges, paid by*            JONAS PETERSON.
*All persons are forbid to harbour or carry her off.*

The *Pennsylvania Gazette*, February 17, 1773.

## TWENTY SHILLINGS REWARD.

*RUN AWAY, the second of this instant February, from the subscriber, in St. George's Hundred, New-Castle county, an Irish servant girl, named BETTY SLONE, but calls herself KITTY OWEN, about 20 years of age, a middle sized woman, with fair hair, fresh complexion, light blue eyes, thin lips, pitted with the small-pox, her hair is very thin, by a spell of sickness that she had, and cut short before, a great singer and talker, and is fond of men; had on, and took with her, when she went away, a black and white linsey petticoat, black quilt, a flannel ditto, a black and white short gown, a purple and white calicoe gown, with ruffles at the sleeves, a dark calicoe short ditto, two 800 shifts, a tow apron, one striped ditto, blue yarn stockings, two pair of shoes, one pair with leather heels, split at the instep and a piece set in, carved metal buckles, a chip hat, with a red ribbon round the crown of it. Whoever takes up said servant, and secures her in any of his Majesty's goals, so that her master may have her again, shall have the above reward, and reasonable charges, paid by WILLIAM READ.*

The Pennsylvania Gazette, February 17, 1773.


RUN AWAY from the subscriber, living in Mill creek Hundred, New-Castle county, an Irish servant man, named JAMES ADAMS; he is about 5 feet 7 inches high, full faced, grey eyed, with an uncommon white in them when he particularly looks at any object, thick lips, and a wide mouth, he wears his own straight fair hair short, is of a swarthy complexion, a thick set fellow, walks close at the knees; had on, when he went away, a lead coloured outside jacket, of homemade cloth, and breeches of the same piece, and a striped worsted under jacket, much wore, an old felt hat, bound with black binding, a pair of black sheep's wool stockings, his jacket had broad metal buttons on it; he has been about five months in the country; he is a weaver by trade, and says he understands something of blue dying and stamping; it is supposed he has made up towards Bucks county, where he has relations, and it is likely he may change his name, and forge himself a pass, as he is a tolerable scholar; he pretends a great deal to religion. Whoever apprehends said servant, and secures him in any of his Majesty's goals, so as his master may have him again, shall have THIRTY SHILLINGS reward, and reasonable charges, *December* 17, 1772.     paid by JOHN JAMES.
.     The Pennsylvania Gazette, February 24, 1773; April 7, 1773.


Wilmington, February 18, 1773.
## FORTY SHILLINGS REWARD.
THIS is to give notice, that a certain JAMES O BRYAN sold to me, the subscriber, in a fraudulent manner, the first of this instant, SIX SHEEP

(which he had stolen from one Charles M'Awley) and for which I paid him. He is about six feet high, pock-marked, speaks with the brogue and lisps, has grey hair, his right leg is much thicker than his left, wears a grey napt short coat, a red double breasted serge jacket, commonly wears linen trowsers, apt to get drunk and sing in company; had on an old wool hat, new shoes, with brass buckles. Therefore, whoever will take up the said O Bryan, and bring him to me, or secure him in any of his Majesty's goals, shall have the above reward, paid by         WILLIAM BROBSON.

*The Pennsylvania Gazette*, February 24, 1773; April 7, 1773.

*Lancaster Goal, February* 11, 1773.
THIS day was committed to my custody, a certain JERRY CLARK, a Negroe MAN, who is advertised in the Pennsylvania Gazette, by Morton Morton, living at Christiana Ferry, New-Castle County, with a reward of Four Dollars for taking up the said Negroe.

Also was committed to my custody, on the 8th day of September, 1772, a certain JAMES HENDERSON, as he called himself, but now confesses that his name is JAMES SHEHEE, and that he is a servant to David Morgan, Esq; near Mr. Jones's tavern, on the Horseshoe road, in Lancaster County. The masters of the said Negroe man, and the other servant, are desired to come, pay their fees, and take them away, or they will be discharged, on paying their own fees, in four weeks from this date, by GEORGE EBERLY, Goaler.

*The Pennsylvania Gazette*, March 3, 1773.

*New Castle, March* 2, 1773.
FIVE POUNDS Reward.
RUN away from the subscriber's farm, near New-Castle, some time in December last past, a Negroe man, named RAGOU, 30 years of age, about 6 feet high, he is a strong hearty fellow, his upper lip turns up; had on, when he went away, a coarse dark grey jacket, with a spotted flannel waistcoat under it, buckskin breeches. It is supposed that he keeps near Newark, or Ogletown. Whoever takes up the said Negroe slave, and secures him in the goal of this county, or brings him to his said master, so that he may have him again, shall have the above reward; or if any person will give proper information against the person, that harbours or entertains him, shall have THREE POUNDS, paid by       RICHARD M'WILLIAM.

*The Pennsylvania Gazette*, March 17, 1773.

TEN DOLLARS REWARD.
*RUN AWAY from the subscribers, living in Salem, a servant man, named* CHARLES GOFF, *a waterman, well known by almost all the watermen in*

*Delaware; he is of a small stature, not exceeding 5 feet 2 or 3 inches high, and proportionably made; he commonly wears a sailor's habit, and talks much of his knowledge in that business; he is a quarrelsome surly fellow, and swears much in conversation, it is probable he will endeavour to get birth on board some vessel to go to sea; all masters of vessels are hereby warned not to employ him, as they shall answer for the same at their peril. The most probable places to get intelligence of him are long the wharffs, of the watermen or sailors, or about Irish-town, in the Southern Liberties. Whoever takes up said Goff, and will return him to his masters, or will secure him in any goal, so that they may get him again, shall receive the above reward, and reasonable charges, from* THOMAS NORRIS, and
March 26, 1773.                THOMAS SINNICKSON.
*The Pennsylvania Gazette,* March 31, 1773.


RUNAWAY,
From Richard Dirrim, living in Dragon Neck, Newcastle
County, on the 5th Instant,
AN INDENTED SERVANT, named JAMES DOGHARTY, about 24 years of age, short straiight black hair, smooth full-faced, round visaged, is addicted to drunkenness and quarrelsome: Had on, when he went away, a light lead coloured coat, grey cloth jacket, an old pair of leather breeches, grey stockings, old shoes half soaled, brass buckles, one of them broke; he took with him a new Russia linen shirt, and two old shirts. Whoever secures him, in any goal, shall receive THIRTY SHILLINGS Reward.
April 21.            RICHARD DIRRIM.
*The Pennsylvania Journal, and the Weekly Advertiser,* April 21, 1773; April 28, 1773.


*Newcastle Gaol, April* 28, 1773.
EIGHTEEN DOLLARS REWARD,
BROKE out of the gaol of this county on Sunday night last, the following persons, to wit. PATRICK M'DANIEL, a servant to JOHN ARMSTRONG, near Wilmington, about five feet seven inches high, short black hair, a down looking fellow, about eighteen years of age; had on an old torn white coat, buckskin breeches, blue ribbed stockings and old shoes. MATTHEW SIMPSON, about five feet six inches high, short dark brown hair, full faced, fresh complexion, a well made fellow and a notorious rogue; had on an old ragged greyish coat, new felt hat, and hat an iron collar on his neck when he broke goal; he served his time (as he said) in or near Lancaster, afterwards became servant to ROBERT JOHNSON, tinker, in Penns Neck, West New-Jersey, who sold him to ADAM LITTLE, in Kent County, Maryland. Also a negro man named POMPEY, who said he was the property of JOSEPH

CROMWELL, living near Deer Creek, Baltimore county; about five feet eleven inches high, a likely well made fellow and a notorious villain; what cloaths he had on were very ragged; had on his legs when he broke gaol a heavy pair of irons. Whoever apprehends and secures the above named prisoners, and lodges them in any of his Majesty's gaols so that the subscriber may have them again, shall have the above reward, or SIX DOLLARS for each, and reasonable charges, paid by
ROBERT MACK, Gaoler.
N. B. Was committed to my custody, a certain ALEXANDER HASLET, who says he belongs to PATRICK GAMBLE, of Chester County; his said master is desired to come and pay charges and take him away.

*The Pennsylvania Packet; and the General Advertiser*, May 10, 1773; May 24, 1773; June 7, 1773.


NEW-CASTLE County, May 7, 1773.
RANAWAY,
From the subscriber, on Monday the 19th of April last,
A NEGRO MAN, named TOM, a likely well-set Fellow, about 24 years of age, 5 feet 9 or 10 inches high, wants two of his upper fore teeth, has a large scar on the right side of his head, and is very talkative: Had on, when he went away, a castor hat, a brown homespun coat, swanskin jacket, blue stuff breeches, ridge and fur worsted stockings a pair of new shoes, and a white shirt; took with him a pair of tow trowsers. Whoever takes up and secures said Negro Man in any gaol, so that his Master may have him again, shall have TWENTY SHILLINGS reward, and reasonable charges, if brought home, paid by ALEXANDER PORTER.

*The Pennsylvania Journal, and the Weekly Advertiser*, May 12, 1773; May 19, 1773.


FOUR DOLLARS Reward.
RUN away from the subscriber's farm, near New-Castle, an Irish servant lad, named GEORGE HENRY, about 20 years of age, about 5 feet 2 or 3 inches high, of a yellowish complexion, has light brown curly hair, large nostrils, and a small scar on his upper lip; takes snuff, and is addicted to lying; had on, when he went away, a half worn blue broadcloth coat, and a scarlet jacket. Whoever apprehends the said servant, and brings him to the subscriber, in New-Castle, shall receive the above reward, and all reasonable charges, *May* 25, 1773. paid by RICHARD M'WILLIAM.

The said servant ran away about a year ago, and was apprehended at Marsh-creek, where it is supposed he will now proceed to; and as he is a weaver by trade, will probably endeavour to get employ in that business.

*The Pennsylvania Gazette*, June 2, 1773. See *The Pennsylvania Gazette*, September 2, 1772; *The Pennsylvania Gazette*, September 1, 1773, and *The Pennsylvania Gazette*, August 17, 1774.


FORTY SHILLINGS REWARD.

RAN AWAY, in the morning of the 22d of this instant, June, from the subscriber, living in Millcreek hundred, and the county of Newcastle, an indented servant man named THOMAS M'DERMOT, of a ruddy complexion, about five feet six inches high, a great pretender to musick, and a good scholar; apt to get drunk: Had on when he went away, an oznabrigs shirt and tow trowsers, both new, an old hat, and new shoes tied with strings: He is about twenty years of age. Whoever takes up said servant, and secures him in any of his Majesty's gaols, or brings him to the subscriber, shall have the above reward, and reasonable charges,
   paid by  JOHN DIXSON.

*The Pennsylvania Packet; and the General Advertiser*, June 28, 1773; July 5, 1773; August 9, 1773.


TEN POUNDS Reward.

RUN away from the subscriber's plantation, near New-Castle, some time in December last, a Negroe man slave, named RAGON, 30 years of age, about six feet high, a strong hearty fellow, was brought up by Thomas Ogle, deceased; had on when he went away, a coarse dark grey jacket, spotted flannel under waistcoat, buckskin breeches, &c. It is supposed that he keeps near Ogletown, or at William Carson's, about 12 miles below New-Castle, where Bird lately kept tavern. Whoever takes up the said Negroe slave, and secures him in the Goal of this County, or brings him to his said master, so that he may have him again, shall have the above reward; or if any one will inform against the person that harbours or entertains him, shall have Five Pounds, paid by   RICHARD M'WILLIAM.

*The Pennsylvania Gazette*, June 30, 1773; July 7, 1773; July 14, 1773; August 4, 1773.


THREE POUNDS Reward.

RUN away, on Friday last, from subscriber, living in Christiana Hundred, New-Castle county, a young Negroe man, named ANDREW; he is about 5 feet 6 inches high, thin visaged, slim made; had on, when he went away, an old lead coloured cloth coat, worn at the elbows, a new flowered flannel jacket, a fine shirt, ruffled at the breast and guards, striped ticken trowsers, home-made white cotton stockings, old calfskin pumps, lately mended, a good raccoon hat; but it is probable he will change his clothes; he has a scar on the left side of his head, and a cut on his leg; plays on the fiddle very well,

and speaks fast and thick when angry. Whoever takes up and secures said Negroe, so that his master may have him again, shall have the above reward, and reasonable charges, paid by
*June* 17, 1773.	JEREMIAH SMITH.
   N. B. All persons following the water, and others, are forbid to entertain said Negroe, at their peril.
   *The Pennsylvania Gazette*, June 30, 1773.


RUN away, the 16th of April last, from the subscriber, near Christiana Bridge, in New-Castle County, on Delaware, a Negroe man, named JAMES, 25 years old, about 5 feet 6 inches high, a small fellow, is very black, and a little marked with the small-pox; he is wide between his two fore-teeth, is this country born, and can play on the fiddle; had on, when he went away, a coarse whitish coloured cloth jacket and breeches, a flaxen under jacket, a half-worn hat, coarse blue stockings, all his apparel is half worn. Whoever takes up and secures said Negroe, so as his master may have him again, shall receive THREE POUNDS reward, paid by
*July* 2, 1773.	ROBERT M'ANTIER.
   *The Pennsylvania Gazette*, July 7, 1773.


### SIX DOLLARS REWARD.
RUN away, last night, from the subscriber, living in St. George's Hundred, New Castle County, an Irish servant man, but calls himself an Englishman, named WILLIAM BUTLER, but probably may change it, a Taylor by trade, a stout well set fellow, wears his own short black hair; had on, when he went away, a check shirt, ozenbrigs trowsers, calfskin shoes, with brass buckles; he stole and took with him a nankeen coat, and breeches not made up, red serge vest, with silver frosted buttons, a pair of buckskin gloves, a furred hat, and a Guinea and an half in gold; he is very remarkable in his face, a sour down look, big mouth, and some black spots under one of his eyes, occasioned by gun-powder. Whoever takes up said servant, and secures him in any goal, so that his master may get him again, shall have the above reward, and all reasonable charges, if brought home,
June 25.	paid by	WILLIAM MOODY.
   *The Pennsylvania Gazette*, July 7, 1773. See *The Pennsylvania Journal, and the Weekly Advertiser*, July 7, 1773.


### SIX DOLLARS REWARD.
RAN-AWAY the 24th ult. from the subscriber, living in St. George's Hundred, New-Castle county, an Irish servant man, (but calls himself an

Englishman) named WILLIAM BUTLER, but probably may change it, a Taylor by trade, a stout well set fellow, wears his own short black hair; had on when he went away a check shirt, Oznabrigs trowsers, calf-skin shoes, with brass buckles. He stole and took with him a nankeen coat and breeches, the breeches not made up, a red serge vest, with silver frosted buttons, a pair of buck-skin gloves, a furred hat, and a Guinea and a half in gold: He is very remarkable in his face, a sour, down look, big mouth, and some black spots under his eyes, occasioned by some gun-powder.—Whoever takes up and secures said servant in any goal, so that his master may get him again, shall have the above reward, and all reasonable charges, if brought home,
July 7.          paid by WILLIAM MOODY.

*The Pennsylvania Journal, and the Weekly Advertiser*, July 7, 1773; July 14, 1773; July 21, 1773. See *The Pennsylvania Gazette*, July 7, 1773.


WHEREAS Mary the wife of the subscriber, having behaved in a most infamous manner, I look upon myself as justified both in the eyes of God and man for leaving her. She lately came from Ireland into America, and lives near Newark in Newcastle county. As I have not cohabited with the said Mary since her coming from Ireland, nor will in future, I hereby forwarn all persons not to trust her, on my account, as I will pay no debts of his contracting.
20*th. July,* 1773.                    ROBERT MITCHELL.

*The Pennsylvania Chronicle, and Universal Advertiser*, From Monday, July 19, to Monday, July 26, 1773; From Monday, July 26, to Monday, August 2, 1773.


RUN away from Captain William Chevers, of the ship Needham, lying at New-Castle, a servant girl, named CATHARINE M'DERMOND, about fifteen years of age, has curled hair; had on, when she went away, a brown stuff gown; it is supposed she will change her cloaths; she is Daughter-in-law to one Whitesides, that is married to said servant's mother, who is gone lower down into Virginia, to her husband; both mother and daughter came in with Captain Chevers about the 12th of July instant, and it is supposed she is gone to Virginia along with her mother. Whoever takes up said servant, and brings her to New Castle, or secures her, so as her master may have her again, shall have Fifty Shillings reward, and reasonable charges,
          paid by WILLIAM CHEVERS, or
in New-Castle.              by Mr. DANIEL M'LONEN,

*The Pennsylvania Gazette*, July 28, 1773. See *The New-York Gazette; and the Weekly Mercury*, August 30, 1773.

EIGHT DOLLARS REWARD.

RAN-AWAY last night, from the subscriber, living in St. George's Hundred, a native Irish servant man, named MICHAEL WHEALLON, but is apt to change his name; is fond of strong drink, and apt to swear and lie; he is about twenty years of age, five feet six inches high, of a fair complexion, down look, stoops much in his walk; stole and took with him one light coloured market coat half worn, one red jacket without sleeves, two white shirts, one check ditto, new felt hat, new shoes and brass buckles; he has been in the country about two years, and at Newfoundland, and it is supposed he will try to get to sea from some seaport town. Whoever takes up said servant and secures him, so that his master may have him again, shall have the above reward, paid by　　BENJAMIN ARMSTRONG.

N. B. All masters of vessels are forbid to carry him off at their peril.

*The Pennsylvania Packet; and the General Advertiser*, August 23, 1773; August 30, 1773. See *The Pennsylvania Packet; and the General Advertiser*, January 18, 1773, *The Pennsylvania Gazette*, January 20, 1773; *The Pennsylvania Journal, and the Weekly Advertiser*, January 20, 1773, and *The Pennsylvania Journal, and the Weekly Advertiser*, August 25, 1773.

EIGHT DOLLARS REWARD.

STOLEN in the night of the 18th inst. (August) from JOHN AIKEN's in Pencader Hundred, Newcastle County, a dark brown HORSE, about fourteen hands high, has a star in his forehead, one eye smaller than the other, a snip on his nose, a white streak on his near side, galled with the gears, a switch tail, is a natural pacer, and had no shoes on; also a bridle, and a saddle with a blue cloth bound with white, and buckskin seat; likewise a silver watch, maker's name William Strong Hale, No. 460. It is supposed they were stolen by a certain JOHN RUSSELL, about 5 feet 7 or 8 inches high, brown complexion, and strait black hair; had on a beaver hat, a suit of snuff coloured fustian cloaths, white thread stockings, and yellow buckles. Whoever takes up the said horse and goods, so that the owner may have them again, and secures the thief in any of his Majesty's gaols, shall have the above reward, or FOUR DOLLARS for the horse only, and reasonable charges,
　　　　　　paid by　　JOHN M'MINN.

*The Pennsylvania Packet; and the General Advertiser*, August 23, 1773.

EIGHT DOLLARS REWARD.

RAN-AWAY the 16th inst. from the subscriber, living in St George's Hundred, a native Irish servant man, named MICHAEL WHEALLON, but is apt to change his name; is fond of strong drink, and apt to swear and lie; he is about twenty years of age, five feet six inches high, of a fair complexion,

down look, and stoops much in his walk; stole and took with him one light coloured great-coat half worn, one red jacket without sleeves, two white shirts, one check ditto, new felt hat, new shoes with brass buckles; he has been at Newfoundland, and in this country about two years, and it is supposed he will try to get to sea from some sea-port town. Whoever takes up said servant and secures him, so that his master may have him again, shall have the above reward, paid by      BENJAMIN ARMSTRONG.
N. B. All masters of vessels are forbid to carry him off at their peril.
*The Pennsylvania Journal, and the Weekly Advertiser,* August 25, 1773; September 1, 1773; September 8, 1773. See *The Pennsylvania Packet; and the General Advertiser,* January 18, 1773, *The Pennsylvania Gazette,* January 20, 1773; *The Pennsylvania Journal, and the Weekly Advertiser,* January 20, 1773, and *The Pennsylvania Packet; and the General Advertiser,* August 23, 1773.

TWENTY SHILLINGS Reward.
RUN-away from the ship Needham, Capt. Cheevers, on the 20th inst, an apprentice lad named John Hutchinson, a lusty young fellow, about 5 feet 6 or 9 [*sic*] inches high, reddish hair, fresh complexion, about 18 years old; had on a check shirt and trowsers, a red handkerchief about his neck, a white jacket with sleeves; is lurking about this city, or may be gone to Philadelphia, looks much like a sailor. Also left the ship at Newcastle, William Makee, alias Kee, and Catharine M'Dermot, Redemptioners; the former left his wife on board, and promised to return after paying a visit to some of his relations at the cross roads near Philadelphia, who he told Capt. Cheevers, would redeem him: He is about 5 feet 6 inches high, thin swarthy complexion, black eyes, went in company with William Armstrong; had on a white coat, (but may change it as he had blue cloaths with him) a white fustian vest, a pale cut wig. Catharine M'Dermot left the ship by making use of her sisters receipt, who, in order to deceive, continued on board till the other had concealed herself; she is a well looking young girl, short but lusty, and no doubt is with her mother and sister, who paid their passages. Whoever takes up any of the above redemptioners, and delivers them to Mr. Daniel M'Lonen, at Newcastle, shall have the above reward for each, though 'tis hoped they will prevent a farther enquiry, by paying their redemption to him, or the subscriber in New-York.
WILLIAM NEILSON.
*The New-York Gazette; and the Weekly Mercury,* August 30, 1773; September 6, 1773; September 20, 1773; *The Pennsylvania Journal, and the Weekly Advertiser,* August 25, 1773; September 8, 1773. See *The Pennsylvania Gazette,* July 28, 1773, for M'Dermot.

*New-Castle, August* 24, 1773.
FOUR DOLLARS Reward.
*RUN away from the subscriber's farm, near New-Castle, this morning, an Irish servant lad, named GEORGE HENRY, about 20 years of age, about 5 feet 5 inches high, of a yellowish complexion, has light brown curley hair, large nostrils, and a small scar on his upper lip, takes snuff, and is addicted to lying; had on, when he went away, a black spotted flannel jacket, and ozenbrigs shirt and trowsers. Whoever apprehends the said servant, so that the subscriber may have hum again, shall receive the above reward, and all reasonable charges, paid by* RICHARD M'WILLIAM.
*N. B. The said servant has been almost three years in the country, and has ran away several times. It is supposed that he has now either a forged pass, or receipt, for the payment of his passage money from Ireland.*
The Pennsylvania Gazette, September 1, 1773; September 8, 1773. See *The Pennsylvania Gazette*, September 2, 1772; *The Pennsylvania Gazette*, June 2, 1773, and *The Pennsylvania Gazette*, August 17, 1774.

*Philadelphia, August* 28, 1773.
FIVE POUNDS *Reward.*
WHEREAS a grey MARE, the property of a certain *William Tate*, was, since last May term, taken in execution by the Sheriff of New-Castle county, which mare has been since feloniously taken out of the stable of *George Gordon*, in Wilmington, by the said *William Tate*, and by him sold to *Adam Ramsower*, Tavern-keeper, in Strawberry-alley, Philadelphia, on the 5th day of July last; the subscribers will pay the above reward to any person or persons, who shall apprehend the said *William Tate*, and secure him in any of his Majesty's goals, so as he may be brought to justice. He is a slender man, about 25 years of age, about 5 feet 7 or 8 inches high, of a fresh and sandy complexion, a little freckled, wears his own hair, speaks remarkably quick, and wants part of the tops of some of his fingers, calls himself of Mill-creek Hundred, New-Castle county, and frequently worked at boring and sawing in a shipyard.
ADAM RAMSOWER, JEREMIAH SMITH.
*The Pennsylvania Gazette*, September 1, 1773.

*New-Castle County, August* 24, 1773.
TWENTY DOLLARS Reward.
*WAS STOLEN, on the 16th instant, out of the pasture of William Patterson, near Christiana bridge, a bay HORSE, about 9 years old, near 14 hands high, a well made horse, in very good order, paces and trots, a hanging mane, switch tail, has neither brand nor ear-mark, has a feather low down on the near side of his neck, and something like one on the offside; a few white hairs*

*in the fore-top, a blackish spot on his wiskers, which was hurt with the cart-saddle; said horse has something of a cramp or lameness in the near hind foot, which may be observed when he is first rode, was shod before. I have great reason to believe the said horse was stolen, by a certain ROBERT JONES, a very great villain and a noted horse-thief, who broke out of Gloucester goal, about 3 years ago, and was then servant to one Allen Gillaspie, of this County; the said Jones was on the plantation when the said horse was stole: He had on a brownish coat, white breeches, brown worsted stockings; he is a lusty strong made fellow, about 35 years of age, about 5 feet 9 inches high, has short brown hair, was born in Ireland, speaks a little on the brogue. Whoever takes up said horse and thief, shall be intitled to the above reward, and for the horse only, ten dollars,*
    *paid by WILLIAM PATTERSON.*
 *N. B. It is supposed the said Jones is gone by way of Carlisle, towards Virginia. August* 24, 1773.
 The Pennsylvania Gazette, September 1, 1773; January 12, 1774; January 26, 1774. Later ads do not have the date at the top. See *The Pennsylvania Journal, and the Weekly Advertiser*, September 1, 1773.

          New-Castle County, August 24, 1773.
        TWENTY DOLLARS Reward.
On the 16th inst. was stolen out of the pasture of WILLIAM PATTERSON, near Christiana Bridge, a BAY HORSE, about 9 years old, near 14 hands high, well made, and in very good order, paces and trots, has a hanging mane and switch tail, has neither brand nor ear-mark, has a feather low down on the near side of his neck, and something like one on the off side, a few white hairs in the fore top, a blackish spot on his weathers, occasioned by a hurt with the cart saddle; he has something of a cramp or lameness in the near hind foot, which may be observed when first rode, and is shod before. There is reason to think said horse was stolen by a certain ROBERT JONES, a very great villain and a noted horse thief, who broke out of Gloucester goal about three years ago, and was then servant to one Allen Gillaspie, of this county. Said Jones was on the plantation the day said horse was stole: Had on a brownish coat, white breeches, brown worsted stockings, is a lusty strong made fellow, about 35 years of age, about 5 feet 9 inches high, has short brown hair, is an Irishman, and speaks a little on the brogue. Whoever takes up said horse and thief, shall be entitled to the above reward, and for the horse only, TEN DOLLARS, paid by WILLIAM PATTERSON.
 N. B. It is supposed the said Jones is gone by way of Carlisle, towards Virginia.

*The Pennsylvania Journal, and the Weekly Advertiser*, September 1, 1773; September 8, 1773; September 29, 1773; October 6, 1773. See *The Pennsylvania Gazette*, September 1, 1773.

TWENTY DOLLARS Reward.

STOLEN, on the night of the 10th ult. out of the pasture of the subscriber, at Christiana Bridge, a bright bay HORSE, 14 hands high, with a long hanging black mane and switch tail, six years old, (but appears to be older) has two colt's teeth in his under jaw, commonly called fitfasts, [*sic*] paces, trots and hand-gallops, and when riding is apt to throw up his nose; had but one shoe, and that on his near fore foot: He is supposed to be stolen by a certain STEPHEN RATCLIFF, a miller by trade, a pale looking man, about 5 feet 6 or 7 inches high, wears his own hair of a brownish colour, had on a light coloured half-worn coat, striped Damascus waistcoat, and blue velvet breeches; he also stole a half-worn saddle, with brass staple buttons before and behind, the stirrup irons jointed in the sides with two rims above, and a narrow leather girth. Whoever takes up said horse and thief, so that the owner may have his horse and saddle, and the thief be brought to conviction, shall receive the above reward; and for the horse and saddle only, THIRTY SHILLINGS, and reasonable charges.

THOMAS SCULLY.

N. B. It is supposed he is gone towards Redstone settlement, as he has a brother and several relations there.

*The Pennsylvania Journal, and the Weekly Advertiser*, September 1, 1773; September 8, 1773.

FIVE POUNDS Reward.

STOLEN from the subscriber, living in Lancaster county, Little Britain township, the 25th of August last, a light BAY HORSE, about 14 1/2 hands high, a natural pacer, shod before, 11 years old last grass, hath no brand nor ear mark, black mane and tail, a very good leader of a team, used with a single line; also a Pinchbeck WATCH, with a china face, and remarkable pictures drawn out on the case, with a steel chain, the seal being broken, as the thief pulled it off the nail where it hung. The said horse and watch are supposed to be taken by one JOHN BROWN, he is about 5 feet 7 inches high, has a down look, swarthy complexion, with his hair cut short; it is supposed he will wear a wig or cap; he has a snuff coloured jacket and breeches, white thread stockings, old shoes, and brass buckles. Whoever takes up said thief, horse, and watch, shall have the above reward, and for the horse only TWENTY SHILLINGS,     paid by     JAMES GILLCREST.

N. B. He says he was born in the Jerseys, near Salem, and now makes his home in Brandywine Hundred; he may perhaps change his name, as he formerly did, from *John Russell* to *John Brown.*
The Pennsylvania Gazette, September 8, 1773.

Newcastle, September 13, 1773.
THREE POUNDS REWARD.
RAN AWAY from the subscriber, living near Newcastle, an Irish servant man named EDWARD M'CALLOGAN, about five feet seven inches high, has a kind of roll in his walk; had on when he went away, a new wool hat, a snuff-coloured cotton jacket with clear buttons, one sky-colour do. a pair of buckskin breeches about half worn, a pair of blue worsted stockings, new shoes with metal buckles, a new white shirt, and a new silk handkerchief. He stole from his fellow-labourer, one Dennis Lafferty, a pass signed by David Finney, Esq; and may probably attempt to travel by that name. Whoever takes up said servant, so that his master may have him again, shall have the above reward, and reasonable charges,
          paid by    PATRICK M'GONNIGLE.
*The Pennsylvania Packet; and the General Advertiser*, September 20, 1773; October 4, 1773. See *The Pennsylvania Journal, and the Weekly Advertiser*, December 22, 1773.

Newcastle Gaol, on Delaware, Sept, 13, 1773.
WAS committed to my care, the following servants and slaves, to wit, JOHN CLEMENTS, says he belongs to John Barkush, near Bush Town, Maryland. A negro man named DICK, speaks very bad English, and says he belongs to John Adams, near Snow-Hill. PETER alias PERO, said he belonged to Jacob Lowry, near Lancaster, but now confesses he belonged to Jacob Peck, near the Gap Tavern, Chester County. GEORGE, a new negro lad, speaks very little English, says his master's name (as well as can be understood) is Moses Lann, and it is supposed by his signs, that his said master lives 100 miles beyond Annapolis. JAMES CONWAY, an Irishman, says he belongs to David Crafford, near Fishing Creek on Susquehanna. On suspicion the two following: JAMES INSELLOW, as he calls himself, a well set fellow, 5 feet 7 or eight inches high, sandy hair, red beard, full faced, large eyes, and is fond of drink. JAMES MOONEYS, as he calls himself, is about 5 feet 7 inches high, much freckled in the face, had on when committed, a light coloured wilton coat, old trowsers, good shoes, and had a new-fashioned cane with some silver mounting on it: They look very suspicious, and are supposed to have changed their names. The masters of the above servants are once more desired to come, pay charges, and take them away in three weeks, otherwise they will be sold out for their fees,
          by ROBERT MACK, Gaoler.

*The Pennsylvania Packet; and the General Advertiser*, September 20, 1773; October 4, 1773; October 18, 1773.

FIVE POUNDS REWARD.
RAN AWAY the 21st day of the Tenth month (called October) 1773, from the subscriber, living near Cantwell's Bridge, in Newcastle county upon Delaware, an Irish servant man named PATRICK GORE, about 21 years of age, five feet nine or ten inches high, of a thin visage pale complexion grey eyes and black hair which he sometimes ties; had on when he went away, a good fur hat, grey coating coat trimed with a figured pewter cap'd button with bone moulds and cat gut eyes, a light coloured cloth jacket without sleeves, an old white shirt with new wristbands not stitched, a pair of velvet breeches lined with shammy, and buttons on the knee-bands, old ribbed worsted hose, darned about the heels, and a pair of good neats leather shoes, with brass buckles: As he took with him near 6*l.* in money, it is likely he may change his stockings, and some other part of his cloathing. He spells badly, but writes a good hand, and understands figures. It is likely he may endeavour to get to Baltimore Town, Philadelphia, or New-York, and try to be clerk, or ship himself for Ireland, as he came from that country about two years ago. Whoever takes up said servant and brings him home, or secures him in any gaol, so that his master may have him again, shall have the above reward,
          paid by    ISAAC STARR.

*Dunlap's Pennsylvania Packet or, the General Advertiser*, November 3, 1773; November 29, 1773; December 27, 1773. See *The Pennsylvania Gazette*, November 3, 1773.

FIVE POUNDS Reward.
RUN AWAY the 21st day of the Tenth month (called October) 1773, from the subscriber, living near Cantwell's Bridge, in Newcastle county upon Delaware, an Irish servant man, named PATRICK GORE, about 21 years of age, about 21 years of age, five feet eight or nine inches high, of a thin visage, pale complexion, grey eyes and black hair, which he sometimes ties; had on when he went away, a good fur hat, grey coating coat, trimmed with a figured pewter capbutton, with bone moulds and cat gut eyes, a light coloured cloth jacket without sleeves, an old white shirt, with new wristbands, not stitched, a pair of velvet breeches lined with shammy, and buttons on the knee bands, old ribbed worsted hose, darned about the heels, and a pair of good neats leather shoes, with brass buckles: As he took with him near 6 l. in money, it is likely he may change his stockings, and some other part of his cloathing. He spells badly, but writes a good hand, and understands figures. It is likely he may endeavour to get to Baltimore-Town, Philadelphia, or New-York, and

try to get to be clerk, ship himself for Ireland, as he came from that country about two years ago. Whoever takes up said servant, and brings him home, or secures him in any goal, so that his master may have him again, shall have the above reward, paid by ISAAC STARR.
*The Pennsylvania Gazette*, November 3, 1773. See *Dunlap's Pennsylvania Packet or, the General Advertiser*, November 3, 1773.

THREE POUNDS REWARD.
*RUN away from the Subscriber, living in St. George's Hundred, New Castle county, an Irish servant man, named DANIEL DURRAH, about 5 feet 3 or 4 inches high, has lately been sick. Had on when he went away, a wool hat, almost new, a blue coat, green jacket, striped ticken breeches, two pair of blue ribbed stockings, new shoes, with Pinchbeck buckles, he took with him, an old grey coat, made whim fashion, and is apt to wear it over his other coat, he is a great tobacco chewer and loves rum. Whoever secures said Servant, and brings him home, shall have the above reward and reasonable charges, paid by WILLIAM CARSON.*
*The Pennsylvania Gazette*, December 1, 1773. See *Dunlap's Pennsylvania Packet or, the General Advertiser*, December 6, 1773.

Red-Lion Hundred, November 27, 1773.
RUN AWAY from the subscriber, living in Red-Lion Hundred, New-Castle county, on the 25th instant, a servant lad, named JOHN COLLINS, born in Ireland, about 5 feet 5 or 6 inches high, dark brown hair, round face, and of a red complexion, strong made, and about 17 or 18 years of age; had on a blue broadcloth coat, and lappelled jacket of the same, old buckskin breeches, yarn stockings, half-worn shoes, and old felt hat. Whoever secures said servant, so that I may have him again, shall receive THIRTY SHILLINGS, from HUGH STEEL.
*The Pennsylvania Gazette*, December 1, 1773.

FIVE POUNDS REWARD.
RAN AWAY from the subscriber, living in St. George's hundred, Newcastle county, an Irish servant man named DANIEL DURRAH, about five feet three or four inches high, has lately been sick: Had on when he went away, a wool hat almost new, a blue coat, green jacket, striped ticken breeches, two pair of blue ribbed stockings, new shoes, with pinchbeck buckles; he took with him an old grey coat, made whim fashion, [*sic*] and is apt to wear it over his other coat; he is a great tobacco chewer, and loves rum. Whoever secures said servant, and brings him home, shall have the above reward and

reasonable charges, paid by     WILLIAM CARSON.
*Dunlap's Pennsylvania Packet or, the General Advertiser*, December 6, 1773; December 13, 1773. See *The Pennsylvania Gazette*, December 1, 1773.

### THREE POUNDS REWARD.

RAN AWAY from his bail, about the latter end of July last, a certain ARCHIBALD M'FARLAND, born in Ireland, and came to this place about a year since; he is a carpenter by trade, about twenty four years of age, and about five feet seven inches high, slim made, with dark brown hair tied behind; had on and took with him, a brown coat, a grey cloth jacket, black breeches, an English castor hat, with sundry other cloaths: he is a little stoop shouldered, of a quick motion of body, flat footed, smooth faced, and of a lively disposition. Whoever secures the said M'Farland in any of his Majesty's gaols, so that his bail may recover him again, shall have the above reward; and if brought to the subscriber, living near St. Georges in Newcastle County, shall have reasonable charges,
    paid by     LAWRENCE HIGGINS.
N. B. It is supposed he is gone towards Baltimore, and that he hath changed his name.
*Dunlap's Pennsylvania Packet or, the General Advertiser*, December 13, 1773.

### THREE POUNDS REWARD.

RAN-AWAY from the subscriber, living in Duck-creek, Kent county upon Delaware, on the first of July last, a negro man called JACK, about nineteen years of age, five feet seven or eight inches high, his teeth broad and then, and stands leaning out of his mouth, one of his upper teeth is turned black; had on when he went away, a pair of long petticoat trowsers, tow shirt, lincey jacket with the stripes across, but it is probable he has changed is cloaths; he was raised near Appoquiminink Bridge, in Newcastle-county, and it is supposed he has made upwards. Whoever takes up and secures said negro, so that his master may have him again, shall have the above reward, and reasonable charges, paid by     SAMUEL TINCH.
N. B. All masters of vessels are forbid carrying him off at their peril.
*Dunlap's Pennsylvania Packet or, the General Advertiser*, December 13, 1773; January 24, 1774.

### Three Pounds, Reward.

RUN-away from the Subscriber, Sept. 8th, 1773, an indented Servant Girl named Mary Kelly, lately from Ireland, but says she has lived 14 Years in London; is about 18 or 20 Years of Age, five Feet six or eight Inches high, stoops in walking, fair Complexion and reddish Hair: Had on when she went away, a little round Man's Hat, green Petticoat, and black stuff Shoes; took with her two short Gowns, one striped blue and white, the other Callicoe with red Flowers; and six Yards of Callicoe not made. Whoever takes up the said runaway Servant, and secures her in any of his Majesty's Goals so that she may be had again, shall be intituled to the above Reward, and if brought home, all reasonable Charges

    paid by me, G. BARNES.
At the Sign of the Harp and Crown, in Wilmington.
*The New-York Gazette; and the Weekly Mercury*, December 13, 1773; December 20, 1773; December 27, 1773; January 3, 1774.

    New-Castle, December 14, 1773.
    FIVE POUNDS Reward.
RAN-AWAY from the subscriber, living near New-Castle, about the first of September last, an Irish servant man named EDWARD M'CALLAGAN, about 30 years of age, 5 feet 7 inches high, chesnut coloured hair, fair faced, has a thick upper lip, stoops a little, walks wide, is knock kneed, and rocks much as he walks: Had on and took with him, a new wool hat, a snuff coloured cotton jacket, and one sky coloured ditto, with small white metal buttons, a pair of half-worn buckskin breeches, blue worsted stockings, new shoes, with metal buckles, a white shirt, and a new cross-barr'd silk handkerchief; but as he is an artful fellow, he may change his cloaths. He stole a pass of one Dennis Lafferty, signed by David Finney, Esq; and may probably pass by that name. Whoever takes up the said servant, and secures him in any goal, so as his master may have him again, shall have the above reward, and if brought home, all reasonable charges,

    paid by PATRICK M'GONIGAL.
*The Pennsylvania Journal, and the Weekly Advertiser*, December 22, 1773; December 29, 1773. See *The Pennsylvania Packet; and the General Advertiser*, September 20, 1773.

# 1774

    TWELVE DOLLARS Reward.
MADE his escape, the 15th of November last, in the afternoon, from the subscriber, one of the Constables of St. George's Hundred, in and for the county of New-Castle upon Delaware, a certain JACOB SADLER, a Bricklayer by trade, about 5 feet 9 or 10 inches high, slim made, has dark short hair, and black eyes, was born in or near Philadelphia; had on, when he went away, a blue coat, and half-worn leather breeches; but, as he had a good many clothes, it would be hard to describe them. He was committed to the county goal of New-Castle, by JOHN JONES, Esq; for want of bail, to

indemnify the Hundred from supporting a bastard child he had got in said Hundred, as also for his breach of promise to the girl. Whoever secures said SADLER in any goal, so that the subscriber can have him again, shall have the above reward, and if brought to New Castle goal, reasonable charges,
   paid by  JAMES HANSON, Constable.
*The Pennsylvania Gazette,* January 12, 1774.

### THREE POUNDS REWARD.

RAN AWAY from the subscriber, an Irish servant man, named JOHN MORGAN, about five feet seven or eight inches high, thin fair hair, very short, pock marked, has a whitish look in his eyes, and speaks with the brogue: Had on, an old felt hat, half worn, bound round with tape, a tow linen shirt, scarlet flannel jacket, made sailor fashion, with a blue one under it, brown cloth breeches, with coarse dirty linen trowsers over them, white yarn stockings, with good shoes and broad rimmed yellow buckles. Whoever takes up and secures said fellow, in any of his Majesty's goals, so that his master may have him again, or brings him home to the subscriber, living in St. George's Hundred, New-Castle County, shall have the above reward and reasonable charges, paid by  WILLIAM CARSON.
*Dunlap's Pennsylvania Packet or, the General Advertiser,* January 17, 1774.

### THREE POUNDS REWARD.

RAN AWAY from the subscriber, living in St. George's hundred, Newcastle county, an Irish servant man named DANIEL DURRAH, about five feet three or four inches high, has lately been sick: Had on when he went away, a wool hat almost new, a blue coat, green jacket, striped ticken breeches, two pair of blue ribbed stockings, new shoes, with pinchbeck buckles; he took with him an old grey coat, made whim [*sic*] fashion, and is apt to wear it over his other coat; he is a great tobacco chewer, and loves rum. Whoever secures said servant, and brings him home, shall have the above reward and reasonable charges, paid by  WILLIAM CARSON.
*Dunlap's Pennsylvania Packet or, the General Advertiser,* January 24, 1774.

       *Kent county, on Delaware, Dec.* 12, 1773.
### TEN DOLLARS REWARD.
RAN AWAY from his bail, the first of November last, a certain HUGH BARRY, an Irishman, by trade a blacksmith, remarkably small, and appears of be very young, but says he is 25 years of age; had on an old blue jacket with new sleeves, a Russia shirt, home-spun trowsers, old shoes, worsted stockings, and an half worn hat: He came in last fall was a year, and his

indenture was assigned over to one James Scott, in Lancaster county, who paid his redemption; as he said he had a wife living at said Scott's, it is supposed he will go there, and from thence to New Virginia. Whoever takes up the said Hugh Barry, and delivers him to the Sheriff of this county or to the Gaoler in Dover, shall have the above reward,
    paid by  PRESTON BERRY.
 *Dunlap's Pennsylvania Packet or, the General Advertiser*, January 24, 1774; February 28, 1774. See *The Pennsylvania Gazette*, March 9, 1774.

      TWENTY SHILLINGS REWARD.
RAN AWAY, on the 30th of January last, from the subscriber, living in Brandywine Hundred, New-Castle County, an Irish servant man, named JOHN MORNE, a smart lively fellow, about 20 years of age, and about 5 feet 2 inches high; a little stoop shouldered, has black hair combed back before, and pretends to be a little hard of hearing; had on when he went away, a fresh coloured cloth jacket, with cuffs on the sleeves, and wooden buttons, an old lincey under jacket, tow shirt, old grey coloured cloth breeches broken in the knees, a new wool hat, two pair of woollen stockings, one of them black, the other blue, one pair of shoes with thongs in them, lately half soaled, and some hob nails in the toes and heels. Whoever takes up said servant, and secures him in any of his Majesty's gaols, so that his master may get him again, shall have the above reward, and all reasonable charges,
    paid by  DANIEL M'BRIDE.
 *N. B. All masters of vessels and others are forbid to harbour or carry him off at their peril.*
 *Dunlap's Pennsylvania Packet or, the General Advertiser*, February 7, 1774; March 7, 1774; April 11, 1774. *The Pennsylvania Gazette*, March 23, 1774. Minor differences between the papers. The *Gazette* omits the line "a little stoop shouldered."

      SIX DOLLARS REWARD.
RUN away from the subscriber, living at White-clay-creek Landing, New-castle county, the 10th instant, an Irish servant man, named HUGH GIBSON, 24 years of age, about 5 feet 7 inches high, has a down look, stoop shouldered, and thin dark brown hair, much given to liquor, and very quarrelsome in his cups, speaks broad, and has been in the army; he had on, and took with him, a coat made of an Indian blanket, a brown worsted and wool jacket, lined with shaloon, too long for him, having been made for a tall man, a striped lincey ditto, blue and white, without sleeves, a pair of buckskin breeches, almost new, linnen shirt, a pair of fulled Germantown stockings, much worn, and a pair of coarse leather shoes, tied with strings, about half worn, Whoever

secures said servant, so that his master may get him again, shall receive the above reward, and reasonable charges, paid by
*February* 12, 1774.              WILLIAM FOOTT.
*The Pennsylvania Gazette*, February 23, 1774.


WHEREAS a certain JOHN M'CONNELL, born in Belfast, in Ireland, by trade a taylor, and worked in December last with Jonathan Willson, at Cantwell's Bridge, in New-Castle County, and borrowed a horse, bridle and saddle, of said Willson, which horse, &c. he rode to Philadelphia, and put up at the Pennsylvania Farmer, kept by Joseph Price, and remained there three days, in which time the said M'Connell sold the said Price his horse, saddle and bridle, alledging that he was in want of money, and had no farther use for him; Therefore, in order to apprehend the said John M'Connell, we, the subscribers, do offer a reward of FIVE POUNDS, to any person who will stop and secure the said M'Connell, in any of his Majesty's gaols, so that he may be brought to justice. He is about five feet six or seven inches high, about twenty years of age, smooth faced, long dark coloured hair, down look, very talkative in company, and remarkably fond of singing a song called the Cheating Landlady; he had on a claret coloured coat, with plain gilt buttons, a scarlet waistcoat, light blue breeches and stockings, and a half-worn castor hat: It is thought he is gone either towards New-York, or Baltimore Town, in Maryland.          JOSEPH PRICE,
                     JONATHAN WILLSON.
*Dunlap's Pennsylvania Packet or, the General Advertiser*, March 7, 1774; March 23, 1774; April 11, 1774.


                         *Kent County, on Delaware, February* 21, 1774.
                         TEN POUNDS Reward.
ABSCONDED from his bail, the first of November last, a certain HUGH BARRY, an Irishman, by trade a blacksmith, remarkably small; and appears of be very young, but says he is 25 years of age; had on an old blue jacket with new sleeves, a Russia shirt, home-spun trowsers, old shoes, worsted stockings, and an half worn hat: He came in last fall was a year, and his indenture was assigned over to one James Scott, in Lancaster county, who paid his redemption; as he said he had a wife living at said Scott's, it is supposed he will go there, and from thence to New Virginia. Whoever takes up the said Hugh Barry, and delivers him to the Sheriff of this county or to the Gaoler in Dover, shall have the above reward,
            paid by    PRESTON BERRY.

*The Pennsylvania Gazette*, March 9, 1774; March 23, 1774. See *Dunlap's Pennsylvania Packet or, the General Advertiser*, January 24, 1774.

*March*, 8, 1774.
THREE POUNDS REWARD.
ABSCONDED from St. George's Hundred, Newcastle County, a few days ago, a certain WILLIAM BRETT, an Irishman, about five feet ten or eleven inches high, has black hair and eyes, and a down look; had on a blossom coloured broadcloth coat and jacket, blue plush breeches, a very old felt hat, which probable he may change, and white ribbed stockings. He took with him a silver watch belonging to the subscriber, which he was to get repaired, the maker's name Wood, London, the number forgot. Whoever secures said BRETT, so that he and the watch may be had again, shall have the above Reward, or FORTY SHILLINGS for the watch only.
BENJAMIN HUFF.
*Dunlap's Pennsylvania Packet or, the General Advertiser*, March 14, 1774; April 11, 1774; April 25, 1774.


TEN POUNDS Reward.
RUN *away, last night, from the subscribers, living in Brandywine Hundred, New-Castle county, two Dutch servant man, one named* John Christopher Busser, *about 21 years of age, a slim fellow, about 5 feet 9 inches high, lightish coloured hair, pockmarked; had on, and took with him, a felt hat, old blue cloth coat, lined with red, lincey jacket, old buckskin breeches, two pair of yarn stockings, and old shoes: The other named* John Brown, *about 20 years of age, a short thick fellow; had on, when he went away, a felt hat, a new coatee coat, of a light coloured cloth, with red lining, and white metal buttons, light coloured cloth jacket, old buckskin breeches, with white metal buttons, one old and one new ozenbrigs shirts, bluish yarn stockings, and half worn shoes, tied with strings. Whoever takes up said runaways, or either of them, so that their masters may get them again, shall have the above reward, or FIVE POUNDS for each, and reasonable charges,*
*paid by* EMANUEL GRUBB, *and* CHARLES ROBINSON.
March 14, 1774.
*The Pennsylvania Gazette*, March 23, 1774. See *Der Wöchentliche Pennsylvanische Staatsbote*, (Philadelphia), April 5, 1774.


*New-Castle, March* 1, 1774.
WAS committed to my custody some time ago, an Irish servant woman, named *Margaret Smith*, and says she belongs to one Thomas Whiteside, of

Chester county. Also a Negroe man, named *JOE*, has a defect in one of his eyes, and says he belongs to one Bastin Cropper, of Accomack county, Virginia. Their masters are desired to come, pay charges, and take them away, in six weeks from the date hereof, or they will be sold for the same, by
      ROBERT MACK, Goaler.
 *The Pennsylvania Gazette*, March 23, 1774; April 6, 1774. See *The Pennsylvania Gazette*, April 6, 1774.

       TEN POUNDS Reward.
                 March 14, 1774.
RAN-AWAY last Night, from the Subscribers, living in Brandywine Hundred, in New-Castle County, Two Dutch Servant Men, one named John Christopher Busser, about 21 Years of Age, a slim Fellow, about 5 Feet 9 Inches high, lightish coloured Hair, pock-marked: Had on and took with him a Felt Hat, old blue Cloth Coat, lined with red, Linsey Jacket, old Buckskin Breeches, two Pair of Yarn Stockings, and old Shoes. The other named John Brown, about 20 Years of Age, a short thick Fellow: Had on when he went away, a Felt Hat, a new Coatee Coat of a light-coloured Cloth, with red Lining and White-metal Buttons, one old and one new Oznabrigs Shirt, bluish Yarn Stockings, and half-worn Shoes tied with Strings. Whoever takes up said Run-aways or either of them, so that their Masters may get them again, shall have the above Reward, or FIVE POUNDS for each, and reasonable Charges, paid by  EMANUEL GRUBB, and
        CHARLES ROBINSON.
 *Der Wöchentliche Pennsylvanische Staatsbote*, (Philadelphia), April 5, 1774; April 19, 1774; April 26, 1774. See *The Pennsylvania Gazette*, March 23, 1774.


BROKE out of the Goal of New-Castle county, on the night of the 26th of March last, the four following persons, viz. *Richard Purcell*, an Irishman, about 21 years of age, 5 feet 10 or 11 inches high, well set, pitted with the small-pox, long black hair; had on a claret coloured coat and waistcoat, of Bath coating, dirty leather breeches, and coarse black stockings; he was convicted here of felony. *Arthur Kelly*, an Irishman, abut 25 years of age, 5 feet 9 or 10 inches high, black complexion, round shouldered, black curled hair, fond of liquor, and a great blackguard; had on an old brown short coat, red under waistcoat, and leather breeches. *John Cain*, committed on suspicion of stealing a saddle in Chester county, the property of Thomas Smedley, about 30 years of age, 5 feet 6 or 7 inches high, well set, smooth faced, short black hair; had on a blue cloth coat and waistcoat, with white metal buttons; had with him a woman, whom he calls his wife, and a child abut 20 months old. *Margaret Smith*, a likely, lusty, broad faced woman,

pitted with the small-pox, short rough black hair, is very talkative, pretends she is with child, and by this time very probably is; her clothes uncertain, but very ordinary; she came from Belfast last summer, with Captain Ewing, was sold to one Mr. Jack, near Lancaster, and says her present master is Thomas Whiteside. Whosoever apprehends the above persons, and delivers them to the Keeper of the Goal of said county, shall have for *Arthur Kelly*, Three Pounds; and for the other three, Thirty Shillings each.
      JOHN THOMPSON, Sheriff.
 *The Pennsylvania Gazette*, April 6, 1774; May 4, 1774. See *The Pennsylvania Gazette*, April 6, 1774, for Smith


      THREE POUNDS Reward.
RUN AWAY from the subscriber, living in Mill-creek Hundred, New-Castle county, an Irish servant boy, named MICHAEL DOHERTY, about 16 years of age, 5 feet 4 inches high, and well set, with strait brown hair, and full broad face, not fresh coloured, but rather of a dunish white or somewhat freckled, a short neck, and big head; had on, when he went away, a felt hat, of this country make, about half worn, a big jacket, not made for him, of light coloured cloth, with mohair buttons, and a flap over the button holes, old shirt, tow trowsers, old shoes, with buckles, and stockings of two colours. Whoever secures said servant, so that his master may get him again, shall have the above reward, and reasonable charges, paid by
*Fourth Month* 5, 1774.      JAMES JACKSON.
 *The Pennsylvania Gazette*, April 20, 1774. See *The Pennsylvania Gazette*, October 4, 1775.


 *RUN away from the Subscriber, living near the Borough of* Wilmington, *on Tuesday, the* 10*th of May Instant, an* Irish *Servant Girl, named* Ann Lester, *about* 30 *Years of Age, of a middle Size, brown Complexion, dark coloured Hair, has her Ears bored, and had Lead in them when she left home: Had on when she went away (but may change her Clothes) a long black and white Calicoe Gown, two striped Linsey Petticoats, one of them new, Shoes and Stockings, a Straw Hat with a brownish Ribbon round the Crown. Whoever takes up and secures said Servant, so as her Master may get her again, shall have* One Dollar *Reward, if taken in* Wilmington, Two Dollars, *if within* 10 *Miles of home,* Three Dollars, *if* 10, *and* Four Dollars, *if* 30 *Miles from home, and reasonable Charges, paid by*  JONAS PETERSON.
*N. B. All Masters of Vessels are forbid to carry her off, or harbour her, at their Peril.*
 *The Pennsylvania Gazette*, May 18, 1774.

RUN-AWAY on Monday the 16th instant, a convict servant man named JOHN NICHOLS, about 5 feet 7 or 8 inches high: Had on and took with him one Oznabrigs shirt, leather breeches, almost new, an old white wilton coat, dark gray fearnought jacket, an under light coloured ditto, blue yarn hose, old shoes and old buckles, and an old felt hat: Also, took with him a black MARE, about 12 hands high, paces. trots, and gallops, & has lost her left eye. The man is of a fair complexion, light coloured hair, very thin, and short on the top. His calling, it is supposed, will be trying to wait on Gentlemen. Whoever secures the said convict servant, so that his Master may have him again, shall have FOUR POUNDS Reward; and a reasonable Reward for the Mare, paid by           JOHN MALLER.
Swan-Creek, May 21, 1774.

*The Pennsylvania Journal, and the Weekly Advertiser*, June 1, 1774; June 8, 1774; June 15, 1774. See *The Pennsylvania Gazette*, June 22, 1774.

*New Castle County, on Delaware, June* 13, 1774.
NOW in the goal of this county, a certain John Phillips, who confesseth that he is the person who made an escape from the Sub-sheriff of York county, in the province of Pennsylvania, and that was advertised in the Pennsylvania Gazette, No. 2330. And two runaway servants, and one Negroe slave, namely, *John Nichols*, who run away (as he says) from John Miller, near Newtown, on Chester river; he had in his custody, when apprehended, a brown Mare, with a saddle and bridle.—*James Linsey*, who confesses himself to be a servant to Messieurs Snowden and Company, of Prince-George's county, in the province of Maryland. A NEGROE LAD, who calls himself ISAAC, and says he belongs to Thomas Welsh, of the county last above named. The masters, or others interested in the prisoners above named, are desired to come, pay charges, and take them away, within six weeks from the above date, otherwise the said prisoners will be sold for their fees, and discharged, by        THOMAS PUSEY, Goaler.
N. B. Also in said goal, John Welsh, and Patrick Morgan, who confess themselves to be runaway servants, belonging to James Black, of Kent county, Maryland.

*The Pennsylvania Gazette*, June 22, 1774; June 29, 1774; August 3, 1774. See *The Pennsylvania Journal, and the Weekly Advertiser*, June 1, 1774, for Nichols.

THIRTY DOLLARS REWARD,
FOR apprehending a certain JOHN HOOKS, who has run away, and taken with him the following articles, viz. one silver watch with the chrystal cracked, one broadcloth coat of a light colour blue mixed with white, one

velvet jacket of a light colour made with a belt, a pair of snuff coloured velvet breeches, a pair of nankeen ditto bound with green tape, a pair of buckskin ditto newly washed, a beaver hat, a pair of pumps and pinchbeck shoe buckles, one bed sheet, a very coarse shirt, also a fine one with uncommon broad neck and wristbands. The said JOHN HOOKS is a well-made fellow, of a yellow complexion and a stuttering speech, dark bushy hair, is about 5 feet 9 inches high, 17 or 18 years of age; had on when he went away, an old wool hat, a coarse blanket jacket, oznabrigs shirt, a kind of black woolen neckcloth about his neck, a pair of dark striped lincey trowsers, strong shoes and no stockings. Whoever secures the said thief and goods shall have the above Reward, or for the goods alone half the Reward, and all reasonable charges, paid by       MARY ARMSTRONG, Blue Dyer,
*June* 15.                            living in Wilmington.
   *Dunlap's Pennsylvania Packet or, the General Advertiser*, June 24, 1777; July 1, 1777; August 5, 1777.


FOUR POUNDS Reward.
RUN away from the subscriber, living in Reedy-Island-Neck, New-Castle county, a Negroe wench, named JUDE, about 5 feet some odd inches high, is very black, full faced, a thick short Neck, square shouldered, and has a remarkable small thick foot, and pretty hollow underneath, and has had one of her feet scalded some time ago, and the skin is a good deal thinner than the other, her fore teeth are a little rotten; she speaks fast and thick; had one, when she went away, a kersey jacket and petticoat, of a yellow colour, a coarse tow shift, a straw hat, and high heeled shoes; she took with her a calicoe jacket and petticoat; she has a small arm, and when detected is very apt to tremble, and be pretty much confounded. Whoever takes up said wench, and secures her, so that the subscriber may have her again, shall have the above reward,      paid by     WILLIAM M'KEAN.
*June* 13, 1774.
   *The Pennsylvania Gazette*, June 29, 1774.


WAS STOLEN,
On the tenth of March last, out of the subscriber's stable
at Back-Creek Landing,
A SMALL chesnut brown MARE, about fourteen hands high, has three white feet, a star in her forehead, trots and gallops: She was stolen by a certain WILLIAM GLENN, who lived then at the subscriber's house, but formerly about Wilmington; he is about six feet high, able bodied, wears a claret coloured coat, pale red jacket, clouded stockings, leather breeches, new shoes and plated buckles: He has lately received some cuts on his head. Whoever takes up and secures the said mare and thief, so that the subscriber may have

the mare again and the thief brought to justice, shall receive THIRTY DOLLARS for the mare, and TWENTY DOLLARS for the thief,
   paid by   THOMAS WIRT.
N. B. He has one grey and one blue eye, plain to be perceived.

 *Dunlap's Pennsylvania Packet or, the General Advertiser*, July 1, 1777; July 8, 1777; August 5, 1777. See *The Pennsylvania Gazette*, March 19, 1777, and *The Maryland Journal and Baltimore Advertiser*, April 22, 1777.

RUN *away, on the 27th of June, from the subscriber, living in the borough of Wilmington, New-Castle county, an Irish servant lad, named Thomas Connely, by trade a barber and hair-dresser, about 5 feet 5 or 6 inches high, of a sandy complexion, grey eyed, wears his hair tied, and has the brogue on his tongue; is apt to get drunk, and very quarrelsome when so; took with him some razors and combs; had on, when he went away, a blue cloth short coat, with a red velvet collar, and yellow cording round the edging, a blue cloth jacket let out at the sides, new Russia drilling breeches, cotton stockings, a coarse wool hat, old turned pumps, and brass buckles. As he can write a tolerable hand, and is well acquainted in this country, it is likely he will forge a pass. Whoever takes up said servant, and confines him in any of his majesty's goals, so that his master may have him again, shall have Ten Dollars reward, and reasonable charges,*
   *paid by* WILLIAM BROBSON.
N. B. *The said servant formerly run away from Robert Wilson, at the Head of Wye river, Maryland, was taken up and put into goal at Philadelphia, and brought from thence in November last.*

 *The Pennsylvania Gazette*, July 6, 1774. See *The Pennsylvania Journal, and the Weekly Advertiser*, July 6, 1774, and *The New-York Gazette; and the Weekly Mercury*, August 15, 1774.

RAN AWAY on the 27th ult. from the subscriber living in the borough of Wilmington, Newcastle county, an Irish Servant Man named THOMAS CONNELY, by trade a barber and hair-dresser, about 5 feet 5 or 6 inches high, of a sandy complexion, grey eyed, wears his hair tied, and has the brogue on his tongue; is apt to get drunk, and very quarrelsome when so; took with him some razors and combs: Had on, when he went away, a blue cloth short coat with a red velvet collar and yellow cording round the edging, a blue cloth jacket let out at the sides, new Russia drilling breeches, cotton stockings, a coarse wool hat, old turned pumps and brass buckles: As he can write a tolerable hand, and is well acquainted in the country, it is likely he

will forge a pass. Whoever takes up said servant and confines him again, shall have TEN DOLLARS reward and reasonable charges
paid by    WILLIAM BROBSON.
N. B. The servant formerly ran away from Robert Wilson, at the Head of Wye River, in Maryland, was taken up, and put into gaol at Philadelphia, and brought from thence about the 4th of November last.    July 6.
P. S. He was taken up last Saturday the 2d inst. at Elizabeth-town Point, and brought back to Prince-ton, from whence he made his escape, next morning. He had taken off the colar from his coat, and sold his jacket.
*The Pennsylvania Journal, and the Weekly Advertiser*, July 6, 1774; July 20, 1774; July 23, 1774. See *The Pennsylvania Gazette*, July 6, 1774, and *The New-York Gazette; and the Weekly Mercury*, August 15, 1774.

FIVE POUNDS Reward.
For taking up an ungrateful Villain and Thief.
RUN away, from the subscriber, a servant man, named WILLIAM MADDEN, was confined in Lancaster goal for the clothes he now wears; by his writing to me his distress, and his honesty, prevailed on me to pay the money and take him out; he is 26 years of age, short black curled hair, was born in Sussex county, and served some of his time Noxontown, and some at Duck-creek; the coat is of a claret colour, with gilt buttons, a short green silk jacket, green velveret breeches, new brown thread stockings, one pair of cotton ditto, a cambrick stock; he is a well made fellow, about 6 feet high, his face much freckled, has the appearance of a mulattoe, his nose turns up, with wide nostrils, his legs all of a thickness, and shins very rotten; some of the things he stole belonged to the lodgers, and as I keep a tavern, will be obliged to pay the owners. Whoever takes up said servant, and secures him, so that his master may have him again, shall receive the above reward, and if brought home reasonable charges,
paid by    PHILIP BACKEN.
*The Pennsylvania Gazette*, July 27, 1774.


FIVE POUNDS Reward for taking up an
ungrateful VILLAIN and THIEF.
RUN AWAY from the subscriber, a Servant Man named WILLIAM MADDEN, about 26 years of age, born in Sussex county, but served his time at Noxon-town and some at Duck Creek; he is a well made fellow, about six feet high, has short black curled hair, his face is much freckled and has the appearance of a mulatto, his nose turns up with wide nostrils, his legs are all of a thickness, and his shins very rotten. Said Madden was confined in Lancaster gaol for the cloaths which he now wears, (by his writing to me, his

distress and his honestly prevailed on me to pay the money and take him out) viz. a coat of a claret colour with gilt buttons, a short green silk jacket, green velveret breeches, new brown thread stockings, one pair of cotton ditto, and a cambrick stock; some of the things he stole belonged to the lodgers in my house, for which I must pay them. Whoever takes up said servant and secures him, so that his master may have his again, shall have the above reward and, if brought home, reasonable charges paid by
July 27.         PHILIP BRACKEN, Tavern-keeper.

*The Pennsylvania Journal, and the Weekly Advertiser*, July 27, 1774; August 3, 1774.


RUN away from the subscriber, living in the borough of Wilmington, in New-Castle county, upon Delaware, the 27th ultimo, an Irish servant lad, named THOMAS CONNELY, by trade a barber and hair-dresser, about five feet five or six inches high, of a sandy complexion, grey eyes, reddish hair, which he wears wear tied; has the brogue in his speech, is apt to get drunk, and is then very quarrelsome; took with him some razors and combs. Had on when he went away, a blue cloth short coat, with a red velvet collar, and corded round the edges; a blue cloth jacket let out at the sides, new Russia drilling breeches; and as he can write a tolerable hand, and is acquainted with the country, it is probable he may forge a pass; for he formely lived at New-York, from whence he went about five years ago to Maryland, and after some time became a valet to Colonel Richard Tilghman, of Queen Ann's County, with whom he went in that character to New-York. He afterwards indented to Robert Wilson, at the Head of Wye River, in Maryland, from whom he ran away, and was put into gaol at Philadelphia, soon after which the subscriber purchased him. He was apprehended the 2d instant at Elizabeth-Town-Point, and brought back to Princeton, from whence he made his escape next morning; he had taken off the collar from his coat, and sold his jacket. Whoever secures said servant in any of his Majesty's goals so that his master may have him again, shall receive TEN DOLLARS reward, besides reasonable charges, paid by       WILLIAM BROBSON.
*Wilmington*, July 29, 1774.

*The New-York Gazette; and the Weekly Mercury*, August 15, 1774; September 5, 1774. See *The Pennsylvania Gazette*, July 6, 1774, and *The Pennsylvania Journal, and the Weekly Advertiser*, July 6, 1774


*Mill-Creek Hundred, New-Castle County, July* 29, 1774.
WHEREAS ANN, the Wife of JOHN BALL, hath eloped from her said Husband, and taken sundry of his Goods, even Wearing Apparel; she has also commenced several Suits at Law with her Neighbours, in order to run him in

Debt; there are therefore to forewarn all Store-keepers, and others, not to trust her on his Account, for he will pay no Debts of her Contracting after the Date hereof. JOHN BALL, Farmer.
*The Pennsylvania Gazette,* August 17, 1774.

*Lancaster Goal, July* 27, 1774.
THIS day committed to my custody, a certain GEORGE HENRY, he is about 20 years of age, about 5 feet 5 inches high, and has blackish hair; had on, when committed, an old red coat, old white striped trowsers, and an old felt hat; he says he belongs to —— M'Williams, Esq; in New-Castle, upon Delaware. Likewise was committed to my custody, a certain LAWRENCE DOWNEY, the 4th day of August inst. he is about 34 or 35 years of age, thin visage, black hair; had on, when committed, an old blanket coat, old brown cloth jacket, leather breeches, white yarn stockings, old shoes, tied with strings; a man of few words; he answers the description in an advertisement of John Roberts, &c. Their masters are desired to come, pay charges, and take them away, in three weeks from this 17th day of August, 1774, otherwise they will be discharged, on paying their fees,
by GEORGE EBERLY, Goaler.
*The Pennsylvania Gazette,* August 17, 1774. See *The Pennsylvania Gazette,* September 2, 1772; *The Pennsylvania Gazette,* June 2, 1773, and *The Pennsylvania Gazette,* September 1, 1773, for Henry.

*August* 25, 1774.
FIVE POUNDS REWARD.
RAN AWAY, from the subscriber, living in the borough of Wilmington, New-Castle County, on Sunday the 21st inst. an Irish servant lad, named CHARLES WALL, by trade a Tanner, about five feet four inches high, about nineteen years old, is a strong well-set artful fellow, with remarkable thick ancles, has lightish brown hair, lately cut, a scar under his chin, pretty subtle, but not talkative unless when in liquor; he can read a little, but not write: Had on and took with him when he went away, a turkey striped jacket with sleeves, and an under jacket of white coating, lined with flannel, one fine shirt, a pair of striped blue and white trowsers, a pair of new shoes with yellow metal buckles in them, a half worn castor hat, bound round with black ribbon, and one round the crown for a band, and a striped blue and white silk handkerchief. Whoever takes up the said servant, and secures him in any of his Majesty's goals, so that his master may have him again, shall have THREE POUNDS reward, and if brought home, the above reward,
paid by CHARLES WHITELOCK.

*Dunlap's Pennsylvania Packet or, the General Advertiser*, August 29, 1774; *The Pennsylvania Gazette*, September 7, 1774; September 21, 1774. Minor differences between the papers. The *Gazette* does not have the date at the top.


*RUN away, last night, from the Subscriber, living in New-Castle hundred and county, near the Red-Lion, an Irish servant man, named JOHN TURNER, about 22 years of age, 5 feet 7 or 8 inches high, of a fair complexion, a little pock pitted, wears his own long fair hair, which he keeps plaited and tied up, and is a pretty good scholar: Had on, when he went away, a coarse tow shirt and trowsers, two linen ditto, a short nankeen coat, a coarse wool hat, old buckskin breeches, new double soaled shoes, with brass buckles, and a pair of worsted stockings. Whoever takes up said servant, and secures him, so that his Master may get him again, shall have THREE POUNDS, if taken in the county, and TEN POUNDS, if taken out of it, and reasonable charges,*
July 6, 1774. paid by JOHN JAQUET.

*The Pennsylvania Gazette*, August 31, 1774. *Dunlap's Pennsylvania Packet or, the General Advertiser*, September 12, 1774.


New-Castle county and hundred, August 18, 1774.
THIS day absconded from his bail, a certain HUGH JONES, a labourer. He is about five feet four inches high, thin vissage, swarthy complexion, down look, a Welshman, speaks fast & bad English, hardly to be understood by them who are not acquainted with him: He had on and took with him a lightish coloured cloath coat, striped trowsers, blue, white, red, and yellow linen trowsers, good shoes, a fur hat, old check shirts, patched on the back with an old check handkerchief, and some new check linen not made up, had very little money with him. He went from New Castle to Philadelphia in Joseph Tatlow's stage, in company with an idle woman, who lived some time in the neighbourhood, and passed for man and wife, and it is likely intends so to do until he is tired of her, as a certain Silver-smith was, who went with the same woman from Wilmington some time ago: The said Hugh Jones was also under an obligation to the Subscriber as a hired servant. Any person securing him in any of his Majesty's gaols, and gives notice thereof to me, shall be entitled to a reward of THIRTY SHILLINGS, and if brought home, reasonable charges, paid by     JOSEPH WOODWARD.

*The Pennsylvania Journal, and the Weekly Advertiser*, August 31, 1774.


NOW in the Goal of the City of Philadelphia, the following runaway servants, viz. *Cornelius Larey,* belonging to James Thomas, in the township of

Uwchland, Chester county, *Michael Buckly*, with an iron collar round his neck. *James Williams*, belonging to Patrick Kelly, Pequea. *John Welch*, belonging to James Welch, Kent county. Their masters are desired to come and pay the charges, and take them away, in three weeks, otherwise they will be disposed of.     PETER ROBINSON, Goaler.
*September 5*, 1774.
*The Pennsylvania Gazette*, September 7, 1774.

### TEN POUNDS REWARD.

RAN AWAY last night, from the subscriber, living in New-Castle Hundred and county, near the Red-Lyon, an Irish servant man, named JOHN TURNER, about 22 years of age, five feet seven or eight inches high, of a fair complexion, a little pock-pitted, wears his own long fair hair, which he keeps platted and tied up, and is a pretty good scholar: Had on when he went away, a coarse tow shirt and trowsers, two linen ditto, a short nankeen coat, a coarse wool hat, old buckskin breeches, new double soaled shoes, with brass buckles, and a pair of worsted stockings. Whoever takes up said servant and secures him, so that his master may get him again, shall have THREE POUNDS, if taken in the county, and if taken out of it the above Reward, and reasonable charges, paid by     JOHN JACQUET.

*Dunlap's Pennsylvania Packet or, the General Advertiser*, September 12, 1774; October 3, 1774. See *The Pennsylvania Gazette*, August 31, 1774.

*September 1, 1774.*
### THIRTY SHILLINGS REWARD.
RAN AWAY from the subscriber, of Wilmington, Newcastle County, a servant lad named MATTHEW MACCHEON, about fifteen years of age: Had on and with him when he went away, one pair of striped trowsers, one tow and one oznabrigs ditto, one striped linen jacket, one pair of shoes, two pair of buckles two coarse shirts, one pair of blue ribbed stockings, one flag handkerchief, one black milled sea hat: He is rather long visaged, out mouthed, fresh complexion, light hair and cut short. He came from Bristol last April with Captain Seymour Hood. Whoever takes up said servant and brings him to the subscriber, or secures him in any goal so that his mistress may have him again, shall receive the above reward,
from MARY HARVEY.

N. B. All masters of vessels are hereby warned not to carry him off at their peril.

*Dunlap's Pennsylvania Packet or, the General Advertiser*, September 12, 1774; October 3, 1774; October 17, 1774. See *The Pennsylvania Gazette*, September 14, 1774.

THIRTY SHILLINGS REWARD.
RAN AWAY on the 27th of August last, from his special bail, living in Pencader Hundred, New-Castle County, WILLIAM PAGE, a shoemaker by trade, about 33 years of age, almost six feet high, a strait fellow, of a dark complexion, wears his own hair of a dark brown colour, tied behind: Had on when he went away, a stocking pattern jacket without sleeves, with orange and green colours in it, the back parts of a blue cloth, a white shirt, a pair of check trowsers, a pair of black grain pumps, a pair of old large plated buckles: It is supposed he is gone to Warwick in Maryland, having a wife there, but not living together agreeable for some years, it is thought he will proceed further. Whoever takes him up and secures him in any of his Majesty's goals shall have the above reward, paid by
JOHN BROWN, and WILLIAM BLACK, Constable.
*Dunlap's Pennsylvania Packet or, the General Advertiser*, September 12, 1774; September 26, 1774; October 3, 1774.

*New Castle, September 5, 1774.*
NOW in the goal of said county, the following persons, viz. A Negroe lad, who calls himself *Prince*, and by an advertisement of Doctor Anthony Yeldall's, in the Pennsylvania Packet, and confession of said Negroe, appeared to be the person therein described. Also a certain *Isaac Jones*, alias *Solomon Isaac*, about 5 feet 6 inches high, black curled hair, dark visage, and lisps when he speaks; was committed as a vagrant: Any person that has any demands against the said *Isaac Jones*, is desired to come, in two weeks from the date hereof, or he will be discharged at that time, on paying his fees. Also a certain *Mary Mentor*, a short thick person, brown hair, red face, and much pitted with the smallpox; supposed to have run from a certain William Kee, of New-Jersey. Also a certain *Michael Jordan*, committed by virtue of an advertisement of William Hopkins, junior. All persons that have any demands against the above persons, are desired to come, in four weeks from the date, or they will be discharged, on paying their fees,
by THOMAS PUSEY, Goaler.
*The Pennsylvania Gazette*, September 14, 1774. See *The Pennsylvania Gazette*, March 22, 1775, for Mentor.

THIRTY SHILLINGS REWARD.
*RUN away from the subscriber, of Wilmington, New-Castle county, a servant lad, named* Matthew Macchoon, *about 15 years of age, had on with him, when he went away, a pair of striped trowsers, one tow and one ozenbrigs ditto, one striped linen jacket, one pair of shoes, two pair of buckles, two coarse shirts, one pair of blue ribbed stockings, one flag handkerchief, one*

*black milled sea hat; he is rather long visaged, out mouthed, and fresh complexion, light hair, and cut short; he came from Bristol last April with Captain Seymour Hood. Whoever takes up said servant, and brings him to the subscriber, or secures him in any goal, so that his mistress may have him again, shall receive the above reward, from*
*Sept.* 1, 1774. MARY HARVEY.
*All masters of vessels are forbid to carry him off at their peril.*
The Pennsylvania Gazette, September 14, 1774. See *Dunlap's Pennsylvania Packet or, the General Advertiser*, September 12, 1774

WILMINGTON, September 13, 1774.
FOUR DOLLARS Reward.
RAN AWAY, on Sunday morning last, from the subscriber, an indented Servant Man named JAMES SAMUEL GORDEN, by trade a jeweller; he is a remarkable little man, smart, well dressed, and of a good countenance; he wears a brown tye wig, but possibly may throw it off: He is endeavouring for New-York, but may possibly make for some other place, as he was taken last Tuesday night at Bristol, in company with a woman he calls his wife, and sent back to Philadelphia alone on board the Burlington boat, from which he made a second elopement: Had on, a short striped jacket or coatee somewhat faded by washing, but possibly may change his dress, as he has a bundle of cloaths with him, among which is a brown coat and a light blue one. Whosoever apprehends said Gorden and secures him, so that the subscriber may have him again, by giving intelligence to Mr. WILLIAM ROSS, in Walnut-street, Philadelphia, shall receive the above reward and all possible charges paid by him. JOHN STOW.
N. B. It is very possible, if he does not take the York road, he will endeavour for Lancaster; if taken there, by applying to Mr. WILLIAM ROSS, tavern-keeper, in said place, shall receive the above reward, &c.
Sept. 21.
*The Pennsylvania Journal, and the Weekly Advertiser*, September 21, 1774.

EIGHT DOLLARS Reward.
*RUN away, on the* 18*th of September last, from the subscriber, living in Mill-Creek Hundred, New-Castle county, an Irish servant man, named* James Swainey, *about* 24 *years old,* 5 *feet* 7 *or* 8 *inches high, black complexion, with long black hair, tied; had on a new suit of grey colsured* [sic] *coating, a jacket of home made Wilton, half-worn, with buttons on the left side, like Eleven-penny bitts, striped linen shirt, black worsted ribbed stockings, new shoes.—He came in the ship Hill, Captain Marshall, from Londonderry, and was landed at New-Castle. Whoever takes up said servant, and secures him,*

so that his master may have him again, shall have the above reward, and reasonable charges, paid by ROBERT KIRKWOOD.
*The Pennsylvania Gazette*, September 28, 1774.

October 5th, 1774.
### THIRTY SHILLINGS REWARD.
RAN AWAY, this morning, from the subscriber, living in Newcastle hundred and county, a servant man named ROGER QUIN, about 24 years old, 5 feet 4 inches high, marked with the small pox, has brown hair; had on and took with him 3 coats, viz. 1 of blue cloth, 1 of wilton much broke at the elbows, and one of white fustain pretty much tarred, 1 blue cloth jacket, 1 brown ditto, and 1 red ditto, 2 oznabrigs shirts, an old pair of neats leather shoes with buckles in them, a pair of blue duffil trowsers, and leather breeches under them, a felt hat bound with black worsted tape: it is thought he is gone by water, as he followed shalloping from Wilmington to Philadelphia, and took with him a shallop's vane. Whoever takes up and secures said servant so that his master may have him again, shall receive the above reward and reasonable charges, paid by JACOBUS HAINES.
*Dunlap's Pennsylvania Packet or, the General Advertiser*, October 10, 1774; October 31, 1774; November 7, 1774.

Newcastle, October 10, 1774.
### THREE POUNDS REWARD.
WHEREAS a certain JOHN MELON, who came into this country in the ship Minerva, Capt. M'Cullough, hired a horse from the subscriber about the 7th of September last, under pretences of going a few miles into the country, but has not since returned: The said MELON has been in this country before, and followed pedling, horse-jockeying, and selling servants; he formerly resided in Charles-Town, Maryland, is well acquainted in several parts of both Maryland and Pennsylvania, and probably is gone to some of the back parts of one or other of the said provinces, he is about 5 feet 8 inches high, 28 years of age, has dark brown hair cut short, and is a little pitted with the small-pox; had on a white fustian coatee and waistcoat, with black velvet breeches: The horse is about twelve hands and a half high, eight years old, his two hind feet and near fore foot white, and is branded with the letter I on the near shoulder. Whoever secures the horse, and the said MELON so that he may be brought to justice, shall receive the above Reward, or for the horse alone, THIRTY SHILLINGS, and reasonable charges,
paid by ROBERT M'ELHERRON.
*Dunlap's Pennsylvania Packet or, the General Advertiser*, October 10, 1774; October 31, 1774; November 7, 1774.

WAS committed to the gaol in Sussex County on Delaware, the middle of February 1773, [*sic*] a negro man who calls himself HARRY, about five feet ten inches high, forty years of age, walks a little lame, and understands something of the carpenters business. The owner is desired to come, prove his property, pay charges and take him away.
       WILLIAM DAVIS, Gaoler.
*Dunlap's Pennsylvania Packet or, the General Advertiser*, October 17, 1774; November 7, 1774; November 21, 1774.


RUN away, from the subscriber, the 12th of September last, from New-castle, the two following redemptioners, viz. *John Mannaughan*, speaks with the brogue on his tongue, about 5 feet 2 inches high, 35 years of age, wears his own black hair, which has a natural curl, of a brown complexion, and is sour looking fellow; had on, when he went away, a new wool hat, a blue cloth coat, striped linen jacket, black thickset breeches, blue yarn stockings, new shoes, with yellow metal buckles, and a good white linen shirt. *Catherine Mannaughan*, about 30 years of age, a low slender woman, of a swarthy complexion, and pretty much pitted with the smallpox; had on, when she went away, a striped linen gown, blue quilted petticoat, a good linen shift, black silk handkerchief, blue yarn stockings, good shoes, and round yellow metal buckles. Whoever takes up said redemptioners, and secures them in any goal, so that the subscriber may get them again, shall have FORTY SHILLINGS reward, or TWENTY SHILLINGS for either, and reasonable charges, paid by JAMES TEAS, Administrator to the estate of *William Glenn*, deceased, in *Middle Octorara*, at Mr. *Joseph Miller's*.
 *The Pennsylvania Gazette,* October 26, 1774.


       FIVE POUNDS REWARD.
RAN AWAY from his bail, on Tuesday the 18th of October last, a certain WILLIAM DELANY, an Irishman, about 5 feet 8 or 9 inches high, of a dark complexion, with black hair tied behind, is fond of strong liquor, and when drunk (which will be as often as he can get rum) is fond of speaking much in his own praise, particularly his great abilities in school-keeping, which he has done for some time in Precipany, near Elizabeth Town, Morris County, New-Jersey, and near Little Gosham, in Orange County, New-York government, and near Duck Creek, Kent County on Delaware: He had on when he went away, a half worn castor hat, a light coloured fustian coat and waistcoat, black stocking pattern breeches, thread stockings, and new shoes with yellow carved buckles. He stole a sorel Stallion, very low in flesh, nine years old, about fourteen and a half hands high, trots and hand gallops when rode, and wheeses much; also a new saddle and striped saddle cloth. Said Delany

served two years with Isaac Decou, Esq; Attorney at Law, in Trenton, New-Jersey, but was obliged to fly from that province for counterfeiting Charles Ogden's hand. Whoever takes up said Delany and the horse, and secures them so that the subscriber may have his horse again, and the thief be brought to justice, shall receive the above Reward, or for the horse alone FIFTY SHILLINGS, with reasonable charges if brought home to Middletown, Newcastle County, on Delaware.

THOMAS SCULLEY.

N. B. It is probable he may change his name and forge a pass, as he writes a good hand.

*Dunlap's Pennsylvania Packet or, the General Advertiser*, November 14, 1774; November 28, 1774; December 12, 1774.

THREE POUNDS REWARD.<br>
Christiana Bridge, 7th. 11 mo. 1774.

ABSCONDED last night from his bail, a certain THOMAS VINER, who is an Englishman, about thirty six years of age, well set, five feet eight or nine inches high, dark complexion, and short black hair; a tanner by trade: Had on and took with him, a suit of new blue broad cloth cloaths, two pair of new calf-skin shoes, two pair of yarn milled stockings, one whereof blue grey colour, the other a redish or flesh colour; a half worn lightish coloured homespun cloath coat with light coloured homespun worsted lining and brown wooden buttons, a new beaver hat and an old beaver ditto, an old pair of leather breeches that has been worn in a tanyard. Whoever takes up said Thomas Viner, shall have the above reward, and if brought to New-Castle gaol, all reasonable charges paid, by   JOHN LEWDEN.

*The Pennsylvania Journal, and the Weekly Advertiser*, November 16, 1774; November 23, 1764. See *Dunlap's Pennsylvania Packet or, the General Advertiser*, November 28, 1774.

FOUR DOLLARS REWARD.

*RAN AWAY from the subscriber living in New-Castle Hundred and county, a servant boy named JOHN RIDDLES, about five feet four inches high, smooth face and long nose, brown hair; had on when he went away, a brown coat, brown jacket and brown breeches, black ribbed stockings, old shoes with brass buckles, and an half worn wool hat. Whoever takes up the said servant, and secures him in any of his Majesty's gaols, shall receive the above reward, and if brought home reasonable charges, paid by Alexander Aiken, in the Hundred aforesaid, or        JAMES M'CLORG.*

*Dunlap's Pennsylvania Packet or, the General Advertiser*, November 21, 1774; December 19, 1774.

*Christiana Bridge, 11th month 7th, 1774.*
THREE POUNDS REWARD.
ABSCONDED last night from his bail, a certain THOMAS VINER, an Englishman, about 36 years of age, well set, about 5 feet nine inches high, dark complexion, short black hair, and a tanner by trade; had on and took with him a suit of new blue broadcloth cloaths, two pair of new calf-skin shoes, two pair of new yarn milled stockings, one pair blue grey and the other reddish or flesh colour, a new beaver hat and an old ditto, a half worn lightish coloured cloth coatee, lined with lightish homespun, with brown wooden buttons, and a pair of old leather breeches that have been worn in a tan-yard, &c. Whoever secures said Thomas Viner in any of his Majesty's gaols, shall have the above Reward, and if brought to New-Castle gaol, all reasonable charges, paid by     JOHN LEWDEN.
*Dunlap's Pennsylvania Packet or, the General Advertiser*, November 28, 1774; December 12, 1774. See *The Pennsylvania Journal, and the Weekly Advertiser*, November 16, 1774.

TWENTY-ONE POUNDS REWARD.
SUPPOSED to be stolen or taken away from the subscriber, by the Master, SAMUEL WORDEN, the sloop Catharine, a new vessel, launched in July last, about 35 feet keel; 17 or 18 feet beam, 5 feet hold, and about 35 tons burthen; her cabin painted blue, with a ship's stern painted blue or green and yellow, two sash windows in the cabbin, one new anchor and cable, rigging all new, one old anchor and cable, a dull painted curtain on her stern, with a new main-sail and jibb, and an old fore-sail; brimstone and turpentine bottom, with a pump directly a midships opposite the cabbin door, painted red. The said SAMUEL WORDEN is about 5 feet 10 inches high, near 45 years of age, of a brown complexion, and made his dwelling at Jones's Creek, in Kent County, on Delaware, where he left a wife; and is supposed to have gone off with a woman from Great Egg-Harbour, who was seen on board about two or three weeks from the date hereof.
Whoever will secure the said Vessel, so that she may be restored to the owner, shall receive FIFTEEN POUNDS; and whoever will secure the Captain, so that he may be prosecuted and brought to justice, shall receive SIX POUNDS, and all reasonable charges,
     paid by     ALEX. RUTHERFORD.
*The Pennsylvania Journal, and the Weekly Advertiser*, November 30, 1774; December 7, 1774.

*Newcastle, December 9. 1774.*
EIGHT DOLLARS REWARD.
Ran Away from the subscriber, the 5th instant, a negro man named

PORTROYAL, forty-one years of age, about five feet seven inches high, a comely well-looking man, of a good countenance, and pretty black, one of his wrists a little crooked, but he does not complain of it in any work: He is well behaved, not given to liquor, appears religious, and can read and write; had on a good beaver hat with silk lining, a blue woollen cap, but had with him also a surtout coat of a cinnamon colour, a light coloured cloth jacket, a swanskin ditto stained with tar, a good white shirt, buckskin breeches, new pale blue ribbed stockings, plated buckles in his shoes, and money in his pocket: He was seen last Saturday in Philadelphia. Whoever takes up and secures said negro, so that his master may have him again, shall have the above Reward, and reasonable charges,
paid by    ROBERT FURNISS.

*Dunlap's Pennsylvania Packet or, the General Advertiser*, December 12, 1774; February 20, 1775. See *The New-York Gazette; and the Weekly Mercury*, December 12, 1774.

New-Castle, December 9, 1774.
FIVE DOLLARS Reward.

RUN away from the subscriber, the fifth instant, a Negro man named Port-Royal, forty-one years of age, about five feet seven inches high, a comely well looking man, of good behaviour, and pretty black, not given to liquor, appears religious, can read and write: Had on a good beaver hat, with silk lining, supposed to be green, a blue, or blue and red woollen cap, but mostly wore a white one, which he had with him. Took with him a surtout coat of a reddish cinnamon colour, a light coloured cloth jacket, a swanskin ditto, stained with tar, a good white shirt, buckskin breeches, new pale blue ribb'd stockings, and old carved plated. He came from Philadelphia in Mr. Skillman's stage waggon to New-York, on Tuesday last. Whoever secures the said Negro so as his master may have him again, shall have the above reward and reasonable charges by applying to Richard Sauce, living in New-York, near the Fly-Market, or to the subscriber,
ROBERT FURNISS.

N. B. He says he is a free man, and once belonged to Mr. Israel Pemberton, in Philadelphia, but it is not true. He pretends to be by trade a brush-maker, which he has done something at.

*The New-York Gazette; and the Weekly Mercury*, December 12, 1774. See *Dunlap's Pennsylvania Packet or, the General Advertiser*, December 12, 1774.

# 1775

*1st Month 2d*, 1775.
THIRTY SHILLINGS REWARD.

RAN AWAY last night, from the subscriber at Brandywine Bridge, near Wilmington, New Castle county, an Irish servant girl named MARGARET STAFFORD, of a low stature and well set, brown complexion and round face, about seventeen years of age; had on and took with her a striped lincey petticoat and old quilt, two striped bed gowns, one lincey and the other linen, two Russia linen shifts, an old cloth cloak of a drab colour, blue yarn stockings, old black stuff shoes, and no head dress except caps, that is known of, but may probably get some, as it is suspected she has some confederate. Whoever takes up said servant and secures her, so that her master may get her again, shall have the above Reward, and reasonable charges,
     paid by  WILLIAM STARR.
*Dunlap's Pennsylvania Packet or, the General Advertiser*, January 9, 1775; January 23, 1775; March 6, 1775.

*New-Castle Goal, December* 12, 1775.
NOW in the Goal of said County the following Persons, viz. Thomas Sloan, belonging to a certain William Finch, of St. George's Hundred, in New-Castle County. John Marshall, who was committed on Suspicion of being a run-away servant, he is about five Feet eight inches high, of a fair Complexion, and fair Hair, a Weaver by Trade, and seems as if crying when he speaks. Thomas Neil, belonging to Samuel Graves; and Edward Coleman, alias Edmund Coleman, advertised by Dennis M'Glaughlin. Also John Curran, committed on Suspicion of being a Runaway Servant; he is about 5 Feet 5 Inches high, fair Complexion and brown Hair, has an effeminate Look; had on and brought with him, a brown Suit of Clothes, a Claret coloured Surtout Coat, bound with green, a Pair of blue coating Trowsers, and a hunting Shirt; he says he served his Time with James Leard, of Augusta County, in the Province of Maryland. Their Masters are desired to come in four Weeks from the Date of this Advertisement, and pay their Fees, otherwise they will be sold for the same,
    by  THOMAS PUSEY, Goaler.
*The Pennsylvania Gazette*, January 11, 1775.

RUN away from the subscriber, near the province bridge, in Kent county, Maryland, an indented servant man, named Redmond Kelly, about 20 years of age, 5 feet 6 or 7 inches high, born in the county of Down, in Ireland, came in with Captain George Anderson last July to New Castle; had on, and took with him, when he went away, a brown coat and jacket, pale blue breeches, brown yarn stockings, new shoes, one white shirt, one check ditto, one brown linen ditto; wears his own brown hair untied, talks pert and squints with one eye, speaks with a brogue on his tongue; had an old felt hat, bound round.

Whoever takes up said servant, so that his master may get him again, shall have Four Dollars reward, and reasonable charges,
        paid by    WILLIAM DAILY.
N. B. All masters of vessels are forbid to harbour or carry him off.
    *The Pennsylvania Gazette*, February 15, 1775.

*Newport, February* 10, 1775.
### SIX DOLLARS REWARD.
RAN AWAY from the subscriber living in Newport, Newcastle county, on Delaware, an Irish servant man, named JAMES WINTERBOTTOM, a sower looking fellow, about 24 or 25 years of age, about 5 feet 6 inches high; he has a round fat face, small eyes, and sandy coloured frizly hair; had on when he went away, a brown coat and jacket, a pair of cotton velvet breeches, with buckles at the knee; and a pair of brown cloth breeches with a button on the knee-band; he has with him 4 white shirts, 3 check ditto, and a womans shirt, marked I. L. he also has a wool hat, bound with tape, is much given to strong liquor and swearing; his left leg has been sore and cured. Whoever takes up said servant, and secures him in any of his Majesty's goals, so that the subscriber may have him again, shall be entitled to the above reward, and reasonable charges, paid by    JAMES LATTIMER.
    *Dunlap's Pennsylvania Packet or, the General Advertiser*, February 20, 1775; March 20, 1775; April 3, 1775; *The Pennsylvania Journal, and the Weekly Advertiser*, February 22, 1775; March 1, 1775; *The Pennsylvania Gazette*, March 1, 1775; March 20, 1775. Minor differences between the papers. The *Gazette* does not have the line "and a pair of brown cloth breeches with a button on the knee-band" and spells the advertiser's last name as "Latimer."

*February* 14, 1775.
### SIX DOLLARS REWARD.
RAN AWAY from the subscriber, living in Kent county, on Delaware, on the seventh day of January, 1774, a servant lad named ENOCH JENKENS, about eighteen years of age, this country born, five feet six inches high, slim made, long visage, hollow eyes, down look, and dark brown hair; his cloaths are uncertain, as he went into Caecil county, Maryland, to his brother John Jenkins, who hired him to William Cochran, and he went away from said Cochran on the first of July last, when he had on a drab coloured coat, snuff coloured waistcoat, coarse homespun shirt and trowsers, old shoes and stockings, and half worn castor hat. Whoever takes up said servant and secures him in any of his Majesty's gaols, so that his master may have him again, shall be paid the above reward by

MORGON BLACKSHEAR.
*Dunlap's Pennsylvania Packet or, the General Advertiser*, February 20, 1775; March 13, 1775; April 3, 1775.


THIRTY SHILLINGS REWARD.
RAN AWAY on the 7th of February last, from the subscriber, living in Newcastle county, an indented servant man named THOMAS M'DERMALD; he came from Ireland with Capt. M'Cutcheon in the year 1772, and has since had for masters James Ray, Joshua Jackson, John Dickson, Peter Robinson, and the subscriber, and has been in Philadelphia gaol: He is about five four or five inches high, red faced, and his nose turns up; had on a thick black and white mixed jacket, with no collar and neither hemmed nor bound round the neck, the sleeves blacker than the body, long trowsers of the same, black stockings, and good shoes. Whoever takes up and secures said servant, so that his master may have him again, shall have the above reward, paid by    JOSEPH OGLE.
*Dunlap's Pennsylvania Packet or, the General Advertiser*, March 6, 1775; March 27, 1775; April 3, 1775.


*Newcastle County, February* 8, 1775.
TEN POUNDS REWARD.
STOLEN from the subscriber, at a public-house near the Road from Annapolis to Baltimore, a sorrel horse, between three and four years old, fifteen hands high, with white fetlocks, and a new saddle, with blue plush housing bound with black leather; also a brown coat, lincey jacket, buckskin breeches, white drawers, three pair of stockings, two pair, of shoes, a silk handkerchief, one short cloth pattern, and two linen shirts. The above were stolen by a certain WILLIAM SHIEN, about five feet six or seven inches high, fresh complexion, black hair tied behind, and has a cut in his foot with an axe; he wore a green jacket with yellow buttons, a home made coat and jacket of a redish colour, a blue surtout coat with a hole burned in the elbow, and a beaver hat; he lived near the Cross Roads in Chester county, but may endeavour to get to Ireland from Philadelphia or New-York. Whoever takes up the said SHIEN, and the Horse, and brings them to JOHN REYNOLDS, in Newcastle hundred, so that I may have them again, shall have a reward of THREE POUNDS if 50 miles from home, FIVE POUNDS in 100 miles, and if 200 the above reward, and reasonable charges if brought home,
paid by    MATTHEW SULLIVAN.
N. B. All masters of vessels are forbid to carry off said Shien at their peril.— He has a French silver face watch, with a piece over the key-hole.

*Dunlap's Pennsylvania Packet or, the General Advertiser*, March 13, 1775.

*Lancaster Goal, March* 10, 1775.
WAS committed to my custody on the 23d day of February last, a certain *Mary Mentor*, alias *M'Kann*, says she is a servant to William Willson, Innholder, in Whiteclay Creek Hundred, New-Castle county, about 5 miles from Newport; she is of low stature, black complexion, and pitted with the smallpox. Her master is desired to come, pay charges, and take her away, in three weeks from the date hereof, otherwise she will be discharged, on paying her fees, by          GEORGE EBERLY, Goaler.
*The Pennsylvania Gazette*, March 22, 1775.

*Baltimore Town, April* 27, 1775.
TWENTY SHILLINGS REWARD.
RAN AWAY from his bail, an Irishman named JAMES MUSGROVE, about thirty years of age, five feet seven or eight inches high, sandy complexion, sandy coloured hair, by trade a painter; had on when he went away, a light coloured coat and grey jacket; his other cloaths unknown. He is very talkative, and much given to drink: He formerly lived at Christiana Bridge, and it is supposed he is done towards Newark, as he has a wife living at John Slater's, near White Clay Creek. Whoever takes up said MUSGROVE, so that the subscriber may have his again, shall receive the above Reward, and reasonable charges, paid by          WILLIAM ROGERS, Hatter.
*Dunlap's Pennsylvania Packet or, the General Advertiser*, May 8, 1775; June 5, 1775.

*New-Castle, April* 29, 1775.
FIFTEEN DOLLARS REWARD
FOR apprehending a runaway JOE, a likely young Negroe SLAVE, this country born, had leave in writing to go Mr. Yeatman's, in the upper part of Christiana Hundred (with whom the said JOE has lived for a number of years last past) on Saturday last, and was to return the Monday following, but has not yet come back to New-Castle; he is a light pale or yellow Negroe, about 5 feet 8 inches high, well proportioned and genteely made, has regular features and a good countenance; he is about 20 years of age; had on, or took with him from Yeatman's his late master, a brown drugget coat, with hair buttons, lined with a country coloured stuff, made of worsted and linen, the coat appears short for him, as he has grown since it was made, a brown lincey jacket, buckskin breeches, tied at the knees with strings, and cut without seams between the thighs, two flaxen shirts, a red and white linen handkerchief, and old felt hat, a pair of brown yarn stockings, two pair of

white thread ditto, one plain the other ribbed, one pair footed with brown thread, a pair of coarse shoes, with hob nails, and a pair of half-worn pumps, with white metal buckles. He is unacquainted with the country, except in some parts of New-Castle and Chester counties; he was seen on the King's road between Wilmington and Chester, on Sunday, the 23d inst. being the day after he went from New-Castle; as he is very artful, it is supposed he will endeavour to go to Philadelphia, New-York or Boston, and will probably change his apparel, and endeavour to pass for a freeman. The above reward will be paid, if he should be taken 60 miles from the town of New Castle, and brought home; *Four Pounds*, if at the distance of 40 miles; *Three Pounds*, if 30 miles; and Two Pounds, if 20 miles, and reasonable charges (including the legal charge under the act of assembly) by JOHN THOMPSON.

*The Pennsylvania Gazette*, May 17, 1775. See *The Pennsylvania Journal, and the Weekly Advertiser*, May 17, 1775.

*Newcastle, April* 29, 1775.
FIFTEEN DOLLARS Reward.
FOR apprehending Joe, a Run-away, a likely young Negro Slave, this country born, who had leave in writing to go to Mr. Andrew Yeatman's, in the upper part of Christiana hundred, (with whom the said JOE had lived for a number of years last past) on Saturday last, and was to return the Monday following, but has not yet come back to Newcastle: He is a light pale or yellow Negro, about 5 feet 8 inches high, well proportioned, and genteelly made; has regular features and a good countenance, and about 20 years of age: Had on and took with him from Mr. Yeatman's, his late Master, a brown drugget coat with hair buttons, lined with a country coloured stuff, made of worsted and linen, (the coat appears short for him, as he has grown since it was made) a brown linsey jacket, buck-skin breeches, tied at the knees with strings, and cut without seams between the thighs, two flaxen shirts, a red and white linen handkerchief, an old felt hat, a pair of brown yarn stockings, tow pair thread ditto, one plain the other ribbed, one pair footed with brown thread, a pair of coarse shoes, with hob-nails, and a pair of half worn pumps, with white metal buckles. He is unacquainted with the country, except in some parts of New-castle and Chester counties; he was seen on the King's road, between Wilmington and Chester, on Sunday the 23d instant, being the day after he went from Newcastle. As he is very artful, it is supposed he will attempt getting to Philadelphia, New-York, or Boston, and will probably change his apparel and endeavour to pass for a freeman. The above reward will be paid, if he should be taken sixty miles from the town of Newcastle, and brought home; FOUR POUNDS, if at the distance of forty miles; THREE POUNDS, if thirty miles; and FORTY SHILLINGS, if twenty miles, and reasonable travelling charges, including the legal allowance under the Act of Assembly,

by JOHN THOMPSON.
*The Pennsylvania Journal, and the Weekly Advertiser*, May 17, 1775; May 24, 1775. See *The Pennsylvania Gazette*, May 17, 1775.

### THIRTY POUNDS REWARD.

RAN AWAY from the subscribers, living in Baltimore county, Maryland, about 12 miles from Baltimore-Town, a white servant Man and a Negro Man, viz. The white Man is named, RICHARD DAWSON, an English convict, came in the country last winter, about fifty-five years of age, was a soldier under the king of Prussia last war, given to liquor, upwards of six feet high, brown hair, round face, fresh coloured, has been hurt in his left thumb, which occasions it to be stiff.—Had on when he went away, an iron collar double rivetted, old castor hat, dark frock much tarred, old dark grey German serge jacket, mended with black linsey, brown role shirt, white full'd cloth breeches, coarse white yarn stockings, and old country made shoes with strings.

SOLOMON, a *Negro*, about 22 years of age, has been in the country about four years, and talks pretty good English.—Had on when he went away, an iron collar, a darby on each leg with a chain to one of them, all double rivetted, a new felt hat, old brown cloth coat, blue cloth jacket line with red, brown role shirt, white full'd cloth breeches, old white yarn stockings, and old country made shoes.—Is it supposed they will make for Boston to the soldiers, as they have often been talking about them, and it is likely they may get their irons off, get other clothes, change their names, and deny their master, as the Negro has always done; has been in Newcastle upon Delaware twelve months and upwards; he went from thence in July last, and got in goal in Somerset county, Maryland, and was brought home in November last; he has been in Philadelphia, he is of middle size, somewhat upon the yellow, has some marks upon one of his cheeks like the small pox, has lost part of the side of his right thumb, that makes the end of it look sharper than the other.

Whoever apprehends them, or either of them, and secures them in any goal, so that their master may have them again, shall have *Twenty Shillings*; if above ten miles, *Forty Shillings*; if above thirty miles, *Three Pounds*; if sixty miles, *Five Pounds*; if two hundred miles, *Ten Pounds*, if five hundred miles, the above Reward, and reasonable charges if brought home, paid by
THOMAS COCKEY, *sen.*     THOMAS COCKEY, *jun.*

*Dunlap's Pennsylvania Packet or, the General Advertiser*, May 22, 1775; June 26, 1775; July 10, 1775; August 14, 1775; September 4, 1775; September 18, 1775. See *Dunlap's Pennsylvania Packet or, the General Advertiser*, July 11, 1775.

TEN POUNDS REWARD.
RAN AWAY from the subscriber, in Christiana Bridge, New-Castle County, on the 23d of April last, an apprentice lad, named GEORGE GRAY, by trade a hatter, 18 or 19 years of age, has two years to serve, about five feet six inches high, has a down look, yellow complexion, with a scar down his nose, very talkative and conceited of his own abilities: Had on when he went away, an olive coloured fustian coat, red vest, nankeen breeches, thread stockings, fashionable shoes, and a pair of very gay carved silver buckles. Whoever takes up said apprentice, and secures him in any of his Majesty's gaols, so that this master may get him again, shall have the above reward and reasonable charges, paid by     JOEL LEWIS.
N. B. All masters of vessels and others are forbid to harbour or carry off said apprentice at their peril.
*Dunlap's Pennsylvania Packet or, the General Advertiser*, May 22, 1775; July 3, 1775.

*New Castle Goal, May* 29, 1775.
NOW in the goal of this county, the following persons, viz. *Thomas Donogho*, about 22 years of age; had on, when committed, a brown coat and swanskin jacket, a wool hat, and buckskin breeches; who says he belongs to Captain Johnston, of Chester-town, in Maryland. Also *William Philiston*, who is advertised by Joseph White, in Bucks county, near New-town. Likewise *Francis May*, who was advertised by John Page and John Bradshaw. Their masters are desired to come, in 4 weeks from the date hereof, pay their charges, and take them away, or they will be sold for the same,     by THOMAS PUSEY, Goaler.
*The Pennsylvania Gazette*, May 31, 1775. See *Dunlap's Pennsylvania Packet or, the General Advertiser*, May 15, 1775, and *Dunlap's Pennsylvania Packet or, the General Advertiser*, June 19, 1775, for May.

*New-Castle, June 5*, 1775.
NOW in the Goal of said County, to wit. A certain *John Alexander*, who was advertised in the Pennsylvania Journal, No. 1694, as a runaway from a certain John Elder, of Lancaster County, on the 7th of May last past. Also a certain Negro Man, named *Will*, who belongs to Isaac Thomas, of Caecil County, Maryland, as he says. Their Masters are desired to come, in four Weeks from the Date, and take them away, or they will be sold for the same,
by THOMAS PUSEY, Goaler.
*The Pennsylvania Gazette*, June 14, 1775.

FOUR DOLLARS REWARD.
RAN AWAY from the subscriber, a certain JAMES MARTIN, who says he was born in Newcastle County, and it is supposed he is or will be some where near St. George's; had on a brown coat and waistcoat of coarse cloth, buckskin breeches, felt hat, and old shoes tied with strings: He took with him a bay Mare, shod before, and is lame in one of her fore feet, an old saddle patched upon the pummel, the bridle tied in a head-piece with a leather thong. Whoever will bring the man or mare to the subscriber, living at ISAAC DAWSON'S tavern, eight miles below down, shall have the above Reward and all reasonable charges, by
   MARK MANLOVE, Constable of Murtherkiln Hundred.
*Dunlap's Pennsylvania Packet or, the General Advertiser*, June 12, 1775; July 31, 1775; August 21, 1775.

FIVE POUNDS REWARD.
RAN AWAY from his bail, living in Red Lion Hundred, New-Castle County, on Delaware, a certain JOHN BRADLEY, aged about twenty-four years, about five feet seven inches high, and in proportion to his heighth, or rather slim, pretty active, speaks with the broague, of a fair complexion, by occupation a labourer, has of late practised ditching and clearing of swamp, and probably would engage in a job of that kind, as he carried off two ditching shovels; had on and took with him when he went away a beaver hat almost new, a new blue lapelled coat, hair buttons with hooks and eyes, a lapelled striped waistcoat, a pair of ticking breeches, worsted stockings, turned pumps with long quarters, and copper buckles: He also stole and took with him, a grey MARE, seven years old, paces and trots, very crooked hind legs, and a switch tail; together with a young MARE COLT, about three weeks old, of a brown dun colour, black mane and tail, with a ratch [*sic*] down its forehead. Whoever takes up said thief and secures him in any of his Majesty's gaols, so that he may be had again, together with the mare and colt, shall have the above Reward, or THREE POUND for the thief, and FORTY SHILLINGS for the mare and colt, and all reasonable charges,
   paid by  MATTHEW WILLIAMSON.
*Dunlap's Pennsylvania Packet or, the General Advertiser*, June 19, 1775; August 7, 1775; August 21, 1775.

THIRTY POUNDS REWARD.
RAN AWAY from the subscriber, living in Baltimore county, Maryland, about twelve miles from Baltimore town, a white servant man and a negro man, viz. RICHARD DAWSON, an English convict, came into the country last winter, about 55 years of age, was a soldier under the King of Prussia last

war, is given to liquor, upwards of six feet high, brown hair, round face, fresh coloured, has been hurt in his left thumb, which occasions it to be stiff: Had on when he went away, an iron collar double rivetted, old castor hat, dark frock, much tarred, old dark grey German serge jacket, mended with black lincey, brown role shirt, white full'd cloth breeches, coarse white yarn stockings, and old country made shoes with strings.

SOLOMON, a negro, about twenty-two years of age, has been in the country about four years, and talks pretty good English: Had on when he went away, an iron collar, a darby on each leg with a chain to one of them, all double rivetted, a new felt hat, old brown cloth coat, blue cloth jacket line with red, brown role shirt, white fulled cloth breeches, old white yarn stockings, and old country made shoes.

Is it supposed they will make for Boston to the soldiers, as they have often been talking about them, and it is likely they may get their irons off, get other clothes, change their names, and deny their master, as the negro has always done; has been in Newcastle upon Delaware twelve months and upwards; he went from thence in July last, and got in goal in Somerset county, Maryland, and was brought home in November last; he has been in Philadelphia, he is of middle size, somewhat upon the yellow, has some marks upon one of his cheeks like the small pox, has lost part of the side of his right thumb, that makes the end of it look sharper than the other.

Whoever apprehends them, or either of them, and secures them in any goal, so that their master may have them again, shall have Twenty Shillings; if above ten miles, Forty Shillings; if above forty miles, Three Pounds; if sixty miles, Five Pounds; if two hundred miles, Ten Pounds, if five hundred miles, the above Reward, and reasonable charges if brought home, paid by THOMAS COCKEY, sen.   THOMAS COCKEY, jun.

*Dunlap's Pennsylvania Packet or, the General Advertiser,* July 11, 1775. See *Dunlap's Pennsylvania Packet or, the General Advertiser,* May 22, 1775.

Wilmington, New-Castle County, July 11, 1775.
RUN AWAY last evening, from the Subscriber, an English Servant Man named JOHN ALDERTON, a Barber by trade, about 22 or 23 years of age, about 5 feet high, broad face, middling long chin, thick set, round shouldered, brown short hair, loves strong liquor, very talkative when drunk, pretends to play on a fife or beat a drum, shaves and dresses hair well, and is very cunning; he arrived at Annapolis in September last, and lived some time near that place; had on, when he went away, a jacket of such stuff as the Negroes generally wear in Maryland, an old wool hat, tow shirt, drilling or Russia sheeting drawers, white thread ribbed stockings, new strong shoes, with black buckles, and a cloth under jacket; he is remarkable for size and appearance, and it is believed he will endeavour to pass for a free man, and offer himself

to some of the militia companies for a fifer or drummer. Any person apprehending said servant, so that his master may get him again, shall have a reward of SIX DOLLARS, if out of this county, and if within this county Five Shillings over and above what the law allows,
paid by    WILLIAM BROBSON, Barber.

*Story & Humphrey's Pennsylvania Mercury, and Universal Advertiser*, July 14, 1775; July 28, 1775; *The Pennsylvania Gazette*, July 19, 1775; August 16, 1775. Minor differences. See *Dunlap's Pennsylvania Packet or, the General Advertiser*, July 17, 1775.

*Kent County, on Delaware, July* 10, 1775.
FIVE DOLLARS REWARD.

RAN AWAY from the subscriber, living on the road leading from Dover to Queen's Town, near the place called Horse-head, on Sunday night, the 2d inst. a servant man named WILLIAM JONES, by trade a gun-lock maker, and very ingenious at any kind of whitesmiths business, and even at blacksmiths work; aged upwards of thirty years, of a middle stature; he went off very well cloathed with sundry sorts of cloaths, and is supposed to have taken plenty of money with him. It is believed he is gone in company with another servant man who is also eloped from a neighbour, (name unknown). Whoever secures said servant in any public gaol, so that his mistress may have him again, or brings him home to her, shall have the above Reward and reasonable charges, paid by    SARAH JONES, Widow.

*Dunlap's Pennsylvania Packet or, the General Advertiser*, July 17, 1775; August 14, 1775; August 28, 1775.

*Newcastle, July* 14, 1775.
EIGHT DOLLARS REWARD.

WHEREAS a certain person who called himself MEAS, on the 6th instant, applied to the subscriber, living in Newcastle, for the hire of a horse to go to Philadelphia, pretending he forgot his pocket-book and some valuable papers there when he left that place in the Port Penn stage, and promised to return the next day, but has not since been heard of, and 'tis believed he has sold the horse: The said MEAS appeared to be a middle aged man, about five feet six or seven inches high, very swarthy and much pitted with the small pox; had on a light coloured wilton coat, black breeches, a regimental round hat with a black ribband round the crown, the rest of his dress unknown: The horse which he got from the subscriber is a dark bay, about fourteen hands high, eight or nine years old, pretty lengthy body, black mane and tail switched, his mane very thick and hangs all on the off side, one fore and one hind foot white, but which uncertain; he paces, trots and hand-gallops, no brand or ear mark: The said MEAS pretends he has a brother in Oxford

Township, Chester County, and is from all accounts, a most notorious villain. Whoever therefore apprehends the said MEAS, and secures him in any of his Majesty's gaols in Pennsylvania or this government, so that the subscriber may have it in his power to secure himself, and also secures the horse so that the owner may get him again, shall receive the above Reward, or for the horse alone FOUR DOLLARS, and all reasonable charges if brought home,
       from    JOHN RIDDLES.
N. B. Was hired with the horse, an almost new saddle with green housings, and an half worn snaffle bridle.
*Dunlap's Pennsylvania Packet or, the General Advertiser*, July 17, 1775; August 14, 1775.


EIGHT DOLLARS REWARD.
RAN AWAY on the 3d inst. (July) from the subscriber, at the new Mills on Brandywine, near Wilmington, an Irish servant man named EDWARD LOW, a cooper by trade, about 5 feet 3 inches high, 24 years of age, has yellow hair, grey eyes, and is fond of strong liquor; had on an old scarlet waistcoat, red striped cotton jacket with sleeves, check shirt, oznabrigs trowsers and old shoes. As he took a sickle with him, it is supposed he will pass for a reaper. Whoever takes up and secures said servant so that his master may get him again, shall receive the above Reward, and reasonable charges, from    GEORGE FORSYTH, Cooper.
*Dunlap's Pennsylvania Packet or, the General Advertiser*, July 17, 1775; August 14, 1775; August 28, 1775.


*Wilmington, New-Castle County, July* 11, 1775.
SIX DOLLARS REWARD.
*RAN AWAY last evening from the subscriber, an English servant man named JOHN ALDERTON, a barber by trade, about* 22 *or* 23 *years of age, about* 5 *feet high, broad face, middling long chin, thick set, round shouldered, brown short hair, loves strong liquor, very talkative when drunk, pretends to play on a fife or beat a drum, shaves and dresses hair well, and is very cunning: He arrived at Annapolis in September, last, and lived some time near that place: Had on when he went away, a jacket of such stuff as the Negroes generally wear in Maryland, an old wool hat, tow shirt, drilling or Russia sheeting drawers, white thread ribbed stockings, new strong shoes, with black buckles, and a cloth under jacket: He is remarkable for size and appearance, and it is believed he will endeavour to pass for a freeman, and offer himself to some of the militia companies for a fifer or drummer. Any person apprehending the said servant, so that his master may get him again,*

shall have the above Reward if out of this county, and if within this county FIVE SHILLINGS, over and above what the law allows, paid by
                WILLIAM BROBSON, Barber.
*Dunlap's Pennsylvania Packet or, the General Advertiser,* July 17, 1775; August 14, 1775. See *Story & Humphrey's Pennsylvania Mercury, and Universal Advertiser,* July 14, 1775.

            *Wilmington, Newcastle County, July* 13th, 1775.
                    FIVE POUNDS Reward.
RUN AWAY from the Subscriber the last evening, A native Irish Servant Man, calls himself JOHN M'GONNEGALL, twenty-two years of age, and five feet seven or eight inches high, thin visage, slim built, gray eyes, light brown hair and wears a club to it; a Barber by trade: had on and took with him, a blue cloth coat and jacket, buckskin breeches, almost new, three shirts, one brown linen, a corded white jacket, striped linen ditto, a pair of red and white striped trowsers, a half worn castor hat, a new pair of black-grain shoes and plated buckles, both his legs sore, one very bad; came from Colerain the last fall: it is thought that the same night he run away he was seen near John Tomlinson's place, on the road leading from Wilmington to Lancaster, in company with another servant man of mine who run away two nights before, (and is now advertised in the papers) and an English woman who came in this spring with Benjamin Taylor, and now a servant to Ellis Mewlin of said county, and it is likely that one of the men and woman may pass for man and wife, if they do not get tired of her and turn her a drift. She is about twenty-one years of age, red faced, low stature and thick built, loves strong drink, and is a great talker, had on, a white diaper bonnet, old patched reddish colour'd gown, red & white strip'd linsey petticoat, a pair of old whitish coloured cloth shoes with metal buckles. Any person apprehending the said John M'Gonnegall, so that his master shall get him again, shall receive the above reward, if out of this county, and if in this county, FIVE SHILLINGS over and above what the law allows; and any person that will apprehend the above described woman, so that her master shall get her again, if out of this county, THIRTY SHILLINGS, and if within the county, what the law allows.—All persons are desired to discover the above Runaways, and as well all other such Runaways, otherwise there will be no such thing as keeping of a Servant.     WILLIAM BROBSON.
                    ELLIS NEWLIN.
*The Pennsylvania Journal, and the Weekly Advertiser,* July 19, 1775; July 26, 1775; *Story & Humphrey's Pennsylvania Mercury, and Universal Advertiser,* July 21, 1775; July 26, 1775; July 28, 1775; August 4, 1775; August 11, 1775. Minor differences between the papers.

THREE DOLLARS REWARD.
RUN away the 17th inst. from the subscriber, living in Brandywine Hundred, a servant lad, named PETER M'COURT, about 17 years of age, 5 feet 4 inches high, of a down look, short black hair; had on, when he went away, a new wool hat, a new brown cloth coat and waistcoat, an old flaxen shirt, tow trowsers, and was bare footed. Whoever takes up said servant, and brings him home, or secures him in any of his Majesty's goals, so that his master may get him again, shall have the above reward, and reasonable charges,
July 25, 1775.      paid by    JAMES M'KEE.
*The Pennsylvania Gazette*, July 26, 1775. See *The Pennsylvania Gazette*, December 6, 1775.


TWENTY SHILLINGS REWARD.
RUN away from the subscriber, living in Brandywine Hundred, New-Castle county, on the 12th of July, 1775, and [sic] English servant man, named JOHN PLATT, a stout, lusty fellow, short brown hair, combed back before, the little finger of his right hand very short, and stands right up; had on, when he went away, an old blue cloth jacket, with stocking sleeves, of near the same colour, coarse homespun shirt, tow trowsers, an old beaver hat, and strong shoes, with Pinchbeck buckles.—Whoever takes up and secures said servant, so that his master may get him again, shall be entitled to the above reward, and reasonable charges, paid by    ADAM WILLIAMSON.
*The Pennsylvania Gazette*, August 2, 1775. See *The Pennsylvania Gazette*, August 16, 1775.


*Wilmington, Newcastle County, Aug. 3, 1775.*
*SIX DOLLARS REWARD.*
*RAN AWAY, last night, from the subscriber, an English servant man, named JOHN HUMBLE, about twenty two years of age, five feet seven inches high; had on and took with him when he went away, a snuff coloured thickset coat and jacket, half worn, striped linen trowsers, buckskin breeches, a small castor hat bound with black ribbond, old shoes with maccaroni plated buckles; his hair long and black, which he wears sometimes tied and sometimes buckled; he is a genteel looking young fellow, came into the country with Capt. Osborn about three months ago. Whoever takes up said servant, and confines him in any of his Majesty's gaols, so that his master may get him again, shall have the above reward, and reasonable charges,*
             *paid by    JOSEPH WARNER.*
*Dunlap's Pennsylvania Packet and the General Advertiser*, August 7, 1775; August 21, 1775; *The Pennsylvania Gazette*, August 9, 1775; August 16, 1775. Minor differences between the papers.

## FOUR DOLLARS REWARD.

*RAN AWAY from the subscriber, living in Red Lion Hundred, Newcastle County, on the 17th of July last, a Negro or Mulatto man slave named BOB, about five feet six inches high, nineteen years of age; he is straight and slim made, with long feet, and resembles an Indian; he is very impudent, and will endeavour to pass for a freeman as he has done once before in Sussex County, and downwards to Somerset: had on an oznabrig shirt, Russia sheeting trowsers, an under lincey jacket without sleeves, neither hat nor shoes unless he got them by stealth: he is suspected of stealing a black horse, about ten years old, as one of the neighbours lost one about the same time. Any person who shall secure him in any of his Majesty's gaols, shall receive the above Reward, and if brought home all reasonable charges,*
        *paid by   GEORGE CLARK.*
*N. B. All masters of vessels are forbid to take him off at their peril.*
    *Dunlap's Pennsylvania Packet or, the General Advertiser*, August 14, 1775; August 28, 1775.

## TWENTY SHILLINGS REWARD.

RUN away from the subscriber, living in Reedy Island Neck, New Castle county, on the 28th of July last, a NEGROE man, named Jacob Purkins, about 26 years of age, 5 feet 9 inches high, or a yellowish colour, he chews tobacco and is very apt to ask any person he sees use it for a chew; he had an iron collar about his neck, when he went away, a pair of old striped holland trowsers, an old felt hat, and an old blue coat. Whoever secures the said Negroe, so as his master may have him again, shall be paid the above reward and reasonable charges,   by   WILLIAM M'KEAN.
    *The Pennsylvania Gazette*, August 16, 1775; September 13, 1775; November 1, 1775. The second and third ads show a reward of forty shillings.

WAS committed to the Goal of Burlington, on the second day of this instant August, a certain JOHN PLATT, an Englishman, who confesses himself to be a Servant to Adam Williamson, of Brandywine Hundred, in New-Castle County, and who is advertised in the *Pennsylvania Gazette*, No. 2432. His Master is desired to come or send immediately, pay Charges, and take him away.      EPHRAIM PHILLIPS, Goaler.
    *The Pennsylvania Gazette*, August 16, 1775. See *The Pennsylvania Gazette*, August 2, 1775.

## FIVE SHILLINGS Reward.

WENT away with his Brother, on the 4th day of February last, with liberty of staying away for the space of two months only, and is not yet returned, an apprentice lad named DAVID CLARK, about twenty years of age, a Shoemaker by trade: He is midling tall, wears his own hair, which is black, and he is marked with the small-pox. Whoever takes up said apprentice, and brings him to his master, living in New-Ark, New-Castle county, shall have the above reward, paid by      JOHN BOGGS.

*The Pennsylvania Journal, and the Weekly Advertiser*, August 16, 1775; August 23, 1775; August 30, 1775.


*Christiania-Bridge 13th of the 8th Month.*
THREE POUNDS REWARD.
RUN-AWAY, last night, from the subscriber, an *Irish SERVANT MAN*, named *CHARLES O'NEAL*, a lusty well made fellow, 5 feet 8 inches high, brownish bushy hair, and is about 20 years of age: Had on, and took away, two pair of shoes, one whereof was dog-skin, a pair of white thread stockings, two pair of old blue and white striped trowsers, course white shirts, pair of almost new leather breeches, a dark coloured fine jean vest lately made out of an old coat, which will appear by part of the button-holes sewed up, a short skirted old light colour cloth coat, new felt hat: Also, took with him several things tied up in a bundle. Whoever takes up and secures said *SERVANT* in any of his Majesty's goals, shall receive the above reward, and reasonable charges, paid by      *JOHN LEWDEN.*

*The Pennsylvania Ledger: or the Virginia, Maryland, Pennsylvania, & New-Jersey Weekly Advertiser*, August 19, 1775; August 26, 1775; September 9, 1775; *The Pennsylvania Gazette*, August 23, 1775. Minor differences between the papers.


EIGHT DOLLARS Reward.
RUN away, last night, from the subscriber, living near Brandywine Bridge, in Brandywine Hundred, New-Castle county, an Irish servant man, named JOHN O'NEAL, who was born near Cork, in Ireland, and speaks English very indifferently; he is about 28 years of age, 5 feet 7 or 8 inches high, well set, has short sandy hair, and a smooth pale face; had on, when he went away, an old castor hat, dark grey coatee, white under jacket, check shirt, linen trowsers, and old shoes, with strings in them: He sailed with Capt. John Blyth, in the Brig John, last June. Whoever secures said servant, so as his master gets him again, shall, if 40 miles from home, have THIRTY SHILLINGS reward, and if 100 miles from home the above reward, and all reasonable charges paid by
*August* 14, 1775.      MARK ELLIOT, junior.

*The Pennsylvania Gazette*, August 23, 1775.

FOURTEEN DOLLARS REWARD.

RAN AWAY from the subscriber, living near the Horse-head, in Kent County on Delaware, on Sunday, the 25th of June last, a servant man, named AARON LOPER, but goes by the name of AARON WALKER, by trade a wheelwright, country born, about 30 years of age, and about 5 feet 8 or 9 inches high, has black hair tied behind and clipped on the top, a large cut on his left wrist with a broad ax, and is a great lover of liquor; had on when he went away, an old wool hat, a fearnought outside jacket, of a lead colour, a home made under jacket with yellow stripes, coarse shirt and trowsers, pale blue stockings, shoes about half worn, and white metal buckles. Whoever takes up said servant and secures him, so as his master may get him again, shall have the above Reward and all reasonable charges,

paid by    THOMAS PROCTOR.

*Dunlap's Pennsylvania Packet or, the General Advertiser*, August 28, 1775; September 11, 1775; October 16, 1775; October 30, 1775; November 27, 1775; *The Pennsylvania Gazette*, August 30, 1775; October 25, 1775; November 29, 1775. Minor differences between the papers. The *Gazette* shows his trade to be "a cart wheelwright" and has "*August* 14, 1775" at the bottom. See *The Pennsylvania Journal, and the Weekly Advertiser*, August 30, 1775.


FOURTEEN DOLLARS REWARD.

RUN-AWAY from the subscriber, living in Kent county, on Delaware near the Horse Head, on Sunday, the 25th of June last, a servant man, named AARON LOPER, but goes by the name of AARON WALKER, about 30 years of age, and about five feet 8 or 9 inches high, country born, by trade a wheel-right, has black hair tyed behind, and clipped on the top of his head, with a large cut on his left wrist, occasioned by a broad-ax, is a great lover of liquor. Had on when he went away, an old wool hat, a fearnought outside jacket of a led [*sic*] colour, a home made under jacket with yellow stripes, coarse shirt and trowsers, pale blue stockings, half worn shoes and white metal buckles. Whoever takes up said servant, and secures him so that his master may have him again, shall have the above reward, and all reasonable charges, paid by me    THOMAS PROCTOR.

*The Pennsylvania Journal, and the Weekly Advertiser*, August 30, 1775; September 6, 1775; October 25, 1775; November 8, 1775. See *Dunlap's Pennsylvania Packet or, the General Advertiser*, August 28, 1775.


New Castle Goal, September 4, 1775.

NOW in the Goal of said County, the following Persons, viz. JOHN CONNOR, a Hair dresser by Trade, who says he belongs to James

Williamson, of Kent County, in Maryland. THOMAS NORTH, born in Oxfordshire, in England, is about five Feet six or seven Inches high, well made, and pitted with the Smallpox; had on, when committed, a wool Hat, a London brown fly Coat, of coarse Cloth, Russia Sheeting Trowsers, and a Pair of coarse Shoes, with Nails in the Heels. WILLIAM MATTHEWS, from Devonshire, in England, of a swarthy Complexion, thin Visage, and brown Hair; had on, when committed, a light blue Waistcoat, spotted in the dying, made in the Sailors fashion with slash Sleeves, a wool Hat, cocked with white Cord, coarse long Trowsers, coarse Shoes, with Copper Regimental Buckles. The two last mentioned Persons say they came in with Captain Thomas Spencer, in the Ship Elizabeth, to Baltimore. Their Masters, if any they have, are desired to come in four Weeks from this Date, and take them away, or they will be sold for their Fees, by    THOMAS PUSEY.

*The Pennsylvania Gazette*, September 6, 1775.


SIX DOLLARS REWARD.

RUN away, last night, from the subscriber, living near Brandywine Bridge, Newcastle county, a servant man, named *Thomas Reiley*, by trade a miller, about 30 years of age, 5 feet 6 inches high, a well set fellow, brown hair, has something of the brogue when he talks; had on, and took with him, a dark brown coat and jacket, a cloth coloured surtout coat, leather breeches, thread stockings, and a good hat; he must have had a bundle with him, as he took all his clothes. whoever takes up said servant, and secures him in any goal, so that his master may have him again, shall have the above reward.
*Sept.* 11, 1775.          JOSEPH TATNALL.

*The Pennsylvania Gazette*, September 13, 1775. See *The Pennsylvania Journal, and the Weekly Advertiser*, September 13, 1775.


SIX DOLLARS Reward.

RUN-AWAY last night, from the subscriber, living near Brandywine bridge, New-Castle county, a servant man, named THOMAS REILY, by trade a miller, about 30 years of age, five feet six inches high, a well set fellow, brown hair, and has something of the brogue when he talks: Had on and took with him a dark brown coat and jacket, a cloth coloured surtout coat, leather breeches, thread stockings, and a good hat; he must have had a bundle with him, as he took all his cloaths. Whoever takes up said servant, and secures him in any gaol, so that his master may have him again, shall have the above reward,     paid by     JOSEPH TATNALL.

*The Pennsylvania Journal, and the Weekly Advertiser*, September 13, 1775; October 4, 1775; October 11, 1775. See *The Pennsylvania Gazette*, September 13, 1775.

*Ninth Month (September)* 24, 1775.
### THREE POUNDS REWARD.

RUN away, last night, from the subscriber, living in Mill creek Hundred, New Castle County, an Irish servant lad, named *Michael Doherty*, about 17 years of age, of a middle stature, has straight brown hair, and broad face; had on, when he went away, a blue broadcloth coat, light coloured jacket, tow trowsers, old shoes, felt hat, half-worn; took with him a light coloured cloth coat and brown ribbed stockings, and an iron grey horse, near 15 hands high, 4 years old, lately galled on the shoulders with the collar, paces and trots very handy.—Whoever takes up said servant and horse, so that the owners may get them again, shall have the above reward, or Forty shillings for one, and reasonable charges, paid by     JAMES JACKSON,
                WILLIAM DIXSON.

Is supposed he has a pass.

*The Pennsylvania Gazette*, October 4, 1775. See *The Pennsylvania Gazette*, April 20, 1774.

### SIX DOLLARS REWARD.

RUN away, on the night of the 24th of September last, from the subscriber, at Christiana Bridge, New-Castle county, an English servant man, named *James Blight Collins*, by trade a Rope-maker, 5 feet 6 inches high, 23 years old, fresh full, smooth face, brown complexion, wears his own hair, a good scholar; had on a blue coat, swanskin spotted jacket, tow trowsers, black stockings, and an old hat; it is likely he will apply to be a school-master, or a clerk. Whoever secures said servant, so that I can get him again, shall have the above reward, and reasonable charges,
           paid by    ROBERT SHIELDS.

*The Pennsylvania Gazette*, October 4, 1775. See *The Maryland Gazette*, October 5, 1775.

### SIX DOLLARS REWARD.

RAN away last night from the subscriber, living at Christiana Bridge, Newcastle county, an English servant man, named James Blight Collins, by trade a rope-maker, about 5 feet 6 inches high, 23 years of age, red full smooth face, brown complexion, wears his own hair, and a good scholar: had on when he went away, a blue coat, spotted swanskin jacket, tow trousers, old hat, and it is likely he will go to Annapolis and apply to be a clerk, or a schoolmaster. Whoever secures him, so that his master may have him again, shall have the above reward, and reasonable charges,
           paid by me,    ROBERT SHIELDS.

*The Maryland Gazette*, October 5, 1775; October 12, 1775; October 19, 1775; November 2, 1775. See *The Pennsylvania Gazette*, October 4, 1775.

EIGHT DOLLARS Reward.

WAS Stolen from the borough of Wilmington, about the first of this instant, a Light Bay HORSE, about 15 hands high, has a large head, a smallish neck and narrow breast, round which the hair was a little chafed off with the edge of a breast-plate, paces well, but has in his trot a kind of hop with the near fore-leg, high hipped and crupper boned, is about 6 or 7 years old, and is a well carriaged horse, has a lump or puff of wind appears (when rode hard) on the near side of his neck, where he is trimmed for the bridle, shod before with steeled shoes.—It is supposed that he was stolen by one Welch, who is advertised, and particularly described by David Cowpland of Chester, for having stolen a small bay horse from him.—Whoever takes up the said horse and secures him so that the owner may have him again, shall have the above reward, and if brought home, reasonable charges
    paid by  JOHN YARNALL.
Wilmington, 20th 11th mo. 1775.

  N. B. 'Tis thought said Welch took him over Dunks Ferry into the Jerseys.

*The Pennsylvania Journal, and the Weekly Advertiser*, November 22, 1775; November 29, 1775; December 13, 1775.


RAN AWAY from the Subscriber, in Newcastle County, on the 14th instant, (November) a servant woman named CATHARINE CARR, about 22 years of age, a middle sized person; had with her when she went away, a gown of stamped linen, a short ditto of purple calico, two striped lincey petticoats, a red shirt, and a black bonnet. Whoever takes up said servant woman, shall have SIX PENCE Reward, and no more,
    paid by  WILLIAM PATTERSON.

*Dunlap's Pennsylvania Packet or, the General Advertiser*, November 27, 1775; December 18, 1775.


EIGHT DOLLARS Reward.

RUN away from the subcriber, at New Castle, on the 19th of August last, a servant newly come from Ireland, went under the name of *Brice M'Whenney*, and sometimes calls himself *M'Kenney*, a thick chunky fellow, about 5 feet 9 inches high, dark complexion and black curled hair; had on sailor's dress, when he went away; it is thought he will pretend to be a deserter from the regulars, as he is capable of teaching the horse and foot exercise. Any person that will secure said servant in any of his Majesty's goals, so as his master may have him again, shall have the above reward, and reasonable charges, paid by JOHN MILES, living in Turbet township, Northumberland county.

*The Pennsylvania Gazette,* November 29, 1775; January 17, 1776; February 28, 1776.

### SIX DOLLARS REWARD.

RAN AWAY from his bail, on Sunday the 19th of November last, a certain JOHN M'CONHUY, about five feet four inches high, twenty-three years of age, has long black hair tied behind, and the top of his nose bit off; had on and took with him, a short blue coatee, a red and blue mixed broadcloth strait coat, white napped jacket, striped silk ditto, old shoes, brass buckles not fellows, and an almost new fur hat. Whoever secures him in any of his Majesty's gaols, so that the subscriber may get him again, shall have the above Reward, paid by       DAVID M'CONHEY,
living near Christiana Bridge, Newcastle County.

*Dunlap's Pennsylvania Packet or, the General Advertiser,* December 4, 1775; December 18, 1775.

### FORTY SHILLINGS REWARD.

RAN AWAY, last night, from the subscriber living in Newport, Newcastle county, a certain JOHN NOWLAND, by trade a saddler, about five feet ten inches high, and has brown hair tied behind, had on, when he went away, a half worn cloth coat of a mixed flesh colour, an olive coloured thickset jacket made in the regimental fashion, a pair of drilling breeches, blue worsted stockings, a pair of new shoes, and a half worn beaver hat, with a white ribband and black rose. Whoever secures him, so that the subscriber gets him again, shall have TWENTY SHILLINGS reward, and if brought home all reasonable charges.

Also ran away, at the same time, a servant lad named WILLIAM ERWIN, about eighteen years old, five feet eight inches high, red hair cut short, full faced, and of a sandy complexion. He had on, when he went away, a beaver hat, a light coloured Wilton coat without lining, whitish jacket, claret coloured breeches half worn, blue yarn stockings, and new shoes with brass buckles. Whoever secures him so that the subscriber gets him again, shall have TWENTY SHILLINGS reward, and if brought home reasonable charges.            CONRAD GRAY.

*The Pennsylvania Evening Post,* December 5, 1775; December 9, 1775; December 16, 1775; December 26, 1775; December 28, 1775; January 2, 1776.

*York-town Goal, November* 24, 1775.

WERE committed into my custody, the following persons, viz. *Joseph Camp,* about 5 feet 8 inches high, an Englishman, about 32 years old; had on, when committed, a grey surtout, an ozenbrigs shirt and trowsers, an old felt hat, and old shoes; he is slim built, has short fair hair, and the crown cut short. *Arthur M'Ginnis*, alias *Peter M'Court*, about 5 feet 4 inches high, an Irish lad, about 17 years old, who says he is a servant to James M'Kee, in Brandywine Hundred, in Wilmington, has short black hair; had on, when committed, an old felt hat, a white cloth jacket, a striped lincey under ditto, a flaxen linen shirt, and tow trowsers. *William Young*, alias *John Thrift*, about 5 feet 10 inches high, slim built, and fair hair; he says he is a servant to Robert M'Kettrick, about 12 miles from Staunton, in Virginia, and says he left his master sometime in January last; had on, when committed, an old wool hat, a brown coating surtout, a white cloth jacket, a pair of trowsers, and old shoes; about 32 years old. Their masters are desired to come, pay the charges, and take them away, in four weeks from the date of advertising, or else they will be sold by MICHAEL GRAYBIL, Goaler.

*The Pennsylvania Gazette*, December 6, 1775. See *The Pennsylvania Gazette*, July 26, 1775.


SIX DOLLARS Reward.

RAN AWAY from the subscriber, living in Newport, Newcastle county, an Irish servant lad named LAURENCE DEMSEY, a tailor by trade, nineteen or twenty years of age, about five feet five inches high, dark coloured hair tied behind, pockmarked, hollow eyes, large mouth and nose, of a morose sour look, very proud and of thick limbs, much given to liquor and quarrelling; had on and took with him, a pair of drilling trousers, a pair of coarse thread stockings, a light blue cloth mended under the right arm with lighter blue and finer cloth, a dark blue sagathy jacket with light blue cloth backs, green breeches and gray stockings, a pair of good shoes and odd yellow buckles, a felt hat cut in the Macaroni fashion, very deep in the crown, a damaskus jacket, two coarse white line shirts, one of them wristed with thick curby cloth, and seams in the back of both. It is very likely he may change his clothes, as he went away with two other lads, and is supposed to be gone to Philadelphia. Whoever secures said servant, so that his master may have him again, shall receive the above reward and reasonable charges.
FRANCES SMITH.

*The Pennsylvania Evening Post*, December 12, 1775; December 21, 1775; December 26, 1775; December 30, 1775.


ON Tuesday the 12th inst, was ran away with, from Cape Henlopen, (being bound out) by the under-mentioned seamen after forcing the subscriber ashore, who was then Master: A SLOOP, called the BETSEY: She is doubled decked, built in Philadelphia; is about four years old; sheathed, black sides, her decks paid with tar and ocre. Had on board 8 hogsheads of rum, 39 barrels of flour, 2 hogsheads of loaf sugar, 100 pounds of chocolate, and 600 pounds of cheese.

GEORGE BUCHANAN, Mate; is about 5 feet 9 or 10 inches high, a native of Scotland, very talkative, smooth faced, long black hair tied behind, about 30 years of age, and has remarkable long legs.

JAMES HERDMAN, about 25 years of age, about 5 feet 10 inches high; from the North of Ireland; a little pock-marked, stout well made, black complection, and short hair.

JAMES HENDERSON, about 5 feet 8 inches high, a native of Scotland; very thick and clumsey, pock-marked, has black curled hair, with some white hairs in his neck, has a remarkable stubb'd nose, and speaks on the North of England Dialect.

PETER M'CALLUM, about 22 years of age and about 5 feet 5 inches high, born in the Highlands of Scotland, smooth faced, with dark brown curled hair, speaks very broken English.

Whoever will stop the vessel and goods, so that the owner may have them again, shall have TWO HUNDRED DOLLARS REWARD, and FIFTY DOLLARS for each of the seamen on conviction,
paid by    PHILIP LACEY.

*The Pennsylvania Journal, and the Weekly Advertiser*, December 20, 1775; December 27, 1775; February 7, 1776.

## 1776

*December* 10, 1775.
EIGHT DOLLARS REWARD.
RAN AWAY from the subscriber, living near the Horse Head, in Kent County, on Delaware, an Irish indented servant man named JAMES LOWERRY, but commonly goes by the name of LAVEREY; he is about five feet seven inches high, by trade a weaver, a good deal pock-marked, pale complexion, black hair commonly tied behind, bold and talkative; had on when he went away, a good felt hat, an old red and white silk handkerchief, two country linen shirts, a blue fulled country cloth coat, an old purple silk jacket, a striped lincey under jacket, old black velvet breeches, old patched trowsers, new blue yarn stockings ringed with white on the tops, white thread ditto, and shoes. Whoever takes up said servant and brings him home, or secures him so that his master may have him again, shall have, if in the country, FOUR DOLLARS, and if out, the above Reward, and all reasonable charges, paid    HENRY ELBERT.
N. B. I bought him of Mr. William Boyce, in Newcastle County.

*Dunlap's Pennsylvania Packet or, the General Advertiser*, January 1, 1776; January 22, 1776; February 5, 1776.

*Newcastle, January* 22, 1776.
WAS committed to the Gaol of this county, on suspicion of being a run-away, a man who calls himself THOMAS BUTLER, about 22 or 23 years of age, 5 feet 6 or 7 inches high, thick set, talks pretty much on the Irish dialect, says he came from Limerick with Capt. Lynch in the fall of 1774, and was brought here the 20th of September last. His master (if any he has) is desired to come and take him away in three weeks from the date hereof, or he will be discharged on paying his fees.—Also, a certain JOHN HETHERINGTON, committed on suspicion of horse-stealing the 14th of October last, and no person appearing last November Court to prosecute, he was detained, but will be discharged on paying his fees if not prosecuted to conviction the third Thursday of February next.
    THOMAS CLARK, Gaoler.
 *Dunlap's Pennsylvania Packet or, the General Advertiser*, January 29, 1776; February 19, 1776. See *The Pennsylvania Gazette*, October 11, 1775; October 25, 1775.

*Lancaster, January* 29, 1776.
WAS committed to my custody on suspicion of being a runaway servant, a certain *Robert Cleghorn*, aged about 14 years, light brown hair, smooth complexion; had on, when committed, a grey coat, old jacket, breeches and stockings, and new shoes; he confesses himself to be a servant to a certain William Price, a Blacksmith, in New-Castle county, who said *Cleghorn* says is a Mulattoe. His master (if any he has) is desired to come or send for him, in three weeks from the date hereof, pay charges, and take him away; otherwise he will be discharged, on paying his fees by
    GEORGE EBERLY, Goaler.
 *The Pennsylvania Gazette*, February 7, 1776; February 28, 1776.


TWENTY SHILLINGS REWARD.
BROKE out of Dover gaol, in Kent County on Delaware, the 2d of January last, a certain WILLIS BROWN, (Mulatto) who passes under the character of a parson and doctor, very talkative, he is about five feet seven or eight inches high; had on when he went away, a brown great coat, a light coloured jacket with sleeves, an old pair of blue trowsers, an old pair of shoes and a hat. Whoever takes up the said Willis Brown and secures him in any of his Majesty's gaols, so that the subscriber may get him again, shall have the above reward, paid by  THOMAS WILD, Gaoler.
 *Dunlap's Pennsylvania Packet or, the General Advertiser,* February 19, 1776; February 26, 1776; March 11, 1776.

*Dover, Jan.* 16, 1776.
WAS committed to the public gaol of the county of Kent upon Delaware, about three weeks past, a certain ISAAC COX, who was some time ago advertised in the public papers, by a certain Eden Smith, of the Jerseys, to have absconded from his bail: This is to give notice to the said Eden Smith, to come and take him away within three weeks from the date hereof, or else he will be sold for his prison charges, by the subscriber.
THOMAS WILD, Gaoler.
*Dunlap's Pennsylvania Packet or, the General Advertiser,* February 19. 1776; February 26, 1776; March 11, 1776.

THREE DOLLARS Reward.
RUN away from the subscriber, in Christiana Hundred, New-Castle county, the 17th of February last, an indented servant lad, named *John Meworthir*, aged 16 years and better, small of his age, he was born in the Welsh tract, he has a down look, brown hair, and very talkative and saucy; had on a deep crowned hat, a dark lead coloured jacket, a pair of buckskin breeches, too big for him and very ragged, brown stockings, old shoes, and an old tow shirt. Whoever takes up said and secures him, so that I may get him again, shall have the above reward, and reasonable charges,
paid by   GEORGE STERN.
*The Pennsylvania Gazette,* March 20, 1776; April 3, 1776.

*Kent County, on Delaware, April* 2, 1776.
*TWENTY SHILLINGS REWARD.*
*RAN AWAY from the subscriber, near Dover, on Monday the 11th day of March last, a mulatto slave named PETER (calls himself Peter Brownberry) about* 40 *years of age, stout and well made, is a native of the West-Indies, has a good countenance, and speaks proper English: Had on when he left home, a felt hat, a tow linen shirt, two jackets, one old the other new, a pair of new breeches of homespun fulled cloth, black and white mixed, and striped across with white, a pair of white yarn stockings and half worn shoes. He has been used to the water, and being well acquainted with the channel in the river Delaware, may attempt to get on board some of the enemy's ships to act as a pilot: The inhabitants along there are requested to be watchful. Whoever secures the said slave so that his master may get him again, shall have the above Reward, and reasonable charges if brought home,*
paid by   *THOMAS IRONS.*
*Dunlap's Pennsylvania Packet or, the General Advertiser,* April 8, 1776; May 20, 1776. See *The Pennsylvania Journal, and the Weekly Advertiser,* April 10, 1776.

Kent County on Delaware, April 2, 1776.
RAN AWAY from the subscriber, near Dover, on Monday the 11th day of March last, a Mulatto Slave, named PETER, (calls himself PETER BROUNBERRY) about 40 years of age, stout and well made: He is a native of the West-Indies, has a good countenance, and speaks proper English: Had on when he left home, a felt hat, a tow linen shirt, two jackets, one old, the other new, a pair of new breeches of homespun fulled cloth, black and white mixed; the breeches across with white, a pair of white yarn stockings, and half worn shoes. He has been used to the water, and being well acquainted with the channel in the river Delaware, may attempt to get on board some of the enemy's ships to act as a pilot; the inhabitants along shore are requested to be watchful. Whoever secures the said Slave, so that his master may get him again, shall have TWENTY SHILLINGS REWARD, and reasonable charges, if brought home, paid by    THOMAS IRONS.
*The Pennsylvania Journal, and the Weekly Advertiser*, April 10, 1776; May 1, 1776; May 15, 1776. See *Dunlap's Pennsylvania Packet or, the General Advertiser*, April 8, 1776.

## EIGHT DOLLARS REWARD.

RUN-AWAY the second of this instant, April, from the subscriber, living in Brandywine hundred, Newcastle county, a Dutch servant LAD, named HENRY NIBBLE, about 20 years of age, about 5 feet 6 or 7 inches high, with light coloured straight hair: Had on when he went away, an half-worn wool hat, an half-worn light coloured cloth jacket without skirts, a new lincey under jacket, black and white coloured, an old tow shirt, buckskin breeches, blue stockings, footed with lighter coloured yarn than the legs, a pair of shoes with strings, lately soaled. Whoever takes up and secures said servant, so that his master may have him again, shall receive the above reward, and reasonable charges paid by    AMER GRUBB.
*The Pennsylvania Ledger: or the Virginia, Maryland, Pennsylvania, & New-Jersey Weekly Advertiser*, April 13, 1776; *The Pennsylvania Gazette*, April 17, 1776; *Dunlap's Pennsylvania Packet or, the General Advertiser*, April 22, 1776; July 29, 1776. Minor differences between the ads. See *The Pennsylvania Gazette*, May 22, 1776; *The Pennsylvania Gazette*, July 3, 1776, and *The Pennsylvania Gazette*, October 9, 1776.

Salem, New-Jersey, March 27, 1776.
THREE POUNDS Reward.
WHEREAS a certain JAMES BELL, about five feet four or five inches high, about 28 years of age, says he taught the light horse in Philadelphia, and at Dover, in Kent County on Delaware, came here, and said he was going to

Philadelphia to buy two stallions, one for Samuel Chew, Esq; at Dover, and the other for himself, and hired a horse of the subscriber, with a half worn saddle; the horse is about 14 hands high, 14 years old, a deep bay, with a star in his forehead, and is lame in stifle joint: Whoever secures the said horse shall have Forty Shillings, and for Bell, so that he may be brought to justice, Twenty Shillings, paid by     GEORGE DUNN.
*The Pennsylvania Gazette*, April 17, 1776.

### EIGHT DOLLARS Reward.

*RUN away, on the 20th of December, 1775, from the subscriber, living in Mill-creek Hundred, New-Castle county, an Irish servant woman, named* Catherine Finnety, *about 22 years of age, a middle sized woman, fair complexion; had on a red and white calicoe gown, a black silk cloak, and a black silk hat.*

*Likewise, from the same person, on the 2d of April, 1776, an Irish servant man, named Joseph Finnety, by trade a Cooper, 5 feet 5 inches high, fair hair, his beard a little sandy; had on a light cloth outside jacket, and a dark brown under jacket, brown velvet breeches; took with him a horse, bridle and saddle, the horse a dark gray, about 14 hands high, 11 years old.*

*Whoever takes up said servants, shall have for the woman Four Dollars, and for the man and horse Eight Dollars,*
    *paid by*   WILLIAM BRACKIN.
*The Pennsylvania Gazette*, April 17, 1776.

Newcastle county, Fourth Month 18th, 1776.
### FORTY SHILLINGS Reward.

RAN away last night, from the subscribers living near Brandywine bridge, two Irish servant women. One named MARGARET FERGUSSON, about forty years of age, tall and lusty, stoops in her shoulders, and has short light or sandy coloured hair. The other named MARY CAULFIELD, twenty-four years of age, of low stature, but thick and strong built, with black or dark brown hair. Had on and took with them, one camblet riding habit faced with blue pelong, one old taffaty gown of a straw colour, one other cotton and linen gown of a light green colour, two callico and one linsey short gowns, three striped linsey petticoats, a black quilt, a gray coating cloak without a cape, each a black bonnet, one low the other high heeled shoes.

Any person securing the said servants so that their masters may have them again, shall be entitled to the above reward, and reasonable charge.
    WILLIAM STARN, and JOSEPH TATNALL.

*The Pennsylvania Evening Post,* April 20, 1776; April 30, 1776. See *Dunlap's Pennsylvania Packet or, the General Advertiser,* April 22, 1776, and *The Pennsylvania Gazette,* April 24, 1776.

*Newcastle County,* 4th month 18th, 1776.
FORTY SHILLINGS REWARD.
RAN AWAY last night, from the subscriber, living near Brandywine Bridge, two Irish servant women, one named MARGARET FORGASON, about 40 years of age, tall and lusty, stoop shouldered, with short light or sandy coloured hair. The other named MARY CAULFIELD, 24 years of age, of low stature but thick and strong built, with black or dark brown hair. Had on and took with them, one camblet riding habit faced with blue peelong, one old taffaty gown of a straw colour, one cotton and linen ditto of a light green colour, two calico and one lincey short gowns, three striped lincey petticoats, a black quilt, a grey coating cloak without a cape, each a black bonnet, one low and the other high heeled shoes, &c. Any person securing the said servant so that their masters may have them again, shall be entitled to the above Reward, and reasonable charges, paid by
WILLIAM STARR, and JOSEPH TATNALL.
*Dunlap's Pennsylvania Packet or, the General Advertiser,* April 22, 1776; July 29, 1776. See *The Pennsylvania Gazette,* April 24, 1776, and *The Pennsylvania Evening Post,* April 20, 1776.

*New Castle County, Fourth-Month* 18, 1776.
FORTY SHILLINGS REWARD.
RUN away last night, from the subscribers, living near Brandywine Bridge, two Irish servant women, one named *Margaret Ferguson,* about 40 years of age, tall and lusty, stoop shouldered, with short light or sandy coloured hair. The other named *Mary Caulfield,* 24 years of age, of low stature, but thick and strongly built, with black or dark brown hair; had on, and took with them, one camblet riding habit, faced with blue peelong, one old taffaty gown, of a straw colour, one other cotton and linen gown, of a light green colour, two calicoe and one lincey short gown, 3 striped lincey petticoats, a black quilt, a grey coating cloak, without a cape, each a black bonnet, one low the other high heeled shoes, &c. Any person securing the said servants, so that their masters may have them again, shall be entitled to the above reward, and reasonable charges,
paid by WILLIAM STARR, and JOSEPH TATNALL.
*The Pennsylvania Gazette,* April 24, 1776; May 12, 1776. See *The Pennsylvania Evening Post,* April 20, 1776, and *Dunlap's Pennsylvania Packet or, the General Advertiser,* April 22, 1776.

RUN away the 21st of March, at night, from the subscriber, living in Millcreek Hundred, New-Castle county, a Dutch servant man, named *Philip Weaver*, about 28 years of age, pretty thick and well set, black haired, marked with the small-pox; had on, and took with him, a grey serge jacket, with sleeves, and an old cloth ditto, new light coloured homespun cloth breeches, with strings at the knees of broad worsted binding, new shoes, two pair of old yarn stockings, a new wool hat, two half worn shirts. Whoever takes up said servant, and secures him, so that his master may get him again, shall have *Thirty Shillings* reward, paid by　　WILLIAM MARSHALL.
　　*The Pennsylvania Gazette*, May 1, 1776.


RUN away on the night of the 25th day of April last, from the subscriber, living in Upper Alloways Creek Township, in the county of Salem, West New Jersey, a servant lad, named JAMES ALLCORN, this country born, about 17 years of age, small of his age, slim built, black straight hair, had on when he went away, a woollen blue cap with some white stripes, an old grey bearskin jacket, with one shirt tore off, a new tow cloth shirt, trowsers of the same, old blue stockings, a pair of old shoes too large for him and been soaled, with brass buckles. Whoever takes up said servant and brings him to his master, or secures him in any goal, so that his master may have him again, shall have five dollars reward, and reasonable charges,
　　　　paid by　　JACOB HOUSEMAN.
N. B. It is supposed he went off with his brother William Allcorn, as he was seen skulking about the plantation some days before, supposed for an opportunity to get him away, and the said William is likewise supposed to be a runaway, as he was a servant not long since to one Mr. Keen, a butcher in Wilmington.
　　*The Pennsylvania Gazette*, May 8, 1776.


　　　　　　　　　FIVE POUNDS Reward.
*RUN away, the 2d of April last, from the subscriber, living in Brandywine Hundred, New Castle County, a Dutch servant lad, named* Henry Nibble, *about 20 years of age, about 5 feet 6 or 7 inches high with light coloured straight hair; had on, when he went away a half-worn wool hat, a half worn light coloured cloth jacket, without skirts a new lincey under jacket, black and white coloured, an old tow shirt, buckskin breeches, blue stockings, footed with lighter coloured yarn than the legs, a pair of shoes with strings lately soaled. Whoever takes up and secures said servant, so that his master may have him again, shall receive the above reward and reasonably charges,*
　　　　　paid by　　AMER GRUBB.

*The Pennsylvania Gazette*, May 22, 1776. See *The Pennsylvania Ledger: or the Virginia, Maryland, Pennsylvania, & New-Jersey Weekly Advertiser*, April 13, 1776, *The Pennsylvania Gazette*, July 3, 1776, and *The Pennsylvania Gazette*, October 9, 1776.


RUN away from the subscriber living near Newcastle, on Friday the seventeenth day of this instant, a pale complexioned negro man, nearly the colour of a mulatto, about twenty-six years of age, and about five feet seven inches high. Had on, when he went away a tow shirt and trowsers, both new, a lead coloured jacket, and old pair of shoes and felt hat nearly half worn. He was born near Indian river, and has frequently run from his former masters to that place. He commonly goes by the name of Jacob Perkins, and without people are very cautious will pass for a freeman.

Any person apprehending him so that his master may have him again, shall receive a reward of three pounds and reasonable charges
paid by    JOHN ANDERSON.
*The Pennsylvania Journal, and the Weekly Advertiser*, May 29, 1776; June 26, 1776; July 17, 1776.


TEN POUNDS REWARD.

Ran away from the subscriber's Plantation in Sussex County on Delaware, on the 8th day of April, 1775; a black Negro Wench, by name SARAH, about 40 years of age, well made, about 5 feet 5 or 6 inches high, with tolerable thick lips and a down look, had remarkable long wool on top of her head: had, and took with her, sundry good home made cloaths. The above Reward will be paid to any person who will deliver the said wench to the subscriber, living in Snow-hill-Town, Worcester County, Maryland, or to Burton Waples, living in Sussex County aforesaid; or EIGHT POUNDS if confined in any goal, so that the subscriber may get her again, will all reasonable charges paid by the public's humble servant,
NATHANIEL WAPLES.

N. B. It is supposed she left the county aforesaid about the letter [*sic*] end of October, or the first of November last, with a Negro fellow, named PETER, belonging to Thomas Robinson of the county aforesaid, who ran away about that time; he is about 20 years of age, a thick well set fellow, and about 5 feet 6 inches high, it is imagined he had about 6 or 10*l.* cash, and well cloathed; he has remarkable hairy temple locks, unless cut off by shaving. It is well know that the said wench was harboured and kept by the fellow aforesaid during the interval aforesaid, and it is supposed she was with child when she ran away, by said fellow, and that they will try to pass for free Negroes, as husband and wife.    N WAPLES.

*The Pennsylvania Journal, and the Weekly Advertiser*, May 29, 1776; June 12, 1776; June 19, 1776; July 17, 1776; August 7, 1776; August 28, 1776; September 11, 1776; September 25, 1776; October 2, 1776. Ads from July 17, 1776 on show her age as "20" and end with "She can read." See *Dunlap's Pennsylvania Packet or, the General Advertiser*, June 3, 1776.


### TEN POUNDS REWARD.

*RAN AWAY from the subscriber's Plantation in Sussex County, on Delaware, on the 8th day of April,* 1775, *a Negro wench named SARAH, about twenty years of age, well made, about five feet five or six inches high, with tolerable thick lips and a down look, had remarkable long wool on her head for a Negro, which she usually tied on the top:* Had on and took with her, sundry good home-made cloaths. The above Reward will be paid to any person who will deliver the said wench to the subscriber, living in Snow hill Town, Worcester County, Maryland, or to Burton Waples, living in Sussex County aforesaid; or EIGHT POUNDS if confined in any gaol, so that the subscriber may get her again, will all reasonable charges
         paid by   NATHANIEL WAPLES.

N. B. It is supposed she left the county aforesaid about the latter end of October or the first of November last, with a Negro fellow named PETER, belonging to Thomas Robinson, of the county aforesaid, who ran away about that time: He is about twenty years of age, a thick, well set fellow, and about five feet six inches high; it is imagined he had about 6 or 8*l.* cash, and well cloathed: He has remarkable hairy temple locks, unless cut off by shaving. It is well know that the said wench was harboured and kept by the fellow aforesaid during the interval aforesaid, and it is supposed she was with child by said fellow when she ran away, and that they will try to pass for free Negroes, as husband and wife.

*Dunlap's Pennsylvania Packet or, the General Advertiser*, June 3, 1776; July 2, 1776; July 22, 1776. See *The Pennsylvania Journal, and the Weekly Advertiser*, May 29, 1776.


*Philadelphia, May* 30, 1776.
WAS committed to my custody, about the tenth day of April last, a certain ANN FRY, supposed to be a runaway servant, belonging to William Kelley, of New Castle. This is to give notice to her master to come, pay charges and take her away, otherwise she will be sold, in three weeks from this date, for the same, by   THOMAS DEWEES, Goaler.

*The Pennsylvania Gazette*, June 5, 1776.

FOUR DOLLARS REWARD.

RAN AWAY from the subscriber, living at Duck Creek Cross Roads, in Kent County on Delaware, on the 8th of May last, an Irish servant girl named ELIZABETH BUCKLY, about twenty-seven years of age, five feet six or seven inches high, much marked with the small-pox, fair hair and complexion, long nose, a good set of teeth, grey eyes, and was born in Corke; had on and took with her, a long purple calico gown, two striped linen short gowns and one lincey ditto, two old black quilts, two lincey petticoats, one flowered lawn apron, one old check ditto, a black bonnet with lace round the edge, a pair of leather shoes and plated buckles, and a red cloth cloak with a cap: She is supposed to have followed the soldiers towards Philadelphia. Whoever takes up the said servant and secures her in any gaol, so that her master may have her again, shall receive the above Reward and all reasonable charge, paid by JOHN FOUDRAY.

*Dunlap's Pennsylvania Packet or, the General Advertiser*, June 17, 1776; July 28, 1776; July 29, 1776.

*June* 17, 1776.

NOW in the gaol of Newcastle, the following run-away servants, viz. JOHN JACOB PLOWMAN, who confesses himself to be an indented servant to a certain James Porter, but cannot tell where his master lives, as he talks the German dialect. JOHN LANGLEY, about nineteen years of age, who says he belongs to Nathan Shepherd, of Cumberland County, West-Jersey. Their masters are requested to come and take them away in three weeks from the date hereof, otherwise they will be discharged according to law.

THOMAS CLARK, Gaoler.

*Dunlap's Pennsylvania Packet or, the General Advertiser*, June 24, 1776; July 1, 1778; July 8, 1776; August 5, 1776.

*Brandywine Hundred, New Castle County, June* 24, 1776.
EIGHT DOLLARS Reward.

RUN away, last night, from the subscriber, living near Wilmington, a Dutch servant lad, named *Henry France Nible*, about twenty years of age, 5 feet 6 or 7 inches high, a chunky well set fellow, fair complexion, light coloured hair, smooth faced; had on, when he went away, an old beaver hat, old light coloured cloth jacket, without skirts, a red and white striped lincey jacket under it, a tow shirt, and two pair of tow trowsers, old shoes, tied with strings; it is probable he may get a pass forged; it is likely he may pass by the name of *Henry France* only; he ran away in April last, and was advertised in the Pennsylvania Gazette, after which he was taken. Whoever secures said servant, so that his master may have him again, shall have the above reward, paid by AMOR GRUBB.

*The Pennsylvania Gazette*, July 3, 1776; July 17, 1776. See *The Pennsylvania Ledger: or the Virginia, Maryland, Pennsylvania, & New-Jersey Weekly Advertiser*, April 13, 1776, *The Pennsylvania Gazette*, May 22, 1776, and *The Pennsylvania Gazette*, October 9, 1776.

### FOUR DOLLARS REWARD.

RAN AWAY from the subscriber, living near Cantwell's Bridge, New-Castle County, on the 4th inst. (July) an apprentice lad named BENJAMIN MERCER, about 19 years of age, 5 feet 2 inches high, well made, a smooth round face, fair complexion, wore his hair tied: Had on and took with him, a blue cloth coat, a striped Damascus vest, a brown stuff ditto, a pair of old buckskin breeches, a pair of white drilling ditto, three home made linen shirts, one new, and one Irish linen ditto, marked I. F. a country made felt hat; by trade a shoemaker, he took a sickle with him. Whoever takes up and secures said apprentice so that his master may get him again, shall have the above Reward and reasonable charges,
        paid by    ROBERT MELDRUM.

N. B. All masters of vessels are forbid to harbour or carry him off at their peril, as it is thought he will endeavour to get on board a privateer.

*Dunlap's Pennsylvania Packet or, the General Advertiser*, July 22, 1776; August 22, 1776.

### TWENTY SHILLINGS REWARD.

RAN AWAY from the subscriber living in the township of East Nottingham, south of the Pennsylvania line and formerly of Chester county, on the 28th day of June, an Irish Servant Girl, named MARGARET SMITH, supposed to be about 26 years of age, about 5 feet high, of a dark complexion, small tender grey eyes, very much marked with the small pox, has made a proactive of running away from her former masters, and was bought out of New-Castle Goal by one David Jenkins, she is supposed to be with child Had on and took with her one brown calimanco quilt, one chintz short gown lines with India calicoe, one white linen handkerchief, a white straw hat and two tow aprons, she may have other cloaths not yet known. Whoever secures said servant, so that her Master may get her again, shall have the above reward and reasonable charges if brought home, paid by    EDWARD PARKE.

N. B. She is very much inclined to smoaking.

*The Pennsylvania Journal, and the Weekly Advertiser*, July 24, 1776; August 28, 1776.

*Kent County, on Delaware, July* 12, 1776.
THREE POUNDS Reward.
RUN AWAY from the subscriber, on the 5th instant, a Negroe man, who calls himself *Moses Graves*, 30 years of age, about 6 feet 1 inch high, slender made, thin visage, smooth face; had on, and took with him, a pale blue coat, only faced, a red coating vest, lined with flannel, it is too large for him, two shirts, and two pair of trowsers, almost new flax and tow, one white shirt and stock, new shoes, and cotton stockings. Whoever takes up the said Negroe, and secures him in any goal, shall receive the above reward, and reasonable charges, paid by     HENRY STEVENS.

*The Pennsylvania Gazette*, July 31, 1776; August 21, 1776; September 4, 1776.


WAS committed to Dover gaol, in Kent county, on Delaware, the 15th instant, a certain salt water Negro, who calls himself SAMBO; he has on a striped woolen jacket with sleeves, a pair of short homespun two trowsers; he is about thirty-five years of age, and says he is the property of James Black.—The master of said Negro is desired to come immediately and pay the charges and take him away, or else he will be sold out for his prison charges.      THOMAS WILD, Gaoler.
N. B. The said Negro has a lump in his forehead, and a large scar on the side of his head.      *June* 27.

*The Pennsylvania Journal, and the Weekly Advertiser*, August 14, 1776.


*York Goal, August 5, 1776.*
*LAST week was committed to my custody, a dark coloured Mulattoe, about 5 feet 9 inches high, strong and well made, aged 24 years in December last; he says he is a freeman, that his name is Jacob Johnston, his mother's name was Darcus Perkins, at Accomack, in Virginia, that she was a white woman, that Mr. Thomas Kirkly, in Kent, and Doctor Ridgley, in Dover, know him to be a freeman, that he laboured in that county about three months in the spring of 1775, from thence he moved to Conestogoe, worked with John and Joseph Miller, from thence to William Read in this county, where he was taken up, &c.*

*Also Thomas Gathen, who saith he run from Lee Masters, at Little Pipe-Creek Furnace, Maryland.*

*Their Masters, if they have any, are hereby desired to come and take them away, in four weeks from the date hereof, or they will be disposed of to pay their fees.*      MICHAEL GRAYBILL, Goaler.

*The Pennsylvania Gazette*, August 21, 1776; August 28, 1776.

Dover, July 29, 1776.

WAS committed the 28th of July, 1776, to Dover goal, in Kent County on Delaware, a MULATTO MAN, who calls himself TIM, tho' very likely, he might have changed his name as he appears to be a great rogue: he says he belongs to John Boon of Maryland: Had on when committed, a snuff coloured cloth coat, tow trowsers, an old white shirt. His master, if any he has, is desired to come, pay charges, and take him away, otherwise he will be sold for his fees, within five weeks from the date hereof.
    THOMAS WILD, Goaler.
*The Pennsylvania Journal, and the Weekly Advertiser*, August 21, 1776; September 4, 1776; September 18, 1776.


FOUR DOLLARS REWARD.

RAN AWAY on the 7th of August last, from the subscriber, living near Middletown, Newcastle, an Irish servant boy named HENRY LIVINGSTON, about sixteen years of age, thick and well set, of a fair complexion, fair hair, a big mouth and thick lips, has a scar on his nose between his eyes, is pretty talkative and can sing middling well; had on when he went away, a home-made tow shirt and trowsers, and an old hat with the crown much torn: It is thought he made towards Philadelphia in order to get on board some vessel, or to make to the camp at York. Whoever takes up said boy and secures him in any gaol, so that his master may get him again, shall have the above Reward, and if brought home reasonable charges,
  paid by   JAMES COCHRAN.
*Dunlap's Pennsylvania Packet or, the General Advertiser*, September 3, 1776.


RUN away from the subscriber, living in St. George's Hundred, a Negroe Man named CUFF, about 22 years of age, 5 feet 6 inches high, had on and took with him two tow shirts, 1 fine linen ditto, 2 pair of trowsers, 1 tow, the other striped linen much worn, a light blue coat mixt with red, a snuff coloured coat, velvet jacket, with clear buttons, a pair of light coloured knit pattern breeches; he is remarkably full eyed, and long hair. Whoever secures said Negroe, so that his master may get him again, shall have Eight Dollars reward, and reasonable charges,
*September* 1.  paid by   WILLIAM READ.
*The Pennsylvania Gazette*, September 4, 1776; September 25, 1776.


RUN away, the 19th day of the First-Month last, from Josiah Hibberd, of East Whiteland township, in Chester county, an indented servant girl, named

*Barbara Abercrombie*, a Scotch woman, she is bulky and well set, of a fair complexion, dark brown hair, about 27 years of age, speaks in the Scotch dialect; had on, and took with her, a short jacket and petticoat, of brown flannel, one petticoat of blue Bristol stuff, a red and white striped lincey ditto, a check apron, two handkerchiefs, one blue and white, the other red and white, a pair of leather heeled shoes, with sundry other things not remembered; she commonly wears a red and white ribbon on a laced cap, is supposed to be in or near Philadelphia, and was advertised some time since in the Evening Post. As I the subscriber have purchased her time of the above named Josiah Hibberd, do therefore offer a reward of *Three Pounds* to any person that will secure her in any goal on the continent, and inform me thereof; or *Four Pounds*, if brought home to my house in Wilmington, in the county of New-Castle, on Delaware, with reasonable expences,
          paid by    CALEB SHEWARD.
*The Pennsylvania Gazette*, September 11, 1776.


          FIFTEEN DOLLARS REWARD.
RAN AWAY from the subscriber's plantation, in St. Georges Hundred, New Castle County, a negro man named BEN; he is about five feet six or eight inches high, well set, much marked with the small pox, and his head grey: Had on and took with him two kersey jackets, tow shirt and trowsers, coarse woollen stockings, old shoes, and an old hat. He has a brother, a free man, who lives near Dover, Kent upon Delaware, and is supposed to have gone that way. Whoever takes up and secures said fellow, so that I may get him again, shall receive FIVE DOLLARS, and reasonable charges if brought home.         Wm. MATTHEWS.
*Dunlap's Pennsylvania Packet or, the General Advertiser*, September 17, 1776.


          *Lancaster Goal, September* 30, 1776.
WAS committed to my custody, a certain Negroe man, who calls himself *William*, and says he is the property of Mr. John Coxon, of Frederick county, Maryland. Also a certain *John Brown*, alias Henry France Nible, supposed to be a runaway servant from Mr. Amor Grubb, by whom he is particularly described in his advertisement. And a certain *Benjamin Simmons*, who confesses himself a servant to Thomas Owings, in Baltimore county, Maryland, by whom he has been advertised the 19th instant. The respective masters of the said servants, and Negroe, are desired to come, in three weeks from the date hereof, pay charges, and take them away, otherwise they will be discharged, on paying their fees,
          by PETER RIBLET, Goaler.

*The Pennsylvania Gazette*, October 9, 1776; October 16, 1776; October 23, 1776. See *The Maryland Journal; and the Baltimore Advertiser*, September 25, 1776, for Simmons. See *The Pennsylvania Ledger: or the Virginia, Maryland, Pennsylvania, & New-Jersey Weekly Advertiser*, April 13, 1776, *The Pennsylvania Gazette*, May 22, 1776, *The Pennsylvania Gazette*, July 3, 1776, for Nible/Nibble.

FOUR DOLLARS REWARD.

RUN-AWAY the 20th ult, from the subscriber living in Kent County, on Delaware, a salt water Negro man named BROWN, talks bad English, about five feet eleven inches high: Had on when he went away, an old white twilled jacket, a brown ditto without sleeves, one striped ditto, a pair of tow trowsers, two tow shirts, a pair of half worn shoes, one felt hat half-worn: It is thought he has crossed over to the Jerseys and tells people that he is free.—Whoever takes up said Negro, and secures him in any goal, or brings him to his master, shall have the above reward and reasonable expences,
 paid by    CHARLES CAHOON.

*The Pennsylvania Journal, and the Weekly Advertiser*, October 9, 1776; October 23, 1776; October 30, 1776.

SIX DOLLARS Reward.

MADE his escape from the goal of the county of New Castle, a Negroe man, named CUFF DIX, belonging to Mark Bird, and by him advertised in the Pennsylvania Journal the 14th of August last; he is an active, well made fellow, and a good hammerman, about 5 feet 5 or 6 inches high, fond of liquor, and stammers a little in his speech; there is an iron ring in one of his ears; he had on a light coloured jacket, and tow shirt and trowsers. He has frequently run away from his master, and often confined in the several goals of the province; as he is an artful fellow, the person apprehending him is desired to take particular care of him; he has often denied his name, and pretends to be a freeman. Whoever secures him, so that he may be had again, shall have the above reward, and reasonable charges.
*October* 11, 1776.          THOMAS CLARK, Goaler.

*The Pennsylvania Gazette*, October 16, 1776; November 6, 1776. See *The Pennsylvania Gazette*, March 12, 1777.

EIGHT DOLLARS REWARD.

RAN AWAY last January, from the subscriber, living in Kent County on Delaware, a Mulatto slave named PETER BROWN, about 45 years of age, 5

feet 8 inches high, chews tobacco; he has passed for a freeman, and worked about Germantown and Schuylkill last spring and summer; in September he was taken up in Germantown and put on board a shallop at Philadelphia to be sent to his master, but made his escape the same night. Whoever takes up said Mulatto and secures him in Dover Gaol, or in Philadelphia Gaol or Work-house, shall receive the above Reward and reasonable charges from
  JAMES HUNTER, Merchant, in Philadelphia,
    or from his master, THOMAS IRONS.
*Dunlap's Pennsylvania Packet or, the General Advertiser*, November 12, 1776. See *The Pennsylvania Evening Post*, November 14, 1776, and *The Pennsylvania Journal, and the Weekly Advertiser*, November 13, 1776.

      EIGHT DOLLARS REWARD.
  RAN AWAY last January, from the subscriber, living in Kent
       county on Delaware,
A MULATTO SLAVE named Peter Brown, about forty-five years of age, five feet eight inches high, chews tobacco; he has past for a free man, and worked about Germantown and Schuylkill last spring and summer, in September he was taken up in Germantown and put on board a shallop at Philadelphia, to be sent to his master, but made his escape the same night. Whoever takes up said Mulatto and secures him in Dover goal, or in Philadelphia goal or work house, shall receive the above reward and reasonable charges from JAMES HUNTER, Merchant, Philadelphia,
    or me, master, THOMAS IRONS.
*The Pennsylvania Journal, and the Weekly Advertiser*, November 13, 1776; November 27, 1776; February 5, 1777. See *Dunlap's Pennsylvania Packet or, the General Advertiser*, November 12, 1776, and *The Pennsylvania Evening Post*, November 14, 1776.


RAN away last January from the subscriber, living in Kent county on Delaware, a Mulatto slave named PETER BROWN, about forty-five years of age, five feet eight inches high, chews tobacco. He has passed for a freeman, and worked about Germantown and Schuylkill last springand summer. In September he was taken up in Germantown, and put on board a shallop at Philadelphia, to be sent to his master, but made his escape the same night. Whoever takes up said Mulatto, and secures him in Dover jail, or in Philadelphia jail or workhouse, shall receive EIGHT DOLLARS Reward, and reasonable charges from James Hunter, merchant in Philadelphia,
    or from his master, THOMAS IRONS.
*The Pennsylvania Evening Post*, November 14, 1776; November 19, 1776; November 28, 1776. See *Dunlap's Pennsylvania Packet or, the*

*General Advertiser*, November 12, 1776, and *The Pennsylvania Journal, and the Weekly Advertiser*, November 13, 1776.

WAS committed to the goal of Dover, in Kent county, on Delaware, a Negro MAN, who calls his name HARRY, about 21 years of age, about 5 feet 6 inches high; has on, a short brown coat, home-spun trowsers, a straw hat, and new shoes: He says he belongs to Sandy Lawson, near Baltimore town. This is to desire the owner to come, pay charges, and take him out, otherwise he will be sold out for his fees, by me     THOMAS WILD, Goaler.
*The Pennsylvania Journal, and the Weekly Advertiser*, November 20, 1776; January 29, 1777.

## 1777

RUN away from the subscriber, living in Newcastle, on the 29th ult. an Irish servant lad, named JAMES M'MULLIN, about 17 or 18 years of age, 5 feet 6 or 7 inches high, made, slender thin visage, brown hair, a remarkable short nose turned up, speaks with the brogue, and has had the ague this long time past; had on when went away, an old brown coat with a red velvet collar, an old blue surtout coat, spotted flannel jacket, tow shirts, claret coloured cloth breeches, a pair of new black stockings and new shoes, one brass buckle, the other tied with a string, and an old beaver hat. Whoever takes up and secures said servant, so that his master may get him again, shall have THREE DOLLARS reward, paid by     JOHN ENOS.
*The Pennsylvania Gazette*, February 5, 1777; February 12, 1777; February 19, 1777.

*New-Castle, March 2, 1777.*
NOW in the Goal of New-Castle on Delaware, a certain NEGROE Man, named *CUFF DICKS*, the Property of Colonel MARK BIRD, of Birdsberry, Berks County, Pennsylvania, who is requested to come, pay charges, and take him away.     THOMAS CLARK, Goaler.
*The Pennsylvania Gazette*, March 12, 1777; March 19, 1777. See *Dunlap's Pennsylvania Packet or, the General Advertiser*, March 18, 1777, and *The Pennsylvania Gazette*, March 19, 1777.

*New-Castle, March 15th, 1777.*
FORTY EIGHT DOLLARS REWARD.
BROKE out of the jail of this county, on Friday night, the 14th instant, the following persons, viz. WILLIAM JOHNSON, 5 feet 9 inches high, fair complexion, long white hair tied behind, one of his foreteeth in his upper jaw lost, the fore and middle fingers of one of his hands off at the first joint, talks

with the Scotch accent; committed for burglary. ROBERT HENRY, 5 feet 10 inches high, well set, born in this country, black hair, by trade a weaver; committed for theft. ARCHIBALD M'MICHAEL, 5 feet 7 inches high, well set, born in Ireland, by trade a taylor; had on a blue coat trimed with red, the buttons marked D. B. committed for assault. A negro man named TOM, 5 feet 11 inches high, very black, large mouth, big feet, small legs, the back of his right hand scar'd [*sic*] where he has been short; committed for theft. A negro man named CUFF DICKS, well set, 5 feet 7 inches high, a small hole in one of his ears large enough to receive the small end of a pipe stem; stammers in his speech. Whoever secures the above-mentioned prisoners in any goal, in the United States, shall receive the above reward, or Eight Dollars for each.         JOHN CLARK, Sheriff.

*Dunlap's Pennsylvania Packet or, the General Advertiser*, March 18, 1777. See *The Pennsylvania Gazette*, March 12, 1777, for Dicks. See *The Pennsylvania Gazette*, March 19, 1777, for all of them.

Back Creek, March 7, 1777.

STOLEN, on Wednesday morning last, out of the Subscriber's Stable, at Back Creek Landing, a small chestnut brown MARE, about 14 hands high, three white feet, a star in her forehead, trots and gallops. She is supposed to be stolen by a certain William Glenn, who formerly lived about Wilmington; he is a man about 6 feet high, able bodied, claret coloured coat, pale red jacket, clouded stockings, leather breeches, new shoes, and plated buckles; has a few cuts lately received on, and wears a handkerchief round, his head. Whoever takes up and secures the said thief brought to justice, shall receive *Thirty Dollars*; for the mare alone, *Ten Dollars*; and for the thief, if punished *Twenty Dollars*, paid by     THOMAS WERT.

*The Pennsylvania Gazette*, March 19, 1777. See *The Maryland Journal and Baltimore Advertiser*, April 22, 1777, and *Dunlap's Pennsylvania Packet or, the General Advertiser*, July 1, 1777.

*New-Castle, March* 15, 1777.
FORTY-EIGHT DOLLARS Reward.

BROKE the goal of this county, on Friday night, the 14th instant, the following prisoners, viz.

*William Johnson*, 5 feet 9 inches high, fair complexion, long white hair, tied behind, lost one of the fore teeth of his upper jaw, the fore and middle fingers of one of his hands off at the first joint, talks with the Scots accent; committed for burglary.

*Robert Henry*, 5 feet 10 inches, dark complexion, long black hair, tied behind, talks much on the Scots accent, committed for burglary.

*William Cochran*, 5 feet 6 inches, well set, black haired, this country born, by trade a Weaver; committed for theft.

*Archibald M'Michael*, 5 feet 7 inches, well set, born in Ireland, by trade a Taylor; had on a blue coat, turned up with red, the buttons marked, D.B.; committed for an assault.

One Negroe Man, named *Tom*, 5 feet 11 inches, a very black, large mouth, large feet, small legs, the back of his right hand scarred, where he has been shot with small shot; committed for theft. Also a Negroe Man, named Cuff Dicks, well set, 5 feet 7 inches, a small hold in one of his ears, large enough to receive the small end of a pipe stem, and stammers in his speech.

Whoever secures the above described prisoners, in any of the goals of the United States, shall receive the above reward, or Eight Dollars each.

JOHN CLARK, Sheriff.

*The Pennsylvania Gazette*, March 19, 1777. *The Pennsylvania Gazette*, March 12, 1777, for Dicks. See *Dunlap's Pennsylvania Packet or, the General Advertiser*, March 18, 1777 for all of them.

*Brandywine Hundred, Third Month* 18, 1777.
ON second day, the 10th instant, a fleshy, likely, dark haired woman, who appeared to be about 25 years of age, supposed to be this country born, came to the house of the subscriber, near Brandywine Bridge, and brought with her for sale a small Remnant of Broadcloth of a snuff colour, and two Remnants of Shalloon, near the same colour, and being questioned how she came by them, she said, her father got them from a Taylor that had broke, and gave £ 3: 10: 0 per yard for the cloth; and upon being examined where she lived, she gave different accounts to different people that asked her; she said she lived beyond Concord, and to other she said it was near Kennet Square, which gave reason to suspect her, and the things were detained until she should give a satisfactory account how she came by them; the day was fixed and is elapsed, and I have not heard from her since; she rode a small bay Gelding, hunting saddle, quilted buckskin seat: This is therefore to request the said young woman to come and take her things away, if she came honestly by them, if not to let the right owner know where to find them; who, upon proving his or their property, and paying charges, shall have them again.

SAMUEL MARSHALL.

*N. B.* I did not take notice of her clothes, only that she had a red short cloak.

*The Pennsylvania Gazette*, March 26, 1777, April 2, 1777.

FORTY DOLLARS REWARD.

STOLEN, on Wednesday morning, the 5th of March, out of the subscriber's stable, at Back Creek Landing, a small chesnut-brown MARE, about 14

hands high, has three white feet, a star in her forehead, trots and gallops; supposed to be stolen by a certain William Glenn, who formerly lived about Wilmington; a down-looking ill featured scoundrel; his eyes are not fellows, one being blue and the other grey; he is about 6 feet high, able-bodied, wears a claret-coloured coat, pale red jacket, clouded stockings, cloth breeches, new shoes, and plated buckles; has a few cuts on his head, lately received, and wears a handkerchief round his head; he will, however, it is probable, endeavour to conceal his wounds. Whoever recovers said Mare, and returns her to the subscriber, or delivers her to Mr. Grant, or to the Printer hereof, in Baltimore, shall receive TWENTY DOLLARS reward, and TWENTY more for apprehending and securing the Thief, so that he may be brought to justice. The reward will be paid by the Printer hereof, or by me
    THOMAS WERT.

 N. B. The Mare, it is said, has, by an exchange, got into the possession of a military officer, in the neighbourhood of Carlisle.

*The Maryland Journal and Baltimore Advertiser*, April 22, 1777. See *The Pennsylvania Gazette*, March 19, 1777, *Dunlap's Pennsylvania Packet or, the General Advertiser*, July 1, 1777.

           Philadelphia, April 9, 1777.
RAN away this morning, from the subscriber, living in Fourth-street, two apprentices; one named THOMAS PEACOCK, born in Pequea township, Lancaster county, about fifteen years of age, near five feet high, pale complexion, and light brown hair cut short; he had on a short brown coatee with gilt buttons, light coloured serge jacket and breeches, dark worsted ribbed stockings, strong shoes almost new, old beaver hat, and an old coarse shirt.

 The name of the other is JOSEPH ENOS, born at New-castle upon Delaware, about thirteen years of age, light hair tied behind, very small, but forward and talkative; he had on a light coloured cloth jacket with wooden buttons and sleeves not quite of the same colour as the body, old brown under vest lined with green, light coloured cloth breeches, one pair of white and another of blue yarn stockings, two new brown linen shirts, and a half worn beaver hat. Whoever secures said boys, so that I get them again, shall have Eight Dollars reward, or Four Dollars for each, and reasonable charges.
    JOHN MARTIN, tailor.

*The Pennsylvania Evening Post*, April 22, 1777.


WHEREAS an indented servant girl named JANE GRAY, belonging to Mr. George Gordon of Wilmington, in the Delaware state, did run away on or about the first instant, and made her escape to this city, where she was apprehended and committed to the workhouse, as she refused to return home.

The subscriber was desired to send her back, but she took the opportunity to make her escape from him on the 25th instant. She is a slim, ordinary face girl, much pitted with the smallpox, about eighteen or twenty years of age, and dark brown hair. She had on a light ground calico gown, linsey petticoat, cross barred silk handkerchief, and a pair of mens shoes. Whoever apprehends said servant, and secures her so that her master or the subscriber gets her again, shall have Eight Dollars reward, and if brought home reasonable charges by George Gordon of Wilmington, or by the subscriber living in Water-street, a little below the Drawbridge.
Philad. April 29.          ALEXANDER GRAHAM.
   *The Pennsylvania Evening Post*, April 29, 1777.


RAN away last Tuesday, from the subscriber living in Cecil county, Maryland, an indented servant man named THOMAS M'SURLEY, born in Newcastle county upon Delaware, about twenty-four years of age, very talkative, rather more than six feet high, slender made, brown curly hair, grey eyes, brown complexion, and one of his feet has been braised [sic] by a cart wheel. He is addicted to liquor, and quarrelsome when drunk. He had a brown and white linsey coat, grey kersey jacket, breeches same as the coat, shirt made of country linen, grey stockings, and an old hat patched behind. Whoever brings him to Samuel Baker, hatter in Second-street, near Market-street, or Thomas May at Elk forge, Maryland, shall have Three Dollars reward and reasonable charges.
May 2.            DANIEL BAYLES.
   *The Pennsylvania Evening Post*, May 3, 1777.


COMMITTED to the goal of Dover, in Kent County, on Delaware, a NEGRO MAN, calls his name LOT, about 40 years of age, very poorly cloathed, and appears not to be in his right reason at times; he says he is the property of ROBERT CONKEY, near the Head of Elk, and this is to desire his master to come and take him out immediately, otherwise he will be sold out according to law, by me       THOMAS WILD, Goaler.
   *The Pennsylvania Journal, and the Weekly Advertiser*, May 7, 1777; June 4, 1777.


RAN AWAY from the subscriber living in Wilmington, a Dutch servant woman named LENA KIME, about thirty years of age, five feet high, thin face, and a scar on her nose; she wears a black bonnet lined with pale red; her other clothes unknown, as she took a good many clothes with her. She is

gone with her husband, who is a servant also, and enlisted with Capt. Bartholomew in the Pennsylvania Fifth battalion, commanded by Col. Francis Johnson. It is posed she is gone to Bristol in order to get to the camp with the soldiers, therefore it is hoped all those that keep the ferries, on Delaware will apprehend said servant, or any other person that secures her in Philadelphia work-house, shall have Eight Dollars reward and reasonable charges.         MOSES BRYAN.
Wilmington, Sixth month 3.
*The Pennsylvania Evening Post*, June 3, 1777.


SIX POUNDS REWARD.
RUN-AWAY on the first day of June instant, three NEGROES, two men and one woman, the property of George Shaw of the city of New-York, tanner. One is about six feet high, or upwards, and goes by the name of JAMES RICHARDS, or RICHARDSON, the other negro named HARRY ROBBINS, of a middling stature, yellow complexion, and mighty complaisant in discourse, but very deceitful and given to liquor. The other a negro woman, of a coal black complexion, named ANN, very nimble and brisk on her feet, but bold and impudent behaviour, born in New-Castle county, on Delaware.

The two negro men have entered into his Majesty's service as waggon drivers, and their names are on the Commissary's books, but are my property. Whoever will take up the said negroes, and bring them to me the subscriber, shall have the above reward, or FORTY SHILLINGS for each, and all reasonable charges,   paid by     GEORGE SHAW.

*The New-York Gazette; and the Weekly Mercury*, June 9, 1777; June 30, 1777.


Cumberland county, West New Jersey, July 22, 1777.
SIXTEEN DOLLARS REWARD.
BROKE goal in January last, and this day made an escape from the subscriber, a certain *ELIAS PAWLING*, was born in said county, about 23 years of age, 5 feet 6 or 7 inches high, full faced, black hair, very clumsy walk; had on, when he escaped, a brown sailor jacket, and an under ditto, near the same colour, of German serge, bound with binding something lighter, homespun shirt and trowsers, an old castor hat; his other clothes unknown; he resided last winter in Slater Neck, in Sussex county, on Delaware, and called himself *Elias Johnston.* Whoever takes up the said prisoner, and secures him in any of the States goals, so that the subscriber gets him again, shall have the above reward, and reasonable charges,
           paid by     JOHN SOULLARD, Goaler.

*The Pennsylvania Gazette*, August 6, 1777; August 20, 1777. See *The Pennsylvania Journal, and the Weekly Advertiser*, August 6, 1777.

Cumberland County, West New-Jersey, July 22.
SIXTEEN DOLLARS Reward.
BROKE GOAL in January last, and this day made an escape from the subscriber, a certain ELIAS PAWLING, was born in said county, about 23 years of age, 5 feet 6 or 7 inches high, full faced, black hair, very clumsey walk; had on when he went away, a brown sailor jacket, and an under one near the same colour of German serge, bound with binding something lighter, homespun shirt and trowsers, an old castor hat; his other clothes unknown; he resorted last Winter in Slater Neck, in Sussex county, on Delaware, and called himself Elias Johnson. Whoever takes up said prisoner and secures him in any of the States Goals, so that the subscriber gets him again, shall have the above reward and reasonable charges,
paid by    JOHN SOULLARD, Goaler.
*The Pennsylvania Journal, and the Weekly Advertiser*, August 6, 1777; August 13, 1777. See *The Pennsylvania Gazette*, August 6, 1777.

Cumberland County, West New-Jersey, August 2[1].
FORTY DOLLARS Reward.
This day made their escape out of the goal of said county, the following persons, viz.
THOMAS RIGGON, born in said county, 5 feet 8 or 9 inches high: Had on when he escaped, a white swanskin vest, with sleeves, another without, of broad cloth, the fore-bodies pale blue, the backs deep blue, a half wore Holland shirt with chitterlins at the bosom, and homespun trowsers, but has other good cloaths, such as wiltin coat and velvet breeches, deep blue thread stockings, much flourished in knitting, wears his hair tied, it is remarkably curled all over his head, has a great impediment in his speech. WILLIAM GLAN, born in said county, but brought up in New-Castle county, five feet nine or ten inches high, thin visage, black hair, down look, slender made. Had on when he escaped, coarse homespun shirt and trowsers, his other cloaths unknown. Whoever takes up said prisoners and secures them in any of the state goals, so that the subscriber gets them, shall be entitled to the above reward, or TWENTY DOLLARS for either of them, and reasonable charges
paid, by    JOHN SOULLARD, Goaler.
*The Pennsylvania Journal; and the Weekly Advertiser*, September 3, 1777.

## 1778

CAME to the subscriber's in Christiana Hundred, Newcastle County, in the Delaware State, about three weeks ago, a Negro man, who says his name is Will; a short thick set fellow, pretends to be a tanner and currier, and can do something at the business; he also says that he belongs to one Isaac Harris, near Frederick Town in Virginia, that said Harris sent him with his son Isaac, who he says was First Lieutenant of Capt. Smith's company; that he was at Mud Island till the fort was destroyed, and was then taken prisoner by the enemy and made his escape from them at Newcastle: He is very lame by a hurt he says he got in the fort, and is almost naked. His master is desired to come, prove his property, pay the charges and take him away.
*April* 10 1778.         WILLIAM UNDERWOOD.
*The Pennsylvania Packet or the General Advertiser*, April 22, 1778; May 27, 1778.

*Dover, Kent County, Delaware State, April* 14.
YESTERDAY was committed to the gaol of this County, a Negro man named LONDON, about five feet five inches high, who says he belongs to Capt. James Young, near Chambersburgh, in Cumberland County, State of Pennsylvania. His said master is desired to send for him, pay charges and take him away.         THOMAS WILD, Gaoler.
*The Pennsylvania Packet or the General Advertiser*, May 6, 1778; June 10, 1778.

*Damascus, Red Lion Hundred, March* 20, 1778.
RAN AWAY from the subscriber this day, a Negro wench named DIDO, about 26 tears of age, a stout well looking hussey; when she went off she wore a striped lincey jacket and petticoat, the rest of his dress unknown. It is supposed some evil disposed persons harbour her in St. Georges or Appoquiniminck Hundreds, as her acquaintance lay most in those neighbourhoods. Punishment of the most rigorous kind will be administered to those who are found to harbour or conceal the above described slave: And a reward of FIFTY DOLLARS will be given to any person who will apprehend and secure the said slave in any gaol in the United States, with every reasonable charge, by         HUMPHREY CARSON.
*The Pennsylvania Packet or the General Advertiser*, May 27, 1778.

*One Hundred and Thirty Dollars Reward.*
BROKE loose and ranaway from the subscriber, from the house of Mr. Buchannan, at the sign of the spotted Leopard, in New-Castle county, one Negro man named LONDON, but changes his name to Daniel Anderson; a

cunning artful fellow, passes for a freeman; he is about 5 feet 5 or six inches high, has some old scars occasioned by cuts on his head; he was once the property of Capt. James Black; was taken out of Dover prison lately, and broke away from the above mentioned Buchannan. Whoever takes up said Negro and secures him in any goal, so that his master may get him again, shall have THIRTY DOLLARS, and reasonable charges; or if brought home to the subscriber, living near Chambersburg, Cumberland county, Pennsylvania, shall have ONE HUNDRED DOLLARS.

Likewise a Mulatto fellow named JOHN HILL, a Methodist Preacher, formerly lived in Charleston, Maryland; he passed the above Negro for a freeman at Capt. Ellis's at the head of Bohemia, and it is thought he harbours in Harford county. Whoever secures the said Mulatto in any goal, so that he may be brought to justice, and gives the subscriber notice, shall have THIRTY DOLLARS reward, and reasonable charges,
May 10th, 1778.     paid by     JAMES YOUNG.
*Dunlap's Maryland Gazette Or the Baltimore General Advertiser*, June 16, 1778.

### TEN DOLLARS REWARD.
RAN AWAY from the subscriber, near Newcastle, in February 1777, a servant man named JOHN M'GARVIY, about 22 years of age; had on when he went away, a white coat, jacket and breeches: He was on board the Oliver Cromwell, the owners or Captain of which vessel are requested not to pay him his prize money, he being my servant.
JAMES EVES.
*The Pennsylvania Packet or the General Advertiser*, August 27, 1778.

### FORTY DOLLARS REWARD.
RAN AWAY from the subscriber, living in Red-Lion hundred, Newcastle county, last October, a Negro man named TOM, about 22 years of age, about 5 feet 8 inches high, the fingers of his right hand are stiff and bending into the palm; he has been seen and spoke with since the British army left Philadelphia. Whoever secures said Negro in any gaol on the Continent, giving the subscriber notice thereof, shall receive the above reward, and if delivered to him at St. Georges, reasonable charges,
            paid by     VALENTINE DUSHANE.
*The Pennsylvania Packet or the General Advertiser*, September 5, 1778; September 15, 1778; September 19, 1778.

*Newcastle, ss.*
### FORTY DOLLARS REWARD.

BROKE Gaol last night, the five following persons, viz. WILLIAM BROWN, an Englishman, thirty six years of age, about five feet seven inches high, fair complexion; had on a blanket surtout coat, sheepskin breeches, yarn stockings and calfskin shoes: He belonged to Capt. Anderson's company at the battle of Germantown, is lame of a wound he received in his foot. EDWARD FOULKE, five feet four inches high, is lame in one of his hands, the fingers very much drawn up: he was committed by John Lea, Esq; for stealing 42 yards of linen from John Augusta, of Christiana hundred. A Negro wench named JENNY NICHOLS, twenty years of age, and slim; had on a yellow stuff short gown, a blue and white lincey petticoat, and has a Negro child with her about ten months old: was committed as a partner with said Foulke in stealing the linen. Negro CESAR, says he belongs to John Page, Kent county; he is very black, has a sour look, about forty-five years of age; had on a white cloth jacket with sleeves, red plush breeches, white yarn stockings, old shoes and one odd buckle; he sometimes wore short petticoat trowsers over his breeches. JIM, a short chunky Negro, about thirty years of age; had on tow shirt and trowsers, a plaid jacket without sleeves; says he lived in Radnor township, and was left free by his motherwill. Whoever takes up and secures said runaways, so that the subscriber may get them again, shall receive the above reward and reasonable charges, at Eight Dollars for either of them, paid by       THOMAS CLARK, Gaoler.
Sept. 11, 1778.

*The Pennsylvania Packet or the General Advertiser*, September 17, 1778; September 24, 1778; September 29, 1778.


TWENTY DOLLARS REWARD.
FOR securing in any gaol so that the owner may get her again, a certain Negro Wench named MARY, a smart, artful huzzey, about thirty years of age, pock marked, can read tolerable well, pretends to be very religious, and talks somewhat on the Irish accent: Had on and took with her, a brown linen short gown, a black and white striped lincey petticoat, tow shift, half worn wooden heel shoes, a black bonnet, one or two check handkerchiefs, and one blanket. She obtained a pass for three days to look for a master, which time has expired five weeks from this date. She ran away about a year ago and passed for a free woman by the name of NANCY, and it is likely she may do the same now, and change her cloaths. Any person securing her as aforesaid, shall be entitled to the above reward, paid by the subscriber at Cantwell's Bridge, Newcastle County.
Sept. 17, 1778.              JOHN ENOS.

*The Pennsylvania Packet or the General Advertiser*, September 29, 1778.

*September 2, 1778.*
### FIFTY DOLLARS REWARD.
RAN AWAY from the subscriber, living in Newcastle County, in the Delaware State, on Tuesday the 1st inst. a certain ISAAC GILES, alias TOLSON, upwards of six feet high, much pitted with the small-pox. Had on took with him a light coloured cloth coat, turned up with red, a white hunting shirt, a pair of new white plush breeches, two or three country linen shirts, a blue cloth jacket belonging to me, lined with persian, and a number of other cloaths unknown, of different kinds. He is supposed to have got between 80 and 100 dollars, mostly continental currency, which I lost early in the morning of that day he ran off, he being the first person that followed me at the time I lost the money. He took likewise Five Pounds, Six Shillings, and Three-pence from a Negro boy of mine, and Fifteen Shillings and Three-pence from one of my overseers, both which sums he promised to return. The above-mentioned fellow lived some time with Doctor James Wyncoop, near Middletown, in the Delaware State, from whom he stole a number of things and made off, and lived as hostler at Newport, Newcastle County, in the Delaware State, with Mr. Isaac Allen, whom he likewise robbed. Any person that will bring to me the above described fellow, shall have the reward above-mentioned, and reasonable charges,
   paid by  DANIEL CHARLES HEATH.
*The Pennsylvania Packet or the General Advertiser*, October 10, 1778; October 17, 1778; November 21, 1778.


*RAN AWAY from Captain Kean, in Wilmington, the night of the 7th of this instant (October) a Negro boy named* JOHN; *he is about sixteen years old and well set, was born in Africa, and speaks unintelligibly: He went off in a brown fustian coatee, with a pale yellow cape, a leather cap and raven duck breeches; took with him a pair of boots and a loose out side coat of a dark grey colour.* FIVE POUNDS *Pennsylvania money, and all charges, will be paid to any person that shall apprehend and deliver the above mentioned Negro to the Honourable* William Henry Drayton, *at Mrs. Hopkinson's, in Walnut street, Philadelphia, Capt.* Kean, *at Wilmington, Mr.* Samuel Purviance, *at Baltimore, the Hon.* Daniel Jennifer, *near Annapolis,*
   *or Mr.* Strode, *at Fredericksburgh, in Virginia.*
*The Pennsylvania Packet or the General Advertiser*, October 10, 1778; November 14, 1778. See *Dunlap's Maryland Gazette; or, the Baltimore General Advertiser*, October 27, 1778.


### FORTY DOLLARS REWARD.
Baltimore, September 22, 1778.

RAN AWAY, on the night of the 21st inst. a Negro Man, named BEN; he is a stout well made young fellow, about 5 feet 8 inches high, about 23 or 24 years of age, has had the small-pox, is a shoemaker, and can do coarse work middling well; he used to go by water in his former Master's time, who lived at Dover, and as he says he has a wife there, he may attempt going that way, if not in some vessel from this Town: he is a good fiddler, takes snuff very frequently, and as he can read and is a smart knowing fellow, he may endeavour to pass for a free man. Had on and took with him when he went away, one pair of coarse trousers of country linen, one check shirt, one white linen ditto, pretty much worn, a blue broad cloth jacket and breeches, the breeches torn behind, one striped linen jacket with sleeves, and double-breasted, an old great coat of country made cloth, of a dirty brown colour, an old hat, and no shoes. Whoever takes up said Negro, and secures him in any gaol, so that his Master may get him again, shall have the above reward, and reasonable charges, paid by       GEORGE HELM.

N. B. The said Negro has a scar on his breast, one over his left eye, and another on one of his hands.—All masters of vessels are forbid taking off said Negro at their peril.

*The Maryland Journal, and Baltimore Advertiser*, October 13, 1778.


TWENTY DOLLARS REWARD.

RAN AWAY about the middle of June last, from the subscriber near Carlisle, in the state of Pennsylvania, a Negro man named BEN, about 26 years of age, five feet eleven inches high, strong made, not very black; had on a short brown cloth jacket, the back parts light coloured, tow shirt and trowsers, am old pair of shoes, a hunting cap bound with yellow tape, a striped silk handkerchief; he also took with him a remarkable large knife; one of his fore fingers is very small. He was formerly the property of a certain Hayes, alias Haset or Haslet, about twelve miles from Dover, in Kent county on Delaware, to which place it is supposed he is gone. Whoever secures said Negro so that his master may have him again, shall have the above reward and reasonable charges, from     ANDREW M'CALISTER.

*The Pennsylvania Packet or the General Advertiser*, October 17, 1778; October 24, 1778.


*October 10th,* 1778.
FIVE POUNDS REWARD.

RAN AWAY from Capt. Kean's, in Wilmington, the night of the 7th Instant, a Negroe boy named JOHN; he is about sixteen years old, short and well set, was born in Africa, and speaks unintelligibly: He went off in a brown fustian coatee, with a pale yellow cape, a leather cap and raven's duck breeches; he took with him a pair of boots, a loose outside coat of a dark grey colour.—

The above Reward, Pennsylvania Money, and all Charges, will be paid to any person that shall apprehend and deliver the above mentioned Negroe to Capt. Kean, at Wilmington, Mr. Samuel Purviance at Baltimore, the Hon. William Henry Drayton at Mrs. Hopkinson's, Walnut street, Philadelphia, the Hon. Daniel Jenifer at Annapolis,
or Mr. Strode, at Fredericksburgh in Virginia.
*Dunlap's Maryland Gazette; or, the Baltimore General Advertiser*, October 27, 1778; November 23, 1778; December 8, 1778. See *The Pennsylvania Packet or the General Advertiser*, October 10, 1778.

ABSENTS himself from the subscriber, living in Wilmington, in the Delaware State, an apprentice lad named SAMUEL CUMINGS, between nineteen and twenty years of age, five feet eight or nine inches high, wore his own brown hair, is of a ruddy complexion, has a modest agreeable countenance, and when he laughs dimples appears in his cheeks: As he has been absent a considerable time, his cloathing is unknown. Whoever takes up said apprentice and brings him to the subscriber, or secures him in any gaol so that his master may get him again, shall receive FIFTY DOLLARS Reward, from JAMES ADAMS.
*N.B.* It is hoped all Printers on the Continent will discourage the proceedings of said Cummings, should he offer his service, by refusing to give him entertainment: And all others are forbid to harbour or conceal him at their peril.           *November 2.*
*The Pennsylvania Packet or the General Advertiser*, November 5, 1778; November 14, 1778; November 19, 1778.

TWENTY DOLLARS REWARD.
RAN AWAY from the subscriber, on Friday night the second of October last, a likely, lusty, young black wench, named DIANA, formerly belonging to Mrs. Ann Griffith; she has large white eyes, and large high breasts: Had on when she went away, a black and white short gown, and petticoat of the same; she took with her two tow shifts, a white corded petticoat, and a plain white jacket gathered round the hips. Whoever will bring the said wench home to the subscriber, living at Black Bridge, Apoquiniminck Hundred, Newcastle County, shall e paid the above reward and reasonable charges, by
ARNOLD NAUDAIN, Jun.
*The Pennsylvania Packet or the General Advertiser*, November 7, 1778; November 17, 1778; January 19, 1779.

*Newcastle County, ss.*
NOW in the gaol of this county, a certain WILLIAM O'BRYAN, on suspicion of being a runaway servant of Jeremiah Moore's, of Fairfax county, Virginia. He is exactly described in the Pennsylvania Packet of the 3d of October, as follows, viz. By trade a weaver, about five feet six inches high, thirty years of age, of a fair complexion, has a ring worm on his face, and is lame in one of this thumbs, which is shriveled and shorter than the other: He has on a blue fustian coat and breeches, striped linen waistcoat, thread stockings, coarse shoes, and a raccoon hat. There is likewise in said gaol, a Negro man who calls himself JACK, says he belongs to Abraham Reister, at the Forks of Gunpowder, Baltimore County: He is about forty years of age, five feet ten inches high, has on an old cloth coat bound with red, tow shirt and trowsers, and old shoes tied with strings. Their masters are desired to come, pay charges and take them away.
Oct. 8.                THOMAS CLARK, Gaoler.
*The Pennsylvania Packet or the General Advertiser*, November 7, 1778.


ONE HUNDRED DOLLARS REWARD.
Newcastle County.
Broke the gaol of this county, on the night of the fifteenth inst. the following persons, viz. JAMES HENNEY, about forty years of age, five feet ten or eleven inches high, stout and well made; had on a light coloured cloth coat and breeches, blue yarn stockings, calf skin shoes, with round steel buckles in them. PETER TRAYNER, by trade a plaisterer, about forty-five years of age, five feet nine or ten inches high; had on a blue linsey coat, claret coloured waistcoat, white linen breeches corded with tow, blue and white yarn stockings half worn, coarse shoes and old felt hat. WILLIAM O'BRYAN, by trade a weaver, about five feet six inches high, thirty years of age, of a fair complexion, lame in one of his thumbs, which is shriveled and shorter than the other; he has on a blue fustian coat, buckskin breeches, striped linen waistcoat, thread stockings, coarse shoes, and an old racoon hat. JOHN DAVIS, about thirty-seven years of age, five feet seven inches high; had on a coarse linen hunting shirt, white flannel waistcoat, old buckskin breeches, blue yarn stockings, coarse shoes, and an old felt hat. JOHN JONES, twenty-three years of age, five feet six inches high; had on a light coloured surtout coat, brown cloth waistcoat, old coarse shoes, a new wool hat that is scolloped. Whoever takes up and secures the above described persons, shall be entitled to the above reward, or Twenty Dollars for each,
paid by    JOHN CLARK, Sheriff.
*The Pennsylvania Packet or the General Advertiser*, November 19, 1778.

# 1779

*Philadelphia, April 27.*
NOW in the Work-house of this city on suspicion of being a run-away, a Negro Wench who is supposed to have come into this city with the British army, or about that time, and has gone by the name of LUCY, alias PEG WALKER; about twenty-two or twenty-three years of age, short and well set, round smooth faced, say she came to town about two years ago with here master, Joseph England, and his wife, from Kent upon Delaware, and that they died soon after in this city without leaving anyone to take care of their effects or her, whereby she thought herself free. Any person to whom she may belong is hereby notified to come, pay charges and take her away in two months from this date, otherwise she will be sold out for the same, by
THOMAS APTY, Work-house Keeper.
*The Pennsylvania Packet or the General Advertiser*, April 29, 1779.


TWENTY DOLLARS Reward.
RUN-AWAY, about the tenth of March last,
A MULATTO man, named JAMES PATTERSON, born in the State of Delaware, about 25 years of age, 5 feet 9 or 10 inches high, has one foot larger than the other, and walks somewhat lame; he has been seen in the district of Southwark lately. Whoever secures said servant, so that his master may have him again, shall have the above reward,
paid by    SAMUEL M'LANE.
*The Pennsylvania Packet or the General Advertiser*, May 19, 1779; June 2, 1779.


ONE HUNDRED DOLLARS REWARD.
STILL *absents himself* from the subscriber, of Wilmington, in the Delaware state, an apprentice lad, named SAMUEL CUMINGS, about 20 years of age, 5 feet 8 or 9 inches high, wore his own brown hair, is of a ruddy complexion, has an agreeable countenance, and when he laughs dimples appear in his cheeks: As he has been away a considerable time, his cloathing is unknown. It is said he has been lately seen in Baltimore town, Maryland, though a report has been industriously spread of his having gone to sea. Whoever takes up said apprentice, and delivers him to the subscriber, in Wilmington, or secures him in New-castle goal, so that his master may get him again, shall receive the above reward—when the fallacious reasons given by the said *Cumings*, in the Pennsylvania Packet, for his transgression, will, by incontestable evidence, be made to appear manifest falshoods, without inserting assertions here which would prove nothing, and when other matters will be settled

before that "authority,"which application should have been made to if such grievances as mentioned had been genuine.
*June* 7, 1779. JAMES ADAMS.
N. B. It is hoped all printers on the continent will discourage the conduct of said *Cumings*, should he offer his service, by refusing to give him entertainment:—And all masters of vessels, and others, are desired not to harbour or conceal him at their peril.
*The Pennsylvania Gazette*, June 16, 1779; June 23, 1779; June 30, 1779.

TWENTY-FIVE POUNDS REWARD.

RAN AWAY from the subscriber, of Bermuda, now at the Fast Landing at Little Duck Creek, on the 22d inst. (June) a Negro man servant called DICK; had on when he went away, a blue jacket, the seams of it covered with white, and a white straw hat: He had a bundle of cloaths, with one or more shirts, so that he may change his dress. Any person that will bring ho, to the subscriber, or to Mr. William Cook at Wilmington, or Mr. Parry at the Fast Landing aforesaid, in my absence, shall receive the above reward, and reasonable charges, paid by BENJAMIN WARD.
*The Pennsylvania Packet or the General Advertiser*, July 13, 1779. See *The Pennsylvania Gazette*, October 27, 1779.

*One Hundred Dollars REWARD.*

RAN AWAY from his bail the 31st last month, July, a certain John Hook, a German, but speaks good English, he is about 21 years of age, five feet five and an half inches high, brown hair tied behind, smooth face, and very sharp chin; had on when he went made his escape, a blue regimental coat, faced with white, a pair linen trowsers, with a pair boots almost new over them, and a sharp cocked hat, which he generally wears with one of the cocks down: Also took with him a pair of buckskin breeches, almost new, tied in a handkerchief, with a shirt. He was seen last Sunday afternoon about 4 miles from the Middle Ferry over Schuylkill. Whoever apprehends the said John Hook, and lodges him in Philadelphia goal, or brings him to the subscriber, living in Mill-Creek hundred, New-Castle county, Delaware State, shall receive the above reward.
*August* 5, 1779, JOHN M'KANNAN.
*The Pennsylvania Packet or the General Advertiser*, August 7, 1779; August 12, 1779; August 17, 1779.


TAKEN up, on Tuesday the 7th of September inst. A NEGRO MAN, who shewed a Girls indenture as his, (it is the indenture of one Mary Mosely, of

Sussex County, and was wrapped in a warrant issued by Burton Waples, Esq; against Richard Mosely, for assaulting John Amwood of Indian River)—The Negro is about 5 feet 6 or inches high, has a scar on his neck, nearly under his left ear; had on an old hat, a check shirt, a flannel under jacket, a blue and white striped homespun over jacket and an old pair of check trowsers, very ragged—As this Negro will not tell his name, but says it is Mary Moslin, though usually called Moses—It is therefore conjectured he has run away from his master, who probably lives near Indian River, as the Fellow came to this City in a vessel from Dover—This is to inform his master, that on application to the Printer, and paying charges he may have him again.

*The Pennsylvania Journal and Weekly Advertiser*, September 8, 1779; September 15, 1779.

ONE HUNDRED DOLLARS REWARD.

RAN AWAY from the subscriber, living near the Trap, in St. George's hundred, Newcastle county, a Negro fellow named GEORGE, formerly the property of William Frazier, of Jones's Neck, near Dover, in Kent county, and well known in that part of the county. The above reward will be given to any person who may secure him in any gaol.

Sould [sic] any person incline to purchase said fellow as he runs, who is young, and active at the farming business, they may know the terms by applying to     THOMAS M'DONOUGH.

*The Pennsylvania Packet or the General Advertiser*, October 5, 1779; October 9, 1779; October 21, 1779.

*New Castle County, October* 10, 1779.

WAS committed to the goal of this county, on the 10th day of July last, a Negroe man named DICK , who confesses he is the property of Capt. James Seemore, of Bermuda, and that he ran away from Capt. Benjamin Ward, when lying at Fast Landing in Kent county, on Delaware. Therefore the said Capt. Seemore or Capt. Ward, or some other person in their absence, is desired to come, pay charges, and take him away in thirty days from the above date, otherwise he will be sold for his fees, by

THOMAS CLARK, Goaler.

*The Pennsylvania Gazette*, October 27, 1779; November 3, 1779; November 10, 1779. See *The Pennsylvania Packet or the General Advertiser*, July 13, 1779.

# 1780

*Dover, Delaware State, Feb.* 6, 1780.
Three Hundred Dollars Reward,

RUN-AWAY, *on the* 22d *of November last, a Negro man, named DANIEL, about 5 feet 4 inches high, has a lively walk, a little bow legged, country born:* Had on and took with him, a brown country cloath coat, an old cotton velvet jacket, a green cloth under ditto, a pair of black velvet breeches, a pair of black knit worsted ditto, both old, and a round hat, his other clothes unknown. Whoever takes up and secures the said Negro, so that his master may have him again, shall receive the above reward, and if brought home, reasonable expences, by    FRENCH BATTELL.

*The Pennsylvania Journal and Weekly Advertiser,* February 16, 1780; February 23, 1780; March 1, 1780; March 8, 1780; March 22, 1780; April 5, 1780; *The Pennsylvania Packet or the General Advertiser,* February 17, 1780; February 22, 1780; March 2, 1780. Minor differences between the papers.

Kent County, Delaware State, Feb. 7, 1780.
*ONE THOUSAND DOLLARS REWARD.*
BROKE OPEN on Sunday evening the 23d of January last, the dwelling-house of the subscriber, in Little-Creek Neck, and the following articles were taken out, to wit: One lead coloured broadcloth coat and breeches, the coat with small oval concave gilt buttons, the breeches with small round convex ditto; one velvet waistcoat nearly the same colour, buttons covered with velvet the same of the waistcoat; one new Holland ruffled shirt, two plain ditto, two cambrick stocks, one pair light coloured clouded worsted stockings, one pair white yarn ditto, one pair shoes and a pair silver shoe-buckles, one round fine new hat, one bandano handkerchief, half a side of soal and half a side of coarse upper leather. The theft was committed by a couple of fellows who ran away from the subscriber the same evening; one of them a low well set black Negro fellow, lately marked with the small-pox, supposed to be about twenty or twenty-one years of age, who called himself DRAPER, but is supposed to have changed his name; the other a young Mulatto fellow about nineteen years of age, five feet ten or eleven inches high, named JOSEPH ARMSTRONG, very artful and subtile, who belonged to the subscriber. Whoever apprehends and secures the above described fellows so that they may be brought to justice and the goods recovered, shall receive the above reward, or FOUR HUNDRED DOLLARS for either of them, and in proportion for what articles may be recovered, paid by
CHARLES HILLYARD, Junior.

*The Pennsylvania Packet or the General Advertiser,* February 22, 1780; March 2, 1780.

*Two Hundred Dollars Reward.*
ABSCONDED from his place of abode, on the sixth of February last, a certain JAMES SHAW, a labourer, a chunky ill-looking fellow, about 5 feet

7 inches high, remarkable for getting drunk, and very abusive when in liquor: He is well known in and about Lancaster and Bettlehausen, by the name of Blue-Lips. At the time of his leaving the subscriber he feloniously took off a piece of fine home spun cloth, of a very light colour, a silver table spoon, London stamp, marked J. M. and a half worn castor hat. Any person or persons securing said SHAW in any goal, so that he may be brought to conviction, and the above articles restored to the owner, shall receive the above reward, or in proportion for any of the articles so returned, or FIFTY POUNDS to any person that will secure him in New-Castle goal,
    paid by  JOHN M'LEAN, New-Castle county.
*The Pennsylvania Journal and Weekly Advertiser*, March 1, 1780; March 8, 1780; March 22, 1780; March 29, 1780.

### THREE HUNDRED DOLLARS REWARD.

RUN-AWAY *from the subscriber, at the Red Lion, in New Castle county, on Friday, the 7th ult. two Negro slaves, one of them a Lad, named Murdy, about 5 feet 5 or 6 inches high, a mulatto, remarkably knock kneed: Had on and took with him, a brown super fine cloth coat turned, greenish coloured cord du roy breeches, a pair of buckskin breeches, two or three shirts, and good shoes. The other a girl, named Rode, about 16 years of age, born in George Town, Kent county, 5 feet 4 inches high: Had on and took with her, a corded white linen short gown, a lincey petticoat, a blue short gown, linen bonnet, two good tow linen shifts, a pair of high heeled shoes, with brass buckles. Whoever takes up said slaves, and secures them in any goal, so that they may be had again, shall have the above reward, and reasonable charges, if brought home, or One Hundred and Fifty Dollars for each of them,*
    paid by  WILLIAM CARSON.
*The Pennsylvania Journal and Weekly Advertiser*, May 12, 1780; May 19, 1780; May 31, 1780.

### Fifteen Hundred Dollars Reward.

RUN away, on the 16th of October last, from the subscriber, living near the Trap in St. George's Hundred, New-Castle County, a Negroe man, named BILL, about 24 years of age, five feet five or six inches high, strait and well made, a right jet black complexion, and speaks good English. He formerly belonged to the estate of Samuel Vance, deceased. It is thought he has an old pass of his father's, who has travelled over most parts of the continent. Whoever takes up and secures said Negroe, so that he may be had again, shall have the above reward, and reasonable charges if brought home,
    paid by  ABEL MILES, or WILLIAM WORKMAN.

*The Pennsylvania Gazette*, May 24, 1780; May 31, 1780; June 28, 1780.

*Millcreek hundred, Newcastle county, Delaware State,*
*May 30, 1780.*
Two Hundred Dollars Reward.
STOLEN from the subscriber on the night of the 21st of this month, A dark bay HORSE, 15 hands high, 7 years old this grass, shod before, is a little hip shot in his near hip, a small star in his forehead, and a snip on his nose. Supposed to be stole by a stranger, his name unknown, wears a blue coat, red jacket, and cloth coloured leggings, half up his thigh; is about 6 feet high, a stout made fellow, swarthy complexion, black hair, inclining to curl, marked with the small pox. Whoever takes up and secures said horse and thief, so that the owner may have his horse again and the thief brought to justice, shall have the above reward, or One Hundred Dollars for the horse only,
paid by   WILLIAM GRAHAM.
*The Pennsylvania Gazette*; June 7, 1780; June 14, 1780; June 21, 1780; June 28, 1780. See *The Pennsylvania Journal and the Weekly Advertiser*, June 7, 1780.


Millcreek Hundred, Newcastle County, Delaware State.
TWO HUNDRED DOLLARS REWARD,
STOLEN from the Subscriber, on the night of the 21st of this month, May, a dark bay HORSE, fifteen hands high, seven years old this grass, shod before, is a little hipshot in his near hip, a small star in his forehead and a snip on his nose, supposed to be stolen by a stranger, his name unknown, wears a blue coat, red jacket, and cloth coloured leggens half up his thigh, a stout made fellow, swarthy complexion, black hair inclining to curl, marked with the small-pox. Whoever takes up and secures the said horse and thief, so that the owner may have his horse again, and the thief be brought to justice, shall have the above reward, or one hundred dollars for the horse only,
paid by   WILLIAM GRAHAM.
*The Pennsylvania Journal and the Weekly Advertiser*, June 7, 1780; June 14, 1780; June 21, 1780. See *The Pennsylvania Gazette*; June 7, 1780.


*Mill-town, Newcastle county, August* 2.
*FIVE HUNDRED DOLLARS REWARD.*
STOLEN from the subscriber, the 26th of July last, a SORREL HORSE, four years old, fourteen hands high, branded on the near shoulder **T B** with a white blaze down his face; was taken by a young man who says his name is WILLIAM STUART. He had on a light coloured great coat, a small round

hat with an old silver band round the crown, striped trousers, thread stockings, and old pumps; is about twenty-one years of age, five feeet seven or eight inches high. He has likewise with him a small bay Horse. Two Hundred and Fifty Dollars will be given for the horse, and reasonable expences; and the above reward for the horse and thief.
     JOHN HERDMAN.
 *The Pennsylvania Journal and the Weekly Advertiser*, August 2, 1780; August 23, 1780; August 30, 1780; October 4, 1780; October 18, 1780.

     *TWO HUNDRED DOLLARS REWARD.*
*RUN AWAY from the subscriber, on the night of the 25th ult. a likely Negro fellow, about 26 years of age, about 5 feet 6 or 7 inches high, well sett, bow legged, can read and write, is a very artful subtile fellow, well acquainted with the country from part of Pennsylvania to North-Hampton county, Virginia, as a waggoner, and it is likley he may pass for a freeman and as a preacher, as he has been in that way for some time amongst the Negroes, (he may make towards the enemy) he had on and took with him, a raccoon hat and perhaps a felt ditto, linen coat, linsey-woolsey working jacket, 2 white shirts, one of about 7 or 8 hundred linen, plain and striped cotton and linen jackets, corded and plain cotton breeches, cotton, thread and yarn stockings, good shoes, he is a shoemaker by trade: had also stocks and a black silk handkerchief; likewise a pinchbeck watch, except he has changed her away, and it is likely he may get a horse. It is supposed he is well furnished with money. The above reward, if brought home to the subscriber, living 12 miles below Dover, Kent county, Delaware State, if taken 50 miles from the subscriber, and Three Hundred Dollars, if exceeding 75 miles, or One Hundred Dollars, if taken up and secured in any goal within the United States, so that the subscriber gets him again, and all reasonable charges.*
*July* 28.     BENJAMIN GIBBS.
 *The Pennsylvania Journal and the Weekly Advertiser*, August 9, 1780.

     Newcastle county, August 2, 1780.
WAS brought to the goal of this county the 4th of July last, GEORGE HOULT, who confesses himself to be a convict servant to William Rhea of Ann-rundal [sic] county, in the state of Maryland, if so his master is desired to come in three weeks from the above date and take him away, otherwise he will be sold for his fees.  THOMAS CLARK, goaler.
 *The Pennsylvania Journal and the Weekly Advertiser*, August 9, 1780.

     *Four Hundred Dollars Reward.*
RAN AWAY from the subscriber, near Duck Creek, on Monday the 14th

inst. (August) a Negro man named JAMES, aged about twenty-three years, a square built well set fellow, about five feet eight inches high, has a scar or two on his breast, and walks rocking, with his toes turning out and his heels in; had on when he went away a good tow shirt and trowsers. It is expected he will endeavour to get to Chester, and from thence cross Delaware over to the Jerseys, he being the same Neegro [sic] that Philip Fitzgerald brought from thence a few years ago. His father is a free Negro and lives in or near Salem, and his wife with Thomas Sharpless in or near Chester aforesaid. Whoever takes up and secures said Negro so that his master may get him again, shall have the above reward and reasonable charges,
    paid by JOHN ANDERSON.
*The Pennsylvania Packet or the General Advertiser*, September 5, 1780.

      Six Hundred Dollars Reward.
STOLEN *from the subscriber, in the night of the 6th instant, a reddish ROAN MARE, about five years ld, [sic] thirteen hands and a half high, trots and canters, has no brand or ear mark, has a small nick in one of her eye whiskers, long switch tail, and long mane, stolen by a certain Nathaniel Chick, born in Ceicil county, Maryland. He had on, a light coloured short coat, small round hat or fur cap, Overalls, and shoes tied with strings. He is remarkably freckled, squints with one eye, and lame in both legs. He picked a man's pocket the same night, the sum of money unknown. Any person or persons securing him in any goal, or brings him to the subscriber in Newcastle, shall have the above reward for the Thief and Mare, or Three Hundred Dollars for the Mare, and reasonable charges.*
    *RANIER PENTON.*
*The Pennsylvania Journal and the Weekly Advertiser*, September 27, 1780.


      *Newcastle county, Nov. 25th, 1780.*
WAS brought to the goal of this county, on the 7th instant, a Negro woman, committed by the named of JENNY, and confesses herself to be the property of Robert Coleman, of Lancaster county, in the state of Pennsylvania, if so, her owner is desired to come within three weeks from this date, pay charges, and take her away, otherwise she will be discharges according to law.
    THOMAS CLARK, goaler.
*The Pennsylvania Journal and the Weekly Advertiser*, December 20, 1780.

## 1781

*Brandywine Hundred, New-Castle County, Jan. 22, 1781.*
One Thousand Dollars Reward.

STOLEN from the plantation of the subscriber, living in Brandywine Hundred, between 5 and 6 miles from Brandywine bridge, in the night of the 16th inst. a likely dark brown MARE, upwards of 14 hands high, about 12 years old, canters well, a natural trotter, has a small star in her forehead, some white hairs in her tail, some saddle-marks, three white spots on her shoulders, and is part blooded. The thief was seen by the neighbours; he had stole a MARE, with a new saddle and bridle from John Long, which mare he rode a few miles, then turned her loose, and stole the above described mare, on which he put Long's saddle and bridle; he is a short set fellow, wore a brown jacket, round hat and white stockings. Whoever secures the mare, saddle and bridle, so as they may be had again, shall have Five Hundred Dollars reward, and Five Hundred Dollars more for the thief, if brought to justice,
   paid by  WILLIAM SMITH, Milwright.

*The Pennsylvania Gazette*, January 24, 1781; January 31, 1781; February 7, 1781.


ONE TON OF BAR-IRON REWARD,
(or the value thereof in currency)

RAN-AWAY from James Sharps, in Sadsbury township, Chester county, on the 10th day of April, 1779, a remarkable likely Negroe Man, very black, named ABEL, about 24 or 25 years of age, 5 feet 10 or 11 inches high, with a mole on one of his cheeks, his clothes unknown; it is supposed he harbours between New Castle and St. George, or about Appquinimink, in Delaware State, as he has some friends that are freemen living in a cedar-swamp in that neighbourhood.

  Whoever takes up said Negroe, and secures him in any goal, or brings him to his master, living in Hopewell-forge, in Lancaster county, shall have the above reward, paid by  PETER GRUBB.
N. B. It is probable he will pass for a freeman, he having got a pass from a free Negroe, named NAT, and may pass by that name.
March 31, 1781.

*The Pennsylvania Gazette*, April 25, 1781; May 9, 1781; May 23, 1781.


Newcastle, April 26, 1781.
Was committed to my custody, a certain NEGROE MAN, who calls himself JACK MARTIN, aged about 23 years, of the stature of five feet six inches, is sprightly and active, and says he belongs to THOMAS WHITE, Esquire,

of Kent county, on Delaware; which said Negroe was tried and convicted here for felony, on the 24th instant, and adjudged to make restitution, to the owner of the goods stolen, to the amount of 6l. 4s. 7d. specie. These are therefore to inform the Master of the said Negro, that unless he comes on or before the first day of June, ensuing, and releases the said slave, by paying the restitution money aforesaid, and the costs of prosecution, the said Negroe will be sold to defray the same, agreeable to an order of the court before whom he was convicted.    SAMUEL SMITH, Sheriff.

*The Pennsylvania Packet or the General Advertiser*, May 12, 1781; May 19, 1781; June 2, 1781.


Fifty Dollars Hard Money Reward.

RUN from Elk Forge, near the Head of Elk, Maryland, the 23d of April, 1781, a negroe man, named DICK, about 27 years old, country born, 5 feet 9 or 10 inches high, thin visage, hollow eyed, streight bodied, and speaks pretty quick. Had on a new felt hat, brick dust coloured English cloth coat, white country cloth vest and breeches, wooden buttons, white shirt, woolen stockings, somewhat milled, and good shoes; he had other clothes with him, and probably may change; he also had plenty of money: He was brought from Sussex county, Delaware State, about 4 or 5 years age, and probably may make that way, or attempt to get to the enemy. Whoever will secure the fellow in any goal on the continent, and give notice to the subscriber, so that he may recover him, shall have the above reward, besides reasonable charges, if brought home.    THOMAS MAY.

*The Pennsylvania Gazette*, May 16, 1781; May 23, 1781


Five Pounds, hard money, Reward.

RAN AWAY from the subscriber, living in New-Castle county, Delaware State, on the 19th of August last, A Mulattoe Slave, named WILL, about 5 feet 9 inches high, a smart lively fellow, marked with the small pox pretty much, likes to play on the violin; his dress unknown, as he lost all his clothes in swimming across St. George's creek, but an old felt hat; is very likely to have got a forged pass for a freeman, and will make for some vessel, or the refugees. Whoever takes up the said fellow and brings him to his master, or secures him in any goal, so that his master may get him again, shall have the above reward, and reasonable charges,
           paid by me,    BENJAMIN BUNKER.

*The Pennsylvania Gazette*, September 5, 1781. See *The Pennsylvania Gazette*, October 10, 1781, *The Pennsylvania Gazette*, October 31, 1781, and *The Pennsylvania Gazette*, November 7, 1781.

*Thirty Hard Dollars Reward.*

RUN-AWAY, on the 19th of August last, from the subscriber, living in New-Castle county, State of Delaware, A Mulattoe Slave, named WILL, about 24 years of age, 5 feet 9 inches high, marked with the smallpox, ties his wool behind, he lost all his clothes swimming across a creek, but an old felt hat; he likes to play on the violin, and loves strong drink; he was raised in the aforesaid county by Captain John Edwards. Whoever takes up the said fellow, and brings him home, or secures him in any goal, so that his master may get him again, shall have the above reward, and all reasonable charges, paid by me   BENJAMIN BUNKER.

*The Pennsylvania Gazette*, October 10, 1781; October 17, 1781; October 24, 1781. See *The Pennsylvania Gazette*, September 5, 1781, *The Pennsylvania Gazette*, October 31, 1781, and *The Pennsylvania Gazette*, November 7, 1781.

Two Half Johannesses Reward.

RAN away from the subscriber, living in New-Castle county, St. Georges hundred and Delaware State, a NEGRO MAN named PETER, about 20 years of age, and about 5 feet 6 or 7 inches high, is marked with the small pox, streight limbed, and well made; was raised in Kent county, Delaware state, by a certain Peter Cooper, and afterwards given to a certain Joseph Berry, and after said Berry's decease, sold by the sheriff of Kent county, as the property of said Berry, to Nehemiah Tilton, at Dover, of whom the subscriber purchased said negro, who ran away from me the 22d of February, in the year 1780: he has been formerly seen in Kent county, but since has been in Philadelphia, and was out the last cruize in the ship Congress, captain Geddes commander, and passed by the name of DICK BUTCHER. Whoever takes up said Negro and secures him in any goal on the continent, or brings him to the subscriber, shall have the above reward.

GEORGE CROW, near Port-Penn.

*The Pennsylvania Packet or the General Advertiser*, October 30, 1781; November 3, 1781; November 10, 1781.

*South Amboy, Middlesex county, Oct.* 15, 1781.

THE Mulattoe Slave (advertised in this Gazette of the 5th September, 1781) named WILL, that run away the 19th of August from Benjamin Bunker, in New-Castle county, is taken up by Capt. James Morgan, and the owner is desired to come and take him away, paying the charges and reward, and proving his property. As there is no goal in this county to secure the said slave, he is desired to come and take him away immediately, there being no certainty of keeping him.

JAMES MORGAN.
*The Pennsylvania Gazette,* October 31, 1781. See *The Pennsylvania Gazette,* September 5, 1781, *The Pennsylvania Gazette,* October 10, 1781, and *The Pennsylvania Gazette,* November 7, 1781.

Fifty Hard Dollars Reward.

THE Mulattoe Slave, named WILL, that run away the 19th of August, 1781, from Benjamin Bunker, in New-Castle county, State of Delaware, was taken up by Captain Morgan, living in South-Amboy, Middlesex county, East-Jersey, has got away from him; he is a smart well made fellow, about 24 years of age, 5 feet 9 inches high, marked with the small pox, and ties his wool behind; he lost his clothes in swimming across a creek, all but an old felt hat; he likes to play on the violin, and loves strong drink. He was raised by Capt. John Edwards, in the above county. Whoever takes up the said fellow, and secures him in any goal, so that his master may get him again, shall have the above reward, paid by     BENJAMIN BUNKER.
*Nov. 6.*

*The Pennsylvania Gazette,* November 7, 1781; November 14, 1781; November 21, 1781. See *The Pennsylvania Gazette,* September 5, 1781, *The Pennsylvania Gazette,* October 10, 1781, and *The Pennsylvania Gazette,* October 31, 1781.

*New-Castle, December 5, 1781.*

WAS brought to the goal of this county, on the second day of this instant, A certain Mulattoe Slave, named JOE,   who confesseth himself to be the property of HENRY HOWARD,   near Northampton Furnace, State of Maryland; if so, his master is desired to come, pay charges, and take him away, within the space of three weeks from the above date, otherwise he will be discharged according to law, by    THOMAS CLARK, Goaler.

*The Pennsylvania Gazette,* December 19, 1781; January 9, 1782.

# 1782

*One Hundred Dollars, Specie, Reward.*

RAN from Elk-Forge, near the Head of Elk, the 23d of April, 1781, Negroe DICK; about 28 years old, 5 feet 9 or 10 inches high, thin visage, hollow ey'd, straight bodied, speaks pretty quick and a little stammering: Had a variety of good clothes with him, and plenty of money; was bro't up to farming, is a very good axman, and handy at most kinds of country work. About 6 years ago was brought from the branches of Nanticoke river, in Sussex county, where he had been brought up, and it is supposed he is now hovering between the bays of Delaware and Chesapeak.

Also ran from the same place, the beginning of Sept. 1777, and joined the British then at Head of Elk, another Negroe named DICK; near 6 feet high, a straight well proportioned fellow, not very black, about 30 years old, apt to smile when speaking, was brought up in Pencader Hundred, New-Castle county, to farming and driving team, at which he is expert, as well as drinking strong liquor.—'Tis thought he is now hovering about Philadelphia, or in the Jersies. Any person securing the above described fellows, or either of them, in any goal, and will give notice to the subscriber, at said forge, so that he may recover him or them, shall have FIFTY DOLLARS for each, and if brought home, reasonable charges.    THOMAS MAY.
N. B. If they return of their own accord, this offence shall be forgiven. *January* 23, 1782.

*The Pennsylvania Gazette,* February 6, 1782; February 13, 1782; February 27, 1782; March 27, 1782; April 17, 1782.

*New-Castle, Feb.* 4, 1782.
WAS committed to the goal of this county, on the fifth day of January last, a young Negroe wench, named HESTER; and confesseth herself to be the property of Elizabeth Ramsey, at or near Octarara. Her mistress or owner is requested to come, pay charges, and take her away within three weeks from the above date, otherwise she will be discharged according to law.
THOMAS CLARK, Goaler.

*The Pennsylvania Gazette,* February 13, 1782; February 27, 1782; March 6, 1782.

RAN AWAY,
From the subscriber, in New-Castle on Delaware,
A LIKELY young MOLATO MAN named STEPHEN, about 18 years of age, born in Somerset county, Maryland, he is about six feet high, and remarkably well made for his age, with particular long feet. Had on when he went away, a black and white country made kersey jacket, new shirt, old white breeches, and a pair of shoes run down at the heel. Went off with the aforesaid fellow, a short black Negro Man, about 23 years of age. Whoever will secure the aforesaid Mulato and Negro, shall have a reward of SIX POUNDS, paid by the subscriber in New-Castle, or WILLIAM GEDDES, Esq. in Philadelphia.
March 1, 1782.            JOHN WITHERED.

*The Pennsylvania Journal and the Weekly Advertiser,* March 9, 1782; March 13, 1782; March 20, 1782; March 27, 1782; March 30, 1782. See *The Pennsylvania Gazette,* March 27, 1782, *The Pennsylvania Gazette,* August 14, 1782, and *The Pennsylvania Journal and the Weekly Advertiser,* November 6, 1782.

SLAVES,
One yellow, the other black,
RUN from New-Castle, in Delaware, the 20th of February, and were seen at Brandywine bridge; their intent must have been New-York or Little-York. The yellow fellow Stephen is about 18 years old, near 6 feet high, well made to his age, remarkable long feet; had on a black and white kersey waistcoat, old white kersey breeches, and new tow shirt. The black fellow Jack is about 22 or 23 years of age, 5 feet 6 or 8 inches high, a great thief; had on a blue coat, black breeches, and took with him an old brown great coat; they were both born in Maryland, and may attempt to pass as freemen, getting a forged pass. The subscriber begs the favour of any persons who may have taken hirelings since the above date, to examine whether the above description answers any of them, or a reward should most chearfully be given any person who might have seen the Negroes attempting to pass through the country, that he might get on their track, but if secured in any goal a reward of Ten Pounds shall be given for their trouble, paid by
WILLIAM GEDDIS, Esq; of Philadelphia,
or JOHN WETHERED, of Delaware.
*The Pennsylvania Gazette*, March 27, 1782; April 3, 1782; April 10, 1782; April 17, 1782. See *The Pennsylvania Journal and the Weekly Advertiser*, March 9, 1782, *The Pennsylvania Gazette*, August 14, 1782, and *The Pennsylvania Journal and the Weekly Advertiser*, November 6, 1782.

Six-Pence Reward.
RAN-AWAY, on the 9th day of August last, an Apprentice GIRL, named CATHARINE DAGNESS, about 14 years of age, well grown of her age, has fair hair: Had on when she went away, a linsey petticoat and bedgown; while bonnet and linen shift. Any person securing said Girl, so that her master shall get her again, shall have the above Reward.    THOMAS M'GILL.
St. George's hundred, Newcastle county, Delaware state, May 6.
*The Pennsylvania Packet or the General Advertiser*, May 9, 1782.

TEN DOLLARS Reward.
RUN away from the subscriber, living in Mill Creek Hundred, New-Castle county, Delaware State, on the 26th of May, 1782, a Negroe MAN, named Peter, about 25 years old, 5 feet 9 inches high, strait and slender built, thin vissage, very smart and active, speaks slow and soft, very submissive; he has a large scar on his left wrist, understands farming and driving team; had on when he went away, a sheeps grey thick cloth coat, an old wool hat, tow linen shirt and trowsers, new shoes and copper buckles, is fond of strong liquor, and very subject to lying; he was born in Bucks county, in Pennsylvania

State, and lived some years with one Jonathan Meredith, a tanner, in Philadelphia; it is supposed he has made for Philadelphia or Bucks county. Any person securing the above described fellow in any goal, so as his master may have notice thereof, shall receive the above reward and reasonable charges, paid by JOHN JAMES.

N. B. All masters of vessels are forbid to carry him off at their peril.

*The Pennsylvania Gazette*, June 5, 1782; June 12, 1782; June 19, 1782; July 24, 1782; July 31, 1782; August 21, 1782; September 25, 1782; October 16, 1782; October 30, 1782; November 13, 1782; *The Pennsylvania Journal and the Weekly Advertiser*, June 5, 1782; June 12, 1782; June 22, 1782; June 26, 1782; July 4, 1782; July 17, 1782; August 28, 1782. Minor differences between the papers. The *Journal* spells the tanner's name "Meridith".

One Shilling Sterling Reward.

RUN-AWAY from the subscriber, living in Wilmington, Delaware State, on Wednesday the 27th of May, an apprentice boy named JOSEPH MACKADOE, about fifteen years old, thin visage, had on a striped jacket, tow trowsers, an old beaver hat.—Whoever brings home the said apprentice, shall have the above reward, and all charges paid,

by WILLIAM JONES, Taylor.

*The Pennsylvania Journal and the Weekly Advertiser*, June 5, 1782; June 8, 1782; June 12, 1782; June 19, 1782; June 26, 1782; July 4, 1782.

SIXTEEN DOLLARS REWARD,

RAN-AWAY from the subscriber on the morning of the eighteenth instant, near Ezekiel Webb's tavern, between Wilmington and Lancaster, four NEGRO Men, one named JACK WHITE, pretty black and grum spoken, pock marked, about 25 years of age, had on a sailors blue jacket, black breeches, white stockings, and a leather cap: another calls himself JACK RICHARDS, remarkable black, about 21 years old, stout made, about 5 feet 10 or 11 inches high, had on a sailors blue jacket, old blue trowsers, and an old hat, and has a stopage in his speach: another named CHARLES JACKSON, a yellow fellow, had on the like jacket and trowsers, and a large old beaver hat, speaks good English, stout made, about 5 feet 8 inches high: the other a black fellow, calls himself FRANK, speaks pritty plain, had on a red coat, old blue trowsers, and a small old hat; 'tis supposed they will try to cross the Delaware in order to get to the enemy, or to offer themselves for sailors. All masters of vessels and others, are hereby forwarned of taking them in, or harbouring them at their peril. Whoever takes up and secures the above negroes, so that their master gets them again, shall have the above

reward, or in proportion for any one of them, and all reasonable charges paid, by me       SAMUEL SAYRE,            June 21.
*The Pennsylvania Packet or the General Advertiser*, June 22, 1782; July 2, 1782.

Five Pounds Reward.

RAN away the 13th of June, 1782, from the subscriber, living in Little Creek hundred, in the state of Delaware, a mulatto man shewing of the indian blood, named LOTT, about forty years old, five feet nine or ten inches high, thin visaged, shews some gray hairs in his beard, he is apt to get drunk, and very abusive when he is so, the forepart of his hair lately trim'd, and bushy behind, had on when he went away, a small round hat half worn, strip'd linen trousers, an under jacket, the fore parts white, the back gray, short blue and white strip'd coatee, a white home spun linen shirt, shoes almost new took with him two pair of tow trousers, and a greyish coat half worn. Whoever apprehends and secures the said servant, so that his master may have him, shall receive the above reward and reasonable charges, by me,
J. WHEILTON.
*The Freeman's Journal: or, The North-American Intelligencer*, July 3, 1782; July 10, 1782; July 17, 1782.

New-Castle, July 5, 1782.

WAS committed to the goal of this county, on the 24th day of June last, the two following Negroe Men, to wit, HARRY, aged about 43 years, 5 feet 7 or 8 inches high; DICK, aged about 34 years, 5 feet 8 or 9 inches high; both confess themselves to be the property of William Luckey, of Montgomery county, and State of Maryland, who is requested to come, pay charges and take them away within three weeks from the above date, otherwise they will be discharged according to law, by
THOMAS CLARK, Goaler.
*The Pennsylvania Gazette*, July 17, 1782; July 24, 1782; August 7, 1782.

SIXTEEN DOLLARS Reward.

RUN away from the subscriber, the 1st of July 1781, in the beginning of wheat harvest, an apprentice LAD, named SAMUEL HYATT, about 5 feet 6 inches high, thin visage, and a remarkable long chin, a midling fair skin under the cloathing, and a very artful fellow, by trade a cart wheel-wright, but has not got his trade fully; had on, and with him, a light coloured cloth homespun jacket, and trowsers of the same, shoes, stockings, shorts and breeches. Whoever takes up said apprentice, and secures him so that his master may have him again, shall receive the above reward, and reasonable charges, paid by THOMAS COOMBS, in Apoquinimy-hundred, and county of New-castle, upon Delaware.

*The Pennsylvania Gazette*, August 7, 1782; September 4, 1782; October 16, 1782.

### SIX POUNDS REWARD.

STOLEN out of the pasture of the subscriber, near New Ark, New Castle county, Delaware State, on the 6th of August instant, A likely young GELDING, four years old last spring, about 14 hands high; he is a yellowish dunn, with a black back, and striped with black round his legs, which is very perceivable; he carries high, and has a tender mouth, trots and hand gallops easy and neat. The person suspected of taking him is a certain Edward Andrewsgold, an Englishman, 5 feet 8 inches high, 21 or 22 years of age, a deserter from Tarleton's legion of horse, a little stoop shouldered, very talkative, a very great liar and swearer; has a little stoppage in his speech, fond of spiritous liquor; has brown curly hair tied behind, wants one of his upper fore teeth, talks very fast and loud. The above reward will be given for the horse and thief, or THREE POUNDS, with reasonable expences, for the horses only, if brought home,

   paid by  JAMES ANDERSON, sen.

*The Pennsylvania Gazette*, August 14, 1782; August 21, 1782; September 4, 1782.

### TEN GUINEAS Reward.

WILL be paid to any person, who will bring to the subscriber his Negroe man STEPHEN. He is a pale fellow, smooth face, down look, about 19 years old, near 6 feet high, straight limbs, but very remarkable long feet; he went from New-Castle last February, in company with a great villain, black Jack, who is now in Chester goal for a robbery, they were chiefly in or near Philadelphia ever since. His dress now unknown, as he changed it soon after his elopement. It is probable the above reward may tempt persons at leisure to make enquiry after him, but if any extraordinary trouble shall be had in the pursuit, it will be chearfully paid by WILLIAM CADDIS, Esq; of Philadelphia, or the subscriber, at New-castle.

August 8, 1782.   JOHN WETHERED.

*The Pennsylvania Gazette*, August 14, 1782; August 21, 1782. See *The Pennsylvania Journal and the Weekly Advertiser*, March 9, 1782, *The Pennsylvania Gazette*, March 27, 1782, and *The Pennsylvania Journal and the Weekly Advertiser*, November 6, 1782.

Delaware state, Wilmington August 12, 1782.
### SIX DOLLARS REWARD.

RAN-AWAY from the subscriber a servant LAD, this country born, aged about 16 years; had on when he went away a broadcloth jacket without sleeves, the skirts of which are cut or tore off even with the pockets, his shirt and trowsers I believe to be tow cloth, his hat a caster. Any person who may apprehend the above described lad, and secure him on any jail, so that I may get him again, shall receive the above reward, and reasonable charges allowed if brought home, by    JONATHAN RUMFORD.
*The Independent Gazetteer*, August 18, 1782.

Wilmington, September 4, 1782.
RAN AWAY from the subscriber, living in Wilmington, on the 20th ult. but since returned home to his mother, and went off again yesterday, an Apprentice Lad, named CARSON DICKESON, 15 years of age, about 5 feet high, by trade a carpenter, has strait light coloured hair, slim made, very talkative, and much given to laughing when in company; has a remarkable scar across his throat, which was burnt when a child; had on and took with him when he went away, two half worn Russia linen shirts, two pair old trowsers, a lead coloured coat, with the pockets inside the skirts, a blue and white linsey jacket, and a white linen jacket with sleeves, one pair buckskin breeches worn one winter, a pair of fustian ditto, one pair of yarn and one pair of old thread stockings, a good pair neats leather shoes, with copper buckles in them, and a felt hat half worn, which he has got bound since he went off. Whoever takes up and secures said apprentice in any goal between Philadelphia, and Baltimore, so that his master may have him again, shall have FOUR DOLLARS REWARD, or TEN DOLLARS if brought home,
        paid by    OBADIAH DINGEE.
N.B. All masters of vessels and others, are forbid to harbour or carry him off at their peril.
*The Pennsylvania Gazette*, September 4, 1782; September 11, 1782; September 18, 1782; September 25, 1782.

Wilmington, October 1, 1782.
ONE DOLLAR REWARD.
RAN-AWAY from his master, an Apprentice BOY, named MATTHIAS VANDIVER, about 5 feet 4 or 5 inches high, down look, short curly hair: had on when he went away, a striped linsey coat, linen trowsers, good shoes, with plated buckles. Whoever secures said Apprentice, and brings him to his master, shall have the above reward.    WILLIAM NASH.
*The Pennsylvania Packet or the General Advertiser*, October 15, 1782; October 22, 1782.

Ten Dollars Reward.
RAN-AWAY on the 3d of October, at night, from the subscriber, living in

Sussex county, Delaware state, a Negro MAN, named HARRY, but may perhaps change his name, born in Kent county, formerly belonging to Mr. Dickinson, is about thirty years of age, nearly 5 feet 8 inches high, a thick sett likely fellow, of a yellow complexion, when drunk looks very ill-natured: Had on and took with him a grey coat lined with white flannel, a white flannel under jacket, three coarse shirts, one pair of tow trowsers, two pair of short breeches, and a pair of large plated shoe buckles, and other articles. Whoever takes up and secures the said Negro, so that his master may get him again, shall have the above reward and reasonable charges paid, by
October 5.        JOHN DAGWORTHY.

*The Pennsylvania Packet or the General Advertiser*, October 24, 1782; November 7, 1782.

Lewes, Sussex County, State of Delaware, Oct. 21, 1782.

WAS committed to my custody, on the 17th inst. (taken in a refugee barge) two negroes, viz, One who calls himself Mine Johnson, born on the Western Shore of Virginia, and says he belongs to a certain Edward Matthews, living on the head of Queen's Creek, and was taken from his said master, about four months ago, he is about nineteen years of age, thick set, and about five feet seven inches high. The other says his name is Samuel Stevenson, a Guinea Negro born, that he belonged to a certain Sarah Baker, (a widow) living in the state of Georgia, between Georgia and Attilmahaw, that he was taken by the enemy about three or four years ago, he is about twenty six years of age, slim built, and about five feet seven or eight inches high. Their masters or owners are requested to come within four weeks from the date hereof, pay the demands against them, otherwise they will be sold for the same.

       Wm. DAVIS, Jailer.

*The Freeman's Journal: or, The North-American Intelligencer*, November 6, 1782; November 13, 1782.

### SLAVES.
#### Twenty Guineas Reward.

RUN-AWAY from New-Castle, last February, two slaves, a black and a yellow; the black is now in Chester gaol. Stephen, a mulatto, near twenty years of age, by this time he may be six feet high, streight limb'd, down look, and by no means forward; his feet is so remarkably long, that the shoemaker that supplies him this fall, may at first view know him.—Also negro Jack, who went off while the British was in Philadelphia. Jack is black, about thirty years old, near six feet high, slender made, his face scar'd in African manner, one of his eyes less than the other; it is probable they may be one the continent, passing for free-men. The above reward, or ten guineas for either

of them, will be paid by William Geddis, Esq. of Philadelphia, or John Wethered, of New-Castle.   Nov 1.
*The Pennsylvania Journal and the Weekly Advertiser*, November 6, 1782; November 20, 1782; November 27, 1782; December 4, 1782. See *The Pennsylvania Journal and the Weekly Advertiser*, March 9, 1782, *The Pennsylvania Gazette*, March 27, 1782, and *The Pennsylvania Gazette*, August 14, 1782.

*Newcastle County, Oct. 26, 1782.*
WAS committed to the gaol of this county, on the 6th day of October, instant, a stout negro man, about thirty-five years of age, five feet, seven inches high, and says his name is Gabriel, and that he is the property of Edward Telfair, formerly of the State of Georgia, who removed his negroes to the back part of Maryland, to Colonel James Johnson's iron works: Therefore his master or owner is requested, to come within six weeks from the above date, and pay charges, and take him away, otherwise he will be discharges according to law, by      THOMAS CLARK, Gaoler.
*The Pennsylvania Journal and the Weekly Advertiser*, November 13, 1782; November 20, 1782; November 27, 1782; December 4, 1782.


RUN AWAY from ISAAC ALLEN, in the city of Philadelphia, on the 4th instant, an indented NEGROE WOMAN, named PHEBE, and took her Child with her, called HANNAH, near three years old. The woman is between 22 and 23 years old, a short, chunky, likely wench, and had a great variety of clothes with her, so that her cloathing cannot particularly described. She is supposed to be secreted some where in Philadelphia, under the name of being free. Whoever takes up said wench and child, and delivers them to ELIJAH WEED, Keeper of the New Goal, shall have FOUR DOLLARS Reward, or if taken in the country, and brought to their master, living in Mill-Creek hundred, New Castle county, shall have SIX DOLLARS Reward, and reasonable charges, paid by     WILLIAM JOHN.
*The Pennsylvania Gazette*, November 13, 1782; January 15, 1783.


*Monckton Park, near Bristol, Bucks, Nov. 13, 1782.*
TWENTY DOLLARS REWARD.
RAN AWAY from the above farm, on the morning of the 5th instant, a young Negro man, named Philip, about 23 years old, but says he is younger, middle size, slender, bow-shin'd or bandy-leg'd; had on a light-coloured short blanket or coarse coat, with a red cape, and red basket buttons, a pair of almost new shoes, white yarn stockings, lately footed. He stole and took with him sundry wearing apparel, which cannot here be described;—he is fond of strong drink,

a fiddle, and dancing, both of which he performs very ill; a great thief and liar; says he has a father and mother with Mr. Ben. Silvester, of Talbot county, Maryland. He was a slave to Mr. Hemphill, of Wilmington, who received one hundred and ten pounds for him last June. To make his time comfortable, his new master made him an indented servant, for a reasonable time, since which he attempted to rob him, and go off to New-York. He was seen last Wednesday near the Red Lyon, on the Bristol road, on his way to Philadelphia, and in Irish-town the same day. Whoever takes up the said Negro, and delivers him to the subscriber, on the above farm, shall receive the above reward, and all reasonable expences.
            ROBERT M. MALCOLM.

N. B. All masters and commanders of vessels are requested not to harbor or carry off said Negro, as they will answer the consequences.

*The Independent Gazetteer*, November 16, 1782; November 19, 1782; November 23, 1782; November 26, 1782.

*November 20, 1782.*
FIVE SHILLINGS REWARD.

RAN away on the 6th of this instant November, from the subscriber, living in Christiana Hundred Newcastle county, an apprentice lad, named SILUS MITCHELL, about 17 years of age, about five feet, eight or nine inches high, slim made, smooth faced, black hair, stoop shouldered; by trade a weaver. Had on when he went away, a light coloured cloth jacket, an old brown under jacket, an half worn wool hat, his shoes almost new. Whoever takes up said lad, and brings him home to his said master, shall have the above reward paid,
            by   SAMUEL LITTLE.

*The Pennsylvania Journal and the Weekly Advertiser*, December 4, 1782; December 7, 1782; December 18, 1782; December 21, 1782; December 28, 1782.

Wilmington, December 26, 1782.
Twenty Dollars Reward.

RAN AWAY on Christmas Eve, from the subscriber, living in Wilmington, New-Castle county, and state of Delaware, a NEGRO Man, named Charles, (formerly London) or may call himself Paul, a spare genteel fellow, about five feet ten or eleven inches high, has a high nose and forehead, very well made, is talkative and bold in appearance, fond of strong liquor. He had on and took with him, an old tow linen shirt, two fine linen ditto, one ruffled, the other plain, one pair old leather breeches, one pair dark yarn stockings, one pair white worsted ditto, a new fine ditto, a scarlet coat and jacket, and old brown round made jacket, lined with tow linen, with wooden buttons, &c. also a brass barrel'd pistol, has been broke at the butt, whoever apprehends and secures the negro, so that his master may get him again, shall receive twenty dollars reward, with all reasonable expences, &c.

DANIEL ADAMS.

*The Pennsylvania Packet or the General Advertiser*, December 31, 1782; January 7, 1783; January 18, 1783; January 30, 1783. See *The Pennsylvania Journal and the Weekly Advertiser*, January 18, 1783.

## 1783

SIXTEEN DOLLARS Reward.

RUN AWAY, the 24th of November last, A likely Negroe Man, named SAUL, of a yellowish complexion, 21 years of age, about 5 feet 11 inches high; had on a country cloth coat of lightish colour, striped jacket, with the stripes across, a pair of long trowsers, striped blue, green and white, a pair of buckskin breeches, one pair of fine woollen stockings of a blue grey, an old fur hat, a home made check shirt, with very pale stripes. Any person apprehending said Negroe, and securing him so that his master may have him again, shall be paid, with reasonable charges, the above reward, by the subscriber, living at Christiana Bridge.

Dec. 23, 1782.          MORTON WELSH.

*The Pennsylvania Gazette*, January 1, 1783; January 8, 1783. See *The Pennsylvania Journal and the Weekly Advertiser*, January 1, 1783.


Sixteen Dollars Reward.

RUN-away the 24th of November last, a likely negro man, named SAUL, of a yellowish complexion, 21 years of age, about five feet eleven inches high; had on a country cloth coat of a light colour, striped jacket, with the stripes across, a pair of long trowsers, striped blue, green, and white, a pair of buckskin breeches, a pair of fine woolen stockings of a blue grey, an old fir [sic] hat, a home-made check shirt, with very pale stripes. Any person apprehending said negro, and securing him, so that his master may have him again, shall be paid, with reasonable charges, the above reward, by the subscriber, living at Christiana bridge.     MARTIN WELSH.

*The Pennsylvania Journal and the Weekly Advertiser*, January 1, 1783; January 4, 1783; January 8, 1783; January 15, 1783. See *The Pennsylvania Gazette*, January 1, 1783.

*Wilmington, Jan.* 7, 1783.

Twenty Dollars Reward.

RAN away on Christmas eve, from the subscriber, living in Wilmington, New-Castle county, and Delaware State, a negro man named Charles, formerly London; a spare genteel fellow, about five feet ten or eleven inches high, has a high nose and fore-head, very well made, is talkative and bold in appearance, fond of strong liquor, has a small scar over one of his eyes. He had on, and took with him, two white linen shirts, one rufled, the other plain, one old tow linnen ditto, one pair old leather breeches, one pair fine white worsted stockings, and one pair dark yarn stockings, a pair of good boots, new shoes, a new fine hat, an old round ditto, a scarlet coat and waistcoat, an old blue cloth great coat, with a white velveret cape, an old brown round made jacket, lined with tow linen, with wooden buttons. Also a brass barrel pistol, has been broke at the butt, and mended. At the same time a negro man, named Sam, belonging to Mr. Gunning Bedford, ran off, with the above-described negroe, and were both seen in the city of Philadelphia. Sam has been since taken up, on board of a brig in the city, and was just going to sea, and it is supposed that Charles will endeavour to make his escape the same way. I am informed he had obtained a pass from a free negroe in this town, by the name of Post, under which pass and name he now passes. All Captains of vessels are forwarned taking the above said negroe off. Whoever apprehends and secures the above-described negro, so that the owner may get him again, shall have the above reward, and all reasonable charges, if brought home, paid by the subscriber.     DANIEL J. ADAMS.

*The Pennsylvania Journal and the Weekly Advertiser*, January 18, 1783; January 22, 1783; January 25, 1783; February 1, 1783; February 5, 1783; February 12, 1783; February 15, 1783; February 22, 1783; March 1, 1783; March 8, 1783; March 12, 1783; *The Pennsylvania Gazette*, January 22, 1783; January 29, 1783; February 5, 1783. Minor differences between the papers. See *The Pennsylvania Packet or the General Advertiser*, December 31, 1782.

### FOUR DOLLARS REWARD.
*Newark, Newcastle County, Jan.* 21, 1783.

WHEREAS a certain JAMES BOGGS, some time ago a residenter at Christiana Bridge, upon the 14th ult. came to the house of the subscriber, in the town of Newark, aforesaid, and in the evening stole away a new MAN's SADDLE. The said Bogs is about 5 feet, 7 or 8 inches high, of a fresh complexion, where he is not known pretends to be much in the mercantile business. He talks much and pretends more, especially when elevated with drink. His cloths are not very certain, as he may change them. Whoever takes up and secures the said Boggs, so that the subscriber may get his saddle, and the offender by brought to justice, shall have the above reward paid by
JOHN MAGUIRE.

The said Boggs is said to be lurking some where about the city of Philadelphia, and searching for an opportunity of going out to sea.

*The Pennsylvania Journal and the Weekly Advertiser*, January 25, 1783; January 29, 1783; February 1, 1783; February 8, 1783.

Twenty Dollars Reward.

RAN-AWAY on the 26th of last month, a Negro Man, named ISAAC, a stout, likely young fellow, about 5 feet, 10 inches high, stoops much in the shoulders and is very talkative: had on and took with him a pair of plush and a pair of leather breeches, a pale blue coat with a red velvet collar, a scarlet waistcoat and another of calf-skin dressed, with the hair on. Whoever takes up and secures said Negro, so that his master may have him again, shall receive the above reward and reasonable charges paid, by the subscriber, living in Jones's-Neck, Kent County, in the Delaware State.
WILLIAM WHITE.         Feb. 3.

*The Pennsylvania Packet or the General Advertiser*, February 6, 1783; February 11, 1783.

TWO DOLLARS REWARD.

RAN AWAY from the subscriber, living in Brandywine hundred, near Wilmington, Delaware state, an Apprentice LAD, named JOHN KILDEAR, about 19 years of age. Whoever takes up said apprentice and brings him to his master, shall have the above reward, but no charges paid.
Feb. 19         WILLIAM ELLIOT, senior.

*The Pennsylvania Packet or the General Advertiser*, February 25, 1783; March 1, 1783; March 8, 1783.

ABSCONDED from his bail, on the 6th of this instant March, a certain JAMES CASKEY, a carpenter by trade, about 30 years of age, 5 feet 7 or 8 inches high, slim made, and has a high nose; wore brown clothes when he absconded, but commonly wears light coloured clothes; his place of residence is Wilmington, but went away from his bail to Philadelphia. Whoever secures the said Caskey, so as the subscriber may get him again, shall have FIVE POUNDS REWARD, and reasonable charges, paid by
                JOHN STEWART, living in Southwark.
N. B. All masters of vessels are forbid to harbour or carry him off.

*The Pennsylvania Gazette*, March 12, 1783; March 19, 1783. See *The Pennsylvania Packet or the General Advertiser*, April 1, 1783.

FIVE POUNDS REWARD.

On the 6th of instant absconded from his bail, March, a certain JAMES CASKEY, by trade a carpenter, about 30 years of age, five feet 7 or 8 inches high, slim made, and has a high nose, wore brown clothes when he absconded, but commonly wears light coloured clothes; his place of residence is Wilmington, but went away from his bail in Philadelphia. Whoever secures said Caskey, so as the subscriber may get him again, shall have the above reward, and reasonable charges, paid by JOHN STEWART, living in Southwark.　　　　March 7, 1783.

N. B. All masters of vessels and others, are forbid to harbour or carry him off at their peril.

*The Pennsylvania Packet or the General Advertiser*, April 1, 1783. See *The Pennsylvania Gazette*, March 12, 1783


ALSO was committed to the same goal, A NEGROE WENCH, about 15 or 16 years of age, who says she belongs to a certain Job Hervey, in Wilmington. Her master is desired to come, in two weeks from this date, prove his property, pay charges, and take her away, otherwise she will be sold.
*Chester, April 7.*　　　　JOHN GARDNER, Sheriff.
*The Pennsylvania Gazette*, April 9, 1783; April 30, 1783.


RUN away from the subscriber, living in Brandywine Hundred, New Castle county, Delaware state, near Grubb's tavern, the sign of the three tuns, a servant lad, named JOHN KINSEY, supposed he will alter his name, near 5 feet high, fair complexion, pitted with the smallpox, had on when he wept away, a grey cloth jacket, homespun shirt and trowsers, a pair of good coarse shoes. Whoever takes up and secures him in any goal, so that his master may get him again, shall receive THREE POUNDS reward, and reasonable charges paid, by　　　　ISAAC GRUBB.

N. B. All masters of vessels and others are forbid to harbour or carry him off, at their peril.　　　　April 26, 1783.

*The Pennsylvania Gazette*, May 14, 1783; May 21, 1783; July 2, 1783.


### TWELVE DOLLARS REWARD.

RAN AWAY on the 27th of last month, a Negro MAN, named SAM, alias SAMUEL THOMSON, about 26 years of age, middle stature: had on when he went off, a light coloured bearskin coat and trousers, and red jacket; has the letters S. T. on one of his arms, and plays on the violin, one of which he has with him; he may possibly have a forged pass. Any person apprehending and securing said Negro Man, so that his master may have him again, shall receive the above reward, paid by GUNNING BEDFORD, esq; at Wilmington, Delaware state, or by GUNNING BEDFORD of Philadelphia.

N. B. All masters of vessels are hereby forbid to carry him off at their peril.

*The Pennsylvania Packet or the General Advertiser*, May 17, 1783; May 24, 1783; June 5, 1783.


WHEREAS a certain *Abraham Albert* (the master shoemaker belonging to the Duc de Lazun's troops, in Wilmington, New-Castle county, Delaware state) did, on the 9th day of this instant, May, sell to me a likely Negro wench, named Bett, about 21 years of age, together with a Mulatto child about eight months old, which wench he said he got with his wife at Boston; but since the said troops went away, says she was born in North-Carolina, and was free: But as I have not understood that any of the slaves were manumited, am of opinion she was taken by some of the British robbers, and fell into the hands of the French troops at the surrender of York-Town.—This is therefore to give notice to her master, if any she has, or any other legally claim to her, to come and prove property, pay charges, and take her.

SAMUEL M'CLINTOCK,

Brandywine hundred, in the county and state aforesaid, May 27, 1783.

*The Pennsylvania Journal and the Weekly Advertiser*, May 28, 1783; June 4, 1783; June 11, 1783; June 18, 1783. See *The Pennsylvania Gazette*, June 4, 1783.


Brandywine Hundred, Delaware State, May 27.

WHEREAS a certain ABRAHAM ALBERT (the Master Shoemaker belonging to the Duke De Lazun's troops, in Wilmington, New-Castle county, Delaware State) did, on the 9th day of this instant May, sell to me, A likely Negroe Wench, named BETT, about 21 years of age, together with a Mulattoe Child, about 8 months old, which Wench he said he got with his wife at Boston; but since the said troops went away, he says she was born in North-Carolina, and was free; but as I have not understood that any of the Slaves in that State were manumitted, am of opinion she was taken by some of the British robbers, and fell into the hands of the French troops at the surrender of York Town. This is therefore to give notice to her master, if any she has, or any other person legally claiming, to come and prove their property, pay charges, and take her away. SAMUEL M'CLINTOCK.

*The Pennsylvania Gazette*, June 4, 1783; June 11, 1783. See *The Pennsylvania Journal and the Weekly Advertiser*, May 28, 1783


RUNAWAY from the subscriber, on the 28th of March last, an apprentice girl, named CATHERINE CROUT, of short stature, with long yellow hair, broad faced, and squints a little; had on, and took with her, an home made

gown, white and yellow, one short ditto of the same, two lincey short gowns, two home spun shifts and two aprons, one black lincey petticoat, one red ditto, a red and white calicoe jacket and petticoat, a linen bonnet of a lye colour, with sundry other articles. Whoever takes up said girl, and secures her, so that her master may have her again, shall receive a reward of One Shilling, paid by      DUNCAN BEARD.
Cantwell's Bridge, May 27, 1783.
 *The Pennsylvania Gazette*, June 4, 1783; June 11, 1783.


WAS found in the possession of Richard Ketchem, late a Capt. of a refugee barge, on Sunday the first day of June inst. a MULATTO BOY, supposed to be nine or ten years of age, and no less than probable belongs to some citizens of these states, and stolen from them by this infamous traitor. Any person proving his property may recover said boy, by applying to the subscribers, at Duck Creek, Cross Roads, Kent county, state of Delaware.
    RICHARD DERRICK.
June 5, 1783. JOHN WATTINGTON. JOSIAH BARLOW.
    JEHU TOWNSEND.
N. B. The boy says his name is Nick.
 *The Pennsylvania Journal and the Weekly Advertiser*, June 28, 1783; July 5, 1783.


☞WHEREAS my Wife MARGARET, during my absence from her, has been guilty of UNCHASTITY, and has had a *base begotten Child* by (as She says) a Man of the name of *Benjamin Hartley*, of Wilmington, in New-Castle County Delaware: These are therefore to forewarn all Persons from trusting her on my Account, as I will not pay any debts of her contracting. *Witness my Hand, this Sixth Day of July,* 1783.
   THOMAS RAWLINGS.
 N. B. Those that RIDE may SHOE; or, He that DANCES may Pay the FIDLER.
 *The Royal Gazette*, July 12, 1783.


      *Wilmington, Newcastle county,* 29*th* of 6*th mo.* 1783.
RUN away from the subscribers, two Apprentice lads, viz. JAMES BOOTH, a cooper by trade, about 19 years of age, 5 feet, some inches high, well set, full faced, dark hair; had on when he went away, a good felt hat bound round the edge, homespun brown linen coatee, striped waistcoat, homespun shirt, check trowsers, and calf-skin shoes. And HENRY GUN, a cedar-cooper by trade, about the same age, 5 feet 8 or 9 inches high, has a stoppage in his speech, long black hair, and commonly keeps it tied; had on when he went away, a lye

coloured striped waistcoat, and under ditto of the same, a pair of homespun breeches, thread stockings, neats leather shoes, a fine shirt, and supposed to have another with him. Any person securing James Booth in any gaol, shall have Forty Shillings Reward, or if brought home Three Pounds, and for Henry Gun, if secured in gaol, Thirty Shillings Reward, or if brought home Forty-five Shillings, and reasonable charges, paid by the subscribers. It is requested for farmers, graziers, coopers and others, to take notice of strangers. All persons are forbid to harbour them, and all masters of vessels are forbid to carry them off at their peril.   HENRY REYNOLDS,
GEORGE WITSIL.
*The Independent Gazetteer*, July 26, 1783; August 2, 1783.


SIXTEEN DOLLARS REWARD.

RAN-AWAY from the subscriber, living near Christiana-bridge, in Newcastle county, in the night of the 11th instant, June, A NEGRO MAN, named NORTH, born in Guinea, and speaks much in that dialect, about 30 years of age, of short stature, slim made, stoop'd shouldered, walks with his toes much out: had on and took with him the following apparel, viz. one black and white coloured cloth coat and jacket, one blue cloth coat, and one coat of fustian with yellow metal buttons, a yellow clouded jacket and a blue ditto lined with yellow, black everlasting breeches, white corded ditto, two wool hats, one of which almost new, cotton, flax, and tow shirts and trowsers, one pair home made striped trowsers, two pair white thread stockings, half worn shoes with large brass buckles. Whoever takes up said Negro Man, and secures him so that his master may have him again, shall have the above reward, and all reasonable charges if brought home, paid by        FREDERICK DEVOU.        June 24.
*The Pennsylvania Packet or the General Advertiser*, July 29, 1783.


SIXTEEN DOLLARS REWARD.

RAN AWAY from Unity Forge, Sussex county, state of Delaware, on the 30th ult. a Negro Man named BEN LATELY, the property of Samuel Lawerty of said place about five feet eight inches high, twenty seven years of age, a well made fellow, very strong and active, of a yellowish hue, his clothes uncertain. Whoever takes up said negro fellow, and secures him in any goal, so that the subscriber can get him again, shall have the above reward, and reasonable charges, if brought home.
JAMES BUCHANAN.
N. B. He probably will pass for a freeman, and is supposed to have a pass.
*The Freeman's Journal: or, The North-American Intelligencer*, July 30, 1783; August 13, 1783.

WAS committed to my custody, on the 19th day of June last, a NEGRO MAN who calls himself *Samuel Moses*, a well set fellow, about five feet, eight inches high, is a little hard of hearing, about 32 years of age; says he belongs to a certain GRIFFIN STIFF, living in or near Northampton Court-house. The owner is desired to come, prove his property, pay charges, and take him again, or he will be sold agreeable to law
*July* 26, 1783.        WILLIAM DAVIS, Gaoler
*Lewes, Sussex County, State of Delaware,*
   *The Independent Gazetteer*, August 16, 1783.


TWELVE DOLLARS Reward.
RAN AWAY from the subscriber, living in Motherkill hundred, Kent county, Delaware state, near the town of Dover, on the 16th inst. A Mulattoe Man, named DICK, about 35 years old, and about 5 feet 2 inches high, middling well set, is left handed, has a scar on his upper lip, pretty long bushy hair, which he combs back on the fore part of his head; he is much addicted to drinking. Had on and took with him, three shirts, two new, two pair of trowsers, one of them blue and white stripe, cross barred, a white linen coat, and a wool hat, pretty much worn. Whoever takes up said fellow, and secures him in any goal, so as his master may have him again, shall have the above reward, and reasonable charges if brought home,
          paid by    GEORGE MANLOVE.
*The Pennsylvania Gazette*, August 27, 1783; September 3, 1783; September 10, 1783.


SIXTEEN DOLLARS REWARD.
RUN away on the night of the 23d instant, from this Borough, a certain JOHN STAKLEN, a Dutchman, by trade a nailer, dark complexion, well set, about 5 feet 7 or 8 inches high, black hair, sometimes clubbed, at other times platted, had on, and took with him, a full suit of deep blue cloth, with mohair buttons, one greenish coloured waistcoat, a wool hat bound, 3 shirts about half-worn, an old pair of white stockings, striped ticken over-alls, a blue and red cap, with a white tassel, one pair of neats leather shoes, one pair of calf skin pumps, one pair broad rimmed brass buckles, one pair scalloped French boots, one small French watch, one pair blue over-all trousers (such as are worn by the French horse) several buttons wanting, and those that are on of various sorts, one pair buckskin ditto, which fit very close to the leg, and are made to tye round the ancle, with narrow black binding, he speaks tolerable English, for the time he has been in the country, is talkative, but particularly so when in liquor.

He stole from the subscriber, one pair saddle-bags, mended at one end, one dark coloured jean coatee, with close cuff sleeves, but since altered, being too small, no pocket flaps, one pair pistols, one large the other small, and several other articles. Whoever takes up the said John Staklen, and brings him to Wilmington, in the Delaware state, or secures him in any goal, so that he may be had, shall be intitled to the above reward and reasonable charges paid by WILLIAM FAWKES.

N. B. The said John Stacklen obtained a pass some time ago from Colonel Craighead; he also had a discharge from the Duke de Lauzun, to whose legion he belonged, until purchased by the subscriber. It is thought he is gone towards Lancaster.

*The Pennsylvania Journal and the Weekly Advertiser*, August 30, 1783; September 17, 1783; September 24, 1783.


RUN away the 17th instant, from the subscriber, an Irish servant man, named DANIEL LAVERTY, (but has since changed his name to SMITH) about 5 feet 8 or 9 inches high, a stout well built man, of a dark complexion, has short hair, and very thick legs. Had on, when he went away, a brown coat, jacket, and breeches; the back of the jacket is white; a fine white shirt and stock, both Irish made, an old large fur hat, white ribbed stockings, and old shoes, half soled, with copper buckles. Whoever takes up the said servant, and secures him in any goal, so that his master may have him again, shall receive EIGHT DOLLARS reward, and if brought home FOUR POUNDS, and reasonable charges, by JOHN AUGUTUS, living in Christiana Hundred, in Newcastle county, state of Delaware. August 26, 1783.

*The Pennsylvania Journal and the Weekly Advertiser*, August 30, 1783.


FORTY DOLLARS Reward.

MADE his escape from the county goal of New Castle, in the State of Delaware, on the night of the 24th instant, a certain Refugee, named Capt. LEVIN TURNER; the fellow is stout and well made, about 5 feet 7 inches high, about 25 years of age, ruddy complexion. Had on when he made his escape, a claret coloured coat, black silk waistcoat and breeches, white thread stockings. Any person apprehending the above described person, and will secure him in any goal in the United States, and give information thereof to the subscriber, residing at New Castle, shall be entitled to the above reward, and reasonable charges, by

New Castle, August 26. THOMAS CLARK, Goaler.

*The Pennsylvania Gazette*, September 3, 1783; September 10, 1783; October 1, 1783; October 8, 1783.

Sixteen Dollars Reward.
RAN AWAY from the subscriber, living in Port Penn, in the Delaware State, the 4th instant, An indented Servant Man, named SAMUEL RICHY, country born, 5 feet 8 or 9 inches high, pretty lusty make, fair complexion; he may probably change his name; was bought out of Philadelphia goal last April; he served part of his time with one Jabez Busby, near Moore's Town, in New Jersey. Had on when he went away, a coarse linen shirt, oznabrigs trowsers, patched on the knees, light blue broadcloth jacket without sleeves, a pair of shoes, with large block tin buckles, and an old hat. Whoever takes up said servant and brings him home, or secures him in any goal, so that his master may get him, shall have the above reward, and reasonable charges
paid, by JAMES READ. Aug. 30.
*The Pennsylvania Gazette*, September 3, 1783; September 10, 1783; September 17, 1783; October 1, 1783.


Chester, September 8, 1783.
WAS taken up, and committed to the goal of Chester county, on the 8th day of this instant, A certain Negroe Man, who calls himself JOE McAULEY, about 5 feet 8 inches high, and about 27 or 28 years of age, says he belongs to a certain Robert Haughy, near Back creek, New Castle county, in the State of Delaware. His master is desired to come, prove his property, pay charges, and take him away, or he will be sold in six weeks from this date.
JOHN GARDNER, Sheriff.
*The Pennsylvania Gazette*, September 10, 1783; September 17, 1783; September 24, 1783. See *The North-American Intelligencer*, September 10, 1783.


WAS taken up and committed to the jail of Chester county, on the 8th day of this instant, a certain Negro Man, who calls himself Joe M'Auly, about five feet eight inches high, and about 27 or 28 years of age, says he belongs to a certain Robert Haughty, near Back Creek, New Castle County, in the State of Delaware; his master is desired to come, prove his property, pay charges and take him away, or he will be sold in six weeks from this date.
Chester, September 8th, 1783.      JOHN GARDNER, Sheriff.
*The North-American Intelligencer*, September 10, 1783; September 24, 1783. See *The Pennsylvania Gazette*, September 10, 1783.


SIXTEEN DOLLARS REWARD.
RAN-AWAY from the subscriber, living near the head of Sassafras river, Kent county Maryland, on the eighth day of July last, a Molatto Fellow, named Shade, about 30 years of age, and about 5 feet 9 inches high, well set and very active,

has a remarkable scar on the right side of his under jaw, occasioned by the kick on a horse, was raised to farming, tho' he pretends to some other kinds of business, as sawing with a whip saw, carpenter work, and moulding of bricks; had on when he went away, white homespun shirt, grey linsey breeches, thread stockings, and good shoes, an under jacket without sleeves, a blue broadcloth coat faced with red, and an old hat. He was raised in Virginia, and thence sold into Sussex county, in Delaware, near Lewes Town, and afterwards to the subscriber; it is supposed he as taken with him two tow shirts, and two pair of tow trousers. Whoever takes up and secures said molatto in any goal, so that his master may have him again, shall receive the above reward, and if brought home, reasonable charges, paid by me,
Sept. 12.          JOHN FRANCIS.
*The Pennsylvania Journal and the Weekly Advertiser*, September 13, 1783. See *The Pennsylvania Gazette*, September 17, 1783.


SIXTEEN DOLLARS Reward.
RUN way from the subscriber, living near the Head of Sassafras River, Kent county, Maryland, on the 8th day of July last, a Mulattoe fellow, named SHADE, about 30 years of age, and about 5 feet 9 inches high, well set and very active, has a remarkable scar on the right side of his under jaw, occasioned by the kick of a horse, was raised to farming, though he pretends something to other kinds of business, as sawing with the whip saw, carpentry and moulding of bricks; had on, when he went away, a white homespun shirt, grey linsey breeches, thread stockings, and good shoes, an under jacket, without sleeves, a blue broadcloth coat, faced with red, and an old hat. He was raised in Virginia, and thence sold into Sussex county, in Delaware, near Lewes Town, and afterwards to the subscriber. Supposed to take with him two tow shirts, and two pair of tow trowsers. Whoever takes up and secures said Mulattoe in any goal, so that his master may get him again, shall receive the above reward, and if brought home reasonable charges,
              paid by    JOHN FRANCIS.
*The Pennsylvania Gazette*, September 17, 1783; October 8, 1783. *The Pennsylvania Journal and the Weekly Advertiser*, September 13, 1783.


New Castle, October 13, 1783.
NOW in the goal of this county, the following Negroe Men, to wit, JACOB, a stout young fellow, about 21 years of age, and confesseth himself to be the property of Nathan Griffith, of the town of Baltimore. SPENCE, a stout well made fellow, about 27 years of age, about 5 feet 10 or 11 inches high, and says he belongs to a certain Mr. Hudson, of Baltimore town, and that he ran away from a Mr. Ridgley's ironworks two years ago. Their master or owners

are requested to come, within three weeks from the above date, and take them away, otherwise they will be discharged according to law.

     THOMAS CLARK, Goaler.

*The Pennsylvania Gazette,* October 15, 1783; October 22, 1783; October 29, 1783.


      EIGHT DOLLARS Reward.
   Mount-Pleasant, Newcastle county, October 6, 1783.

RAN away from the subscriber on the first day of September last, but did not leave the neighbourhood till the 21st, a negro Man, named STEPH, very black, about 5 feet, 8 or 9 inches high, slim made, and knock kneed, has lost some of his fore-teeth, has a scar on the back of his right hand, and is about 23 years of age, and is much addicted to lying and running away. Had on when he went away a half worn wool hat, a brown cloth coat, half worn, new shoes with old brass buckles, thread stockings and linen breeches; but it is likely he may change his dress and name. It is thought he has taken the road for New-York. Any person that will secure the above negro in any jail, so that the owner may have him again, shall have the above reward and reasonable charges if brought home, by   RICHARD GRIFFITH.

*The Pennsylvania Journal and the Weekly Advertiser,* November 1, 1783. See *The Pennsylvania Gazette,* December 3, 1783.


      New Castle, November 24, 1783.

WAS committed to the goal of this county, on the 16th of this instant, a certain SAMUEL FLETCHER, in company with JOHN HAMER, on suspicion of horse stealing, and both were indicted, tried, and Fletcher being found guilty of the felony, received his punishment according to law, and Hamer being acquitted, was remanded to goal, as being a person suspected of committing divers felonies within the commonwealth of Pennsylvania; and it is alledged that the said John Hamer was proscribed by that name in the public papers of said commonwealth. Therefore any person or persons knowing him to be the same, is hereby requested to appear at any time before the 22d day of December next, and have him removed, otherwise he will be discharged, by   THOMAS CLARK, Goaler.

*The Pennsylvania Gazette,* December 3, 1783; December 10, 1783; December 17, 1783.


    Mount Pleasant, New Castle county, Nov. 20, 1783.

RAN AWAY from the subscriber, about the first of September last, A Negroe Man, named STESS, 23 years of age, about 5 feet 8 inches high, light and

slim built, about 5 feet 8 inches high, light and slim built, somewhat knock-kneed, one or more of his fore teeth out, has a scar on the back of his right hand; it is thought he has a brown coat on, linen breeches, thread stockings, with country made shoes; he appears to be an orderly, mannerly fellow, and a great Methodist, and will endeavour to pass for a free man: it is thought he has gone towards New York, but perhaps may be skulking about the wharves at Philadelphia, in order to get a passage. Any person that will secure him in any goal, so that the subscriber may get him again, shall have EIGHT DOLLARS Reward, if taken within the state of Delaware, and if out of the state, TWELVE DOLLARS, with all reasonable charges,
    paid by RICHARD GRIFFITH.
N.B. All masters of vessels and others are forbid to harbour or carry him off at their peril.
 *The Pennsylvania Gazette*, December 3, 1783; December 10, 1783; December 17, 1783. See *The Pennsylvania Journal and the Weekly Advertiser*, November 1, 1783.

## EIGHT DOLLARS REWARD.

RAN away from the subscriber, living near Middletown, in Newcastle county, and state of Delaware, on the 12th instant, a Negro man named Tom, but has since changed his name to Jack, aged about 20 years, about 5 feet 6 or 7 inches high. Had on when he went away, a short white coat with wooden buttons, and no pocket flaps, a mixed brown cloath jacket, without sleeves, and laerd before, a pair of old buckskin breeches, white yarn stockings, and double soaled shoes. He is a well-made fellow, very black and smooth-faced. He has been seen one mile above Wilmington, and it is thought he will either endeavor to get on board some outward bound vessel, or else to cross the country, toward New London cross roads, as he has a mother in that neighbourhood. Whoever takes up said fellow, and secures him in any goal, so that his master may get him again, shall have the above reward, and reasonable charges paid by  HARMANUS SCHEE.
N. B. He says he was set free by Mr. Thomas Rothwell, on account of his turning Methodist.    Dec. 21.
 *The Pennsylvania Journal and the Weekly Advertiser*, December 31, 1783; January 3, 1784.

# INDEX

Abercrombie, Barbara, 327
Abraham, Hannah, 190
Adair, John, 143
Adams, Daniel, 365
Adams, Daniel J., 366
Adams, George, 76
Adams, Hans, 207
Adams, James, 207, 251, 255, 345
Adams, John, 267
Adams, Mr., 163
Adams, Thomas, 112
Adamson, James, 250
Aiken, John, 262
Albert, Abraham, 369
Alderton, John, 301, 303
Alexander, Daniel, 181
Alexander, James, 183
Alexander, John, 299
Alford, Thomas, 86
All, Robert, 183
Allcorn, James, 320
Allcorn, William, 320
Allen, Aaron, 66
Allen, Isaac, 363
Allen, Willam, 124
Allen, William, 241
Allfree, Thomas, 48
Allison, Samuel, 87
Allmark, Elizabeth, 125
Aloan, Mary, 27
Alpden, Matthias, 25
Alton, William, 26
Ambruster, Matthias, 80
Amwood, John, 346
Anders, William, 227, 230
Anderson, Captain, 339
Anderson, Daniel, 337
Anderson, David, 126, 129
Anderson, George, 293

Anderson, James, 88, 134, 242, 360
Anderson, John, 321, 351
Anderson, Joseph, 209, 210
Anderson, Thomas, 11
Anderson, William, 36
Andrew, Richard, 241
Andrews, John, 113
Andrews, Mr., 111
Andrews, William, 230
Andrewsgold, Edward, 360
Anslow, Thomas, 71
Anthony, Elizabeth, 22
Apty, Thomas, 344
Armitage, James, 13
Armour, William, 54
Armstrong, Benjamin, 262, 263
Armstrong, Cornelius, 228
Armstrong, James, 147
Armstrong, John, 257
Armstrong, Mary, 114, 115, 279
Armstrong, William, 107, 152
Arrowsmith, Benjamin, 158
Arthur, Robert, 61
Auckintack, Alexander, 185
Augusta, John, 339
Augutus, John, 373
Backen, Philip, 281
Bailey, Isaac, 217
Baird, Robert, 18
Baity, Patrick, 233
Baker, Samuek, 334
Baker, Sarah, 362
Baker, William, 252
Balis, Daniel, 191
Ball, Andrew, 103
Ball, John, 282
Balvaird, Jannet, 59
Bambridge, John, 172, 175
Bandy, Andrew, 60

Bandy, Richard, 60
Banning, John, 222
Barber, Peter, 4
Bargain, Ann, 17
Barkush, John, 267
Barlow, Henry, 84
Barlow, Josiah, 370
Barnes, Elizabeth, 196
Barnes, G., 271
Barr, Thomas, 33
Barry, Hugh, 272, 274
Barry, Mathias, 4
Barry, Robert, 95
Bartholomew, Capt., 335
Bartley, Thomas, 146
Basil, Robert, 32
Bateman, Samuel, 134
Battell, French, 347
Battell, William, 5, 8, 17
Baxter, James, 44
Bayard, Widow, 229
Bayles, Daniel, 334
Beady, John, 66
Beard, Duncan, 370
Beate, Isaac, 197
Bedford, Gunning, 366, 368
Beech, Thomas, 185
Beeks, William, 22
Belcher, James, 198
Bell, James, 317
Bellach, James, 195
Bennett, James, 39
Bennett, John, 54
Bennett, Margaret, 140
Bentley, George, 102
Berry, Benjamin, 11, 14, 15, 16
Berry, Betty, 229
Berry, Elizabeth, 215
Berry, Joseph, 354
Berry, Preston, 273, 274
Berry, William, 34, 47
Bevan, Joshua, 44
Beverton, Samuel, 92

Biays, Matthew, 195
Bickham, Sanders, 229
Bickley, Sam., 48, 49
Bickley, Samuel, 41, 43, 44, 48
Bilderbank, Joseph, 234
Bimpson, Henry, 80
Bird, Mark, 328, 330
Bird, Mr., 259
Bishop, Henry, 72, 75
Bishop, Thomas, 182
Black, Charles, 166, 170
Black, James, 106, 278, 325, 338
Black, William, 286
Blackshear, Morgon, 295
Blacksher, John, 133
Blackwood, S., 199
Blackwood, Samuel, 199
Blair, Captain, 90
Blaney, William, 214
Bleany, William, 221, 222
Block, Richard, 201, 203, 206
Blue, Uriah, 72
Blunt, Samuel, 110
Blyth, John, 307
Boardley, John Beale, 197
Boggs, Elizabeth, 122
Boggs, James, 366
Boggs, John, 307
Boggs, Joseph, 41
Bolden, Nathan, 246
Bolton, Thomas, 215
Bond, Captain, 5
Bond, Thomas, 56
Bonham, Ephraim, 241
Boon, John, 326
Boon, William, 157
Boort, Jonathan, 106
Booth, James, 370
Booth, John, 56
Borell, Andrew, 136
Borrough, Joseph, 128
Boss, Edward, 168
Bouchell, Doctor, 227

Bouchell, Sluyter, 227
Boucher, James, 77
Bowen, John, 41
Bowen, William, 181
Bowle, Joseph, 45
Bowman, William, 119, 185
Boyce, Boaz, 73, 87
Boyce, William, 314
Boyd, John, 117
Boyl, Michael, 167
Bracken, Henry, 191
Bracken, Philip, 282
Brackin, William, 318
Bradford, Samuel, 250
Bradley, John, 300
Bradshaw, John, 299
Bradshaw, William, 73
Braidy, Patrick, 233
Braken, Henry, 246
Brann, Andrew, 149
Brannen, Michael, 73
Bratten, George, 74
Bratten, James, 133, 134
Brett, William, 275
Brewer, Edward, 108, 109
Brice, Lawrence, 119
Bridges, Edward, 37
Briggs, Joseph, 41
Briscow, Isaac, 172
Britt, Daniel, 74, 173
Brobson, William, 256, 280, 281, 282, 302, 304
Brockenbrough, John, 212
Broker, Eustatius, 101
Broom, James, 112
Browen, William, 242
Brown, Eleanor, 183
Brown, Godfrey, 106
Brown, James, 123, 198
Brown, John, 164, 188, 189, 266, 275, 276, 286
Brown, Michael, 21
Brown, Patrick, 119
Brown, William, 106, 129, 139, 339
Bryan, Andrew, 188
Bryan, Elizabeth, 224
Bryan, John, 6, 191
Bryan, Moses, 335
Bryant, Honor, 110
Buchanan, George, 314
Buchanan, James, 371
Buchanan, William, 217
Buchannan, Mr., 337
Buckingham, John, 51
Buckley, John, 125
Buckly, Elizabeth, 323
Buckly, Michael, 285
Bullen, John, 245
Bumgardain, Mrs., 198
Bunker, Benjamin, 353, 354, 355
Burk, Richard, 4
Burke, Thomas, 192
Burn, Captain, 215
Burnet, William, 168
Burns, James, 68
Burns, William, 207
Burroh, Joseph, 126
Burroughs, Joseph, 225, 226
Burton, William, 35
Busby, Jabez, 374
Bush, David, 37, 107
Busser, John Christopher, 275, 276
Butler, Thomas, 315
Butler, William, 260, 261
Caddis, William, 360
Caddle, James, 81
Cahoon, Charles, 328
Cahoone, James, 15
Cain, John, 276
Caldwell, James, 244
Caldwell, Joseph, 166, 246
Calley, John, 106
Callsey, William, 7

Camble, James, 203
Camp, Joseph, 312
Campbell, Duncan, 61
Campbell, John, 81
Canby, James, 87
Canby, Thomas, 90, 94, 96
Cane, Abel, 18
Cannan, Matthew, 115, 164, 179
Cannan, Michael, 194
Cannon, James, 174
Cannon, Matthew, 176
Cantwell, Richard, 11
Carabery, Terence, 150
Carberry, Hugh, 93
Carlisle, Joseph, 86
Carr, Catherine, 311
Carr, Peter, 103
Carr, Robert, 130
Carril, Patrick, 55
Carroll, John, 55, 168, 176, 197
Carsan, Mr., 45
Carsan, Richard, 105
Carson, Charles, 170
Carson, Humphrey, 337
Carson, James, 173
Carson, Mr., 148
Carson, William, 259, 269, 270, 272, 348
Carter, John, 124, 239
Carter, William, 40, 149
Carty, Cornelius, 107
Caruther, Nathaniel, 3
Carvel, Jacob, 212
Caskey, James, 367
Cast, Henry, 154
Caten, Robert, 119
Caten, Thomas, 119
Caudon, Duncan, 229
Caulfield, Mary, 318, 319
Cavenor, Charles, 43
Chalmers, James, 26
Chalmers, Jenet, 26
Chamberlain, John, 62, 63

Chambers, John, 230
Chambers, Mathew, 45
Charlton, William, 79
Chattin, James, 186
Cheevers, Capt., 263
Chestnut, James, 81
Chevers, William, 261
Chew, Samuel, 318
Chick, Nathaniel, 351
Chubb, George, 151
Chubb, William, 151
Clare, Peter, 5
Clark, David, 307
Clark, George, 157, 306
Clark, Hugh, 66, 69
Clark, James, 97
Clark, John, 72, 75, 95, 96, 160, 225, 331, 332, 343
Clark, Robert, 20
Clark, Thomas, 38, 315, 323, 328, 330, 339, 343, 346, 350, 351, 355, 356, 359, 363, 373, 376
Clarkson, John, 168
Claxton, James, 39
Clay/Clayton, Joseph, 28
Clayton, James, 126
Clayton, John, 102
Cleary, Robert, 81
Cleghorn, Robert, 315
Clemens, Eleanor, 190
Clement, David, 86
Clements, John, 267
Clemmons, Edward, 220
Clemson, Thomas, 52
Cleneay, Samuel, 156
Clenfay, William, 229
Clingan, William, 133, 134
Clinton, Thomas, 151
Cloyd, David, 24
Cobourn, Joseph, 82
Cochran, David, 198, 199
Cochran, James, 207, 326

Cochran, Moses, 230
Cochran, William, 294, 332
Cockey, Thomas, Jr., 298, 301
Cockey, Thomas, Sr., 298, 301
Cockran, James, 200
Colburn, Captain, 172
Coldren, James, 79
Cole, John, 248, 249
Colegate, Richard, 52
Coleman, Edward/Edmund, 293
Coleman, Robert, 351
Colesberry, Swain, 125
Colesberry, Swen, 126
Colesbery, Swen, 128
Colesbury, Henry, 142
Colesbury, Swen, 130
Colgan, James, 138
Collings, John, 97
Collins, James Blight, 310
Collins, John, 269
Collins, Thomas, 61, 65, 158
Collister, Daniel, 162
Colsberry, Swen, 129
Con, John, 195
Conaway, Cornelius, 123
Conely, Briant, 50
Coner, Morris, 132
Conkey, Robert, 334
Connely, Thomas, 280, 282
Conner, Charles, 74
Conner, Patrick, 59
Connolin, Patrick, 74
Connor, Charles, 70
Connor, Jeremiah, 90
Connor, John, 85, 116, 308
Connor, Michael, 229
Conolly, Mary, 67
Consiglio, Francis, 182, 185
Conway, James, 267
Conway, William, 185
Conyngham, Mr., 119
Cooch, Thomas, 91, 94

Cooch, Thomas, Jr., 245
Cook, John, 120, 121, 122
Cook, Richard, 8
Cook, Walter, 108
Cook, William, 345
Coombs, Thomas, 360
Cooper, Peter, 354
Cormely, Robert, 41
Corsa, William, 153
Cortney, Ann, 79
Cosway, James, 34
Cotter, James, 158
Coulton, John, 49
Coulton, Marmaduke, 1
Cowan, Henry, 176, 179
Cowden, Philip, 199
Cowpland, David, 311
Cox, Isaac, 230, 231, 316
Cox, William, 1
Crafford, David, 267
Craghead, George, 136
Crapper, Levin, 192, 193, 204, 205
Crips, Andrew, 191, 236
Crips, Matthew, 192
Croane, Mary, 191
Croker, John, 20
Cromel, Mary, 106
Cromwell, Joseph, 258
Cronkelton, James, 229
Cropper, Bastin, 276
Crosby, John, 150
Crout, Catherine, 369
Crow, George, 80, 354
Crummell, Mary, 103
Cumings, Samuel, 344
Cummings, Mr., 181
Cummins, James, 116
Cunningham, Henry, 186
Curran, John, 293
Currey, George, 146
Curtis, Jehu, 4
Custolow, John, 127

Dagness, Catharine, 357
Dagworthy, John, 362
Daily, Brian, 195
Daily, John, 209, 220
Daily, William, 294
Dalton, Richard, 84
Darlington, William, 22
Davey, Mr., 45
Davies, James, 80
Davies, William, 98
Davis, Alexander, 77
Davis, David, 166
Davis, Elijah, 155
Davis, John, 343
Davis, Mr., 178
Davis, Thomas, 229
Davis, William, 68, 238, 241, 289, 362, 372
Dawes, Edward, 82
Dawson, Isaac, 300
Dawson, Richard, 298, 300
Day, John, 35, 235
Decamp, Jacob, 197
Decou, Isaac, 290
Delany, William, 289
Dellum, Josiah, 220
Delong, John, 139
Demerist, Elias/Haley, 35
Dempsy, Vallentine, 6
Demsey, Laurence, 313
Denn, Murtha, 83
Dennis, Richard, 130, 188
Denny, Christopher, 254
Denny, Walter, 24
Dent, Lawrence, 35
Dereckson, Zachariah, 144
Derrick, Richard, 370
Devenny, Cornelius, 194
Devou, Frederick, 371
Diamond, Margery, 245
Dickenson, John, 254
Dickeson, Carson, 361
Dickinson, Mr., 362

Dickson, James, 248, 249
Dickson, John, 295
Dickson, Samuel, 103
Diggens, Mary, 200
Dingee, Obadiah, 361
Dirrin, Richard, 257
Dixon, Thomas, 135
Dixon/Dixsen, Robert, 35
Dixson, John, 259
Dixson, William, 310
Dobbins, John, 162
Dodd, John, 44
Dodds, John, 250
Dogharty, James, 257
Doherty, Michael, 277, 310
Dolan, John, 249
Donaldson, Thomas, 72
Donnally, Felix, 167
Donogho, Thomas, 299
Doran, Bryan, 153
Dorsey, John, 220
Dorthety, Daniel, 152
Dougherty, Captain, 148
Dougherty, Hugh, 219
Dougherty, John, 174
Douglass, John, 133, 134, 178
Dowdall, Andrew, 20
Dowdle, Thomas, 127
Downey, James, 47
Downey, Lawrence, 283
Downing, James, 27
Downing, John, 202
Downing, Thomas, 35
Downon, John, 145
Downs, Mary, 148
Doyle, John, 215
Doyle, Michael, 47
Doz, Andrew, 201
Draper, Alexander, 19
Draper, William, 29
Duchee, Anthony, 45
Duddley, James, 21
Duell, John, 138

Duff, Henry, 123
Duff, Mr., 81
Duff, Thomas, 159, 181, 182
Duffore, Joseph, 154
Dummond, Duncan, 7
Dunabour, George Michael, 96
Dunavin, Robert, 177
Dunbar, Weldon, 220
Duncan, Bridget, 8
Dunlap, Peter, 114
Dunn, George, 318
Dunn, William, 83
Durborow, Hugh, 15
Durrah, Daniel, 269, 272
Dushane, Anthony, 40
Dushane, Isaac, 147
Dushane, Valentine, 60, 65, 107
Dushane, Valentine, Jr., 63
Dushen, Garret, 23
Dutton, Joseph, 197
Dyal, William, 250
Eakin, Alexander, 152, 153
Eberly, George, 256, 283, 296, 315
Eccles, John, 81
Ecklin, David, 99, 101
Edgar, Captain, 166
Edger, John, 187
Edonovan, Patrick, 44
Edwards, James, 105
Edwards, John, 71, 354, 355
Egan, Roger, 207
Egburts, James, 79
Elbert, Henry, 314
Elder, John, 299
Eleazer, David, 137
Elliot, Mark, 159
Elliot, Obadiah, 80, 91
Elliott, Joseph, 203
Elliott, Mark, Jr., 307
Elliott, Obadiah, 203
Elliott, William, 367
Ellis, Capt., 338

Elsey, John, 79
Emmit, Abraham, 150
Emory, John, 227
Emson, Thomas, 31
Endless, John, 112
England, Joseph, 84, 344
English, David, 87
English, Robert, 98
Enoch, Benjamin, 190
Enos, John, 330, 339
Enos, Joseph, 333
Enos, Samuel, 162
Erwin, William, 312
Evance, John, 49
Evans, David, 81
Evans, George, 127
Evans, John, 3, 49
Evans, Mr., 38
Evans, William, 146, 147
Everet, John, 214
Eves, James, 338
Eves, Samuel, 11, 14, 15, 16
Ewing, Captain, 277
Ewing, Henry, 176
Eyers, Martha, 226
Faries, Robert, 92
Farquhar, Alexander, 29
Farrall, James, 220
Farrel, Edmond, 5
Farrow, James, 102
Faulkner, Richard, 99
Fawkes, William, 373
Fee, Agnes, 87
Ferguson/Fergusson, Margaret, 318, 319
Ferrel, Eleanor, 150
Ferrell, Patrick, 235
Ferson, Henry, 103
Few, Daniel, 104
Few, James, 83
Field, James, 210
Finch, William, 293
Finly, David, 25

Finnety, Catherine, 318
Finnety, Joseph, 318
Finney, David, 267
Finney, John, 34
Fitzgerald, John, 64, 185
Fitzgerald, Mary, 71
Fitzgerald, Philip, 351
Fitzgerald, Rowland, 3
Fitzpatrick, John, 90
Fitzpatrick, Peter, 59
Fitzpatrick, Philip, 94, 95, 96
Fleming, John, 133, 134
Fletcher, Samuel, 376
Floyd, William, 177
Flynn, Patrick, 101
Folwell, Goldsmith Edward, 62
Foott, William, 232, 274
Foran, John, 213
Ford, Benjamin, 28
Forgason, Margaret, 319
Forrist, Samuel, 46
Forsyth, George, 303
Forwood, Jacob, 171
Foset, David, 244
Foster, David, 165
Foudray, John, 323
Foulke, Edward, 339
Fowler, John, 39
Fraim, Robert, 231
Frame, Alexander, 6
France, Henry, 323
Francis, John, 375
Francis, Thomas, 99, 101
Fray, William, 103
Frazier, William, 346
Freeland, Nazareth, 233
French, Aves, 8
French, Col., 14
Fry, Ann, 322
Fryer, John, 14
Fullam, Walter, 247
Fulton, James, 105
Fulton, Robert, 197

Furbee, Michael, 127
Furniss, Robert, 292
Fussell, Capt., 153
Gallaspey, William, 252
Gallaway, John, 18
Galloway, Samuel, 184
Gamble, Patrick, 258
Ganduett, John, 107
Gantbony, Peter, 105
Gardner, Archibald, 139
Gardner, John, 368, 374
Garland, Nicholas, 143
Garretson, John, 144
Garriston, John, 118
Gathen, Thomas, 325
Gausling, John, 149
Gearran, Thomas, 237
Geddes, Captain, 354
Geddes, William, 356
Geddis, William, 357, 363
George, Thomas, 48
Getteys, Archibald, 143
Getteys, Samuel, 143
Gibbs, Benjamin, 350
Gibbs, James, 7
Gibson, Alexander, 137
Gibson, Hugh, 273
Giffen, Matthew, 225
Gilaspy, Patrick, 174
Gilder, Tobias, 111
Gile, Patrick, 95
Gilespy, John, 64
Gill, Patrick, 83
Gillan, Edward, 60
Gillaspie, Allen, 265
Gillaspy, Patrick, 173
Gillcrest, James, 266
Gillespie, Allan, 148
Gillespie, Allen, 213, 217, 219, 240
Gillespie, Patrick, 170
Gillespy, Patrick, 166
Gilpin, Thomas, 56

387

Gilpin, Vincent, 149, 161
Glasford, Hugh, 113
Glen, William, 336
Glenn, William, 279, 289, 331, 333
Godard, William, 234
Goff, Charles, 256
Goforth, John, 195
Gold, Elizabeth, 172
Golden, William, 233
Goldsmith, Daniel, 63
Gonne, Henry, 24
Goodfellow, Joseph, 208
Gooding, Abraham, 52
Gooding, John, 2, 34, 40, 154
Gorden, James Samuel, 287
Gordon, George, 239, 264, 333
Gordon, John, 161
Gordon, Robert, 38
Gordon, William, 171
Gore, Patrick, 268
Gore, Thomas, 246
Goure, John, 6
Grachams, Francis, 57
Graham, Alexander, 334
Graham, Francis, 58, 70
Graham, John, 73
Graham, William, 153, 349
Grant, John, 173
Grant, Mr., 333
Graves, Samuel, 293
Gray, Conrad, 164, 224, 312
Gray, George, 299
Gray, Isaac, 102
Gray, Jane, 333
Gray, John, 171
Graybil, Jacob, 236
Graybil, Michael, 313
Graybill, Jacob, 155
Graybill, Michael, 325
Green, Stephen, 112
Green, Thomas, 51

Griffin, George, 68
Griffin, William, 240
Griffith, Gideon, 56
Griffith, Nathan, 375
Griffith, Richard, 376, 377
Grimes, Francis, 63
Grub, George, 16
Grub, Nathaniel, 88
Grubb, Amer, 317, 320
Grubb, Amor, 323
Grubb, Emanuel, 275, 276
Grubb, Isaac, 368
Grubb, John, 67
Grubb, Nathaniel, 102
Grubb, Peter, 352
Gudding, Abraham, 14
Gun, Henry, 370
Gylese, John, 224
Hadley, Joseph, 79
Hadly, Simon, 9, 10
Haggerty, Michael, 185
Haily, John, 244
Haines, Jacobus, 288
Haines, Nathan, 212
Hains, Cornelius, 145, 221, 231, 237, 238
Hains, Jacobus, 90
Hale, William Strong, 262
Hall, John, 118, 142
Hall, Peter, 42
Hall, Richard, 13, 124
Hall, Robert, 214
Hamelon, Mary, 181
Hamer, John, 376
Hamilton, Alexander, 183
Hamilton, Andrew, 61
Hamilton, James, 94, 157
Hance, John, 60
Hanley, Dudley, 76
Hanson, James, 272
Hanson, Thomas, 42
Harburn, John Frederick, 197
Harding, James, 168, 169

Harding, John, 50
Hargrace, George, 22
Harison, Sapins, 5
Harly, Manus, 70
Harper, Henry, 242
Harris, Barney Couzens, 130
Harris, Isaac, 337
Harrison, Philip, 104
Harrison, Samuel, 30
Hart, John, 16
Hart, Mary, 181
Hart, Patrick, 242, 243, 247
Hartin, Patrick, 140
Hartley, Benjamin, 370
Hartley, William, 24
Harvey, Alexander, 135, 142, 148, 149, 150, 151, 153, 154, 158, 161, 165, 168, 169, 172, 174, 175, 178, 182
Harvey, Mary, 285, 287
Harwood, John, 246
Haslet, Alexander, 258
Haughey/Haughty, Robert, 374
Hawks, Jane, 224
Hawks, Mary, 224
Hawksford, John, 44
Hawthorn, John, 47
Hay, David, 158, 159
Hay, William, 113
Healy, Cornelius, 127
Healy, Thomas, 119
Heany, Henry, 125
Hearsha, John, 250
Heath, John, 54
Helm, George, 18, 341
Hemphill, Mr., 364
Hemphill, William, 211
Henchy, Joseph, 78
Henderson, James, 256, 314
Henderson, John, 70, 74
Henderson, William, 184, 211
Hennen, John, 90
Henney, James, 343

Henrickson, Peter, 18
Henry, George, 78, 247, 258, 264, 283
Henry, John, 13
Henry, Robert, 331
Heran, John, 177
Herdman, James, 314
Herdman, John, 350
Hersey, Isaac, 83
Hervey, Job, 368
Hetherington, John, 315
Hewes, Isaac, 214
Hewes, William, 186
Hibberd, Josiah, 326
Hicklen, William, 30
Hicklin, James, 89
Higgins, Lawrence, 270
Hilburn, Robert, 223
Hill, Benjamin, 44
Hillyard, Charles, Jr., 347
Hinchmam, James, 220
Hines, Jacobus, 98, 150
Hiron, John, 195
Hirons, Charles, 231
Hodge, William, 85
Hodgen, Robert, 197
Hodgins, Mr., 9
Hodson, Samuel, 36, 37
Hofman, Ludwick, 92
Holderness, John, 178
Holland, Francis, 229
Holland, William, 229
Holme, Thomas, 236
Holt, Mr., 38
Homes, Richard, 43
Hood, Seymour, 285, 287
Hooke, John, 345
Hooks, John, 278
Hopkins, Edward, 57
Hopkins, Patrick, 59
Hopkins, William, Jr., 286
Horan, John, 124
Hoult, George, 350

Houseman, Jacob, 320
Housman, John, 28
Howard, Henry, 355
Howel/Howell, William, 24
Howell, Daniel, 64
Howell, Lewis, 31
Howell, Nicholas, 1
Howell, Reynold, 52
Hoyd, Thomas, 89
Hudson, Mr., 375
Huey, John, 32
Huff, Benjamin, 275
Hugh, William, 3
Hughes, John, 65
Hughes, Samuel, 174
Hugill, George, 46
Hugins, Jacob, 124
Humble, John, 305
Humphreys, Thomas, 121
Humphries, Abraham, 63
Humphries, Thomas, 120
Hunloke, Thomas, 41
Hunter, James, 329
Hunter, Mary, 129
Hunter, Mr., 158, 159
Hustin, James, 167
Huston, James, 187
Hutcheson, John, 39
Hutchings, James, Jr., 248, 249
Hutchinson, John, 263
Hutchison, John, 51
Hyatt, Samuel, 359
Hynes, John, 5
Imlay, Joseph, 113
Inglis, John, 101
Ingram, Abraham, 44
Insellow, James, 267
Irons, Thomas, 316, 317, 329
Isaac, Solomon, 286
Jack, George, 197
Jack, Mr., 277
Jack, Robert, 219
Jackson, Charles, 358

Jackson, James, 277, 310
Jackson, Joshua, 295
Jacquet, Christiana, 248
Jacquet, John, 285
James, James, 69, 72
James, John, 127, 252, 255, 358
James, Richard, 22
James, Thomas, 78
Janaury, Elizabeth, 211
Janvier, Isaac, 177
Jaques, Joseph, 138
Jaquet, John, 115, 118
Jenkens, Enoch, 294
Jenkins, Capt., 34
Jenkins, David, 324
Jenkins. John, 294
Joel/Joell, Captain, 133, 134
John, David, 64
John, Thomas, 8
John, William, 363
Johns, Anne, 11
Johns, Thomas, 11
Johnson, Alexander, 150
Johnson, Elias, 336
Johnson, Francis, 335
Johnson, James, 12, 27, 363
Johnson, John, 190, 210
Johnson, Robert, 257
Johnson, Thomas, 28
Johnson, William, 330, 331
Johnston, Captain, 299
Johnston, Elias, 335
Johnston, Jacob, 246
Johnston, James, 102
Johnston, Randle, 102
Johnston, Thomas, 85
Jolley, Andrew, 42
Jones, Amos, 91
Jones, Benjamin, Jr., 232
Jones, Edward, 19
Jones, Evan, 18
Jones, Griffeth, 1
Jones, Hugh, 284

390

Jones, Humphrey, 105
Jones, Isaac, 286
Jones, J., 231
Jones, James, 101
Jones, Jehu, 197
Jones, John, 67, 130, 131, 208, 209, 210, 271, 343
Jones, Morgan, 19
Jones, Mr., 39, 256
Jones, Owen, 16
Jones, Robert, 103, 213, 265
Jones, Samuel, 185
Jones, Sarah, 302
Jones, William, 223, 302, 358
Jordan, Michael, 286
Juquat, John, 68
Justis, Andrew, 132
Kairns, Jane, 234
Karling, Thomas, 133, 134
Karree, Robert, 133, 134
Kearns, John, 82
Keay, John, 178
Kee, William, 286
Kee, Willian, 263
Keen, Mr., 320
Kelley, George, 71
Kelley, William, 157
Kelly, Arthur, 129, 277
Kelly, Daniel, 38
Kelly, Hugh, 67, 76
Kelly, John, 28, 97
Kelly, Martin, 151
Kelly, Mary, 270
Kelly, Patrick, 285
Kelly, Redmond, 293
Kelly, Timothy, 175
Kelly, William, 108, 109, 110
Kenny, Edward, 9, 10
Kerlan, Patrick, 49
Ketchem, Richard, 370
Keyll, John, 2
Kildear, John, 367
Kime, Lena, 334

Kincoval, Josiah, 50
King, Capt., 6
King, Henry, 197
King, John, 215, 221, 222
King, Thomas, 91
King, William, 178
Kinkaid, Andrew, 169
Kinley, James, 157
Kinsey, John, 368
Kirkly, Thomas, 325
Kirkpatrick, Catharine, 72
Kirkpatrick, Samuel, 110
Kirkwood, Robert, 288
Kittle, John, 151
Knight, Joseph, 17
Kollock, Jacob, 92
Kollock, Mr., 38
Lacey, Philip, 314
Lafferty, Dennis, 267, 271
Langley, John, 323
Lann, Moses, 267
Larey, Cornelius, 284
Lathim, Mr., 125
Latimer, James, 234
Lattimer, James, 294
Lattomus, James, 187
Lauzun, Duc de, 369, 373
Laverey, James, 314
Laverty, Daniel, 373
Lavery, John, 240
Lawden, Richard, 7
Lawerty, Samuel, 371
Lawrie, Daniel, 89
Lawson, Diana, 112
Lawson, Sandy, 330
Lay, Abraham, 31, 34
Lea, John, 339
Lea, Joseph, 235
Leacy/Leary Cadry, 215, 216
Leard, James, 293
Lee, Purmott, 208
Lee, Shadrach, 131
Lee, William, 195

Lefferty, Catharine, 71
Lefferty, James, 71
Leitler, Thomas, 219
Lemmon, Jacob, 178, 182, 201, 202
Lemmon/Lemon, Richard, 216
Lennon, Thomas, 155, 243
Leonard, Darby, 178
Lester, Ann, 277
Lettimore, John, 77
Levett, Charles, 13
Levick, Clayton, 156
Levick, William, 117
Levingston, Philip, 197
Lewden, John, 290, 291, 307
Lewellin, David, 208
Lewis, Ellis, 7
Lewis, Jacob, 62
Lewis, Joel, 299
Lewis, John, 244
Lewis, Moses, 29
Lewis, Robert, 57, 92, 101
Lewis, Stephen, 19
Lewis, Thomas, 43, 82
Linsey, James, 278
Liston, Ann, 254
Little, Adam, 257
Little, Archibald, 69
Little, Samuel, 364
Little, Thomas, 217
Littler, Joshua, 96
Littler, Thomas, 218
Livingston, Henry, 326
Llewelin, John, 210
Lloyd, Henry, 178
Lock, John, 128
Lockerman, Vincent, 78
Lockhart, John, 127
Loe, Thomas, 26
Logue, John, 75
Lolar/Lolor, Mark, 66, 68
Long, Abraham, 61
Long, George, 122, 126

Loper, Aaron, 308
Love, Andrew, 36
Lovelock, Richard, 41
Lovett, Charles, 14
Low, Edward, 303
Lowdon, Hugh, 3
Lowerry, James, 314
Lowry, Jacob, 267
Luckey, William, 359
Luff, Caleb, 115
Lunan, Alexander, 85
Lunn, Thomas, 230
Macanoully, Denish, 1
Maccheon/Macchon, Matthew, 285, 286
MacClean, John, 248
MacClure, Nathan, 24
MacCurdey, Alexander, 24
MacDaniel, John, 6
Macgunnigan, Edward, 54
Macilvaine, Captain, 176
Mack, Robert, 218, 221, 229, 235, 242, 244, 258, 267, 276
Mackadoe, Joseph, 358
Mackey, John, 232
MacMullen, James, 24
Macpherson, Captain, 231
Macquire, John, 11
Madden, William, 281
Magee, Samuel, 143
Magil, Daniel, 1
Maglaery, Thomas, 152
Maguire, John, 366
Makee, William, 263
Malcolm, Robert M., 364
Malcom, Captain, 233, 236
Maller, John, 278
Manlove, Boaz, 212
Manlove, Ebenezer, 160
Manlove, George, 171, 372
Manlove, Mark, 300
Manlove, Matthew, 157
Mannaughan Catherine, 289

Mannaughan, John, 289
Marker, David, 222
Marley, Adam, 77
Marrow, John, 207
Marshall, Captain, 287
Marshall, David, 46
Marshall, John, 293
Marshall, Samuel, 332
Marshall, William, 230, 320
Martin, Jack, 352
Martin, James, 95, 300
Martin, John, 333
Martin, Thomas, 188
Masters, Lee, 325
Mathews, James, 56
Matthews, Edward, 362
Matthews, George, 111
Matthews, Polly, 229
Matthews, Thomas, 100
Matthews, William, 309
Matthews, Wm., 327
May, Charles, 3
May, Francis, 299
May, Thomas, 334, 353, 356
McAnalty, William, 88
McAnaly, Martin, 234
McAntier, Robert, 128, 260
McAwley, Charles, 256
McBay, Andi, 189
McBride, Daniel, 273
McBride, James, 239
McBride, Thomas, 23, 119
McBride, William, 149
McCallagan, Edward, 271
McCallion, Hugh, 236
McCallogan, Edward, 267
McCallum, Peter, 314
McCane, Michael, 124
McCarlin, James, 40
McCarter, Charles, 30
McCartey, John, 61
McCarty, Alice, 183
McCarty, Capt., 182

McCarty, Captain, 96
McCarty, John, 110
McCay, Mary, 148
McClane, John, 167
McClane, Patrick, 38
McClaskin, Arthur, 107
McClean, John, 167, 186
McClellan, Jean, 86
McClement, Andrew, 59
McClintoc, Samuel, 148
McClintock, Samuel, 369
McClorg, James, 290
McClure, Catherine, 209
McClure, William, 237
McColgan, Edward, 228
McColgan, Patrick, 170
McCollister, Margaret, 39
McCollough, John, 138
McColum, John, 50
McCombs, Jacob, 241
McConhey, David, 312
McConhuy, John, 312
McConnell, James, 66, 144
McConnell, John, 274
McCourt, Peter, 305, 313
McCuley, Robert, 148
McCullough, Capt., 288
McCullough, James, 240
McCullough, John, 141
McCully, Robert, 169
McCurdey, James, 2
McCutcheon, Capt., 295
McDaniel, James, 95
McDaniel, John, 228
McDaniel, Patrick, 257
McDermald, Thomas, 295
McDermed, Robert, 223
McDermond, Catharine, 261
McDermont, John, 179, 204
McDermot, Catharine, 263
McDermot, Thomas, 259
McDermott, John, 197
McDonnald, John, 172

McDonough, Thomas, 346
McDowel, Ephraim, 40
McDowell, Andrew, 122
McDowell, George, 210
McDowell, John, 27
McDowell, Joseph, 69
McDowell, Joshua, 176, 191, 194
McDowell, William, 7
McDuff, John, 158
McElherron, Robert, 288
McEntire, Nicholas, 51
McFarland, Archibald, 270
McFarland, John, 50
McFee, Robert, 47
McFilie, James, 122
McGarviy, John, 338
McGaugty, Andrew, 135
McGill, Thomas, 128, 357
McGinnis, Arthur, 313
McGlaughlin, Dennis, 293
McGloughlin, Amos, 161
McGonigal, Patrick, 271
McGonnegal, Patrick, 228
McGonnegall, John, 304
McGonnigle, Patrick, 267
McGradie, James, 155
McGuire, Bartholomew, 70
McGuire, Nicholas, 30
McGuire, Patrick, 39
McIlvaine, James, 79
McIlvaine, William, 189
McKann, Mary, 296
McKannan, John, 345
McKay, Charles, 115
McKean, Thomas, 199
McKean, William, 279, 306
McKee, Andrew, 226
McKee, James, 305, 313
McKenney, Brice, 311
McKettrick, Robert, 313
McKever, James, 250
McKillip, Randall, 164

McKinley, James, 125
McKnight, James, 150, 247
McLane, Samuel, 344
McLane, Thomas, 114
McLaughlin, James, 90, 98, 232
McLaughlin, William, 173
McLean, John, 348
McLoghlin, Dennis, 98
McLone, Patrick, 38
McLonen, Daniel, 261, 263
McLonen, Robert, 116, 151
McMechen, William, 177
McMichael, Archibald, 331, 332
McMinn, John, 262
McMullen, James, 183
McMullin, James, 330
McNealy, Patrick, 151
McPeters, John, 155
McPherson, Captain, 128
McQue, John, 138
McRabbie, John, 40
McSurley, Thomas, 334
McSwine, James, 163
McVaugh, Archibald, 174
McWhenney, Brice, 311
McWhiggon, Lawrence, 232
McWhorter, William, 233, 236
McWilliam, Mr., 283
McWilliam, Richard, 107, 247, 256, 258, 259, 264
McWilliams, Richard, 183
Means, Samuel, 197
Meas, Mr., 302
Meldrum, Robert, 324
Melon, John, 288
Men, unnamed, 2, 9, 17, 40, 41, 54, 64, 76, 146, 170, 175, 176, 184, 218, 349, 352, 361
Mendenhall, Stephen, 184, 186
Mentor, Mary, 286, 296
Meque, John, 157
Mercer, Benjamin, 324
Mercer, Frances, 104

Meredith, Jonathan, 358
Meredith, Joseph, 219
Meredith, Owen, 20
Meshefrey, John, 203
Metcalf, Jacob, 22
Metere, Andrew, 180
Mewlin, Ellis, 304
Meworthir, John, 316
Middleton, Robert, 133
Mifflin, George, 18
Mifflin, John, 208
Miles, Abel, 348
Miles, John, 311
Miligen/Milighen, John, 191, 193
Millar, George, 92
Miller, Alexander, 166, 170
Miller, Capt., 141
Miller, Charles, 54
Miller, John, 114, 133, 134, 278, 325
Miller, Joseph, 289, 325
Mills, John, 172
Mills, William, 227, 230
Mines, Francis, 59
Mines, John, 42
Minshall, Griffith, 82, 92
Mitchell, John, 97, 142, 158
Mitchell, Mary, 261
Mitchell, Robert, 261
Mitchell, Silus, 364
Moles, Oliver, 185
Mollen, Mr., 45
Money, John, 214
Monro/Monrow, George, 49, 67, 82, 85, 99, 104
Montgomery, Alexander, 88, 141
Montgomery, John, 89, 153
Montgomery, Thomas, 89, 97
Moody, Thomas, 194
Moody, William, 260, 261
Moon, Edward, 200
Mooneys, James, 267

Moor, Benjamin, 22
Moor, John, 156
Moor, Richard, 5
Moorand, John, 170
Moore, Alexander, 150
Moore, Elizabeth, 214
Moore, James, 76
Moore, Jeremiah, 343
Moore, John, 180
Moore, Thomas, 17
Moore, William, 56
Morgan, Captain, 355
Morgan, David, 117, 256
Morgan, James, 355
Morgan, John, 224, 272
Morgan, Mary, 200
Morgan, Patrick, 278
Morgan, Thomas Spry, 172
Morne, John, 273
Morris, Michael, 235
Morris, William, 117
Morrison, John, 185
Morrison, Matthew, 87
Morrow, John, 156, 157, 194
Morton, John, 166
Morton, Morton, 256
Morton, Thomas, 161
Mosely, Mary, 345
Mosely, Richard, 346
Mott, Richbell, 94
Moulsdale, James, 234
Mounteer, William, 191
Mourton, William, 33
Muheaw, William, 184
Mullagan, John, 220
Mulvehill, Hugh, 86
Murphey, Robert, 180
Murphy, Daniel, 208, 210
Murphy, Dennis, 175, 176
Murphy, Margaret, 6
Murphy, Morgan, 65
Murphy, Thomas, 146
Murry, Timothy, 6

Musgrove, James, 296
Musgrove, Joseph, 132
Nagel, George, 213
Nash, William, 361
Naudain, Arnold, 243
Neal/Neil, Mary, 89
Negroes, Abel; Abraham, 115; Andrew, 259; Ann, 335; Armstrong, Joseph, 347; Bazil, 158, 159; Beck, 59; Ben, 110, 152, 327, 341; Berry, 34; Bess, 105; Bett, 369; Bill, 348; Blake, Harman, 229; Bob, 240, 306; Briens, Cudjoe, 163; Bristol, 226; Bristor, 225; Brounberry, Peter, 317; Brown, 328; Brown, Peter, 328, 329; Brown, Willis, 315; Brownberry, Peter, 316; Butcher, Dick, 354; Caesar, 31, 37, 142; Cap, 94; Cato, 22, 185, 234; Cedo, 236; Cesar, 56, 67, 339; Chade, 374; Charles, 175, 244, 364, 365; Clark, Jeremiah, 240; Clark, Jerry, 256; Cuff, 215, 326, 328; Daniel, 347; David, 19; Dick, 60, 63, 65, 78, 112, 161, 168, 169, 178, 267, 345, 346, 353, 355, 356, 359, 372; Dicks, Cuff, 330, 331, 332; Dido, 337; Draper, 347; Duffee, George, 219; Edward, Daniel, 186; Esther, 212; Francisco, William, 142; Frank, 160, 164, 358; Gabriel, 363; Garrison, Joseph, 221; George, 118, 138, 139, 140, 267, 346; Graves, Moses, 325; Gregg, 80; Hannah, 363; Harry, 60, 192, 193, 204, 205, 289, 330, 359, 362; Hester, 356; Hill, John, 338; Hoburn, James, 107; Hughes, Thomas, 172; Hugill, George, 45; Hugill, William, 45, 46; Hugin, Rose, 33; Isaac, 278, 367; Ishmael, 243; Jack, 61, 153, 174, 192, 229, 244, 270, 343, 357, 360, 362; Jack, Whitehall, 61; Jacob, 168, 375; James, 110, 227, 242, 260, 351; Jane, 174; Jem, 110, 175; Jenny, 351; Jim, 117, 339; Joe, 171, 225, 227, 276, 296, 297, 355; John, 135, 136; Johnny, 22; Johnson, Mine, 362; Johnston, Jacob, 325; Jude, 279; Judith, 108; Julius, 159; Jupiter, 216; Kate, 89, 119; Lamme, Ned, 163; Lamy, Ned, 156; Lately, Ben, 371; London, 337, 365; Lot, 334; Lott, 359; Lucy, 344; Mary, 339; McAuley/McAuly, Joe, 374; Miller, Francis, 131; Miller, John, 125; Ming, 106; Montgomery, John, 178; Moses, 346; Moses, Samuel, 372; Murdy, 348; Nan, 243; Nancy, 339; Nat, 352; Ned, 51, 79, 107; Nichols, Jenny, 339; Nichols, Johm, 278; Nick, 370; North, 371; Null, 168; Parkeson, John, 242; Patterson, James, 344; Peg, 192, 193, 204, 205; Perkins, Jacob, 321; Pero, 267; Peter, 111, 267, 321, 322, 354, 357; Phebe, 363; Philip, 363; Pompey, 133, 172, 257; Portroyal/Port-Royal, 292; Post, 366;

Negroes, Price, William, 315;
Prince, 286; Prince Orange,
227; Prudence, 229; Purkins,
Jacob, 306; Ragon, 259;
Ragou, 256; Rane, 94;
Richards, Jack, 358;
Richards/Richardson, James,
335; Rode, 348; Sam, 69, 91,
94, 112, 155, 366; Sambo,
325; Sarah, 321, 322; Saul,
365; Shade, 375; Sharper, 116,
151, 205, 206; Sharper, John,
243; Shirley, George, 62; Sip,
88; Solomon, 298, 301;
Spence, 375; Spencer, 229;
Steph, 376; Stephen, 56, 356,
357, 360, 362; Stess, 376; Sue,
119; Thomson, Samuel, 368;
Tim, 326; Toby, 5; Tom, 111,
153, 187, 229, 258, 331, 332,
377; Toney, 119, 254;
Toppen, 121; Negroes,
unnamed, 10, 12, 23, 44, 63,
81, 90, 93, 99, 112, 113, 134,
151, 165, 173, 182, 212, 350,
368; Walker, Peg, 344;
Wenyam, James, 52; White,
Jack, 358; Will, 121, 299, 337,
353, 354, 355; Williams,
Joseph, 8; Wilson, William,
129
Neil, Rhody, 110
Neil, Thomas, 293
Neilson, William, 263
Nemins, Robert, 191
Nemins, William, 191
Nesbitt, Mr., 119
Nevins, Isabella, 57
Newberry, Widow, 22
Newland, John, 60
Newlin, Ellis, 304
Newlin, Joseph, 140
Newnan, William, 190

Newport, Benjamin, 158
Nibble, Henry, 317, 320
Nible, Henry France, 323
Nicholls, John, 97
Nichols, Benjamin, 19
Nichols, John, 278
Nieman, Zachariah, 234
Niven, David, 27
Nivin, Robert, 49, 64
Nixon, Thomas, 52
Noads, Thomas, 211
Norris, Captain, 220
Norris, Thomas, 257
North, Thomas, 309
Nowland, John, 312
Noxon, Thomas, 26
O'Bryan, William, 343
O'Bryan, James, 255
O'Bryan, William, 343
O'Caden, Patrick, 47
O'Dennysey, Laughlin, 55
O'Donnelly, John, 148
O'Dough[ir]t, Rger, 9
Ogden, Charles, 290
Ogle, Joseph, 295
Ogle, Thomas, 66, 85, 99, 101, 152, 259
Ogorman, Owen, 148
Oharro, Catherine, 175
O'Herrin, James, 226
O'Loug, Dennis, 23
O'Neal, Charles, 307
O'Neal, John, 307
O'Neal, Mary, 89
O'Neil, Hugh, 32
Osborn, Capt., 305
O'Shocknecy, Thomas, 212
Ouldisworth, Stephen, 4
Owen, George, 155
Owen, Kitty, 255
Owen, Owen, 30, 33
Packom, Timothy, 18
Page, John, 299, 339

Page, William, 286
Palmer, John, 62
Parke, Ann, 201
Parke, Edward, 324
Parke, Hugh, 111, 195
Parke, Thomas, 4, 120, 131
Parker, Mr., 11
Parks, Andrew, 157
Parks, George, 248
Parr, Samuel, 21
Parr, William, 186
Parry, Mr., 345
Partridge, James, 235
Partrige, James, 223
Paterson, James, 58
Patterson, Jacob, 141
Patterson, James, 58
Patterson, Mr., 5
Patterson, William, 27, 118, 139, 140, 223, 225, 251, 264, 265, 311
Pattison, John, 108, 109
Pawling, Elias, 335, 336
Peacock, Thomas, 333
Pearce, James, 244
Peck, Jacob, 267
Peele, Andrew, 197
Pendegrass, John, 57
Penrose, John, 242
Penton, Ranier, 351
Perkins, Caleb, 30, 130, 131
Perkins, Darcus, 325
Perkinson, John, 97
Peterson, Jacob, 141
Peterson, Jonas, 254, 277
Petterson, Jacob, 141
Philimon, Jacob, 215
Philiston, William, 299
Phillips, Ephraim, 240, 306
Phillips, John, 79, 278
Phillips, William, 231
Phipps, Stephen, 233
Pierce, Robert, 128
Piercy, John, 75
Pike, Stephen, 220, 237
Pits/Pitts, David, 36, 37
Platt, John, 305, 306
Platt, Samuel, 190
Plowman, John Jacob, 323
Poleson, Jasper, 84
Pollien, Mr., 111
Popham, James, 188, 189
Porter, Alex., 206
Porter, Alexander, 205, 258
Porter, James, 323
Porter, Samuel, 169
Powel, James, 48
Powell, John, 57
Preden, Catherine, 111
Price, David, 52
Price, Edmund, 244
Price, James, 185
Price, John, 137
Price, Joseph, 274
Price, Samuel, 189
Price, Widow, 56
Price, William, 162
Priestman, Joseph, 201, 202
Proctor, Thomas, 308
Proger, Edward, 78
Prosser, John, 47
Provost, Major, 110
Purcell, Peter, 180
Purcell, Richard, 276
Purday, John, 182
Purday, Mary, 182
Pusell, John, 48
Pusey, Caleb, 68, 79
Pusey, Thomas, 185, 207, 212, 214, 215, 218, 278, 286, 293, 299, 309
Pye, Robert Richard, 249
Quin, Roger, 288
Rachford, John, 28
Radmont, Henry, 46
Ralston, Paul, 204

Ralston, Samuel, 51
Ramsey, Elizabeth, 356
Ramsower, Adam, 264
Randolph, Peyton, 124
Rankin, Captain, 197
Rankin, George, 158, 162
Rankin, Michael, 233, 236
Rankin, Moses, 89, 95, 97
Raredon, Daniel, 118
Ratcliff, Stephen, 266
Ratcliffe, Charles, 121
Ratlidge, Thomas, 137
Rawlings, Margaret, 370
Rawlings, Thomas, 370
Ray, James, 295
Rayman, Jonathan, 20
Read, Charles, 12
Read, Christian, 17
Read, George, 125, 202
Read, James, 374
Read, John, 14, 20, 27, 56, 141
Read, Mr., 125
Read, William, 8, 9, 255, 325, 326
Read, Wm., 10
Redick, Catherine, 135
Redman, Anthony, 196
Redman, Catharine, 196
Reed, Ithiel, 93
Reed, James, 250
Reed/Read, John, 50
Reel, Mary, 106
Rees, John, 114, 116
Rees, William, 226
Reese, John, 162
Reiley, Patrick, 220
Reiley/Reily, Thomas, 309
Reily, James, 38
Reister, Abraham, 343
Rendels, Hugh, 63
Rennalds, Henry, 107
Rew, Joshua, 243
Reynolds, David, 155

Reynolds, Henry, 225, 251, 371
Reynolds, John, 295
Reynolds, Lawrence, 5
Rhea, William, 350
Rice, Samuel, 188, 189
Richard, Francis, 148
Richardson, Edward, 43
Richardson, Isaac, 133, 134
Richardson, Joseph, 212
Richey, John, 81
Richy, Samuel, 374
Riddles, John, 290, 303
Ridgely, Doctor, 325
Ridgely, Mr., 375
Ridgeway, John, 102
Riggon, Tague, 227
Riggon, Thomas, 336
Roany, Margaret, 245
Robbins, Cornelius, 197
Robbins, Harry, 335
Roberts, Daniel, 22
Roberts, John, 22
Roberts, Robert, 22
Robertson, Robert, 240
Robeson, William, 163
Robinson, Charles, 275, 276
Robinson, Daniel, 28
Robinson, Francis, 223
Robinson, George, 45, 46
Robinson, James, 159
Robinson, John, 85
Robinson, Peter, 285, 295
Robinson, Robert, 103
Robinson, Rudeman, 155
Robinson, Samuel, 40
Robinson, Thomas, 184, 197, 321, 322
Robinson, Valentine/Valantine, 33, 37, 45, 46
Rock, George, 56
Rodeney, Caesar, 111
Rodgers, William, 43
Rodman, John, 73

Rodney, Caesar, 105
Rodney/Rodeney, Daniel, 32
Rogers, Edward, 248, 249
Rogers, Grace, 115, 118
Rogers, Thomas, 41
Rogers, William, 296
Rolston, Paul, 197
Ross, John, 96
Ross, William, 287
Rotheram, Joseph, 84
Rothwell, Jacob, 144, 145
Rothwell, Thomas, 377
Rowan, William, 142
Rowland, Samuel, 62
Rudullph, Hance, 61
Rumford, Jonathan, 361
Russell, John, 252, 262, 267
Ruth, Joseph, 230
Ruth, Samuel, 174
Rutherford, Alex., 291
Rutherford, Alexander, 239
Ryan, John, 98, 194
Ryan, Mary, 98
Ryan, Richard, 132
Ryan, Thomas, 72, 75
Sadler, Jacob, 271
Sadler, Joseph, 168
Sands, Thomas, 102
Sauce, Richard, 292
Saunders, James, 191
Sauter, Jacob, 160
Sauter, John, 160
Saven, Thomas, 215
Sayre, Samuel, 359
Schee, Harmanus, 377
Schluter, John, 84
Scholefield, David, 195
Scott, Alexander, 175
Scott, James, 273
Scott, John, 99
Sculley, Thomas, 290
Scully, Thomas, 266
Sebley, Richard, 211

Seemore, James, 346
Seers, William, 73
Selthridge, William, 38
Senix, James, 132
Shafter, Henry, 62, 63
Shankland, John, 25, 26
Shankland, Joseph, 121
Sharp, John, 102
Sharpless, Thomas, 351
Sharps, James, 352
Shaw, George, 335
Shaw, James, 154, 347
Shaw, John, 151
Sheehan, John, 197
Shehan, John, 228
Shehee, James, 256
Shelley, Mr., 56
Shennan, John, 9
Shennan/Shrennan, John, 8
Shepherd, Nathan, 323
Sheward, Caleb, 327
Shields, Robert, 310
Shien, William, 295
Shippen, Edward, 112
Sigfreidusalrichs, Peter, 84
Silver, Patrick, 46
Silvester, Ben., 364
Simkin, John, 75
Simpson, Matthew, 257
Simson, James, 198
Singleton, John, 99, 148, 183, 189
Sinnickson, Thomas, 257
Sinton, William, 3
Skanlon, William, 39
Skillman, Mr., 292
Slater, Robert, 170, 209
Slauter, Joseph, 32
Sloan, Thomas, 293
Slone, Betty, 255
Smedley, Thomas, 276
Smith, Anne, 135
Smith, Capt., 337

Smith, Conrad, 177
Smith, Daniel, 373
Smith, David, 169, 185
Smith, Eden, 316
Smith, Frances, 313
Smith, James, 106
Smith, Jeremiah, 165, 260, 264
Smith, John, 21
Smith, Jonathan, 86, 215
Smith, Margaret, 234, 275, 276, 324
Smith, Richard, 218, 249
Smith, Samuel, 172, 180, 189, 353
Smith, Spencer, 110
Smith, Thomas, 17
Smith, William, 7, 93, 352
Snodgrass, William, 175
Snowden, Mr., 278
Soullard, John, 335, 336
South, Thomas, 197
Spafford, John, 91, 94
Sparling, John, 65
Spearing, John, 222
Spencer, Thomas, 309
Spencer, William, 28
Springer, John, 105
Stafford, Margaret, 293
Stahl, Augustine, 85
Staklen, John, 372
Stalcop, Andrew, 190
Stalcop, Hannah, 190
Stanley, Mary, 135
Stapler, John, 251
Starn, William, 318
Starr, Isaac, 268, 269
Starr/Starn, William, 293, 319
Stedham, Tobias, 192
Steel, Alexander, 76, 234
Steel, Hugh, 269
Steel, James, 20
Steel, Thomas, 61
Stenson, James, 198

Stern, George, 316
Stevens, Henry, 137, 226, 325
Stevenson, Samuel, 362
Stevilen, John, 30
Stewart, Archibald, 81
Stewart, John, 367, 368
Stidham, Cornelius, 180
Stiff, Griffin, 372
Still, John, 66
Story, John, 166
Stow, John, 287
Stuart, William, 349
Sullivan, Jeremiah, 75
Sullivan, Matthew, 295
Sullivan, Timothy, 12
Sutherland, Thomas, 190
Sutter, Peter, 163
Sutton, John, 114
Sutton, William, 142
Swainey, James, 287
Swainey, Luke, 209
Sweney, James, 163, 184, 186
Swetman, James, 157
Sykes, James, 4, 6
Tarrant, Thomas, 18, 21
Tate, Anthony, 51
Tate, William, 264
Tatlow, Joseph, 284
Tatnall, Joseph, 309, 318, 319
Taylor, Benj., 34
Taylor, Benjamin, 304
Taylor, Capt., 149
Taylor, Captain, 41
Taylor, Emanuel, 41
Taylor, John, 88, 248
Taylor, Joseph, 147
Teas, James, 289
Teernan, John, 221
Telfair, Edward, 363
Tharp, John, 244
Theadford, Walter, 66
Thetford, Walter, 46, 55, 76
Thomas, Catherine, 175

Thomas, Edward, 16
Thomas, Griffith, 132
Thomas, Isaac, 299
Thomas, James, 284
Thomas, John, 218
Thomas, Joseph, 27, 155, 175, 192, 220
Thomas, Reas, 65
Thomas, Thomas, 30, 33
Thompson, George, 133, 134
Thompson, John, 93, 99, 100, 102, 103, 107, 108, 110, 111, 112, 277, 297, 298
Thompson, Samuel, 42
Thompson, William, 65
Thomson, J., 81
Thomson, John, 106
Thornton, Francis, 115, 118
Thrift, John, 313
Tiday, William, 220
Tilden, Charles, 42
Tilghman, Richard, 282
Tilton, Nehemiah, 354
Tinch, Samuel, 270
Tizdel, Henry, 127
Tobin, Thomas, 242, 243
Toby, Cornelius, 18
Tolbot, Thomas, 189
Tomlinson, John, 304
Tomson, James, 2
Tool, Mary, 93
Toppam, Christopher, 33
Tottan, Thomas, 136
Townsend, Jehu, 370
Townsend, Joseph, 147
Trayner, Peter, 343
Trenchard, Curtis, 252, 253, 254
Trimble, John, 36
Troth, Henry, 90
Tucker, John, 119
Tuder, Henry, 165
Tuffo, Henry, 1
Turner, Daniel, 229

Turner, John, 285
Turner, Levin, 373
Turner, Mr., 81
Turner, Stephen, 207
Tussey, William, 77
Underhill, John, 217
Underwood, Joseph, 32
Underwood, William, 132, 337
Vanable, Joseph, 3
Vanbebber, Captain, 117
Vanbebber, Henry, 134
Vanbeeber, Henry, 114
Vance, Samuel, 348
Vandike, David, 177
Vandiver, Matthias, 361
Vandyke, David, 176
Vandyke, Frederick, 68
Vanlier, Dr., 194
Vaughan, Jonathan, 151
Veghte, Nicholas, 205
Veight, Nicholas, 192, 193, 204
Viner, Thomas, 290, 291
Waffen, William, 71
Wainrite, Ann, 59
Wainwright, Nancy, 98
Wakely, Mr., 96
Walkens, Henry, 92
Walker, Aaron, 308
Walker, James, 86, 167, 187
Walker, Ralph, 156, 163
Wall, Charles, 283
Wall, Hannah, 211
Wall, Henry, 186
Wall, Patrick, 91
Wall, William, 42
Wallace, Josiah, 129, 139
Waller, William, 67
Walton, John, 38
Waples, Burton, 321, 322, 346
Waples, Nathaniel, 321, 322
Ward, Benjamin, 345, 346
Ware, David, 227
Warner, Joseph, 204, 305

Wasson, Ann, 245
Waters, William, 43, 218
Watson, John, 21
Watson, Mary, 215
Watson, Widow, 13
Watters, William, 217
Wattington, John, 370
Way, John, 201, 203, 206
Weatherspoon, David, 138
Weaver, Philip, 320
Webb, Ezekiel, 358
Weed, Elijah, 363
Weir, James, 133
Welch, Christopher, 66
Welch, James, 285
Welch, John, 285
Welch, Morris, 69
Welch, Mr., 311
Welch, Richard, 161
Welch, Thomas, 105
Weldon, William, 146
Wells, Henry, 230
Wells, James, 106
Wells, Susannah, 35
Welsh, Captain, 159
Welsh, John, 278
Welsh, Martin, 365
Welsh, Mary, 69
Welsh, Morton, 365
Welsh, Nicholas, 69
Welsh, Thomas, 278
Wert, Thomas, 331, 333
Westward, Edward, 83
Wethered, John, 357, 360, 363
Wharton, Charles, 192, 193, 204, 205
Wheallon, Michael, 262
Whealon, Michael, 252, 253
Wheatly, Abigail, 124
Wheilton, J., 359
Whitaker, Conrad, 78
White, John, 142
White, Joseph, 299

White, Patrick, 75
White, Robert, 146
White, Thomas, 352
White, Townsend, 109
White, William, 367
Whitehead, James, 97
Whitelock, Charles, 283
Whitely, Abigail, 117
Whitely, Anthony, 88
Whiteside, Thomas, 275, 277
Whitesides, Mr., 261
Whitley, Anthony, 106
Whitside, John, 20
Whittet, William, 2
Wilby, Henry, 223
Wild, Thomas, 315, 316, 325, 326, 330, 334, 337
Wiley, William, 234
Wilkin, David, 67
Wilkinson, Thomas, 197
Willard, Joseph, 53
Williams, Cornelius, 1
Williams, David, 102, 200, 206, 241
Williams, George, 237, 238
Williams, James, 32, 285
Williams, John, 41, 144, 145, 190
Williams, Robert, 103
Williams, Thomas, 9, 75
Williamson, Adam, 305, 306
Williamson, James, 309
Williamson, Matthew, 300
Willington, Lieutenant, 110
Willis, Joel, 252
Willson, Hugh, 199
Willson, John, 5
Willson, Jonathan, 274
Willson, William, 296
Wilson, Charles, 137, 211, 249
Wilson, Christopher, 195
Wilson, Hugh, 196, 198
Wilson, James, 162, 198

Wilson, John, 48, 137
Wilson, Joseph, 82
Wilson, Nicholas, 83, 96
Wilson, Robert, 280, 281, 282
Wilson, Sarah, 200
Wilson, William, 83, 168
Wingate, Henry, 29
Winsant, Jane, 165
Winterbottom, James, 294
Winterton, John, 173, 174, 235, 244
Wirt, Thomas, 280
Withered, John, 356
Witherspon, David, 56
Witherspoon, Mr., 162, 200, 227
Witherspoon, Thomas, 160, 164, 198
Witsil, George, 371
Women, Bridget, 8; unnamed, 104, 116, 129, 139, 146, 156, 191, 287, 332
Wood, Abraham, 62
Wood, John, 212, 241
Wood, Joshua, 66

Woodcock, William, 95
Woodland, Jonathan, 55
Woods, Joseph, 144
Woods, Samuel, 146
Woodward, John, 284
Worden, Samuel, 291
Workman, William, 349
Worms, Daniel, 99
Wotterson, John, 166
Wright, Hugh, 168
Wright, John, 178, 181
Wynkoop, Cornelius, 22
Yarnall, Abraham, 143
Yarnall, John, 311
Yeates, Joseph, 207
Yeatman, Andrew, 297
Yeatman, Mr., 296
Yeatman, Thomas, 7
Yeats, Harmon, 196
Yeldall, Anthony, 286
Young, James, 51, 337, 338
Young, John, 179
Young, William, 252, 253, 313